THE COLLECTED WORKS OF
MAHATMA GANDHI

Owing to the antiquity and rarity of this book, certain pages are regrettably absent, and readability is compromised due to the blurring of the original text. If you possess any insights regarding the availability of these missing sections, kindly inform us. Your assistance is crucial in ensuring the completion of this significant work for the benefit of future generations.

THE COLLECTED WORKS OF
MAHATMA GANDHI

MOHANDAS KARAMCHAND GANDHI

GYAN

Published by

GYAN

Gyan Publishing House
5, Ansari Road
Daryaganj, New Delhi-110002
Phone: 011-47034999, 9811692060
E-mail: books@gyanbooks.com

Distribution Network
gyanbooks.com
India, USA, Canada, UK, Australia

ISBN: 978-93-6780-595-4 (PB)

First Published, 1927

2nd Impression 2025

Printed at: Gyan Press, Delhi.

THE COLLECTED WORKS OF MAHATMA GANDHI
Author: MOHANDAS KARAMCHAND GANDHI

THE COLLECTED WORKS OF MAHATMA GANDHI

XXXII

(November 1926 - January 1927)

THE COLLECTED WORKS OF MAHATMA GANDHI

XXXII

(November 1926 - January 1927)

THE PUBLICATIONS DIVISION
MINISTRY OF INFORMATION AND BROADCASTING
GOVERNMENT OF INDIA

PREFACE

The period—November 5, 1926 to January 20, 1927—covered by this volume was a relatively quiet one. There was a lull in political activity and Gandhiji, enjoying freedom from incessant touring and public speaking, could devote his time to things that concerned him more—spinning and khadi, anti-untouchability and anti-drink work, Hindu-Muslim unity and cow-protection—besides attending to the immense volume of letters that poured in from all quarters.

But most of all it was a period of inward searching and pondering over spiritual values. One such question that exercised Gandhiji's mind at this time was that of stray dogs. The issue, as he put it, was "whether in consonance with the principle of ahimsa, it may be a duty to kill certain dogs under certain circumstances when no other alternative is possible. I submit that it may be and I hold that there cannot be two opinions in the matter" (p. 42).

Apparently there were two opinions. Those who held more formal notions of non-violence wrote indignant letters. In the series of articles under the title "Is This Humanity?", begun in the preceding volume and concluded in this, Gandhiji answered the critics and provided a lucid exposition of the principle of ahimsa as he understood it. "All action," says Gandhiji, "is tainted inasmuch as it presupposes *himsa.* And yet we free ourselves from the bondage of action through action itself . . . And this *himsa* . . . must be the lowest minimum, must be rooted in compassion, must have discrimination, restraint, detachment at its back, and must lead us every moment onward to the path of ahimsa. . . . The religion of ahimsa consists in allowing others the maximum of convenience at the maximum of inconvenience to us, even at the risk of life. Everyone has to determine for himself the amount of inconvenience he is capable of putting up with. . . . Religion, even as the soul, is both one and many" (pp. 380-1).

Pride of place in this volume goes naturally to the "Discourses on the *Gita*", the finest fruit of his sabbatical year in the Ashram. An apt introduction to this informal masterpiece is provided by the critical account of Shrimad Rajchandra with which the volume opens. It was this friend who in 1893-94 helped Gandhiji to resolve his doubts about his mother-religion, assured him that no other religion has its "subtle and profound thought, its vision of the soul or its charity" and thus restored to him his peace of mind. What Gandhiji sorely needed at the time, and what Rajchandra's answers to his questions (Appendix I) and the books sent by him provided in ample measure, was a spiritual motive and experience, a hope and glimpse of *moksha* in this very life, which would make it worth one's while to practise the higher ethics of utmost responsibility for oneself and freedom for others. One of the books recommended and sent by Rajchandra, the *mumukshuprakarana* of the *Yoga Vasishtha*, prescribes a strong sense of *purushakara* (human endeavour) in facing world problems, and also self-examination and critical analysis at every step of experiences as they come. If, when the ideas of Maitland and Tolstoy came to Gandhiji, he was ready to accommodate and apply them within the framework of his ancestral Vaishnavism, it was because he had already been "converted" to *mumukshutva*, by the wise counsel of Rajchandra. This "serious call" to a life of *moksha*-oriented dharma is the only conversion which Gandhiji considered legitimate and which every true religion expects at some stage from its adherents.

Though for various reasons Gandhiji declined to accept Rajchandra as a guru in the traditional sense he was grateful to the Jain philosopher for the counsel to cling to one's own faith, to respect other faiths and in due course to transcend all faiths which were like "so many walled enclosures in which men and women were confined". While studying the excellence of each faith and explaining it to the followers of that faith, the genuine seeker finds that "after a certain stage is reached the Shastras give no help; experience alone helps then" (p. 12). Beyond this stage every Shastra becomes a fetter hindering further progress. Since every accepted faith has thus to be transcended in experience, "everyone may, following his own faith, win his freedom, that is, *moksha*, for to win *moksha* means to be perfectly free from attachments and aversions" (p. 13).

In the "Discourses on the *Gita*" there are repeated references to the Bible, the Koran, *Pilgrim's Progress* and the works of Rajchandra himself, all of which show Gandhiji's readiness and ability to handle the *Gita* not as a sectarian scripture but as a manual of universal religion and pure ethics "which persons belonging to all faiths can read" (p. 350).

Gandhiji's interpretation of the *Gita*, as indeed of the entire epic, is *adhyatmic* or anagogical. The war described by Vyasa is no external or historical event, but a vivid poetic representation of the invisible conflict raging within each one of us. "It tells of the

. . . Pandavas in our minds who are battling with the Kauravas in it. . . . Krishna is the *atman* in us, who is our charioteer. We can win only if we hand over the reins of the chariot to him" (pp. 108-9).

By this surrender of the reins to Krishna within, by thus internalizing and enthroning the ideal person pictured in Ch. II, the autonomy of the individual, his freedom of choice and responsibility for effort, is strengthened rather than weakened. "The *Gita* does not decide for us. But if, whenever faced with a moral problem, you give up attachment to the ego and then decide what you should do, you will come to no harm" (p. 109). To measure our progress in disinterestedness, "our yardstick is the ability to see others as ourselves" (p. 374). Progress here is far from easy, but one is helped to "see others in oneself by seeing them and oneself in God" (p. 249). In this process of identification, the first step is identification with Arjuna so that the Lord's words to him are felt to be meant for us.

Hence the central importance, even in our public prayer, of 'practising the presence' of the *sthitaprajna* described in Ch. II. "We recite these verses daily so that we may understand their meaning and be guided by them" (p. 127). The ideal person is as a seed sown in one's heart and growing freely there in response to all the predicaments it passes through. The scripture, even the *Gita*, is soil which our mind, as the germinating seed, uses creatively, choosing what ingredients it needs and ignoring the rest. How and how far one should follow the scripture in solving the conflicts of dharma confronting one depends on one's temperament and training. While it is open to all to revel in the poetry of the *Gita* (pp. 233, 292), the earnest seeker should observe *yama* and *niyama* and other rules of discipline, should acquire *adhikara* or fitness, before taking up the study of the *Gita*. To look for ethical guidance there "without having equipped oneself in this manner . . . would be like taking up a study of botany without ever having seen plants" (p. 103). In other words, Gandhiji's approach to the *Gita* is functional and practical, not academic and theoretical. Its enthralling poetry is not a way of escape from life's problems, but an inspiration to follow strenuously the conduct it prescribes for eradicating the ego. We should study and understand the *Gita* "not merely to satisfy our curiosity but with the aim of putting its teaching into practice . . . We should leave alone what we cannot put into practice. It is a misuse of our intellectual energy and a waste of time to go on reading what we cannot put into practice" (pp. 227-8).

Unerringly Gandhiji puts his finger on the *Gita's* 'secret', its whole meaning and purpose, which is to transform or destroy the ego, the separate shape or shadow to which we cling. "There is only one spiritual evil, with only one cause and one remedy. To explain this oneness an extreme example is used. If one's kinsmen deserve to be killed, they ought to be killed. . . . We can follow truth only in the measure that we shed our attachment to the ego" (pp. 106-7). Arjuna's despondency arises not from reluctance to killing as such, but from reluctance to killing one's kinsmen.

In Discourses 41-45 which enlarge the meaning of *yajna*, Gandhiji is only exercising the liberty of interpretation permitted by the orthodox schools. As circumstances change and men become more enlightened, "sons should enrich the legacy of their fathers". One can well imagine a time when a wise man "will mean by the spinning-wheel not an article made of wood but any type of work which provides employment to all people" (p. 154).

In this expanded meaning, *yajna* means "any action performed with a view to public good" (p. 155). And so the cherishing of the gods (Ch. III. 11) means that "we should serve the humblest human beings, even those whom we never see, with respect and honour and looking upon them as gods and not as our servants; we should, in other words, serve the whole world" (p. 156). At the same time Gandhiji's restrained comments on II. 52-3 and IV. 17 show how anxious he is to avoid, in these lay talks, any revolutionary departure from tradition. What is significant in Gandhiji's approach is not originality but an earnest resolve to interrelate and harmonize faith and conduct.

With Gandhiji religion was no formal profession, it was a moral effort and spiritual experience embracing faith and conduct, action feeding knowledge and knowledge illuminating action. Hence karma was not mere ritual or prescribed action. "Activity of every kind is karma" (p. 351). "Even the decision to stop breathing is karma. Even the refraining from karma is karma" (p. 148). ". . . the very process of living is a form of karma . . . no one can escape doing karma" (p. 206).

Since karma is thus inescapable, what the *Gita* does is to integrate it with *jnana* and *bhakti*. "The *Gita* does not give the central importance to karma, nor to *jnana* nor to *bhakti*. . . . Karma, *jnana* and *bhakti*, all three are essential, and each in its place is of central importance" (p. 351). *Jnana* and karma are both excellent, but neither can be practised without the other. It is only knowledge that burns up the bonds of karma and converts it into *akarma*. But this knowledge must "sink from the intellect to the heart", must be directly experienced. Food in the vessel or even food in the stomach will not satisfy hunger; "it is only when it is digested in the stomach and converted into blood that we may say that our hunger is satisfied" (p. 219).

And for our *swadharma*, the daily bread which can thus be used to satisfy our spiritual hunger, one need not go searching. It is there waiting for us, "the work which falls to our lot from hour to hour" (p. 369). It comes to us naturally and "grows and expands on its own. We can satisfactorily perform only our dharma, that which lies before us" (p. 365). The strenuous, intelligent and disinterested pursuit of *swadharma* is *karmayoga*, "a royal road, easy to follow. It is the sovereign yoga" (p. 119).

This spiritual *sadhana*, indeed the sovereign yoga, is no special religious action; it is "very much concerned with practical life. A dharma which does not serve practical needs is no dharma, it is *adharma*. Even cleaning of latrines should be done in a religious spirit" (p. 152). But the *Gita*'s karma is "not karma done under compulsion; it must be prompted by . . . knowledge" (p. 352).

When karma is done knowingly and voluntarily and for the sake of the *atman*, it is in reality *akarma*. "If we can renounce the fruits of karma, that is, work only for others, then we may work like horses. On the other hand, when working for ourselves, we should be like a piece of inert matter, have no interest in the work at all. This is a state of the heart, an attitude of mind" (p. 216).

Yajna being work for the benefit of others, "violence committed for the sake of *yajna* is not violence" (p. 353). It is the *yajna bhāvanā* that converts karma into *akarma* and even violence into non-violence. As illustrations of such non-violence Gandhiji cites Harishchandra preparing to cut his wife's throat, a surgeon performing an operation, a compassionate passer-by severing finally a half-cut head (p. 179). *Akarma* means, in practice, reducing the degree of violence involved in each karma (p. 353). "Karma done in the spirit of *yajna*, that is, for the benefit of others, does not bind" (p. 355).

The objection to violence arises not from dogmatic ethics, but from simple psychology. It is our natural human sensitivity which inhibits violence. "The desire to end the suffering of others is . . . *mahaswartha* [the supreme self-interest]" (p. 257). Let us frankly recognize that all our work is prompted by self-interest. But what is self-interest? "If this self-interest is the interest of the *atman*, then one's work is for the benefit of others. All the activities of such a person will be prompted by the motive of service" (p. 365).

The sight of injustice or underserved suffering stirs us to our depths and causes mental confusion and despondency. "We shall not be cured till we feel a crisis. The experience is like the pangs of childbirth. . . . one feels born again" (p. 362). Instead of turning rabid and attacking others, the non-violent reformer looks inward, recognizes the common humanity of all involved in the given situation, and goes through *tapas* for redeeming one's 'opponents' as well as oneself. In this struggle against evil while befriending all those caught in it, power comes from meekness which mobilizes instead of disintegrating our human strength, physical, intellectual and moral. Physically each one of us is nothing in this vast universe, "in this universe of stars, suns and planets" (p. 376). To overcome this helplessness even the awakened intellect feels powerless. Then Yogeshwara Krishna, the Self abiding in the heart of every being, whispers: "Your intellect by itself will not serve you. You will need to do yoga, karma-yoga" (p. 363).

The evil that once maddened us now acquires a new meaning; it assumes a less substantial and more remediable shape. It existed because we supported it. If we withdraw that support, it will collapse. The world, with all its good and evil, is as much in us as we are in it. "Evil cannot by itself flourish in this world. It can do so only if it is allied with some good" (p. 97). On a total view, "it is not wickedness but goodness which rules the world" (p. 192). Not only that; it is God who permits evil, it is He that appears as Ravana and calls man to heroic action. Evil exists so that in resisting it man may perform *tapas*, gain patience and purity of mind and so grow in knowledge. The example of King Janaka and the teaching of Shri Krishna should prevail over our own experience. "We are imperfect human beings and deduce imperfect principles from our imperfect experience" (p. 364). The truth taught by these masters of action and nobly interpreted by Gandhiji, not only in these 218 informal talks, but in his whole long life, is that the way of karma leads to *jnana*, that sustained, disinterested action and honest self-examination starve the ego out of existence and bring on the joyous realization that "this whole universe exists in God" (p. 218) and that "all selves are one" (p. 280).

NOTE TO THE READER

In reproducing English material, every endeavour has been made to adhere strictly to the original. Obvious typographical errors have been corrected and words abbreviated in the text generally spelt out. Variant spellings of names have, however, been retained as in the original.

Matter in square brackets has been supplied by the Editors. Quoted passages, where these are in English, have been set up in small type and printed with an indent. Indirect reports of speeches and interviews, as also passages which are not by Gandhiji, have been set up in small type. In reports of speeches and interviews slight changes and omissions, where necessary, have been made in passages not attributed to Gandhiji.

While translating from Gujarati and Hindi, efforts have been made to achieve fidelity and also readability in English. Where English translations are available, they have been used with such changes as were necessary to bring them into conformity with the original.

The date of an item has been indicated at the top right-hand corner; if the original is undated, the inferred date is supplied within square brackets, the reasons being given where necessary. The date given at the end of an item alongside the source is that of publication. The writings are placed under the date of publication, except where they carry a date-line or where the date of writing has special significance and is ascertainable.

References to Volume I of this series are to the August 1958 edition. References to *An Autobiography* cite only the Part and Chapter, in view of the varying pagination in different editions.

In the source-line, S.N. stands for documents available in the Sabarmati Sangrahalaya, Ahmedabad; G.N. refers to those available in the Gandhi Smarak Nidhi and Sangrahalaya, New Delhi; C.W. denotes documents secured by the Collected Works of Mahatma Gandhi.

The Appendices provide background material relevant to the text. A list of sources and a chronology for the period covered by the volume are also provided at the end.

ACKNOWLEDGEMENTS

For material in this volume, we are indebted to the Sabarmati Ashram Preservation and Memorial Trust and Sangrahalaya, the Navajivan Trust and the Gujarat Vidyapith Granthalaya, Ahmedabad; the Gandhi Smarak Nidhi and Sangrahalaya, New Delhi; Shri G. D. Birla, Calcutta; Smt. Vasumati Pandit, Surat; Shri Parasram Mehrotra, New Delhi; Smt. Mirabehn, Gaaden, Austria; Smt. Tehmina Khambhatta, Bombay; Shri Mahesh Pattani, Bhavnagar; Shri G. V. Ketkar, Poona; Shri Hari-ichchha Kamdar, Baroda; Mrs. Lumsden, Ontario, Canada; Smt. Radhabehn Chowdhari, Calcutta; Smt. Gangabehn Vaidya, Bochasan; Smt. Sushilabehn Gandhi, Phœnix, Durban; Shri Kanubhai Mashruwala, Akola; Shri Dahyabhai M. Patel, Ahmedabad; Shri V. G. Desai, Poona; the publishers of the books—*Bapuna Patro–4: Manibehn Patelne*, *Gandhijinu Gitashikshan*, *Hand-spinning and Hand-weaving*, *Shrimad Rajchandra*; and the following newspapers and journals: *Aaj*, *Amrita Bazar Patrika*, *The Bombay Chronicle*, *Forward*, *The Hindu*, *The Hindustan Times*, *The Leader*, *Navajivan*, *Sabarmati*, *The Searchlight* and *Young India*.

For research and reference facilities, we owe thanks to the All-India Congress Committee Library, the Gandhi Smarak Sangrahalaya, the Indian Council of World Affairs Library, the Research and Reference Division of the Ministry of Information and Broadcasting, New Delhi; the Sabarmati Sangrahalaya and the Gujarat Vidyapith Granthalaya, Ahmedabad and Shri Pyarelal Nayyar, New Delhi; and for assistance in photo-printing documents, to the Photo Division of the Ministry of Information and Broadcasting, New Delhi.

CONTENTS

1. *PREFACE TO "SHRIMAD RAJCHANDRA"*

November 5, 1926

INTRODUCTION

When Shri Revashanker Jagjivan, whom I regard as an elder brother, asked me for a foreword to this[1] edition of Shrimad Rajchandra's[2] letters and writings, I could not refuse his request. As I tried to think what I could say in such a foreword, I felt that it would serve two purposes if I gave the few chapters of my reminiscences of Rajchandra which I wrote in the Yeravda jail[3]: one, that as my attempt, though incomplete, was undertaken purely in a spirit of religious devotion, it might help other *mumukshus*[4] like me, and two, that those who did not know Shrimad Rajchandra in life might know a little about him and so find it easier to understand some of his writings.

The chapters which follow leave the story incomplete. I do not think that I can complete it, for, even if I get time, I do not feel inclined to go much further than the point where I left off. I, therefore, wish to complete the last chapter, which had remained unfinished, and include in it a few things.

In these chapters I have not touched upon one aspect of the subject which I think I should place before the readers. Some people assert that Shrimad was the twenty-fifth Tirthankar[5]. Some others believe that he has attained *moksha.* Both these beliefs, I think, are improper. Either those who hold them do not know Shrimad or their definitions of Tirthankar or liberated soul are different from the commonly accepted ones. We may not lower the standard of truth even for the sake of those whom we love dearly. *Moksha* is a condition of supreme value. It is the highest state of the *atman*[6]. It is so rare a condition that to attain

[1] Second edition. It cannot be ascertained when the first edition was published.

[2] Rajchandra Ravjibhai Mehta

[3] Gandhiji was in this jail from March 1922 to February 1924.

[4] Seekers after *moksha,* deliverance from phenomenal existence as the supreme end of life

[5] A soul that has risen to perfection and teaches the way to others. Jains believe in 24 such Tirthankars, of whom Mahavira, a contemporary of the Buddha, was the last.

[6] The self

it much more effort and patience are necessary than, say, for emptying the sea drop by drop with a blade of grass. A perfect description of that state is impossible. A Tirthankar will naturally command, without seeking them, the powers which belong to the state immediately preceding *moksha*. One who has attained freedom while still living in this body will suffer from no physical disease. In a body untroubled by desire there can be no disease. There can be no disease where there is no attachment. Where there is desire there is attachment and while there is attachment *moksha* is impossible. Shrimad had not attained the total freedom from attachment which should characterize a *mukta purusha*[1] or the *vibhuti* which belongs to a Tirthankar. He had such freedom and such powers in a much larger measure than the ordinary man or woman, and so in common speech we may describe him as one who was free from attachment or who possessed superhuman powers. I am sure, however, that Shrimad had not attained to the perfect freedom from attachment which we attribute to a *mukta purusha* or acquired the *vibhuti* which we believe that a Tirthankar would manifest. I do not say this with the intention of pointing out any shortcoming in a great character worthy of our highest reverence; I say it in order to do justice both to him and to the cause of truth. We are all worldly creatures, whereas Shrimad was not. We shall have to wander from existence to existence, whereas Shrimad may have only one life more to live. We are perhaps running away from *moksha*, while Shrimad was flying towards it with the speed of wind.

This was no small achievement. Even so, I must say that he had not attained the supreme state so beautifully described by him. He himself said that he had come upon the Sahara in his journey and that he had failed to cross the desert. Shrimad Rajchandra, however, was a rare being. His writings are the quintessence of his experiences. Anyone who reads them, reflects over them and follows them in his life will find the path to *moksha* easier; his yearning for sense-pleasures will become progressively weaker, he will become disinterested in the affairs of this world, will cease to be attached to the life of the body and devote himself to the welfare of the *atman*.

The reader will see from this that Shrimad's writings are meant only for those who are qualified to study them. All readers will not find them interesting. Those who are inclined to be critical will get material for criticism. But those who have faith

[1] A liberated person

will find these writings of absorbing interest. I have always felt that Shrimad's writings breathe the spirit of truth. He did not write a single word in order to show off his knowledge. His aim in his writings was to share his inward bliss with his readers. I am sure that anyone who wishes to free himself from inner conflicts and is eager to know his duty in life will gain much from Shrimad's writings, whether such a reader is a Hindu or belongs to another faith.

And, hoping that the few reminiscences of Shrimad's life which I have written down will help the reader who is qualified to read his writings, I give them here as part of this Foreword.

SOME REMINISCENCES OF RAYCHANDBHAI

Chapter 1: Introductory

Today is the birth anniversary of the late Shrimad Rajchandra, whose reminiscences I have started writing, that is, it is the *Kartiki Purnima*[1], Samvat 1979. I am not attempting to write a biography of Shrimad; such an attempt is beyond my capacity. I do not have with me the material needed for a biography. If I wanted to write one, I would spend some time in his birth-place, the port of Vavania[2], examine the house in which he lived, see the places which were the scenes of his childhood play and wanderings, meet his childhood friends, visit the school which he attended, interview his friends, disciples and relatives and gather from them all information which was likely to be useful; only after I had done all this would I start writing the biography. But I have not visited these places or become acquainted with such persons.

And now I have begun to doubt even my capacity for writing these reminiscences. I remember to have remarked more than once that, if I had the time, I would write such reminiscences. One of his disciples, for whom I feel the highest respect, heard me say this, and I have undertaken this attempt mainly to satisfy him. I would be happy, in any case, to write these reminiscences of Shrimad Rajchandra, whom I used to call Raychandbhai or the Poet, out of my love and respect, and explain their significance to *mumukshus*. As it is, however, my attempt is merely intended to satisfy a friend. To be able to do justice to these reminiscences

[1] The full-moon day of *Kartika*; the day corresponded to November 4, 1922.

[2] In Saurashtra

of his life, I should be well acquainted with the Jain way, which I must admit I am not. I will, therefore, write them from an extremely restricted point of view. I will content myself with a record of my memories of him and of the events in his life which had left an impression on me, and with a discussion of what I learned from those occasions. The benefit which I thus derived, or some benefit similar to that, will perhaps be derived by the reader who is a *mumukshu* from a perusal of these reminiscences.

I have used the word *mumukshu* advisedly. This attempt at writing my reminiscences is not intended for all classes of readers.

Three persons have influenced me deeply, Tolstoy, Ruskin and Raychandbhai: Tolstoy through one of his books and through a little correspondence with him, Ruskin through one book of his, *Unto This Last*—which in Gujarati I have called *Sarvodaya*,—and Raychandbhai through intimate personal contact. When I began to feel doubts about Hinduism as a religion, it was Raychandbhai who helped me to resolve them. In the year 1893, I came into close contact with some Christian gentlemen in South Africa. Their lives were pure, and they were devoted to their religion. Their main work in life was to persuade followers of other faiths to embrace Christianity. Though I had come into contact with them in connection with practical affairs, they began to feel solicitude for my spiritual welfare. I realized that I had one duty : that until I had studied the teachings of Hinduism and found that they did not satisfy my soul, I should not renounce the faith in which I was born. I, therefore, started reading Hindu and other scriptures. I read books on Christianity and Islam. I carried on correspondence with some friends I had made in London. I placed my doubts before them. I entered into correspondence with every person in India in whom I had some trust, Raychandbhai being the chief among them.[1] I had already been introduced to him and a close bond had grown between us. I had respect for him, and so I decided to get from him everything he could give. The result was that I gained peace of mind. I felt reassured that Hinduism could give me what I needed. The reader will have some idea of how much my respect for Raychandbhai must have increased because of his being responsible for this result.

Nevertheless, I have not accepted him as my guru. I am still in search of one, and so far my feeling in regard to everyone

[1] *Vide* Appendix I.

whom I might think of as a guru has been "No, not this". One must have the requisite qualification to come upon a perfect guru, and I cannot claim to have it.

CHAPTER 2

I was introduced to Raychandbhai in July 1891, on the very day on which, returning from England, I landed in Bombay. At this time of the year the sea is stormy. The ship, therefore, had arrived late and it was already night. I stayed with Dr. Pranjivan Mehta, Barrister, now the well-known jeweller of Rangoon. Raychandbhai was his elder brother's son-in-law. The doctor himself introduced me to him. On the same day I was also introduced to Jhaveri Revashanker Jagjivandas, another elder brother of his. The doctor introduced Raychandbhai as "a poet", and added, "though a poet, he is in our business. He is a man of spiritual knowledge and a *shatavadhani*"[1]. Someone suggested that I should utter a number of words in his presence, saying that no matter to what language they belonged he would repeat them in the same order in which I had uttered them. I could not believe this. I was a young man, had just returned from England, and was a little vain, too, of my knowledge of languages; in those days I was under the powerful spell of English. Having been to England made a man feel that he was heaven-born. I poured out all my store of knowledge, and first wrote out words from different languages—for how possibly could I afterwards remember them in their due order? I then read out the words. Raychandbhai repeated them slowly one after another and in the same order. I was pleased and astonished, and formed a high opinion about his memory. This was an excellent experience to break a little the binding spell of English on me.

The Poet did not know English at all. At the time I am speaking of, he was not more than twenty-five. His study in the Gujarati school was not much either. And even then he possessed such a powerful memory and such knowledge, and was respected by everyone round him! I was all admiration. The power of memory is not sold in schools. Knowledge, too, can be acquired without going to school if one wants it—is keen on it—and one need not go to England or elsewhere to command respect, for virtue is always respected. I learned these truths on the very day I landed in Bombay.

[1] One who can pay attention to a hundred things simultaneously

The acquaintance with the poet which began on this occasion grew over the years. Other persons possess a powerful memory, and one need not be dazzled by it. Knowledge of the Shastras, too, is found in plenty in many. But such persons, if they have no real culture, can give us nothing of value. A combination of powerful memory and knowledge of the Shastras will have real worth and will benefit the world only if they exist along with genuine culture of the heart.

CHAPTER 3: VAIRAGYA[1]

When shall I know that state supreme,
When will the knots, outer and inner, snap?
When shall I, breaking the bonds that bind us fast,
Tread the path trodden by the wise and the great?

Withdrawing the mind from all interests,
Using this body solely for self-control,
He desires nothing to serve any ulterior end of his own,
Seeing nothing in the body to bring on a trace of the darkness of ignorance.

These are the first two verses of Raychandbhai's inspired utterance at the age of eighteen.

During the two years I remained in close contact with him, I felt in him every moment the spirit of *vairagya* which shines through these verses. One rare feature of his writings is that he always set down what he had felt in his own experience. There is in them no trace of unreality. I have never read any line by him which was written to produce an effect on others. He had always by his side a book on some religious subject and a note-book with blank pages. The latter he used for noting down any thoughts which occurred to him. Sometimes, it would be prose and sometimes poetry. The poem about the "supreme state" must have been written in that manner.

Whatever he was doing at the moment, whether eating or resting or lying in bed, he was invariably disinterested towards things of the world. I never saw him being tempted by objects of pleasure or luxury in this world.

I watched his daily life respectfully, and at close quarters. He accepted whatever he was served at meals. His dress was simple, a dhoti and shirt, an *angarakhun*[2] and a turban of mixed

[1] State of disinterestedness towards worldly things

[2] A tight-fitting coat of relatively thin cloth, fastened with laces

silk and cotton yarn. I do not remember that these garments used to be strikingly clean or carefully ironed. It was the same to him whether he squatted on the ground or had a chair to sit on. In the shop, he generally squatted on a *gadi*[1].

He used to walk slowly, and the passer-by could see that he was absorbed in thought even while walking. There was a strange power in his eyes; they were extremely bright, and free from any sign of impatience or anxiety. They bespoke single-minded attention. The face was round, the lips thin, the nose neither pointed nor flat and the body of light build and medium size. The skin was dark. He looked an embodiment of peace. There was such sweetness in his voice that one simply wanted to go on listening to him. The face was smiling and cheerful; it shone with the light of inner joy. He had such ready command of language that I do not remember his ever pausing for a word to express his thoughts. I rarely saw him changing a word while writing a letter. And yet the reader would never feel that any thought was imperfectly expressed, or the construction of a sentence was defective or the choice of a word faulty.

These qualities can exist only in a man of self-control. A man cannot become free from attachments by making a show of being so. That state is a state of grace for the *atman*. Anyone who strives for it will discover that it may be won only after a ceaseless effort through many lives. One will discover, if one struggles to get rid of attachments, how difficult it is to succeed in the attempt. The Poet made me feel that this state of freedom from attachment was spontaneous to him.

The first step towards *moksha* is freedom from attachment. Can we ever listen with pleasure to anyone talking about *moksha* so long as our mind is attached to a single object in this world? If at any time we seem to do so, it is only the ear which is pleased, in the same way, that is, as we may be pleased merely by the musical tune of a song without following its meaning. It will be a long time before such indulgence of the ear results in our adopting a way of life which could lead towards *moksha*. Without genuine *vairagya* in the mind, one cannot be possessed with a yearning for *moksha*. The poet was possessed by such yearning.

[1] Cushion

CHAPTER 4: BUSINESS LIFE

He is a true *Vanik*[1] who never speaks an untruth,
He is a true *Vanik* who never gives short measure,
He is a true *Vanik* who honours his father's word,
He is a true *Vanik* who returns the principal with interest.
Good sense is the *Vanik's* measure, and the king's measure his credit.
Should the *Vania*[2] neglect business, suffering like a forest fire spreads far and wide.

SHAMAL BHATT

It is generally believed that the spheres of practical affairs or business and spiritual pursuits or dharma are distinct from and incompatible with each other, that it is madness to introduce dharma into business, for we should succeed in neither if we made any such attempt. If this belief is not false, there is no hope for us at all. There is not a single concern or sphere of practical affairs from where dharma can be kept out.

Raychandbhai showed through his life that, if a man is devoted to dharma, this devotion should be evident in every action of his. It is not true at all that dharma is something to be observed on the *Ekadashi*[3] day or during the *Paryushan*[4], on the *Id*[5] day or on a Sunday, in temples, churches or mosques, but not in the shop or the king's court; on the contrary, Raychandbhai used to say and hold, and demonstrated through his own conduct, that such a belief amounted to ignorance of the nature of dharma.

The business in which he was engaged was that of diamonds and pearls. He carried it on in partnership with Revashanker Jagjivan Jhaveri. He also ran a cloth shop side by side. I formed the impression that he was completely upright in his dealings. I was accidentally present sometimes when he negotiated a deal. His terms were always clear and firm. I never saw any 'cleverness' about them. If the other party tried it, he immediately saw through it, and would not tolerate it. On such occasions, he would even knit his brows in anger, and one could see a flash of redness in his eyes.

Raychandbhai disproved the prevalent idea that a man who is wise in the sphere of dharma will not be wise in the affairs of practical life. He displayed the utmost vigilance and intelli-

[1] A community traditionally engaged in trade and commerce
[2] Same as *Vanik*
[3] Eleventh day of the each half of the lunar month
[4] A week devoted by Jains to fasting and self-purification
[5] A day observed as sacred by Muslims

gence in his business. He could judge the worth of diamonds and pearls with the utmost accuracy. Though he did not know English, he was quick in following the general substance of the letters and telegrams received from his agents in Paris and took no time to see through their tricks. His guesses generally turned out to be correct.

Though he displayed such vigilance and intelligence in his business, he was never impatient or felt worried about his affairs. Even when he was attending the shop, some book on a religious subject would always be lying by his side and, as soon as he had finished dealing with a customer, he would open it, or would open the note-book in which he used to note down the thoughts which occurred to him. Every day he had men like me, in search of knowledge, coming to him. He would not hesitate to discuss religious matters with them. The Poet did not follow the general, and beautiful, rule of doing business and discussing dharma each at its proper time, of attending to one thing at a time. Being a *shatavadhani*, he could afford to violate it. Others who might seek to emulate him would fare as a man trying to ride two horses at the same time. Even for a man who is wholly devoted to dharma and is completely free from attachments, it would be best always to concentrate on what he is engaged in at the moment; in fact that would be the right thing for him to do. That would be a sign of his being a man of yoga. Dharma requires one to act in that manner. If any work, be it business or something else, is a worthy activity, it ought to be done with single-minded attention. For a *mumukshu*, inward meditation on the self should be as spontaneous and continuous as breathing. He should not cease from it even for a moment. But even while meditating on the self, he should be totally absorbed in the work he was doing.

I do not mean to say that the Poet did not live in this way. I have said above that he used to display the utmost vigilance in his business. I did, however, form the impression that the Poet exacted more work from his body than he should have done. Could it possibly mean imperfection in his yoga? It is a principle of dharma that one should even lay down one's life in discharging one's duty. But to undertake work beyond one's capacity and look upon it as one's duty is a form of attachment. I have always felt that the Poet did have this highly subtle attachment in him.

It often happens that man accepts work beyond his capacity through spiritual motives and then finds it difficult to cope with it. We look upon this as virtue and admire it. But looked at from a spiritual point of view, that is, from the point of view of dharma, there is every possibility that the motive behind such work springs from a subtle form of ignorance.

If we are no more than instruments in this world, if it is true that we are given this body on hire and that our highest duty is to attain *moksha* through it as quickly as we may, then we must certainly give up everything which may serve as an obstacle in our path—that is the only true spiritual attitude.

Raychandbhai himself had explained to me, in a different form and in his own wonderful manner 'the argument I have advanced above. How, then, did he come to take upon himself certain tasks which worried him and brought on severe illness on him?

If I am right in believing that even Raychandbhai was temporarily overcome with spiritual ignorance in the form of a desire to do good, the truth of the line "All creatures follow their nature, what then will constraint avail?"[1] is very well illustrated in his case, and this is all that it means. There are some who use these words of Krishna to justify self-indulgence; they altogether pervert their meaning. Raychandbhai's *prakriti* took him into deep waters despite himself. To undertake work in this manner may be an error, but it may be considered so only in the case of one who is nearing perfection. We, ordinary men and women, can do justice to a good cause only if we become mad after it. We shall close this argument here.

It is also sometimes believed that religious-minded men are so simple that everyone can deceive them, that they understand nothing about worldly affairs. If this belief is true, then the two avatars, Krishnachandra and Ramachandra, should be looked upon not as incarnations but as mere ordinary men of the world. The Poet used to say that it should be impossible to deceive a person of perfect spiritual knowledge. A person may be religious-minded, that is, may be moral in his life, but may have no spiritual knowledge. What is required for *moksha*, however, is a happy combination of moral life and spiritual knowledge which is the result of one's own experience. In the presence of one who has acquired such knowledge, hypocrisy and fraud cannot keep their mask for long. Untruth cannot flourish in the presence of truth. In the presence of non-violence, violence ceases. Where the light of

[1] *Bhagavad Gita*, III, 33

honesty shines, the darkness of deception vanishes. The moment a man of spiritual knowledge devoted to dharma sees a deceitful man, his heart melts with compassion. How can one who has seen the self in him fail to understand another person? I cannot say that the Poet always demonstrated this truth in his life. People did occasionally cheat him in the name of religion. Such instances do not prove any flaw in the principles, but suggest how very difficult it is to acquire spiritual knowledge of absolute purity.

Despite these limitations, I have not observed in anyone else such a beautiful combination of practical ability and devotion to dharma as I did in the Poet.

CHAPTER 5: DHARMA

Before we examine Raychandbhai's life of dharma, it is necessary to discuss the nature of dharma as explained by him.

Dharma does not mean any particular creed or dogma. Nor does it mean reading or learning by rote books known as Shastras or even believing all that they say.

Dharma is a quality of the soul and is present, visibly or invisibly, in every human being. Through it we know our duty in human life and our true relation with other souls. It is evident that we cannot do so till we have known the self in us. Hence dharma is the means by which we can know ourselves.

We may accept this means from wherever we get it, whether from India or Europe or Arabia. Anyone who has studied the scriptures of different faiths will say that the general nature of this means as expounded in them is the same. No Shastra in any religion says that we may speak untruth or follow it in practice, nor that we may commit violence. Stating the quintessence of all Shastras, Shankaracharya said: "*Brahma satyam jaganmithya*."[1] The Koran-e-Sharif says the same thing in different words when it asserts that God is one and alone, and that nothing beside Him exists. The Bible says: "I and my Father are one." All these are different statements of the same truth. But imperfect human beings, expounding this one truth through their various understandings, have erected veritable prison-houses from which our minds have to escape. We, imperfect human beings, try to go forward with the help of others less imperfect than we, and imagine that beyond a certain stage there is no further way to go. In truth

[1] The *Brahman* alone is real, the world of appearance is false.

it is not so at all. After a certain stage is reached, the Shastras give no help; experience alone helps then. Hence sang Raychandbhai :

> That state the Blessed one who has attained perfection of knowledge sees in his vision,
> But cannot describe in words;
> I have fixed my eyes on that supreme state as my goal,
> But at present it is an aspiration beyond my power to realize.[1]

Ultimately, therefore, it is the *atman* which wins *moksha* for itself.

Raychandbhai has expounded this essential truth in numerous ways in his writings. He had made a deep study of a number of books on dharma. He could follow Sanskrit and Magadhi languages without any difficulty. He had studied Vedanta, as also the *Bhagavata* and the *Gita*. As for books on Jain religion, he used to read every such book that he came across. His capacity for reading and absorbing was inexhaustible. He found one reading enough for grasping the substance of a book.

He had also read in translation the Koran and the Zend-Avesta.

He used to tell me that he was inclined towards Jain philosophy. He believed that the *Jinagamas*[2] contained the perfection of spiritual knowledge. It is necessary that I should state this view of his. I look upon myself as altogether unqualified to express an opinion on it.

Raychandbhai did not, however, lack respect for other faiths. He even felt admiration for Vedanta. A *vedantin*[3] would naturally take the Poet to be a *vedantin*. In all his discussions with me, he never told me that if I wished to attain *moksha* I should follow a particular dharma and no other. He advised me only to pay attention to my actions. When we discussed what books I should read, he took into consideration my personal inclination and the early family influences on me and advised me to continue the *Gita* which I was then reading. Other books which he suggested were *Panchikaran*, *Maniratnamala*, the chapter on *Vairagya* in *Yogavasishtha*, *Kavyadohan* Part I, and *Mokshamala* composed by himself.

[1] Probably through a slip of memory, Gandhiji has here brought together the first two lines of stanza 20 and the first two of stanza 21.

[2] Sacred books of the Jains

[3] Follower of Vedanta

Raychandbhai used to say that the different faiths were like so many walled enclosures in which men and women were confined. He whose one aim in life is to attain *moksha* need not give exclusive devotion to a particular faith.

> Live as you will,
> Attain to Hari anyhow.

This was Raychandbhai's principle too, as it was Akha's[1]. He was always bored by religious controversy and rarely engaged himself in it. He would study and understand the excellence of each faith and explain it to the followers of that faith. Through my correspondence with him from South Africa, too, this is the lesson which I learned from him.

My own belief is that every religion is perfect from the point of view of its followers and imperfect from that of the followers of other faiths. Examined from an independent point of view, every religion is both perfect and imperfect. Beyond a certain stage, every Shastra becomes a fetter hindering further progress; but, then, that is the stage reached by one who has transcended the *gunas*. If we follow Raychandbhai's point of view, no one need give up his faith and embrace another. Everyone may, following his own faith, win his freedom, that is, *moksha*, for to win *moksha* means to be perfectly free from attachments and aversions.

MOHANDAS KARAMCHAND GANDHI

[From Gujarati]
Shrimad Rajchandra

2. *LETTER TO G. D. BIRLA*

Diwali [*November 5, 1926*][2]

BHAI GHANSHYAMDASJI,

I was very much pleased to have your long letter. I had heard slanderous remarks made about you. I did not believe them, but your letter has completely satisfied me. They said that you took work by giving Rs. 500[3] instead of a hundred. From what you have written, I have nothing to say.

[1] A Gujarati poet of the 17th century

[2] The reference to addressee's proposed trip to Geneva suggests that the letter was written in 1926. Diwali fell on November 5 in that year.

[3] Perhaps a slip for Rs. 50

As for Geneva, I must advise you to be patient. I see no great benefit in your going there. If the experience of the West is necessary, go on your own. You will have many occasions to go. But my inner self says it is not today. In the end you should do what your conscience dictates.

Yours,

MOHANDAS GANDHI

From a copy of the Hindi: C.W. 6137. Courtesy: G. D. Birla

3. *MESSAGE TO "FORWARD"*

As heirs to the great legacy left by him[1], he must deserve it by our action.

Forward, 6-11-1926

4. *IS THIS HUMANITY?–V*[2]

[*November 7, 1926*][3]

A friend writes a long letter mentioning his difficulties and pointing out what Jainism has to say to him, a *shrawak*, in the matter. One of his questions is:

> You say that if we can neither take individual charge of roving dogs nor have a *pinjrapole* for them, the only alternative is to kill them. Does that mean that every roving dog should be killed, although it may not be rabid? Don't you agree that we leave unmolested all harmful beasts, birds and reptiles, so long as they do not actually harm us? Why should the dogs be an exception? Where is the humanity of shooting innocent dogs whenever they are found roving? How can one wishing well to all living beings do this?

The writer has misunderstood my meaning. I would not suggest even the destruction of rabid dogs for the sake of it, much less that of innocent, roving dogs. Nor have I said that these latter should be killed wherever they are found. I have only suggested legislation to that effect, so that as soon as the law is made, humane people might wake up in the matter and devise

[1] C. R. Das

[2] For the first four articles of the series, *vide* Vol. XXXI. Originally written in Gujarati, the articles were translated into English by Mahadev Desai.

[3] The articles are placed according to the dates of their publication in *Navajivan*.

measures for the better management of stray dogs. Some of these might be owned, some might be put in quarantine. The remedy, when it is taken, will be once for all. Stray dogs do not drop down from heaven. They are a sign of the idleness, indifference and ignorance of society. When they grow into a nuisance, it is due to our ignorance and want of compassion. A stray dog is bound to take to his heels if you do not feed him. The measure that I have suggested is actuated no less by a consideration of the welfare of the dogs than by that of society. It is the duty of a humanitarian to allow no living being aimlessly to roam about. In performance of that duty it may be his duty once in a way to kill some dogs.

Here is another question:

> I agree that the dogs are sure to be killed by man whenever they become a menace to society. But you say, 'To wait until they get rabid is not to be merciful to them.' This means that every dog is potentially rabid and that therefore it should be killed as a matter of precaution. I met a friend from the Ashram who assured me that you did not mean this, and that you had suggested it only as a last resort when dogs had become a menace. This is not clear from your articles. Will you make it clear?

My previous articles and my answer to the first question leave nothing to be cleared. I must explain what I mean when you say that you cannot wait on until the dog gets rabid. Every stray dog is harmful. The harm is [not] confined to cities alone and it must stop. We do not wait until the serpent bites us. The rabies of the dog is concealed in its capacity to bite. A friend has sent me figures of cases of hydrophobia treated in the Civil Hospital, Ahmedabad:

Period	Cases from the city	Cases from the district	Total
Jan. to Dec. '25	194	923	1117
Jan. to Sept. '26	295	695	990

These figures must alarm everyone who is interested in the welfare of the community, especially if he is a humanitarian. I admit that all the cases may not have been of hydrophobia. But it is difficult to say whether a dog is or is not rabid, and many run in fear to the hospital, because most dogs are found to be rabid afterwards. There is only one remedy to relieve them of this fear and it is not to allow dogs to roam about.

I was in England 40 years ago when effective measures were taken to stamp out rabies. There were, of course, no stray dogs there. But even for the dogs which had regular owners, an order was passed that dogs found without collars with the name and address of the owner thereon and without muzzles would be killed. The measure was taken purely in the public interest. Practically the next day all the dogs in London were found to be with collars and muzzles. It was, therefore, necessary to kill only a very few. If anyone thinks that the people in the West are innocent of humanity, he is sadly mistaken. The ideal of humanity in the West is perhaps lower, but their practice of it is very much more thorough than ours. We rest content with a lofty ideal and are slow or lazy in its practice. We are wrapped in deep darkness, as is evident from our paupers, cattle and other animals. They are eloquent of our irreligion rather than of religion.

Here is a third question:

> You have different definitions of religion for the individual and for society. But why should not religion in both cases be the same? The ideal ought to be the same for both. That it may be impossible to carry it out is a different matter. For, even in case of the individual, only the occasion can show how far he has been able to carry out his ideal in practice. You yourself have said that your ideal is to save even a cruel animal at the risk of your life, but you could not say what you would actually do when faced by such an animal. There is no reason why society should not similarly have a lofty ideal and leave the individuals free to practise it according to their capacity.

My definition of religion for the individual and for society is the same. The ideal must always be the same, but the practice I have conceived to be different in the case of the individual and the society. Truly speaking, practice differs in case of every individual. I do not know of two men having the same extent of the practice of ahimsa, though their definition of ahimsa is the same. The extent of practice in case of society is the average of the different capacities of its members. Thus, for instance, where a section of the society is milk-arian and the other fruitarian, the practice for the society extends to the use of milk and fruit.

The writer next sets out two Jain doctrines as follows:

> Jainism is based on the doctrine of *syadvada*—manysidedness of reality. As is aptly said: 'No absolute rule is correct; only the relative rule is the correct rule.' Which means that an act which may be described as *himsa* under certain circumstances may be ahimsa under other circumstances. Man should always use his discrimination

in determining his conduct. There are two classes of Jains. Sadhus (the monks) and *shrawaks* (the laity). Their code of conduct is thus defined: The sadhu is always non-violent. He may not eat to save himself, may not cook for himself, may not walk even a step for his own purpose—all his activity is for the welfare of the community and it should be as harmless as possible. He has to avoid the 42 infringements laid down in the Shastras. The sadhu is described as *nirgrantha*—free from bonds. So far as I know there is no sadhu today who can satisfy the definition of a sadhu given above.

The *shrawak* may not kill or injure any living being, except when it is essential for himself. He is a worldly man and he cannot take his humanity farther than this. So if 20 per cent compassion is expected of the sadhu, 1.25 per cent is expected of the *shrawak*. If the latter goes beyond the measure expected of him he approaches the state of a sadhu, but *as a shrawak* nothing more is expected of him.

I knew the substance of this distinction. I am quite conscious that the Jain doctrine is not contrary to the opinion I have expressed in these articles. If the Jains accept the interpretation given above, the opinion expressed by me can be deduced from it. But whether they accept it or not, I humbly submit that my opinion is capable of being, and has been, independently justified.

Young India, 11-11-1926

5. *ABOUT MADHADA ASHRAM*

Bhai Shivji had sent to the newspapers a statement in reply to my article[1] regarding Madhada Ashram and himself. This statement he has now sent to me for publication; but as it has already appeared in the daily newspapers, I see no need to publish it here. However, as a certain portion of it referring to his relations with me is of interest to the public, I give below my reply to it.

I was sad to read Bhai Shivji's statement. He has adopted the proverbial method of the thief attacking the warder.

There are no differences of opinion between Bhai Shivji and myself. But I have formed a certain opinion regarding his character and his management of affairs on the basis of Shivji's own confessions. This opinion I conveyed to the executive committee of the Kathiawar Political Conference, and I proposed, as I felt

[1] *Vide* Vol. XXXI, pp. 470-2.

bound, to publish it in the *Navajivan.* But before I did so, I wrote to Bhai Shivji, so as to avoid any injustice being done to him. The question before me was whether I should or should not publish my opinion about Bhai Shivji. This cannot be described as a difference of opinion.

It was certainly I who suggested the idea of the *Panch.* That was for Bhai Shivji's satisfaction and not for mine. There are no allegations against me. Being a public worker I had the duty of making an inquiry into the charges against a colleague. I started the inquiry and, as it was being made, I kept Bhai Shivji informed about it. Finally, I had a meeting with him, and in view of the confessions which he then made there remained nothing more for me to do. Bhai Shivji was found guilty on his own admission. When the case was placed before the committee of the Conference on the same day, and when it became imperative for me to publish it in the *Navajivan,* Bhai Shivji changed his attitude.

If Bhai Shivji or any of his friends wish to know from me the details of the confessions made by Shivji, together with the details of the inquiry that I had made, then I am willing to write to them these details. Bhai Shivji and his friends are at liberty to publish my correspondence with them or with others on this matter. I do not wish to bore the readers by publishing it myself.

I must, however, say that Bhai Shivji's behaviour in every respect, after my inquiry about him, has confirmed my opinion against him. First, I was the judge and others were the complainants. They had given money to Bhai Shivji. When my viewpoint became unacceptable to Bhai Shivji, even I was declared to be a complainant. Now Bhai Shivji, in his statement, seems to consider me at fault. But he and all those who are interested in the social workers obeying more or less the rules and regulations of morality, and who desire faultless management of public funds should know that the proposal to appoint the *Panch* was for the benefit of Bhai Shivji. He is still guilty in my opinion. His lapses are grave and he has confessed most of them. The *panchnama*[1], which I could never have signed, was drawn up, as far as I know, by Bhai Shivji himself. By issuing this statement Bhai Shivji has added salt to the wound and made his guilt worse.

[From Gujarati]

Navajivan, 7-11-1926

[1] A written statement announcing the appointment of arbitrators

6. LETTER TO BANARASIDAS CHATURVEDI

Kartika Sud 3, 1983 [November 8, 1926]

BHAI BANARASIDASJI,

I have your letter. I like the idea of your going to S. A. but the purpose of it does not seem very justifiable to me. If you want to earn your livelihood by going there and writing for the newspapers, the purpose will not be served by your going to South Africa. It will be better if you write a book or take up a job in order to earn money.

Yours,
MOHANDAS GANDHI

From a photostat of the Hindi: G.N. 2574

7. LETTER TO JAMNALAL BAJAJ

Kartika Sud 3, 1983 [November 8, 1926]

CHI. JAMNALAL,

I have your letter. I had completely forgotten the election affair. I see no difficulty in your doing what you think proper. I have written to everyone concerned that I can never participate in it. I would not approve of it if you have to visit many places. It would harm your health.

Ba is completely well, so there is no need to worry. Let us see what happens when I come. There must be many candidates. I intend to bring Lakshmidas with me so that he may have a change.

Blessings from
BAPU

From a photostat of the Gujarati: G.N. 2876

8. LETTER TO SYED ZAHIRUL HAQ

SABARMATI,
November 10, 1926

DEAR FRIEND,

I thank you for your letter.[1] It may flatter my pride, but I hope I have none. I am conscious of my unfitness and limitations. If there was the slightest chance of successful intervention, my seclusion would not deter me. But I see none. I therefore remain still and pray.

The spinning-wheel is not dearer to me than precious lives. I take to it as a child to its mother's breasts, because I believe it to possess the capacity of saving millions of lives from penury and degradation. I commend it to you.

Yours sincerely,

The Hindu, 19-11-1926

9. LETTER TO C. RAJAGOPALACHARI

November 10, 1926

MY DEAR C. R.,

Your letter. The dogs are giving enough food for *Navajivan*. They have also increased the sale of postage stamps. And it is all to the good.[2]

Chhotalal leaves for your place on 16th. So he thinks. He won't be happy till he gets there. He is a beautiful, restless soul. Work, work, work.

I think you should come to Wardha. It is a long journey but, if you can at all spare yourself, do come. Not to go to Gauhati is a sound decision.

[1] Syed Zahirul Haq of Barh, Patna, had, in an open letter dated October 25, 1926, drawn Gandhiji's attention to the communal riots in Howrah on the occasion of Durga Puja and appealed to him to "leave your Ashram and rescue the people as a saviour of the nation from the deep ditch they are going to fall into". The 'open letter' as well as Gandhiji's reply was published in *The Hindu* under the caption: "Hindu-Muslim Disharmony: Mahatmaji's Reply to Call for Intervention". The correspondence was also published in *The Searchlight*, 26-11-1926.

[2] The reference obviously is to the series of articles published under the title "Is This Humanity?". *Vide* Vol. XXXI.

I think with you about the agricultural commission. I hope to write something next week.

Devdas was here for a day. He has gone to Panchgani to replace Pyarelal who has gone to Punjab to nurse a cousin of his.

Yours,
BAPU

From a photostat: S.N. 19728

10. LETTER TO V. L. PHADKE

Kartika Sud 5, 1983, November 10, 1926

BHAI MAMA,

I have not been silent of purpose. I have written about that portion of your letter which called for a note. I shall start the series of articles and I shall send you the portion about Godhra before publishing it. I think there should be no objection to purchasing the Ramachandran water-lift[1]. Some difficulties have, however, arisen in securing it. I have helped you as much as I could.

Blessings from
BAPU

From a photostat of the Gujarati: G.N. 3816

11. PROSTITUTION OF IDEALS

I extract the following from a letter on the remarriage of child widows:

> In your reply to B., Agra, in the *Young India* of September 23,[2] you say that child widows should be remarried by their parents. How can this be done by those parents who perform *kanyadan*, i.e., who give their daughters in marriage according to Shastric injunctions? Surely, it is impossible for parents who have most solemnly and by religious rites renounced all claims on their daughter in favour of their son-in-law to give her in marriage after his death to another person. She may of her own accord remarry if she will, but since she was given by her parents

[1] A large-size bucket contrivance devised by Shri Ramachandran of Agriculture College, Madras, for drawing water from wells with the help of only one animal

[2] *Vide* Vol. XXXI, p. 443.

> as a gift or donation (*dan*) to her husband, no one in the world after the death of her husband has any right to give her in marriage. And for the same reason she herself does not possess any right to remarry. She would, therefore, be faithless and a traitress to her dead husband if she remarried without his express consent given at the time of his death. From a logical point of view, it is thus impossible for a widow—be she child, young or old—who was married according to *kanyadan* system, which is prevalent amongst most *sanatanis*, to remarry unless her husband had given her permission to do so. A true *sanatani* husband cannot, however, brook the idea of giving such permission. He will rather fain agree to his wife's becoming *sati*, if she can or, at any rate, will like her to spend the rest of her life in devotion to his memory or, which is the same thing, in devotion to God. In this he will solely be actuated by the desire or sense of duty to help the preservation of the high ideals of Hindu marriage and widowhood, which are complementary to and not independent of each other.

I regard this kind of argument as prostitution of a high ideal. No doubt the correspondent means well, but his over-anxiety about purity of woman makes him lose sight of elementary justice. What is *kanyadan* in the case of little children? Has a father any rights of property over his children? He is their protector, not owner. And he forfeits the privilege of protection when he abuses it by seeking to barter away the liberty of his ward. Again, how can a donation be made to a child who is incapable of receiving a gift? There is no gift where the capacity to receive is lacking. Surely *kanyadan* is a mystic, religious rite with a spiritual significance. To use such terms in their literal sense is an abuse of language and religion. One may as well take literally the mystic language of the *Puranas* and believe in the earth being a flat dish sustained on the hood of a thousand-headed snake and Divinity lying in soft ease on an ocean of milk for his bed.

The least that a parent, who has so abused his trust as to give in marriage an infant to an old man in his dotage or to a boy hardly out of his teens, can do is to purge himself of his sin by remarrying the daughter when she becomes widowed. As I have said in a previous note[1], such marriages should be declared null and void from the beginning.

Young India, 11-11-1926

[1] *Vide* Vol. XXXI, pp. 377-81.

12. *HANDLOOM* v. *SPINNING-WHEEL*

It seems now to be generally recognized that India, having more than 71 per cent of her population as agriculturists most of whom are idle for nearly six months in the year, needs a supplementary industry and that that industry to be universal can only be hand-spinning. But some contend that hand-weaving is better because it is more remunerative and, therefore, a better proposition.

Now let us understand this argument in some detail. It is said that hand-weaving gives about eight annas per day as against one anna from hand-spinning. Therefore, if a person works for only two hours per day, he will earn from hand-weaving two annas against one pice in the same time from hand-spinning. It is added that one pice would be no economic attraction to anybody and that, if hand-weaving could be presented to the people, it would be wrong to ask them to do hand-spinning *instead.* The protagonists of the handloom contend further that there is no difficulty about getting as much mill-spun yarn as may be required for India's needs, and, finally, they say that even for the sake of keeping alive hand-weaving, which has hitherto defied the competition of weaving-mills, it should be pushed with vigour and determination. Some of the protagonists of hand-weaving even go so far as to say that the hand-spinning movement is mischievous in that it turns people's attention away from the possible industry of hand-weaving and misleads them into supporting an impossible industry which has died of its own inherent weakness.

Let us test this specious-looking argument.

In the first instance, hand-weaving is not a practicable proposition as a supplementary industry, because it is not easy to teach, it has never been universal in India, it requires several hands to work at, it cannot be done during odd moments. It has been and can only be generally an independent occupation and is in the majority of cases the sole occupation like shoe-making or smithy.

Moreover hand-weaving cannot be universal in the same sense that hand-spinning can be. India needs 4,661 million yards of cloth per year. A weaver weaves on an average three quarters of a yard per hour of rough khaddar. Therefore, if all foreign, indigenous or mill-made cloth could be excluded, at the most nine million weavers working at the rate of two hours per day would be required to produce the whole of our annual requirements. If it be contended that not so many weavers but so many families would be occupied, then the two annas for two hours would have to be distributed among many, thus materially reducing the earnings of the individual per day.

Now let us consider the possibilities of spinning. We know that it was at one time the *universal* supplementary industry of India. Millions have not yet forgotten the art and tens of thousands have even now spinning-wheels in their homes. Hand-spinning is therefore capable of immediate and limitless extension. And as it has been found that ten spinners supply one weaver, against nine million weavers ninety million spinners would be able to add to their earnings what to them will be a material and welcome addition, i.e., at least 25 per cent of their income. I have assumed the very high figure of 40 rupees per year per head to be the average income. Unlike weaving, spinning may be interrupted any moment and, therefore, it can be done during all odd moments. Spinning is learnt easily and quickly and the spinner begins to draw some thread from the very commencement.

Moreover, it is wrong to rely upon an unfailing supply of mill-yarn. Hand-weaving and mill-weaving are not complementary propositions. They are mutually antagonistic, the tendency of weaving mills, like all machinery, always being to displace the product of the hand. If, therefore, hand-weaving could become a supplementary industry on a large scale, it would have to be solely dependent on mills which would naturally squeeze the last pie from the weaver for the supply of yarn and would scrap it at the first opportunity.

On the other hand, hand-spinning and hand-weaving are mutually complementary, as can be today proved from the experience of the existing spinning depots. Even as I write, I have letters from co-workers saying that in their centres they have to send away weavers for want of yarn.

It is little known that a vast number of weavers of mill yarn are in the hands of *sowcars*, and they must be, so long as they rely upon the mill product. The village economy demands that the weaver should receive his yarn not from the middleman but from his fellow-worker the farmer.

Again, so far as can be ascertained, there are at present some twenty lakhs of weavers at work. Every additional loom means an outlay of at least Rs. 15. Every additional wheel need not mean more than Rs. 3½. The Khadi Pratishthan pattern costs only

Rs. 2½. And, at a pinch, even an improvised *takli* which need not cost anything can be impressed into service.

Thus, the spinning-wheel appears to be the only foundation on which satisfactory village life can be constructed. It is the centre round which alone it is possible to build up village reorganization.

But it is said that one pice per two hours is no economic attraction to even the poor villager. In the first place, the wheel is not meant for, it is not now presented to, any person who has a more remunerative employment. How is it that thousands of women are today walking a few miles daily or weekly to receive raw cotton and the few pice for the yarn they deliver? If a loom were suggested to them, they would not take it up, they would not have the time or the ability for it. Town-dwellers have no notion of the gnawing poverty of the masses of India. Let us not talk of the machine age in their case. The machinery of Manchester has robbed them of the butter to their bread which the wheel was, for it has been replaced by nothing else equal to it or better. For these, therefore, the spinning-wheel is their only hope.

I do not here examine the more ambitious but chimerical proposals for agricultural improvements. There is room enough for them, I have no doubt. But that is a matter of time and education, whereas the ever-growing poverty demands an immediate remedy which the wheel alone supplies. The wheel does not displace or disregard possibilities in the shape of such improvements. It is a prelude to them. Wherever it has gone, it is affecting the lives of villagers in a variety of ways and it enables the townspeople to establish a living contact with the villagers and their villages.

"If hand-spinning is all you say, how is it that it has not already been universally adopted ?", asks the critic. The question is quite fair. The answer is simple. The message of the wheel has to be carried to a people who have no hope, no initiative left in them and who would, if left to themselves, starve and die rather than work and live. Such was not the case before, but long neglect has made laziness a habit with them. That laziness can only be removed by the living contact and example of men of character and industry plying the wheel before them and by gently showing them the way. The second great difficulty is the absence of a ready market for khaddar. I confess that it cannot for the time being compete with mill-cloth. I will not engage in any such killing competition. The capitalist may for capturing the market sell his calico for nothing. The manufacturer whose only capital is labour cannot afford to do so. Can there be any competition between the dead artificial rose, however symmetrical it may be, and the living rose whose two petals will not be alike, or can there be any competition between a wax statue of Cromwell and the living one? Khaddar is a living thing. But India has lost her eye for the real art and is, therefore, satisfied with the glossy exterior. Revive the healthy national taste for khaddar and you will find every village a busy hive. As it is, the resources of khaddar organizations are taxed to the utmost in order to create a market for the article. The marvel is that in spite of heavy odds against it, the movement is making headway. Over twelve lacs worth of khaddar was sold only last year. But it is nothing to boast of when one thinks of what needs to be done.

I have thus summarized the case for the spinning-wheel as a supplementary industry as against the handloom. Let there be no confusion of thought. I am not against the handloom. It is a great and thriving cottage industry. It will progress automatically if the spinning-wheel succeeds. It is bound to die if the wheel fails.

I invite criticism of the argument and shall gladly retrace my steps if the argument or the facts cannot be sustained.

Young India, 11-11-1926

13. COW-PROTECTION

A correspondent writes:

> As most of the Hindus intuitively feel that the cow should be protected at all events, I too do so. I had witnessed the miserable sight of starving cows in their prime of life, being sold in lots, to Mussalman hide merchants in the famine-stricken areas of the Ceded Districts.
>
> The Hindu scriptures alone seem to have enjoined cow-protection on its followers. I have been trying to understand the philosophy of it. If the cow has to be protected purely from selfish motives, on account of its continuous utility from its birth till after its death, cow-protection should have become universal and not confined to Hindus alone, for, mankind by instinct is selfish. If, on the other hand, it has to be protected on account of its meek and harmless nature, there are other animals as the sheep and deer which also equally require human protection. What then is the special virtue in the cow, exclusively known or useful to the Hindu, over other domestic animals at any rate? If Hindus, not excluding the vegetarian and orthodox sections, are entitled to kill buffaloes, goats, sheep, etc., for, purposes of food or sacrifice, what right have we to resent Mussalmans killing the cow for sacrifice or

food? Would not the appeal of the Hindus to the Mussalmans to protect the cow be more reasonable and effective, if we Hindus ourselves gave up animal killing for food or sacrifice?

There is much to be said in favour of the argument adopted by the correspondent. But man does not govern himself by logic. He is a complex being; therefore, a multiplicity of considerations act upon him and move him to do or to refrain from doing things. Logically speaking, therefore, a Hindu who protects the cow should protect every animal. But taking all things into consideration, we may not cavil at his protecting the cow because he fails to protect the other animals. The only question, therefore, to consider is whether he is right in protecting the cow. And he cannot be wrong in so doing if non-killing of animals generally may be regarded as a duty for one who believes in ahimsa. And every Hindu, and for that matter every man of religion, does so. The duty of not killing animals generally and, therefore, protecting them must be accepted as an indisputable fact. It is then so much to the credit of Hinduism that it has taken up cow-protection as a duty. And he is a poor specimen of Hinduism who stops merely at cow-protection when he can extend the arm of protection to other animals. The cow merely stands as a symbol, and protection of the cow is the least he is expected to undertake. But, as I have shown already in my previous writings, he is failing even in this elementary obligation.

The motive that actuates cow-protection is not 'purely selfish', though selfish consideration undoubtedly enters into it. If it was purely selfish, the cow would be killed as in other countries after it had ceased to give full use. The Hindus will not kill the cow even though she may be a heavy burden. The numberless *goshalas* that have been established by charitably-minded people for tending disabled and useless cows is in a way an eloquent testimony of the effort that is being made in the direction. Though they are today very poor institutions for the object to be achieved, the fact does not detract from the value of the motive behind the act.

The philosophy of cow-protection therefore is, in my opinion, sublime. It immediately puts the animal creation on the same level with man so far as the right to live is concerned. But it is no part of Hinduism to prevent by force cow-slaughter by those who do not believe in cow-protection. Hindus will bring the Mussalmans and the rest of the world to their way of thinking only by living the religion of ahimsa as fully as it is humanly possible.

They must rely upon the working of the great principle in their own lives and making its effective appeal to the outer world. They will not convert the latter by force of arms. They certainly can by force of ahimsa. We little realize the matchless potency of ahimsa when it is thoroughly put into active operation.

Young India, 11-11-1926

14. TAKLI IN SCHOOLS

Dr. Profulla Chandra Ghosh of Khadi Pratishthan sends me the following notes on the introduction of *takli* in schools:[1]

I congratulate the authorities in charge of the Malikanda national school. A spinning-wheel is any day superior to the *takli* for obtaining a larger quantity of yarn. And I have never intended to give absolute preference to the *takli* over the wheel. But I have little doubt in my mind that, in the large number of schools we have, the *takli* yields better results than the spinning-wheel as has been amply shown by general experience. The reasons are obvious. School-rooms are too small to accommodate the spinning-wheels for all the boys and girls. Secondly, even if room could be found, they are far too expensive compared to the *takli*. Thirdly, the wheel frequently goes out of order and neither the school masters nor the pupils are able to set them right in a moment. Once the wheel goes out of order, it often takes a long time to repair it. It is not possible to supervise the work of a large number of boys spinning at the wheel. On the other hand, the *takli* is incredibly cheap. It can be worked by thousands at a time. It can be handled even in a crowded room requiring practically no space for its accommodation. It rarely goes out of order and when it does, it can be instantaneously replaced. *Takli*-spinning can be supervised no matter how many pupils engage in the operation. The quantitative result of mass spinning on the *takli* is on the whole more satisfactory than on the wheel. But having said all this in praise of the *takli*, needless to say I can have no objection to any school taking up the wheel in preference to the *takli* if it can overcome the objections mentioned by me.

Young India, 11-11-1926

[1] Not reproduced here. The correspondent had argued, giving figures about the progress in spinning on the charkha by boys of the national school at Malikanda, Dacca, that it could not be said that *takli* was always to be preferred to the charkha in schools. That could be done only in the case of the younger boys who could not ply the charkha.

15. NOTES

KHADDAR AND GOVERNMENT SERVANTS

A correspondent says:

> Some of the Government servants are terribly afraid to purchase hand-spun and hand-woven cloth when our hawkers approach them. They are under the impression that they should not purchase khaddar, yet the Bombay Government is openly appealing to the people to encourage Indian industries. Can you say whether the Madras Government servants are allowed to purchase hand-spun and hand-woven cloth without fear of the Government?

I wish I could answer the question. But I have not the power. It is however inconceivable to me that any Government should proscribe the use of hand-spun and hand-woven cloth. It is possible to conceive the insistence on a form of dress, but certainly not the kind of cloth to be used. It is painful to find that there are Government servants who labour under imaginary fears. I have seen many Government servants making free use of khaddar without let or hindrance. If I was a servant of the Madras Government, I should unhesitatingly wear khaddar unless there was positive prohibition to the contrary in which case I should resign.

KHADI WORK AND VOLUNTEERS

Dr. Hardiker has sent me the programme of the work to be done by the Karnatak Branch of the Hindustani Seva Dal. I take the following from the copy before me:

> The organizers and workers of the Karnatak Branch of the Hindustani Seva Dal met at the Dal Office, Hubli, on the 13th, 14th and 15th October, 1926, with Mr. Hoskoppa Krishnarao in the chair and after full discussion passed the following resolutions regarding the future programme of work to be undertaken by them:
>
> *Resolution* 1: This meeting of the organizers and workers of the Karnatak Dal resolves that they should concentrate their attention on the following programme:
>
> (a) To sell khaddar worth Rs. 40,000 (forty thousand) in Karnatak within seventy-two appointed days beginning from the 1st of February 1927 to the 13th midnight of April 1927 (including the National Week), under a scheme to be settled finally by Dr. Hardiker and Mr.

Hoskoppa Krishnarao, in consultation with Mahatma Gandhi, Sjts. G. B. Deshpande and S. V. Kowjalgi.

Note: The commencement of work under this item has to be postponed to 1st February, 1927, in view of the Assam Congress necessitating the Dal's concentrated activities at Gauhati during the preceding period commencing from the middle of November.

This is a good khadi programme. The Dal will have done well if it is carried out. Let me point out from my own experience and that of co-workers that khadi work will not flourish unless the principal workers know the science of ginning, carding, spinning and can distinguish between the different varieties of cotton and know genuine khadi from the spurious article. Khadi work to succeed evokes all the best that is in one. I shall watch the progress of the programme with considerable interest. There was another resolution passed by the Dal inviting me to visit the Province next year during the sale days. I should not give much credit to the volunteers if they expect to sell only 40,000 worth of khaddar with me as one of the sellers. The members should know that I put a fairly high price on my presence. They will have to put before me a more attractive programme than they have prepared if they are to draw me. And they must know that I am but one bride with many suitors to please. And as I do not believe in polyandry, the winner will have to offer a tempting dowry. It would be well for them therefore not to build any hope on my going to Karnatak early next year.

Khadi amongst Non-Brahmins

A correspondent writes:

> You will be glad to learn that the non-Brahmins of Nipani are taking a keen interest in khadi. It is the one platform on which Brahmins and non-Brahmins are uniting. There was a large meeting on the 23rd of October. It was a good meeting. Mr. Rawan was present at the meeting and he gave his whole-hearted support to khadi although he said that he continued to abide by the non-Brahmin party's programme of work. A khadi bhandar was opened at Nipani. This was chiefly due to the exertion of Sheth Mulji Sicca of Cutch. He has promised to sell khaddar at cost price. The non-Brahmin friends seem to be convinced that the question of growing poverty of the masses, which term includes non-Brahmins, cannot be solved without the universal use of khadi. The Nipani leaders therefore feel that it is not enough to be hostile to khadi but it is necessary to encourage khadi by all available means.

I congratulate the non-Brahmin friends of Nipani upon their decision, and hope that they will organize khadi work so as to place it on a stable basis.

SPINNING IN SCHOOLS

The following report about the progress of spinning in the schools under Guntur Municipality will be read with interest:

> The number of schools is 35.
>
> Girls' schools 9 and boys' schools 26. There are 454 girls and 363 boys. The number of girls spinning is 70 and that of boys 60. 15 charkhas are supplied to the boys' schools and 17 to the girls' schools. During the year the boys have spun 24,000 yds. and the girls 26,000 yds. The boys' yarn weighs 118 *tolas* and the girls' yarn 130 *tolas*. The Municipality purchased 3 maunds of slivers for Rs. 46-8-0. The yarn is in the Municipal office. About 100 of the pupils wear khadi. The number of all the teachers is 87. Out of them 30 are women and 57 are men. Almost all wear khadi. 63 give yarn to the A.I.S.A. One is also a Congress member under the yarn subscription rule.
>
> Rs. 500 worth of khadi was purchased.
>
> Spinning is taught in 10 schools at present. Hindi was being taught in 10 schools but was discontinued owing to an adverse resolution of the Municipal Council.
>
> Khadi is being freely distributed to *Panchama* boys and poor boys. Caste teachers are working in *Panchama* schools and *Panchama* teachers are teaching in schools where high-caste Hindus are studying.
>
> Holidays are being granted on the occasion of the birthday or anniversary of the national heroes.
>
> All teachers are able to spin. Their yarn is in the Municipal office. A charkha has been supplied to every teacher. About two maunds of slivers are used by the teachers.
>
> The other employees of the Municipality are about 100 and almost all of them wear khadi.

SPINNING DURING THE WAR

A Mombasa correspondent sends the following extracts from *My Reminiscences of East Africa* by General Von Kettow-Vorbeck, showing the possibilities of spinning under stress:

> Notwithstanding the great amount of booty taken at Tanga, it was evident that, as the war seemed likely to be prolonged, the stocks in the Colony would become exhausted. The natives at New Moschi began all of a sudden to wear silk; this was by no means a sign of special extravagance; the stocks of cotton clothing in the Indian shops were simply

coming to an end. We had seriously to think of starting manufactures ourselves, in order to convert the abundant raw material into finished products. A curious existence now developed, reminding one of the industry of the Swiss family Robinson. Cotton fields existed in plenty. Popular books were hunted up, giving information about the forgotten arts of hand-spinning and weaving; white and black women took to spinning by hand; at the missions and in private workshops spinning-wheels and looms were built. In this manner, in a short time, the first useful piece of cotton cloth was produced. After various trials, the most suitable dye was obtained from the root of a tree called Ndaa, which imparted a brownish-yellow colour, very inconspicuous both in the grass and in the bush, and therefore, specially suitable for uniforms.

Would that we considered India to be in a state of war and refrained from using foreign cloth and even Indian mill-made cloth. All argument against the possibility of hand-spinning will then vanish like smoke. And are we not in a state worse than war when we have proof positive that millions of the inhabitants of India are living in semi-starvation?

"ALL FOR THEE"

A kind Tamil friend sends me for my day of silence quotations that do one's soul good to read. I do not give in *Young India* quotations except when there is an association about them and when they are relevant. In the collection the friend has sent me I find the following very appropriate verses from George Herbert:

Teach me, my God and King,
    In all things Thee to see,
And what I do in anything,
    To do it as for Thee.

A servant with this clause
    Makes drudgerie divine;
Who sweeps a room as for Thy laws,
    Makes that and the action fine.[1]

I give one more equally appropriate. It is from Ruskin:

When we build, let it be such a work as our descendants will thank us for; and let us think, as we lay stone on stone, that a time is to come when stones will be held sacred because our hands have touched them, and that men will say as they look upon them: See! this our fathers did for us.

[1] This is not, however, the first time Gandhiji had come across these lines. He commended them to Esther Faering in a letter on March 17, 1920. *Vide* Vol. XVII.

Public life would be much purer than it is if we would do everything in the name of the King of kings and not for self but for posterity.

Young India, 11-11-1926

16. A CORRECTION

It gives me great pleasure to be able to publish this correction.[1] The notes in question were prepared, as I have already stated, first by one co-worker and then recast by another. They had to be done in a hurry. Needless to say, none of the writers had the slightest intention of comparing the two institutions. The object was merely to show the steady reduction in khaddar prices. The correction made by Satis Babu is welcome and enforces the argument advanced by the writers who had to depend upon the figures they could then lay hands upon. I am glad too to be able to give the readers the corrected and increased sales of the Pratishthan.

Young India, 11-11-1926

17. LETTER TO DR. K. K. KURUVILLA

SABARMATI,
November 11, 1926

DEAR FRIEND,

I have your letter. I do remember the correspondence with Dr. Paret. In my opinion, his course is clear. He must persist in picketing in spite of the notice. If he has the backing of public opinion, he will be able to do the picketing. If he has not, he will have to go to jail. And his imprisonment must ultimately bring success. But before taking the step, he should

[1] Not reproduced here. This came from Satis Chandra Das Gupta and pointed out in a letter of November 2, 1926, in the light of figures, the unfairness of the comparison of the Khadi Pratishthan with the Abhoy Ashram, made in the article "Charkha as the Only Cottage Industry" in *Young India*, 28-10-1926.

cultivate public opinion and make it clear to the Government that he has no intention of resorting to violent picketing.

Yours sincerely,
M. K. GANDHI

DR. K. K. KURUVILLA
MARTHOUSE SEMINARY
KOTTAYAM

From a microfilm: S.N. 19732

18. LETTER TO SATIS CHANDRA DAS GUPTA

November 12, 1926

DEAR SATIS BABU,

I feel your pangs from this long distance and, therefore, dread to write to you and still more to ask you to do anything outside your beat.

But the work I am asking you to do may be a little welcome diversion. Do go to Capt. Petaval's Institute in Bagbazar silently and see what it is. Is there anything in it? He is most insistent and wants me to advertise his movement. I have no faith in it or him.[1] Lest I may be doing him an injustice, I want you to guide me. You will see that now he has Dr. Ray with him.

You must come out of the Slough of Despond and be joyful even though everything may seemingly go wrong. You saw the liberty I took with your letter about the prices.[2]

How is Hemprabha Devi doing? She must write to me at least once a fortnight. Has malaria abated in your colony?

Can you attend on 23rd?

With love,

Yours,
BAPU

From a photostat: G.N. 1563

[1] *Vide* "Letter to J. W. Petaval", 12-11-1926.
[2] *Vide* the footnote to "A Correction", 11-11-1926.

19. LETTER TO C. VIJAYARAGHAVACHARIAR

[*November 12, 1926*][1]

DEAR FRIEND,

Your welcome letter. I cannot plead guilty to the charge that I am partial to the North and indifferent to the South. I do not know that I shall have much to say about the Congress deliberations, even if I go there. I shall want to occupy the position I did in 1915-18, my work being confined to my special subjects. Somehow or other, the councils do not interest me. And what is going on makes me sad.

How are you keeping?

Yours sincerely,

C. VIJAYARAGHAVACHARIAR
ARAMA
SALEM

From a photostat: S.N. 19730

20. LETTER TO H. B. TEJUMAL

[*November 12, 1926*][2]

DEAR FRIEND,

To quote from scriptures will not help you. Draupadi's prayer is a celebrated instance. If one has faith in one's prayer, I have not a shadow of a doubt in my mind that it can move mountains. Faith and proof are contradictory acts. Hence illustrations are of little avail. The only thing is to pray whether one gets an answer to one's prayer or not. Prayer should never be directed to a selfish object.

Yours sincerely,

SJT. H. B. TEJUMAL
MEDICAL PRACTITIONER
NEW SUKKUR
SIND

From a photostat: S.N. 19731

[1] From the addressee's letter dated November 17, 1926 (S.N. 12083).
[2] Based on the S.N. register

21. LETTER TO J. W. PETAVAL

SABARMATI,
November 12, 1926

DEAR FRIEND,

I am thankful for your persistence. Please continue. Some day I shall understand you and your scheme better. You are getting, on your spinning, enough help. Pray, therefore, let me watch your activity in silence. Some day I must visit your institution in person.

Yours sincerely,

CAPTAIN PETAVAL
POLYTECHNIC INSTITUTE
BAGBAZAR
CALCUTTA

From a microfilm: S.N. 19733

22. LETTER TO GIRI RAJ KISHORE

November 12, 1926

DEAR FRIEND,

I have your letter. You may come. But I warn you again. I may simply give you a corner in my verandah for your abode. There may be no intellectual work for you at all and there may be all labour including, of course, sanitation work, water carrying, etc. You may be put on spinning or the like for eight hours per day.

You may be called upon to do your own cooking and, in no case, should your expense exceed Rs. 15 per month. Several here do it for less than Rs. 10.

If this attracts you, you will be happy here, not otherwise.

Yours sincerely,

GIRI RAJ KISHORE
ROHTAK

From a microfilm: S.N. 19734

23. LETTER TO MURLI PRASAD AMBARTHA

November 12, 1926

DEAR FRIEND,

Khaddar is advocated not for the ruin of Manchester but for the uplift of the masses.

Mills can give employment only to a few lacs. Millions of people in partial unemployment must have an industry brought to them. The wheel is the only such industry. The question of cost cannot be allowed to affect an industry which is a vital need. Dear khaddar is therefore economically cheaper than cheap khaddar. It is possible to clothe India through khaddar in a year's time. It is impossible to do so through mills. The latter cannot do it under 20 years at least.

Yours sincerely,

SJT. MURLI PRASAD AMBARTHA
C/O B. GOKUL PRASAD
VAKIL
MORADPORE P.O.
PATNA

From a microfilm: S.N. 19735

24. LETTER TO IDA MILLER

November 12, 1926

DEAR FRIEND,

I have your letter. M. Roniger will, I think, be translating *The Story of My Experiments with Truth.*

Yours sincerely,

FR. IDA MILLER
XIII BAUMGARTENSTRASSE, 53
VIENNA

From a photostat: S.N. 19736

25. LETTER TO MULCHAND AGRAWAL

Kartika Sud 7, 1983 [*November 12, 1926*]

BHAISHRI MULCHANDJI,

I have your letter. I have respect for traditional ceremonies but as place, time and circumstances change, so does the nature of traditions. I am neutral as regards the thread and other ceremonies.

I believe in *varnashrama* but these days both [*varna* and *ashrama*] seem to have vanished. We have all become Sudras. There were never five *varnas*.

The process of spinning is merely a *yajna* and open to all; but one who performs it for the sake of livelihood is a Vaisya. From the point of view of vocation it is a teacher, only if he works without wages is he a Brahmin.

Yours,

MOHANDAS GANDHI

From a photostat of the Hindi: G.N. 764

26. LETTER TO BEHRAMJI KHAMBHATTA

Friday [*November 12, 1926*][1]

BHAISHRI KHAMBHATTA,

Chi. Devdas says that both of you wish to come and stay here with some of your friends but that you are feeling shy. There is no reason to feel so. Come without hesitation whenever you wish to. There will be some congestion, but I shall put you up somewhere. Your health, I hope, is excellent. We shall discuss Mr. Eddy's book when you come. I have already given some thought to it.

Blessings from

BAPU

BHAI BEHRAMJI KHAMBHATTA
275 HORNBY ROAD
FORT, BOMBAY

From a photostat of the Gujarati: G.N. 6587

[1] The postmark bears the date 13-11-1926. Friday fell on November 12.

27. LETTER TO SRI PRAKASA

[*November 13, 1926*][1]

DEAR FRIEND,

I have your letter. The dogs you refer to I do not regard as a nuisance though even in their case I would make their life less precarious than it is. But there are dogs in a city like Ahmedabad who are a danger to society, who are ill cared for and who are not wanted. If they cannot be cared for or otherwise kept as we would be kept, they should be killed rather than that they should be specimens of living death.

I hope to deal with the khaddar question in *Y.I.*

Yours sincerely

SRI PRAKASA
SEVASHRAMA
BENARES CANTONMENT

From a microfilm: S.N. 19729

28. LETTER TO VASUMATI PANDIT

Saturday [*November 13, 1926*][2]

CHI. VASUMATI,

I have your two letters. I have no worry if you keep well. I can bear your coming here sooner or later. I cannot bear it if your health breaks down. You must certainly be acquainted with Vikram, Indravadan's brother. He wishes to stay in the Ashram. What have you to say about this?

Devdas was here for a day and then he left for Panchgani.

Blessings from
BAPU

CHI. VASUMATI DHIMATRAM
C/o AMBALAL MATHURADAS
PALIAD-VEDA
P.O. DANGARVA

From the Gujarati original: C.W. 472. Courtesy: Vasumati Pandit; also S.N. 9220

[1] Based on the S.N. register
[2] From the postmark

29. *LETTER TO TULSI MAHER*

Saturday, Kartika Sud 8, 1983 [*November 13, 1926*]

CHI. TULSI MAHER,

I got your letters. I read some of them to the Ashramites. The dream was good. I cannot tell you more than what you heard in it. It would be enough if that much is accomplished. Hope your health is good. Are there cows and buffaloes in Nepal? The paper on which you have written is hand-made. Is it made there or is it imported? What is the price? Bhansali's forty days of fast will be over on Monday. His health is excellent.

Blessings from
BAPU

From a photostat of the Hindi: G.N. 6528

30. *IS THIS HUMANITY?–VI*

[*November 14, 1926*]

A friend has sent a long letter containing a number of questions and raising a number of difficulties. He has also sent me his copies of *Navajivan* with profuse marginal notes on this series of articles. Some of his questions have been already answered in these pages. Without reproducing here the rest of his questions, I propose merely to give my answers.

I think I have been considering the whole question quite dispassionately. I do not think I could be accused of any partiality for *himsa* or for my own peculiar views in the matter. My partiality is all for truth which I seek to find out through ahimsa. It is my conviction that it cannot be found out in any other way. The question in dispute for me is not whether truth is our goal or not, nor whether ahimsa is or is not the only way to it. There is no possibility of my ever doubting these fundamental principles. The question before me is about the practice of these principles. Every day I see fresh aspects opening out to me. There is every possibility of my making mistakes in the practice of ahimsa and, though I am taking every precaution possible to avoid them, it is possible that I may err occasionally. Let not friends, therefore, impute partiality to me when I cannot agree with them. Let them believe me to be unconsciously in error and bear with me. I now proceed to give the answers.

1. The question to solve is not what is hydrophobia and how to treat it.

2. The municipality or the Government will find a remedy not in accordance with ahimsa but with what they conceive to be public interest. The Mahajan can find the right remedy if they are truly non-violent. Government will never subscribe to the absolute principle of non-destruction of animals (dogs in the present case). Municipalities have members belonging to different faiths and different communities. They cannot, therefore, be expected to insist on a non-violent remedy.

3. The duty of finding a non-violent remedy is the Mahajan's. It is a mistake to think that the Mahajan is blameless or helpless.

4. For the purpose of the discussion, I make no distinction between a rabid dog and a man who has run amuck and is in the act of dealing death. Habitual violence is a disease. The habitually violent man goes on in his murderous career only because he is beside himself. Both a rabid dog and a rabid man are worthy of pity. When they are found in the act of injuring others, and when there is no other remedy than to take their life, it becomes a duty to do so to arrest their activity. The duty is all the greater in case of a votary of ahimsa.

5. I have never meant that everyone should own a dog. What I have said is that the dogs should in no case be ownerless. Not that the owned dogs will be immune, but the owners will be responsible for them if they are diseased or get rabies.

6. The ownerless stray dogs are not innocent as lambs. They were never so. Owned dogs are generally so. The purpose of the present controversy is to make all the dogs innocuous.

7. I have never suggested that roving dogs should be killed wherever found. I have suggested enabling legislation in the interest of the dogs themselves. That will make humanly inclined people alive to their sense of duty and they will then either own dogs or find out some other remedy and thus make the existence of stray dogs impossible. In refusing alms to the beggar, the purpose is not to starve him, but to teach him self-help, to make him a man. The duty of killing dogs arises in the circumstances and to the extent I have indicated in the previous articles. To say that it is a sin to extirpate dogs is not to contradict me. For I have never expressed a contrary opinion.

8. It is idle to discuss whether Mr. Ambalal's conduct was or was not proper, or whether my opinion about it was or was

not correct. The public is not in full possession of the details of the incident. The broader question of ahimsa is the main issue, and to bring in Mr. Ambalal in the discussion is to cloud the issue.

9. The issue is: Whether, in consonance with the principle of ahimsa, it may be a duty to kill certain dogs under certain circumstances when no other alternative is possible. I submit that it may be and I hold that there cannot be two opinions in the matter. There may be a difference as to whether particular circumstances justify the act. The consolation for a votary of ahimsa lies in the fact that, from his standpoint, such circumstances can only be rare.

10. But I can see one difference of opinion that must for the time being remain. In the letter under consideration as also in many others, I see that there is an instinctive horror of killing living beings under any circumstances whatsoever. For instance, an alternative has been suggested in the shape of confining even rabid dogs in a certain place and allowing them to die a slow death. Now, my idea of compassion makes this thing impossible for me. I cannot for a moment bear to see a dog, or for that matter any other living being, helplessly suffering the torture of a slow death. I do not kill a human being thus circumstanced because I have more hopeful remedies. I should kill a dog similarly situated, because in its case I am without a remedy. Should my child be attacked by rabies and there was no hopeful remedy to relieve his agony, I should consider it my duty to take his life. Fatalism has its limits. We leave things to Fate after exhausting all the remedies. One of the remedies, and the final one to relieve the agony of a tortured child, is to take his life.

But I shall not labour this point. What to my mind is impotence of the votaries of ahimsa is an obstacle to a true understanding of this dharma. I hope therefore that those who differ from me will for the present bear with me.

So much about the thoughtful letter of a friend. I shall now deal with an angry letter. The letter says:

> You have been so much under the Western influence that you have learnt to think it proper to kill lower beings for the sake of man. It is better for you to confess your error and apologize to the world. You should have made up your mind in this matter after exhaustless [*sic*] sifting. Instead, you have passionately taken sides and discredited yourself.

This is the least offensive sentence I have picked up from letters of this type. I submit I have not formed my opinion without much deliberation. It is not an opinion I have recently formed. Neither is it hasty. One should not let one's so-called greatness come in the way of the formation of opinion, otherwise one cannot arrive at truth.

I do not think that everything Western is to be rejected. I have condemned the Western civilization in no measured terms. I still do so, but it does not mean that everything Western should be rejected. I have learnt a great deal from the West and I am grateful to it. I should think myself unfortunate if contact with and the literature of the West had no influence on me. But I do not think I owe my opinion about the dogs to my Western education or Western influence. The West (with the exception of a small school of thought) thinks that it is no sin to kill the lower animals for what it regards to be the benefit of man. It has, therefore, encouraged vivisection. The West does not think it wrong to commit violence of all kinds for the satisfaction of the palate. I do not subscribe to these views. According to the Western standard, it is no sin, on the contrary it is a merit, to kill animals that are no longer useful. Whereas I recognize limits at every step. I regard even the destruction of vegetable life as *himsa*. It is not the teaching of the West.

Argumentum ad hominem has no place in a discussion of principles and their practice. My opinions should be considered as they are, irrespective of whether they are derived from the West or the East. Whether they are based on truth or untruth, *himsa* or ahimsa, is the only thing to be considered. I firmly believe that they are based on truth and ahimsa.

Young India, 18-11-1926

31. *VAUTHA FAIR*

Fairs are held all over our country. At some place or other annual fairs are held. All sorts of people come to these fairs from nearby places. For the big fairs people come from every part of India.

Such a fair is held every *Kartiki Purnima* at Vautha in Dholka taluka. On behalf of the District Congress Committee, Shri Dahyabhai has been rendering service there, with the help of a small band of volunteers, for the last several years. This year, too, he has published an appeal for volunteers. Last year and the year before I had intended to attend this fair but could not. This year, too, to my great regret, I am not able to go. But

I recommend that those who wish to do social service should go there. Even in the fairs organized for religious purposes, evil practices have grown rampant. Cheats go to such fairs and deceive simple people. Many kinds of immorality are practised there and gambling and other vices encouraged. Volunteers can definitely effect some reform by going there. I hope that those who can spare some days will go there and render all possible services.

[From Gujarati]

Navajivan, 14-11-1926

32. LETTER TO GERTRUDE GROGAN

November 14, 1926

DEAR FRIEND,

I like your earnest letter.[1] When, if ever, God wants me to go to America, He will open the way for me and guide my steps.

Yours sincerely,

MISS GERTRUDE GROGAN
BARNARD COLLEGE
NEW YORK

From a photostat: S.N. 19737

33. LETTER TO RAMESHWARDAS PODDAR

Kartika Shukla 9, 1983 [November 14, 1926]

BHAI RAMESHWARJI,

We have no other way but Ramanama. Chant Ramanama and never be disheartened.

Yours,
MOHANDAS

From a photostat of the Hindi: G.N. 188

[1] On October 15, 1926, the correspondent had written of America's need of spiritual guidance and added: "It takes a man of your great insight to furnish it. For the sake of those in America who feel a need for you, come, oh Mahatma, and you will be assured of a sincere welcome" (S.N. 10830).

34. *LETTER TO FEROZE*

November 15, 1926

DEAR FRIEND,

Your letter. There is no royal road to the control of passions. Constant endeavour and constant waiting upon God are the two things needed.

Yours sincerely,

FEROZE
V. CHAKWANO
P.O. PHALIA
(GUJRAT DISTRICT)
PUNJAB

From a microfilm: S.N. 19738

35. *LETTER TO FELIX VALYE*

November 15, 1926

DEAR FRIEND,

Mr. Pickthall[1] asks me for an article or a message for your magazine. I have not a moment to spare for writing an article. What message shall I send you save to say that my nationalism is intense internationalism ? I am sick of the strife between nations or religions.

Yours sincerely,

DR. FELIX VALYE
HOTEL RICHMOND
GENEVA

From a photostat: S.N. 19739

[1] Marmaduke Pickthall, sometime editor of *The Bombay Chronicle*

36. LETTER TO JAMNALAL BAJAJ

Monday [*November 15, 1926*][1]

CHI. JAMNALAL,

I get your letters regularly. Kamala is well and happy now.

There is no need to come specially to attend the meeting of the Charkha Sangh. I hope you are having rest there. If you are not, you should run away to some other place.

Read the wires. I found all the replies satisfactory.

Bhansali's fast of forty days will end today. He will break his fast tomorrow morning. His strength has been very well maintained. He has not taken any service from anyone.

I hope to start from here on the 2nd December.[2] Who will accompany me has not yet been decided.

Devdas has gone to Panchgani because of Mathuradas. Pyarelal had to go to the Punjab because of his sister.

It was necessary for Soniramji to undergo an operation and his mother and others were not willing to have the operation done anywhere except in Rangoon.

Champabehn is here. She has not been entrusted with any responsibilities.

Blessings from
BAPU

From a photostat of the Gujarati: G.N. 2877

37. LETTER TO LALAN PANDIT

THE ASHRAM,
November 15, 1926

BHAISHRI LALAN,

I am not aware of any violence in my language. Calling a hypocrite a hypocrite is no violence but perhaps there is violence in not calling him so. What would we call a serpent? If my son is worthless and if I describe him using good epithets, I would be

[1] From the reference in the letter to Bhansali's fast, it is clear that it was written on the Monday following November 13, 1926; *vide* "Letter to Tulsi Maher", 13-11-1926.

[2] To go to Wardha; Gandhiji reached there on December 4.

guilty of untruth, and in my humble opinion untruth in any form is violence. In calling a worthless person worthless there is no violence, but unedifying behaviour on our part towards him is violence. I do not read the *Bombay Samachar*.

Vandemataram from
MOHANDAS

BHAI LALAN PANDIT
C/o SHETH CHHOTALAL MALUKCHAND
HATHIBHAINI BAHARNI VADI
AHMEDABAD

From a microfilm of the Gujarati: S.N. 19962

38. LETTER TO DEVCHAND PAREKH

[*November 15, 1926*][1]

BHAISHRI DEVCHAND,

It is good that Bhai Fulchand[2] took pity on you. But I can't afford to do so. Who can do the copying for me? Therefore you have to read my handwriting.

I received your letter only today, therefore I have sent a telegram to Porbandar saying that the March dates would suit me.

We cannot drag Malaviyaji [to the conference][3]. Besides, what will he speak in the Khaddar Conference ?[4] I prefer Jaisukhlal Mehta or Vallabhbhai Patel. It is worthwhile if men are drawn through interest in work. What can they do if they come only because of big names.

These are my personal views only. What you all decide is to be accepted as the right thing.

I shall definitely start from here on the 2nd December.

When I shall return is in God's hand. It should not be surprising if I return only at the time of the Conference. So take from me in the current month whatever work you wish me to do.

[1] From the postmark

[2] Fulchand Kasturchand Shah

[3] For holding the session of the Kathiawar Political Conference

[4] This was to be held along with the Kathiawar Political Conference at the same place; *vide* Vol. XXXI, p. 532.

Tell Bhai Fulchand that his letter will be discussed when he comes here.

BAPU

[PS.]

I am returning the letter in English.

From a photostat of the Gujarati: G.N. 5721

39. TELEGRAM TO MADHOJEE, MANDAL MANTRI, NIMKHAR[1]

[On or after *November 15, 1926*]

I MUST NOT INTERFERE.

GANDHI

From the original: C.W. 4964 b. Courtesy: Parasram Mehrotra

40. INTRODUCTION TO "HAND-SPINNING AND HAND-WEAVING"

SABARMATI,
November 16, 1926

It will be remembered that early last year Sjt. Revashanker Jagjivan Mehta, the Joint Treasurer of the National Congress, announced a prize of Rs. 1,000 for the best essay on spinning. The judges appointed were Sjts. Ambalal Sarabhai, Shankerlal Banker, Maganlal Gandhi and myself. Sixty other essays were received. After much deliberation, the judges decided to distribute the prize between Professor S. V. Puntambekar, at present of the Benares Hindu University, and Sjt. N. S. Varadachari. The essay that is now being presented to the public is the result of the joint effort of these two winners who were requested to amalgamate their essays and give a joint production. It is difficult to say how far the effort is an improvement upon the originals. But workers in the vast field of hand-spinning will find ample material in the following pages to strengthen their position and I should be much surprised if the sceptic does not find enough food for reflection.

The authors have applied themselves to an examination principally of the following propositions:

[1] This was sent in reply to a telegram dated November 15 reading: "Kindly wire whom you prefer Birla or Sriprakasa. Congress work suffering."

Are there millions in India who require a supplementary occupation, the majority being idle for want of it during at least four months in the year? Is hand-spinning the only supplementary occupation and, if it is, can it be easily taken up by the people? Is it possible to sell khaddar woven from hand-spun yarn among the people in the teeth of the competition offered by foreign and Indian mills?

The readers will find that the authors have endeavoured to give an affirmative answer to all these important questions. Is it not the duty of everyone who wants to see an amelioration in the condition of India's masses carefully to read what the authors have stated and to support the khaddar movement if they accept their conclusions? Let them denounce it as a waste of effort, if they can dare controvert the facts adduced by the authors.

M. K. GANDHI

Hand-spinning and Hand-weaving

41. LETTER TO N. S. VARADACHARI

THE ASHRAM,
SABARMATI,
November 16, 1926

MY DEAR VARADACHARI,

Here is the preface[1]. It should be quite in time. If you have to suggest any improvement, do not hesitate to make the suggestion. You may write your own preface and call it foreword or call this foreword and call yours a preface if you like writing one. You will see that the essay is free from error.

Yours sincerely,

From a copy: S.N. 11246

[1] *Vide* the preceding item.

42. *LETTER TO KANAK CHANDRA SHARMA*[1]

[*November 16, 1926*]

I have your letter and the piece of khaddar.

KANAK CHANDRA SHARMA
[SECRETARY AND ACCOUNTANT
A. I. S. A.
NAVGONG
ASSAM]

From a microfilm: S.N. 11247

43. *LETTER TO BRIJKRISHNA CHANDIWALA*

Kartika Sud 11 [*November 16, 1926*][2]

BHAI BRIJKRISHNA,

It was only due to lack of time that I could not reply to your letter earlier. Do come when you feel like coming and go whenever you wish. I want to offer you whatever consolation I can.

Devdas came here and went off to Panchgani.

Blessings from
BAPU

From a photostat of the Hindi: G.N. 2351

44. *LETTER TO MUNNALAL G. SHAH*

Kartika Sud 11 [*November 16, 1926*][3]

BHAISHRI MUNNALAL,

I have your letter. One who tries to observe *brahmacharya*, truth, non-violence, non-thieving and non-possession, who believes that untouchability is sinful, who labours without feeling any fatigue, who thinks it is his dharma to clean latrines, who controls

[1] The reply is scribbled on an undated letter reporting the position of khaddar production work in Navgong district and making suggestions for improved cotton cultivation.

[2] Devdas went to Panchgani in 1926. *Kartika Sud* 11 fell on November 16.

[3] The postmark bears the date 18-11-1926. *Kartika Sud* 11, however, fell on November 16.

the palate and spins and cards daily and wears pure khadi, only such a person may stay in the Ashram.

Vandemataram from
MOHANDAS

SHRI MUNNALAL GANGADAS SHAH
BURHANPUR

From a microfilm of the Gujarati: S.N. 19964

45. FLOWERS FROM THE POET'S GARDEN

Mrs. Blair—daughter of the late W. C. Bonnerjee—sends me the following translation made specially for her by Mrs. Pramatha Chaudhuri, the Poet's niece. Mrs. Blair says:

> She wrote them out for me in Bengali as I wanted a helpful saying for everyday reference such as one can get in English. She selected these quotations from addresses given by the Poet from time to time at Santiniketan. The addresses were written down at the time the Poet gave them, but I do not think they have been printed. I liked the quotations so much that I got them put into English.

I am sure the readers of *Young India* will like to treasure these flowers from the Poet's garden.

> The centi-petalled lotus of Love, depending on the stalk of Self, gradually unfolds itself petal by petal from the self to the family, from the family to society, from society to one's country, from one's country to humanity, from humanity to the Universal Spirit, from the Universal Spirit to the Supreme Spirit, thereby accomplishing its process of evolution.
>
> He whose intellect cannot perceive law and order in the working of the universe is incapable, ineffectual and defeated in every department of life.
>
> They who succeed in the field of material power do so by aggrandizing themselves, whereas they who succeed in the spiritual sphere do so by sacrificing themselves.
>
> Because when a man attempts to see the whole thing at once he sees it indistinctly, therefore he first breaks it up into parts, and then fits them all into a whole.
>
> In proportion as India lost mastery over Nature by giving over-emphasis to the spiritual side, so she is now required to pay the penalty for it.
>
> The work that we do from necessity or want, that work is our bondage; but the work that we do out of joy is not bondage; that work is freedom.

We realize perfect joy in proportion as we are able to harmonize knowledge, love and work in ourselves.

He who desires to be master of the house must be stricter than all others in obeying the discipline and rules of the house.

When the mind is not prepared to receive ideas, then words do not reveal their full meaning to the irreverent listener.

Life's mission is a very difficult one, its field is very large, its laws are very difficult to understand, its activities are very various, its sacrifices are very hard to make.

The lamp cannot conceal its own light within itself.

As stagnant water is ever afraid of being polluted by dirt, so today captive India, through fear of pollution, continually raises forbidding walls in order to cut herself off from all connection with the outer and larger world, and keeps even sun and air at a distance.

It is only when we daily draw purity from the source of our character, that words and ideas come to our help.

Man has built up his life on three great planes, the material, the religious, and the spiritual.

We give the name of desire to that external force which attracts our efforts to things outside us.

As external things are the aim of desire, so are inward motives the aim of will.

In all this vast Universe, and throughout this great life of humanity, it is impossible that we should not acknowledge Him at all anywhere.

When the ties of desire are severed, then earth, sky and water, living creatures and inanimate objects, beasts and men,—all become filled with bliss, and there is no limit to joy.

That I have come and stood in the midst of this vast universe is a most wonderful event, there is nothing more momentous than it.

There is joy even in the endeavour after realization, let alone the state of fulfilment.

To what an incalculable extent do we waste our strength throughout the day in futile talk and in futile deeds?

It is only when we want to turn towards God that we are able to realize how strong is the attraction of this godless life that we have built up for ourselves.

As the final aim of every tree is to bring forth fruit, so the final aim of this world-tree is to bring forth the perfect man.

Dwelling in the midst of this world, God only gives of Himself; He takes nothing. And when our soul can partake of this nature of God, then will it attain Truth.

Young India, 18-11-1926

46. SPINNING AS DEATHBED CONSOLATION

Two versions have been published in *Young India* of the story in which the brave Buddhist wife asks her dying husband to dismiss all anxious worldly thoughts out of his mind and to die a peaceful death as she knows how to spin and will maintain the children as well as herself by that means, one in 1921 and the other during the current year. But they were either inaccurate or incomplete. Having since looked up the Pali original, I translate below the first, and part of the second paragraph in Section XVI, *Chakkampata* (*Saraniya-Vagga*) of the *Anguttara-Nikaya*, a canonical work of the Buddhists:

"The householder Nakulapita was dangerously ill and very much worried. Then Nakulamata, his wife, addressing him, said, 'You should not now give yourself to anxious thought even for a moment. It is very painful that a person should die with anxious thoughts weighing upon his mind, and the Lord Buddha has censured such a kind of death. Perhaps you are afraid that when you are no longer with us, I shall not be able to feed the children and maintain the household. But your fears are groundless, as I am skilful in spinning cotton and in dressing hair (This second expression is not quite clear to me. I wish some Pali scholar throws more light upon it. V. G. D.) and will, therefore, have no difficulty whatever in providing for children as well as myself when you are away. Therefore please dismiss all disturbing thoughts out of your mind.

" 'Again perhaps you apprehend that when you are no more I might contract a second marriage. But you must drive away any such fear, seeing that we have for the last sixteen years lived a life of chastity though married, and maintaining a household. Please let your mind be at perfect peace.' "

V. G. D.

From this note I have removed the original text as I hardly think the readers of *Young India* want the original texts, Sanskrit or other. But I must not omit the following remark that V.G.D. made under the texts removed.

It is a great pity that all Pali texts are published in the Latin script although Fausboll of Copenhagen, the Danish editor of the *Jataka*, haughtily observes:

"I have continued to transliterate the Oriental into Latin characters and shall continue to do so in all I publish of Pali, for it is my conviction that the fine Latin characters must not only henceforward be applied to languages which have no literature and to literatures which have hitherto not been published, but also that they one day will supersede all other characters when Europeo-American civilization has, like a lava, laid itself over all other civilizations and made them into Herculaneums and Pompeiis." I wonder how the Buddhist patrons of the Pali Text Society enjoy the fine prospect pictured in the above.

Young India, 18-11-1926

47. *THE ARTS OF KINGS AND QUEENS*

A correspondent who has personal experience of the service that the spinning-wheel is rendering sends me the following from Ruskin's *Sesame and Lilies*:[1]

> Begin with the first—the lord of them all—agriculture. . . .
>
> Then, after agriculture, the art of kings, take the next head of human arts—weaving, the art of queens, honoured of all noble Heathen women, in the person of their virgin goddess—honoured of all Hebrew women, by the word of their priest king—'She layeth her hands to the spindle, and her hands hold the distaff; she stretcheth out her hand to the poor. She is not afraid of the snow for her household, for all her household are clothed with scarlet. She maketh herself covering of tapestry; her clothing is silk and purple. She maketh fine linen and selleth it, and delivereth girdles to the merchant.' What have we done in all these thousands of years with this bright art of Greek maid and Christian matron? Six thousand years of weaving and have we learnt to weave? Might not every naked wall have been purple with tapestry, and *every feeble breast fenced with sweet colours from the cold*? What have we done? *Our fingers are too few, it seems, to twist together some poor covering for our bodies.* We set our streams to work for us, and choke the air with fire, *to turn our spinning-wheels*—and are we clothed yet? Are not the streets of the capitals of Europe foul with the sale of cast clouts and rotten rags? Is not the beauty of your sweet children left in wretchedness of disgrace, while with better honour, nature clothes the brood of the bird in its nest, and the suckling of the wolf in her den? And does not every winter's snow robe what you have not robed, and shroud what you have not shrouded; and every winter's wind bear up to heaven its wasted souls, to witness against you hereafter, by the voice of their Christ: 'I was naked, and you clothed me not?'

and remarks

> Scathing indictment indeed, but how fervently he pleads for the spinning-wheel. If he could say this of an admittedly rich country like

[1] Only excerpts are reproduced here.

Europe, how much more should it be true of a country like India, proved beyond question to be poorer?

Young India, 18-11-1926

48. SOUTH AFRICAN SITUATION

Here are extracts from a letter from Mr. Andrews after his arrival in Durban:

> It is good to get here again, and though it has been a difficult time on the voyage, I am so thankful that I came on and did not delay longer. There are any amount of things here to be settled and other things to put straight before the delegation arrives, and it will take every moment of my time to get through.
>
> Today I have had the warmest possible welcome and Rawat's Bioscope was crowded this evening at the 'welcome'. I am staying with Sorabji at 19, 1st Avenue. The house at 110, Field Street, is all pulled down and the site sold to Europeans!
>
> The days have been crowded to the full and it is almost impossible to avoid it as I had expected. There was a very serious smallpox outbreak in the Indian quarters and every single smallpox case was that of an Indian. The mortality was as high as 25% and it was of a very virulent type. There were vicious letters in the Press abusing Indians for insanitary habits, etc. The one thing to do was what you did in Johannesburg and after getting vaccinated myself (without which I could have done nothing at all), I got the Medical Officer to let me visit the Indians who were kept in quarantine daily, and did everything I could to pacify them. Also we met and formed an Indian Health Committee and decided to work under the doctor's orders and he has already set us to work. At once, as soon as this was announced the whole tone of the Press changed and we have been praised where before we were being blamed. Altogether it is going to work out for the best.
>
> I have had time now to consider things fully and get hold of the situation. There is no doubt that if we can get the best public opinion on our side in the next few weeks, we shall get a good Press and materially help the Conference by creating a favourable atmosphere beforehand. It has been rather difficult to persuade them not to have a big demonstration just at the time of the Conference, thinking it would 'impress' them. I have been explaining to them that some good solid work [like] clearing out the dirt from insanitary quarters would 'impress' far more than all the demonstrations and speeches in the world.

> At the same time, the last thing I should wish is that things should go to the other extreme and get slack and lazy and indifferent. What is needed is to direct the excitement and energy into a right channel. I have consulted the best Europeans who are sympathetic and they all say that the hartal and Day of Prayer which we held about a year ago was extraordinarily impressive in the right sense of the word and no one felt it to be provocative. They felt that Indians were doing the right thing in their own way and doing it well.

The reference to the sale of the property in Field Street revives oldest memories. It was one of the oldest properties of which a long lease was purchased by the late Haji Aboobakr Amod,—one of the earliest Indian merchants to settle in South Africa. The property was sublet to the late Parsi Rustomjee who had possession of it till his death. It was more a public place than a private store—most informal Indian gatherings were held there. It was the place where the most important decisions were taken. It was there that Gokhale used to pass much of his day time. It was there that Andrews worked. It sheltered the rich and the poor. It had become a real dharmsala. On the expiry of the lease the Durban Town Council refused to renew the lease and advertised the property for sale subject to the prohibition of Indian bids. The Durban Town Council knew the (to the Indians) sacred character of the place, but the knowledge could not save the property from passing into European hands. Hence the reference to it by Mr. Andrews and the note of exclamation.

His presence there at this juncture is indeed a godsend. The unfortunate outbreak of smallpox might easily have created a panic both among Europeans and Indians. The former might have taken dangerously drastic measures and the latter might have become paralysed with fear. The prompt measures taken by Mr. Andrews averted what might have developed into a calamity.

That godly man's presence is likely to turn the scales in favour of the settlers. And though not much may be expected of the Conference, he is certainly creating the proper atmosphere for a calm and just consideration of the intricate problem.

Sir Mahomed Habibulla's deputation has a heavy responsibility on its shoulders. It has the solid backing of unanimous public opinion. Let us hope for the best.

Young India, 18-11-1926

49. *SPINNING IN MUNICIPALITIES*

It is only by accident that I get information about spinning in the schools under Municipalities and Local and District Boards. If the chairmen or secretaries of Municipalities and Local and District Boards who are in the habit of seeing *Young India* will kindly send the information about the introduction and progress of spinning in those schools, it will be possible to get accurate statistics about the output of yarn in such schools and the number of boys and girls spinning.

Young India, 18-11-1926

50. *CONDITIONS OF PACIFIC STRIKES*

A friend sends me an extract from *No More War*, an organ of the British Pacifists. I copy from the extract the following conditions Mr. A. Fenner Brockway lays down as a test of a pacific strike:

1. A strike in protest of social evils which destroy human life can be as much an act of pacifism as a strike against war. (Starvation wages kill as many human beings as are killed by guns.)
2. If it be said that "constitutional" means could be used to end these evils, the same can be said of war. Our "constitutional" machinery is inadequate. The voters two years ago had neither wage reductions nor war in mind.
3. If it be said that a strike (and particularly a general strike) against wage reductions is an effort to "coerce" the nation or the Government, the same can be said about a general strike against war. As a matter of fact, neither has any promise of success unless the greater part of the nation supports it.
4. It is not accurate to liken a strike to an economic blockade. So far as there is danger of hunger, it would be the strikers themselves who would suffer first. In actual fact, in the recent General Strike, the T.U.C. (Trade Union Congress) was prepared to co-operate in maintaining life and health. The Government refused co-operation.
5. *The determining factor as to whether a strike is pacifist or not* is the spirit from which it springs. A strike against war in which the motive was hatred of members of the Government rather than of war and which represented a spirit which might be transformed into civil war, would not be

> an act of pacifism, nor would a strike against wage reductions animated by hatred of the employers or of members of the Government, or by anti-social feeling. But both are acts of pacifism when inspired by the spirit of protest against the evils themselves.
>
> 6. Whilst it is admitted that a non-pacifist spirit occasionally showed itself in the utterances, and still more rarely in the acts of strikers, I have not the least hesitation in saying that the dominant motive in the Great Strike was that of self-sacrificing moral protest and not anti-social force or personal hatred. It was this which gave it spiritual power; in this the secret of the wonderful self-discipline of the men was to be found.
>
> A pacifism which can only see the cruelties of occasional military warfare and is blind to the continuous cruelties of our social system is worthless. Unless our pacifism finds expression in the broad human movement which is seeking not merely the end of war, but our equally non-pacifist civilization as a whole, it will be of little account in the onward march of mankind. The spirit of life will sweep on, quite uninfluenced by it.
>
> The No More War Movement will fulfil its purpose just in so far as it recognizes this.

I would only add to these admirable conditions one more test. A pacific strike must be limited to those who are labouring under the grievance to be redressed. Thus if the match manufacturers, say, of Timbuctoo, who are quite satisfied with their lot, strike out of sympathy for its millhands who are getting starvation wages, the match manufacturers' strike would be a species of violence. They may and should help in a most effective manner by withdrawing their custom from the millowners of Timbuctoo without laying themselves open to the charge of violence. But it is possible to conceive occasions when those who are not directly suffering may be under an obligation to cease work. Thus if, in the instance imagined, the masters in the match factory combine with the millowners of Timbuctoo, it will clearly be the duty of the workers in the match factory to make common cause with the mill-hands. But I have suggested the addition purely by way of illustration. In the last resort, every case has to be judged on its own merits. Violence is a subtle force. It is not easy always to detect its presence though you may feel it all the same.

Young India, 18-11-1926

51. NOTES

RAMACHANDRAN LIFT

Numerous letters have been received both by Mr. Ramachandran and me regarding the Ramachandran Animal Power Lift. Some ask to be supplied with the lift at once, others ask pertinent questions about it. Mr. Ramachandran has left all the letters with me. The lift is patented. The inventor has no lift ready to supply. He has to get it manufactured. He has not the means to attend to many orders with despatch. I am, therefore, trying to secure facilities for rapid manufacture. The inventor has proceeded to Madras to attend to his affairs and prepare to give his whole time to the supervision of manufacture and putting up the lift. I, therefore, urge the correspondents to be a little patient and await the necessary arrangements that must be made before a supply can be commenced. An endeavour is being made to nationalize the manufacture and to secure the lowest possible quotations for the lift.

Correspondents will forgive me for not replying individually to their letters. I deal below with some of the points raised by them:

1. If the arrangements that are pending go through, I hope to publish a diagram with the letterpress.

2. The parts are not at all complicated; on the contrary, the plan is incredibly simple. It is undoubtedly designed to answer village requirements.

3. Small lengths of rails, pulleys and wire ropes have to be supplied from cities.

4. The lift should last several years. The bucket and the rope may require more frequent replacement.

5. So far as I can see, an ordinary village blacksmith should be able to attend to such repairs as may become necessary.

6. The lift must be fixed by a skilled mechanic. The weights, the incline, etc., have to be adjusted. The rails must be truly laid. The pulley must be in its proper position. But I understand that a man with ordinary intelligence can be easily and quickly trained to fix the lift with its appurtenances. The mechanic will have to be paid his travelling expenses, etc. These details are now being attended to.

7. The most economical way is to use a heavy male buffalo, the heavier the animal, the larger the quantity of water it will carry without any exertion.

8. The empty trolley is carried up by the weight of the bucket.

9. The bucket is as a rule 40 lbs. in weight, the trolley 100 lbs.

10. The lift can be employed for any depth, even 125 ft., i.e., it is capable of being used wherever the ordinary *mhote* can be.

KHADI SALES

During the period of probation the problem of the sale of khadi is as great as, if not greater than, that of production. Hitherto, the sales have not kept pace with production. The best-managed province for sales is undoubtedly Bengal. The tone set by the Khadi Pratishthan,— the creation of Dr. Ray and his lieutenant Satis Chandra Das Gupta—has been kept up by the organizations that have grown up there. Bengal has also striven with considerable success to manufacture according to local needs. This is sound economy. The method has enabled the workers to come and keep in touch with the buying middle class at the one end and the manufacturing poor class at the other. The consequence is a steady improvement in texture, variety and pattern and in prices from the buyer's point of view. The remarkable fact about the growing cheapness of khadi is that generally the reduction in prices has not meant a corresponding reduction in wages of carders, spinners and weavers, but has been due to better knowledge and greater efficiency.

The latest instance of organized sales comes from Sylhet. Sjt. Dhirendranath Das Gupta has been managing only a small khadi centre at Kulaura near Sylhet. He reports that he sold during the Puja holidays only over Rs. 2,600 worth of khadi.

Though there is no doubt that in the other provinces, too, considerable improvement has been made as in Bengal, the sales have not been so methodically organized as there. Bihar is trying to come very near Bengal. But the workers all over the provinces should devise methods of stimulating sales. The experiences of Mr. Bharucha and other veterans should be pooled and schemes with variations suiting the various provinces should be devised and put into operation. Hawking and peripatetic exhibitions have come to stay. There is danger of all these schemes being top-heavy if the minutest details are not worked out. There are some stores in the different parts of India which from this standpoint should perhaps be closed. A store costing Rs. 500 per year and selling no more is one that is fit to be closed. There is gross mismanagement or ignorance about it.

The True Spirit

A correspondent writes:[1]

For me this correspondent is a member, in spirit, of both the organizations. Technically he will become a member by producing the yarn of his own spinning before a deputy of A.I.S.A. in his district, and sending the equivalent price of the yarn. For some, even to send that amount is not possible. They can then remain members in spirit and enroll themselves as volunteers sending a report of their work from time to time and holding themselves ready to do any service that may be required of them and that they may be capable of rendering.

Temperance Reform

For some time past some Christians of Travancore have been earnestly striving to put down the drink habit by working from within, i.e., by seeing and speaking to the people given to the habit. They are trying to organize picketing with the intention of warning the visitors to the liquor dens. The simple procedure seems to have frightened the Travancore authorities. The District Magistrate at Kottayam has served a gagging notice upon Dr. Z. M. Paret who is a well-known Christian in Travancore and, so far as I know, whose non-violent spirit has never been questioned. This is the notice:

> Whereas it has been made to appear to me from reports received from the District Superintendent of Police, Kottayam, that you are making speeches inciting people to do picketing before liquor shops and to commit other form of lawlessness and that speeches are likely to cause breaches of the peace and bring the authority of Government into contempt, I do hereby strictly order and enjoin you under Section 26 of the Regulation IV of 1905 not to make any speech, harangue or address from this day in any part of this District of Kottayam.

The notice begs the question by describing every speech advising picketing as an incitement. What the "other form of lawlessness" there can be is not made clear in the order. Thus in Travancore if the Magistrate's order correctly interprets its law, a premium is put upon the vice of drunkenness. Not only does a State provide facilities for drink but it also prevents reformers from resorting to

[1] The letter is not reproduced here; it stated the writer's difficulty, in view of his financial position, to pay subscriptions to the A.I.S.A. and the All-India Cow-Protection Association, despite being a spinner and weaver.

the only effective and peaceful method of directly approaching the drunkards and appealing to them not to give way to temptation. I hope that the law of Travancore is faultless and that the District Magistrate has erred in his interpretation. The interpretation should be tested in a higher court. In any case, the reformers' duty is clear. If the law is at fault they must move for its repeal. And if all effort to set it right fails, their peaceful picketing must go on even at the risk of being imprisoned, taking care to avoid enlisting as volunteers persons who cannot restrain themselves under provocation. It is worthy of note that the gag is perpetual.

Is It Hyper-suspicion ?

> My fears at the very outset that the Agricultural Commission is merely a British commercial enterprise for selling agricultural implements is being confirmed by reports of meetings held in England.

This is an extract from a letter of a correspondent who weighs every word he writes, has no malice in him, and is at present not much interested in politics. I have reproduced the extract because I have shared the fear myself. It is possible that the fear is an echo of my own distrust and that the Commission is a well-meant effort to probe the bottom of the agricultural condition of the people of India. I would be delighted to discover that my fear or suspicion was wholly unjustified. But whilst it lasts and is shared by others, it is much better to express it than to harbour it secretly.

Only the other day, I reproduced an extract from a letter received from another correspondent who was a visitor to the Exhibition. He had gone with a bias in favour of the Exhibition. But he could not help giving an involuntary expression to his feeling that "the centre of attraction in the Exhibition was agricultural implements and machinery which the peasantry would never use." Indeed, he went further and said, "Some of the machinery was fit only for the scrap heap." He knew what he was talking about, having handled machinery on a fairly large scale. He thought that many things were allowed to be exhibited which had not been tested and guaranteed. An exhibition to be instructive and profitable should contain nothing that is not tested. Simple credulous people going there finding in flaring headlines preposterous claims on behalf of machines would naturally buy them and on finding them to be useless rue the day when they purchased them. The wise and just thing, however, is to suspend one's judgment and to keep an open mind till the report of the Commission is out.

Widows and Widowers

A correspondent writes:

> I have carefully read the correspondence "A Catechism" and your replies published in the *Young India* dated 14th October '26.[1] While answering the first question of the correspondent on page 357 in para first in the concluding portion, you say, "I should any day subscribe to a reform in the Hindu Law making sinful the remarriage of a widow or a widower who voluntarily married after maturity."
>
> In my opinion, a reform of this kind in the Hindu Law will be disastrous and to a large extent affect the moral standard of the society as a whole. For instance if a man or a woman married after maturity and unfortunately happens to lose either his wife or her husband after some days of married life, do you mean to say that the man or the woman should not be allowed to remarry even though a great desire of enjoying married life is left unfulfilled, for the only reason that the man or the woman concerned married after maturity? If a reform of this kind is made in the Hindu Law, I am afraid the man or the woman will find out some immoral way of gratifying his or her unsatisfied desire and there will be a wholesale moral corruption in the society. I therefore think that this question should entirely be left to the discretion of the man or woman concerned.

My reply to the catechist was a challenge to man who is the law-giver. He will not allow his liberty to be restricted. My reply, therefore, is an attempt to show that what is considered desirable for man should be equally so for women and that, therefore, a widow should have the same discretion as a widower about remarriage. Moreover, the Hindu Law is not inelastic like the laws made under the British Constitution. It will be noticed that I have deliberately used the word 'sinful' instead of criminal. A crime carries with it punishment imposed by a man-worked State. A sin is punishable only by God or one's conscience. And I do think that, if Hindu society would rise to the level I have aimed at in my answer, it will be a great gain for it and humanity.

What Is Khaddar?

A friend enquires whether the following definition of a 'Congressman' given in *The Leader* is a correct definition:

> Those who do not use 'pure' khaddar, i.e., khaddar woven by themselves out of yarn spun by themselves, have no right to call themselves Congressmen and should not be treated as such.

[1] *Vide* Vol. XXXI.

The correct definition is given in the body of the Congress resolutions. But for the sake of those who have no time to refer to the Congress resolutions, I may state that it has never been contemplated that the cloth to be used by Congressmen has to be woven by themselves. As a matter of fact, neither has the khaddar yarn to be spun by the members. The spinning test is totally apart from the wearing of khaddar, and it is purely voluntary. Whereas the wearing of khaddar is compulsory, the only thing needful is that the khaddar should be hand-spun and hand-woven—it does not matter by whom spun and woven. The yarn spun by the member need not form any part of the khaddar he wears. It is surprising to me that at this time of the day it is necessary to explain the meaning of khaddar. The appropriate question, however, would be how many Congressmen are wearing such pure khaddar as it is defined in the Congress resolution and not as in the quotation.

THE NECESSITY OF TESTING YARN

I have often laid stress upon the necessity of testing all the yarn that is spun either by volunteers or paid spinners. It does not mean that the yarn should be tested every day. But a periodical test is necessary if we are to improve the strength and evenness. These pages have also shown how a testing plant can be improvised without any difficulty. I hope that khadi centres will introduce this much-needed reform.

Young India, 18-11-1926

52. LETTER TO VASUMATI PANDIT

THE ASHRAM,
Thursday, November 18, 1926

CHI. VASUMATI,

I have your letter. You may come to Wardha. You have not given me the news that I had specially asked for about your health. Ramdas left today after staying for two days. Haribhai[1] has come today. He and Kusum[2] will go to Broach tomorrow.

Blessings from
BAPU

From a photostat of the Gujarati: S.N. 9221

[1] Haribhai Desai of Broach; he had worked for some time as Gandhiji's secretary during the initial period of the Sabarmati Ashram.

[2] Wife of Haribhai Desai

53. LETTER TO REVASHANKER J. MEHTA

Kartika Sud 14 [November 18, 1926][1]

REVERED REVASHANKERBHAI,

I have your letter. It would certainly be very good if Jamnalal did do the work of the school.

Please let me know how much money can be invested in the [Ramachandran] lift. Do not have any qualms in regard to the matter. I have never wished to know anything about finances and therefore I may unknowingly make a bold demand. It is for you to check such a demand. If I know for certain that you will, then only will I not hesitate to make demands on suitable occasion.

Good that you have decided to go to Deolali. There is no harm if you send Dhiru[2] here provided he likes to come. It will be no burden to me. The weather is very good at present. It is not possible for me to go to Deolali and now there is no need either.

Regards from
MOHANDAS

From a photostat of the Gujarati: G.N. 1260

54. LETTER TO BAPUBHAI NARANJI VASHI

Kartika Sud 14, 1983, November 18, 1926

BHAISHRI BAPUBHAI,

I am giving in *Navajivan* the reply[3] to the last paragraph of your letter. I do not wish to give there the reply to the rest of your letter.

Every Hindu should have nothing but respect for Rishi Dayanand's[4] life. *Satyartha Prakash* is disappointing but it is better not to search and find out why it is so. We should exalt the virtues of great men. We may take note of their imperfections, if any, but a devotee should not probe into their causes.

[1] Reference to addressee's Deolali trip indicates that the letter was written in 1926; *vide* "Letter to Revashanker J. Mehta", 25-11-1926.

[2] Addressee's son

[3] Not traceable

[4] Dayanand Saraswati, author of *Satyartha Prakash* and founder of the Arya Samaj

I have deliberately decided not to give extracts from *Satyartha Prakash*. The person for whose sake I wished to give the extracts has already called on me. I showed him the extracts. If, further, I were to give the extracts [in *Navajivan*], this great man would be maligned, and his virtues lost sight of and a controversy might start; hence I decided not to give them.

I find the use of the word 'Arya' artificial. Whatever may be the origin of the word 'Hindu', it carries naturally that meaning which is forced into any other word.

By birth we all are low. It is only when we acquire virtuous qualities that we become *dwijas*[1]; this is the purport of one verse. Others emphasize the importance of birth. Each view is valuable from its respective point of view. We take birth according to the *sanskaras* of our previous births. New *sanskaras* modify them to some extent. There is humility and conservation of strength in allowing ourselves to be known as we are born.

What we call *prarabdha* is nothing but the fruit of deeds in our previous births. Human efforts mean our attempts to make desirable changes therein. Sometimes one acts in opposition to the other, while at other times they run together harmoniously. Hence it cannot be said that one is always stronger than the other. We cannot disregard *prarabdha*; we cannot give up human effort. This explains the importance attributed to effort free from attachment.

Vandemataram from
MOHANDAS

From a microfilm of the Gujarati: S.N. 19965

55. LETTER TO G. D. BIRLA

Kartika Sud 14, 1983 [*November 18, 1926*]

BHAI GHANSHYAMDAS,

I have your letter. Regarding Geneva I have given my opinion a few days ago at your Kashi address.

It appears from Deviprasadji's letter that you are bound by promise. If such is the case the question of going or not going does not arise. As it is, you ought to go.

Yours,
MOHANDAS

From a photostat of the Hindi: C.W. 6138. Courtesy: G. D. Birla

[1] Twice-born

56. LETTER TO PARAMESHWARA DIAL GUPTA

November 19, 1926

DEAR FRIEND,

I do not propose specifically to deal with your questions in *Young India*. I have in the past dealt with such difficulties and may do so incidentally in the series I am writing.

I do not regard Rama and Krishna as historical characters as depicted in the books. Ravana represents passions, as Kauravas represent the evil in us. The burden of the *Ramayana* and the *Mahabharata* is to teach ahimsa.

I do not accept everything related in the *Mahabharata* as gospel.

If you will reread my writings on ahimsa, you will not find any contradiction between the passages quoted by you.

If a man cannot defend his country by non-violent means, he will be justified in using violent means rather than surrender in a cowardly manner.

I do say that truth must be told at any cost. But one is not always bound to disclose facts.

Yours sincerely,

PARAMESHWARA DIAL GUPTA
CHRIST CHURCH COLLEGE
CAWNPORE

From a photostat: S.N. 19740

57. LETTER TO SATYANAND SARASVATI

SABARMATI,
November 19, 1926

DEAR FRIEND,

I have your letter. I believe Rajendra Babu to be incapable of doing anything mean. But if you give me permission to send your letter to Rajendra Babu, I would secure his explanation.

I do not repent of my estimate of Mussalmans.

Yours sincerely,

SWAMI SATYANAND SARASVATI
C/o B. N. SINHA
SAMASTIPUR
B.N.W. RY.

From a photostat: S.N. 19742

58. LETTER TO DEVCHAND PAREKH

[*November 19, 1926*][1]

BHAISHRI DEVCHAND,

I have your letter. We should not put Dr. Pranjivan to inconvenience[2]. But we can have Revashankerbhai[3]. Would you like Nanabhai Narsinhprasad? Do you want Jamnalalji? We have the big problem of English, otherwise we could have Rajagopalachari. Would you like to have Kripalani? But I should suggest that you choose a real lover of khadi. I think we should look at the work of a man rather than his name. I have received your wire. The 30th will suit me.[4]

BAPU

From a photostat of the Gujarati: G.N. 5705

[1] From the postmark

[2] By offering him the presidentship of the Kathiawar Political Conference

[3] Revashanker Zaveri, brother of Dr. Pranjivandas Mehta

[4] For holding the meeting of the Executive Committee of the Kathiawar Political Conference

59. *LETTER TO BEHRAMJI KHAMBHATTA*

Friday [*November 19, 1926*][1]

BHAISHRI BEHRAMJI,

I have your letter. You may come whenever you can. I will start from here on the 2nd December. It is not certain when I shall return to the Ashram. I had come to know from Devdas that you were in danger of getting leucoderma. Even if you get it, what does it matter? There is no need to worry or be perturbed about it. I assume that you have enough spiritual understanding to be able to live cheerfully even if you have leucoderma. We can talk about this if you come earlier.

Mrs. Eddy's book is ordinary. It contains nothing new. Her language has a certain strangeness about it. That lady may have some ability but I found that she was misusing her knowledge. The cure for suffering lies in bearing it. Man should never use his spiritual strength to cure his suffering. If Jesus used his spiritual power to cure the sick, that does not mean that all of us should start using our spiritual power to cure ourselves. If we adopt remedies to cure the body, which is perishable, they, too, should be physical.

Hence a sick person should pray to God thus:

"O God! this illness is the result of my sins committed knowingly or unknowingly. Deliver me from my sins and give me the strength to bear this suffering."

If a sick man thinks that he is not sick, it is a kind of delusion. He is a true man who knows that he is sick but remains unaffected by his suffering. A sick person should analyse himself and, realizing that his body and soul are distinct, understand their true relation and the meaning of *moksha*.

I strongly advise you to leave off Christian science. You may, if you wish, certainly try ordinary remedies for your ailment, or do nothing and have faith in God. That's the golden mean. Take simple treatment and develop the power of endurance.

If you have anything to say to me in this matter, please do. I have certainly not read Mrs. Eddy's book as carefully as you

[1] Mahadev Desai, writing to the addressee on November 21, and apparently referring to this letter, asked: "Have you received Bapu's letter regarding Christian science?" The letter, therefore, appears to have been written on the preceding Friday which was November 19.

are likely to have done. I have just glanced through it. If I have done her an injustice, it has been done unknowingly. But how can I hide from you the impression it has made on me?

And, therefore, the last point is that, whatever my views, you should weigh them and do what your conscience tells you. We ourselves bind or free us. Others merely advise and keep away.

Blessings to you both.

BAPU

From a photostat of the Gujarati: G.N. 7534

60. LETTER TO HARJIVAN M. VYAS

Kartika Purnima 1983 [*November 19, 1926*]

BHAISHRI HARJIVAN,

I have your letter. My viewpoint is entirely different as regards both your questions.

Mill cloth may or may not contain any fat, but on account of the use of that cloth the fat of millions is being sucked and therefore its use should be given up.

If, while refining foreign sugar, bone dust is used, there is no reason to believe that it is not used in sugar made in our country. But it is good if we make the least use of sugar and such other things.

If we examine minutely how everything is made we shall surely find some sort of defect. So a thoughtful person will make do with the fewest things, and will give up using foreign goods even of good quality when local substitutes are available.

Vandemataram from
MOHANDAS GANDHI

BRAHMACHARI HARJIVAN MANISHANKER VYAS
ZAMKA, P.O. BAGASRA, BHAYANI
KATHIAWAR

From a microfilm of the Gujarati: S.N. 19967

61. LETTER TO SATISH CHANDRA MUKHERJEE

November 20, 1926

DEAR SATISH BABU,

I was delighted to have your long letter. But I was sorry to learn that you had malaria and that Krishnadas had unhappy experiences. You must please take care of yourself and have Krishnadas by your side. I hope you will continue to let me hear from you both about yourself and Krishnadas.

I am thankful for your profitable criticism. I shall deal with some of the points in the series I am writing. Greatest good of the greatest number is a doctrine which I think cannot be defended on the ground of ahimsa. Ahimsa insists on the greatest good of all. My defence of the destruction of the dogs is no doubt partly utilitarian and a concession to and an admission of our weakness. But destruction of suffering animals is defended on the highest ground of religion.

Yours sincerely,

SATISH CHANDRA MUKHERJEE
C/o S. C. GUHA
DARBHANGA

From a microfilm: S.N. 19743

62. LETTER TO JAMNALAL BAJAJ

Kartika Vad 1 [November 20, 1926][1]

CHI. JAMNALAL,

I have your letter. May you live long and may your purity grow. No one in this world is free from imperfection. We can only strive to get rid of it. You are making an effort in that direction. A person who makes an honest effort knows no fall. This is the divine pledge.

We shall now meet on the 4th. I intend to go *via* Tapti Valley [Railway]. Shastriar arrives tomorrow.

Blessings from
BAPU

From a photostat of the Gujarati: G.N. 2878

[1] The postmark bears the date, "23-11-1926", Wardha, where the addressee received it.

63. IS THIS HUMANITY?–VII

[*November* 21, 1926]

Some of my correspondents do not seem to realize the fundamental consideration underlying my suggestion for the destruction of dogs under certain circumstances. Thus, for instance, I have not made the suggestion in a purely utilitarian spirit. The utility to society incidentally accrues from the act, but the principal consideration is the relief of the long drawn-out agony of the creatures whose present condition it is simply impossible for me to tolerate. In the articles in this series, there has not been even the remotest suggestion that man has the right of disposal over the lower animals and that he may, therefore, kill them for his own comfort or pleasure. One of the writers betrays a strange confusion of thought when he says that the characteristic of an exalted soul is that he remains unaffected by the misery around him. He is callous, rather than exalted, who has not learnt to melt at others' woe, who has not learnt to see himself in others and others in himself. Intense longing for the happiness of others was the mother of the discovery of ahimsa. And the sage who was the embodiment of compassion found his soul's delight in renouncing his own physical comfort and stopped killing for his pleasure the dumb creation about him.

A correspondent reminds me of the advice given me by Shri Rajchandra when I approached him with a doubt as to what I should do if a serpent threatened to bite me.[1] Certainly his advice was that, rather than kill the serpent, I should allow myself to be killed by it. But the correspondent forgets that it is not myself that is the subject-matter of the present discussion, but the welfare of society in general as also of the suffering animals. If I had approached Raychandbhai with the question whether I should or should not kill a serpent writhing in agony, and whose pain I could not relieve otherwise, or whether I should or should not kill a serpent threatening to bite a child under my protection, if I could not otherwise turn the reptile away, I do not know what answer he would have given. For me the answer is clear as daylight and I have given it.

A studious correspondent confronts me with some verses from

[1] *Vide* Vol. I, p. 91.

a Jain philosopher and asks if I agree with the position taken up in them. One of the verses says:

> One should not kill even beasts of prey in the belief that by killing one such, one saves the lives of many.

Another says:

> Nor should one kill them out of a compassionate feeling that if they were suffered to live longer they might sink deeper into sin.

The third verse says:

> Nor should one kill distressed creatures presuming that one would thereby shorten the length of their agony.

To me the meaning of the verses is clear. And it is this that a particular theory should not be the spring of action in any case. You may commit *himsa*, not in order that you thereby realize in practice a pet theory of yours, but because you are driven to it as an imperative duty. Work which spontaneously comes to one's lot, or action without attachment, in the words of the *Gita*, is the duty of a seeker after *moksha*. Confine your energy to work that comes your way, I conceive the Jain philosopher to say, never seek fresh fields of activity. The verses, to me, define the mental attitude of detachment that should govern one's action in cases where *himsa* seems to be imperative and unavoidable.

But I have arrived at my present views independently of any authority, though originally they may have been drawn from various sources, and I submit that they are in perfect consonance with ahimsa, even though they may be proved to be contrary to the teaching of the philosopher.

Young India, 25-11-1926

64. *KHADI FROM YAJNA YARN*

A member of the All-India Spinners' Association writes as follows:

> Khadi is woven from the yarn received from the members and then it is sold. How are the proceeds utilized? Would it be wrong if this khadi was supplied to the poor at a cheaper rate, charging only the weaving expenses, etc.? What advantage do you find in the present system? I wish you to clarify this matter through *Navajivan*.

I think that this question has already been answered once. The *yajna* yarn is received in a very limited quantity—and though its quality is improving day by day and so irregularly that it can just cover the expenses of collecting and storing. Hence the khadi made from this yarn is sold at ordinary rates. Sufficient khadi to meet the demands of poor people is produced neither from *yajna* yarn nor from any other yarn. But the *yajna* yarn amply feeds the poor. The khadi that is produced out of the yarn spun by the poor costs more per yard than mill-made cloth. Yet the middle and the rich classes are trying to ensure the success of the art of spinning by purchasing it. When this *yajna* which is now being performed on a small scale becomes widespread, khadi will be given almost free to the poor, while the rich and the middle classes will wear khadi available at low price. At present the yarn received by the Spinners' Association satisfies the sentiment which when developed will fulfil the material need. If the Spinners' Association has no members and if [for membership] there is no condition of good spinning, then there would be no one carrying on khadi work as at present. Thus even though the poor are not enabled to wear khadi made of yarn received by the Spinners' Association, yet they derive all the benefits of its activities. The very existence of the Spinners' Association is for the benefit of the poor.

[From Gujarati]
Navajivan, 21-11-1926

65. *NOTES*

Late Shri Lallubhai Asharam

Who will not feel grieved at the death of Sir Lallubhai Asharam? He was the glory of Gujarat. All are praising him with one voice for his sense of justice. I had very little personal acquaintance with him; but I hear praises of his character from every quarter. Sir Lallubhai possessed the rare combination of knowledge, wealth and character. Every Gujarati, every Indian can be proud of him and emulate his good qualities. May God grant strength and courage to the members of Sir Lallubhai's family to bear this great calamity.

Khadi-hawking in Kathiawar

I have written earlier that the Khadi Institution at Amreli has produced khadi in large quantities. My view is that this khadi should be consumed in Kathiawar itself. It is our misfortune that khadi has to be hawked. If khadi is consumed locally then the energy spent by the hawkers in selling it can be utilized for increasing production. The production is not done for fun, but for the sake of giving work to unemployed women. Those Kathiawaris who realize this should make full use of the khadi produced in Kathiawar. This is a service to India and this is real economics. It would be doing service to the whole world if all of us would shoulder our individual responsibilities. Society is crushed because its members have to carry others' burdens. If a few rich would cease riding on the shoulders of the poor, then the burden on the poor would be lightened. But the world will always have the rich and the poor. And so there arises the duty of doing service to the poor. We may not have the strength to live like the poor, but all of us can.

This explains why it is essential for us to spin. If we wear the khadi which is spun and woven by the poor, it would be a service to them to that extent.

We should begin this service with our next door neighbours. So the khadi produced in Kathiawar must be purchased, in the first instance, by Kathiawaris themselves.

This khadi may be found expensive, coarse, or not durable. But I hold that it ought to be purchased in spite of these defects. The *chapatis* made by a mother though thick, ill-shaped and expensive are preferable to the beautiful round and cheap *chapatis* of Delhi.

Following this line of thinking, Abbas Saheb will again start khadi-hawking in Kathiawar. Starting on the 19th, the programme is as follows:

Gondal	19, 20
Dhoraji	22, 23, 24
Ranavav	26, 27
Manavadar, Batwa	1, 2, 3, 4
Mangrol	4, 5, 6
Junagadh	10, 11
Jetpur	20, 21, 22
Upleta	24, 25
Porbandar	28, 29, 30
Verawal	7, 8, 9
Jamnagar	12, 13, 14

It is my earnest hope that at all these places the people will welcome him and his co-workers and help them in selling off the khadi.

I should like to say that much better khadi is produced at present than that sold four years ago; it is thinner, more durable and cheaper. With the passage of time and with due encouragement, it will be still better and cheaper. It is in our hands to bring this about.

[From Gujarati]

Navajivan, 21-11-1926

66. LETTER TO C. F. ANDREWS

November 22, [1926][1]

MY DEAR CHARLIE,

I have just got your cable about prayer day[2]. I am forwarding it to Sarojini and writing a strong backing leader in *Young India*.[3] The whole Ashram will join you that day in your prayers. I hope to be that day in Wardha. I shall be with you in spirit that day though the body will be there with Vinoba and Jamnalalji.

Shastri[4] was here yesterday. We had a long and quiet chat.

Please remember there can be no response from our side to any scheme of repatriation, voluntary or otherwise. We are bound to look after all returned immigrants. But that can be no part of any scheme. Any such agreement will immediately make repatriation compulsory in substance though not in law.

I hope you are getting *Young India* regularly. I do deal with S.A. matters almost in every issue. The coming number will deal with Colonial-born Indians. It is an appeal to them not to ask for any differential treatment.

Hope you are keeping good health.

The elections here have saturated the atmosphere with poison.

With love,

Yours,

MOHAN

From a photostat: G.N. 967

[1] The original did not bear the 'year'. This is inferred from the reference to the article about Colonial-born Indians published under "Notes", 25-11-1926.

[2] To be observed on December 19, the Sunday following the arrival of the Government of India delegation in South Africa for the Round Table Conference. *Charles Freer Andrews*, p. 222, has: The proposal was welcomed everywhere; in India, Gandhi and Dr. Westcott the Metropolitan commended it to their people; in South Africa, under the leadership of the Deans of Cape Town and Johannesburg English Christians joined with Indians in prayer, and Dr. da Plessis of Stellenbosch issued a similar call to the Afrikaander people.

[3] *Vide* "A Day of Prayer", 25-11-1926.

[4] V. S. Srinivasa Sastri

67. LETTER TO SATIS CHANDRA DAS GUPTA

November 22, 1926

DEAR SATIS BABU,

I have your two letters. No one who reads your letter about Capt. Petaval can accuse you of want of humour. For conciseness and biting sarcasm, the letter is not to be improved upon.

Your letter about Prafulla Babu makes me intensely grieved. I wish you had given me the cause for this sudden change. What is he now going to do? It does mean much to me that a man of Kshitish Babu's silent enthusiasm can be closely drawn to me, i.e., the movement.

You must not lose your equanimity on any account whatsoever. Read over and over again that part of "Ayodhya Kand" which deals with the banishment of Rama. It is enough to make anyone rejoice in suffering. What though even the whole world should desert so long as your own faith does not desert you? Khadi if it has truth in it and true representatives will survive many more shocks. You must come to Wardha early and pass a few quiet days there.

Of course you will tell me to write to Prafulla Babu, if you think it necessary.

Here is a letter from Abhoy Ashram for publication. Please tell me what to do with it. I am telling Suresh Babu that I am sending it to you before publishing it.

Hemprabha Devi's letter is sweet.

With love,

BAPU

From a photostat: G.N. 1564

68. LETTER TO HEMPRABHA DAS GUPTA

Monday [November 22, 1926][1]

DEAR SISTER,

I am very happy to have your letter. You must always write to me.

I do not know the reason why Prafulla Babu left. Such things will keep on happening in the world. You are right in saying that in suffering the soul blossoms. This is the teaching of all religions.

I am relieved to know that all of you are now keeping good health.

Blessings from
BAPU

From a photostat of the Hindi: G.N. 1615

69. LETTER TO C. RAJAGOPALACHARI

November 22, 1926

MY DEAR C.R.,

I have your letter. I knew when I wrote the article[2] on hand-weaving *v.* hand-spinning, that those whom I had in view would be little touched by it. But I could see that there were many who thought like them. They might understand the position. If I ever see the Viceroy, I do not expect to fare better with him. Two pice per day sticks in the throat. Acceptance of the wheel means a revolution in one's outlook.

Well, you have Chhotelal there. I hope you will succeed in making him positively gay. I should even countenance his marriage, if I could make him shake off his moodiness. I will propose a vote of thanks to you at the next meeting of our newly-formed board, if you can renew him and make him think of others besides himself.

Sastri passed a pleasant afternoon with us yesterday. He

[1] It appears this letter was written on the same day as the one to Satis Chandra Das Gupta, *vide* the preceding item.

[2] *Vide* "Handloom *v.* Spinning-wheel", 11-11-1926.

asked to be shown the Ashram and he looked at everything with interest.

Pethick-Lawrence tells me he had a nice time with you.

With love

Yours,
BAPU

[PS.]

What about Wardha?

From a photostat: S.N. 19744

70. LETTER TO RAVISHANKER G. ANJARIA

Kartika Vad 5 [November 23, 1926][1]

BHAISHRI RAVISHANKER ANJARIA,

I have looked over your questions. Blind faith surely destroys the soul. Moreover, this is not a subject which requires you to believe in someone. It is therefore proper that everyone should decide for himself with the help of his own discretion.

You will not find in my article anything to the effect that all stray dogs are in a miserable plight.

Nor have I stated anywhere that all dogs might bite or catch rabies.

Nor have I suggested at any place destruction of the canine race.

I would never suggest violence for the sake of utility. In my opinion, where there is no dharma there is no utility.

But those who needs must destroy dogs can easily busy themselves with checking cow-slaughter like others who try to put an end to cow-slaughter though they think nothing of destroying vegetation. Whether the killing of a dog is unavoidable is to be decided on the merits of each individual case. Do not the Hindus who kill goats abjure cow-slaughter?

A man who looks to his own happiness and continually commits violence in quest of it knows not his dharma.

Have no fear that my articles would shake non-violence off its foundations.

Why should we not regard the deliberate breeding of dogs as unnecessary as we do that of mosquitoes and the like?

[1] The reference to the two articles about killing rabid dogs which had appeared in *Navajivan*, 10-10-1926 and 17-10-1926, suggests that the letter was written in 1926.

I do not endeavour to preach violence; I only intend to deprecate false non-violence. In fact, we have been committing grave violence in the name of non-violence. And I find that in these circumstances we cannot readily understand true non-violence.

I have no doubt that my view is based on true non-violence. I can, therefore, wait in patience. Do not be uneasy as I am not likely to ask you or anyone else to kill a dog or any other creature.

Vandemataram from
MOHANDAS

DOCTOR SAHEB RAVISHANKER GANESHJI ANJARIA
MANGROL
KATHIAWAR

From a microfilm of the Gujarati: S.N. 19968

71. LETTER TO JANAKDHARI PRASAD

THE ASHRAM,
SABARMATI,
November 24, 1926

DEAR JANAKDHARI BABU,

I have your letter. I was grieved to hear of your fever and happy to learn at the same time that you have pulled through.

I do not feel inclined to make time for reading the literature about the 'Coming of the World Teacher', because it would not carry conviction to me. If a great teacher comes down to the earth, he would leave his mark whether we recognize him or not. So long as we believe in and worship God with all our heart, we are on the safe ground. He will make our way clear to whatever we should do.

Yours sincerely,

JANAKDHARI PRASAD
GANDHI VIDYALAYA
HAJIPUR

From a microfilm: S.N. 19746

72. LETTER TO F. W. PETHICK-LAWRENCE

THE ASHRAM,
SABARMATI,
November 24, 1926

DEAR MR. LAWRENCE,

I was delighted to receive your letter.[1] Friends had really prepared me for receiving you and Mrs. Lawrence at the Ashram and I was looking forward to your visit here. I am sorry you were not able to come. I shall certainly be delighted to meet you at Gauhati if I come there. There is just a likelihood of my being unable to attend the forthcoming Congress. I shall know more fully during the second week of December.

I shall be in Wardha near Nagpur between 4th and 20th December.

I, indeed, remember having had the privilege of lunching with you in London when I was there on the South African Deputation.

Yours sincerely,

F. W. PETHICK-LAWRENCE, ESQ.
C/o GREAT EASTERN HOTEL
CALCUTTA

From a photostat: S.N. 19747

73. LETTER TO J. W. PETAVAL

THE ASHRAM,
SABARMATI,
November 24, 1926

DEAR FRIEND,

I have your letter. In order to know something about your activity as distinguished from your writings, I asked a kind friend in Calcutta to see your place.[2] The enclosed is an extract from his

[1] Writing from Adyar on November 16, Pethick-Lawrence who, along with his wife, was then visiting India, had recalled Gandhiji's visits to them in London many years ago, and hoped to meet Gandhiji again at the Gauhati Congress the following month (S.N. 10840).

[2] *Vide* "Letter to Satis Chandra Das Gupta", 12-11-1926.

letter.[1] You, will, therefore, see that I am in my own way trying to study your movement. Let me feel my way to it in the manner I know.

Yours sincerely,

From a microfilm: S.N. 19748

74. LETTER TO DEVCHAND PAREKH

Wednesday [November 24, 1926][2]

BHAISHRI DEVCHANDBHAI,

I have your letter. There will be accommodation for as many as will come. We shall consider the cases of Hakim Saheb, Dr. Ansari and others. If you arrive on Monday evening, it will be all right.

BAPU

From a photostat of the Gujarati: G.N. 5710

75. NOTES

ADDRESS TO SASTRI

Ahmedabad honoured itself by using the occasion of the Rt. Hon. Sastri's private visit to present him with an address and a purse. It is worthy of note that persons belonging to all parties joined the function. Would that such occasions were often seized to demonstrate our oneness in spite of our political or religious differences and also to promote mutually courteous and friendly intercourse among different groups.

COLONIAL-BORN INDIANS

I have received a letter on behalf of colonial-born Indians of South Africa chiding me for "absolutely forgetting them". The letter says:

> Our only desire is that we should receive only one message from you. I am sure you will not refuse this our last request to you.

I appreciate the affection underlying this rebuke. There is a strong tie binding the colonial-born Indians to me. But there was no special message that I could think of sending to them. The majority of my messages are sent through the weeklies that

[1] *Vide* "Letter to Satis Chandra Das Gupta", 22-11-1926.
[2] The postmark bears the date, 25-11-1926, Sabarmati.

I am editing. And the pages of *Young India* and Gujarati and Hindi *Navajivan* are full of messages to the settlers and their descendants in South Africa. Though I do attend to a great deal of private correspondence, force of circumstances has obliged me to restrict it to its utmost limit and treat these weeklies as a vehicle for correspondence. These weeklies, as a friend once reminded me, are not newspapers but views-papers, for the transmission of my views such as they are. They have also received messages through C.F. Andrews. But these friends want me to send them a special message through the Rt. Hon. Srinivasa Sastri. I know what this request means. The letter reminds me of the days when Gokhale was in South Africa. The colonial-born Indians knew my connection with Gokhale and they rightly expect me to use Srinivasa Sastri as a vehicle for all my thoughts and sentiments. Colonial-born Indians and other friends in South Africa will certainly have their heart's content through Srinivasa Sastri.

I am writing these notes before meeting him. We shall have discussed the whole of the South African question not only in its relationship to the things that the Union Government can or cannot do, but also to the things that the Indians, including the colonial-born, can and cannot do. But one thing I would say to the latter publicly. Let them beware of the tendency to cut themselves away from the settlers who were not born there and of asking for special privileges by reason of their own South African birth. Let them remember that they are, and remain, Indians in every sense of the term in spite of their South African birth and that, therefore, their duty is to throw in their lot completely with the former and work with them in every possible way. They will, by so doing, serve themselves and the country. Let them remember the work that they did so selflessly and bravely as members of the Stretcher Bearer Corps in 1899 during the Boer War and during the protracted satyagraha struggle between 1906 and 1914. Never was there then a whisper of their cutting themselves adrift or asking for special privileges. They have a great future before them if they will seize the occasion. They can become a living link between South Africa and India, if they will but represent the best of India and assimilate the best of the Western civilization that they come in contact with and as it is represented there by the best Englishmen and the best Boers.

A Tissue of Misrepresentations

A friend sent me some time ago an article written about me in *The Nineteenth Century and After*. I glanced through it, but it contained so many misrepresentations that I did not think it worth while reading it through, nor did I feel inclined to contradict the many falsehoods contained in it. Those who would credit them were not likely to be affected by any contradiction from me. But now a law student who, from the tone of his letter, has felt deeply hurt by the article, which he does not believe, wants me to deal with two specific statements. They are:

> In one of the schools which owed allegiance to Gandhi, a high-caste parent refused co-education of his son with the out-caste, and a high-caste teacher refused to teach a low-caste boy. The question was referred to Gandhi who upheld the high-caste men. That he said he would have helped the untouchables if he could does not excuse him.
>
> The papers of the time published statements to the effect that Gandhi was busy over his work of collection in Bombay and could not come just then, etc.

They are both false. Those who know my work about untouchables know that I have resisted, at the risk of losing friendships and donations to public causes, any attempt to discriminate against untouchables in national institutions. There is half truth in the statement about Chandpur. I did not go there when the trouble broke out. But the reason given by the writer is utterly devoid of truth. I am not omnipotent. I have only a limited sphere of work. I apply myself to the task that comes to me. I go only where I am wanted and where I regard myself competent to render some service. Thus I do not now run to places where Hindus and Mussalmans fight, not because I do not want to go or am preoccupied, but because I feel powerless. Nor do I rush wherever labour troubles occur, even though I may be invited. The work I was then doing had nothing to do with my not going to Chandpur. If I had felt the call I would have gone at all cost.

The law student and others who are interested in me will do well not to be disturbed over misrepresentations regarding me. They are the lot of public workers. My reputation will not suffer by mis*representations*. It certainly will when I am guilty of mis*conduct*. No whitewashing will then save it. But today my withers are unwrung even though a German friend tells me that a German paper accuses me of having promoted a film company. The innocent writer does not know that I have never once been to a cinema and refuse to be enthused about it and waste God-given time in spite of pressure sometimes used by kind friends. They tell me it has an educational value. It is possible that it has.

But its corrupting influence obtrudes itself upon me every day. Education, therefore, I seek elsewhere.

The Wheel in England

A correspondent writes:

> I give below some extracts from *Village Industries* by J. L. Green:
>
> "Spinning and weaving, too, have been revived here and there as an auxiliary occupation. A good example of what may be done by enthusiasm in this direction exists at Willey, one of the beautiful villages for which Surrey is famous. A few years ago Miss Margaret Lieth, one of the youngest lady inhabitants of the village, commenced a weekly spinning and weaving class in a large comfortable room in her garden, and by her example and energy, she has managed to get practically the whole village interested in the work.
>
> "A third example is the spinning and weaving industry at Winterlow, where several men and women are employed in their own homes and in a weaving-shed."
>
> If the charkha is not out of place in England how much less is it in India?

This extract but emphasizes the titbits (often quoted in these pages). Sjt. Balaji Rao of Coimbatore has been assiduously collecting to demonstrate the universality of the life-giving industry.

Khaddar and Madras Government

Sjt. C. V. Rangam Chetti addressed the following letter to the Madras Government:

> I have the honour to bring to your kind notice that some of the Government servants are terribly afraid to purchase hand-spun and hand-woven cloths when our hawkers approach them. They are under the impression that they should not purchase these cloths. You are aware that the Bombay Government is openly appealing to the people to encourage Indian industries. In last summer Rs. 800 worth of khaddar was sold by my hawkers at Ooty. Most of the purchasers are Government servants. I have the honour to request that you will be good enough to let me know whether Government servants are allowed to purchase hand-spun and hand-woven cloths without fear by the Madras Government.

To which the following reply has been received by him:

> The honorary Manager, All-India Spinners' Association (Andhra Branch), is informed that the Government have no reason to suppose that either the fear or the impression referred to exists among those in their service.

I congratulate both the parties and I hope that if there are Government employees who refuse to buy khadi for fear of Government, they will shed their fear and their foreign garments.

Young India, 25-11-1926

76. A DAY OF PRAYER

C. F. Andrews has sent me the following characteristic cablegram:

> Executive decided observe December nineteenth day prayer forthcoming Conference. Churches co-operating. After widest consulting best European sentiment feel step likely much appreciated. Advise Sarojini.

He is an intensely godly man and, therefore, a man of prayer. His politics are guided, coloured and ennobled by his prayers. Prayer with him is no empty formula. It is with him intense and incessant communion with God and waiting upon Him for guidance in his daily work great and small. No work that is done in His name and dedicated to Him is small. All work when so done assumes equal merit. A scavenger who works in His service shares equal distinction with a king who uses his gifts in His name and as a mere trustee. Unlike as among us very imperfect beings, in His Durbar the motive rather than the act itself decides its quality. We infer the intention from the act. He, knowing the intention as much as the act, judges the act according to the intention.

And Andrews, because his intentions are the purest possible, believes that God will ensure his success. He has every reason for his belief. For he has hitherto succeeded where others have failed. No one knows the history of Andrews's many unseen services. Those the public see are by no means the most significant or fruitful, not to mention contemporary events. Who knows, for instance, how he influenced the many beneficial decisions of Lord Hardinge? Truly with him, his "left hand knoweth not what his right hand doeth".

This good man has made his own this South African matter to which he was first appointed by Gokhale. He thinks and prays about it intensely. He had prepared me by a previous letter for the cable I have given to the public. He has infected the Indians with his belief in prayer. I know them all and I must own that many have accepted his advice purely as a matter of form or to please him or to make political capital out of the event. But I know that there are some who have endorsed his proposition with absolute sincerity. The sincerity of the few will cover the insincerity or the indifference of the many.

The Dutch element of South Africa is religious according to its own lights. In South Africa, therefore, in times of famines or locust visitations, there are days officially appointed for humiliation and prayer. It is then no wonder that Andrews has found the best European sentiment ranging itself round a proposal which has its seat, not in his brain but in his heart. But he is not easily satisfied. He wants an adequate response from India and her public bodies. He wants no resolutions, he does not ask for money, he wants a melting of our hearts. He wants us, if we will, to look Godward. He wants us to seek help from God.

Andrews has become an Indian because he is an Englishman. He wants to rule not by force but by love. And love ever identifies itself with the loved one. He believes that the reputation of European humanity is at stake in South Africa. So much tribulation has been suffered in South Africa that in his opinion, the future of the relations between Asiatic and coloured races and the European will largely depend upon the deliberations of the forthcoming Conference, which is mainly a result of his efforts. He wants divine blessings on these deliberations and asks our co-operation [in] invoking them. Let no one ask what is prayer and where and who is God. Both prayer and belief in God are supremely acts of faith. Let those, therefore, who have that faith respond to the appeal of this English Indian.

Prayer is a result of realization of our helplessness and our final reliance upon God to the exclusion of all else. We are surely conscious of our helplessness. On the eve of his departure, the Rt. Hon. Srinivasa Sastri has called the Indian cause which he is going to espouse a 'desperate cause'. Let us then pray on the 19th if we have faith in God. All Hindus, Mussalmans, Christians, Parsis, Jews and others can join if they will. Though we may know Him by a thousand names, He is one and the same to us all.

Young India, 25-11-1926

77. CURIOUS IDEAS[1]

This is a joint production from the teachers of a Board High School. It is therefore a somewhat representative and responsible document. But for this character the letter bears, I should not have published it. The campaign against untouchability and other social and religious reforms is bringing to light grotesque and subtle ideas held even by men of learning. The defence offered by the teachers of gross superstitions shows how argument follows conviction, and, therefore, shows what a small place argument holds in any great movement. It is the example of the reformer that matters. And when that example assumes power by being proof against misrepresentation, calumny, and persecution even to the point of death, the reform spreads. So will it be with untouchability and the like. But let us evaluate these teachers' arguments for a while.

In the first instance, they have chosen a bad analogy. I do not know that people are afraid to approach me or to touch me. On the contrary, whenever I travel, I am embarrassed by the over-attention of crowds wanting to touch me. They will not leave me alone even while I am taking my bath.

Secondly, if our untouchable countrymen are afraid to touch the higher-caste men, surely it is not because of the latter's greater purity, but because they have been taught not to touch them and because of the knowledge that any attempt to touch would be followed by abuse or worse.

Thirdly, the inferiority, in point of character, of the untouchables is an unwarranted assumption. Class considered, probably they are in no way inferior to the others for truthfulness, purity and other public and private virtues, which under favourable circumstances they have been capable of exhibiting as fully as any.

It is a misuse of the doctrine of previous birth to argue that these people will require generations before they can come up to the level of the so-called high-castes. The *Gita* teaches us that it is as open to an untouchable as to a learned pundit to attain salvation

[1] These ideas were embodied in a joint statement, not reproduced here, in which the authors had questioned the wisdom of Gandhiji's anti-untouchability campaign, pleaded for *sattvic* food, suggested that Gandhiji should take to the yoga of the *rishis,* and persuade some of his followers to live and work in villages.

in the existing birth. If the high-castes are really higher, they should have no fear of association with the untouchables. For the latter can only gain by such superior contact without the former becoming in any way degraded especially when they mix among the untouchables for the sake of service and not for the sake of mere sociableness in which there is mutual give and take of vice and virtue. I do not become contaminated by entering a public house if I enter it as a reformer with the intention of weaning the drunkard from his habit as I would be contaminated if I entered a public house with a friend to keep him company and without any preconceived determination of resisting the temptation that the public house or the friend may place in my way.

Equally strange is the argument of the teachers regarding the influence of food on character. I am a keen food reformer, many friends consider me to be fanatical in my zeal for food reform and for reducing one's food to the simplest terms possible. But I know that the teachers are attaching importance to food out of all proportion and the influence it exerts upon character. If public work were to be suspended till public workers were found who would avoid all condiments and subscribe to a rigid food formula, there would be no public work done. One can only press the advantages of a simple, frugal and non-stimulating diet upon workers. But one dare not stop all public activity till that reform has been achieved. The mischievous habit that has grown up of measuring religion and conduct in terms of food is highly detrimental to the growth of a sound religious sense. For these worthy teachers would even postpone the overdue marriage reform, till people begin to take what they are pleased to call *sattvic* food. There is no doubt whatsoever that there is a vital connection between diet and self-restraint. At the same time, innumerable instances are on record of people being in the habit of taking ordinary food and still keeping themselves under restraint. Those who are trying to exercise self-restraint find out for themselves the value of regulating the demands of the palate. It would be wrong, therefore, to make of dietetic reform an indispensable condition for other reforms.

As for the removal of the cruel practice of child-marriage let the teachers and those who think like them know that there are people who, in spite of their rigidly simple diet, find it most difficult to curb their animal passions. After all is said and done, "the mind is its own place, and in itself can make heaven of hell, a hell of heaven". And why is there all this morbid anxiety about female purity? Have women any say in the matter of male purity? We hear nothing of women's anxiety about men's chastity. Why should men arrogate to themselves the right to regulate female purity? It cannot be superimposed from without. It is a matter of evolution from within and, therefore, of individual self-effort.

As to the results of practice of yoga and non-violence, I cannot subscribe to the claim made by the teachers on behalf of those who take to non-violence and yogic practices. Even the most advanced among them cannot override the irrevocable and immutable laws of nature. They are as much bound by them as any of us. God Himself has reserved no right of revision of His own laws nor is there any need for Him for any such revision. He is all-powerful, all-knowing. He knows at the same time and without any effort the past, the present and the future. He has, therefore, nothing to reconsider, nothing to revise, nothing to alter and nothing to amend.

Non-violent people and yogis do undoubtedly develop certain powers. But they are all within the realm of Universal Law. I do not resort to any yogic practice firstly, because I have inward peace without it (It may be wrong on my part to be content with my present lot.) and, secondly, because I have not found a person whom I could implicitly trust and who could teach me the proper yogic exercises.

As for the movement towards villages, many of my co-workers are already working in the villages. But I confess that it is an uphill task. I own that it is not possible for everybody to be able to settle down in a village because he has the will.

Young India, 25-11-1926

78. KHADI WORK IN TAMIL NADU

The following carefully prepared report[1] of khadi work in Tamil Nadu for the past twelve months will be studied with interest. It shows slow but steady progress in every branch of the work. The reduction in the selling price by 25 per cent is a

[1] Not reproduced here. The report covered the work of 64 khadi organizations in 13 Tamil districts for the period October 1925—September 1926. It gave figures to show that, whereas production through private agencies was increasing, direct production through A.I.S.A. had decreased. It also gave figures to show that prices had been reduced, quality had improved and sales had gone up, and described efforts being made to seek the co-operation of local bodies in introducing hand-spinning in schools.

good gain, though part of it is no doubt due to the fall in the price of cotton. The quality of khadi has perceptibly improved. One feature of the sales is that three fourths of the khadi is now being sold locally. This was not so in the initial stages. The hawking scheme is largely responsible for this healthy improvement. The report draws attention to the ignorant and extraordinary Government resolution which prohibits introduction of hand-spinning in schools where hand-weaving is also not taught and which thus renders the introduction of hand-spinning all but impossible. The ignorance of the framer of the resolution is on a par with that of a noted economist who thinks he has demolished hand-spinning all the while knowing it only as hand-weaving.

Young India, 25-11-1926

79. *LETTER TO C. VIJAYARAGHAVACHARIAR*

THE ASHRAM,
SABARMATI,
November 25, 1926

DEAR FRIEND,

I have your letter.[1] Did I not say in my first letter that I am not sure of attending the Congress this year for the simple reason that I do not know whether I can [be] of any service? At the same time, I shall not certainly avoid going there if my absence is at all likely to be misunderstood. But I shall consult friends when this wretched election fever has subsided.

My attitude towards Hindu-Muslim unity is a fixed thing. I want it without the slightest bargain and I shall strain every nerve to secure it.

Yours sincerely,

From a photostat: S.N. 12087

[1] In his letter of November 17, Vijayaraghavachariar had likened Gandhiji to "sandalwood which perfumes the hand that crushes it and would yield none of its fragrance to gentle touches" and hoped that Gandhiji would solve the Hindu-Muslim problem at the Gauhati session of the Congress (S.N. 12083).

80. LETTER TO L. R. PANGARKAR

THE ASHRAM,
SABARMATI,
November 25, 1926

DEAR FRIEND,

I have your letter. I deeply appreciate it. I cannot give you any idea of how much I avoid writing and speaking on all kinds of subjects that are referred to me. But on some matters when reference is made, it is impossible for me to avoid speaking or writing, even at the risk of losing popularity and more. When saying what you feel is relevant, if you do not say it you are guilty of untruth. I cannot very well alter the whole course of my life by suppressing the truth rather than the telling of it because relevant.

Yours sincerely,

L. R. PANGARKAR, ESQ.
NASIK CITY

From a microfilm: S.N. 19749

81. LETTER TO REVASHANKER J. MEHTA

Thursday [November 25, 1926][1]

RESPECTED REVASHANKERBHAI,

Received your letter. The matter about the [Ramachandran] water-lift is clear to me. I feel that we ought to keep an eye on Dhiru's diet.

I shall leave this place for Wardha on the 2nd. I have chanced upon the postcard Chi. Ratilal[2] wrote to a diamond merchant asking for diamonds. He has not much judgment. He admitted

[1] From the postmark

[2] Son of the addressee's brother, Dr. Pranjivandas Mehta

[having done that] when I spoke to him. Both have returned from Dhoraji[1].

Pranams from
MOHANDAS

SHRIYUT REVASHANKER JAGJIVAN MEHTA
ROSEDALE
DEOLALI

From a photostat of the Gujarati: G.N. 1265

82. A LETTER[2]

THE ASHRAM,
Thursday, November 25, 1926

BHAISHRI,

I have your letter. I have no doubts about the importance of agriculture. But I do not know of any other means apart from the charkha for promoting agriculture.

Vandemataram from
MOHANDAS GANDHI

From a microfilm of the Gujarati: S.N. 19969

83. LETTER TO G. D. BIRLA

Kartika Krishna 6, 1983 [*November 25, 1926*]

BHAISHRI GHANSHYAMDASJI,

I got your telegram. I am sorry to tell you that my last letter to you was sent to revered Malaviyaji's address. It only said this: The reason why I oppose your going to Europe is that you should go as a free person. Copies of such letters are not kept. But this was the purport. It is a different matter if you had promised and are morally bound to go.

Yours,
MOHANDAS GANDHI

From the Hindi original: C.W. 6139. Courtesy: G. D. Birla

[1] A small town in Saurashtra
[2] Addressee not known

84. LETTER TO LILAVATI

Kartika Krishna 6, 1983 [November 25, 1926]

CHI. LILAVATI,

There is no better *mantra* than Ramanama. In this age and in this country there can be no *yajna* better than that of the charkha.

MOHANDAS

From a photostat of the Hindi: G.N. 6277

85. TELEGRAM TO PRESIDENT, CONGRESS, KHAGARIA[1]

[SABARMATI,
On or after *November 26, 1926*]

NOT INTERFERING ELECTIONS. ALL CHARGE HANDED SWARAJISTS.

GANDHI

From the draft: C.W. 4964. Courtesy: Parasram Mehrotra

86. DISCOURSES ON THE "GITA"[2]

[1]

February 24, 1926

This verse[3] provides the key to the study of the *Gita*. It is both a prayer and a stipulation. It says, "Whatever you may be,

[1] This was sent in reply to a telegram from the addressee received in Sabarmati on November 26, 1926 which read: "Printed copies telegram purpor[ting] your saying voting Congressmen sinful published here confusing Council voters. Wire...publication actual facts."

[2] The talks were given at the Satyagraha Ashram, Ahmedabad, during morning prayers over a period of nine months from February 24 to November 27, 1926. Notes were taken by Mahadev Desai and Punjabhai, an inmate of the Ashram. These were edited by Narahari Parikh and published in book form in 1955 under the title *Gandhijinu Gitashikshan*.

[3] The verse in question was recited by Narayan Moreshwar Khare, music teacher at the Ashram.

whether Vishnu or Siva, if you are free from attachment and aversions, I bow to you."

The *Mahabharata* is not history; it is a *dharma-grantha*[1]. Who can ever describe an actual event? A man cannot exactly describe even a drop of water seen by him. God having created him so weak, how can he describe an actual event perfectly? In this battle, moreover, the warriors were, on the one side, the sons[2] of Dharma, Vayu, Indra and Ashvinikumars and, on the other, a hundred brothers[3] all born at the same instant. Have we ever heard of such a thing actually happening? Duryodhana[4] rode on the chariot of *adharma*[5], and Arjuna[6] that of dharma. The battle described here is, therefore, a struggle between dharma and *adharma*. Sanjaya[7] is a man of devotion. The battle takes place far away from where he is, and he cannot see it; Vyasa[8], therefore, endows him with divine vision so that he can see what is happening. And what does this signify? Only this: that the epic describes the battle ever raging between the countless Kauravas and Pandavas dwelling within us. It is a battle between the innumerable forces of good and evil which become personified in us as virtues and vices. We shall leave aside the question of violence and non-violence and say that this *dharma-grantha* was written to explain man's duty in this inner strife.

[2][9]

Chapter I

February 25, 1926

Quite a few such blind men[10] live within us. This is not a battle which took place so many thousand years ago; it is one which is raging all the time, even today.

[1] Work treating of religious and ethical questions

[2] Yudhishthira, Bhima, Arjuna, Nakula and Sahadeva whose fatherhood has been attributed to the five gods listed

[3] The Kauravas

[4] Eldest of the Kauravas

[5] The opposite of dharma

[6] Third among the Pandavas, the central figure in the epic

[7] Who saw and reported the battle to the blind King Dhritarashtra, father of the Kauravas

[8] Author of the *Mahabharata*; he himself figures in some of the episodes described in the epic.

[9] This talk covers the first three verses of Chapter I.

[10] The reference is to Dhritarashtra.

Duryodhana tells Dronacharya[1] that his own pupil, Dhrishtadyumna[2], has planned the deployment [on the Pandava side]. They are, on both sides, his pupils, to whom he has imparted the same knowledge. But it depends on themselves whether they use that knowledge well or ill.

[3]

February 26, 1926

I displayed my ignorance, not knowledge, on the first day.[3] But there is much in the *Gita* for anyone who, though ignorant of grammar, aspires after *moksha*. It is stated in the *Gita* itself that everyone, whether a woman, a Vaisya or a Sudra, can acquire spiritual knowledge if they have devotion to God. All the same, learning should not be slighted. To understand any matter, one must have the knowledge which comes from learning. If any one of you had committed the mistake which I did, I would not have overlooked it.

Well, then, the battle-field described here is primarily the one inside the human body. Does the *Gita* then prohibit physical fighting altogether? No; fighting there may well be. But here the physical battle is only an occasion for describing the battle-field of the human body. In this view the names mentioned are not of persons but of qualities which they represent. What is described is the conflict within the human body between opposing moral tendencies imagined as distinct figures. A seer such as Vyasa would never concern himself with a description of mere physical fighting. It is the human body that is described as Kurukshetra, as *dharma-kshetra*[4]. It does become that when used in the service of God. The epithet may also mean that for a Kshatriya a battle-field is always a field of dharma. Surely a field on which the Pandavas too were present could not be altogether a place of sin.

[1] The Brahmin preceptor who had taught the Pandavas and the Kauravas the art and science of war

[2] Brother of Draupadi, wife of the Pandavas

[3] That is, on February 25, 1926. Gandhiji had made a mistake while splitting a vowel combination (*pashya* + *etam* in I. iii).

[4] Field of dharma

Bankimchandra[1] says that it is doubtful whether Draupadi had five sons. It is, however, difficult to decide. Karna[2] had the Sun-god as father. Every one of the characters had a miraculous birth. Whether out of compassion for Duryodhana, or because he was generous-hearted, Karna joined the former's side. Besides Karna, Duryodhana had good men like Bhishma[3] and Drona also on his side. This suggests that *evil cannot by itself flourish in this world.* It can do so only if it is allied with some good. This was the principle underlying non-co-operation, that the evil system which the Government represents, and which has endured only because of the support it receives from good people, cannot survive if that support is withdrawn. Just as the Government needs the support of good men in order to exist, so Duryodhana required men like Bhishma and Drona in order to show that there was justice on his side.

[4][4]

February 27, 1926

This pair of words can be interpreted in two different ways: *aparyapta* may mean (1) boundless, limitless, or (2) inadequate, insufficient; and *paryapta* may mean (1) limited or (2) adequate, sufficient. The meaning will depend on what we believe to be the feeling in Duryodhana's heart. Of the two meanings of *aparyapta*, I have accepted "inadequate", "insufficient". It has appealed to me from my earliest days. What Duryodhana felt was that their army, protected by Bhishma, was not sufficiently strong, whereas the Pandava army, protected by Bhima[5], was; for grandfather Bhishma loved both sides and Duryodhana had, therefore, a secret fear that he might not fight with his whole heart.

[1] Bankimchandra Chatterjee (1838-1894); Bengali poet and novelist; author of *Krishnacharitra*—a book which Gandhiji had read during his imprisonment in Yeravda.

[2] Eldest son of Kunti, begotten by the Sun-god before she was married to Pandu. Karna was abandoned by her and brought up by a charioteer, was honoured by Duryodhana who gave him a place in his court.

[3] Uncle of Pandu and Dhritarashtra; to enable his father Santanu to marry Satyavati, he renounced his claim to kingship and pledged that he would never marry.

[4] This talk covers verses 10 to 16 dwelling chiefly on verse 10.

[5] The second of the Pandavas

[5]

February 28, 1926

The use of Sanskrit for prayers is a mere form; the real aim is to let the meaning of dharma sink into one's heart. Simple like a villager that I am, why should I insist on reading the *Gita* myself? Why should Mahadev refuse to do that?[1] Why did I take this upon myself? Because I have the necessary humility. I believe that we are all imperfect in one way or another. But I know well enough what dharma means, and have tried to follow it in my life. If I have somewhere deep in me the spirit of dharma and loving devotion to God, I shall be able to kindle it in you. But one cannot light a piece of stone. Only those of you who have some oil and wick in them will light their lamp with this match-stick of mine; only those who have something in them will profit from this discussion.

Our pronunciation should be such that the recitation of the verses would immediately please the mind. I committed a grammatical error yesterday. In the clause *shankham dadhmau pratapavan*[2], I explained *pratapavan* as being in apposition to *shankham*. It should be applied to Bhishma, the grandfather. But my Sanskrit is no better than a villager's. I am not so proficient in it that, if I commit an error, it would be immediately felt by my ear, would jar on it.

Sanjaya is proceeding with his description of the conches which are being blown in the Pandava camp.

Kairmaya saha yoddhavyam:[3] Arjuna is asking, not whether it is necessary that he should fight, but against whom he has to fight. If he did not wish to fight, he would have told Krishna so on the previous day itself. He had no aversion to fighting as such. In fact, he had obtained Yudhishthira's[4] permission and secured weapons from Indra that he might fight. Krishna would have, in that case, asked Arjuna to go to Duryodhana and win him over. But that was not the case. Arjuna had fought even during the exile. He had fought when King Virat[5] was attacked by Duryodhana. He was always prepared to fight. His question,

[1] Gandhiji had remarked that Mahadev Desai knew better how to read the verses and explain the meaning, and the latter had demurred.

[2] The valiant one blew his conch; I, 12.

[3] Against whom I must fight; I, 22.

[4] The eldest of the Pandavas

[5] With whom the Pandavas lived in disguise during the last year of their exile

therefore, was who they were against whom he would be fighting. We should always bear this in mind.

[6]

March 2, 1926

Arjuna requests Shri Krishna to station his chariot between the two armies, so that he may see the warriors on the field.

He sees that all of them are relatives and friends, whom one cannot easily bring oneself to kill.

Arjuna says: "I do not see any good in killing one's kinsmen." The stress here is on "kinsmen". He says:

> I would not fight against them, even for the kingdom of the three worlds; how could I, then, fight against them for a few clods of earth?[1]

Because he has asked for only five villages as the Pandavas' share. He repeatedly asks how he can be happy after killing his kinsmen. All his arguments are summed up in the question: *Kairmaya saha yoddhavyam* ? He is unhappy, not at the thought of killing, but at the thought of whom he was required to kill. By putting the word "kinsmen" repeatedly in his mouth, the author of the *Gita* shows into what darkness and ignorance he has sunk. Arjuna has been arguing from a practical point of view and Shri Krishna, it is hinted here, will try to meet that very argument.

The world will blame a person even for going to a court against his relations. Arjuna is shaken in his whole being, but it is not as if Shri Krishna wanted him to cast off this weakness of his forthwith. If, while seeking to follow the path of good, we do not eschew something which even in practical life we are required to eschew, dharma would cease to be dharma. In our daily life we avoid doing things out of fear of society. In this case, it is not merely a question of avoiding something which even ordinary people would avoid; it is a question of killing hundreds of thousands of men. How could Arjuna bring himself to do that? He had no need to go to Krishna for an answer to the question. If he could have approached us, even we could have told him: "Do not fight." When the dharma laid down for even this *kaliyuga*[2] requires us to refrain from unnecessary fighting, we should ask why Arjuna thought it necessary to put the question to Shri Krishna and why the two had such a long discussion. We can, therefore, understand the teaching of the *Gita* aright only if we

[1] *Bhagavad Gita*, I, 35

[2] Age of strife

give careful thought to the author's aim and the attendant circumstances. These last verses, however, are of great importance, for the entire argument which follows is based on them; we shall discuss them tomorrow.

[7]

March 3, 1926

What people would generally do in their common dealings is regarded as good. If we see anyone here, or elsewhere, who renounces a right in regard to worldly matters and forgives even strangers, not to speak of relations, we would think of him as a good man. If we desist from beating up a thief or any other felon, do nothing to get him punished but, after admonishing him and recovering from him the stolen article, let him go, we would be credited with humanity and our action would be regarded as an instance of non-violence; a contrary course would be looked upon as violence. How is it, then, that Shri Krishna stops Arjuna from advancing such an argument? How can we explain a plainly contrary teaching in *Bhagavad Gita*? Why does Shri Krishna describe Arjuna as cowardly and weak?

The *Bhagavad Gita* is consistent from the first to the last verse. That is why we meditate on its teaching and hope to discover from it the path to *moksha*. We should, therefore, think whether Arjuna's argument is valid or contains some flaw.

As though he were digging up a mountain to discover a mouse, Shri Krishna[1] describes the *Gita*, at the conclusion of each chapter, as an Upanishad, as a *Yogashastra*[2] and as *brahmavidya*[3] and describes this particular one as a chapter on Arjuna's despondency.

It is important to consider what Arjuna's question was and what the circumstances were in which he raised it. Having got his chariot stationed between the two armies, he said he wanted to see who those men were against whom he would be fighting. His reason is, for the time being, clouded. He has lost his nerve. All that has gone before shows that Arjuna is a great warrior and that, when starting out to fight, he does not, like Dharmaraja[4], hesitate and ask all manner of questions. In the past, he never hesitated even when he had to fight against relations. Even during their fourteen years' exile, he gave free expression to his

[1] Evidently, this is a slip for Vyasa, author of the *Mahabharata*.

[2] A treatise on yoga

[3] Knowledge concerning the *Brahman*, the Absolute

[4] Yudhishthira

hatred for the Kauravas before Dharmaraja; what is more, victory in the battle depends entirely on him. Bhima is physically strong and daring, but he lacks Arjuna's power. In their preparations for the battle during the fourteen years' exile, the other brothers always placed Arjuna at their head. When there was a battle outside Viratnagar, Arjuna, who had been living there in disguise wanted to be led to the place of fighting. Why does a man, who loves fighting to this extent, want his chariot to be stationed between the two armies and to see who the warriors are on the other side? He knows every one of them well enough. Why does he argue with Shri Krishna and tell him all that he does? He could have left the place immediately. Arjuna has a smaller army—an army of seven *akshauhini*[1] as against the Kauravas' of eleven. Let us suppose that Arjuna flees the battle-field. Though his enemies are wicked people, are sinners, they are his relations and he cannot bring himself to kill them. If he leaves the field, what would happen to those vast numbers on his side? If Arjuna went away, leaving them behind, would the Kauravas have mercy on them? If he left the battle, the Pandava army would be simply annihilated. What, then, would be the plight of their wives and children? I publish in *Navajivan* a narrative of the European War, and there is a reason for this. It reminds us of the battle of the *Mahabharata*. I give the narrative so that readers may know the ruin which such a war brings on a whole people. If Arjuna had left the battle-field, the very calamities which he feared would have befallen them. Their families would have been ruined, and the traditional dharma of these families and the race would have been destroyed. Arjuna, therefore, had no choice but to fight. This is the meaning of the battle in crude physical terms; I shall discuss later what it would be if the battle-field were taken to be the human being.

I will tell you tomorrow what I said when I discussed the *Gita* in Phœnix[2].

[8]

Chapter II

March 4, 1926

Shri Krishna tells Arjuna: Shake off this faintncss of heart and arise. His state of mind is imagined to be like that of Chris-

[1] A division of the army comprising 1,09,350 foot-soldiers, 65,610 horse-soldiers, 21,870 chariot-soldiers and 21,870 elephant-soldiers

[2] Settlement near Durban, which Gandhiji had founded in 1904

tian in the Slough of Despond. Why does Krishna say this to Arjuna, who is in fact ready to forgo everything?

When I was in London, I had talks with many revolutionaries. Shyamji Krishnavarma, Savarkar[1] and others used to tell me that the *Gita* and the *Ramayana* taught quite the opposite of what I said they did. I felt then how much better it would have been if the sage Vyasa had not taken this illustration of fighting for inculcating spiritual knowledge. For when even highly learned and thoughtful men read this meaning in the *Gita*, what can we expect of ordinary people ? If what we describe as the very quintessence of all Shastras, as one of the Upanishads, can be interpreted to yield such a wrong meaning, it would have been better for the holy Vyasa to have taken another, more effective, illustration to teach sacred truths.

He has drawn Arjuna and Shri Krishna so vividly that we are inclined to regard them as historical figures. The historian-author, moreover, gives the histories of cities, communities and individual characters and claims that he is describing a battle in which the best men of his age took part. I said how much better it would have been if the revered Vyasa had not adopted the method which he did. This, you may say, was impertinence on my part. But what should one seeking to serve truth do? What must one do if one sees an error? It is not wrong to draw attention, in all humility, to what one feels to be an error. This thought remained in my mind for many years. Then I thought I should read the *Mahabharata*. I decided to do so, that I might understand the atmosphere of the age in which the *Gita* was written and feel the good and the evil influences at work in that age. I read in jail a Gujarati version of the *Mahabharata* which I could get there. I saw that Vyasa did not believe that fighting was wrong. The illustration which he has taken is a very beautiful one. Just as in Aesop's *Fables* and in *Panchtantra*, the authors have created conversations among birds and animals to impart moral teaching, so in the *Mahabharata* virtues and vices are personified and great moral truths conveyed through those figures. The description of the battle serves only as a pretext. The *Mahabharata* itself was not composed with the aim of describing a battle. In the *Gita*, the author has cleverly made use of the event to teach great truths. If the reader is not on his guard, he may be misled. The very nature of dharma is such that one may easily fall into error if one is not vigilant. Anyone rashly imitating Prahlad would do

[1] Vinayak Damodar Savarkar

something very wrong. This is the reason for the injunction against the reading of the Shastras by one without qualification. It is not easy for any person to solve the problems of dharma which may face him. He will not succeed till he has made himself fit by observing the *yama-niyamas*[1] and similar other rules of discipline. To take up a work like the *Gita* without having equipped oneself in this manner is the surest way of falling into the Slough of Despond. It would be like taking up a study of botany without ever having seen plants.

The author has used the word *Gudakesha* for Arjuna. It means one who has conquered sleep, who is always vigilant. We should, therefore, think carefully about this illustration of the battle. The first thing to bear in mind is that Arjuna falls into the error of making a distinction between kinsmen and outsiders. Outsiders may be killed even if they are not oppressors, and kinsmen may not be killed even if they are. My son, even if a drunkard, would inherit my property. I would write in *Navajivan* about another's son if he was wicked, but would not treat my own son in that manner. The *Gita* says, "No, this is not right. We have no right to point an accusing finger at others. We should point out the lapses of our own people first." Arjuna was Dronacharya's best pupil. Bhishma had actually showered love on him as if he had been his first-born. Arjuna should be ready to kill either of them. It has become his duty to non-co-operate with both, for they have joined the wrong side. Should it become necessary to cut off, with a sword, one's father's head, one must do so if one has a sword and is a Kshatriya, and if one would be ready to cut off anyone else's head in similar circumstances. Shri Krishna, therefore, asks Arjuna to free himself from ignorant attachments in this world. How should I act as editor of *Navajivan* ? Would it be right for me to proclaim with beat of drum the theft committed by an outsider's child and say nothing about a boy of my Ashram, who may have misbehaved in the same way? Certainly not. The *Gita* permits no distinction between one's relations and others. If one must kill, one should kill one's own people first. Shri Krishna asks Arjuna: "What is this you are saying about people being your relations?" The *Gita* wants to free him from this ignorant distinction of some people being his relations and others not. He has resolved to kill. It was not right, then, that he should shrink from killing particular individuals. It was not with any selfish motive that he had gone out to kill. Ravana

[1] Rules of moral discipline and religious observances

deserved to be killed by Rama. Why did not the latter take cover behind such wise talk? He knew well enough that Ravana could do no harm to Sita. But he did not argue with himself in that manner. We never say that he fought for the sake of Sita; we believe that he fought in order to kill Ravana.

Even if we believe in non-violence, it would not be proper for us to refuse, through cowardice, to protect the weak. If Arjuna had forgotten the difference between kinsmen and others and had been so filled with the spirit of non-violence as to bring about a change of heart in Duryodhana, he would have been another Shri Krishna. Actually, however, he believed Duryodhana to be wicked. I might be ready to embrace a snake, but, if one comes to bite you, I should kill it and protect you. Arjuna has two courses open to him: he should either kill Duryodhana and others, or else convert them. In the circumstances, Arjuna's laying down arms would mean the annihilation of all those on his side. His refusal to fight would bring on a disaster. Thus, Vyasa has taken the right illustration. A person who believes in fighting and does not regard it as violence, though it is violence, is here being asked to kill.

[9]

March 5, 1926

The question which Arjuna asks Shri Krishna is not whether it is right for him to kill. His question is whether it would be right to kill his kinsmen. This question arises out of bias. Bhishma and Drona, a kinsman and an honoured person, stand vividly before his eyes. How can he kill them? To a person whose dilemma is not concerning violence and non-violence but is only about whom he may kill, our commonsense can give only one answer. But a godfearing man like Arjuna should pause and reflect before acting. Only a person with deep understanding can solve the rather fine problem whether he should go on with the recitation of *gayatri*[1] or run to the help of someone who is crying out in distress. To a godfearing man, the problem would present no difficulty. The author of the *Mahabharata* has discussed such delicate issues on almost every page of the epic. He has taken instances from the lives of individual characters and drawn lessons from them. Some of the instances may well have been incidents of history, but he has treated them as poets and

[1] Vedic prayer to Sun-god for illumination

seers have always treated such incidents. English poets, too, have written plays and poems with historical figures as subjects. The author of the *Mahabharata* raises, for instance, the question whether the sage Vishvamitra had secretly eaten beef[1] and whether one should accept food offered by a chamar. The author has, thus, discussed problems of three kinds.

[10]

March 6, 1926

From today we begin the argument of the *Gita* and shall not, therefore, be able to go as fast with the verses as we have been doing.

"Accept innocent happiness, innocent joy, whatever the source," said Raychandbhai. Accordingly, we may derive a variety of meanings from the verses of the *Gita.*

The argument addressed to Arjuna begins with the eleventh verse[2], and continues right up to the last chapter. Shri Krishna starts with the distinction between the *atman*[3] and the body, for that is the first step to spiritual knowledge. We must first know certain definitions, then alone can we proceed. Arjuna is represented as a seeker, as a man who believes in the *atman* and observes the disciplines of *yama-niyama*, and so Shri Krishna starts giving him the knowledge of the *atman.* One becomes entitled to ask questions and seek illumination only if one has observed *brahmacharya*[4] and always followed truth, and only then will one's questions deserve to be answered. Arjuna has this fitness; he has the genuine spirit of submission and humility.

We have not yet fully discussed the premise on which the argument of the *Gita* is based. Yesterday we were discussing Arjuna's plea that it is wrong to kill one's kinsmen, not that it is wrong to kill at all. He was asked to forget the distinction of kinsmen and outsiders. The Hindu Shastras say that non-violence is the supreme dharma. The question, therefore, whether or not it is right to kill does not arise. Only an atheist would raise such a question. Arjuna has observed the disciplines of *yama-niyama*, among which ahimsa is placed first. But ahimsa is an ideal which it is impossible to realize to perfection. It may be possible

[1] The story is told in the Shanti Parva of the *Mahabharata.*

[2] Of Chapter II

[3] The self, unidentifiable with any one aspect of human individuality

[4] Celibacy, as an expression of perfect control of all the senses

to realize it in thought, but not in action. Shankaracharya[1] has said that one seeking *moksha* should have far greater patience than one who would try to empty the sea, drop by drop, with a blade of grass. One must have equal patience for realizing the ideal of perfect non-violence. It is impossible in this body to follow ahimsa fully. That is why *moksha* is laid down as the supreme end of life. Violence is inescapable. While the eyes wink and nails have to be pared, violence in one form or another is unavoidable. Evil is inherent in action, the *Gita* says further on. Arjuna did not, therefore, raise the question of violence and non-violence. He simply raised the question of distinction between kinsmen and others, much in the same way that a fond mother would advance arguments favouring her child.

The *Bhagavad Gita* traces all maladies to their one source. A physician treats different diseases with different remedies. But, on the basis of researches in medical science, physicians are now coming to the conclusion that, though diseases seem different from one another, in the final analysis they are one. The cause is one, and so is the cure. Similarly, Shri Krishna says that there is only one spiritual evil, with only one cause and one remedy. To explain this oneness, an extreme example is used. If one's kinsmen deserve to be killed, they ought to be killed; and one must not hesitate even if the entire world were likely to be destroyed in consequence. It is not only Arjuna's right but his duty to act in this manner. To his question whether one ought not to make an exception in regard to relations, he gets an unambiguous answer. The principle, thus, admits of no exception, just as there can be no exception in the matter of following truth, for truth is God and, if exceptions were admitted in regard to it, God also would be sometimes truth and sometimes not-truth. Thus the rule in this instance admits of no exception.

Shri Krishna tells Arjuna that he is talking specious wisdom. The *Gita* does not teach the path of action, nor of knowledge, nor of devotion. No matter how well one cultivates *vairagya* or how diligent one is in performing good actions or what measure of *bhakti*[2] one practises, one will not shed the sense of "I" and "mine" till one has attained knowledge. One can attain self-realization only if one sheds this attachment to the ego. It is possible only for

[1] 780-812; philosopher and teacher of Vedanta. He travelled all over the country and established a number of *mathas*. His works include commentaries on the *Bhagavad Gita* and the Upanishads and many hymns.

[2] Devotion

a person who has succeeded in doing so. In English, 'i' is a vertical line with a dot[1] above it. Only when this 'I' is done away with can one attain self-realization. A man's devotion to God is to be judged from the extent to which he gives up his stiffness and bends low in humility. Only then will he be, not an impostor, but a truly illumined man, a man of genuine knowledge. The *Gita* does not advocate any one of the three paths; I have from my experience come to the conclusion that it has been composed to teach this one truth which I have explained. We can follow truth only in the measure that we shed our attachment to the ego.

It is to teach this that Shri Krishna has advanced the beautiful argument of the *Gita*.

[11]

March 7, 1926

As every human being passes through childhood, youth and so on to old age, so also does he or she meet death. The phrase *dehantarprapti*[2] used here does not mean a new body or another life, for what is being discussed here is the fear of death, not that of a new life.

[12]

March 9, 1926

We feel afraid only so long as we take the rope to be a serpent. Likewise, if we know the natural stages of growth of the body, we shall not grieve over death. In order to help Arjuna to overcome his agitation, Shri Krishna tries to explain to him the difference between the *atman* and the body.

> O Kaunteya, contacts of the senses with their objects bring cold and heat, pleasure and pain; they come and go and are transient. Endure them, O Bharata.
>
> O noblest of men, the wise man who is not disturbed or agitated by these, who is unmoved by pleasure and pain, he alone is fitted for immortality.[3]

[1] Gandhiji uses the word '*shunya*' for 'dot'. The suggestion is that one progresses on the spiritual path in the measure that one travels towards this *shunya* or zero.

[2] Passing into another body; II, 13

[3] II, 14 and 15. The translation of this and other verses from the *Gita* is reproduced from Mahadev Desai's *The Gita According to Gandhi*.

Any being who is not subject to the impressions of senses will never experience fear. It is these impressions which are responsible for the feelings of happiness and misery. Someone has said that the muscles of a man who is angry become thirteen times as tense as when he is normal, and of a man who is laughing nine times as tense. That is, one spends more energy when one is angry, and one whose energy is thus wasted cannot attain to immortality. The cultivation of this state requires practice. We can even say of a person who has attained to it that he is God. Once a sannyasi, an impostor, paid a visit to Phœnix. He asked me to recite any verse from the *Gita* which I knew. I recited this one. During the early days of my legal practice, I was on one occasion very much troubled in my mind. I then went out for a walk. I was very much agitated. I then remembered this verse, and the very next moment I was almost dancing with relief. We should identify ourselves with Arjuna and have faith that Shri Krishna is driving our chariot. Thus, the meaning of the *Gita* on the commonsense level is that, once we have plunged into a battle, we should go on fighting. One ought not to give up the task one has undertaken. In this way, the illustration used should not be pointless or inadequate and a wise man should not read a wrong meaning in it either.

Vyasa's own intention was something different. He wanted to write the *Mahabharata* in such a way that even little boys and girls would study it, remember the virtuous characters in it and learn to keep away from people like the wicked characters in the epic. His aim was to strengthen the finer impulses in us and help us to overcome the evil ones. Before the women, too, he held up the example of Draupadi and thus taught them that they should, when threatened with danger, roar like lionesses and protect their honour. Draupadi could do this and rouse Arjuna, Yudhishthira and Bhima. The author of the *Mahabharata* has raised woman to a great height through his epic. The chief aim of the epic, however, is to represent the most invisible of all invisible wars. It tells of the Arjuna and other Pandavas in our mind who are battling with the Kauravas in it. The moral problems which confront one in this inner war are far more difficult than those of a physical war. An error in the sphere of practical action will at the most result in the destruction of this perishable body, but the result of an error in this inner invisible war will lead to perdition. The most painful punishment is appointed for evil intention. In the course of time, Pandavas and Kauravas are bound to be forgotten. They will most certainly be forgotten when this Age ends. We should not delude ourselves with the belief that they will continue to be remembered for ever. This Age of ours was preceded by many others. Even when all of them are forgotten, this war in our heart will go on. The *Gita* shows how we may emerge safe from it. The Krishna of the *Gita* is not the person who, when the hour of his death arrived, fell to a hunter's arrow, and Arjuna is not that person from whose hand the Gandiva bow slipped. Krishna is the *atman* in us, who is our charioteer. We can win only if we hand over the reins of the chariot to him. God makes us dance, like the master in a puppet show. We are smaller than even puppets. We should, therefore, trust everything to God, as children to parents. Let us not eat uncooked stuff. Let Krishna the cook prepare and give us what food of grace He wills for our *atman*.

The *Gita* does not decide for us. But if, whenever faced with a moral problem, you give up attachment to the ego and then decide what you should do, you will come to no harm. This is the substance of the argument which Shri Krishna has expanded into 18 chapters.

[13]

March 10, 1926

The verse[1] beginning with the phrase *matrasparsha* applies to sleeping as much as to waking. We have to make ourselves conscious machines. We should cultivate such perfect concentration that, like a man asleep, we are aware of nothing else. Hazrat Ali told his people to draw out the arrow from his body while he was praying, for at that time he would be totally absorbed in devotion to God. One cannot say that such a thing could be done when one was asleep, for one would not be able to fall asleep at all when the body was pierced with an arrow. A person who can be totally absorbed in every task on hand, as Hazrat Ali could be in prayer, who lives in such a state of self-absorption all the twenty-four hours of the day, will attain to immortality.

Shri Krishna now explains why the impressions of the senses are unreal:

> What is non-Being is never known to have been, and what is Being is never known not to have been. Of both these the secret has been seen by the seers of the Truth.[2]

[1] II, 14
[2] II, 16

That which never was cannot exist, and that which exists cannot cease to exist. Even the sun is transient, coming into existence and vanishing. The candle both exists and does not exist, for, when it is burnt up, its substance dissolves back into the five elements. Everything which has a name and a form ceases one day to exist in that particular mode, though it does not cease to be as a creation of God.

[14]

March 11, 1926

The *jnanis,* the men of knowledge, have discovered what exists and what does not exist. Name and form are brittle as glass. The *jnanis* know what is implied in the difference between existence and non-existence. We only know one simple thing: God is, nothing else is.

We shall breathe life into the Ashram by laying down our own lives. Its lands and buildings may disappear, but the spirit we inform it with will never perish.

> Know that to be imperishable whereby all this is pervaded. No one can destroy that immutable Being.[1]

Know that this Bodiless One, which can lift many Govardhan mountains on its little finger,[2] is imperishable.

Avyaya means that which cannot be spent.

[15]

March 12, 1926

> These bodies of the embodied one who is eternal, imperishable and immeasurable are finite. Fight, therefore, O Bharata.[3]

Aprameya means that for which there can be no evidence, that is, no evidence in the sense in which smoke is regarded as evidence of fire.

Therefore fight, O Bharata. If we argue that since all bodies are perishable, one may kill, does it follow that I may kill all the women and children in the Ashram ? Would I have in doing so acted according to the teaching of the *Bhagavad Gita,* merely because their bodies are perishable? We believe the watchman

[1] II, 17

[2] Shri Krishna as a boy is said to have lifted the Govardhan mountain on his little finger.

[3] II, 18

to have been mad because he had killed a person; if, however, he were to cite this verse of the *Gita* to justify what he did, we would call him wicked. What, then, shall we say of a person who mouths these seemingly learned arguments and then commits wickedness? To know the answer to this, we should go back to the First Chapter. Arjuna had said that he did not want even the kingdom of gods if he had to kill his kith and kin for that. But he is bound, in any case, to kill them, for he has accepted the dharma which requires him to kill. This verse with the word *yudhyasva* applies to him, but it does not apply to others. In this verse, Shri Krishna wants to free Arjuna from his ignorant attachment. When Harishchandra was required to kill a virtuous woman like Taramati[1], his eyes fell on her *mangal-sutra*[2] and [recognizing her], he held back. He would not have done so if it had been some other woman. In this case Shri Krishna would have told him that it was his duty to kill her. He would say to Harishchandra: You have lost your wits; you have killed people in the past and now you shrink from killing the woman because of your attachment for her as your wife. You would thus betray your dharma. He would tell Harishchandra that his body as well as his wife's was perishable. If a person would cut his own throat rather than another's, then Krishna would tell him that he could kill others as a duty.

Shri Krishna advances another argument.

> He who thinks of This (*Atman*) as slayer and he who believes This to be slain, are both ignorant. This neither slays nor is ever slain.[3]

The *atman* neither kills nor is killed. This argument can be advanced only to a person . . .[4] It is like putting the cart before the horse. As that is impossible, so the body, if it sought to drive the *atman*, would never succeed. If anyone says that it can, he does not know what he is talking about.

[16]

March 13, 1926

Suppose that your father was a teacher,[5] that you and . . . misbehaved in the same way and your father punished . . . but

[1] Harishchandra's wife

[2] Ornament carrying black or purple coral beads worn as a symbol of the married state

[3] II, 19

[4] Some words have been missing here in the source.

[5] This was addressed to a child in the audience.

not you; would that be right?[1] Arjuna did not understand what even a child like you does. Shri Krishna told him all this long argument of the *Gita* just to explain this.

He who is afraid kills. He for whom there is no death will not kill.

Those who come to the prayer meeting but do not follow the readings from the *Gita* should be regarded as not attending the prayers. We shall have truly welcomed the guest who has arrived at our place only if we receive him into the home with love, help him to wash, offer him a clean seat and serve him the best food prepared for ourselves, and ourselves eat only what remains after he has finished. We shall have welcomed him, shall have acted truthfully, only if we act in this manner. But if one frowns at the guest, does not speak to him with love, places before him a dirty, unwashed plate and serves stale food, fails to ask him if he would have another helping and then claims to have welcomed him and offered him a meal, one would have done nothing of the sort but would in fact have insulted the guest. Such conduct, therefore, would be a violation of truth. Rotten and foul-smelling food or food which has been left over ought not to be offered even to a beggar. If at all we wish to offer food to a beggar, we should offer clean grain. If we would rather give him nothing, we should tell him so discreetly. This would be acting truthfully. We can thus, by exercising our discrimination, decide what is truthful and what is not.

> This is never born nor ever dies, nor having been will ever not be any more; unborn, eternal, everlasting, ancient. This is not slain when the body is slain.[2]

This *atman* was never born and will never die; it is not as though it ever was not and may not be again. The author has used a separate epithet to indicate each of these several aspects. The *atman* is unborn, eternal and ancient. Everyone knows it. The body perishes, but it does not. One generation knows of it from another. It is a thing that all parents must have explained, or ought to explain, to their children.

> He who knows This, O Partha, to be imperishable, eternal, unborn, and immutable—whom and how can that man slay or cause to be slain?[3]

The *Gita* has been composed not in the form of aphorisms, but so as to be carried in the mind from moment to moment.

[1] The child replied to this in the negative.

[2] II, 20

[3] II, 21

It was written not for the learned, but for all the four castes, —rather, all the eighteen castes—to read and understand. It was written for the Sudras, the Bhangis[1], and for women—in fact, for all classes. If the author has used a variety of epithets for a subject, though all of them mean the same thing, it is simply in order that we may grasp what he wants us to understand—in the same way that a mother explains a point to her children over and over again in different words.

[17]

March 14, 1926

> As a man casts off worn-out garments and takes others that are new, even so the embodied one casts off worn-out bodies and passes on to others new.[2]

Would I be ready to change this body for another, unless I would give up a worn-out one and have a fresh one ? If the eyes cannot see, the ears cannot hear and the palate cannot relish food, would a person wish to live on bed-ridden, or die?

> This no weapons wound, This no fire burns, This no waters wet, This no wind doth dry.[3]

Weapons cannot cleave it. If we strike the air with a weapon, can we hurt it? The *atman* is subtler even than air. Fire cannot burn it, nor can water wet it; how can air, then, ever dry it? Having described the *atman* thus, the author gives an appropriate epithet to indicate each of its several aspects:

> Beyond all cutting, burning, wetting and drying is This—eternal, all-pervading, stable, immovable, everlasting.[4]

More epithets again: eternal, all-pervading, stable, immovable and everlasting. The verse which follows states the same thing.

> Perceivable neither by the senses nor by the mind. This is called unchangeable; therefore, knowing This as such, thou shouldst not grieve.[5]

Such is the *atman*, Krishna says and you should not, therefore, grieve over anyone's death. Why should you, then, grieve over the death of your relations ?

[1] Community regarded as untouchables attending to scavenging work
[2] II, 22
[3] II, 23
[4] II, 24
[5] II, 25

[18]

March 16, 1926

What do you call the thing which protects us against the sun?[1] Likewise, there is a word, *aja*, to designate that which was never born, and another, *achhedya*, to designate that which cannot be pierced.

Shri Krishna takes Arjuna slowly from darkness to light. Have you seen the *atman*?[2]

It is so naughty that it dwells in us and yet we cannot see it. It is the deer that even Ramachandra would not be able to kill. Ramachandra is omnipotent, and so he could kill only that which deserved to be killed.

Having argued thus, Shri Krishna says: "But suppose that the *atman* has none of these attributes. What of it ? What even if it is born and dies again and again? All the more reason why you should not grieve over death."

> And if thou deemest This to be always coming to birth and always dying, even then, O Mahabahu, thou shouldst not grieve.
>
> For certain is the death of the born, and certain is the birth of the dead; therefore, what is unavoidable thou shouldst not regret.[3]

He who dies is certain to be born again. We ought not to grieve over what is inescapable, what cannot be helped.

[19]

March 17, 1926

> The state of all beings before birth is unmanifest; their middle state is manifest; their state after death is again unmanifest. What occasion is there for lament, O Bharata ?[4]

All beings were unmanifest before birth and will again become unmanifest after death. Birth and death are God's concern. He alone, therefore, knows their mystery. Even doctors have failed here, for they cannot create a body. "Who am I, whence do I come? Am I destined to rise to heaven?" The *atman* becomes incarnate in birth. We can see this, the middle stage. Men who have thought over these problems have asserted that, for bestowing and taking away life, God does not require even a fraction of

[1] The question was addressed to a child who replied: *chhatri*, an umbrella.
[2] The question was again put to a child who answered in the negative.
[3] II, 26 and 27
[4] II 28

the time that is required for drawing and erasing a circle on the blackboard. No mathematician can ever calculate the measure of that time.

Tatra ka paridevana. Why, then, grieve? This is the great mystery of God. As a magician creates the illusion of a tree and destroys it, so God sports in endless ways and does not let us know the beginning and the end of his play. Why grieve over this?

> One looks upon This as a marvel; another speaks of This as such; another hears thereof as a marvel; yet having heard of This none truly knows This.[1]

Some wise men see the *atman* as a thing of wonder and some describe it so. Others hear it so described but cannot understand what it is. Such is our pathetic state. There can be no end to describing God's greatness, so mysterious is His sport.

Finally, Shri Krishna sums up:

> This embodied one in the body of every being is ever beyond all harm, O Bharata; thou shouldst not, therefore, grieve for anyone.[2]

"O Arjuna, this *atman* which dwells in everyone's body can never be killed." The body's death is like the breaking of a piece of glass. This cycle of birth and death goes on for ever and ever.

[20]

March 18, 1926

The theft which took place today[3] provides a lesson in the application of the *Gita*. Where there is possessiveness, there is violence. We have to guard things which we think are ours; when we give away a thing to someone, this possessiveness disappears since we no longer regard that thing as ours. All things in the world belong to us, but we are indifferent towards them and do not lose any sleep on their account. In the same way, we should think that the things we keep in the Ashram belong to others as much as to us, and so remain indifferent towards them. The other way is the way of violence, of Satan. That is not the way we have chosen. Ours, however, is a mixed way at present. We have adopted the principle of collective possession, and individual possession is restricted to a minimum. Krishna tells Arjuna to give

[1] II, 29
[2] II, 30
[3] In the Ashram

up this possessiveness, and through these two characters Vyasa tells us to do so.

After discussing the problem from the spiritual point of view Shri Krishna considers it from the mundane point of view. He tells Arjuna what his duty in the practical world requires.

> Again, seeing thine own duty thou shouldst not shrink from it; for there is no higher good for a Kshatriya than a righteous war.[1]

A Kshatriya has no duty higher than that of fighting in a righteous war. Why is the war described as righteous? Because it is not of Arjuna's seeking. He was happy enough in his home, but he was challenged by Duryodhana. The war came to him without his seeking, and had as it were opened the door of heaven to him.

Proceeding, Shri Krishna talks about one's good name in the world:

> The world will for ever recount the story of thy disgrace; and for a man of honour disgrace is worse than death.[2]

If a person who has accepted cleaning of latrines as his work wearied of it, saying that it was a Bhangi's work, Shri Krishna would tell him that he was betraying his dharma, that he would lose his good name, that people would for ever talk ill of him. For a man who has a good reputation in society, its loss is worse than death. Arjuna, Shri Krishna said, would give the great warriors a ground for accusing him of having fled from the battlefield in fear. He sums up this part of the argument with the following verse:

> Hold alike pleasure and pain, gain and loss, victory and defeat, and gird up thy loins for the fight; so doing thou shalt not incur sin.[3]

The argument in this verse is not practical, but spiritual.

[21]

March 19, 1926

The verse about "pleasure and pain" is not addressed to Arjuna alone but to all of us. "You will incur no sin by killing your kinsmen." —this is said repeatedly in the *Gita*. If a person remains unconcerned with defeat or victory, knowing that they are a part of life, he commits no sin in fighting. But we should also

[1] II, 31
[2] II, 34
[3] II, 38

say that he earns no merit. If we seek merit, we shall also incur sin. Even the best thing has an element of evil in it. Nothing in the world is wholly good or wholly evil. Where there is action there is some evil. If Harishchandra had felt any doubt in his mind, what would a holy sage have told him? "Cut your wife's throat; you will incur no sin." If a person learns to make no distinction between gain and loss, pleasure and pain, he would rarely be tempted to commit a sin.

If we had blamed the thieves and regarded them as very wicked men, we would have been filled with rage and wanted to kill them.

We can do without beating of drums over a birth, but it is difficult not to grieve over a death. If we thus cultivate an attitude of indifference and learn to check anger, we shall one day succeed in freeing ourselves from these pairs of opposites.

The argument in the *Bhagavad Gita* falls into three parts: (1) "Whence this weakness in you?" (2) Arjuna's questioning; (3) Krishna awakening his intellect and explaining to him how the *atman* and the body are separate things. Then follow the practical considerations.

What is one to do? How is one to proceed having known that the *atman* is different from the body? This is the fourth stage in the argument.

> Thus have I set before thee the attitude of Knowledge; hear now the attitude of Action; resorting to this attitude thou shalt cast off the bondage of action.[1]

The word *sankhya*, it has been said, is somewhat confusing. It may be so for the learned, it is not so for us. All that Shri Krishna means is this: "I explained the matter to you from a theoretical point of view. I pointed out the difference between the *atman* and the body. Having explained this to you, I will now put the argument with reference to yoga. Yoga means practice. After understanding this, you will have to translate your knowledge into action in the manner I shall explain." The word yoga is used repeatedly in the *Gita*. It explains how to act. "If you understand this," Shri Krishna says, "you will escape from the bondage of action."

[1] II, 39

[22]

March 20, 1926

There is much disputation concerning the meaning of the verse which we took up for discussion yesterday, as will be evident to anyone who makes a deep study of the *Gita*. I however feel that you should follow the rule that I have followed. It does not matter if that seems like making a virtue of our weakness. We should not involve ourselves in disputations about the meaning of Shastras. Bishop Butler was a man of great learning, but he took a pledge never to enter in a religious controversy. An atheist happened to be on a visit [to England]. The Bishop could have argued with him. But he wrote to a friend saying that he would not enter into any discussion with the atheist. It was possible, he said, that he might not be able to answer an argument of the latter on the instant. It was also possible, he added, that his reasoning might have no effect on others, in which case he would produce on them a wrong impression. It was therefore better, he said, to remain quiet. The atheist was free to question any belief. Why enter into any argument, about the existence of God, which was self-evident?

Raychandbhai once thought that he could do good to the world through his gift of attending to a hundred things simultaneously. If, he thought, he gave demonstrations of that gift in the Town Hall in Bombay, with a High Court judge presiding over the function, people would be converted and seek the welfare of their soul. After two or three days, he felt doubts about the wisdom of such a demonstration. It would be, he thought, a display of his own attainments, but would prove nothing about the power of God. Accordingly, he wrote a letter of apology and said that he had decided not to give the demonstration, but did not wish to explain why.

A person may say about Siva: 'He may be naked, He may wear human skulls round his neck, but He is my God, I want no other.' We may say the same thing in regard to this verse. *Sankhya* may mean any number of things. I have explained the idea to the best of my understanding and I have set you thinking. Now I shall demonstrate a practical application. Its many explanations may be of interest to learned men; they are not for us. We wish to study so that we may learn to be servants and devotees of God, may see God. To see God we do not have to enter into disputes. At the moment these children make my world. I wish to awaken their thought, entertain them and explain things to them. I have no aim beyond this. Every day we recite:

What is non-Being is never known to have been,
And what is Being is never known not to have been.

If, despite that, we act as if the unreal was the real, to what purpose do we recite the verse?

At every moment we have to decide whether a particular action will serve the *atman* or the body. We cannot, however, break open the cage of the body, and so we must simultaneously follow *vidya*[1] and *avidya*[2].

And now follows a verse which explains how a person who tries to put this teaching into action is saved.

> Here no effort undertaken is lost, no disaster befalls. Even a little of this righteous course delivers one from great fear.[3]

No sin is incurred by those that follow the path of action. A beginning made is not wasted. Even a little effort along this path saves one from great danger. This is a royal road, easy to follow. It is the sovereign yoga. In following it, there is no fear of stumbling. Once a beginning is made, nothing will stand in our way.

Only yesterday I wrote to a friend and told him that he suffered not from fistula but from something else. I advised him to keep repeating Ramanama. What one does in this way never goes in vain. How would it have helped him if I had advised him to have a *yajna*[4] performed? He would not have got a genuine priest to conduct the *yajna*. There would be many other difficulties. Nor would I advise him to go to Jagannath Puri[5] and make such and such an offering to such and such a deity. What if following my advice, he became an atheist? If, instead, he got smitten with love for Rama, he would be saved from a great fear. He suffers from a mental disease and should become free from attachments. He should constantly think on Rama. Doctors, too, advise us not to think of the disease from which we may be suffering.

This is a very important verse. It contains the profound idea that nothing done is ever lost, that there is no sin there, only safety. This is the royal road, the right angle. All right angles are of 90 degrees. This path is the path of truth. There is no harm, no fear of destruction, in following it. On the other hand,

[1] Knowledge [2] Ignorance; for Gandhiji's meaning here, *vide Isopanishad.*
[3] II, 40
[4] Sacrifice
[5] A centre of pilgrimage in Orissa

a person who argues whether it is right to tell a lie in order to save a cow or to eat meat to save one's life, can never be sure where he will end up.

[23]

March 21, 1926

Three points, tests or conditions are mentioned for proving that the *atman* is different from the body. We can act every moment on the assurance: in this path no effort is ever lost. What can we do right now which will never be lost? What can we think of? There is only one reply, that we must follow the prayers, and that too with perfect concentration.

Ramaswamy Aiyar once addressed a meeting in Bombay in the early days of non-co-operation. Khadilkar[1] said then that among all political activities there was only one which satisfied all the three conditions. That activity yields immediate result; there is no obstacle to its progress; and there is the advantage of being saved from the fear of loss of sixty crores of rupees.

Shri Krishna explained the same thing over again in the verse which follows:

> The attitude, in this matter, springing, as it does, from fixed resolve but one, O Kurunandana; but for those who have no fixed resolve the attitudes are many-branched and unending.[2]

O Arjuna, the resolute intellect here is one-pointed. Along this path which I shall explain to you, one must hold one's intellect so firm that there is no wavering. The actions of a man whose intellect is not fixed on one aim, who is not single-minded in his devotion, will branch out in many directions. As the mind leaps, monkey-fashion, from branch to branch, so does the intellect. A person who clings to his life will seek help from any *vaid* or saint or witch-doctor whom he meets. Similarly, a monkey will fly from branch to branch and ultimately meet an untimely death, the victim of a sling-shot. The mind of a person of uncertain purpose grows weak day by day and becomes so unsettled that he can think of nothing except what is in his mind at the moment. In present-day politics, there is no good at all and plenty of evil, for it is full of flattery and one is not protected from dangers, but, on the contrary, surrounded by them. It does

[1] Presumably, Krishnaji Prabhakar Khadilkar, a scholar, journalist, dramatist and public worker of Maharashtra

[2] II, 41

not help us to realize the *atman*; in fact we lose our soul. We lose our dharma, we lose the capacity for good works, lose both this world and the other. If, on the other hand, we can have faith in this spinning-wheel movement, we can serve the world, be happy ourselves, can live safe from a great danger, that is, can live without fear of those who would hold us down. We also secure, simultaneously, a means of ensuring our welfare in the other world. If a person who takes up this work does not seem to be of a fixed mind, you may conclude that he is not following the royal path.

It is only if we have the faith in our hearts that we are all one, though we exist as separate beings, it is only then that we can feel a sense of equality. Otherwise, even two leaves are not equal.

The next three verses describe the man whose intellect is not resolute.

[24]

March 23, 1926

A person who is of fixed mind in a small matter can be so even in a big matter. If he is asked to make an ellipsoid of clay and concentrate on it, he would do so. In trying to concentrate on any object, one is likely to be distracted by all manner of troublesome thoughts. A person to whom this happens may be described as one whose intellect is not fixed on one aim. One who would succeed in the yoga of works must be of a fixed mind in small matters as well as big.

Now follows the description of an intellect not fixed on one aim. In describing it, Vyasa has run down the Vedas as he has done nowhere else. So many things were interpolated into the Shastras in the course of time, but we have gone on believing that everything in them is divinely inspired. By doing this, we make ourselves mere pedants. *Veda* means to know. That which helps us to acquire the knowledge of the *Brahman*, which provides us the best means of acquiring such knowledge, that is the Veda.

> The ignorant, revelling in the letter of the Vedas, declare that there is naught else; carnally-minded, holding heaven to be their goal, they utter swelling words which promise birth as the fruit of action and which dwell on the many and varied rites to be performed for the sake of pleasure and power; intent, as they are, on pleasure and power their swelling words rob them of their wits, and they have no settled attitude which can be centred on the supreme goal.[1]

[1] II, 42, 43 and 44

Ignorant people, that is persons who are learned and yet devoid of knowledge, utter flowery speech, that is speech which is attractive, on which blossom new flowers every day. Men who wrangle over the meaning of the Vedas; men filled with endless desires (men who have many wishes and teach others to be like them); men who are ever thinking of heaven (who are merely for enjoyments, who always talk of enjoying even this world thoroughly and paint glowing and attractive pictures of life in heaven and) who assert that there is nothing beyond heaven; who always say that our actions in life unfailingly bear appropriate fruits and persuade people to perform innumerable rituals to secure enjoyments and win greatness (there are people who say these things even today.); who advise us to propitiate a great many gods and so make us feel helpless; who induce us to offer fanciful prayers to imaginary gods and turn us away from prayer to the God of all gods—such men push us deeper and deeper into quagmire. The fancies and thoughts which often trouble our minds are also evidence of an intellect branching out in many directions. Even in small matters, we can say, our intellect is not resolute. It will be resolute only if we fix our minds on one purpose and cling to it with discrimination, only if we work without looking for immediate results. At present, whether in politics or social reform we leap from one branch to another. I began with the illustration of a ball of earth and told you that, even if we concentrate on that, we can realize the *atman*.

I was once asked by someone why I had not succeeded in realizing the *atman*. I told him that for me the means themselves stood for such realization. The fact that such a question was asked is enough to suggest that the person who put it would not understand the humility which inspired my reply and would approach many others with the same question. This same condition prevailed in Vyasa's time. How can we expect that a person who is attached to enjoyments of the senses and possession of power, whose mind has been led away by all manner of attractive words, will have a resolute intellect? *Samadhi* means fixing the mind on God. How can one's intellect remain fixed and motionless in such a state? The mind of a person who is not satisfied with a lakh which he has earned and hopes to earn ten lakhs the next day, who, addressed as a *Mahatma* this day, hopes to be so addressed ever afterwards—the mind of such a person is distracted by all manner of thoughts and attractive visions. His mind will not be plain white, like khadi; he is ever wanting to dress his mind, as fashionable women do their bodies in many-coloured saris with borders of various designs. Such a person can never be devoted to God. Only he who has a spirit of extreme humility, who has the faith of Faithful[1], can be said to have a resolute intellect.

[25]

March 24, 1926

We saw yesterday that those who hanker after enjoyments and power can never fix their intellect on one aim. Only a person like Hazrat Ali who is completely absorbed in God can succeed in doing so. Only a person whose *chitta*[2] has become absolutely purified, whose mind has expanded and awakened to light, has become as clear as a mirror, can have in his stainless mind, a vision of God. If any sound emanates from such a person it can only be that of the name of Rama. After explaining this, Shri Krishna described the pedantic student of the Vedas. He now sums up the idea of the three verses in one:

> The Vedas have as their domain the three *gunas*[4]; eschew them, O Arjuna. Free thyself from the pairs of opposites, abide in eternal truth, scorn to gain or guard anything, remain the master of thy soul.[3]

The Vedas treat of the three *gunas*; you rise above them. (But this is not true. If it is, the Vedas would not be God's word. Shri Krishna is here talking about the Vedas as expounded by the ritualist pedants. The statement, therefore, gives only one side of the truth. The Vedas which utter *neti neti*[5]—there is nothing except truth—those Vedas are ever the objects of reverence for us. We can cite verses from the *Gita* itself and that it tells us to accept the Vedas as thus understood.)

Arjuna is asked to be above the pairs of opposites, which means to be indifferent to happiness and suffering. He should act in the fighting between the Kauravas and the Pandavas as if he was not personally involved in it. He should be *nityasattvastha*, which means that his mind should always remain steadfast. He should be *niryogakshema*, that is, give up all thought of acquiring, holding and defending possessions. But one must preserve one's body, at any rate. Arjuna should, therefore, cultivate detachment in that respect. He should cease to concern himself with yoga and *kshema*

[1] In *Pilgrim's Progress*
[2] Mind-stuff
[3] II, 45
[4] *Sattva*, *rajas* and *tamas*, modes of being
[5] "Not this, not this"

and live in the *atman*. He should live always thinking that he is not the body, not an entity with a name and a form, that he transcends these.

> To the extent that a well is of use when there is a flood of water on all sides, to the same extent are all the Vedas of use to an enlightened *Brahman*.[1]

What may be found in a tank will also be found in a big lake. He who knows the *Brahman* will know everything else. He possesses occult powers, too, for the knowledge of the *Brahman* is the perfection of these powers. The three *gunas* are dealt with in the Vedas; he who rises above them attains to the knowledge of *Brahman*. The person who has the throne will not covet a position of civil or police authority. He who has reached the Gangotri[2] has known the Ganga. We get from the former all the benefit we would from the latter, and in addition the person taking his abode near the Gangotri is away from the crowd and lives unattached to the pairs of opposites. Near the Hoogli, the Ganga water is turbid, but it is fresh and clear near Rishikesh and Hardwar. The higher one ascends towards the top, the greater the purity and cleanliness.

(Some interpret this verse in a different way, but we shall not go into that.)

After this introduction, Shri Krishna tells Arjuna that the sovereign yoga which he wished to explain to the latter was this:

> Action alone is thy province, never the fruits thereof; let not thy motive be the fruit of action, nor shouldst thou desire to avoid action.[3]

Your right is to work, and not to expect the fruit. The slave-owner tells the slave: "Mind your work, but beware lest you pluck a fruit from the garden. Yours is to take what I give." God has put us under restriction in the same manner. He tells us that we may work if we wish, but that the reward of work is entirely for Him to give. Our duty is to pray to Him, and the best way in which we can do this is to work with the pickaxe, to remove scum from the river and to sweep and clean our yards. This, certainly, is a difficult lesson to learn. The relationship between the slave-owner and his slave is an unhealthy one. It is based on [the owner's] self-interest. That between the lion and

[1] II, 46
[2] Source of the Ganga in the Himalayas
[3] II, 47

the goat is of the same character. But man is ever rushing into the mouth of God. A wise man does so consciously and deliberately, and tells God that he wishes to be His slave, and not the world's. The more God seems to reject him, the more he strives to be near Him. This verse is intended to describe this peculiar relationship. The eye-lids certainly protect the eyes, but they do not do so with conscious intention. They protect the eyes by reflex action. The relationship between God and man is similarly spontaneous. Mirabai has sung: "By a slender thread has Hari tied me to Him, and I turn as He pulls the thread." The relationship between us and God is of the kind described here. The thread is slender, and a single one besides.

Ma karmafala, etc., means: "Do not act so as to be the cause of your suffering fruits of action; do not be attached to action; or be over-eager to do anything. Think that everything is done by Me. What reason do you have to believe that you do things?" So, if it is God's will that we must die, He will destroy us; if such is not His will, He will arrest the hand raised against us.

[26]

March 25, 1926

Ma te sangostvakarmani: In reading this yesterday, I said *karmani* instead of *akarmani*, for that is how I have always read this verse. *Akarma* means all work which falls outside the sphere of one's duty. "You should not," Krishna says to Arjuna, "feel tempted to take up such work, feel drawn to work which is not your duty."

> Act thou, O Dhananjaya, without attachment, steadfast in Yoga, even-minded in success and failure. Even-mindedness is Yoga.[1]

Work without attachment, being established firmly in yoga. Yoga means renouncing the fruit of action. It means not desiring the fruit of work which is *akarma*. We should do no work with attachment. Attachment to good work, is that too wrong? Yes, it is. If we are attached to our goal of winning swaraj, we shall not hesitate to adopt bad means. If a person is particular that he would give slivers to me personally, one day he might even steal them. Hence, we should not be attached even to a good cause. Only then will our means remain pure and our actions too.

Proceeding, Shri Krishna says: One should be even-minded in success and failure. In other words, one should dedicate to

[1] II, 48

Krishna all that one does, surrender oneself completely to Him. The person who has an equal mind towards all things may be described as one established in yoga. Krishna explains the same idea further:

> For action, O Dhananjaya, is far inferior to unattached action; seek refuge in the attitude of detachment. Pitiable are those who make fruit their motive.[1]

Work done without the yoga of intellect is extremely harmful. One should, therefore, seek refuge in intellect. "Intellect" means a resolute intellect. Having once made a decision there is no arguing the matter further. Anyone who works for reward is a *kripan*, that is, a person deserving our pity.

[27]

March 26, 1926

A person without a fixed purpose has an unsteady mind. Bhartrihari[2] has described many forms of this weakness of mind.

> Here in this world a man gifted with that attitude of detachment escapes the fruit of both good and evil deeds. Gird thyself up for yoga, therefore. Yoga is skill in action.[3]

A person who is firmly yoked to his intellect, an intellect which is resolute, who is totally merged in it and who is a yogi, such a one renounces [the fruit of] work both good and bad, that is, is disinterested towards either. Shri Krishna, therefore, asks Arjuna to be a yogi. Yoga means nothing but skill in work. Anyone who wants to decide whether he should or should not do a particular thing, should seek a yogi's advice. This is why it is said that where there is a prince of yogis like Shri Krishna and a bowman of prowess like Arjuna, prosperity and power follow as a matter of course.

> For sages, gifted with the attitude of detachment, who renounce the fruit of action, are released from the bondage of birth and attain to the state which is free from all ills.[4]

Yogis renounce the fruits of work, and are freed from the bonds of birth. How can a person who has awakened to the truth about his body ever die? Such a one attains to immortality.

[1] II, 49

[2] A celebrated poet and grammarian of ancient India, who is said to have been the brother of King Vikramaditya

[3] II, 50

[4] II, 51

> When thy understanding will have passed through the slough of delusion, then wilt thou be indifferent alike to what thou hast heard and wilt hear.[1]

When your intellect, Shri Krishna tells Arjuna, has crossed the slough of delusion, you will become disinterested towards all that you may have heard in the past or that may seem to you worth hearing in future; that is, you will remain indifferent.

> When thy understanding, distracted by much hearing, will rest steadfast and unmoved in concentration, then wilt thou attain Yoga.[2]

When your intellect, once perverted by listening to all manner of arguments, is totally absorbed in the contemplation of God, you will then attain to yoga. When a person is firmly established in *samadhi*[3] he is filled with ecstatic love and, therefore, can be completely indifferent to this world.

[28]

March 27, 1926

Arjuna now asks how we may know the man established in *samadhi* from his speech. "Speech" means outward sign. The food which the *Gita* offers is different from what one's mother gives. Before Mother *Gita*, the earthly mother stands no comparison. He who has the *Gita* always engraved in his heart and keeps it there till the moment of death, will attain to *moksha*. A boy who gives himself to daily worship of the *Gita* will be another Dhruva or Sudhanva. We recite these verses daily so that we may understand their meaning and be guided by them.

[29]

March 28, 1926

"You are my arm," Shri Krishna tells Arjuna. "It is I who make it move." We say, likewise, in our morning prayers: "You it is that makes our senses function." One who is ever patient and works with single-minded attention to the task on hand may be described as a yogi skilled in action.

[1] II, 52
[2] II, 53
[3] The eighth stage in yoga

[30]

March 30, 1926

> When a man puts away, O Partha, all the cravings that arise in the mind and finds comfort for himself only from *atman*, then is he called the man of secure understanding.[1]

He who banishes all bad desires arising in his mind may be described as a *sthitaprajna*[2]. We add the word "bad" because here in the Ashram we engage ourselves in ceaseless work and we cannot ask a cripple to get up and walk. Though, of course, ultimately we arrive at a stage when we should banish all desires, even the desire to see God, for to a person in that stage all action becomes spontaneous. After one has seen God face to face, how can the desire to see Him still remain? When you have already jumped into the river, the desire to do so will no longer be there. Our desire to see God ceases when we are lost in Him, have become one with Him.

We would be ill if we remained in a river the whole day. Anyone who sleeps all the twenty-four hours will fall ill, and so also anyone who eats all day long. There is not a single thing in the world which we can go on desiring perpetually. It is because of this that we have the problem of happiness and misery. The more often we desire a thing, the stronger our desire becomes every time. The more we satisfy desires, the more urgent they become. That is also true about our daily discussions of the *Gita*. Though I cannot make them very interesting, those who really wish to follow them will find their desire becoming daily stronger. No one, of course, will fall ill because of that. Or, maybe, we need not consciously desire a thing which we always want. The sun rises and sets every day; we do not consciously wish that it may. He who has overcome his desires completely, should be natural in all his actions, as walking and similar movements of the body are natural.

There is only one desire in life which is good and the desire for the means to realize it is also good.

Who can succeed in banishing desires in this manner? He whose self abides content in itself is known as a *sthitaprajna*.

Whenever we hear anyone speaking about God, we should forget everything else and attend to his words. A person such as described above, if he is attending a reading of the *Ramayana* or the

[1] II, 55

[2] One who is of steadfast intellect

Gita, will be completely absorbed in following them. He will never feel it a strain to rise even at four in the morning.

The state in which the self abides in itself in serene content is the same as described by Narasinh Mehta[1] in this line in a poem of his: "The *Brahman* dancing in sportive play in front of the *Brahman.*" The poet here expresses the very same truth. The *Brahman* has all its joy through the *Brahman* in the company of the *Brahman*. The slave can never conceive of his existence without his master. A person who has the name of another on his lips all the twenty-four hours will forget himself in the latter. The *atman*[2] becomes the *Paramatman*[3] in the same manner. The *atman* may be a ray of the *Paramatman*, but a ray of the sun is the sun itself. Apart from God, we can have no existence at all. He who makes himself God's slave becomes one with God.

The state described here is not that of a person who lives self-satisfied, surrounding himself with possessions of all kinds. We should learn to be content in ourselves. The means and the end should become one. But who can find joy in the self through the self? One can do that by learning to work in a new spirit. One who takes opium before going to bed will not sleep well, but the man who sleeps in the natural course will sleep in peace, his mind abiding in God.

The verses which follow are by way of an explanation of this verse. Self-help does not consist merely in not seeking help from others; it consists in not needing such help.

If children have faith, they can live as a *sthitaprajna* does. They have their parents and teachers to look after their needs. They have, therefore, no need to take thought for themselves. They should always be guided by their elders. A child who lives in this manner is a *brahmachari*, a *muni*, a *sthitaprajna*. He is so in the sense that he does what he is asked to and carries out every instruction. Such a child could even become Prahlad.

[31]

March 31, 1926

The verse[4] beginning with *prajahati* can never mean that we may remain as we are. If that were the meaning, the second line would have no place in it. The man who lives contented in the

[1] A 15th-century saint-poet of Gujarat
[2] The individual self
[3] The Universal Self
[4] II, 55

self through the self will give up all desires, but one can live in such a state only if the desire to become better, to grow spiritually awakens in one. Anyone who wants to live in such a state must give up everything which is likely to obstruct his effort. If all that we do is merely to indulge in fancies, like Shaikhchilli[1], it would be better not to think at all, neither good thoughts nor bad. The road to hell is paved with good intentions. That is why it is said that one may cast into a river a ton of thoughts and cling to an ounce of practice.

(I have read in an English book that a boy who eats till he is full cannot preserve celibacy. One should not overload one's stomach.)

> Whose mind is untroubled in sorrows and longeth not for joys, who is free from passion, fear and wrath—he is called the ascetic of secure understanding.[2]

The man who does not feel depressed by suffering, is not overcome by suffering (knowing that suffering is always the effect of some cause), who is indifferent amid pleasures and is no more subject to attachments, fear and anger—such a person may be described as *sthitadhi*, that is, one whose intellect remains steadfast and is never caught in a whirlpool.

> Who owns attachment nowhere, who feels neither joy nor resentment whether good or bad comes his way—that man's understanding is secure.[3]

The man who has withdrawn interest from all objects, given up desire for them, who is unconcerned, indifferent in good or ill chance, who is neither pleased nor annoyed by anything—such a person's intellect is steadfast. Shri Krishna gives an illustration of this:

> And when, like the tortoise drawing in its limbs from every side, this man draws in his senses from their objects, his understanding is secure.[4]

The man who holds in his senses to prevent them from going out to their objects, as the tortoise draws in his limbs and holds them as if under a shield, has an intellect which is steadfast. Only that man who voluntarily holds in his senses may be known as completely absorbed in God. When our senses seem to move out

[1] Day-dreamer
[2] II, 56
[3] II, 57
[4] II, 58

of our control, we should think of the tortoise. The objects of the senses are like pebbles. If we hold in the senses, the pebbles will not hurt, that is, if we hold under control our hands, our feet, our eyes, and so on.

[32]

April 1, 1926

Shri Krishna now explains how the senses may be held back from their objects.

> When a man starves his senses, the objects of those senses disappear from him, but not the yearning for them; the yearning too departs when he beholds the Supreme.[1]

Only a person who denies the body the food it craves for will cease to be troubled by his senses. The senses of a well-fed man always keep awake, but they lose all their power when he stops eating. The Shastras say that, if a man's appetites are not under his control, it would be best for him to fast. We are enjoined to fast during the Ramadan and the extra lunar month of the Hindus to discipline the senses. Suppose that I have decided to go to the city and see a play; if, however, I have been fasting on that day, I would feel disinclined to go. If our senses cannot be controlled we should undertake a fast; if they cannot be controlled fully, we should give up food altogether. This is what the first half of the verse means.

And now about the second half:

The appetites subside, but our pleasure in the objects of senses remains. If a person who is fasting feels that his life is secure, he will not suffer because of the fast, but ordinarily desire for food persists. During a fast, impure desires will probably subside, but one gets impatient for the fast to end. Unless the desire for food disappears completely, the fast will not endure. The desire for sacrifice will not endure without renunciation. When we have an opportunity to enjoy anything, we find that our physical appetites become strong again. This, of course, does not mean that we should not occasionally give up things for a temporary period. We should certainly give up anything we can give up.

In the first half, we are told that we should curb impure desires by fasting; but fasting alone does not yield the required result. Something more is needed. If we see God, our instinctive desire for objects of senses will also subside. This last thing confronts us

[1] II, 59

with a problem. Until one's pleasure in objects of the senses has disappeared, one cannot become established in *samadhi*, and until one has become so established one will not succeed in overcoming desires.

How to solve this problem? We should persevere in our effort. We should, slowly and gradually, learn to feel God's presence in the depths of our heart. We should, occasionally, banish the very thought of eating and feel that it would be much better that our body should perish than that we should be enslaved by pleasures. One does not, of course, achieve self-conquest by committing suicide. It is the desires which need to be conquered. Anyone who eats to keep alive his body may certainly eat, but he should stop eating if he finds that eating food rouses his appetites. If he can be patient when fasting, they will subside completely. He may, when they have subsided, ask for milk or water if he wants these for keeping himself alive. It is said about Lord Buddha that he once fainted because he had been fasting. At that time, a woman came and placed a few drops of milk on his lips. Did the milk rouse his appetites? No; on the contrary, he realized God soon after.

The purport of this verse is that we should fast for self-purification. But the Shastras tell us that, while fasting, we should wish with all our strength for freedom from desire. If, in addition, we also yearn to see God, then only will our fasting bear fruit. If we desire that our appetite should subside, it is in order that we may see God. When we are fasting, our one desire should be to see God. Our appetites stand in the way, and so we must weaken their hold on us. After a person has seen God, it is all one to him whether he eats or does not eat. Vinoba told me a story about Chaitanya[1], that a lump of sugar placed on his tongue remained there undissolved, like a stone. The reason for this was that his pleasure in objects of sense had completely died away. I have said that it is not the palate, but the mind, which feels pleasure. If a man's pleasure in objects of sense has disappeared, if he has become established in *samadhi*, or if he is suffering from a disease like jaundice, nothing placed on his tongue will dissolve. Thus, the man who has turned away from pleasures and the man who is stricken with disease ultimately reach the same state, one voluntarily, the other against his will.

Chaitanyadeva felt all the time that it was God's grace which sustained him and that if he should eat at all, it must be only that he may see God one day. To see Him one should completely

[1] A 16th-century religious reformer of Bengal

conquer one's appetites, and even the instinctive pleasure one feels in objects of sense must subside. This verse provides the key to such a state. To curb the appetites, we should stop eating, that is, deny our senses their food. When they have no occasion to function, they will be denied their food. If, after this, we take the next step and concentrate our attention on attaining self-realization, our instinctive pleasure in objects of sense will subside completely. The man who attains such a state will be in the same condition as Janaka[1].

[33]

April 2, 1926

We shall proceed with the verse we took up yesterday. It is a very important verse. I kept thinking on it the whole day. Four or five hundred years ago, in Europe and Arabia they attached great importance to mortification of the flesh. In the time of the Prophet, prayer, fasting and keeping awake at night were considered essential for subduing the *nafas* (this is a very good word denoting the sense-organs collectively; it also means desire). The Prophet was often awake till two or three after midnight, and was never particular when and what he ate. It was not merely that he kept the *roza* fast. That was necessary for everyone to keep, even for people engrossed in worldly affairs. The Prophet, however, undertook a *roza* fast every now and then. While one is keeping this fast, one is not permitted to take water during daytime, but after sunset it is absolutely necessary that one must drink some water. The Prophet, however, did not apply this rule to himself, and so an associate of his told him: "Since you do not eat, we too will not eat." The Prophet's reply was: "No, you should not fast. God sends you no such food as He sends me." Silenced by the reply, the questioner slapped himself on the face and left, thinking: "We, others, observe the *roza* because he falls into ecstasies and asks us to fast, but in actual practice we only make a fuss." To the Prophet, fasting brought happiness, for it was an occasion when he could live constantly in the presence of God. His food consisted of dates. Just as in countries where people drink every home has a vineyard, so in Arabia there are date-palms near every house, and when the Prophet wished to eat he plucked a few dates from these trees. Some others who lived with the Prophet and served him also ate dates. The little flour

[1] Philosopher-king, famous in the Upanishads as a knower of Reality and master of desireless action

that was ground for them was also coarse. He used to keep awake for such long hours that the Bibisaheb would wait impatiently for him to lie down to sleep. Besides keeping awake thus, he would withdraw himself into solitude so that he might subdue the senses and be blessed with a vision of God. Jesus did likewise. He lived in solitude, fasted for forty days and subjected his body to the utmost mortification. At the end of forty days, he felt that he heard a mysterious voice, that God was talking to him and that the veil which hid God from him had lifted. Those who followed him taught the same thing. There has been a tradition of fasting and prayer in Europe right to the present day.

And then came Luther in Germany. He said that the others had misinterpreted the texts, and that their lives were all deception. As the sun moves westward, darkness follows close behind it, reaching almost as far as the sun but not quite; in the same way, hypocrisy follows close behind holiness. Luther saw through all this. He plainly saw the superstitions and hypocrisies which flourished in monasteries. It is a strange law of nature that once men become accustomed to a certain thing they continue to do it through sheer inertia. In those days, they even burnt people alive. Those who believed in mortifying the flesh thought it their duty to curb the senses and to kill others who did not do so. Observing these evils, Luther went to the opposite extreme. After all, whatever the evils associated with external practices, it is only through self-control that one can see God. The Protestants, however, believed that there was nothing but hypocrisy in the Catholic practices, and so they destroyed a most potent means of realizing God. Because this means harmed some people, it does not follow that it harms all. But they believed that it did.

In India, too, this wind is blowing at present. It is often said that control of the senses is difficult to achieve, but in truth it is not so. This is not only my present belief; I held it even when I was conducting my experiments. Three things are essential for control of the senses: (1) faith; (2) a conviction of the necessity of subjugating the senses, so strong that we would persist even if we were all alone in this belief; (3) food is body's nourishment, a means of keeping it alive, but it is also the cause of the senses becoming turbulent and, therefore, when it ceases to serve the purpose of nourishing the body, eating should cease. When steam fails to make the engine run, when the pipe through which it flows is rusted, its supply ought to be stopped. A wise engineer would know that, if this supply were not stopped, the engine could burst. The position with regard to food and the body is identical, and, therefore, if feeding the body results in the senses becoming turbulent, we should stop eating. As, however, our instinctive pleasure in food will not disappear when we stop eating, we should also pray for God's grace. We have a poem in which we say that we should pray for God's forgiveness for the thousand sins which we commit. We are drawn to these sins against our will, we slip into them slowly and gradually without consciously wishing to commit them. We should pray for God's mercy so that we may be forgiven the many thousand sins of this kind. Hence, if anyone is convinced that he ought to kill his physical appetites, he does nothing wrong in fasting. If he has faith, it will certainly be rewarded. If it is not rewarded, God's promise to man will be falsified; but our experience is that this never happens. One must not shrink from a fast of ten or twenty or fifty days. Gibbon[1] never made any statement without first verifying its truth. He has mentioned Catholics fasting for as many as fifty days. They had certainly mastered the senses to that degree. In this miserable age, people become impatient if they get no result in five days. Let no one think that our pleasure in objects can be quickly destroyed. If it is not destroyed and the man can control himself no longer, he may eat, but he should not accept defeat. He should start a fast again. This readiness to stake one's all and perish is bound to be rewarded with victory. The man will ultimately win but only if he perseveres after failing ten or even twenty times. There is such great beauty in this effort, and that is why I advise it. What is followed in the Roman Catholic Church is also enjoined in Islam. The people who at present do evil things in the name of Islam have little understanding of it. Those, on the other hand, who go on praying in their obscure homes, certainly realize God. They give up all indulgences. One cannot indulge in pleasures and live a life of renunciation at the same time. If we understand the truth that we eat only to give the body its hire, then we are fit to understand the *Gita*.

One more point (which I will not elaborate today). It is, that the author of the *Gita* has categorically laid down the principles. We shall find no error in them if we examine them in the abstract, but when we try to put them into practice we experience difficulties. But I will take up this point later.

Having told Arjuna this with regard to cravings of the senses, Shri Krishna proceeds as in the next verse:

[1] Edward Gibbon (1733-94); author of *The History of the Decline and Fall of the Roman Empire*

> For, in spite of the wise man's endeavour, O Kaunteya, the unruly senses distract his mind perforce.[1]

However much an intelligent man may strive, the senses are restless, they shake his self-control and forcibly draw his mind towards their objects; they draw even a *jnani*[2] after them. The senses are like uncontrollable horses. If the rider is not vigilant and the reins are not all right, there is no knowing where they will carry him. "A monkey, and drunk besides"[3], that is how it will be.

> Holding all these in check, the yogi should sit intent on Me; for he whose senses are under control is secure of understanding.[4]

"The *sthitadhi*, having controlled all his senses, will rest wholly absorbed in Me. Anyone who strives in this manner and succeeds in holding his senses under control, such a one is a *yogi*."

Thus Shri Krishna shows how to become a *sthitaprajna*.

[34]

April 3, 1926

I explained yesterday that, in order that our pleasure in the objects of senses may subside completely, fasting, *bhakti*[5], prayer and vigils are necessary. But the pleasure [in objects] will not disappear till we have realized God. The question is, can it disappear completely while the body is there? I have come to the conclusion that no one can be called a *mukta* while he is still alive; one may be said at the most to have become fit for *moksha*. When we speak of Janaka as a *muktatma*, the word *mukta* is used in a general sense and the term means that he was a man who would attain deliverance after his death, that he would not have to be born again. It is doing violence to the meaning of words to say that a man has attained deliverance even while he lives in the body, for the necessity for deliverance remains so long as connection with the body remains. A little reflection will show us that, if our egoistic attachment to ourselves has completely disappeared, the body cannot survive. If we have no wish at all to keep the body alive, it must cease to exist. If we but move our hand the mind

[1] II, 60
[2] A man of spiritual knowledge and illumination
[3] A Gujarati saying
[4] II, 61
[5] Devotion to God

is bound to move too. If, now, we would completely withdraw the mind from the body, the latter should become "as the burnt silken thread, only the form surviving". Some attachment is bound to persist while our bodies are capable of motion. Scientists remove air from a bottle, but a little of it remains in it. The air becomes more and more rarefied, and only a scientist would know that there was any inside. Similarly, our pleasure in objects does not disappear completely while the least degree of association with the body persists, as signified by its movements. Moreover, as long as we commit even a little violence, *moksha* is not possible, and the slightest movement of the body involves some violence. Even if the body is lying completely motionless, its functioning involves some violence, however little it may be. There is violence even in the act of thinking, and so long as that is so man cannot attain a state of perfect self-realization, his mind cannot even comprehend such a state.

Thus, the cravings of the senses die away only when we cease to exist in the body. This is a terrible statement to make, but the *Gita* does not shrink from stating terrible truths. Truth does not remain hidden because it is not stated. *Moksha* is the supreme end, and even yogis can experience it only in contemplation. We must, therefore, say that the Dweller in the body cannot be free while He dwells in it. The prisoner is in jail and the king promises him that he will be released; but till he is actually released he cannot be said to have come out of the cage.

He can only imagine his condition after release. In the same way, if there is anyone waiting to receive and greet the *atman* on its release, he cannot do that as long as it remains imprisoned in this cage of the body.

And this cannot but be so. How can it be otherwise than that the state after release will be different from the state before it?

Truth is so profound and great a thing that, as we think more and more about it, we realize that to have a direct experience of it, we should completely shed our attachment to the body and yearn every moment for *moksha*. As we think of *moksha* in this light, its value in our eyes should daily increase. If it is the most important thing in life, it should be clear to us that it cannot be attained while we live in this body. Till the gate of the body prison has opened, the fragrance of *moksha* is beyond our experience. Whether terrible or not, this is the truth.

We need not spend much thought or indulge in intellectual exercises over this problem. Once we are decided on the end, we should concentrate our attention on the means; if they are right, the end is as good as attained. If we have trust in our father, we may rest assured that we shall get our share in his property and need not ask him whether he has made a will. Similarly, we need not argue about this matter. The thing is like Euclid's straight line. No one in the world has as yet succeeded in drawing a perfect right angle, but we can construct buildings with the help of instruments which approximate to a right angle. Likewise, we can only conceive the state of *moksha*. We can conceive a perfect straight line only when we erase the straight line before us; similarly, we can attain deliverance only when we leave the body.

> In a man brooding on objects of the senses, attachment to them springs up; attachment begets craving and craving begets wrath.
>
> Wrath breeds stupefaction, stupefaction leads to loss of memory, loss of memory ruins the reason, and the ruin of reason spells utter destruction.[1]

Dwelling constantly on objects of sense-pleasure produces attachment for them. Shri Krishna here explains the order in which withdrawal from sense-objects is to be accomplished. If we constantly think about having a certain object, the mind will become strongly attached to the thought of its possession, and this in turn will grow into a passionate desire to possess it so that the object takes still greater hold of our mind. Attachment produces impatience and passion gives rise to anger. When we fail to get the object of our desire, we become angry. As it recedes from us, we get angry with others. Anger clouds a man's vision, so that he loses his judgment and forgets what he is. "Who am I, and from whence?"—he forgets to ask. If he could but recollect, would he not realize what was proper and what was not proper for him? The man who forgets what he is loses his power of discrimination. Such a person is as good as dead. Quite a few persons mount the gallows with perhaps a smile on their face. But they depart from this world and have no future in the other. Thus, through constant dwelling on objects of sense the man is ultimately destroyed. He as good as commits suicide. It is not merely that his body perishes; he will not rise from his fallen state for many lives to come. One should, therefore, crush the craving of sense the moment it arises. The first thing to do is to get over the habit of dwelling on objects of sense-pleasure in our imagination.

[1] II, 62 and 63

For that purpose, one should constantly think on God, should live as it were in a state of *samadhi*.

[35]

April 4, 1926

> But the disciplined soul, moving among sense-objects with the senses weaned from likes and dislikes and brought under the control of *atman*, attains peace of mind.[1]

He who lives with his senses no longer subject to attachments and aversions and perfectly under his control becomes fit for God's grace. When a man's ears, nose, eyes, and so on, go on performing their functions naturally without conscious willing on his part—the winking of the eyelids does not need to be willed, there must be some disease if it is otherwise—we say of such a person that his sense-organs, having become free from attachments and aversions, function spontaneously.

What is the natural work of the ear? We describe a man as established in *samadhi* when his *atman* abides in serene content in itself. His senses must be under his perfect control. The ears of a man whose mind has become one-pointed must have become the servants of his *atman*. Actually, however, we are the slaves of our senses. From this slavery we must win swaraj for the *atman*. The ears should in fact listen only to the divine music of the *atman*. They would not, then, hear even the loud beating of drums. While the *atman* dwells in this body, it should live as the latter's master and god, and use the senses to do only their natural work. Such a person has no charm for Panditji's singing; he attends only to the praise of God.

As Sanjaya had been given the gift of divine vision, so there are divine eyes and ears behind our bodily eyes and ears. The person who is ruled by his *atman* will have the gift of inner senses and will not need the outer ones. These latter are always subject to some degree of attachment and aversion. Our hands may be cut off, but they will not move on their own—such should be the degree of our self-control. There was once a great bishop[2] in England who held out his hands to be burnt first. Hazarat Ali did not feel the pain of the arrow, for his mind was absorbed in the contemplation of God. The man who has not sold himself to

[1] II, 64

[2] Presumably this refers to Thomas Cranmer (1489-1556), Archbishop of Canterbury, who was burnt at the stake.

his senses as their slave, but has made himself God's slave has no right to ask for a reward from Him in the form of His grace. He who has become God's slave will, instead of trying to be a master in this world, believe even while he suffers God's lashes that they are for his good. Why do we pray to God to breathe greater life into us? God had His own interest—a divine interest—in creating man and that is that the latter should so live that he would not seek pleasures of the senses, but would devote himself entirely to His contemplation and service.

This is the principle. In daily life, one should choose the best that is possible for one. If a man is incapable of hearing the divine song in him, he may listen to good songs sung by others. He should do work which would make him feel in tune with his *atman*. As long as we must use our moral judgment, we should choose what is good and shun what is evil. We shall then succeed in making the senses do their natural work. For one who lives in this way,

> Peace of mind means the end of all ills, for the understanding of him whose mind is at peace stands secure.[1]

When God's grace descends on us, bringing us peace, all our suffering ends. Who can harm him who is protected by Rama? He on whom God daily showers His grace has all his sufferings destroyed. The intellect of a man whose *chitta* has become calm and whose only thought is of God, stands secure and is protected against error. Shri Krishna now describes a condition the opposite of this:

> The undisciplined man has neither understanding nor devotion; for, for him who has no devotion there is no peace, and for him who has no peace whence happiness?[2]

The meaning is that the man who has not become one in God, who is not a yogi established in *samadhi*, lacks the faculty of intellect altogether. One who is unsteady has an intellect which is many-branched; of what good is such an intellect? It feels no devotion, it does not utter Ramanama. He who lacks devotion and does not meditate on God, how can he attain peace? The man who is filled with devotion sits in single-minded contemplation of God, but the other man who has no peace, how can he be happy?

[1] II, 65
[2] II, 66

[36]

April 6, 1926

Before we resume our reading of the *Gita*, let us apply to our practical situation what we have already learnt. Today is the sixth[1], the day of India's awakening. I look upon it as a day of religious awakening, though ordinarily it would be regarded as a day of political significance. On that day we had kept a fast, bathed in a river and gone to temples; Muslims had offered prayers in mosques and Parsis in their fire-temples. Who can say how many of them were sincere? At that time, of course, everyone seemed to be sincere. That was the day on which we started satyagraha. We commenced civil disobedience in the evening by selling copies of *Hind Swaraj*[2]. All, Hindus, Muslims and Parsis, seemed to have gone crazy on that day. Today, too, we have kept a twenty-four hours' fast. We should understand the aim behind it. The aim is to bring about spiritual awakening in us. Our aspiration to go from untruth into truth, from darkness into light, is not something for the distant future; it is immediate. For us, non-violence and truth are symbolized in the spinning-wheel. It may be made only of wood, but if we see in it the *chintamani*[3] then it becomes the *chintamani*. It is intelligent to regard the spinning-wheel to be what it is, but it is more intelligent to regard it as the *chintamani*. If even the dullest can see God in a clod of earth, what may we not see in the spinning-wheel ?

What is wrong, if we see swaraj in the spinning-wheel ? Our idea, therefore, does not violate dharma. We should understand this when we keep a fast and spin. The Satyagraha Ashram will go on doing its work even when the rest of the country goes to sleep. And we shall, as I have said, get swaraj through the spinning-wheel. The *Bhagavad Gita* says that women, Vaisyas and Sudras, all classes of people, can win freedom. In the same way, all of us can do this. Whether or not we are stout and well-fed, we can do this work if we are strong in mind. Let us, therefore, cultivate firmness of mind; if we do not let the senses distract the mind, we can become fit for satyagraha.

[1] April 6, 1919 was observed throughout India as a day of protest against the Rowlatt Bills: *vide* Vol. XV, pp. 183-8.

[2] Published in 1909 and proscribed in March 1910 by the Government of Bombay 3; *vide* Vol. X.

[3] A fabulous gem that fulfils all the desires of its owner

Let us now take up the verse which we are to discuss today.

> For when his mind runs after any of the roaming senses, it sweeps away his understanding, as the wind a vessel upon the waters.[1]

A pleasure-loving man wastes his time in aimless wandering; he must have new suits of clothes every day, he eats and drinks what pleases his palate and goes about dressed in finery. If one of his pleasure-loving senses is so undisciplined that it seeks gratification anywhere and anyhow and if his mind is totally enslaved by this one sense, it will drag his intellect behind it as the wind drives a ship before it in the sea and wrecks it on a rock or runs it aground. Thus the man whose senses are completely out of his control and whose mind is totally enslaved by one of them will be ruined through gradual stages explained earlier as the consequences of attachment. If the mind is enslaved by even a single sense, one is lost.

> Therefore, O Mahabahu, he, whose senses are reined in on all sides from their objects, is the man of secure understanding.[2]

The man whose senses are under his control and are kept away from their objects is a man established in *samadhi*.

> When it is night for all other beings, the disciplined soul is awake; when all other beings are awake, it is night for the seeing ascetic.[3]

In conclusion, Shri Krishna gives the mark of a *sthitaprajna* in one verse. He is awake when it is night for other human beings, and when other human beings and all the creatures seem to be awake, it is night for the ascetic who sees.

This should be the ideal for the Satyagraha Ashram. Let us pray that we may see light when all around us there is darkness. If we are brave, the whole world will be brave; as in our body, so in the universe—this is how we should feel. We should thus be ready to take upon ourselves the burden of the whole world, but we can bear the burden only if we mean by it doing *tapascharya*[4] on behalf of the entire world. We shall then see light where others see nothing but darkness. Let others think that the spinning-wheel is useless, and believe that we cannot win swaraj by keeping fasts. We should tell them that we are sure we shall get it; for, as the *Gita* says, *yavanartha udapane*[5], that is, if through

[1] II, 67
[2] II, 68
[3] II, 69
[4] Voluntary suffering as moral discipline
[5] A reference to II, 46

fasts and similar practices we can obtain the position of a liveried servant in God's Kingdom, why cannot we secure such a position in our swaraj? The world will tell us that the senses cannot be controlled. We should reply that they certainly can be. If people tell us that truth does not avail in the world, we should reply that it does. The world and the man established in *samadhi* are like the west and the east. The world's night is our day and the world's day is our night. There is, thus, non-co-operation between the two. This should be our attitude if we understand the *Gita* rightly. This does not mean that we are superior to others; we are humble men and women, we are a mere drop while the world is the ocean. But we should have the faith that, if we succeed in crossing to the other shore, the world, too, will. Without such faith we cannot claim that the world's night is our day. If we can achieve self-realization through fasting and spinning, then self-realization necessarily implies swaraj.

[37]

April 7, 1926

Yesterday, we learnt an important mark of the *sthitaprajna*. What seems light to other people is darkness to the yogi. For instance, we tell a great number of people that they should eat sparingly, but a man who has spent his days in devotion to God will immediately understand that, if he eats full meals every day, it will be a hindrance to his life of devotion. Such a yogi, therefore, will keep himself alive on very little food while other people go on feasting on delicacies. But he will not parade his self-control. Narasinh Mehta ridiculed in his song renunciation, knowledge, meditation, etc., and gave the palm to the *gopi's* love, but this sounds strange to people in the modern age. The truth is that those whom the world knows as yogis are not really yogis, nor what the world describes as the four modes of liberation[1] or as spiritual enlightenment are such in fact. These phrases are used merely to deceive the world. The man who really lives a life of contemplation will outwardly seem a man of the world. His mind may be absorbed in God all the hours of the day, but he will move in the world like other men. He will not go about trumpeting that he lives a life of contemplation. The *gopis* in their love go on dancing, for, knowing that their love is pure, they are not

[1] Namely, attaining *salokya* (the world of God), *samipya* (nearness to God), *sarupya* (the form of God), *sayujya* (union with God)

afraid of the world's censure. Mira said that she paid no heed to what the world said, since she had not left her husband but only wished to discover the true meaning of devotion to one's husband. Gopichand[1] is living in a palace of gold. He is looking admiringly at his body, which is exuding the fragrance of *abir*[2] and *gulal*[3], and his face is lit up with a smile of joy. And then, it happens, tears drop from the eyes of Mainavati[4] who is watching him from the balcony above. Gopichand wonders from where the water-drops can come, seeing that there are no clouds in the sky. Mainavati explains to him that his body which he so admired will one day perish, it will be covered with wrinkles, the teeth in the mouth will loosen and come out and the eyes will see no more. What will his body avail him, she asks, if he were to die just then? She has wasted her whole life, but he has time yet to escape and save himself. Is it likely that a mother would give such advice? What the world prizes highly seemed of little worth to this mother, for she was a woman of spiritual wisdom. As the earth rotates on its axis, once every twenty-four hours we are hanging with our feet up and heads down. We can move about in this position because the earth pulls us towards itself like the ants moving on the surface of a lump of sugar. We, the ants on the earth, do not know that the latter is round and is in constant motion. The spiritually enlightened man and the yogi know the hidden truth of these things and tell us what is unreal. What the world takes as real is unreal to them. What it describes as darkness, they will describe as light. The yogi has an inner vision which is different from the world's. The body should live as prisoner of the *atman*. It should function entirely under the latter's control.

> He in whom all longings subside, even as the waters subside in the ocean which, though ever being filled by them, never overflows—that man finds peace; not he who cherishes longing.[5]

The sea, though being ever added to, remains confined within its bounds; it stands where it has always stood despite countless rivers emptying their waters into it. The man in whom evil impulses and desires subside in the same manner is a yogi. The man who is a slave of desires, whose senses are for ever being

[1] A king in Hindu mythology who by his renunciation displayed the purest love for his mother

[2] & [3] White and red powders

[4] Gopichand's mother

[5] II, 70

allured by their objects, such a person is not a yogi. He is a yogi who is like the sea, who is not like a rivulet or a brook which soon overflows and soon dries up. Christian[1], too, was a yogi and a man of contemplative life. His voice sounded but one refrain. A man, whose mind is constantly absorbed in God, whether he is bathing or eating or drinking, how can he feel evil desires? Like the sea, he is ever full. Rivers and streams fall into it and come to rest, and their waters are cleansed of their dirt. If this dirt spread out in the sea-water, would the latter be as clear as it is? We actually go to a sea-coast to enjoy its fresh air. In like manner, every evil desire subsides and disappears in the sea of a yogi's mind.

> The man who sheds all longing and moves without concern, free from the sense of 'I' and 'mine'—he attains peace.[2]

Such peace may be experienced by a man who has given up all cravings and lives untroubled by desires. He attains to it by shedding the consciousness of "I" and "mine". He alone is a true yogi who never feels "I am doing this".

> This is the state, O Partha, of the man who rests in *Brahman*; having attained to it, he is not deluded. He who abides in this state even at the hour of death passes into oneness with *Brahman*.[3]

The *brahmi* state is that in which we realize the *Brahman*. Having attained it, we are never overpowered by the darkness of ignorance again. It has already been said that objects of sense lose all attraction for us when we have seen God. Similarly, here again Shri Krishna sums up the argument by saying that, having attained to the *brahmi* state, a man never falls again into delusion. A person who is in this state at the moment of his death attains *brahma-nirvana*[4]. This statement can mean either of two things: one, that he will attain to the *Brahman* if he is in that state at the moment of death, and, two, that he will attain eternal peace if he always lives in such a state, right up to the moment of death. If a man who has lived a wicked life till now takes to a good life from tomorrow, there is nothing he will lack. But it will not avail a man to have been good all his life if in his last days he becomes wicked. That man, then, may be said to be good who remains so till the last day of his life. That is why it is said: "Call no man

[1] In *Pilgrim's Progress*
[2] II, 71
[3] II, 72
[4] Absorption in the *Brahman*

good till he is dead." However good a man may have been, he may yet weaken in his old age and worry over his children and his social affairs. We may know that a man has attained *moksha* only if he died in the *brahmi* state.

The nirvana of the Buddhists is *shunyata*[1], but the nirvana of the *Gita* means peace and that is why it is described as *brahma-nirvana*. We need not concern ourselves with this distinction. There is no reason for supposing that there is a difference between the nirvana mentioned by Lord Buddha and the nirvana of the *Gita*. Buddha's description of nirvana and this other description of nirvana refer to the same state. A number of learned men have shown that the Buddha did not teach a doctrine denying the existence of God. But all these are pointless controversies. What can we say about a state which is so different from anything known in our life that we cannot describe it even when we have attained to it? If it is agreed that our bodily existence is not a thing to be cherished, all these other controversies are unmeaning.

This is the end of Chapter II. *Sthitaprajna* means a person who has become completely free from attachments and aversions.

[38]

[Chapter III]

April 8, 1926

The Chapter which we completed yesterday is known as Sankhyayoga. We saw that, after discussing the distinction between the body and the *atman*, Shri Krishna told Arjuna that he had explained the Sankhya view, that is, analysed logically the distinction between the body and the *atman*. This did not help Arjuna to know it in his own experience, but he grasped it intellectually. Arjuna's duty of fighting was explained to him, but only so far as it could be done with the help of argument. Shri Krishna then explained yoga to him, that is, the method of acting in a disinterested spirit. This led to the discussion concerning the *sthitaprajna*.

From the last verse of Chapter II, it would seem that Shri Krishna had nothing further to add. Indeed, if Arjuna had not again put a question to him, there was really nothing for him to add. The *brahmi* state includes *bhakti* too. But in view of the natural tendency in everyone to let his desires rule his reason, truth has to be repeated often so that it may be made more clear. If an

[1] Nothingness

unenlightened man decides for himself, he usually decides in favour of worldliness. Therefore he has to keep on repeating to himself that he is the *atman*, for it is not a truth experienced by him at all hours of the day. A son who has no doubt in his mind at all need not tell his mother that he is her son. The repetition of Ramanama and *dwadashmantra*[1] are for people who have not had self-realization. After release from the body, the man who explains and the man who listens, the two will be one. So long as the body exists, the problems of the means [of attaining *moksha*] will remain; that is why Vyasa expanded the *Gita* this length. There is nothing in it which is not contained in the verses which we recite at the time of our evening prayers. Vyasa has placed before readers a divine truth through the *Gita*. Whether Sankhya or yoga, sannyasa or the life of the house-holder, all these paths are essentially one. Action and inaction mean the same thing, this is the substance of the *Gita*'s teaching. Since these different paths are so mixed up with one another, we should understand their essential identity if our one aim is to know God and realize the unreality of all else. The way to know Him is not to sit cross-legged, but to work in a disinterested spirit.

A man does not become a yogi because he is known to have performed a thousand *yajnas* or made huge gifts. We have to take into account whether he was free from attachment to the ego, whether he willingly turned [in Mira's words] as God pulled him with a slender thread, whether he worked accordingly, and so on. Vyasa wants to tell us that a yogi should offer up to God everything he does, whether it be good or indifferent, should look upon Him as the sole author of everything. And so he makes Arjuna ask Krishna:

> If, O Janardana, thou holdest that the attitude of detachment is superior to action, then why, O Keshava, dost thou urge me to dreadful action?
>
> Thou dost seem to confuse my understanding with perplexing speech; tell me, therefore, in no uncertain voice, that alone whereby I may attain salvation.[2]

First, Shri Krishna put forward the logical argument, and then he described the marks of the *sthitaprajna*. He also explained that yoga meant *karmasu kaushalam*[3]. Arjuna complains that

[1] Literally, sacred formula of twelve syllables: *Om Namo Bhagavate Vasudevaya*

[2] III, I & 2

[3] Skill in action

Shri Krishna has confused his judgment by such contradictory advice, and requests him to tell him some one thing clearly and definitely.

> I have spoken, before, O sinless one, of two attitudes in this world —the Sankhyas', that of *jnanayoga* and the yogis', that of *Karmayoga*.[1]

[39]

April 9, 1926

Arjuna tells Shri Krishna: I cannot judge what is good. At moments I feel that I should fight, and then again I feel that a *sthitaprajna* should have no work to do.

> Never does man enjoy freedom from action by not undertaking action, nor does he attain that freedom by mere renunciation of action.[2]

Merely by refusing to work, one can never experience the state of *naishkarmya* (freedom from experiencing results of action), or attain to *moksha*.

We shall meet this word karma again and again in the *Gita*. What can it mean? It must have, of course, a restricted meaning. But it will help us to understand the relevant verses in the *Gita* if we take the word in its broadest meaning. Karma means any action, any bodily activity or motion. In the *Gita*'s definition of the word, however, karma includes even thought. Any motion, any sound, even breathing, are forms of karma. Some of them we cannot avoid performing. Some of them we perform as a matter of necessity, some others are involuntary. The divine in us urges us on to the path of good, and the demoniac to that of evil. Even if the man is good the demoniac element in him drives him to evil courses. Another man may be wicked, but the divine element in him forces him to follow good. Thus action is impelled by nature, or is the result of compulsion or volition. How do you say, Shri Krishna asks Arjuna, that you will not work? You will not stop riding the horses of your fancies. Even sannyasis are helpless, let them say what they will. Even the decision to stop breathing is karma. Even the refraining from karma is karma. It will not, help one, therefore, to attain to the state of *naishkarmya*. Renunciation of action and the state of *naishkarmya* should come spontaneously.

[1] III, 3
[2] III, 4

> For none ever remains inactive even for a moment; for all are compelled to action by the *gunas* inherent in *prakriti*[1].[2]

No one can cease from karma even for a moment. To listen and not to listen, both are forms of karma. *Sattva, rajas* and *tamas*, the three forces or modes of *prakriti*, drive everyone to action, whether he will or no. A *tamasik* man is one who works in a mechanical fashion, a *rajasik* man is one who rides too many horses, who is restless and is always doing something or other, and the *sattvik* man is one who works with peace in his mind. One is always driven to work by one or another of these three modes of *prakriti* or by a combination of them.

> He who curbs the organs of action but allows the mind to dwell on the sense-objects—such a one, wholly deluded, is called a hypocrite.[3]

Anyone who curbs the organs of action outwardly but dwells all the time on the objects of sense and gives free rein to his fancies, and then believes that he has attained to *naishkarmya*, such a person is sunk in ignorance and his claim is mere hypocrisy. A person who gets his hands tied up but in his mind strikes the enemy, does in reality strike, though outwardly he does not seem to do so. He does not get the pleasure of actually striking, but certainly experiences the fruit of doing so. Please do not misunderstand what I have said. It does not mean that there is no scope for effort or striving, nor that, in that case, we had better act as we feel inclined to. We are constantly thinking of doing something or other, but reflection also helps us in restraining our hands. There can be no hypocrisy in ceaselessly fighting the enemy who holds us in his grip. The point of the verse is that there should be no contradiction between thought and action. It is hypocrisy to yearn inwardly for an object and outwardly keep away from it. It is not hypocrisy if, despite one's best efforts, one does not succeed in always remaining vigilant, for the evil habit has had a long hold over us. Only, one should not merely try but also wish to remain vigilant. Hence, it is wrong for anyone who mentally dwells on objects of sense and outwardly shuns them to describe himself as a sannyasi or yogi. The psychological effects of our actions in past lives cannot be wiped out all

[1] Cosmic energy, as distinguished (in the Sankhya philosophy) from *Purusha*, the Cosmic Consciousness, witness of the action of *prakriti*

[2] III, 5

[3] III, 6

at once. Waves of desire will continue to rise. They will drench us again and again, but one day they will leave us dry. If someone forces me to take up and hold a lamp in my hand, I can say that I did not hold it, for I was not willing to do so. If a person is forced to do anything, his action is not his. For instance, a person who is forced to let off a gun is not a murderer. On the other hand the man who supplied him the powder and planned everything is a murderer. If the man who actually fires the shot does so of his own free will, he too is a murderer. In this way, there should be concord between thought and action. Where this is absent, it is difficult to judge to whom to attribute intention and to whom action. We kept a fast oh the sixth; if, however, we dwelt in our minds the whole day on the pleasure of eating, our fast was no fast. On the other hand, a person is not a hypocrite if, though tempted to eat, he suppresses the desire every time he feels it and so keeps struggling all the time. The man who does evil things has no hope. But he who struggles against evil thoughts will tell himself that he would die rather than let himself do an evil thing; he will go on fighting against his evil thought. The *brahmachari* between whose thoughts and actions reigns perfect harmony and who is always pure in mind deserves the highest reverence. It is the nature of the mind to be ceaselessly active, thinking of one thing or another. He who strives ceaselessly to restrain it is sure to win the battle. It is not as if he never gratified sex-urge, but he does so with discrimination. He is a true sannyasi and yogi between whose thoughts and actions there is such complete harmony that he is not even aware that he observes *brahmacharya.* He should be a man who has made himself a eunuch. If the person is a woman, she should not be conscious at all of being a woman. The man's impotence should not be the incapacity of disease; he should have voluntarily cultivated it. He should become completely free from desire, should become incapable of doing evil. Even a vigilant man may fall, but ultimately he will win complete freedom from desire. A man who remains non-violent in action will in time become free even from the desire to strike anyone.

There is no outward difference between a fool and a wise man. The former has no pretensions. The latter wants to be taken as a fool. Outwardly the behaviour of the two will seem alike. The man whose mind is active with intense energy will appear dull. The earth rotates with such great speed that it seems to be stationary. There is no reference here to the idea of *shunya.* Buddha's nirvana was also not *shunya.* There is only a seeming inertness.

[40]

April 10, 1926

We saw yesterday that a man, while himself remaining in the background, may provide the means of killing and get someone else to do it, and thus become guilty of the heinous sin of murder. His guilt is even greater than that of the person who actually kills. Yudhishthira went to Drona and Bhishma and asked them: 'What is this you have decided to do?'[1] They replied that it was their stomach which had forced them. This means that a slave or servant, being unable to oppose his master's wishes, is less guilty than the latter. The person, on the other hand, who plots a murder and gets someone else to execute the plot is far more wicked than the latter. He is a hypocrite, moreover, as the verse explains.

Proceeding, Shri Krishna explains the opposite manner of acting:

> But he, O Arjuna, who keeping all the senses under control of the mind, engages the organs in *karmayoga*, without attachment—that man excels.[2]

The first point is that one should go on doing karma through the respective organs of action, and the second is that one should hold the same organs under one's control. Shri Krishna has thus divided the physical organs into two classes. The ten organs are the sentries. Five of them function as spies and the other five carry out orders. Hands, feet, etc., belong to the latter class. If the eyes, the nose and other sentries of their class do not remain under our control, we can stop using them. We can curb them every moment. Holding them under control, we make the sentries of the other class carry out orders. He is the best man who controls the functioning of his organs in this manner and works without attachment. A man who gets angry cannot be described as non-attached, he is, in truth, strongly attached.

> Do thou thy allotted task; for action is superior to inaction; with inaction even life's normal course is not possible.[3]

One should do the appointed work, the task which has been assigned to one, for action is superior to inaction. No one can

[1] They had agreed to fight on the side of the Kauravas though they knew that justice was on the side of the Pandavas.

[2] III, 7

[3] III, 8

cease completely from action even for a moment. If that is so, it is better that we work of our own free will. Why need we consult anyone for doing *niyata* karma, that is, for doing work specially meant for us? For, we cannot even keep our bodies alive without working.

> This world of men suffers bondage from all action save that which is done for the sake of sacrifice; to this end, O Kaunteya, perform action without attachment.[1]

Yesterday I explained the meaning of the word karma. Similarly, we should discuss the meaning of *yajna* too. Some learned students of the Shastras believe that the *Gita* is not concerned with work like a cobbler's or like spinning, that is, with work which we do in our practical life. By karma they mean such things as ritual offering of food to the manes, and exclude spinning and weaving from its definition. But the *Gita* is very much concerned with practical life. A dharma which does not serve practical needs is no dharma, it is *adharma*[2]. Even cleaning of latrines should be done in a religious spirit. A man of such spirit will ask himself, as he does the work, why there should be so much foul smell. We should realize that we are full of evil desires. The excreta of a person who is suffering from a disease or is full of evil desires are bound to emit foul smell. Another person who does not do this work in a religious spirit but shirks his duty will remove the contents anyhow, and not clean the bucket; such a man does not do the work as a religious duty. He has no compassion in him, nor discrimination. Thus, dharma is certainly connected with practical life. We have, therefore, accepted a broad definition of karma, and will accept an equally broad definition of *yajna*. We will discuss this tomorrow.

[41]

April 11, 1926

As we have the word *yajna* in our language and the practice is enjoined in our dharma, so the Bible and the holy books of the Jews too have each a corresponding word, and an idea similar to that of *yajna*. We find three things in the Koran: (1) animal sacrifices, on the Bakr-i-Id day; (2) it refers to a practice which also obtained among the Jews, a father sacrificing his son—Ibrahim does this; and (3) Ramadan, which is a form of sacrifice, that

[1] III, 9

[2] The opposite of dharma

is, parting with or giving up something which is dear to us. In the same way, we see in the Bible the meaning of the term sacrifice expanding after Jesus. He told the people that they could not realize their aim by this sacrifice of animals, that for performing a sacrifice in the right sense of the term they would have to do much more than kill animals. He told them that it was not a sacrifice to destroy other lives, that one should give one's own life as sacrifice. With that idea, he sacrificed his own life for the eternal welfare of the world, for its spiritual welfare, for washing away its sins and not merely for feeding the people. Among the Hindus, too, the practice of human sacrifice was prevalent at one time. Then followed animal sacrifice. Even today, thousands of goats are sacrificed to Mother Kali. *Yajnas* are also performed for securing the fulfilment of many worldly desires. The root word in the English term "sacrifice" had a good meaning; it meant "to sanctify". In Sanskrit, *yaj* means "to worship". In the Old Testament, the word for *yajna* means "to renounce". But the underlying idea, that all actions performed for the good or service of others are forms of *yajna*, will be accepted by everyone. Maybe our motive in sacrificing an animal is that of public good, for instance, securing rainfall. The motive in this may be that of public good, but it is not a true sacrifice in which we kill other creatures. We may tell ourselves that we have made a sacrifice in paying for the goat, but the crores of other Hindus are not likely to share that belief.

In Gujarat, too, we find this practice prevails in places. A buffalo is sacrificed on the Dushera Day[1]. Our reason, however, tells us that there is no sacrifice in this, that we do not really worship God by doing this. However, the belief underlying this practice, too, is that we serve public good through it. We should, therefore, include two points in the definition of *yajna*: it is something which is done to serve others' good, but without causing suffering to any creature. We serve the good of the world by refraining from causing suffering to other creatures, because we shall refrain from doing so only if we cherish the lives of other creatures as we do our own, only if we believe that the body is transient. If we interpret correctly the word *yajna* as it is used in the *Gita*, we shall find no difficulty in understanding its teaching and living in accordance with it. We can perform a *yajna* with the mind as much as with the body. Of these two

[1] The tenth day of *Asvina*, the month in the Hindu Calendar roughly corresponding to October

meanings of *yajna*, we should accept that which suits the context every time.

We need not go into why in the past people performed—or even at the present time do perform—animal sacrifice. We shall answer the question in one or two sentences. Man selects for his food what is available in his environment. What objection, moreover, can there be from people's point of view to anything done for public good which is not in itself regarded as sinful? Where people believe that the rains will not come unless some person or creature is sacrificed, no hesitation is felt in performing such a sacrifice. As man's beliefs become more enlightened, the meanings, which people attach to certain words also become more enlightened. Even if Vyasa had defined the words which he used, we would ask why we should accept the meanings given by him. For instance, non-co-operation has come to mean much more than we at first intended it to mean. There is no harm in our enlarging the meaning of the word *yajna*, even if the new meaning we attach to the term was never in Vyasa's mind. We shall do no injustice to Vyasa by expanding the meaning of his words. Sons should enrich the legacy of their fathers. Why should we object if anyone regarded the spinning-wheel with greater sentiment than what we seek to create in the people about it? It is quite possible that in future people may see harm in the spinning-wheel, may come to think that no one should wear cotton clothes at all, because they do harm. They may, for instance, believe that clothes should be made from fibres extracted from banana leaves. If people should come to feel that way, anyone who still clings to the spinning-wheel would be looked upon as a fool. A wise man, however, will mean by the spinning-wheel not an article made of wood but any type of work which provides employment to all people. That is also the case with regard to the meaning of the term *yajna*. Thus, we may, and should, attach to it a meaning not intended by Vyasa.

> Together with sacrifice did the Lord of beings create, of old, mankind, declaring:
>
> "With this may you cherish the gods and may the gods cherish you; thus cherishing one another may you attain the highest good.[1]

We should think carefully what the term god, too, means. Who are god Indra and other gods? Who are the god of water and the god of woodlands? There was an argument once over one

[1] III, 10 & 11

of the verses in our morning prayers, whether it was proper to worship Saraswati conceived as a figure with hands and feet. Just as it was explained at the time that Saraswati was not a goddess living somewhere far away in the clouds, so are Indra and others not gods living in the heavens; they symbolize the forces of nature. If only we take the thirty-three crores of gods in whom we believe to stand for man, we would serve our own good and also that of the whole world, of all the creatures in it. The gods symbolize the different forms of energy, the forces which sustain the universe. Even the belief in terrible gods does not deserve to be dismissed. The power of God in all its three aspects—creative, protective and destructive—is beneficial, but we do not understand the real meaning of these three aspects because of our limited knowledge. The *Nagapanchami* day is observed to save ourselves from harm by snakes. It is not right to observe any such day to appease snakes. And so also about ghosts and spirits. What are ghosts? They are merely creatures of our imagination. Our aim should be, instead, to worship the sustaining energy of God, to worship it in all its aspects.

[42]

April 13, 1926

We cannot give any arbitrary meaning to the term *yajna*. We can adopt only a meaning which is consistent with the use of the word in the *Gita*. We may draw all possible conclusions from the principles of geometry, but they should be such as Euclid would not question or oppose. We do no injustice to the poet in going beyond his meaning. Any purpose which a well serves will be served by a lake too. If water can be used for a good purpose, it can also be used for an evil purpose. We can destroy a dam and thereby render innumerable fields useless. So the meaning which we have attached to the term *yajna*, namely, any action performed with a view to public good, is not inconsistent with the use of the term in the *Gita*.

"This world suffers bondage from work unless it is work done as *yajna*"; in this verse, the word *yajna* can also be interpreted to mean Vishnu and the worshippers of Siva may take it to mean Siva. In other words, any work dedicated to God helps one to attain *moksha*.

"Along with *yajna* the Lord created men." Which type of *yajna* is meant here? Does the term have any special meaning? I think it has. The reference here is not to mental or intellectual work. Brahma[1] did not ask human beings to multiply and prosper merely by working with their minds; what He meant was that they should do so through bodily *yajna*, by working with the body. Scriptures of other religions enjoin the same thing. The Bible says: "With the sweat of thy brow thou shalt earn thy bread."[2] Thus bodily labour is our lot in life; it is best, then, to do it in the spirit of service and dedicate it to Shri Krishna. Anyone who works in that spirit all his life becomes free from evil and is delivered from all bonds. Such a person is like a soldier in the King's army, who is content to carry out orders. He is as worthy as the General. Both have equal value in God's eyes, for He looks only to the attitude. Arjuna's arrows availed him not when Krishna was no longer by his side, and he was robbed by a Kaba[3]. The verse, commencing with *sahayajna* then, talks of bodily *yajna*, of a kind, moreover, through which gods and men would serve each other's needs. By gods we may understand all living beings or God's sustaining energy. Gods are the invisible forces. So long as a person has someone in sight for whom he works, he is not engaged in service; real service consists in working for those whom one does not know personally. The thirty-three crores of gods belong to the world of imagination. Children cannot even conceive this number. We cannot take in with our eyes so many beings assembled at one place, nor count them. We cannot see these gods, as we see our children, and yet we cultivate a living relationship with them. By and by, the sphere of our service will enlarge itself to embrace the whole world. We have thus left aside the word gods and interpreted the verse to mean that we should serve the humblest human beings, even those whom we never see, with respect and honour and looking upon them as gods and not as our servants; we should, in other words, serve the whole world.

This verse tells us that we should undertake bodily labour to do service. Man simply cannot live without such work. If he had not violated this law, he would not suffer as much as he does, the rich would not have become masters of immeasurable stores of wealth and the millions would not be suffering in poverty. God is a great economist. He is omnipotent. We cannot refrain completely from storing things for future use. But God never stores, for he can destroy and create the universe with a mere thought. He

[1] The Creator
[2] Gandhiji said this in English.
[3] A highway robber

wants us, therefore, to provide only for each day. If we want anything the next day, we must labour for it. He has warned that we are doomed if we do not labour, if we do not bend the body and work with it. He has commanded that we should willingly endure every kind of suffering. If we honour this law in our life, there would be no hunger and no sin or immorality in this world. Evil desires will never disturb a man who labours all the twenty-four hours for the good of the world (I say twenty-four hours because one keeps working even in sleep.). If the labourers in the world were filled with evil desires as we are, the world could not last. The rich seek all kinds of luxuries. If the workers, too, did that, where would the world be? In the West, nowadays the idea has come to prevail that men and women are born to gratify all their desires. *Adharma* is being propagated. If people worked with the shovel or pick-axe, would they be disturbed with evil desires? We should submit ourselves, therefore, to this restraining law. If we do our bodily *yajna* properly, all will be well with us, we shall advance the good of our *atman* and of the world, our mind and body will be ruled by our *atman* and we shall be filled with serene peace. It can be said that such a person, even though acting, does nothing.

I cannot understand the idea that one can perform a *yajna* by lighting a few sticks. It does not do to say that doing so purifies the air. There are many other ways of purifying the air. Why should we at all pollute the air? It is always pure. It is we who pollute it. But this is not the aim behind a *yajna*. When the Aryans first came to this country, they tried to civilize the non-Aryan races. Maybe the idea of *yajna* was originally conceived for the uplift of the latter. There were big forests in those days, and it may have been regarded as everyone's duty to help in clearing these forests, for it was a social necessity. And because this work was regarded as a duty, it came to be looked upon as a means of attaining *moksha*. Innumerable ceremonies were devised, all of which required the lighting of fire. If these *rishis*[1] had lived in the desert of Sahara, they would have conceived of *yajna* as refraining from cutting a single twig, as planting of trees or drawing a certain quantity of water. In burning wood in this age, we misuse the capital of our forefathers; or we show ourselves witless pedants by understanding the thing in a literal sense. If we think of the matter now, we shall see that burning sticks is no longer a form of bodily *yajna*. If we would under-

[1] Literally, seers

take any such *yajna* in this age and in this country, it is spinning, the reason being the same as in the instance I cited of the forests. At that time, the very thought of cutting trees for wood in a forest might have shaken a man with fear; but the man who had faith would have started the work straightway, for the person who had asked him to do it was inspired with absolute conviction. Such a man of faith would simply go on cutting trees (Recall the instance of Stevenson and the ditch near Manchester. He asked people to go on and on filling it with earth.) If the order for cutting down trees had not gone out, snakes and poisonous air would have remained of course. Someone has said that a true idea is born in the mind of one person who acts upon it, and thus, it starts on its career. If you employ the right means, the end is certain to follow. All that is necessary is to make a start. A man of faith will go ahead with his work, undeterred by difficulties. He knows no such thing as failure. Let the world believe in failure, he would say, I do not know what it is. This is what is meant by disinterested work. Such a person hopes for nothing, and works in patience; he resorts to no scheming and is never in too much hurry for the result.

[43]

April 14, 1926

We discussed yesterday the meaning of the term *yajna*. Using one's limbs, labouring, working for others' good, these ideas follow from this one verse. What is meant by saying that mankind was created along with *yajna*? As we cannot escape the cycle of birth, old age and death, so also bodily labour is our lot in life from which there is no escape. But what actually happens is that man becomes self-centred and follows his own wishes in every matter, or works in order that he may be able to indulge in pleasures. But the world cannot go on thus, and if the world cannot go on, the individual who behaves in this manner also cannot live. Man is born a helpless creature. The child needs someone—a mother-god or father-god—to look after it. Man is born dependent, and dies in dependence. Freedom is a state of the mind. A man can describe himself as *swadhin*[1] only to the extent that he feels so, for he can say that he submits himself to a law of his own free will. But there are laws disregard of which would make government impossible; a man cannot, however, commit a crime and escape its consequences. Not only that, the relations of the person

[1] Dependent on oneself

committing a crime also suffer with him. A crime ultimately proves as harmful to its author as the swallowing of raw mercury. Man is, thus, dependent on others in all things. He is his own master in only a few matters. It is, therefore, best for him to do everything in the spirit of *yajna*. *Yajna* was created simultaneously with us, so that we may serve the gods and the latter may serve us. If we let ourselves be ruled by them, they, too, will be ruled by us. The right *yajna* for this age is the *yajna* of spinning. We should, however, think of *yajna* only in its primary meaning which we have discussed. All other forms of *yajna* follow from that. Our most important activity is eating and drinking. Even our body is born as a slave. If we learn to keep it alive exclusively for the good of the *atman*, we should attain *moksha*. The body is meant to be spent for the good of the *atman* and of the world. Different men act in different ways, and if we believe in what the law terms "a legal fiction", that the king does no wrong, then the king also becomes good. If today the Princes are wicked, so are their subjects. In these other matters too, we keep up some legal fictions. We entertain such a fiction about the spinning-wheel, too, that through it we establish a bond with the world, having abandoned the old fiction that we establish such a bond by burning sticks and pouring ghee into the fire.

It is not recently that I have come to attach this meaning to *yajna*; I have understood it in that sense ever since I first read the *Gita*. What I read about the Russian writer Bondoref's [views on] "bread labour"[1] only confirmed my idea, but the idea was with me from the beginning and has grown stronger with years. The Russian writer has stated one side of the truth. We understand the other side too. We now understand the idea of bread labour better, for by *yajna* we do not mean labour as a means of livelihood. Thanks to the associations which the term calls up, we do not restrict *yajna* to mean this and no more. Labour in this context means bodily labour. He alone should eat who has laboured for twelve hours. Anyone who sincerely wants to observe *brahmacharya*, to preserve purity and to be free from evil desires, must engage himself in bodily labour. People who do physical work are not subject to the sway of such desires as much as we are. Maybe they are dull in mind; but it is better to be dull in mind than to be a prey to evil desires. The world would go on even if there were no intelligent men and women in it, but it would be nowhere if all people refused to do physical work. We

[1] Gandhiji uses the English expression.

have exercised our intelligence in acknowledging the law of bodily labour. The one universal form of such labour is agriculture and it should, therefore, be looked upon as *yajna.*

> "Cherished with sacrifice, the gods will bestow on you the desired boons." He who enjoys their gifts without rendering aught unto them is verily a thief.[1]

The gods, gratified by *yajna*, that is, by your work for the service of others and your bodily labour, will grant you the means to gratify your desires; that is, the gods in the form of society will grant them to you. Anyone who receives what they give but offers nothing to others is a thief. He is a thief who does not do bodily labour for society.

> The righteous men who eat the residue of the sacrifice are freed from all sin, but the wicked who cook for themselves eat sin.[2]

Those holy persons who eat only what is left behind after the *yajna* is over become free from all sins. They who first offer to society, to Shri Krishna, what they get to eat, live free from sin. But those who cook food only for themselves, who work only for selfish ends, take in nothing but sin when they eat. That is why one should regularly and daily perform *yajna*, make a sacrifice, of which body labour is the foundation. The greatest *yajna* consists in observing the very first commandment of God, the commandment with which every human being is sent into this world.

> From food springs all life, from rain is born food; from sacrifice comes rain and sacrifice is the result of action.[3]

If people did nothing, there would be no rains, which means that there would be no rains if people did not perform *yajna.* Work which is necessary must be done. But people are simply not ready to exert themselves and plant trees. Rains are plentiful in forests. But there they are of no benefit to human beings; in fact they do terrible harm. They do not do that after human beings start working in those forests. Cherapunji has the heaviest rainfall in the world, but what good does all that rain do? (Of course, the rainfall there serves as a standard of comparison for rainfall in other parts of the world, but that is a different matter.)

In this verse, the *Bhagavad Gita* enunciates the principle explained by scientists that there can be no rain in regions barren of vegetation.

[1] III, 12
[2] III, 13
[3] III, 14

[44]

April 15, 1926

Know that action springs from *Brahman* and *Brahman* from the Imperishable; hence the all-pervading *Brahman* is ever firm-founded on sacrifice.[1]

This verse is a little difficult to understand. "You should know," Krishna says to Arjuna, "that karma springs from *Brahman*, and the latter from *yajna.*" In an annotated *Gita* found in Bihar, karma is explained as *Brahman*, and a little below, the latter is explained as the source of the universe, as that which fills the entire universe, and from which arise Brahma, Vishnu and Siva, or, in other words, as that which we describe as dwelling in the hearts of all creatures, that which is the common element of belief among all faiths and sects.

It is true that *Brahman* springs from *yajna*. Wherever we find anyone filled with the spirit of renunciation, anyone whose *atman* abides in serene content within itself, who suffers when others suffer and who practises the supreme *yajna* of maintaining a sameness of attitude towards all, there we may be sure that *Brahman* is present. But there is one thing, whether about this *yajna* or any other, namely, that it should not be so performed as to cost the body nothing. Dharma is not to be followed with tender regard for one's body. That is dharma in following which one suffers in the body to the limit of one's endurance. There is no *yajna* for him who is not ready to mortify his body. What right does a person have who undertakes bodily labour for the sake of the world—if there are thirty-three crores in India, there must be billions in the whole world, and if to these we add the insects and other forms of life, then each of us is but one hair on the body as compared with the total number of living creatures in the world—what right does such a person have to feel that he works for the world? If all my hairs were to be plucked off, I would die, but one hair lost means nothing. If we look round in the world, we shall see that the whole of it is within us. If we forget which is the hair and which the world, we shall come to feel one with the world. We shall then spend this body in the service of the world all the hours of the day.

All this talk about knowledge is because of the body; otherwise, for an unembodied one, how can there be any question of knowledge? The highest knowledge of all in the world is knowledge of the self. Moreover, the idea of a human being

[1] III, 15

having no body exists only in our imagination. Mortification of the body, therefore, is the only means of self-realization and the only *yajna* for everyone in this world. We are all labourers. If the rich would look upon themselves as labourers as much as the people who work with their bodies are labourers, the latter would get all that they want. They would then feel quite satisfied with their condition and devote themselves whole-heartedly to their work. If the working men, however, deliberately claim that they are the equals of their masters, they are sure to come to grief. If we follow the methods of the British in running our government when we have swaraj, we would be behaving as masters. But we wish to give up the ways of masters and turn ourselves into workers. If, while working as labourers, we learn to be detached and make ourselves ciphers, we would come out of the darkness of night. This is the idea in the verse containing the phrase eternally founded in *yajna*.

But, then, who is the Brahma mentioned in the first verse of this group? Who, again, are Vishnu and Siva? I do not look upon them as distinct Beings. We may take them to represent aspects of God or His powers. They are represented in the *puranas* as being different from other gods. All that is partly right and partly wrong. They imagined all these things because they wanted to teach people dharma somehow. In truth, there is no such Being as Brahma or Siva. The only reality is the neuter *Brahman*. But as God is conceived of as doing nothing, it was imagined that this universe comes into existence out of Brahma. If I destroy a man's belief in a Brahma with four faces, in what way do I enlighten him? How will that profit me? If such a person asks me whether I share his belief, I will tell him that I do not. But others who believe in a personal God should be free to do so. And so Brahma means the active energy of God. In fact in Tilak Maharaj's *Gita*, Brahma is explained as *prakriti*; I will say, then, that *prakriti* is Brahma. Whatever our belief, what we have to understand from all this is that in every *yajna* God's presence may be felt, and that, where there is no *yajna* of body labour, God, too, is absent, though, of course, we believe that God is present everywhere. Human beings go on working with their bodies and that keeps the cycle going. I have no doubt at all that the Imperishable here means God.

> He who does not follow the wheel thus set in motion here below, he, living in sin, sating his senses, lives, O Partha, in vain.[1]

[1] III, 16

Such a person's life is a burden on others. The earth rotates ceaselessly all the twenty-four hours of the day, and anyone who merely rests on it doing nothing lives to no purpose. One who is always engaged in *yajna* is not subject to the binding effects of karma. But he who, disinclined to work, pleads *aham Brahmasmi*[1] in justification of his idleness, is stated by the *Gita* to be living in sin. This is what Narasinha Mehta meant when he wrote that those who renounce the world will not win deliverance and those who enjoy life will. Here, "those who enjoy life" means all the people in the world who labour with their bodies and "those who renounce the world" means the incorrigible idlers.

I have explained the wheel in this verse to mean the spinning-wheel. I look upon it as the means of supreme *yajna* in this age. He who plies it will have lived worthily, will have won the battle of life.

[45]

April 16, 1926

Yajna means any activity for the good of others.[2] A man works for the good of others when he spends his body in their service. If we look upon our body as the property of the world and use it so, we would retain our control over it but always keep it clean, would not let it be eaten up by white ants. All this, however, should be done in a spirit of dedication to God. It would give us profound happiness if in using it we act as its trustees or guardians. A watchman who serves as one who held his body as a trust may assure us that he would be constantly seen coming to our house, and that this fact by itself was enough to keep off thieves, and if we have trust in such effect of his name we might let this Rama[3], this watchman, go, grant him *moksha*. Similarly, [we should have faith that] any physical labour undertaken in the spirit of service will produce rain.

That is a poet's explanation[4] and it is correct. The word *yajna* comes from the root *yaj*, which means "to worship", and we please God by worshipping Him through physical labour. What should we do if we want rain over a desert? We should plant trees

[1] I am *Brahman*; one of the four "great utterances" in the Upanishads

[2] A member of the audience had asked Gandhiji how *yajna* could produce rain.

[3] A general name for servant, current among Gujaratis in Bombay

[4] A child in the audience had said that their service through physical labour would please God.

there. We should plant trees in any region over which we want rain, and cut them down in those regions where it rains in excess.

The original intention behind the idea of *yajna* was that people should do physical work. We forgot the root and came to concern ourselves with branches and leaves, believing that by pouring oblations into fire we perform a *yajna*. In the old days, it was necessary to cut down trees and burn up the wood in order to clear the land. What was the idea in the pupils approaching their teachers wood in hand? Cutting down trees and burning wood had become a form of *yajna*. At the present time, spinning has become a *yajna*. If water was scarce and we had to fetch it from a distance of two miles, fetching water would be a *yajna*.

Laborare est orare—Work is worship. We can connect this dictum with the idea in this verse.

[46]

April 17, 1926

If we use our intellect for serving others, would that also not be a form of *yajna*? This verse does not say that all forms of *yajna* produce rain. It only says that without *yajna* there can be no rain. That does not mean that all forms of *yajna* can produce rain, just as it is not true that all edible things can support life.

It may be asked what connection there can be between the facts of physical life and spiritual matters? The laws which hold in the spiritual world hold also in the phenomenal world. All the rules which concern the physical body have the welfare of the *atman* as their aim. That should be our primary aim in all our physical activities. We must turn away from everything which does not help us to attain self-realization. One thing, of course, is true. Just as bodily labour undertaken with a view to service will produce rain, so the employment of our intellect in the service of others will promote the welfare of the world.

How do we explain the fact that sometimes *yajna* fails to produce rain? An effect follows a chain of causes, all of which are not visible to us. Besides *yajna*, many other favourable circumstances have to be present. We have no ground for believing that a given action must always produce a given effect. There may have been a thousand other factors which had contributed to the appearance of that effect on a previous occasion.

No event or action is without its effect. Was the earthquake in Japan at the end of the last war the result of Divine wrath?

The explanation given by . . .[1] was that when man becomes cruel, nature too may become so. There is, however, no question of cruelty on the part of nature. How can we regard anything which is pure justice as cruelty? Man does everything through pride. Not so God. To attribute cruelty to Him is to measure Him with a yardstick which we apply to human beings. This is the point of view which produced philosophical atheism. How can we turn God into a human being? From another point of view, He certainly acts, for he bestows life and consciousness. It is He who is ever active and does everything, hears without ears and sees without eyes. It is not correct to believe that an earthquake may be punishment for sin. Why should we believe, either, that an earthquake is a punishment? If a nation is sunk in sin and God wants to save it, He might send an earthquake with that aim. If I wish to commit an immoral act, a most heinous one, and if God sends a snake to bite me in order to prevent me from doing what I intend, would that be His wrath? He does that in order to save me. Take the story of Nala and Karkotak. Karkotak told Nala that if he did not transform him into an ugly figure, he, Nala, would perish with the advent of *Kaliyuga*. Similarly, we should not believe that possession of a kingdom is necessarily the reward of holy merit earned by our goodness. God's ways are inscrutable. We should be afraid of answering all such questions. We may answer simply that we do not know. Of course, we can know God's laws, we have a right to ask what they are. But a wise man restrains his curiosity and tries to know only as much as is necessary for attaining self-realization. Even in that sphere, there ought to be a limit somewhere. Even scientists have not been able to discover how the soul comes into being. I do not find it impossible to imagine that one day man will be able to prevent earthquakes, just as he is able to change the courses of rivers. But the power to bring about such changes is a trivial matter. The laws of physical nature pale into insignificance when compared with those of the *atman*, for the former concern only the world of name and form. It is wise not to have too much curiosity regarding them. We may know what is necessary for us in order to offer praise to God, and, having acquired enough for that purpose, we should have no more curiosity in such matters.

[1] The name is omitted in the source.

[47]

April 18, 1926

But the man who revels in *atman*, who is content in *atman* and who is satisfied only with *atman*, for him no action exists.[1]

He has no interest whatever in anything done, nor in anything not done, nor has he need to rely on anything for personal ends.[2]

There is nothing for such a person to do; not that he does nothing, but it makes no difference to him whether he does or does not do it. He is equally unconcerned in either case. He has no end to pursue through other beings.

It may seem to us that both the verses say the same thing. If we do not think carefully, we shall probably feel that they contradict the verses which precede them. It was said in one of them that anyone who refused to work the rotating wheel was a sinful and indolent man. Here, on the other hand, it is said with reference to the man living contented in the *atman* that there is nothing for him to do. It may seem, but it is not, a paradox to say that one who works in the spirit of service will live contented in his self and there will be nothing which he wants to do. If we place an ant on a ball and keep the latter rotating, there will be nothing for the ant to do but to rest where it is, content with itself. It will tell itself that the ball was rotating, and itself with it, and that was enough. If, now, an ant-hill was provided inside the ball and it was necessary for the ant to move and reach it, it would say that it would be moving inside a rotating ball and have to exercise no choice in doing so. What duty can a prisoner have? He merely carries out orders. The man who lives in the self makes himself the slave of the self. He carries out the orders of the self, and, therefore, has his happiness in the self and lives contented in it. (If the prisoner I referred to just now was a satyagrahi, he would say that he would go on listening carefully to this master, the self, and so win it over.) If he is all the time absorbed in listening to the voice of the self and acts so as to conform to the turning wheel, what would be there for him to do? Tolstoy states somewhere this same thing, that man in his foolishness boasts that he will do this and he will do that, that he will relieve the suffering of people in distress and so on. But it will be enough, says Tolstoy, if this person comes down from off the backs of the people he is sitting on. The people on whose backs he is riding, they have nothing to do. We

[1] & [2] III, 17 & 18

are riding on the backs of the poor. There is nothing we need do, except get off their backs—if, that is, we follow only the voice of the self inside. There is nothing for us to do because we are not even aware of doing anything when we do it spontaneously.

Thus, the man who refused to do *yajna* was described earlier as *indriyarama*,[1] as an incorrigible idler, and another who is ceaselessly employed in work is described as one who is content in the self. He works so much, and that spontaneously, that there is nothing for him to do.

I understand better than Panditji himself the point of the question[2] which he put. How is it that the *Gita* talks about rain ? In a discussion about spiritual matters, everything must be about the *atman*. This is probably what he has in mind. The *Gita* leads the reader on to worms and insects, to birds and animals, and so on finally to rain, and tells him that, if people do enough physical work, they will get as much rain as they need. We can infer some such general principle from its teaching.

Can rain have any connection at all with whether we lead sinful or virtuous lives? It may have, but we do not know how. If we understand a part of the whole, then we shall understand the whole. We know something about the world of invisible things if we understand the visible world. For instance, if we make it a practice to walk long distances, the *atman* within us too will be governed by the rhythm. If, thus, we understand how we should act in one matter, we shall also know how to act in other matters. For this purpose, too, there is a rule we can follow, and that is that we should discover a principle or a law which has no exception. For instance, water is water only if it contains one part oxygen and two parts hydrogen. This law has no exception, in the same way that a right angle must have ninety degrees, neither more nor less. If, therefore, we know what the "wheel thus set in motion"[3] is, in accordance with the rule explained above that a principle should have no exception, we shall experience no difficulty. Shri Krishna has explained here a law of physical nature first and then, through it, a spiritual law.

[1] III, 16

[2] How could *yajna* produce rain?

[3] *Vide* translation of III, 16.

[48]

April 20, 1926

Therefore, do thou ever perform without attachment the work that thou must do; for performing action without attachment man attains the Supreme.[1]

The verses here have different meanings, but it is not that one verse applies to the enlightened man and the other to the man yet striving for enlightenment. One and the same verse can be understood to apply to both, in the same way that the *Gita* as a whole can be interpreted to refer to both the types of war, the outer and the inner. This verse, therefore, means that we may say of a person whose attachment to the ego has disappeared that there is no karma for him, that he may do something and yet do nothing.

For through action alone Janaka and others achieved perfection; even with a view to the guidance of mankind thou must act.[2]

When Janaka was informed that his city was burning, he merely said: what if it is burning? The man who is directing the operations of a fire brigade can go on giving directions only if he keeps himself where he is. Can he leave his place of duty if he is told that his town or his house is on fire? He has completely given up thinking about himself. The person who follows the maxim, "Honesty is the best policy", exchanges a diamond for a cowrie. If the man who follows truth does so with the hope that he will thereby succeed better in his business, his truthfulness will be a cause of bondage for him, but it will be the cause of his deliverance if he follows it for the sake of *moksha*. Anyone who acts in this manner is a yogi, for yoga means skill or wisdom in action. He who does all these things with a selfish motive is a mere stone; he who does them for the highest end is like Jada Bharata[3], though, in the end, he does attain illumination. The line "Live as you like"[4] applies to him. For that, however, the person should go on working ceaselessly. "He intends nothing

[1] III, 19

[2] III, 20

[3] His story is told in the *Bhagavat*. An illuminated soul from his birth, outwardly he lived as an imbecile, indifferent to all slights.

[4] The first line of a verse from Akha, a 17th-century Gujarati poet, whom Gandhiji often quotes

to serve other ends".[1] This can be said only of one who has cleansed himself completely of the ego.

> Whatever the best man does is also done by other men; what example he sets, the world follows.[2]

People will adopt the standards which such a person sets. They will always observe what the eminent do. To what extent does Gandhi follow truth in life? Even the thoughts in which a great man indulges will produce an effect. His is a lame truthfulness who speaks truth as a matter of policy, but he who is truthful in his thoughts will act aright though he be dumb. Every thought of such a person is bound to come true. He is the ideal man whose actions, speech and thought are in harmony with one another. Everyone will follow him. This is the reason why I have placed the spinning-wheel before people; if there are any who devote themselves to it whole-heartedly, all will follow them. If those who worship an image of clay can realize God, why not a person who spins in this spirit?

[49]

April 21, 1926

Today is Ramanavami Day[3]. On this day we have a reading from the *Ramayana* for two hours and, in the morning, there is a discourse on the incarnation of Rama. People fast, or take only one meal or eat only fruit. We shall put into practice what we have learnt from the *Gita* by celebrating the Ramanavami today in this manner. I am faced with a conflict of duties. Though I am in the Ashram, I may not be able to join in the celebration. There is another duty I have to discharge. Pandit Motilal has written to me and asked me to send for a certain person and discuss some matters with him. I shall, therefore, be in the Ashram but engaged in discussions with him; when the *Ramayana* is being read, I shall be busy looking after the preparations for his lunch. All this is wrong. If I had become totally absorbed with all these activities in the Ashram and made it a rule to join in every celebration as I unfailingly attend prayers at four in the morning, I would have told Motilalji that today being Ramanavami I would

[1] A line from Rajchandra, who had exercised a profound influence on Gandhiji's thinking in his early years

[2] III, 21

[3] The birth-anniversary of Rama on the ninth day of the bright half of *Chaitra*, a month corresponding to April-May

be able to free myself only for half the day. But I do not yet have such firmness of mind, and, therefore, cannot act in that manner. It would not seem natural in me to do so. But I should let the Ashram advance in that direction. So long as we have not become truly civilized, we are half animal and half human. If we could be complete men, our lives would be devoted wholly to the pursuit of goodness. I often feel that, as your leader, I should set an example in every matter. But I cannot do so unless there is complete harmony between my thought, speech and action. You should, of course, go on with the usual programme. Keep a fast and have a reading from the *Ramayana*. Please bear with my deficiency, and see that you do not follow this weakness of mine after I am dead. My inability today to remain firm is not part of my normal nature. But it is my duty, I owe it to you, to present myself to you as I am.

I shall take no time now, speaking on Rama's life; I shall speak about it when readings from the *Ramayana* begin soon after the rest period is over.

Just now I shall only say that we should make it our aim to spread among the people a realization of the holy power of Ramanama[1]. Which is the Rama of the *Ramadhun*[2] that follows the *bhajan*[3]? Is he the Rama of Tulsidas or Valmiki, or the Rama whose birth-anniversary falls today? Are these Ramas different from one another, or are they the same Rama? We shall understand all this if we reflect carefully over the matter. I shall have to leave some of these points. I can only follow my own sentiment in this matter. Let everyone dwell today on the thought that Ramanama will save us. I still feel troubled in my mind sometimes. When I worry over my work, like other people, I start repeating Ramanama. I sometimes keep thinking about the *Gita* and the meaning of particular verses when I retire for the day; I start repeating Ramanama, then fall asleep, for I know that it is my duty at that time to sleep. If we wish to fill the whole world with the power of Ramanama, it is not by constantly repeating the sounds *ra* and *ma* that we can succeed; we must ceaselessly think on God. If the mind is disturbed by all kinds of evil thoughts or if we get angry, we should start repeating Ramanama. If our aim is to use Ramanama to deceive the country so that it may follow us, it is a very wicked thought. For us

[1] Repeating the name Rama as a sacred formula

[2] A song for group singing, with frequent repetition of the name 'Rama'

[3] Devotional song

Ramanama is a boat for crossing to the other shore. We should, therefore, put it in the proper place, enveloped with sweet fragrance. I was once presented with a copy of the Koran. Haji Habib told me that it could be kept with proper care only at his place, and nowhere else, for they would put it above other books and touch it with their hands only after washing them properly. This, he said, I might not do. In this way man envelops in fragrance the thing which is dear to his heart. God will certainly be displeased with the man who keeps the Koran in the holiest place but his mind in an unholy place.

We should thus give a wide meaning to Ramanama. We should extract the utmost benefit from anything to which our heart is drawn.

[50]

April 22, 1926

> Whatever the best man does is also done by other men; what example he sets, the world follows.[1]

We should learn from this verse that if young people follow the bad example of their elders, it is the elders who should be blamed.

> For me, O Partha, there is naught to do in the three worlds, nothing worth gaining that I have not gained; yet I am ever in action.[2]

For whom should one cook, for one already full or for one fasting? For others, of course. To Shri Krishna, the whole world is a guest, and he loves all the creatures in it (and he must, for the world is his creation!). People look upon me as Purushottam, says Krishna, so I must observe proper measure in everything, otherwise the universe would perish.

> Indeed, for were I not, unslumbering ever to remain in action, O Partha, men would follow my example in every way.[3]

I have to be busy every moment to see that the world goes on, for I am its ruler, I am the master of the ceremonies. Since I make the world dance as I will, I am also called Natavar[4]. This ruler of the world cannot afford to sleep by day or by night, nor can he rest from work.

[1] III, 21
[2] III, 22
[3] III, 23
[4] The Supreme Player

> If I were not to perform my task, these worlds would be ruined;
> I should be the cause of chaos and of the end of all mankind.[1]

I must, says Krishna, keep the fire burning the whole day, otherwise there would be confusion in the social order, and, I would be responsible for the destruction of society.

We work so that we may please God, and if we give up doing that the people will observe no discipline, will refuse to work and feel completely lost.

> Just as, with attachment, the unenlightened perform all actions, O Bharata, even so, but unattached, should the enlightened man act, with a desire for the welfare of humanity.[2]

One must work just as ignorant people do, except that they work with attachment. We, too, must take up a pick-axe and work like them. A wise man should be as industrious and work as hard as others; only, he should work for the good of the world, disinterestedly and without attachment. (If you spin for the poor without attachment to your work, you will serve your own good and theirs). If you work in this spirit, you are a man of spiritual knowledge and, though working, are doing nothing. Does a person who has kept the *ekadashi*[3] fast commit a sin by attending to cooking? He or she cooks, in a disinterested spirit, for children and guests.

[51]

April 23, 1926

> The enlightened may not confuse the mind of the unenlightened, who are attached to action; rather must he perform all actions unattached, and thus encourage them to do likewise.[4]

A wise man should not confuse the judgment of ignorant people who are attached to the work which they do, should not, for instance, ask them to go without a thing because we can do so. Shri Krishna has said a little earlier that if he did not work for the people, there would be confusion of *varnas* in society. He says the same thing in this verse in different words. If Arjuna took any unexpected step, people would not understand his intention and might do something which he had never wanted them to do. He had asked those hundreds of thousands of men

[1] III, 24

[2] III, 25

[3] The eleventh day in either half of the lunar month

[4] III, 26

to assemble there ready for battle. How could he, now, cause confusion in their minds? He should, therefore, go on doing his duty in the spirit of yoga, unattached to the fruits of his work, and inspire others to work likewise.

> All action is entirely done by the *gunas* of *prakriti*. Man, deluded by the sense of 'I', thinks 'I am the doer'.[1]

The man who is sunk in ignorance believes in his pride that his actions are his, whereas they are prompted by his nature, by *sattva*, *rajas* and *tamas*. (Anyone who says that he bats his eyelids is either a fool or suffering from a disease of the eye. He does not wink his eyes really, he harms them.) But he who acts as if he were a mere witness of his actions will win admiration for everything he does. The work done by a person without much ability but also without attachment to his ego will produce better results than that done by another who is attached to his ego. Take the example of a state ruled by a king and his minister. The latter works within the framework of the administrative set-up. In just the same way, we are pilgrims in this world and obey the laws of the world. If we lay claim to what we are prompted by our nature to do, we sow confusion in the minds of the ignorant. We should realize that we are no more than servants bound to carry out another's orders, and should voluntarily act as if we were slaves. Mira described herself as being a slender thread, because she submitted to her nature. She used the phrase "slender thread" because she had submitted herself to God's will so completely that there was no question of her resisting. He who eats simply to give the body its hire will not think of pleasing his palate. Anyone who lives in accordance with this law will forget his ego completely, surrender to Krishna everything he does.

[52]

April 24, 1926

The verse which we shall discuss today presents a problem, for its meaning has been completely perverted. It is interpreted without any reference to the context. There was a libertine in Rajkot. He used this verse to justify his dissolute life. He was a student of the shastras and could cite appropriate Sanskrit verses, on occasion, and so enjoyed a good status in society. He used to say that nature followed its own urges and that, therefore, he was not to blame, that he was untouched by either sin or virtue.

[1] III, 27

> But he, O Mahabahu, who understands the truth of the various *gunas* and their various activities, knows that it is the *gunas* that operate on the *gunas*; he does not claim to be the doer.[1]

He who classifies *gunas* and karma into their sub-divisions, divides them into their different types and then analyses each, and so arrives at the truth about them will know that everything is the result of *gunas* acting upon one another and will not get involved in their activities through attachment to them. The impostor I mentioned used to say that *prakriti* was God's *maya*[2], and he was not responsible for her actions. If, however, we understand the meaning which the term *prakriti* bears in the preceding verse, we shall see that there was nothing we need do of our own choice. Only that person who has ceased to be attached to any work can say, like King Janaka, that he is not responsible for the actions of his *prakriti*. But the man who is full of ignorant attachment and thinks little cannot take cover behind this verse. The point of this verse is, in the extremely difficult business of running this world, in the running of this intricate machine (the very thought of which is sufficient to make one's head spin), what is there that I can do? What strength have I? I dare not touch a single part of it. Anyone who considers carefully how this world is kept going will see that the different *gunas* are ceaselessly active and doing their work. Let us take the small example of the spinning-wheel. Suppose for a moment that the spindle became conceited. Its part in the working of the wheel is quite small. It has no motion of its own, and if it believed itself or the string to be the source of the motion, it would commit a grievous error. If it decides to become bent, it would produce a discordant note while rotating. It might feel that, instead of rotating monotonously, it was now moving in a novel manner, but it would soon lose its place. When dying, it might perhaps realize that it had made a terrible mistake, that its pride had cost it its very life. Let us suppose now that the spindle has no such pride. It will then think that its motion was not its own, that it contributed nothing to the spinning, the string did its work and the wheel did its. It might then say that the *gunas* operate on the *gunas* and that it was of no interest to itself how they worked. I must work, the spindle would tell itself, as a mere slave, otherwise I and my relations would be ruined.

[1] III, 28

[2] A term in Vedanta; it means the illusory world of phenomena and also the creative energy which projects that world.

It would then feel no pride and would no longer be carried away by foolish notions. We could say of such a spindle that it had learnt wisdom. The same argument applies to human beings. No one can go on indulging himself and then argue that his conduct was the result of the *gunas* doing their work according to their nature. We would come to grief if we made wrong comparisons. If, pointing to the example of an animal, we, too, act as it does, we would become animals. A man, on the contrary, must bear in mind that he is a human being, and that he resembles animals up to a point and no more; that is, he resembles them in respect of the physical needs of sleeping, eating, breeding, etc. The man who decides that he need not eat and sleep as animals do, that he need not, like a dog fight for a piece of bread, such a person will reflect deeply and, having discovered the truth, always live as a mere witness. The animal instincts will not have completely disappeared, but he will realize, if he has understood the law which rules human life, that he must not be a slave to sleep, food and sex, that, in other words, the laws of animal life do not apply to him. As soon as he has understood the laws of *prakriti*, he will see that they are the basis of the laws governing human life. In regard to the machine of his body his only right, he now sees, is to maintain a disinterested attitude towards it. He will not, then, touch anything unclean with his hand or see it with his eyes. Such a person will become free from bondage to the body and be able to say that in all his actions it is the *gunas* which act according to their nature, that the ears do their work of hearing, the eyes of seeing, and so on. He will act like the spindle in our example as if he were inert matter with no will of his own. His body will function mechanically. It will then indulge in immorality no more than a log of wood does. By its nature, the human body is but a corpse and, by itself, is as sinless as a log. The senses will not do evil of themselves, so long as the mind which controls them does not wish to do evil. He who has discovered the law of human life will study the working of the *gunas* and act accordingly like the man who prints after setting the types carefully. The types which have become worn out have to be melted back into metal and cast again, and then reset; in like manner, the man who is guided by the truth that in all matters it is the *gunas* which do their work will make himself completely inert, doing nothing on his own.

[53]

April 25, 1926

The senses are not just 16,000[1], their number is infinite. If we make them dance as we wish, instead of ourselves dancing as they wish, we would be the directors of the drama of life. In the first Chapter, even the evil-minded Duryodhana asks his warriors to remain in their positions and protect the patriarch Bhishma. If, likewise, we protect the director of the drama, who dwells within us, play our part in accordance with his instructions, the director would not become weak.

> Deluded by the *gunas* of *prakriti* men become attached to the activities of the *gunas*; he who knows the truth of things should not unhinge the slow-witted who have not the knowledge.[2]

This world is *maya*, it is a rotating wheel, and, therefore, those who are sunk in darkness remain attached to *guna* and karma. Those who are under the spell of the *gunas* of *prakriti* are swayed by all kinds of desires, yield to grief and ignorant attachments. The man of knowledge should not unsettle the ignorant, he should not lift him from one place and put him in another. For instance, says Shri Krishna to Arjuna, you are on a battlefield, ready for fighting, and so are these others; you have now chanced to learn some wisdom, but you should not, because of that, shake others from their beliefs. If anyone of us should suddenly become enlightened with profound knowledge, it does not mean that he would be able to change all others immediately. He is a fool who seeks to change overnight other people who are following their own ways in life. This, of course, does not mean that, where the system itself is bad, we should not try to reform it. That would be a complete perversion of this idea.

[54]

April 27, 1926

> Cast all thy acts on Me, with thy mind fixed on the indwelling *atman*, and without any thought of fruit or sense of 'mine' shake off thy fever and fight![3]

After explaining all this—after explaining what karma is and why one should do it—Shri Krishna tells Arjuna that, dedi-

[1] Lord Krishna is believed to have ruled over 16,000 senses, which are represented as His queens.

[2] III, 29

[3] III, 30

cating every action to Him, having purified his mind, fixed it on his *atman* and emptied it of all desires, and without entertaining any thought of gain, he should go on doing karma (not that, Shri Krishna explains, he should win a kingdom and enjoy it but) as a matter of duty and irrespective of whether or not he was likely to benefit. (We should, for instance, get up at four in the morning as a matter of duty without thinking whether it will do us any good). You should, Shri Krishna says, shed your attachment to the ego and work—that is, work with the thought that you are not the doer of the karma and its fruit is not meant for you to enjoy, acting as if you were a piece of inert matter like the spindle of the spinning-wheel and like the wick of a lamp which goes on burning by itself. If I did not bring into existence all the factors necessary for the burning of the lamp, how would the wick burn? The wick was shut up within the cotton pad. How did that cotton know that it would one day be made into a wick? It was spun and twisted and then made into a wick. If Arjuna wanted to be like the wick, to think of himself as the *atman* within and not his body, he must learn to shed his attachment to the ego and empty himself of all desires. By first choosing good against evil and then becoming unattached to either, one can transcend both. So long as we dwell in the body, it functions according to its nature. We should live in accordance with this truth, otherwise we shall invite moral ruin. We should, therefore, aim at the highest. The same is true about our aspiration for *moksha*. One who is already in water no longer desires to jump into it. If it were true that in water we melt away, we would not at all want to jump into it. Just then, however, *moksha* was not Arjuna's goal, nor did he aspire after it or hope for it. We should have as our ideal a state unaffected by hope or desire though, of course, our present state is that of human beings full of desires. Being in a state unaffected by desire is the same as having the absolute conviction that we shall attain *moksha*. This idea of a state unaffected by desire is to be understood both in regard to our spiritual aspiration and the needs of the body, that is, both in regard to the ultimate goal and practical concerns. In regard to the former, there is no question of being affected by desire. The man who is incapable of doing evil, what interest can he have in good and evil? It is not true that, after the evil in one is completely destroyed, one is able to do good. We only imagine that it is so. When a person never feels the urge to use a sword, how can we attribute non-violence to him? This is a scientific truth, and not poetry; it states a principle concerning the *atman*. Be in such a state, Shri Krishna tells Arjuna, that is, be perfectly still in your mind, and fight. This idea that one should learn to act like inert matter occurs at many places in the *Mahabharata*. Why did Shri Krishna ask them to place an iron image of Bhima before Dhritarashtra?[1] He made everyone his instrument, and then asked them to place an iron image of Bhima—what does all this mean? He asked Arjuna to become passion-free and fight, that is, to banish all impatience and anxiety from his mind and then fight. I would kill a snake or flea or bug only if I am angry or annoyed.

We shall discuss tomorrow what Krishna meant when he asked Arjuna to "fight".

[55]

April 28, 1926

Shri Krishna asked Arjuna to banish all impatience and anxiety and then fight. When he said "fight", he meant that Arjuna should do what he regarded as his duty. If we could know every time what we should do, if everyone's duty, in a given situation was evident to him, all of us would have the same ideas of duty. But that is not so. On the contrary, we have to reflect to discover what our duty is. We have to apply numerous tests and then only do we see what our duty is. That is why Shri Krishna asks Arjuna to be passion-free and do his duty. One can do one's duty only if one banishes all impatience and anxiety in regard to it. Anyone who has lost control over his speech-organs will seem to talk in a disconnected fashion. The fact is that all of us talk in that manner. An Italian has described all human beings as mad. If we were not mad, we would not indulge in all this vain prattle; though, even when prattling, we prefer to prattle in one way rather than another. Since, therefore, we must make a choice at every step, Arjuna is asked to do his duty without being over-excited about it, that is, without attachments and aversions. We need not doubt the intentions behind the actions of a mother who has ceased to make any distinction between her own child and another's. Freedom from attachment and aversion is the first step towards understanding one's duty. Following this line of thinking to its logical conclusion, we would see that a non-violent man is one who is free from attachments and aver-

[1] At the end of the fighting, the blind Dhritarashtra wanted to embrace Bhima, but Shri Krishna saw that he wished to crush Bhima in his arms and so advised an iron image of Bhima to be placed before the king.

sions. For instance, Harishchandra saw the auspicious necklace round Taramati's neck and recognized it. He saw that he had to cut off the dear head of her whom he adored. You will ask me how this is an illustration of non-violence. Violence does not consist in the act of cutting off someone's head; it consists in the motive behind the act. How if we knew that Harishchandra would have preferred to kill himself rather than kill Taramati? Suppose it had been the King's order that, if the *Chandal* could not bring himself to kill the person before him, he could kill himself, Harishchandra would have certainly preferred to put the knife to his own throat. But he was given no such choice. He had actually brought down the knife and it was then that the gods held back his hand.

Take another instance, that of a doctor who has to carry out an operation. The doctor who operated upon me was all kindness. Even if he was not, he did not in any case wish to harm me. If the doctor was called upon to amputate someone's leg, he would certainly not derive pleasure from the operation. His only motive would be to help the patient. Not only the doctor, but the patient too knows that the amputation is for his benefit. Thus operations involve the use of all kinds of knives and lancets, but they involve no violence.

A third instance. Let us suppose that a man has had his head half cut and it is hanging loose from the neck. He signs to passers-by and requests them to kill him so that he might be spared the suffering. Most passers-by, let us suppose, take no notice and go on. One, however, stops and looks at the man, sees his suffering and realizes that his death is certain. This person, then, may surely sever the head completely and end his suffering. This, too, is non-violence. It is so because the passer-by was not prompted by any selfish motive in what he did.

We hear in our country many persons advance such arguments to justify killing, but they are insincere; those, for example, who kill snakes are cowards. They are afraid of dying themselves, and their only thought in killing a snake is to save themselves from being bitten by it. The violence involved in killing a snake may be pardonable, but violence there certainly is. There is violence (may be pardonable violence) in killing even a person who is the most wicked of men in the eyes of the world, for killing him will not make the world a happier place, and those who kill him do not do so because they are really concerned about his welfare. If one person is out to destroy the entire world, and all the people in the world prefer to be destroyed rather than kill him, it is possible that that person will be terrified by the violence he would have perpetrated, and after that there would be no more violence[1] in the world.

Thus, to be *vigatajvara* means to be without aversions and attachments. One may even commit violence then. If anyone, deceiving himself, commits violence in the name of non-violence, of course he would not attain *moksha*. There is a possibility of *moksha* for one who commits violence but knows that he does so, but there is none for the hypocrite.

And so Shri Krishna said, "Cast all thy acts on Me."[2] He thus asked Arjuna to fulfil a number of conditions and then to fight.

> Those who always act according to the rule I have here laid down, in faith and without cavilling,—they too are released from the bondage of their actions.[3]

To do one's duty means to fight and struggle. Since every karma involves a choice, there is necessarily a struggle. Even though caught in this way between opposites, you will have transcended them if you dedicate every action to Krishna, do everything without attachment or aversion, have faith in God and present every karma as a gift to Him. If you believe God to be the author of all you do, you will be touched neither by sin nor by virtue. God comes down in the form of Vaman[4], with an appealing face like a mother's, and begs us to trust everything to Him. He who accepts my teaching, says Shri Krishna, and acts accordingly, without attachments and aversions and without partiality to anyone, is not bound by the effects of any karma.

[56]

April 29, 1926

> But those who cavil at the rule and refuse to conform to it are fools, dead to all knowledge; know that they are lost.[5]

[1] The source has 'non-violence', evidently, a slip.

[2] III, 30

[3] III, 31

[4] One of the incarnations of Vishnu. He begged from the demon King Bali as much ground as he could cover in three steps and, on the request being granted, covered Heaven and Earth in two steps and claimed the King's head for the third.

[5] III, 32

> Even a man of knowledge acts according to his nature; all creatures follow their nature; what then will constraint avail?[1]

This verse has been taken to mean that a wicked person can never reform himself. An instance of this is provided here by . . .[2]; she lies there away from us, and how can we persuade her to change her ways? But, then, the aspiration to realize God is also part of human nature. The beast's nature is merely to feed and sleep. It cannot meditate on Rama every morning, but man is different. Ramdas Swami[3] exhorted people never to depart from the path of virtue, the path of the highest virtue. But this verse says something altogether different; (all creatures follow their nature). If a person has the nature of an animal, how far will another succeed, try as long as he might, in reforming that person? How long can we keep such a person suppressed? What can we do to a person who refuses to behave better than an animal? I could have hit that girl with my sandals, but it would have made her more obstinate still. One day, however, she may feel Rama's grace and, remembering this incident, reform herself. This verse is not intended to discourage a man from struggling against his nature. One must of course struggle to improve oneself. But should some other person tell us day in and day out that we remain as beasts and do not improve, there is bound to be a quarrel every time. Take the example of a teacher and a pupil. If the pupil himself tells the teacher that the latter should cane him or box his ears whenever he did anything wrong, the teacher should certainly do that.

Yesterday, we mentioned three illustrations of non-violence. This is one more instance of it. Pupils such as the one in this illustration control themselves and are also controlled by others. Our minds may be disturbed by innumerable evil desires, but we do not welcome them, as we do not welcome a disease which may attack us. Our natural desire is to get well, and the doctor, therefore, is free to put any restrictions on us; the patient will thank him for doing so. But what good will it do to punish a person who does not himself wish to change? Anyone who has ceased to be a human being and behaves like a beast cannot be reformed by others, true though it is that Rama dwells in his heart too. Of course, one should never despair of being able to improve oneself. But how can outward self-control help a man

[1] III, 33
[2] The name is omitted in the source.
[3] A 17 th-century religious reformer of Maharashtra

to whom wickedness has become second nature? His release can come only with death. Ravana told Mandodari[1] that he was an enemy of Rama, that he wished to die. And die he did, through his own sins.

Nigraha means trying to control oneself or others. One may try to control a friend, or one's wife or sister or pupil, if they wish to reform themselves. But what can we do if they oppose us? What can even an emperor do to a person who has abandoned all shame? No one will succeed in his efforts to reform such a person.

We can offer satyagraha only against a person who has some love in his heart. We can control another only if there is mutual love between us; where there is no such love, the only course for us is non-co-operation with the other party. Tulsidas advised non-co-operation with the wicked.

[57]

April 30, 1926

Men believe in their pride that they can imprison others and beat them into submission. But we know that thefts and murders have not stopped. What, then, should one do? Everyone should look after himself. This verse certainly does not mean that one should not try even to control oneself, for we have already read: holding all these in check, the yogi should sit intent on Me.[2] The senses are so powerful that trying to control them taxes our energy to the utmost and involves us in violent struggle against ourselves. Shri Krishna tells Arjuna there that he who controls them—passionately beats them down into submission and reins them in, as we do a horse—we do no violence in using the whip thus—and sits meditating on Him, self-controlled, is a man established in *samadhi*. A little later, he says: therefore Mahabahu, he whose senses are reined in on all sides from their objects. . . .[3]

Nigraha means another person trying to impose discipline on us. Addressed to Arjuna, the verse means: "If you believe that you can control your army, you should understand that it will not obey you, for it does not think as you do, its heart is set on fighting. By running away from battle, you will be instru-

[1] His wife

[2] II, 61

[3] II, 68

mental in the warriors forsaking the traditional duty of their caste and being guilty of conduct unworthy of themselves."

> Each sense has its settled likes and dislikes towards its objects; man should not come under the sway of these, for they are his besetters.[1]

Attachment and aversion are an inseparable pair. The senses feel either the one or the other towards their objects. We should not be swayed by them, for they are the thieves trying to rob the *purusha*[2] within us. They are ever after us, go where we will, and rob us of all our earnings. There is thus the fullest scope for human striving; in fact, it is one's duty to strive. Having done that duty, one may console oneself with the preceding verse; struggling tirelessly, we may tell ourselves that we can go no further than our nature permits. But taking up such an attitude does not help us. We must continue to struggle ceaselessly. We should continue till we reach the breaking point and that with the conviction that we are bound to succeed. Any man or woman or child who takes cover behind the preceding verse and stops struggling will be a thief in God's eyes. The line, "seeking pearls, men plunge into the sea, reckless of their lives,"[3] describes the spirit of desperate earnestness in striving.

> Better one's own duty, bereft of merit, than another's well-performed; better is death in the discharge of one's duty; another's duty is fraught with danger.[4]

We should strive to the best of our ability in our own sphere of work, but waste no effort on anything which lies outside it. It would be dangerous for us to go and live in a mansion in Bombay, but it would be a sign of our being happy if we are content to live here in the Ashram.

[58]

May 1, 1926

To speak the truth is a dharma common to all. But there are special duties, that is, duties which pertain to individuals. Suppose that one's job is to clean lavatories. Such a person should not envy another whose job is to keep accounts. The man who cleans lavatories as carefully as he does the utensils in his home

[1] III, 34
[2] In Sankhya philosophy, the inner witness watching the play of *prakriti*
[3] From a poem by Pritam, a Gujarati poet, (1720-98)
[4] III, 35

observes his dharma in the truest manner. It would not be right for Arjuna to think of retiring to a forest and spending his days telling beads on the rosary. His duty was to fight and kill. Retiring to a forest may be the right course for a *rishi*, it was not so for Arjuna. Even if the dharma meant for Arjuna seemed less worthy, for him it was the best. Why should he, Shri Krishna asks him, talk egotistically, acting like the proverbial dog who believed that he was drawing the heavily-laden cart? He assures Arjuna that, if there was any sin in the latter following his dharma, the responsibility for that would be His, Krishna's. During the years which Ramachandra spent in the forest, Bharat did not himself rule the kingdom as king but acted as the former's representative. Ramachandra's sandals were placed on the throne and Bharat carried on the administration in Ramachandra's name. There was not a moment when he was not absorbed in thinking on Rama. Similarly, Shri Krishna asks Arjuna why he thought that, if he won the battle, the kingdom would be his. If he had no wish to enjoy the fruits of his effort, it was actually his dharma to fight and win the kingdom. He should act only as an instrument.

> Then what impels man to sin, O Varshneya, even against his will, as though by force compelled?[1]

We shall discuss Shri Krishna's reply tomorrow.

[59]

May 2, 1926

How is it that a person is often driven to a wrong path against his or her will?

> It is Lust, it is Wrath, born of the *guna—rajas*. It is the arch-devourer, the arch-sinner. Know this to be man's enemy here.[2]

The reply, according to Shri Krishna, was simple. When the child refuses to go to school, is simply unwilling to go, what is the reason? He refuses to go because he wants to run away with a bad play-fellow or because he is planning some mischief. Thus, one cause is *kama*[3]. It is man's evil thoughts which drive him to evil deeds. The second cause is anger. We get angry when we do not get the thing we want. Anger has its source in *rajas*. These two great enemies of man drive him to sin. The reign of *kama* is

[1] III, 36
[2] III, 37
[3] Desire

different in its effect from the reign of Rama. Those who prosper under Rama's reign understand the sport of God which this creation is. Those, on the other hand, who are swayed by desire and anger will see, in the creation, not Rama's sport, but Satan's. Like Kumbhakarna[1] *kama* is ever waiting, open-mouthed, for its prey. When its appetite is not satisfied, its victim is filled with anger. Know, Shri Krishna tells Arjuna, that this is your enemy. Since the two are twins, He has used the singular pronoun *enam*.

> As fire is obscured by smoke, a mirror by dirt, and the embryo by the amnion, so is knowledge obscured by this.[2]

If there is any smoke, it stays only for a while. As soon as it has gone, the fire gives full heat. The mirror will have to be cleaned, and only then will it give service, provided of course we know that the thing is a mirror. But the foetus covered by the placenta can do nothing about it, it cannot even cry. The man who is under the sway of desire and anger passes through these three stages.

> Knowledge is obscured, O Kaunteya, by this eternal enemy of the wise man in the form of Lust, the insatiable fire.[3]

This *kama* harms, like an enemy, even a man of spiritual knowledge.

[60]

May 4, 1926

> The senses, the mind and the reason are said to be its seat; by means of these it obscures knowledge and stupefies man.
>
> Therefore, O Bharatarshabha, bridle thou first the senses and then rid thyself of this sinner, the destroyer of knowledge and discrimination.
>
> Subtle, they say, are the senses; subtler than the senses is the mind; subtler than the mind is the reason; but subtler even than the reason is He.[4]

Shri Krishna now explains the various stages. It is true indeed that the senses are powerful—they control the body. The mind is stronger than the senses and the intellect stronger than the mind. But stronger still than the intellect is the *atman* which dwells in the body. The senses, the mind and the intellect, these three are the dwelling places of desire and anger. But the *atman* in you,

[1] Ravana's brother in the *Ramayana*, a voracious eater who slept for days at a stretch

[2] III, 38

[3] III, 39

[4] III, 40, 41 & 42

Shri Krishna tells Arjuna, is higher than all of them. If we seize the house in which the enemy lodges, we shall be able to kill him, or he will leave the place and run away. Occasionally, one may forget Him who is the Lord over these three, but that need not worry us, since the moment we think about that Lord we shall be able to overcome all of them.

> Thus realizing Him to be subtler than the reason, and controlling the self by the Self (*Atman*), destroy, O Mahabahu, this enemy—Lust, so hard to overcome.[1]

"Subduing the *atman* by the *atman*" means overcoming the baser, the demoniac impulses in the mind through the *atman*, that is, through the godward impulses; in other words, Arjuna should, Shri Krishna tells him, master his egotistic instincts by striving for spiritual welfare and, assured that his real self was more potent than the intellect, he should storm the fort and seize it. The senses are the gate-keepers and the mind is the minister. What the senses tell the mind is reported by the latter to the intellect, and the intellect decides and issues its order. If, however, we regain the sovereignty which is rightfully ours, then we would be able to subdue the mind, the intellect and the senses whom at present we have accepted as our masters, as in our country we have accepted foreigners as our masters and believe that we get the food we eat because of them.

Our *atman* should be vigilant day and night. One whose *atman* is so awake will not have dreams in his sleep. But we are bound to have them if we are slaves of sleep. Shri Krishna thus assures Arjuna that, if he keeps constant watch, he will be harassed neither by thieves coming in from outside nor by those that dwell within. If we do not establish our rule over the body, it will yearn for things which we do not approve of and we shall forfeit our authority over it.

[61]

May 5, 1926

If we wish to deal worthily by even the most wicked person, we should assume that he has no evil intention. He is bound to have good feelings somewhere deep in his heart. The *atman* never gets angry. It remains unattached and unmoved. If we cannot overcome desire or anger in us even in some measure, we should tolerate them when they invade us.

[1] III, 43

No one has yet succeeded in laying down a universal rule about how we should act towards a thief. We should, however, bear in mind that however we act we should be inspired by love for him. We must think and find out how we may win him over with love. We should assume that it is not in human nature to steal. Even as rational beings we should be convinced that there is no human being in the world who is beyond all hope of change. Love is a kind of force of attraction. Science tells us that even dust has the property of attracting other things. Even a particle of dust possesses some kind of power of attraction; that is why Mirabai sings about the bond of love. That bond is much stronger than that of a slender thread can ever be.[1] Why should we be filled with passion or get angry whenever we lose anything?

Such is the yoga described in this third chapter. There is ceaseless movement and change. We cannot choose but work with the body as ceaselessly as the ball of this earth rotates. What is the way, then, of saving ourselves from work? The *Gita* replies that, by shedding all attachment and aversion, we escape the fruits of our actions.

[Chapter Four]

> I expounded this imperishable yoga to Vivasvan; Vivasvan communicated it to Manu, and Manu to Ikshvaku.
>
> Thus handed down in succession, the royal sages learnt it; with long lapse of time it dwindled away in this world, O Parantapa.[2]

We are doing things every moment, but it is God who has placed us on his wheel and is moving it like a potter, producing ever new shapes. "This yoga was known from the beginning of time, but has perished in this age. People have forgotten the art of working without attachment and aversion. Were it not so," Shri Krishna said, "I would not have had to be a witness to this battle."

> The same ancient yoga have I expounded to thee today; for thou art My devotee and My friend, and this is the supreme mystery.[3]

The highest truth may be imparted only to a *bhakta*[4], for such a person will serve the world's good.

[1] Mirabai's lines read: Hari has tied me with a slender thread/And I turn as He pulls me.

[2] IV, 1 & 2

[3] IV, 3

[4] A devotee of God

[62]

May 6, 1926

Shri Krishna says,

This yoga, "was known in ancient times, I taught it to Vivasvan, he taught it to Manu, and Manu taught it to Ikshvaku." At this Arjuna wonders. You and I, he says, live in the present age, and you say you taught this to people in former times; how can that be?

> Later was Thy birth, my Lord, earlier that of Vivasvan. How then am I to understand that Thou didst expound it in the beginning?
>
> Many births have we passed through, O Arjuna, both thou and I; I know them all, thou knowest them not, O Parantapa.[1]

When we sing about the succession of births for human beings through 84,00,000 living forms, we refer to our having had countless lives before the present one, and we state our inference that death is only a change from an old house into a new one. But it is only a person who remembers his previous lives that can say this with certainty. Shri Krishna states categorically that, being a yogi, he remembered his previous existences but that Arjuna could not remember his. He could say this; we cannot.

> Though unborn and inexhaustible in My essence, though Lord of all beings, yet assuming control over My nature, I come into being by My mysterious power.[2]

The Hindu belief in avatars may present a difficulty to some of us. Avatar means descent. Our descent means God's descent too, for He is present in every creature and in every object. All this is His *maya*. All concrete things—our body, the material objects, all these—exist at definite points in space and time, but the *atman* was not born in time, it pervades all space and exists through all time. We do not know it by direct experience. If we wish to understand the principle known as God, either with the help of reason or through faith, we should first know the *atman*. What is it? So long as we live in ignorance, it is more distant than even the sky, but in our awakened state we cannot say that it is removed from us by even so much as an inch. It is that through which we came into being and through which we exist; if you believe that you are that, then "I" and "you" are identical—but only a person devoid of egotism can assert that.

[1] IV, 4 & 5

[2] IV, 6

"I" and "you" are identical in the sense in which the ring and chain are in the final analysis but gold. Name and form are only for a moment; while things have them, they are no more real than a mirage. That into which things merge when they cease to have name and form is ever the same.

And so Krishna says:

"Though I was never born in time, though I am the Lord of all creatures, I incarnate Myself and am born as a human being."

This is the essential nature of the *atman*. If we realize this truth, we would always act in conformity with that nature; we then act, though born as human beings, as if we were never born. If the *atman* in each of us is identical with the *atman* in everyone else, one *atman* born in a body means all of them born, and all others born means that one born too. This is a difficult idea to grasp. "This is *maya*," says Shri Krishna, "and through it I incarnate Myself in this world time and again."

We can follow reason only up to a point. What, then, does avatar mean? It is not as if God comes down from above. It would be right to say, if we can say it without egotism, that each one of us is an avatar. The *atman* in every body is as potent as the *atman* in any other, though outwardly we see differences. In our awakened state all are one, though in our ignorant state we may seem separate existences. In real truth, there are not several, there is only one.

If we constantly reflect over this essence named the *atman*, we shall regard no one as an enemy to be killed and shall have nothing to get angry about. We shall then see that anyone who hits us hits himself too.

When Krishna says that He incarnates Himself as a human being, he only uses the idiom of common speech. God never incarnates Himself as an *atman* and is never born as a human being. He is ever the same. When, from our human point of view, we see special excellence in some individual, we look upon him as an avatar. In God's language there is no such word as avatar; it exists only in the language of human beings.

[63]

May 7, 1926

Arjuna asked Shri Krishna how He could have expounded this yoga to other people of olden times, to which Shri Krishna replied that they had had many previous existences, which He remembered but Arjuna could not. He added that, though He was not subject to birth and change, though He was the Lord who dwelt in the hearts of all creatures, He submitted to the action of *prakriti*, which was His creation, and through the power of his *maya* came down to live on the earth.

He then proceeds to explain in what circumstances God incarnates Himself as a human being.

> For whenever Right declines and Wrong prevails, then O Bharata, I come to birth.[1]

In these lines Shri Krishna held out an assurance to the entire world. If God remained inactive when dharma was eclipsed, man would be helpless. In this *Kaliyuga*, all human efforts produce results contrary to what was intended. Hindus and Muslims, for instance, continue to fight among themselves. Can anyone prevent this? I was passionately eager to do such penance that they should never fight. But all my efforts failed. Does that mean that this fighting will go on for ever? Assuredly not. Will God let human beings overindulge their senses with impunity? He tells us that He will tolerate our self-indulgence within limits, for He knows that we would weary of it. I will tolerate, He says, a little fighting and will not incarnate on the earth just because of that. But when men recognize no limits in fighting, demolish temples and kill people indiscriminately, that would mean eclipse of dharma. That would be wickedness in the name of dharma, it would mean the spread of *adharma* and disorder. Do not, God says to comfort men, give way to despair when such things happen. "It is good," He says, "that you feel helpless at such a time, for by making you feel so I humble your pride." We remember what Surdas[2] says: "I have tried my strength in one way and another, till I am weary and can do no more; you must save me now;" that is how man thinks in his pride, that he will do this, and he will do that, but God humbles his pride. Man, however, has this promise from the Lord. He need not despair and feel that, if he fails in some task, it will not be done. Let him have faith that God will have it done. So the Lord has said in these lines that, whenever necessary, He comes down to live on the earth, and sets everything right. If He did not do that, He would not enjoy our worship and reverence. What dishonour can there ever be for a man who lives as God's slave? It is the slave's master who will be judged from the manner in which the slave

[1] IV, 7

[2] A 16th-century saint-poet of Northern India

lives. Is it, therefore, ever likely that God will let dharma be eclipsed? If *adharma* prevails, God will forfeit our reverence and worship. He has, therefore, no choice but to incarnate Himself as a human being.

> To save the righteous, to destroy the wicked, and to re-establish Right I am born from age to age.[1]

Shri Krishna has told us that we do nothing, nor does He. Who, then, destroys the wicked, and how are they destroyed? It is God's inviolable law that karma never fails to produce its effect. We can say that a human being may be able to counteract the effects of karma, and yet assert that karma never fails to produce its effect. The point is not that a person may not have to suffer the fruits of his actions, but that, if he cultivates non-attachment, even while in fact suffering the fruits of action, he would not inwardly feel that he suffered them. But suffer them he must. No karma is ever forgiven. It is, therefore, the wickedness of the wicked which destroys them. When, in this world, one human being kills another, the former is only an instrument. Arjuna was a bowman of prowess and a brave warrior. When he killed his enemies, it was not his strength which prevailed against Duryodhana. The latter was destroyed by his own sins. Hence the saying, "The pot of sin is bound to break one day." If it was true that God comes down from above and destroys the wicked, He would be as much under the sway of ignorance as we are. But that is not what happens. If we have faith and understand God's law, we would be sure that the wicked would be destroyed through their own sins.

Destruction of the wicked does not mean their physical destruction. Physically, both the wicked and the virtuous perish. It may be that a *bhakta* will pass away in the prime of his youth, and a wicked person will live up to the age of 76; shall we say that this was an instance of God's injustice? Kesar Bhagat was bitten by a serpent yesterday and died; should we, therefore, believe that he was a wicked man? In fact he was a good man; he was, though a mere labourer, a *bhakta* and a man of upright character. We would be punished with degradation if we believed that a man must have been wicked because he died early.

Yes, it is true in one sense that the good do not die, for we sing their glory ever afterwards. Everyone sings the glory of Rama, but no one of Ravana. If we think of him still, it is in

[1] IV, 8

order that we may keep ourselves free from his sins, run away from them. On the contrary, if we sing the virtues of a man and assimilate them, let them sink into our very soul, they are bound to become stronger in us day by day. Virtues never die. If we see the contrary in the world, that is but God's *maya.* It is true that virtues are cultivated with effort, and that vices require no such effort; but ultimately vices perish and virtues prosper. The appearance to the contrary is the effect of *maya.* If that were not so, what is said here about "destruction of the wicked" would not be true.

Shri Krishna does not mean here physical destruction of the wicked. While the *vasana*[1] with which a man died exists, he cannot but be born again. It is stated, it is true, that a good man will not be born again, but only if he rises above the plane of *gunas.* There is, beyond the *gunas* of good and evil, a state which is characterized by no *guna.* It is not an undesirable state, but a desirable one. It is the state of *moksha,* a state which endures for ever. But the assurance which God holds out here is not that goodness never perishes, but that evil most certainly does. When evil seems to prevail in the world, He, the Witness within, manifests Himself and shows that in truth it does not, shows it by the example of His own life. When evil spreads in the world, some persons, inspired by God, feel in their hearts that it is not enough for them to be a little good, that they must do *tapascharya* and be exceptionally good, so good that people would look upon them as perfect manifestation of the Divine in man. That is how Shri Krishna came to be worshipped as the fullest avatar. God has in these verses assured man that whenever dharma is eclipsed and the reign of *adharma* spreads, He comes into the world to protect the good, to destroy the wicked and restore the rule of dharma. This means that dharma is never destroyed. Shri Krishna did not say that while the wicked are destroyed, the good are not. He himself passed away, and that too meeting an untimely death.

If we take a total view, we shall see that it is not wickedness but goodness which rules the world. The wicked can prevail only when they number crores, but goodness will rule when embodied to perfection even in one person. Non-violence has been described as so powerful that all forces of violence subside in its presence. Under its influence, even beasts forget their nature. Even

[1] Desire clinging to one's self even after the death of the physical body

one good person can change the world. Such a one enjoys an empire over people's hearts; we do not, because we follow goodness only as best we may. The type of good man I have mentioned has but to send a message, and people will do what he wants them to do, such is the power of goodness. Where wickedness prevails, there is disorder in every field of life, but where goodness rules, order prevails and people are happy. They are happy not in the sense that their material needs are satisfied but in the sense that they lead virtuous and contented lives. As for material possessions, some men have crores of rupees and yet live a distracted life; that is no sign of being happy.

This verse, then, means that when *adharma* spreads, some men undertake *tapascharya* and, through their *tapascharya*, generate goodness in the world. Even the wicked bow in reverence before goodness. Its power is felt by beasts too. This can happen even in the present age. Anyone who has completely shed hatred and ill will, who has succeeded in making his life a perfect embodiment of truth, can command everything in life. He does not have to ask that anything be done. He has only to wish and the wish will be fulfilled.

God does not have to be born and to die, to incarnate Himself on earth as a human being. It is but His *maya* that we see in the world. That *maya* is described here and we are reassured that wickedness prevails only for a while but goodness endures for ever. We should, therefore, cultivate goodness in ourselves and see that we do nothing whereby we may become wicked.

[64]

May 8, 1926

God destroys evil and restores goodness by inspiring man's heart with noble ideals. On the balance goodness must prevail in the world, otherwise the world would perish. We see that a family in which evil increases is ruined, like, for instance, the Yadava race, which perished. It had taken to evil ways. Though a man like Krishna dwelt among them, the Yadavas took to immorality and drinking, fought among themselves and were killed. Even a strong and self-willed man whom no one dares attack will sooner or later fall at someone's hands; this is so true that no member of the Yadava race survived. When there is so much evil in the world that on the balance there is more of it than good, that their sum is a minus quantity, the destruction of the world is certain. The body endures only so long as there is vitality in it; in the same way, the world would perish if at any time there should be less of goodness and more of evil in it. That is why the Lord said that He appeared in the world in every age.

> He who knows the secret of this My divine birth and action is not born again, after leaving the body; he comes to Me, O Arjuna.[1]

Is there any reason why such a person should not merge into God? He would see that his body was perishable, and that it was not worthwhile to waste his energy on it. Was it not better, he would ask himself, to strive to realize the immortal *atman*? The *atman* is confined in the cage of this body, held in the prison of the body like a criminal. All of us have committed a crime, so to say, and are, therefore, imprisoned in the body; witness, for instance, Tulsidas and Surdas saying in their poems that there was no greater sinner in the world than they. We sin from the moment we are born, and that is why we are born again and again. Being confined in the cage of this body, we cannot soar as high as we wish. But we can do so if we reflect over the mystery of God's incarnations and actions in the world of men. If we realize the truth about the *atman* which is a lion, we shall become lions. How can we realize that truth? To explain that, Shri Krishna says:

> Freed from passion, fear and wrath, filled full with Me, relying on Me, and refined by the fiery ordeal of knowledge, many have become one with Me.[2]

"Those who know the mystery of God's incarnations and actions become free from attachments, from fear and anger," says Shri Krishna. "They become absorbed in Me. (If you open their hearts, you will find the image of Rama inside.) They live in complete surrender to Me. Purified by knowledge and *tapascharya* they have become as I am, have lost themselves in Me." Shri Krishna has explained here how we may know that a person has understood the mystery of God's incarnations and actions.

[65]

May 9, 1926

> In whatever way men resort to Me, even so do I render to them. In every way, O Partha, the path men follow is Mine.[3]

[1] IV, 9
[2] IV, 10
[3] IV, 11

In other words, people reap as they sow. As the quality of your *bhakti*, so is its reward. If there is any motive behind your *bhakti*, if you seek anything through it, you will get what the quality of your *bhakti* entitles you to. You will get, not what you wish to get, but what you deserve to get. We may wish to become God, but that does not mean that we shall become God. We shall get only that which we have earned by our manner of life. We shall get what we deserve. If you walk a distance of four miles, you will get only what is at the end of it. If you eat *kariatu*[1] to have a purge, it does not mean that the effect will follow. *Kariatu* will at the most cure a mild fever. If you swallow castor oil and then wish that you should get no motion, you cannot have it so. This is the meaning of the line: In whatever way men resort to Me, even so do I render to them.

Shri Krishna then says: *mama vartmanuvartante manushyah Partha sarvashah.*

"Everyone follows a path which leads to Me." This verse has a history behind it. When Tilak Maharaj was alive, he had cited this verse in the course of a discussion about violence and non-violence. I had argued that we should bear with a person who might have slapped us. In reply, he cited this verse to prove that the *Gita* upheld the principle of "tit for tat". That is, we should act towards a person as he acts towards us. I cling to the reply which I gave to him then.[2] I had argued that this verse could not be used in support of his contention. We should not act towards a person as he acts towards us. If he is bad to us, we may not therefore be bad to him. This verse merely lays down God's law. Shri Krishna says that He will worship a person as the latter worships Him. That means, we reap as we sow. One cannot do evil to others and expect good for oneself. Man has no right to return two slaps for one. But a principle quite the opposite of this prevails in the world, and as education spreads the position becomes worse. Uncivilized people may return two slaps for one, may fight back when attacked, and among them the relation of father and son may not be always sweet. If, however, a father behaves as a civilized man, he would use wisdom and endure the son's misconduct in patience, and so teach him to behave with humility. If the son is good, then he would suffer his parents' weaknesses in patience, and that is the better way of the two. We prefer the second to the first. Besides, we read in the preceding verse about

[1] Chiretta

[2] *Vide* Vol. XVI, pp. 490-1.

the type of man who can realize God. It says that those serene persons who are *vitaragabhayakrodhah*, that is, who are free from all attachment, fear and anger, realize God. The present verse cannot contradict that one, but completes its meaning. The previous verse says that a person who yields to attachment and anger will not realize God. If one yields to anger, one will reap the fruit of anger. We are thus taught not to yield to anger but to banish attachment, fear and anger from us.

In the second line, therefore, the Lord says that men are governed by His law. He means that law, the law of karma, which rules the world. We can truly say that God is law. God created His law and left the world to its governance, reserving to Himself no right to interfere with its operation. He then told men to decide for themselves whether they would or would not continue to be born in the world, as though making the position clear to them in advance so that they might not blame Him afterwards.

If we worship God, He would be pleased; but it does not mean that, if we do not worship Him, He would be displeased and would change His law. The law is immutable. Ishvar[1] is not a ruler though literally the word means "a ruler". But, then, since God does nothing, he suffers nothing either. He neither acts nor suffers the consequences of action. He stands apart, detached. We have given free rein to our imagination and employed all manner of epithets to describe God, and we quarrel about Him needlessly. Take the instance of the Jain and the Vedanta philosophies. According to the latter, all things are pervaded by God, whereas the former holds that no such being as God exists. We adopt a third attitude,—one which is the right one for laymen to adopt—namely, that God both exists and does not exist. God is not a ruler; He is all-pervasive, He is life, He is unconditioned and devoid of form. His rule consists in the rule of His law. No one has questioned the existence of His law. Not a single school of philosophy has done so. That law is of course a living law. If we equate it with God, recognize that it is God, people will then have no reason for quarrelling. That is the implication of this verse.

The principle of "You will reap as you sow" is part of even man-made law. Anyone who steals is punished. Even a thief has to submit to the law. He is not a rebel. The person who defies a law with deliberate intention to do so is an outlaw, but the murderer who is punished for his crime is not an outlaw. We become

[1] God

outlaws when we commit civil disobedience, for our disobedience is deliberate. Those who commit civil disobedience, and do so deliberately, are also outlaws, but the person who steals in abject helplessness is still ruled by the country's law. In the same way, man too is ruled by God's law, whether he submits to it willingly or not. That immutable truth is stated in this verse:

> Those who desire their actions to bear fruit worship the gods here; for in this world of men the fruit of actions is quickly obtainable.[1]

Every desire bears its proper fruit. So long as any desire is left in us, we cannot escape the round of birth and death. If we strive for yogic powers, our effort will certainly be rewarded, though not necessarily in the manner described in books on yoga. Chanting a *mantra*[2] is not necessarily rewarded in exactly the same way as described in the Shastras. Men try to discover God's laws, they conclude that certain actions will have certain results. If they get hold of the truth, may be there will be some efficacy in the *mantras* which they employ; but, then, even self-seeking and insincere men use this method. Or, it may be that the ceremonies accompanying the chanting of the *mantra* were not correctly performed; if so, the hoped-for result would not follow. I do not know anything about *mantras* for counteracting the effects of snake-bite, but there may be something in these claims. Some persons assert that we still know very little about the laws underlying the efficacy of such *mantras*. In this age they are discovering the laws of the visible world, but the number of such laws is infinite. Shall we ever succeed in discovering them all? Similarly, there are laws governing the invisible world too. In future, the laws of that world—the powers of the mind—may also be discovered. *Mantras* originated in the discovery of such laws. But, like the hypotheses about the visible world, the principles behind particular *mantras* may or may not be true and, according as they are true or not, the *mantras* may succeed or fail.

The author of the *Gita* knew this and, therefore, advised us to take no interest at all in these things. If we go after them, we may perhaps have our desires fulfilled, and so he said that people who hanker after worldly success worship various gods. But that, he said, will profit them little in the end. It will not increase the sum of happiness in the world. If, however, we decide to work in a spirit of disinterested service, we would not concern ourselves with *mantras*, nor shall we be required to study innume-

[1] IV, 12

[2] Formula with magical efficacy

rable Shastras. Just one little Shastra will suffice, the practice of *bhakti*—Ramanama. We shall not even have to study the whole of the *Gita*, it will suffice if we understand its substance. We should find out and take the place appointed for us in this world-machine created by God. A man who has no desires, how well his work shines! We suffer because of our innumerable desires. People do not keep to their places of duty and that creates disorder and confusion in the world. That man who, instead of being absorbed in his work, is always discontented has not found his right place in the world-machine. If even in a family every member is discontented, the family would be disrupted. In similar circumstances there would be chaos in a country's government, too. If everyone working in this world-machine seeks a reward for his work and, therefore, constantly changes the spheres of his work, there will be no order anywhere; the condition of such a person is like that of one who wastes himself in pleasures and then runs about in search of tonics and pills. With our minds full of cravings, we run after things in the world. While our attachment to the ego remains, we shall never taste the sweet ambrosia of Self-knowledge. The *Gita*, therefore, tells us that if, giving up attachment to the ego, we attend to the best of our ability to the task which has fallen to our lot, an emperor's work and that of one who cleans lavatories will be esteemed of equal worth in God's court. There, King Janaka and the man who cleaned lavatories in his palace have an equally honoured place. Suppose, however, that a present-day ruler and Janaka's Bhangi were to present themselves in God's court at the same time, in all likelihood, the Bhangi would be given an exalted place and the ruler would be left out. In God's court a man with a crown is not esteemed as of greater worth than one who has nothing on his head. The latter will be regarded worthy of a crown while a man with a jewelled crown will receive no attention. Hence the *Gita* says that he who works without attachment to the ego works best and becomes qualified for *moksha*.

[66]

May 11, 1926

The order of the four *varnas*[1] was created by Me according to the different *gunas* and karma of each; yet know that though, therefore, author thereof, being changeless I am not the author.[2]

[1] Divisions of society

[2] IV, 13

"I have," Shri Krishna says, "created four *varnas* on the basis of character and work." These are Brahmin, Kshatriya, Vaisya and Sudra. What should be the character of a Brahmin? What is distinctive of him? He is a Brahmin who knows *Brahman*, who lives most in the consciousness of God. And a Brahmin's work in life is to teach and help people to realize God. Besides this particular gift, he will also have the qualities of character which mark the other *varnas*. The Kshatriya's special dharma is protection of society. He should, above all, be a brave man. The Vaisya occupies himself with commerce. That is his special dharma. If he did not follow it, perhaps the world would not go on as it does. The Sudra's special dharma is service. If he combines with his service the spirit of *yajna* or the motive of public good, he will win the reward of his life. There is here no question of higher and lower. If we regard the person who cleans lavatories as lower and another who reads the *Gita* as higher, that will be the end of us. The majority in the world are engaged in the work of service. If a man combines the spirit of *yajna* with such work, he will be a *mumukshu*. A Sudra is expected to have humility, but humility does not mean abjectness. He serves no one except God.

Anyone for whom action is a necessity is subject to continual change. God is spotless and without form. He has no need to sleep or eat and drink. He does not move, and yet it is He who does everything. The weather expert will tell us that the storm was produced by changes in atmospheric pressure, but as he looks back for antecedent causes, he will reach a point beyond which he will not be able to go. God is an expert law-maker, for He is the author of all laws, though, being perfect, He is under no necessity to act or do anything. He never violates His law. God is present in everything that exists and, therefore, He and His law are one. He is spirit. That is, His law is spirit, it is God Himself. He is, and also is not, the doer of things. Since the universe displays some order in its running, we may assume that God is the author of that order. But the Lord has told us here that He is its author and yet is not its author—that is His mystery beyond human understanding.

Actions do not affect Me, nor am I concerned with the fruits thereof.[1] "Fruits of action do not cling to me, for I have no desire for them," says Shri Krishna. Once a machine is set in motion, every part in it works automatically. When we have

[1] IV, 14

learnt to function in this manner, like a machine, we shall have gained the true end of human effort. We shall then be fit for direct realization of God.

[67]

May 12, 1926

God works like a machine. He is His law. He is the author of law and He it is who administers it. What perfect order this represents! There is never a question of His suspending His law or of deciding to uphold it. The machine has been going on from eternity. God's law exists and has been in operation since the time that He came into being, if we can say such a thing about Him. We indeed conceive such a necessity for Him. He never suffers the effects of karma, for He has no wish to be fulfilled through any karma. Every part in a machine goes on working ceaselessly; it is the man behind the machine who operates it. In regard to God, we also imagine that He is Himself the machine and its operator. Can anyone say of a machine that it suffers the effects of karma or has any wish to be fulfilled through karma? A machine simply goes on working. If, in the same manner, we become totally immersed in our work, so that we are one with our work, we lose ourselves in that work. But, then, we should first ascertain our duty. The man of lust loses himself in his lust, so much so that he becomes the very embodiment of lust. Even simple contact with such a person is dangerous. We should not lose ourselves in our passions in that manner. Our duty is to strive for self-realization and we should lose ourselves in that aim. Such a person can never be disturbed by evil desire and, at last, he becomes one with God. If we lose ourselves in God, become machines, make ourselves as clay in God's hands, is it any wonder that we may become one with Him? We should lose ourselves in God so completely that we do not remain separate from Him at all. This verse explains how we can do so. It is to explain this that the Lord says here that karma has no effect on him, for he desires nothing through karma.

"Anyone who knows this truth about Me is never bound by karma."[1] How can he be? He who knows God's law will work but will desire nothing through work. Why do we feel the strain of work? Because, as we work, we remain attached to the "I" within us; were it not so, we would never feel impatient or worried. We should be so absorbed in our work that we do not even

[1] IV, 14

notice the time when we should stop it. We should thus work on like machines. I once saw a beautiful painting in a Roman Catholic Church, the work of a gifted painter. It is the time of prayer. Women have been working in the fields, pickaxes in hand. As one of them was about to dig with her pickaxe, the bell tolled for prayer and the pickaxe fell from her hand, she bent her body as though kneeling for prayer and started praying. The poet—for the painter is a poet—had imagined the woman as working like a machine. For these women work was worship. There is a saying in Latin which means that bodily labour is a form of worship. Anyone who believes that it is so will automatically kneel down at prayer time. A person who has resolved that he will always get up at four will roll up his bed as the clock strikes four. If such a person misses praying at prayer time, he will feel weary and oppressed and will not be able to concentrate on any work.

A person who works with such devotion, how can he suffer the effects of karma? That is, he never feels the strain of work. He is ever fresh. There are so many who cannot be happy unless they are working. They never feel the need to stop work for a moment and stretch themselves for rest. If any visitors interrupt them in their work, they feel miserable. Such persons never feel the effects of karma.

The man of lust loses himself in his lust, but he wearies of his indulgence because he seeks pleasure from it. Anyone who seeks pleasure is bound to weary of it sooner or later. If a person indulges his palate, he cannot but fall ill; he is bound to suffer from some disease. But what disease can he suffer from who never indulges his palate, who does not eat for enjoyment? One should do the task on hand without expecting pleasure from doing it, do it merely as one's duty. He who approaches his work in this spirit, who desires nothing through it, will not have to suffer the effects of karma. God does not suffer the effects of karma though He controls this vast machine. The signs which indicate that we suffer such effects are the need we feel for food and water and the wearing out of our bodies. God is ever awake. We are awake for some time and then sleep, we eat and feel hungry. But God, though He is ever awake, does not have to make an effort to keep Himself awake, He does not sleep and does not eat. Though He acts, He does nothing. Behind every act of ours, there is a trace of egotism and attachment to the "I",—an action of the will. We will to act, we have to do so, before we do anything. God keeps awake for ever without a moment's interruption. We cannot do so. If, however, we keep such a state before us as our ideal, we can do the best work. That is why Shri Krishna said: yoga is skill in action.[1] That is, the man who is firmly established in yoga always does better work than one who is restless and impatient in his work.

> Knowing this did men of old, desirous of Freedom, perform action; do thou, then just as they did—the men of old in days gone by.[2]

The seekers of *moksha* in old days knew this truth and worked in such a spirit. To realize God means to work like God, with single-minded devotion and ceaseless vigilance. Though living in the human body, we should imitate God as much as we can. "Our forefathers did this. You too," Shri Krishna tells Arjuna, "should act in the same manner" (Man is ruled by vows. God has no need to take any. Everyone should resolve that he or she will not fall asleep here. You ought not to give me pain by dozing here.). How is it that Arjuna thought about dharma when he was required to kill his relations? Shri Krishna, therefore, rebuked him and said that he should not think on those lines, for in old times people worked without thinking of any reward for work. If one works in that spirit, one is not bound by the effects of karma. "Think how I act," says Shri Krishna. "I create society with its four classes, but I am not bound by the effects of karma, for I remain unattached." "You too," He tells Arjuna, "should act in that manner."

You, students, should study with the same devotion as the *brahmacharis*[3] of old days. They bore themselves in such a manner that, though mere boys, they seemed to be grown-up, mature men. I speak of more than forty years ago. I distinctly remember that, at our place, in the absence of the priest his young son read the *Bhagavata*, and he read it very well indeed; so good was the education he had received at home. He must have been barely fifteen. Those whom we describe as *brahmacharis* today must behave as the *brahmacharis* of old did. You should sit upright, like a pole. Practise prayers for a whole month, and then you will discover that you are making some progress. What is the meaning of your feeling restless as you sit here? What is the good if you feel that, when you leave this place, you will get back into bed?

"Do your work and leave the responsibility to me," says Shri Krishna. "What is it you can do? Everything is done by me. Left

[1] II, 50

[2] IV, 15

[3] Students attached to preceptors in hermitages

to yourself, you will remain slumbering. On your own, you do only evil. You cannot say that I incline you to remain slumbering or to do evil. I inspire you to do only good. It is Satan who inclines you to remain slumbering, to abuse people, to behave disrespectfully to others and to cheat people in the name of spinning."

[68]

May 13, 1926

> 'What is action? What inaction?'—here even the wise are perplexed. I will then expound to thee that action knowing which thou shalt be saved from evil.[1]

"I will explain to you what right karma is and, having understood it, you will save yourself from evil, from the round of birth and death."

Our eyes are closed with bandages, like those over the eyes of the bullock in the oil-press. These bandages are not eternal, but we let them stay because we have grown used to them as natural, as fear is natural to us. There was a lion cub who, having always lived among goats, would tremble with fear like a goat. Then a real lion happened to meet him, and he held a mirror before him. The cub roared, and escaped from the company of the goats. This cub had not been forced to put a bandage over its eyes, the bandage had just grown of itself. In the same way, everyone of us has the bandage of ignorance grown over the eyes, and we do not know that it is not our dharma to live in evil, to submit to the round of birth and death. Our dharma is to rise ever higher until at last we can rise no more. We can have no rest till we have reached the goal. There will be eternal peace when we have reached it, that is, the peace of *moksha.* If you are on the top of the Himalayas, you are certain to fall from there, the top itself will crumble one day. It will crumble because it is ever changing. There is no changing in the state of *moksha* and no falling from there. *Moksha* means destruction of the shackles of birth and death, getting out of that round, it means deliverance from evil. If we meet a worthy guru, and he loosens the bandage of ignorance over our eyes and holds before us the mirror of knowledge, we would know what we are, would know whether we deserve to go from birth to birth or are fit for something else. In truth we deserve better than to follow this round, we belong to a higher station. We shall become fit for that station

[1] IV, 16

when the darkness of ignorance has vanished. The Lord told Arjuna that He would show the way by following which he could save himself from evil, that his actions till then were only a means of binding him. Shri Krishna wished to help Arjuna to deliver himself from that bondage, but what could He have taught him if the latter had not questioned Him eagerly, had not shown that he thirsted for knowledge, if he had not told Him: "I am like one sunk in ignorance; I do not know what my duty is; I have faith in you; show me what my dharma is?"

> For it is meet to know the meaning of action, of forbidden action, as also of inaction. Impenetrable is the secret of action.[1]

One should know what karma is, what *vikarma*—that is, forbidden karma—is, what *akarma*—that is, ceasing from karma—is. The truth about karma is a deep mystery.

> Who sees inaction in action and action in inaction, he is enlightened among men, he is a yogi, he has done all he need do.[2]

The aim of this verse is to show that one who does karma may still not be doing anything. I have already in a previous discourse mentioned my own example and told you that if I worked with attachment to my ego there were occasions when I would become mad. But things go on and leave me unaffected because I do everything merely as my duty. Even if every boy here were to leave me, I would not shed one tear. I would, on the contrary, dance with joy like Narasinh Mehta and sing "Happy am I that the net is no more". If we work in such a disinterested spirit, we can follow the example of the Lord who said that, though He had created society with its four classes, He was not their creator. That is so because of the principle that one may do karma and still not have done it.

We are caught in the motion of the wheel of this world. Our duty is to work ceaselessly as a part of this machine. We should spend every minute of our waking life in doing work which has fallen to our lot, and do it as if we are impatient over it and yet not be so, be calm in fact. The bullock that keeps the water-wheel in motion goes round and round, but no bucket falls from its place. If it were not a bucket but our heart in that place, it might even fall off; the bucket, however, does not fall off, it remains in its place, calm. We should be filled with such calm. On the other hand, if our heart is agitated, we may rest from

[1] IV, 17
[2] IV, 18

work but shall not have ceased from action, we would still be working. The bonds tighten round such a person and there is but misery in store for him. If he believes that those who let themselves be entangled in the affairs of life weave bonds of karma round them and that he himself is free, he will be under a delusion, for every thought is a form of karma. That is why the Lord has said that the truth about karma is a deep mystery. Those who do karma through their thoughts load themselves with burdens so heavy that they will never be able to throw them off. On the other hand, the man who becomes absorbed in work, does it as duty, and, if he finds that he cannot do a particular thing, leaves it alone,—such a person weaves no bond of karma round him.

Last evening, I rebuked . . .[1] and other boys. On that, . . .[2] told me that there was harshness in my voice and asked me if it was not a sign of anger in me. I said that I was not God. I only strive for perfection, but I am not fit to be anyone's guru. I am full of desires, and so, when I am excited, my voice is naturally raised. If I had succeeded in banishing every desire from me, I would be able to do as much work as I am doing now, but my voice would ever be the same. I aspire to reach such a state. It is true that sometimes my voice is raised and there is a little flash of anger in my eyes. This is the state Arjuna had in mind when he asked the Lord how a person is overcome with evil desire against his will.[3] I am still swayed by desire and anger. I say this to illustrate the truth that we cease from karma in the measure that we do karma without any thought of its fruit. If I run away from a task in despair, if I get upset or raise my voice because . . .[4] does not listen to me, I weave the bonds of karma round me. Having undertaken a duty, having agreed to look after some children entrusted to me and sharing the responsibility of bringing them up, how can I now run away from the task? If I retire to the heights of the Himalayas and live there in peace, I would be indulging my body in idle comfort and weave round myself the bonds of karma. I must, therefore, remain in the midst of these responsibilities, and win *moksha* through them. If I become free from anger and shake off ignorance, if I become more vigilant and alert, I would be doing no karma even when occupied in some karma. This illustration explains both the ideas, of a person

[1], [2] & [4] The names are omitted in the source.
[3] III, 36

doing no karma even when occupied in karma and of another who, though he believes that he is doing no karma, is in fact weaving the bonds of karma round himself.

Everyone should apply this illustration to himself, forgetting all about me as an individual. I have mentioned my own example merely in order to explain that we are all imperfect. I say, not merely out of modesty or as a matter of form, but with detachment, that I am imperfect. This is not my modesty, but the simple truth. When I am completely free from the sway of desire and anger, you will always see me calm, more so than you see me today. I am striving to be free from these. I feel that one day I shall attain such a state of calm.

In this age, we do not have the means with which to measure ourselves. The *Gita* was composed to help us. It says that we should work like machines and pour out our life in our work.

[69]

May 23, 1926

We should think further about the first line of the verse[1] beginning with *karmanyakarma*.

We saw in a previous verse that no human being ceases from karma altogether even for a moment. That means that the very process of living is a form of karma. Eating, speaking, thinking, sleeping, all these are forms of karma (. . . .[2] said that, when he retired to that place to seek peace, he had tried to stop even thinking, for thinking, too, is a form of karma.). Thus, no one can escape doing karma. Still the *Gita* distinguishes between karma and *akarma*, between the yogi and ordinary human beings, between night and day, and explains that the involuntary processes in the body are not karma; that is, even though we do such karma, we weave no bond round us through it. I have an aim in this discussion of the *Gita*, and that is that children should understand some of the ideas and act accordingly, and, therefore, the discussion is certainly a form of karma for me. If I had accepted the work of teaching and if explaining the *Gita* came naturally to me, then this very work would perhaps deserve to be described as *akarma*. Even so, the idea of *akarma* is like the Euclidean definition of a straight line, and the work of explaining the *Gita* would be *akarma* only in a relative sense. Karma

[1] IV, 18

[2] The name is omitted in the source.

becomes relatively *akarma* when it is undertaken for the service of others, for the sake of our higher good. We may be said to eat and breathe with that aim only if we have voluntarily and deliberately dedicated our body to the service of Shri Krishna. He who lives with the knowledge that his body is not his, that God makes it dance as He wills, may be said to have realized God. All karma done in that spirit is *akarma*. Anything else, though seeming *akarma*, is in truth karma. A yogi may have ceased riding fancy's horses, and still his *samadhi* may be a form of karma for him if he has sought it for better health. Some persons suffering from consumption learn to enter into such *samadhi*; it is plain that their aim in doing so is to cure themselves of their disease. Their karma in this case is not inspired by the motive of higher good. Only that karma is so inspired in which our aim is realization of God and nothing else, when this aim, too, is pursued with spontaneous naturalness. The person who is inspired by it is not in the least conscious of it. In all that he does, there is only the yearning for realizing God and no other thought. Such a person loses the very consciousness of his body, as the *gopis* did. Even those who are possessed by lust lose the consciousness of their bodies, but they go to hell because they have given themselves up to the pursuit of lust and do not yearn to see God. When such a person, after he has had enough of pleasure, experiences the joy of devotion to God, he realizes that this latter joy is far superior to the pleasure he got by giving himself up to lust, that by losing himself in the pleasure of lust he grew weaker, whereas by losing himself in the joy of God he was filled with strength. After this experience, he is no more negligent in work but learns to be proficient in it. He who does everything for the sake of the higher good and dedicates all his work to God has ceased from karma. Just as the judge dispenses justice and the hangman hangs the condemned man in the name of the king, so if we feel that in this empire of the universe we are God's slaves and are prompted by Him to do what we do, all our actions will be for our higher good.

> He whose every undertaking is free from desire and selfish purpose, and he who has burnt all his actions in the fire of knowledge—such a one the wise call a *pandita*.[1]

That person whose undertakings are never inspired by selfish desire or personal aims but are altogether spontaneous, whose

[1] IV, 19

karmas have been burnt up by the fire of knowledge (everything that exists and will cease has life in it, which means that a piece of stone has life in it, but, though it does no karma it has no knowledge either)—such a person will not be like a stone in regard to karma but, on the contrary, may do all manner of karma and will still have his karmas burnt up by the fire of knowledge. For instance, this earth created by God is in unceasing motion and yet seems at rest; it seems so though it is spinning with a speed which would make us giddy if we could see it. When typing on a typewriter has become mechanical work with the typist, the finger will alight on the right letter even when he is not looking at the keyboard; he who is able to work in such spontaneous manner and is fully alert, like the typist, in everything he does, may be described as the Buddha.

[70]

June 2, 1926

We may be doing much work, but without any consciousness that we are working.[1] We wish to know the *atman* dwelling in this human body—wish to know it directly so that its knowledge may become a part of our being as it was with Sudama[2]. An experienced carpenter will make a board effortlessly, whereas one with only a theoretical knowledge of the craft will not be able to make one. He who has learnt to work effortlessly in this manner goes on working mechanically and still remains detached. The verse beginning with *yasya sarve samarambhah*[3] describes the character of such a person. We do not have to make any effort for winking the eye; all our actions should become spontaneous like this. Anyone who has acquired control over his thoughts to this degree will never have an evil thought; such a person will move in the world as if he was no more than a corpse. He will seem so to us because he has no desire and no aim, is not subject to attachments and aversions; he is a man who has ceased from karma.

This work of explaining the *Gita* which I am doing is prompted by a personal motive, the wish to see that the boys understand it.

[1] The remark was prompted by the sight of a mad man who came towards the meeting, muttering the word "Prabhu", God.

[2] An indigent Brahmin friend of Krishna

[3] IV, 19

> He who has renounced attachment to the fruit of action, who is ever content, and free from all dependence,—he, though immersed in action, yet acts not.[1]

He who has given up desire for the fruits of karma, who is ever contented, not more so at one time and less at another time, who is always satisfied with what he has—such a person may be ever so deeply engrossed in work but in truth he does nothing. As Narasinh Mehta has said, an ascetic and a perfectly chaste woman do not know the pleasure of earthly love; if any such person were to come and see us plying the charkha all the hours of the day, he would think that we had become mad, that we were so occupied with work that we paid no attention to performing daily worship. But, according to the *Gita*, we can say that we were doing no work, for we had no selfish aim in our work and did it simply as our dharma, did it merely because of our faith [in the value of spinning]. With scepticism all round us, to go on spinning with the faith that it would bring swaraj indicates the state of unvarying inner content in which we live. This is true, of course, of only those people who attribute all this power to the charkha and devote themselves whole-heartedly to it.

> Expecting naught, holding his mind and body in check, putting away every possession, and going through action only in the body, he incurs no stain.[2]

He alone does not feel the body to be a burden who hopes for nothing, whose mind is ever steady and who has completely given up the desire for possessions. How does this become possible? The body, too, is a kind of property which we possess. We should so use it that we would not mind its perishing today rather than tomorrow. If we cultivate such an attitude, we would not feel the body to be a burden. Ladha Maharaj had given up all concern with this particular form of property, the body, and kept repeating the name Siva all the hours of the day; anyone who works in that spirit, with the sole aim of giving the body its hire and not for the sake of pleasures, may be doing karma all the time and still he stores up no sins.

[1] IV, 20
[2] IV, 21

[71]

June 3, 1926

That person who is described as doing *shariram* karma does not have to suffer the fruits of karma. This does not mean that his karma bears no fruit, but only that he seeks none. In other words, he does not attribute the karma to his *atman*. For instance, I listen to the *Gita* being read out. I should do so with humility, for listening to it is my duty; the fruit of listening to it will follow of itself, whether we think of it or not, in the same way that a seed which has been sown grows by itself into a tree. This seed has no ego. We are animals to the extent that we have some needs in common with them, but in certain respects we are different from them. The consciousness that we do things should disappear from us. A person who writes his diary every day does not think about how much his hand worked during the day; in that way all our work should be done mechanically.

Even an action which one took to be most virtuous karma may turn out to be sin. Supposing one is born a prince through the virtue of meritorious work, how does it profit one? What good is there in being born a prince ? To be born poor and to be born a prince, these are two extremes of the same state. We say that we should try to make do with less sleep, and that may seem contrary to the teaching of the verse we are discussing. But we make the effort in order that by and by sleeping less may become natural to us, just as we try to rise above *rajas* and *tamas* by engaging ourselves in *sattvik*[1] activity.

Shariram karma means karma for keeping the body alive. Observance of *brahmacharya* and other rules has become difficult for us because we pamper the body too much. We have made difficult what should be quite natural to us. It is not natural for human beings to violate *brahmacharya*. We seek pleasures because we live as if the body and the *atman* were identical. If, instead, we look upon the body as only a material object and think merely of keeping it alive somehow, we would not run after pleasures. How can we be ever disturbed by evil desires if we look upon our body as the temple of the *atman*? Should anyone maintain himself merely by doing half an hour's writing every day? No. Anyone who does so is a thief. The mind works for the *atman*, and so does the body, but we ought to undertake physical labour to maintain the body. Even the work of teaching cannot serve as a

[1] Characterized by *sattva*

means for this purpose. Only agriculture or similar work can count as work for the sake of the body.

> Content with whatever chance may bring, rid of the pairs of opposites, free from ill will, even-minded in success and failure, he is not bound though he acts.[1]

He who is satisfied with what he gets in the ordinary course of things, who has risen above the pairs of opposites, such as happiness and suffering, has no ill will in him and bears an equal mind towards success and failure, is indifferent towards them or is not affected by them—such a person does not dance with joy on getting something which is welcome to him and does not start lamenting his lot when disagreeable things happen—he may do karma and still be not doing it, that is, will not be bound by the effects of his karma.

> Of the free soul who has shed all attachment, whose mind is firmly grounded in knowledge, who acts only for sacrifice, all karma is extinguished.[2]

That person who works without attachment is free, that is, he is not bound by the effects of karma. He whose mind has become steady through knowledge and who always works in the spirit of *yajna* has all his karmas burnt up in the fire of knowledge.

It would be far better that we die than that we eat merely to serve ourselves. That is, if we cultivate a state of mind such that we eat and drink in order that we may serve God, serve the *atman*, that is, eat and drink in the spirit of *yajna*, then we shall have ceased from karma.

[72]

June 4, 1926

If we recite certain verses thousands of times over and over again and with faith, they acquire great power for us. A Muslim should not tire of reciting *kalamas*[3] and a Hindu should not tire of reciting the *gayatri* or of repeating Ramanama or the *dwadash mantra*.

[1] IV, 22

[2] IV, 23

[3] The creed of Islam as expressed in the verse from the Koran: There is no God but Allah and Mohammed is His apostle.

I have discussed today's verses at great length with Vinobaji, too, but I am not sure of their meaning. The *Gita* was composed after the time of the Vedas, and the different sects have tried so to interpret its teaching that it may support their own tenets. It is too much to believe that the *Gita* condemned Vedic rituals. I have, therefore, tried again and again to get a meaning which would not conflict with the Vedic practices. Not that this was necessary for myself. My task is to find in them a meaning that would satisfy you. The teacher of the *Gita* did not lay down that those who came after him should always read in it only the meaning which he himself had in mind. Now, it says that every karma done in the spirit of *yajna* leaves no effects behind it. Any action done without reference to one's own interest is a form of *yajna*. The next verse follows as a consequence from this, and also explains the manner of doing such *yajna*.

> The offering of sacrifice is *Brahman*; the oblation is *Brahman*; it is offered by *Brahman* in the fire that is *Brahman*; thus he whose mind is fixed on acts dedicated to *Brahman* must needs pass on to *Brahman*.[1]

That which is thrown into the *yajna* is *Brahman* and so is the oblation (*arpan* has been interpreted to mean all the materials used for the purpose of the *yajna*). If that oblation is thrown by *Brahman* into the fire which is also *Brahman*, it is bound to act as *Brahman*. Anyone who relates all his karmas to *Brahman* will merge into the latter. How can a person who sees God in every aspect of a *yajna* have to suffer the fruits of karma? He becomes both the ladle used in the *yajna* and the oblation poured out by its means. He looks upon God as a potter and offers himself as clay to Him and lets Him make from it any pot He pleases. The verse thus explains how there may be *akarma* in karma.

[73]

June 5, 1926

Shri Krishna now explains the different types of *yajna*:

> Some yogis perform sacrifice in the form of worship of the gods, others offer sacrifice of sacrifice itself in the fire that is *Brahman*.[2]

I have been told by Vinoba that there is support in the Vedas for the view that a person who has attained to knowledge of the *Brahman* need not worry about performing *yajna*. One who has

[1] IV, 24
[2] IV, 25

made his life itself a long *yajna*, why should he undertake any other *yajna*?

A woman who is nearly blind has come among us. She has a fine voice and sings *Raghupati Raghav Raja Ram*. She is a Tamilian. She has come here with her husband's permission. She appears intelligent. We should feel that anyone who serves her performs a *yajna*. Such service serves our higher good. But to a person who performs a *yajna* by means of a *yajna*, that is, who has made his whole life a *yajna*, doing a *yajna* comes most naturally. Such a person is ever engaged in doing *yajna* with ceaseless vigilance. He identifies himself with all creatures in their suffering. The meaning here is not that he gives up doing *yajna*. Rather, it becomes his very nature to engage himself in *yajna*, just as it is natural for God to dwell in the heart of the basest of human beings. Some persons make a sacrificial offering of sense organs, hearing and others, into the fire of self-control; that is, they stop hearing with their ears, speaking with their tongues, savouring food and drink with the palate and seeing with their eyes. Others make a sacrificial offering of sound and other objects of sense into the fire of the sense-organs. Here the process is reversed. Since we cannot stop our ears altogether, we should hear only what is good. Since we cannot keep our eyes shut for ever, we should use them only to see the glory of God everywhere. This is what is meant by saying that some persons sacrifice the objects of sense into the fire of the organs of sense.

[74]

June 6, 1926

When Kishorelal was living apart from others in a cottage, he tried to cultivate self-control. He was disturbed by the noise of passing trains while reading the *Jnaneshvari*[1]. I made the suggestion to him that he should block his ears with pieces of rubber. But he got used to the situation and declined to use any such pieces.

But what about children? The only course for them [in such circumstances] is to take measures to stop the functioning of the organ in question, for the state of inward concentration is not easy for them to cultivate. That is how we should act in regard to sound and other objects of sense.

Proceeding, Shri Krishna says:

[1] Commentary on the *Gita* by Jnaneshvar, a Maharashtrian saint of the thirteenth century

> Others again sacrifice all the activities of the senses and of the vital energy in the yogic fire of self-control kindled by knowledge.[1]

Others stop the functioning of all sense organs, stop even the movement of *prana*, that is, breathing, make themselves motionless and enter into *samadhi*, become firmly established in the *atman* and, lighting this yoga with the fire of knowledge, make a sacrificial offering of all the organs into it.

If a person cannot control his mind by any other means, he may adopt this way. Or one may get angry with oneself and stop the functioning of all one's organs. Some persons become angry with themselves because they do not succeed in their efforts to observe *brahmacharya.* Those who sail to the North Pole sacrifice money in millions over and over again, without getting disheartened. The man who tries to observe *brahmacharya* but fails in his efforts becomes desperate and undertakes an indefinite fast, resolving in his mind that he will not let any organ of the body function because, so long as even one of them is functioning, his mind revels in evil thoughts; he, therefore, decides that it is best to stop all organs from functioning. This is lighting up the fire of the yoga of control of the *atman.* This is no mere *samadhi* of the body, it is *samadhi* illumined by knowledge. A man striving for success in *brahmacharya* suffers pain as a woman in labour does. If a person cannot bear obstruction to his efforts to cultivate self-control, we see that he gets upset. This is why I often say that such a person is like a milch cow and that we should bear his kicks.

> Some sacrifice with material gifts; with austerities; with yoga; some with the acquiring and some with the imparting of knowledge. All these are sacrifices of stern vows and serious endeavour.[2]

There are people in this world who perform the *yajna* of money (who let their wealth be shared by others). Some others perform *tapas*[3] and imprison the monkey which is our mind. Some others, still, practise yoga or devote themselves regularly to holy studies, to the study of the Vedas. Some perform the *yajna* of the pursuit of knowledge. They do not read, but devote themselves to reflection and meditation. Ascetics who put themselves under strict vows perform a *yajna* in that manner.

[1] IV, 27
[2] IV, 28
[3] Austerities

[75]

June 8, 1926

> Others absorbed in the practices of the control of the vital energy sacrifice the outward in the inward and the inward in the outward, or check the flow of both the inward and the outward vital airs.[1]

Some throw *pranavayu*[2] as sacrifice into *apanavayu*[3], while others hold the latter in the former. Some others still hold both. All these are practitioners of *pranayama*[4].

> Yet others, abstemious in food, sacrifice one form of vital energy in another. All these know what sacrifice is and purge themselves of all impurities by sacrifice.[5]

[76]

June 9, 1926

> Those who partake of the residue of sacrifice—called *amrita* (ambrosia)—attain to everlasting *Brahman*. Even this world is not for a non-sacrificer; how then the next, O Kurusattama ?[6]

To strive and conquer desire is also a form of *yajna*. The *Gita* teaches us to look upon all activities for *paramartha*[7] as forms of *yajna*. *Paropakar* means working for others; but the idea that we work for others is only an illusion. We always work for ourselves. We shall attain deliverance only if we work exclusively for our higher self. All activities for *paramartha*, therefore, aim at one's own good.

Coming back to the verse, those who consume what remains after the *yajna* is over, that is, those who utilize for themselves only the time which remains after they have completed the *yajna*, enjoy *amrita* and attain to the timeless *Brahman*. The person who has done no work during the day but, like a heifer idling in mud, has spent his time in bed, steals the sleep which he enjoys at night. The man who does no *yajna* can win nothing in this world; what then can he win in the other world? He is lost in both.

[1] IV, 29
[2] Vital air in the lung
[3] Vital air in the abdomen
[4] Breath control
[5] IV, 30
[6] IV, 31
[7] Literally, the Supreme good; the term also means altruism.

[77]

June 10, 1926

The verse which we have been discussing has a wide meaning. It means that we should eat only after all others have had their food. So long as the embodied soul lives in this world, it has no choice but to have relations with others. To become disinterested in the body, therefore, means that one should devote oneself exclusively to the service of others so that one may attain the *Brahman* beyond time. We should be as impatient to attain it as a lost sheep is to get back to its fold. Those who, on the contrary, live only for themselves prosper neither in this world nor in the next. Therefore, Shri Krishna tells Arjuna: stop thinking of some people being and others not being your relations. If you may kill any people, you should kill these too.

> Even so various sacrifices have been described in the Vedas; know them all to proceed from action; knowing this thou shalt be released.[1]

One meaning given to this verse is that there are these different types of *yajna* in the sight of the *Brahman* [*sic*]. This interpretation omits any reference to the Vedas, for the *Gita* has actually denounced them. And, moreover, the verses[2] in question are found nowhere in the Vedas. Ordinarily, of course, the verse should mean this: "The Vedas describe these different types of *yajna*. You should know that all of them exist through karma; only so can you win *moksha*." After explaining the meanings of karma and *akarma*, the Lord makes it clear in this verse that it is simply impossible for anyone to live without doing karma. That of course does not mean that a state of *akarma* is impossible. Every karma done for the good of the *atman*, though it appears to be karma, is in reality *akarma*. If we can renounce the fruits of karma, that is, work only for others, then we may work like horses. On the other hand, when working for ourselves, we should be like a piece of inert matter, have no interest in the work at all. This is a state of the heart, an attitude of mind. Anyone who cultivates that attitude towards everything he does, sleeping, eating, drinking or cleaning the lavatory, will attain to *moksha*.

The words *evam bahuvidhah* in this verse mean that the different types of *yajna* are enumerated only as illustrations. Others can

[1] IV, 32

[2] That is, the verses in the *Gita* enumerating the different types of *yajna*; IV, 24 to 30

also be included if they satisfy the *Gita*'s definition of *yajna*.

> Knowledge-sacrifice is better, O Parantapa, than material sacrifice, for all action which does not bind finds its consummation in Knowledge (*jnana*).[1]

The person who performs the *yajna* of knowledge makes a greater sacrifice than another who performs the *yajna* of money, for the *yajna* of knowledge includes everything, money and all other things. Knowledge covers everything which exists in the world, without reference to the distinction between living and non-living. If we understand the terms *dravya*[2] and *jnana* in a wide sense, a *yajna* of knowledge includes *yajna* of every kind of *dravya*. Anyone who imparts the highest knowledge to us, convinces us to the very depth of our being that the body is not the *atman*, performs a very great *yajna* indeed.

[78]

June 11, 1926

> The masters of knowledge who have seen the Truth will impart to thee this Knowledge; learn it through humble homage and service and by repeated questioning.[3]

"You can obtain this knowledge," Shri Krishna tells Arjuna, "by bowing before a guru in utmost humility, —by prostrating yourself before him, fuel in hand,—by serving him and by frequent questioning, by harassing him with questions, and in no other way. The enlightened ones who have seen the truth will impart this knowledge to you."

[79]

June 12, 1926

> When thou hast gained this knowledge, O Pandava, thou shalt not again fall into such error; by virtue of it thou shalt see all beings without exception in thyself and thus in Me.[4]

"When you have received that knowledge," proceeds Shri Krishna, "your understanding will never again be clouded by the darkness of ignorance and you will make no distinction like that

[1] IV, 33
[2] Any material; in a restricted sense, the term means "money".
[3] IV, 34
[4] IV, 35

between kinsmen and others, you will learn to regard all beings with an equal eye so that you will see them all as existing in you and in Me; in other words, for you everyone will be a kinsman. The entire universe is filled by Me, and, therefore, you will see Me in all objects. When the 'I' in you has melted away, then it will be *jale Vishnu, sthale Vishnu, Vishnu Parvatamastake*[1] for you." Once we have realized that this whole universe exists in God, how can there be any problem of violence and non-violence for us? We would feel even thieves and tigers to be ourselves. Till we feel in that way, we may be sure that we have not attained to a state of knowledge at all.

[80]

June 13, 1926

Can we claim that we have the knowledge described in the verse which we have been discussing? Suppose that we learn in one day to recite it; do we then become seers of truth ? Do we become so when we teach that verse to others? Of course not. We cannot have this knowledge merely by talking about it. We understand with our reason that the universe is the same as ourselves, but we can only imagine what that means. We cannot grasp the idea or feel its truth. The moment we leave this place, we shall treat all others as different from us. Only that person in whom this idea has sunk from the intellect to the heart—even an intellectual nincompoop can have a heart which is an ocean of compassion—can feel its truth in direct experience. Shri Krishna says to Arjuna: "When I say that men of knowledge will impart this knowledge to you, I do not mean that they will convince your reason; I mean that they will awaken in you the faith that it is so. You will then realize that it is because of your reason that you see things as separate from one another, that in truth they are one." God, ourselves and all objects in the universe are in essence one Reality. Even God vanishes and we have only *neti, neti*. When a person has realized this, his ignorance will have completely vanished.

> Even though thou be the most sinful of sinners, thou shalt cross the ocean of sin by the boat of knowledge.[2]

[1] "Vishnu in water, Vishnu on land and Vishnu on the tops of mountains"

[2] IV, 36

"Even if you are the most wicked of sinners," says Shri Krishna, "you will cross the sea of darkness and ignorance with the ship of knowledge"—crossing the Swayambhu-Raman[1] sea of *moha*[2], sang Raychandbhai.

Hunger cannot be satisfied by the knowledge that there is food in the vessel, or even when that food is swallowed down into the stomach; it is only when it is digested in the stomach and converted into blood that we may say that our hunger is satisfied.

> As a blazing fire turns its fuel to ashes, O Arjuna, even so the fire of Knowledge turns all actions to ashes.[3]

First, knowledge was compared to a ship, and now it is compared to fire. It burns up the bonds of karma.

[81]

June 15, 1926

For me, the *Gita* is the ship, not because it is a learned work but because I have liked it, it has appealed to me in my old age, or because some verse in it has been a great support to me, put it any way you like.

Man does not live by bread alone, whereas the lower creatures need only food to live. Anna Kingsford used to say that men seemed like tigers and snakes. Certainly, the lower creatures are as brethren to us. We all come from the same source. But they need only food to live, whereas man lives by performing *yajna*. Everyone performs *yajna* in one way or another. The spinning-wheel is one type of *yajna*. Prayers, too, are a *yajna* for us. They represent a mode of spiritual cleansing. Till we have performed that *yajna*, we should feel uneasy inside us. Only those who attend to these readings of the *Gita* in that spirit, not others, may be said to be really interested in it. If we were not thus interested in these readings, we would engage a teacher more learned than even Vinoba and with his help, study the *Gita* in order to learn Sanskrit or be honoured as pundits in society. Instead, we join these prayers in order that they may sustain us in our life. Man's need for prayer is as great as his need for bread. A bad man will use his ears to hear evil of others and see sinful things, but

[1] The name given in Jain literature to the farthest sea, which was believed to be so vast that no one could cross it

[2] The state of delusion in which the self takes the phenomenal existence as real

[3] IV, 37

the good man says that, had he a thousand eyes and ears, he would use them to contemplate the vision of God for ever and to hear devotional songs, and employ his five thousand tongues to sing His praises. It is only after I have prayed here every day that I feel the bliss of having tasted the *amrita* of knowledge. For that man who wishes to be a real human being, dal and *roti* are not his food. They count little to him. His real food is prayer. On Sundays, I used to lie in bed till late in the morning, and in vain would Ba[1] try to get me out of it. She used to spoil my mornings, which was not right. Many women do this sort of thing. They should not. Actually I had an excuse for what I did, for in those days I did not pray (as I do now). Even so, I tell you of my mistake. Sleeping for longer hours on Sundays did not make me the less drowsy on Mondays. You are *brahmacharis*. You ought to get up in time and attend prayers every day. You may excuse yourselves from other duties, but never from prayers. You should cultivate such a state of mind that for half an hour you will have only one thought in your mind, and no other. Everyone should set apart some time in this manner for reflection. It provides an opportunity to feel one with all living creatures. That is enough for today by way of introduction to the *Gita*.

[82]

June 16, 1926

> There is nothing in this world so purifying as Knowledge. He who is perfected by yoga finds it in himself in the fulness of time.[2]

We see nothing in this world as holy as this knowledge (The purest *yajna*, therefore, is the *yajna* of knowledge.). He who has become fit for *moksha* through the practice of yoga comes to this knowledge in the course of time by his own effort. That knowledge is realization of the self. As soon as this realization is attained, all the burden of this body and of karma will melt away.

> It is the man of faith who gains knowledge—the man who is intent on it and who has mastery over his senses; having gained knowledge, he comes ere long to the supreme peace.[3]

Anyone who has unshakable faith will win deliverance with the help of Ramanama only. Parents purposely give their children the names of the Lord. That also may save them. That person

[1] Kasturba Gandhi
[2] IV, 38
[3] IV, 39

who is for ever devoted to the Lord, who is self-controlled and who can fall into sleep any time he chooses, who has perfect control over every sense, attains this knowledge and soon wins peace—*moksha* through it.

[83]

June 17, 1926

We do a sum in mathematics with the help of our reasoning faculty. It does not matter whether or not we have faith in mathematics. But, for spiritual knowledge, faith is essential. Does a child have to train his intellect in order to love its mother or father? An illiterate mother loves her child with her heart. We may have a love relationship of any kind with God. The poet has presented to us only a few aspects of Divine love. A person who has no conception of the vast sea may be given some idea of it by telling him of rivers and streams.

> But the man of doubt, without knowledge and without faith, is lost; for him who is given to doubt there is neither this world nor that beyond, nor happiness.[1]

That person who does not value knowledge, who lacks faith, that is, who is a sceptic, will perish. He prospers neither in this world nor in the other.

> He who has renounced all action by means of yoga, who has severed all doubt by means of knowledge—him self-possessed, no actions bind, O Dhananjaya![2]

"Therefore," Shri Krishna says, "the doubt in your heart, born of ignorance, destroy it with the sword of knowledge and take up yoga—karmayoga[3]—and get ready."

[84]

[Chapter V]

June 18, 1926

> Thou laudest renunciation of actions, O Krishna, whilst at the same time thou laudest performance of action; tell me for a certainty which is the better.[4]

[1] IV, 40
[2] IV, 41
[3] The yoga of disinterested work
[4] V, 1

Shri Vyasa uses the figure of Arjuna to make it clear that he wrote the *Mahabharata* only as a *yajna* and that those who read it for their spiritual good would also be performing a *yajna*.

[85]

June 19, 1926

When can we say that a person who is eating is, nevertheless, not eating? Can we say that because, while eating, he absent-mindedly puts a morsel into his nostril? Anyone who thinks about play while he is eating is merely inattentive; we cannot say that he is disinterested in eating. But a person may be eating with proper attention and yet we may say of him that he is, nevertheless, not eating. Of whom can we say this ? Of one who eats as though he was performing a *yajna*, who offers up his action of eating to Shri Krishna, who eats with the feeling that he does so in obedience to the Lord's command. Or, such a person may also tell himself that it is not he, but his body, that is eating—the *atman* does not eat, or drink or sleep; he will then eat to serve others, to serve the lame, the crippled and the afflicted. That will be service of God, for God who dwells in the afflicted is also like them. That person's karma of eating will be in truth *akarma*, and will not bind him. If we aspire to be good, we must ceaselessly work to serve others, serve them in a perfectly disinterested spirit. We should not serve anyone with the hope that he, too, will serve us one day, but we may serve him because the Lord dwells in him and we serve that Lord. If we hear anyone crying in distress for help, we should immediately run to him and help him. We should help the Lord crying in distress. After doing what was needed, we should feel that it was all a dream. Would the Lord ever cry in distress? In this way, all our acts of service will seem to us as dreams.

Those who offer delicacies to the Lord before partaking of them, do they really perform an act of dedication to Shri Krishna ? No, they don't. They themselves eat those delicacies. They do not eat them in the spirit of *yajna*. If a person offers the best part of such dainties to others to eat and himself eats only the indifferent items which remain behind, we may describe him as *yajnashishtamritabhuj*[1].

> Renunciation and performance of action both lead to salvation; but of the two, *karmayoga* (performance) is better than sannyasa (renunciation).[2]

[1] One who eats the *amrita* left behind in a *yajna*; IV, 31

[2] V, 2

[86]

June 20, 1926

When Shri Krishna said *nehabhikramanashosti*[1], He assured us that no effort undertaken to follow dharma is ever wasted. Man cannot completely refrain from karma, and therefore, it is easy for everyone to follow karmayoga. Renunciation of karma, on the other hand, is a difficult matter, for it requires knowledge, whereas karmayoga can be followed even by an ordinary person. To retire into a cave in the Himalayas and sit there for ever doing nothing—it is extremely difficult to succeed in such an effort. It is a hard task to cultivate such stillness that one would not be tempted by anything even in one's thoughts. The Lord, therefore, tells us that karmayoga is a better path, since the other one is beset with obstacles and is likely to encourage hypocrisy, while the karmayogi runs no such risk.

> Him one should know as ever renouncing who has no dislikes and likes; for he who is free from the pairs of opposites is easily released from bondage.[2]

Why should a karmayogi be looked upon as superior to a sannyasi? A karmayogi is necessarily a sannyasi. But a karmayogi of what type? One who has no ill will, who desires nothing and is ever devoted to his duty, who is not affected by the pairs of opposites, easily becomes free from the binding effects of karma.

> It is the ignorant who speak of *sankhya* and yoga as different, not so those who have knowledge. He who is rightly established even in one wins to the fruit of both.[3]

Sankhya here means sannyasa and yoga means karmayoga. Men of little understanding think them to be distinct from each other, but not so the wise. In truth, they are two sides of the same coin. Anyone who becomes established in either reaps the fruit of success in the other too.

A thing at rest and another in intense motion seem alike. The earth, for instance. Rest and motion are a pair of opposites. But he who remains unaffected by such opposites reaps the fruit of both.

[1] In II, 40
[2] V, 3
[3] V, 4

> The goal that the *sankhyas* attain is also reached by the yogis. He sees truly who sees both *sankhya* and yoga as one.[1]

The state which is attained through *sankhya*, that is, through renunciation of karma, is attained by the karmayogi too. He alone has true knowledge who understands that *sankhya* and karmayoga are the same thing. That is, if we consider the essence of the two, we shall find no difference between them at all. Hence work done in the spirit of *yajna*, done without egotism for our higher good and for the service of others, has a place in both.

[87]

June 22, 1926

Karma means work which circumstances make it necessary for us to undertake, not that which we do of our own choice. We should feel that we need not even pray for *praninam artinashanam*[2] or wish to work ceaselessly with that aim. When the 'I' in a person has vanished and he has merged into God, he feels no need to pray for anything. He will do only such work as circumstances make necessary for him. If he has no inclination of his own, only the purest type of work will come to him, and he will do it with the feeling that Narayana[3] does everything. When Harishchandra got ready to put the knife to his wife's throat, was it really Harishchandra who was acting? It was the Lord who prompted him to act as he did, and Harishchandra only carried out His order. The unhappy man, he had made himself a mere servant. Having made ourselves servants of the Lord, it is not for us to choose what we shall do and what we shall not. We should do any work which comes to us and at the same time leave the burden of such work to Narayana to shoulder.

> But renunciation, O Mahabahu, is hard to attain except by yoga; the ascetic equipped with yoga attains *Brahman* ere long.[4]

For him who has not learnt to offer all his actions to Shri Krishna, sannyasa is extremely difficult to practise. The truth is that sannyasa is impossible to practise except through karmayoga. Really speaking, therefore, sannyasa is karmayoga, and nothing

[1] V, 5

[2] "End to the suffering of all creatures", from the verse:
I do not desire a kingdom nor that I may go to heaven or win liberation.
I only desire that the suffering of all creatures in pain may end.

[3] Vishnu

[4] V, 6

else. He who has become free from attachments and aversions, who has shed the 'I' in him, has become a true sannyasi.

> The yogi who has cleansed himself, has gained mastery over his mind and all his senses, who has become one with the *atman* in all creation, although he acts he remains unaffected.[1]

He who is established in yoga soon attains the *Brahman*. Anyone who successfully follows karmayoga becomes established in yoga. He who has become pure, he whose evil impulses have all been burnt away and become reduced to a burnt thread in which only the twists of the original material are visible, will act mechanically in everything he does. That of course does not mean that he pays no attention to what he is doing; it only means that he has no egotistic feeling that he himself is doing anything, though the thread which he draws out will be as straight as that drawn by a machine. An unthinking person works mechanically and the Lord's servant, too, does merely what he is asked to do. But he does not work for payment and, therefore, his work shines out, whereas the hired labourer's work does not shine out as he works for money. No supervisor is required to keep watch over a Lord's servant at work. Outwardly, he seems dull, but inwardly he ever lives in the *Brahman*. He will have all the virtues of a machine and none of its defects. Besides, the man who lives in the *atman*, who has subdued the demons in him and mastered the senses, who sees himself in all creatures and all creatures in himself, will make no distinction between relations and others. He will ever live as a servant of all, and will partake only of what remains after others have had their share. Of such a person it can be said, *kurvannapi na lipyate,* that he works, but is not bound by the effects of karma.

> The yogi who has seen the Truth knows that it is not he that acts whilst seeing, hearing, touching, smelling, eating, walking, sleeping, or breathing.
>
> Talking, letting go, holding fast, opening or closing the eyes—in the conviction that it is the senses that are moving in their respective spheres.[2]

These two verses are a commentary on the preceding verse. The man who knows the Truth acts as if he himself did nothing. Whether seeing or hearing, smelling, eating, walking, lying down to sleep, breathing, speaking, parting with or accepting anything, winking—in all these he will feel that it is his senses which are

[1] V, 7
[2] V, 8 & 9

functioning according to their nature. Such a person acts but does not do anything. A yogi can take up this attitude, and so can a rogue, as also a devotee of the Lord. He who has consecrated his heart to the Lord will feel no desire to do anything for himself. Even when he retires to sleep, he will say that it is his body which will fall into sleep. The functions of the body are not evil in themselves. We make them so. If the body works without interference by us, it will emit nothing but fragrance. We can thus take it as a mathematical truth that our work will tend to evil in proportion as we are conscious of the 'I' in us and it will tend to good in proportion as we shed that 'I'.

[88]

June 23, 1926

If we keep loudly reciting the two verses which we have been discussing, we do not become yogis thereby. We should cultivate such a state that we wholly cease to be conscious of the 'I' in us. Only that person can apply these verses to himself who is always completely absorbed in the task on hand, whose every action is dedicated to Shri Krishna and who seeks no benefit for himself from anything he does. If he uses his ears, it is to hear praise of God. If he uses his eyes, it is to have *darshan*[1] of the Lord. Nor does he ever suffer. Whenever anything happens which might cause him pain, he would think that the pain was not felt by him. 'If,' he would tell himself, 'I forget the 'I' in me when suffering this pain and think of Rama, no one would be able to know that I had been stung by a scorpion.' He would feel that it had stung his body and that there was a red spot on it, that is all. He works mechanically, and still everything he does shines out. His actions grow ever more beautiful. He never tires of work, never feels upset and confused.

> He who dedicates his actions to *Brahman* and performs them without attachment is not smeared by sin, as the lotus leaf by water.[2]

Shri Krishna says this to guard against anyone making unworthy use of the preceding two verses. Such a person remains untouched by sin, as the lotus leaf remains untouched by water. The term "sin" is used here in a wide sense, and covers both sin and virtue. Such a person does not have to suffer the consequences of either sinful or virtuous action. He goes on working,

[1] Sight of an object, place or person regarded as holy

[2] V, 10

but remains unaffected by work. Leaves of other plants get wet and decay, but the lotus is not moistened by water.

> Only with the body, mind and intellect and also with the senses do the yogis perform action without attachment for the sake of self-purification.[1]

The yogis work, but only with their bodies, with their minds or their intellectual faculties or their senses, and feel that they themselves are not working since they work without attachment and with the aim of self-purification. To work with this aim means to dedicate one's work to the *Brahman*.

We worked for self-purification in 1921, but afterwards strayed from that path and so found ourselves in difficulties.

He who works for self-purification goes on working with his machine in a disinterested spirit.

> A man of yoga obtains everlasting peace by abandoning the fruit of action; the man ignorant of yoga, selfishly attached to fruit, remains bound.[2]

Renouncing the fruits of karma, the yogi wins the peace which is the reward of faith and devotion, the peace which brings *moksha*, —the peace enjoyed by the man established in *Brahman*. That is not the peace of a stone or the peace which the unthinking man enjoys, or that which the man of lust absorbed in the pursuit of lust enjoys for a while; it is the peace of the man established in *Brahman*, the bliss which belongs to the *atman*.

The man who is not established in yoga stays in the grip of desire. He who works under the sway of ignorance must be a man attached, that is, one who is bound through attachment to fruits of work or with the snake-like coil of expectation and sense-cravings. When a snake is provoked, it can coil round us and crush us to death, but at the most it breaks our bones. To Mirabai, however, the snake in front of her seemed Shaligram[3] dancing. At the worst it would have harmed her physically, but the snake which bites the man of lust destroys his very soul.

[89]

June 24, 1926

We should understand the meaning of the words of the *Gita* not merely to satisfy our curiosity but with the aim of putting its

[1] V, 11
[2] V, 12
[3] Shri Krishna

teaching into practice. In my case, the constant reading of the *Gita* has filled my life with prayer. We should leave alone what we cannot put into practice. It is a misuse of our intellectual energy and a waste of time to go on reading what we cannot put into practice. I have to say this because of a complaint Shri Vinoba has made. As the students do not go to bed early, they find it difficult to rise early and their health suffers. The students complain that the teachers, too, do not retire early but keep awake talking till midnight. This does not accord well with the spirit in which we have been reading the *Gita*. We should be *sarvabhutatmabhutatma*[1] or *atmavat sarvabhuteshu*[2]. For the sake of our neighbour, we should desist from making noise or, if we talk, talk in low whispers, as thieves do. I, too, should retire early in the evening. What does the phrase *brahmanyadhaya karmani*[3] mean? God does not arouse him who does not wish to wake up. That means that we should adjust ourselves to the weakest limbs in society; or eliminate them, destroy and burn or bury them. If we are not ready for this, we should not exert ourselves to reform or raise any class of people.

> Renouncing with the mind all actions, the dweller in the body, who is master of himself, rests happily in his city of nine gates, neither doing nor getting anything done.[4]

The self-controlled man, that is, the man established in the *atman*, mentally renounces all karma and lives in peace. To renounce all karma mentally means to make the mind indifferent to them, to withdraw it into an attitude of detachment towards work and feel that we are not doing what we are engaged in, that it is God who impels us to do it. Surely we do not feel, as we breathe, that we are breathing. We have mentally renounced that karma. It becomes necessary to breathe with a conscious effort of mind only when natural breathing is obstructed. At all other times, it goes on mechanically. The *atman* dwells, ever at rest, in this body with nine doors[5], doing nothing and causing nothing to be done. Though it may be working or acting to make others work, it will not be doing so if it has mentally renounced karma.

[1] Who sees his *atman* as one with the *atman* in every creature; in V, 7
[2] Who sees himself in all creatures
[3] In V, 10
[4] V, 13
[5] Eyes, ears, nostrils, mouth and two organs of excretion

[90]

June 25, 1926

This life is a play proceeding before us. If we devote ourselves to our work without taking interest in the play or letting our mind be distracted by it, we would be *karmasannyasis*[1]. Suppose that a prisoner is asked to attend and witness another being whipped. He attends without any interest. His eyes see what is happening, but his mind may not be attentive. I would see a thing to which I become a witness by chance, but I would leave the place without stopping even a moment longer.

We recognize relationships, that this is a son and that is a brother, regard it as our duty to see that the bonds endure, and act accordingly—in all this we are involved with our minds. There is no mental renunciation of karma.

> The Lord creates neither agency nor action for the world; neither does He connect action with its fruit. It is nature that is at work.[2]

The Lord says: "Ultimately I am the Creator of all beings. That means that, when you see I see, and when you do not see I, too, do not see."[3] That is [His] nature. This is a truth before which speech fails.

We may assert, from different points of view, that God is the Doer, and also that He is not.

If you withdraw interest from the functioning of your senses, they will never feel any strain and you will not feel exhausted. Of course, some exhaustion you will always feel, since complete annihilation of the 'I' sense is impossible. We discussed yesterday the idea that we should speak not of "self-realization" but of "self-purification". Self-purification is to be achieved through the body. We act through the *atman* to the degree that we have to act through the body. In truth, however, the *atman* does nothing, nor does it cause anything to be done.

[91]

June 26, 1926

When God the Artist painted this human eye, He so made it that the *atman* should shine through it. He certainly could not have intended it to cast lustful glances. The function of the eye

[1] Those who have renounced action

[2] V, 14

[3] The second sentence is placed within brackets in the source.

is to ensure the safety of the body and to see God. What are the thoughts which come to your mind when you look upon the image of Hanuman? Of *brahmacharya*, *bhakti* and service. And of strength, for he was Ramachandra's servant and Ramachandra always gives his servants the strength they need. In this way the moment we look at anyone's eyes we should be able to see the *atman* behind.

> The Lord does not take upon Himself anyone's vice or virtue; it is ignorance that veils knowledge and deludes all creatures.[1]

Man's real nature is to serve others and to work for self-purification, and so we should not cherish the 'I' in us. This is why it is said here that God does not take upon Himself anyone's sin.

> But to them whose ignorance is destroyed by the knowledge of *atman*, this their knowledge, like the sun, reveals the Supreme.[2]

When a man's ignorance, which envelops the knowledge in him, has been destroyed by that knowledge, the light of God is revealed to him. God is the witness of all that occurs. The idea that we should live in obedience to Him, act only as prompted by Him—that is knowledge. We can experience its truth directly only when all the twists in the heart have straightened out and the *atman* alone shines there forever.

[92]

June 27, 1926

When the night in one's mind has turned to dawn, one comes in the presence of God.

> Those whose intellect is suffused with That, whose self has become one with That, who abide in That, and whose end and aim is That, wipe out their sins with knowledge, and go whence there is no return.[3]

He whose intellect has become fixed on the Lord, who has merged in Him, who is exclusively devoted to Him and who ever lives absorbed in Him, who has dedicated his all to the Lord and trusts to Him alone, such a person, attains deliverance; the sins of such a one are washed away by knowledge.

[1] V, 15
[2] V, 16
[3] V, 17

> The men of Self-realization look with an equal eye on a Brahmin possessed of learning and humility, a cow, an elephant, a dog and even a dog-eater.[1]

Pundits, that is, men of knowledge, see all things with an equal eye. They have the same regard for a Brahmin rich in learning and gentleness, for a cow, an elephant, a dog or a *Chandal.* They feel that the *atman* in each of these is identical with the *atman* in themselves. The only difference is that in some the *atman* is enveloped by layers upon layers of ignorance, and in others these layers have fallen off. What was said earlier, that the yogi sees himself in others, means the same thing as this. Ganga water in separate vessels is Ganga water after all.

> In this very body they have conquered the round of birth and death, whose mind is anchored in sameness; for perfect *Brahman* is same to all, therefore in *Brahman* they rest.[2]

They have conquered the world on this very earth, in this very life, who are equal in mind to all human beings, who have no taint of impurity in them, who abide in God and live ever devoted to Him.

When can we say of a person that he is *samadarshi*? Can we say so of that man who would give equal quantities to an elephant and an ant? Indeed no. We can say it of him who gives to each according to his or her need. A mother will give nothing to her child who is ill and will give another who is well as much as he can eat. A person who is filled with the spirit of non-violence, with compassion, will so act that the world will say of him that he behaved towards all as if they were himself, did justice to all; that he gave water to him who needed water and milk to him who needed milk.

No one can be like God, absolutely free from impurity and equal towards all. One can, therefore, become *samadarshi* only by losing oneself in Him.

[93]

June 29, 1926

Let us describe some instances of equal regard for all. One is that of the elephant and the ant. Second, if an enemy and a friend arrive at his place together, both hungry, the *samadarshi* will offer food first to the enemy. He would feel that to be jus-

[1] V, 18
[2] V, 19

tice. He would be afraid lest there be some hatred for the enemy lurking in his heart, and he would satisfy him first. The friend, too, would appreciate his motive.

A pundit[1] does not mean one who is merely learned, but one who is both learned and wise. If anyone warns him that feeding an enemy would be like giving milk to a snake, he would cite in reply this verse from the *Gita* and say that he was a man of faith, that his father was a lover of the *Gita* and so was he, that they had never come to harm by following its teaching. 'Why should I, therefore, not continue to do so?,' he would ask.

One rule of swadeshi is that in serving people we should give priority to those who live near us. There is also an opposite rule, that we should serve first those who are distant from us and then those who are near us. Near in the first rule means physically near, and distant in the second rule means distant from us mentally. Both may mean the same thing. An enemy may be physically near and distant mentally; we should, despite his being distant, serve him first.

The reason behind this rule of swadeshi is that we cannot reach all human beings in this world. If you ignore your neighbour and seek to serve someone living far away, that would be pride on your part.

We display good manners, culture and learning in serving first those who are mentally distant from us.

> In this very body they have conquered the round of birth and death, whose mind is anchored in sameness; for perfect *Brahman* is same to all, therefore in *Brahman* they rest.

Those who follow this rule in their conduct have won the battle of this life. They hold enemy and friend in equal regard. The enemy is the elephant and the friend is the ant of our illustration.

We should make ourselves like that with which we wish to be one. If we wish to lose ourselves in *Brahman*, we must become *samadarshi* as *Brahman* is.

> He whose understanding is secure, who is undeluded, who knows *Brahman* and who rests in *Brahman*, will neither be glad to get what is pleasant, nor sad to get what is unpleasant.[2]

[1] The reference is to V, 18.

[2] V, 20

[94]

June 30, 1926

> He who has detached himself from contacts without finds bliss in *atman*; having achieved union with *Brahman* he enjoys eternal bliss.[1]

The person, who has become liberated into unity with *Brahman* and who is not attached to the objects of his outgoing senses, experiences true happiness in his *atman*. One can have peace only by remaining unattached. It is impossible to prevent the impact of sense-impressions; that is why Shri Krishna speaks of the need to become unattached. If we constantly meditate on the holy feet of Rama, the impact of external impressions will have no effect on us. The *atman* that is united in yoga with *Brahman*, that is, which has attained to the state of *samadhi* in which it merges into *Brahman* and abides in it for ever, such an *atman* enjoys undying bliss.

> For the joys derived from sense-contacts are nothing but mines of misery; they have beginning and end, O Kaunteya; the wise man does not revel therein.
>
> The man who is able even here on earth, ere he is released from the body, to hold out against the flood-tide of lust and wrath,—he is a yogi, he is happy.[2]

Shri Krishna is repeating here what he has already explained in Chapter II.

> He who finds happiness only within, rest only within, light only within,—that yogi, having become one with Nature, attains to oneness with *Brahman*.[3]

That yogi who finds his happiness and his peace within him, who does not need external objects to make him happy, who is ever self-absorbed and is inspired by the light which shines within him, such a yogi has merged into *Brahman* and attains nirvana in it.

We should read the *Bhagavad Gita* in order that its poetry may be revealed to us.[4] There are two types of nirvana. One is destruction of one's body, after which, however, the necessity of being born again and again remains as ever. The other nirvana is *brahmanirvana*, which is a state of void. But the void is in regard to the external world; within it is all bliss of illumination.

[1] V, 21
[2] V, 22 & 23
[3] V, 24
[4] This sentence is in square brackets in the source.

> They win oneness with *Brahman*—the seers whose sins are wiped out, whose doubts are resolved, who have mastered themselves, and who are engrossed in the welfare of all beings.[1]

Rishis who are sinless and pure attain to *brahmanirvana*. *Rishis* of what description? Those whose doubts have vanished, who hold their *atman* a prisoner (have control over it) and who rejoice in the good of all creatures.

Such a *rishi* can bear ill will to no one. He is ever ready to serve the welfare of even the most wicked. He serves the whole world. A person can become the very embodiment of selfless service only if Rama dwells in his heart. Anyone who is earnestly concerned for the good of another cannot bear any real suffering on the part of the latter. We have heard of fathers who get cholera if their sons are infected by it, though of course their concern was only for their sons. A father may not be happy with his son, and still he cannot bear when the latter suffers. A *rishi* like this would be moved to profuse tears by the suffering of others, and he would strive ceaselessly to end it.

[95]

July 1, 1926

Sarvabhutahite ratah: We have an instance of this in the story of Yudhishthira and his dog.[2] We should not merely cure the fever of a member of our family, but try to discover the cause of the fever from which the whole world is suffering and remove that cause. All beings in the world are sunk in ignorance.

Do you know anything about the *atman*? Perhaps a little. Well, a *rotla*[3] is unbaked before it is baked.[4]

The cause of disease is not in the stomach, it is indulgence of the palate, and the cause of that, again, is the mind.

> Rid of lust and wrath, masters of themselves, the ascetics who have realized *atman* find oneness with *Brahman* everywhere around them.[5]

Those yogis who are free from desire and anger, whose minds have become steady and who are ever absorbed in their *sadhana*[6],

[1] V, 25

[2] In the *Mahabharata*, Yudhishthira refused to enter Heaven unless a dog that followed him was also allowed to go, with him.

[3] Thick, round cake of unleavened bread, made of coarse millet

[4] This paragraph is placed within brackets in the source.

[5] V, 26

[6] Single-minded effort for self-realization

who have realized the self, are always and in all circumstances in a state of *brahmanirvana.*

> That ascetic is ever free—who, having shut out the outward sense-contacts, sits with his gaze fixed between the brows, outward and inward breathing in the nostrils made equal; his senses, mind, and reason held in check; rid of longing, fear and wrath; and intent on Freedom.[1]

Outward action is a symbol of inner action. It is not enough that breathing is regular and the eyes are focused on a point between the brows; these actions should be symbols of an inner state.

The first verse here runs on into the second one.

> Knowing Me as the Acceptor of sacrifice and austerity, the great Lord of all the worlds, the Friend of all creation, the yogi attains to peace.[2]

Since God is the Friend of all creatures, why need such a person fear Him?

Since He accepts all service and all our karmas, they can never be fruitless. In dedicating everything to Him, we necessarily act without thought of self. And we are convinced in the heart of our hearts that nothing that we do will remain fruitless.

[96]

Chapter VI

July 2, 1926

The last chapter raised the question, "Of sannyasa and karmayoga, which is superior?" Shri Krishna has tried to answer the question, but the problem is not one which can be easily solved. The personal God and the impersonal *Brahman,* both are real; and likewise he who rests in absolute peace and he who is ceaselessly occupied in work, both are right, for the sannyasi is in fact working and the other one who is always working rests in absolute peace. One person may feel that there is nothing he need do, that he is already in the presence of God; such a person can cease from work. He who has free access to the king's court, what more need he do? When the subjects themselves know the king's will and carry it out, what work need the king do? It would surprise the subjects only if he came forward to work. I have still to remind you again and again that you should not doze here, that you should be attentive, and so on; but a day

[1] V, 27 & 28
[2] V, 29

will come when it will not at all be necessary for me to do this, for all of you will have then learnt to work methodically. It is, therefore, right and proper that at present I keep telling you these things and take interest in these matters; it will be equally right if, by and by, I stop doing so and let myself rest in peace.

But Arjuna does not say yet that he has understood the point, and so Shri Krishna takes up the same argument again in Chapter VI.

> He who performs all obligatory action, without depending on the fruit thereof, is a sannyasi and a yogi—not the man who neglects the sacrificial fire nor he who neglects action.[1]

He who deposits all his works in God's treasury, and goes on doing his duty without looking for reward—for, as we know, God is the enjoyer of *yajna* and *tapas*, —is both a sannyasi and a yogi. But that person who never lights the fire for *yajna*—originally it was an act of public service to keep a fire burning in the home for performing a *yajna*—or never works, is neither a sannyasi nor a yogi. Such a person would in fact be a prince of idlers.

> What is called sannyasa, know thou to be yoga, O Pandava; for none can become a yogi who has not renounced selfish purpose.[2]

Shri Krishna says: "Know that yoga is the same thing that the learned describe as sannyasa. For you, it is not sannyasa to run away from the battle; sannyasa for you lies in fighting—it is I that enjoy a *yajna*—for the person who has not renounced personal motives for action can never be a yogi. Sannyasa is not something which can be demonstrated outwardly; it is a matter of the spirit within. The restless play of desires and fancies should cease; only then can one be a sannyasi."

[97]

July 3, 1926

> For the man who seeks to scale the heights of yoga, action is said to be the means; for the same man, when he has scaled those heights, repose is said to be the means.[3]

For the *muni* who aspires to master yoga, the only means is work (For yoga has been defined as skill in action.). If a person lets himself be beaten for a long time on the anvil of work, some

[1] VI, 1
[2] VI, 2
[3] VI, 3

day he may be shaped into a yogi. For him who has established himself in yoga, who has attained to a state of spiritual equipoise, whose mind has become steadfast, for such a person the right means [of continuing in this state] is *shama*, that is, resting in peace.

The argument here is the same that we discussed yesterday. Today, I have to try and explain my meaning in different ways. To succeed in my effort, I have to see that my meaning sinks into you, so that you understand it as clearly as I do. This effort is a kind of yoga and will be rewarded with success. When you learn to understand my meaning through a mere gesture, then the right means for us will be silence. A factory is filled with noise the whole day, but, when the time for closing it arrives, complete peace reigns in it. That machine required the means of work in order to be a yogi; afterwards, peace became the means. That is how a well-ordered machine acts. Such peace is not the peace of the grave or the peace of lethargy or inertness; it is the peace of conscious life, the peace of the sea.

> When a man is not attached either to the objects of sense or to actions and sheds all selfish purpose, then he is said to have scaled the heights of yoga.[1]

When a person remains unattached to objects of the senses or to work, but uses his senses and works in a detached spirit, such a person, then, who has renounced all personal motives for work, is said to have established himself in yoga.

> By one's Self should one raise oneself, and not allow oneself to fall; for *Atman* (Self) alone is the friend of self, and Self alone is self's foe.[2]

You can win *moksha* only by your own effort. Today, we simply act as enemies of our *atman*. The *atman* is self-effulgent, and so it must win its freedom by its own effort. Who can light the divine sun? He rises into freedom as soon as it is dawn. He comes, established in yoga, and sinks into peace in the evening (But does the sun really sink into peace? Shall I have sunk into peace even when I die?).

[98]

July 4, 1926

In our ordinary language we say that God grants freedom to the *atman*, for we do not know how to express the idea in any

[1] VI, 4
[2] VI, 5

other way. But can the *atman* ever merge in God except through its own power? It has all the attributes of God, and that is why it can merge in Him. As the *atman* is self-effulgent, so is God. A thing cannot merge in something else with unlike attributes. We are advised to take care and see that our *atman* does not destroy itself, for it is in the power of the *atman* to do so, though, of course, it cannot annihilate itself completely because it is imperishable. The man who says "I am an atheist" contradicts himself in that very statement. We cannot add a single moment to the life of this universe, and so also we can never succeed in destroying the *atman*.

> His Self alone is friend who has conquered himself by his Self; but to him who has not conquered himself and is thus inimical to himself, even his Self behaves as foe.[1]

While we live, there are two sides in us: the demoniac and the divine, the God-like and the Satanic. So long as this strife goes on, it is our duty to fight Satan and protect ourselves. In the war between gods and demons, it is the former who always win in the end. When the world is no more, God will laugh and ask where Satan was. The *atman* of the atheist acts as his enemy. The truth is that the *atman* of each of us does so, thanks to the evil of *kaliyuga*.

> Of him who has conquered himself and who rests in perfect calm the Self is completely composed, in cold and heat, in pleasure and pain, in honour and dishonour.[2]

That person who has overcome the lower self in him and who is ever unperturbed, in heat or cold, pleasure or pain, honour or dishonour,—any praise or censure given to us is like a stream which flows away towards God and disappears—the *Paramatman* in such a person becomes *samahita*[3]. Even in him who is the very image of unquiet, who is filled, not with non-violence, but with violence, who is not truthful but untruthful—even in such a one the Supreme Self abides in perfect equipoise.

[1] VI, 6
[2] VI, 7
[3] Gandhiji has not indicated the meaning which he attaches to it.

[99]

July 6, 1926

We can say that the *atman* dwells in perfect equipoise when what is outside of us is a reflection of what is within. It will not do if the body is erect but the mind is not so. Today our minds are not erect. The dog has four legs, and we have two, and yet our minds behave like those of four-legged creatures.

> The yogi who is filled with the contentment of wisdom and discriminative knowledge, who is firm as a rock, who has mastered his senses, and to whom a clod of earth, a stone and gold are the same, is possessed of yoga.[1]

Jnana here means listening to readings from the Shastras, meditating over them, studying them, and *vijnana* means realizing the *atman* in direct experience. *Jnana* is understanding through reason, and *vijnana* is that knowledge which sinks through reason into experience. *Jnana* is knowledge obtained from the Shastras, whereas *vijnana* is knowledge which is part of one's experience. Non-violence will have become direct experience for us in this sense when our whole life comes to be permeated with the spirit of compassion, when non-violence manifests itself in us in its true essence. That boy who comes to feel compassion as his own experience will to that extent have purified himself, or attained knowledge of the self.

He whose *atman* is filled to perfect contentment with such *jnana* and *vijnana*, who dwells firmly like *kuta*—he is a *kutastha* that is, who endures blows, as the anvil does without ever breaking into pieces, remains unshaken in the midst of even extreme suffering—who has subdued his senses completely, such a one may be described as a yogi who has attained freedom. He has become united with God, has become inwardly purified. To such a yogi, clay, stone and gold, all are equal. All three come from earth. Earth which has hardened is stone. Gold, silver, diamonds, sapphire, all these are transformations of earth. But they are all without any worth—everyone of them is but dust. If we shed greed, we would look upon all these articles with the same eye.

> He excels who regards alike the boon companion, the friend, the enemy, the stranger, the mediator, the alien and the ally, as also the saint and the sinner.[2]

[1] VI, 8
[2] VI, 9

He who has the same regard for friend and foe, for one who deserves to be hated and one who is a kinsman, for the sadhu and the sinner, as he would have for clay and gold, he may be said to have won the battle of this life. The same law applies to the world of the living which applies to the world of inert matter. As clay and gold are ultimately the same substance, so the sadhu and the sinner are ultimately one.

The sadhu and the sinner are forms of the same reality. They are both manifestations of the *atman*. The layer of uncleanliness has disappeared from over the sadhu's *atman* and is becoming ever thicker over the sinner's. We shall have risen above the ordinary level only when we learn to have equal regard for either. Tulsidas has shown by his example how we can do that.

> Let the yogi constantly apply his thought to *atman* remaining alone in a secluded place, his mind and body in control, rid of desires and possessions.[1]

A yogi should constantly live in solitude and be in union with the *atman*. To live in solitude means to withdraw the mind from the outside world. He who lives by himself and seeks to control his mind should shed all desires and, having renounced all possessions, yoke the *atman* to the *Paramatman* in contemplation. Renunciation of possessions includes renunciation of the desire for possessions too. He who practises *japa*[2] in solitude in the hope of winning a kingdom is no yogi. A man who possesses a few lakhs of rupees may be less acquisitive than another who daily gives away money in charity and sacrifices wealth but is constantly thinking of money.

[100]

July 7, 1926

Rahasi[3] means in a quiet place free from noise and *ekaki*[4] means living by oneself. One can live in solitude and by oneself even in the midst of the bazaar in Ahmedabad.

Even so, one must have physical solitude. One can go to a cremation ground and, thinking on the perishable body, experience the feeling of solitude. *Yatachittatma*[5] means one who is free from physical or mental restlessness. A man can make do with

[1] VI, 10

[2] Constant repetition of a name or formula believed to have spiritual power

[3], [4] & [5] In VI, 10

a mere *langoti*[1], which even a flying kite may bring him. Can anyone, however, do without some possessions for the comfort of the body? We should supply the body its minimum needs and not seek to multiply them. If we go on multiplying bodily needs, we shall ever be going from birth to death and from death to birth. So long as the turban is there, we may use it but we should not buy another to replace it; likewise, we may look after the body, but only to supply its minimum needs. We shall not then have to be born and to die again and again. *Atmanam yunjita*[2] means yoking the *atman* to the *Paramatman*, fixing it on the *Paramatman.*

> Fixing for himself, in a pure spot, a firm seat, neither too high nor yet too low, covered with *kusha* grass, thereon a deerskin, and thereon a cloth.[3]

One should place a seat in a holy spot—*desha* may mean even "country", for it was supposed that Bharat was *karmabhumi*—a country in which people engage themselves in *karma* with ceaseless vigilance is a *karmabhumi*—whereas one is born in other countries to enjoy the fruits of one's actions (though India is no longer such a country today)—one should place a firm seat, neither too high nor too low. One should spread out *kusha* grass and *ajin*, and then cover the spot with a piece of cloth. *Ajin* means deerskin. This is mentioned because in those days deer used to be hunted. A yogi devotes himself to his practice for quite a long time. He should, therefore, protect himself carefully lest he should feel cold and his limbs become cramped. He should place himself on such a seat and remain there motionless.

> Sitting on that seat, with mind concentrated, the functions of thought and sense in control, he should set himself to the practice of yoga for the sake of self-purification.[4]

[101]

July 8, 1926

I gave a wrong meaning yesterday to the phrase *yatachittendriya*[5]. To control the activity of the *chitta* and the senses means

[1] Codpiece
[2] In VI, 10
[3] VI, 11
[4] VI, 12
[5] In VI, 12

to restrain such activity. *Yogah chittavrittinirodhah*[1]. If the waves are continually rising, we describe the sea as stormy. There is no essential difference between the sea and the waves in it. All souls are like waves in water, that is, they are but different forms of that water. We need not ask why we should let waves rise in ourselves. Human beings conceive God as a kind of doll; respectable people even make gold images of Him. All this goes on. The rising of a wave means being born, and the wave subsiding means death. Telling himself this, a man may become steady in mind and let the wave of desire subside in it. Patanjali tells us that if we restrain the waves from rising, we shall know whether the master of the *chitta* is desire or whether it is God. Expanding the phrase *chittavriti*, Shri Krishna spoke of *chitta* and *indriyas* in this verse.

> Keeping himself steady, holding the trunk, the neck and the head in a straight line and motionless, fixing his eye on the tip of his nose, and looking not around.
>
> Tranquil in spirit, free from fear, steadfast in the vow of *brahmacharya*, holding his mind in control, the yogi should sit, with all his thoughts on Me, absorbed in Me.[2]

[102]

July 9, 1926

These four verses describe processes of yoga. I remember to have read in jail that they would take not less than six months to learn. These processes are physical actions, and we cannot be certain that everyone will profit from them. The body and the mind, however, are so difficult to control that in our country people attach special importance to these processes. When such ideas are given importance in theory, all kinds of experiments are undertaken, as, for instance, climbing Dhavalgiri as a holy effort. Two Italian boys had decided to tour round the whole earth walking. They were just young boys. They were happy with what they had undertaken. When I asked them what they hoped to learn from their tour, one of them got very angry. They would acquire a venturesome spirit, from which they themselves would profit, but in other ways they would have simply thrown away their lives. The same is true about *pranayama* and other processes which have been mentioned. There is no fraud behind them,

[1] "Yoga is controlling the activity of the mind"—Patanjali in *Yogasutra*.
[2] VI, 13 & 14

and no intention to impose on people; they are a means of fixing our mind on God. If I resolve to observe silence even when in the midst of a bazaar, why should I let my mind be distracted by the noise around me? Similarly, while attending these prayers, too, we are at once in the midst of society and in solitude.

> The yogi, who ever thus, with mind controlled, unites himself to *atman*, wins the peace which culminates in *Nirvana*, the peace that is in Me.[1]

We may attain the peace which follows our merging in *Brahman* if we are good children of God.

> Yoga is not for him who eats too much, nor for him who fasts too much, neither for him who sleeps too much, nor yet for him who is too wakeful.[2]

Yoga is not meant for the person who eats too much. He will not succeed in his efforts for spiritual discipline. Nor will the person who eats nothing, who takes a vow of total abstinence from food, succeed in his yoga. Similarly, the man who sleeps or keeps awake too long also will not succeed.

It should be borne in mind that this is said in continuation of the preceding four verses. It is true that anyone who eats or sleeps too much can achieve nothing. Some persons live merely on the physical level; they can achieve nothing worth while. But the converse requires a little thinking about. He who has undertaken spiritual discipline but cannot bear hunger will be in the same mental condition as the starving millions in the country. He will not be able to provide his *chitta* the nourishment it needs and so he will not succeed in fixing his thoughts on God. And the same is true about keeping awake.

There is no fear that anyone here intends to abstain from food or to keep awake too long in this manner. This verse refers to a person who imposes such discipline on himself for progress in yoga. But a person who, however hard he tries, cannot acquire control over his senses, whose eyes always open to cast lustful glances and whose other senses, too, crave indulgence—let such a person certainly undertake long fasts, even if his body should perish in consequence. He should do nothing for outward show. We look upon truth as the chain which binds us all together here. Any of us here who fasts will not deceive himself. He may fast if he feels that he cannot curb his cravings in any

[1] VI, 15
[2] VI, 16

other way. An idea has come to prevail nowadays that in this world one must satisfy one's desires. Hence my advice to you that you should not spare yourself any harshness in striving for self-purification. If a person loves to boast about secretly gratifying his eye, ear or palate, it would do him much good to take any number of vows to curb the body and cultivate vigilance. If we wish to, we can certainly control the senses. But we do not wish to do so, and then look for excuses. The *Gita* advises such persons not to eat or sleep too much.

The four verses we have discussed describe a method which serves as a kind of help like that with which a child may learn to walk. They advise one to follow the golden mean. Having adopted such a method, one's effort should be to do or to die. If people sacrifice so much to discover the North Pole, will it be too much if we lay down our lives in the effort to discover the North Pole of the *atman*?

[103]

July 10, 1926

Shri Krishna advised moderation in the beginning, the avoiding of excess in all matters. It is only by and by that one can judge what constitutes excess. He said, therefore, that in the beginning one should proceed slowly.

A time may come, however, when we shall not feel as excess what may seem to be so to an ordinary person. When a person is distracted by innumerable evil impulses and feels himself helpless to curb them, he may employ satyagraha against his body and against God. We should scrupulously practise non-violence towards others, but we would come to grief if we adopt it in dealing with our body. Against our body we must employ non-co-operation. That is, we must begin by non-co-operating with the evil impulses in our heart. We must tell the body that we have been paying it hire in the form of food for working as our watchman, but that we have decided to stop paying it from today because it is not doing its duty properly. We may pay rent only for a house which serves to protect us, of which the roof does not leak and the walls are not dilapidated. Why pay for a house which is rotten inside? The other one with a leaking roof and dilapidated walls can be repaired, but what can we do with a house the air in which has become poisoned? Thus, if the body does not fulfil the conditions of our leasing it, we have a right to go on an indefinite fast.

> To him who is disciplined in food and recreation, in effort in all activities, and in sleep and waking, yoga (discipline) becomes a relief from all ills.[1]

The man who avoids excess, what does he gain? He who is regular in food, rest and so on, who acts with due moderation in everything, who is moderate even in his sleep, will find that his practice of yoga ends all his suffering.

> When one's thought, completely controlled, rests steadily only on *atman*, when one is free from longing for all objects of desire, then one is called a yogi.[2]

When the mind has come under our complete control, when it is easily restrained by us, when it is fixed constantly on the *atman*, that is, acts in everything in obedience to the *atman*, when it has become completely disinterested, that is, become free from all desires, then the person may be said to be established in yoga.

> As a taper in a windless spot flickers not, even so is a yogi, with his thought controlled, seeking to unite himself with *atman*.[3]

The condition of the yogi who is regularly practising yoga and who has acquired control over his mind is like that of a lamp in a windless place, which does not flicker. If we are unsteady in mind, the storm of the cravings of the senses blows out the *atman* as a breeze blows out the lamp. As the latter gets its food from air, so the *atman* gets the food it needs through the senses and the mind. The lamp gets its food from air which is motionless; likewise the *atman* gets nourishing food from the mind if we keep the air of its impulses still.

> Where thought curbed by the practice of yoga completely ceases, where a man sits content within himself, *atman* having seen *atman*.[4]

When the impulses in a person's mind have subsided and the mind is filled with peace, when through the practice of yoga the mind has come under one's control and its impulses have subsided, when the person sees the *atman* through the *atman*, that is, when his mind has become absorbed in the *atman* and he lives for ever content in the *atman*,—such a person has become a yogi.

[1] VI, 17
[2] VI, 18
[3] VI, 19
[4] VI, 20

[104]

July 11, 1926

Watt discovered that if we collect steam and let it escape through a pipe, it will draw a load of any weight. Similarly, those boys who restrain all their outgoing impulses and concentrate them in one direction will be able to carry any weight on their shoulders. How much, then, would we benefit if we restrain all these impulses and let them subside and be transformed into devotion to God.

> Where he experiences that endless bliss beyond the senses which can be grasped by reason alone; wherein established he swerves not from the Truth;[1]

When compared with the highest bliss—the bliss which abides for ever—the pleasures of the senses are but momentary. That bliss cannot be felt through the senses, it can be experienced only by the intellect. If a person has perceived with his intellect the reality which God is, if he has understood with it his duty and then yoked himself to the chariot of God, if, shaking off lethargy, he has entered his name in God's office for duty—such a person will never be shaken from his purpose.

A person whose mind has become fixed in this manner does not cease even for a moment to be conscious of the reality which is God. He is a yogi.

> Where he holds no other gain greater than that which he has gained; and where, securely seated, he is not shaken by any calamity however great;[2]

Having attained this state, the person does not even dream that he can gain anything better still. Such a condition is possible only if one thinks about nothing but Ramanama even in one's dreams, if one has worked the whole day in a disinterested spirit of service. If we have not spent the night in sound sleep, if we have had a bad dream, we may understand that our mind is still full of greed, attachment, etc. He whose mind does not sleep at all during any hour of the day is firmly established in yoga, he is single-minded in his devotion.

I once saw in Pretoria jail a Negro who had a mind so strong, like a demon's, that he never shrank back, no matter how much he was flogged. The yogi's mind, however, becomes like a

[1] VI, 21
[2] VI, 22

god's; his skin glows and the mind never wavers. If the mind of a person who dwells in solitude is wandering in all directions, though physically alone he lives amidst a crowd.

> That state should be known as yoga (union with the Supreme), the disunion from all union with pain. This yoga must one practise with firm resolve and unwearying zeal.[1]

What has been described as yoga means complete absence of suffering. The state beyond happiness and suffering cannot be described in words. We speak of it as peace. When we are in that state, we are said to be in yoga. We should establish ourselves in such yoga with a determined mind, without getting tired of the effort.

[105]

July 13, 1926

Anyone who depends for his happiness on external circumstances makes it plain that in fact he does not want to be happy. In the end such a person becomes unhappy. But he who feels neither happiness nor misery—we should throw both into the river Sabarmati—if we become glad on getting something which is to our liking and feel miserable when we get something which we do not like, either state of mind is bad—he who rises above both happiness and misery has achieved yoga. Yoga means absence of suffering, never feeling miserable. If anyone abuses us, we should lay the abuse at God's feet. Likewise, if anyone praises us, the praise too we should lay at His feet. This is the meaning of non-possessiveness. He is a yogi who cultivates such a state of mind and feels himself as light as a flower.

> Shaking oneself completely free from longings born of selfish purpose; reining in the whole host of senses, from all sides, with the mind itself;
>
> With reason held securely by the will, he should gradually attain calm and with the mind established in *atman* think of nothing.[2]

Such a person is a yogi; that is, he escapes from the dualities of happiness and suffering.

> Wherever the fickle and unsteady mind wanders, thence should it be reined in and brought under the sole sway of *atman*.[3]

[1] VI, 23
[2] VI, 24 & 25
[3] VI, 26

Proceeding, Shri Krishna explains in different words the idea of the preceding verses. He has asked Arjuna to fix the mind on the *atman*. What more can He say? But He tries to explain the idea still more clearly.

One should withdraw the mind from any object or thought to which it wanders, hold it in check and bring it under the control of the *atman*.

The speed of air can be measured by a meteorologist and that of electricity by a scientist. But no machine has yet been invented to measure the speed of the mind. It is unsteady and restless. We should withdraw it from every direction in which it flies and fix it in the right place, that is, in the *atman*.

> For, supreme bliss comes to this yogi, who, with mind becalmed, with passions stilled, has become one with *Brahman*, and is purged of all stain.[1]

Such a yogi, whose mind has become stilled, whose *rajasik* impulses, whose egotism and pride, have all completely subsided, and who has become merged in *Brahman*—such a yogi will experience the supreme bliss.

> The yogi, cleansed of all stain, unites himself ever thus to *atman*, easily enjoys the endless bliss of contact with *Brahman*.[2]

The yogi who has thus learnt to yoke his *atman* constantly [to God], who has been purified of his sins, who has felt the contact of *Brahman*, enjoys everlasting bliss.

> The man equipped with yoga looks on all with an impartial eye, seeing *atman* in all beings and all beings in *atman*.[3]

He who is established in yoga, who looks upon all with an equal eye, sees himself in all other creatures and all other creatures in himself—such a yogi with an equal eye for all can enjoy the bliss of merging in *Brahman*.

[106]

July 14, 1926

The verse which we took up yesterday is an important one. The yogi is not one who sits down to practise breathing exercises; he is one who looks upon all with an equal eye, sees other creatures in himself. Such a one attains *moksha*. To look upon all

[1] VI, 27
[2] VI, 28
[3] VI, 29

with an equal eye means to act towards others as we would towards ourselves. That idea is explained still further in the following verse.

> He who sees Me everywhere and everything in Me, never vanishes from Me nor I from him.[1]

"He who sees Me everywhere and sees all creatures and objects in Me, I am never absent from such a person. He is always dear to Me, he is never far from Me,"—as Hanuman was never far from Ramachandra.

[107]

July 15, 1926

It is not easy to see all creatures in ourselves. The key with which to achieve this is given in the next verse, and that is, that one should see others in oneself by seeing them and oneself in God. As ice becomes what it is from water, so we have all come from the same water and shall turn again into that water. The hailstone which realizes that it is water in substance will feel itself as water. God and God's *maya* are one; what distinction, then, can there be between a Brahmin, a *Chandal* and a Sudra? That is why the sage Bharadwaja asked Rama whether the latter had killed Ravana or only his own *maya*. Rama is never absent from us and we are never far from Rama.

> The yogi who, anchored in unity, worships Me abiding in all beings, lives and moves in Me, no matter how he live and move.[2]

"The yogi," says Shri Krishna, "who worships Me the dweller in all creatures, who, after merging in *Brahman*, feels that he is *Brahman* and that the world exists in *Brahman* and who worships Me with that feeling, such a yogi, though ever engaged in outward activities, lives in Me."

As they say, "walking with unsteady steps on the earth but fixing the mind on the sky", so a person who has his eyes always fixed on the sky of his heart dwells in God every moment, whether walking or eating or drinking, or in any condition whatever. There are impostors who claim that, though they may indulge in immoral pleasures, they are still yogis. They tell us that, being victims of *maya*, we may hold that some things are permitted and others forbidden, but that they themselves are

[1] VI, 30
[2] VI, 31

bound by no rules. If we ask them to exchange their gold for our stone, they will not agree. They will answer that they are learned men and the gold had better be with them. But about the actions of a person who has banished all evil from his heart, the world will say—he himself will not claim it—that though doing karma he dwells in God.

> He who, by likening himself with others, senses pleasure and pain equally for all as for himself, is deemed to be the highest yogi, O Arjuna.[1]

He who acts towards others as if they were himself will meet their needs as if they were his own, will do to others what he would to himself, will learn to look upon himself and the world as one. He is a true yogi who is happy when others are happy and suffers when others suffer.

Only that person who has reduced himself to a cipher, has completely shed his egotism, can claim to be so. He alone may be said to be such a person who has dedicated his all to God. But this is a difficult state to achieve, and so Arjuna puts a question.

> I do not see, O Madhusudana, how this yoga, based on the equal-mindedness that Thou hast expounded to me, can steadily endure, because of fickleness (of the mind).[2]

When we are travelling in a train, we cannot see clearly the things outside. That is how it is.

> For fickle is the mind, O Krishna, unruly, over-powering and stubborn; to curb it is, I think, as hard as to curb the wind.[3]

Arjuna says: "O Krishna, the mind is fickle, it unsteadies the heart, it is strong, and obstinate in its fickleness. We can see this truth if we can curb it, but it is as difficult to curb it as it is to curb air."

> Undoubtedly, O Mahabahu, the mind is fickle and hard to curb; yet, O Kaunteya, it can be held in check by constant practice and dispassion.
>
> Without self-restraint, yoga, I hold, is difficult to attain; but the self-governed soul can attain it by proper means, if he strive for it.[4]

[1] VI, 32
[2] VI, 33
[3] VI, 34
[4] VI, 35 & 36

[108]

July 16, 1926

We may have studied the *Gita* with great care and attention, but we can achieve nothing if we lack strength of heart. We should strive for self-purification in respect of all our attachments. We should overcome ignorant attachments and carry out self-purification. Arjuna has become a bridge between Shri Krishna and the world. Possessing such knowledge and after having enjoyed the privilege of Shri Krishna's company for so long a time, he should have no question to ask. It is for the benefit of the world that he puts all the questions.

> If one, possessed of faith, but slack of effort, because of his mind straying from yoga, reach not perfection in yoga, what end does he come to, O Krishna?[1]

He who does not persevere in his effort to be a yogi, who does not strive hard enough, who has faith but whose mind has wandered away from yoga—he may have retired into a secluded spot in a forest but his thoughts dwell in the world without—what becomes of such a person who has failed to reach the goal of his yoga? Does he rise or does he fall?

> Without a foothold, and floundering in the path to *Brahman*, fallen from both, is he indeed not lost, O Mahabahu, like a dissipated cloud?[2]

A person may have read a number of books and been struggling for some spiritual progress. But afterwards he thinks and tells himself: "No, I feel inclined to retire into solitude and put my head in God's lap and offer satyagraha to him." One, however, who has let his mind wander in all sorts of ways and has become full of doubts perishes like a scattered cloud. He becomes like a jug without a bottom. Because he has strayed from the path towards *Brahman* which he has been following, does such a person perish?

> This my doubt, O Krishna, do Thou dispel utterly; for there is to be found none other than Thou to banish this doubt.[3]

[1] VI, 37
[2] VI, 38
[3] VI, 39

[109]

July 17, 1926

Shri Krishna answers this question with a solemn assurance.

> Neither in this world, nor in the next, can there be ruin for him, O Partha; no well-doer, oh loved one, meets with a sad end.[1]

Shri Krishna says: "No, Arjuna, such a person is destroyed neither in this world nor in the other, for a weak yogi who strives half-heartedly is certainly not destroyed. No one who strives for good ever comes to harm." In these words, Shri Krishna assured the whole world that He would always welcome those who sought Him as persons engaged in a good effort, no matter with what energy they pursued their aim. Every action bears fruit and in particular no effort for realizing God is ever wasted. A person making such an effort never falls, but always rises. If he has faith, what does it matter if he cannot strive with determination? Whatever his achievement, he will be counted as a soldier in God's army.

> Fallen from yoga, a man attains the world of righteous souls, and having dwelt there for numberless years is then born in a house of pure and gentle blood.[2]

Such a person rises, after his death, to the world which men of good deeds attain and, after dwelling in it for a long time, is born in a family of men who are holy and possess *shri*—that is, men who enjoy God's grace, not necessarily possess riches—for it is difficult for one born in a rich family to practise yoga or chant Ramanama. Is Vishnu, with whom dwells Lakshmi, believed to be the Lord of Lakshmi because He owns a mint? No. Lakshmi means *bhakti*. The sage Agastya may be described as a man who enjoyed *shri*, for he had obtained from Shiva the boon of *bhakti*. Shri Krishna ate a dish of green leaves offered by Vidura[3]. It is in the family of such a person that one who has fallen from the path of yoga, a weak yogi who none the less has faith, is born.

> Or he may even be born into a family of yogis, though such birth as this is all too rare in this world.[4]

[1] VI, 40

[2] VI, 41

[3] Character in the *Mahabharata* known as "the wisest of the wise"; he gave good advice to both the Pandavas and the Kauravas, but in the war he sided with the former.

[4] VI, 42

Or he is born in the family of a wise yogi. Born in such a family, he learns to have an equal mind in all things right from his childhood. *Bhakti* is a daily practice in the family of such a yogi. We may say that Sudhanva and Narad were so fortunately born.

> There, O Kurunandana, he recovers the intellectual stage he had reached in his previous birth, and thence he stretches forward again towards perfection.[1]

He acquires in this family the state of equal-mindedness which I explained to you. He acquires in this life the state which he had failed to acquire in his previous life, whether or not he remembers his effort in that life.

In Italy, there is an eight-year-old boy who plays on the Sitar [*sic*] as if he was born with the skill.

Similarly, if a boy of eight can look upon all with equal regard, we shall conclude that that is the effect of his mode of life in a previous birth. He will then strive further in the same direction and ultimately reach his goal.

> By virtue of that previous practice he is borne on, whether he will it or not; even he with a desire to know yoga passes beyond the Vedic ritual.[2]

Because of his experience in the previous life, such a person is spontaneously drawn towards God. He who is a yogi and yearns for knowledge crosses the *shabdabrahman*, that is, goes beyond the endless forms of karma and rituals enjoined in the Vedas, not beyond the karma which we undertake with a view to service or in a disinterested spirit but beyond the karma prompted by personal motive and activities undertaken for the sake of various personal gains.

> But the yogi who perseveres in his striving, cleansed of sin, perfected through many births, reaches the highest state.[3]

Persevering in his effort, such a yogi destroys the effects of his sins and, succeeding in his aim after many lives, attains *moksha*.

[1] VI, 43
[2] VI, 44
[3] VI, 45

[110]

July 18, 1926

The capital of self-purification acquired in this life will never be wasted.

> The yogi is deemed higher than the man of austerities; he is deemed also higher than the man of knowledge; higher is he than the man engrossed in ritual; therefore be thou a yogi, O Arjuna![1]

Shri Krishna says: "I ask you to be a yogi, for the yogi is superior to the person who performs *tapascharya,* and he is considered superior even to the man who is a *jnani.* Here *jnani* does not signify a person who is merely learned in Shastras or is wise in practical affairs. The yogi is superior also to one who spends all his time in rituals and similar pursuits. You should, therefore, be a yogi."

> And among all yogis, he who worships Me with faith, his inmost self all rapt in Me, is deemed by Me to be the best yogi.[2]

Among all classes of yogis, the best of course is the one who has faith in God. As the rays of the moon are the only thing which will make the *chataka* bird happy, so nothing is as effective as constant repetition of the Lord's name for ending man's threefold suffering in this world.

A Swami from Pushkar Raj[3] once came to visit me. He asked me: "Why have you taken up the spinning-wheel now in your old age?" In a region in which water is scarce, anyone who digs with a shovel—digs for water so that he may serve others—is repeating Ramanama though he may not be literally doing so, and reaps the fruit of repeating it. There are many in the world for whom food is the only *Brahman.* It is dharma to undertake physical labour and make such a starving person labour too, till he can get food. That sannyasi put his question to me, but he did not know that I was practising *akarma* through karma.

In this sixth chapter, Shri Krishna has explained how one may cultivate the spirit of sacrifice through work; he has explained the means of learning self-control. As the method, however, is difficult to practise—though it is not essential that everyone should follow it—, the question is raised whether a person who fails in such an effort does not get the worst of both the worlds. Replying,

[1] VI, 46

[2] VI, 47

[3] A holy place in Rajasthan, sacred to *Vaishnavas*

Shri Krishna says: "No; nothing done with a spiritual motive is lost."

[111]

Chapter VII

July 20, 1926

> Hear, O Partha, how, with thy mind riveted on Me, by practising yoga and making Me the sole refuge, thou shalt, without doubt, know Me fully.
>
> I will declare to thee, in its entirety, this knowledge, combined with discriminative knowledge, which when thou hast known there remains here nothing more to be known.
>
> Among thousands of men hardly one strives after perfection; among those who strive hardly one knows Me in truth.[1]

That is, this knowledge is of supreme worth and not everyone can acquire it.

> Earth, Water, Fire, Air, Ether, Mind, Reason and Ego—thus eightfold is my *prakriti* divided.
>
> This is My lower aspect; but know thou My other aspect, the higher —which is *Jiva* (the Vital Essence) by which, O Mahabahu, this world is sustained.[2]

[Shri Krishna says to Arjuna,] "There is also another *prakriti* of Mine which you may call *para prakriti*. It exists in living creatures, and is superior to the *prakriti* in inert matter; through it the entire universe exists."

[112]

July 21, 1926

We should regard an enemy as one with us. We should reflect how we wish someone who is afraid of us to behave towards us. Even if it is in his power to cut us to pieces, we want him to be fair to us. If we have imprisoned someone, we should not put him under greater restraint than necessary, though he may be our enemy. In any case, we cannot torture him to death. This is no more than the law of the world. Even obeying that law, though we fear snakes and do not wish to die, we also want to complete the reading of the *Gita* and to acquire the highest

[1] VII, 1, 2 & 3
[2] VII, 4 & 5

knowledge, to serve a few people in the world and bring the spinning-movement to success, to work in the cause of cow-protection. With this aim, we may wish to protect ourselves. I don't wish to suggest that you cruelly tortured the snake. But certainly you did not simply lift it and remove it elsewhere. This is a difficult matter. We may catch a snake and remove it, but should do so gently. We should not inflict pain on it. We should think on this matter not because Kishorelalbhai wants us to do so, but because we want to put the teaching of the *Gita* into practice. We should certainly not beat up a snake for our pleasure. We must not derive pleasure from tossing a kitten. This is ignorance and cruelty. Even a child should think how he or she would feel if someone treated him or her in the same manner.

Why does the *Gita* counsel us to treat *Chandals* and *Bhangis* in the same manner as we do others?

We should actually feel towards them in the same manner. It is in vain that one reads the *Gita* if one does not try to live in such a spirit. We should not get pleasure in torturing snakes and other creatures like them. We catch a snake and hold it tight with sticks, but we may do this because we have no choice in the matter. Our attitude should be the same as when we take special care of the body and even pamper it, but feel how much better it would be if we did not do this. We should adopt a fixed attitude of mind, that in such matters we should do the minimum necessary and no more. Do not tell yourselves that you will think about these matters when you have white hair on your heads. You must make the best use of your youth right now. As Lord Krishna said, among thousands only one person strives for self-realization, that is, for self-purification, and among the thousands who strive only a rare person comes to a right knowledge of Him. Hence we should strive hard and long. We should look upon ourselves as those exceptional persons among thousands. We should try to become philosophers. We should aspire to be the rare individuals among those thousands, and hope that we shall succeed.

> Know that these two compose the source from which all beings spring; I am the origin and end of the entire universe.[1]

Shri Krishna says: "The *apara prakriti*, the soul that lives in the visible world, and the *para prakriti*, the invisible world, believe

[1] VII, 6

these to be the cause of all creatures that live. For I am the source of the whole universe, and am that in which it subsides. That is, I am the cause of creation and destruction. Do not think, therefore, that you kill anyone."

> There is nothing higher than I, O Dhananjaya; all this is strung on Me as a row of gems upon a thread.[1]

"As the beads are held together by the string, so this universe is held by Me."

> In water I am the savour, O Kaunteya; in the sun and the moon I am the light; the syllable AUM in all the Vedas; the sound in ether, and manliness in men.
>
> I am the sweet fragrance in earth; the brilliance in fire; the life in all beings; and the austerity in ascetics.[2]
>
> Know Me, O Partha, to be the primeval seed of all beings; I am the reason of rational beings and the splendour of the splendid.[3]

[113]

July 22, 1926

> Of the strong, I am the strength, divorced from lust and passion; in beings I am desire undivorced from righteousness.[4]

"I am the strength of the strong, but that strength which is used without selfish motive or attachment. Such was King Janaka's strength. I am the *kama* in creatures which is not contrary to dharma." "Kama not contrary to dharma" means the desire for *moksha*, or the desire to end the suffering of creatures.

If we desire to end the suffering of others, our suffering, too, will end. This is true in the ordinary sense of the words. But in Sanskrit the desire to end the suffering of others is described as a *mahaswartha*[5]. It means interest in the *moksha* of all creatures. Anyone who feels such a desire would be striving hard for his own *moksha*.

> Know that all the manifestations of the three *gunas*, *sattva*, *rajas*, and *tamas*, proceed from none but Me; yet I am not in them; they are in Me.[6]

[1] VII, 7
[2] VII, 8 & 9
[3] VII, 10
[4] VII, 11
[5] Literally, supreme self-interest
[6] VII, 12

We say that we should offer up everything to God, even evil. The two, good and evil, are inseparable, and so we should offer up both. If we wish to give up sin, we should give up virtue too. There is possessiveness in clinging even to virtue.

We say of the physical Rama that he both had and did not have a body. He had contradictory attributes, he was personal God and impersonal *Brahman*, he had attributes and was beyond attributes. For the evil, God is evil. He is in truth the very image of compassion, but He cannot violate His law and so we say that He destroys evil.

> Befogged by these manifestations of the three *gunas*, the entire world fails to recognize Me, the imperishable, as transcending them.[1]

Truly speaking, even those who are ruled by *sattvik* impulses may be said to be under their power because of their ignorance.

> For this My divine delusive mystery made up of the three *gunas* is hard to pierce; but those who make Me their sole refuge pierce the veil.[2]

It is said in the *Bhagavat* that in *kaliyuga* anyone who constantly repeats *Om namo Bhagavate Vasudevaya* will cross this sea of becoming and reach the other shore. This is true of Ramanama, too.

> The deluded evil-doers, lowest of men, do not seek refuge in Me; for, by reason of this delusive mystery, they are bereft of knowledge and given to devilish ways.[3]

[114]

July 23, 1926

> Four types of well-doers are devoted to Me, O Arjuna; they are, O Bharatarshabha, the afflicted, the spiritual seeker, the material seeker, and the enlightened.[4]

My worshippers whose actions are ever the holiest fall into four classes, says Shri Krishna. They are: (1) those in distress, (2) those who yearn for *jnana* or seek *moksha*, (3) those who worship Me for worldly benefits, and (4) the *jnanis* who worship God as His servants and seek nothing from Him. They tell God that it was simply their duty, as His subjects, to worship Him, and that

[1] VII, 13
[2] VII, 14
[3] VII, 15
[4] VII, 16

it made no difference to them whether or not He rewarded them.

> Of these the enlightened, ever attached to Me in single-minded devotion, is the best; for to the enlightened I am exceedingly dear and he is dear to Me.[1]

Among them all, the *jnani*, who always lives in union with Me, yoked with Me, calls upon Me "*tunhi, tunhi*"[2] and lives as a *bhakta*, keeps repeating My name as if he was reciting a *kalama* from the Koran, is the best.

Mirabai was a great devotee of the Lord, but she belonged to the class of *jnanis*. "I am," Shri Krishna says, "very dear to such *jnanis* and they to Me. We are thus like the lover and the beloved."

> All these are estimable indeed, but the enlightened I hold to be My very self; for he, the true yogi, is stayed on Me alone, the supreme goal.[3]

All these four classes are noble people, though maybe some of them believe in *mantras* and worship God through them. Is it not better that, instead of spending their time in sin, they should worship God?

Is not a man who begs before the king's palace better than another who enters it to rob? The self-respect of a suffering man is fully preserved only if he approaches the king and no one else for help. There are people in the world who, when they suffer, seek succour not from God but from others. The Lord, therefore, is certainly pleased when people go to Him. "All these are certainly worthy men," says Shri Krishna, "but of them all the *jnani* is My very soul, Myself as it were. He who has yoked himself to Me has risen to the highest state."

> At the end of many births the enlightened man finds refuge in Me; rare indeed is this great soul to whom 'Vasudeva is all'.[4]

After many lives, the *jnani* seeks refuge in Me. "After many lives" means after a long and hard struggle. Such a person is always saying, not with his tongue merely but with his very heart, that this whole universe is a manifestation of Vasudeva[5]. A mahatma of that greatness is very rare.

[1] VII, 17
[2] "Thou, Thou"
[3] VII, 18
[4] VII, 19
[5] Vishnu

> Men, bereft of knowledge by reason of various longings, seek refuge in other gods, pinning their faith on diverse rites, guided by their own nature.[1]

Selfish men whose minds are clouded by all kinds of worldly desires and who seek the help of witch-doctors worship lower deities. Some, for instance, vow to make a gift of so much rice or so many coconuts to the Mother-goddess at Khodiar; they obey their nature and worship her in that manner.

We may say that Ladha Maharaj belonged to the class of men who are driven by suffering to worship God, but he may also have been a *jnani*. We do not know his mental state.

[115]

July 24, 1926

> Whatever form one desires to worship in faith and devotion, in that very form I make that faith of his secure.[2]

If they think that they of their own accord worship the gods whom they do, they are ignorant. They do not get their faith from those deities. What help can a mere courtier give to one who has direct access to the king? For instance, Sudama went straight to Shri Krishna, and then the courtiers' attitude towards him changed. Such a person need not worship any other deity.

> Possessed of that faith he seeks to propitiate that one, and obtains therethrough his longings, dispensed in truth by none but Me.[3]

If there were many independent deities who could act on their own, there would be no God.

> But limited is the fruit that falls to those short-sighted ones; those who worship the gods go to the gods, those who worship Me come unto Me.[4]

Short-sighted worshippers of gods reap perishable fruits. Only one type of person wins deliverance. Those who worship the lower gods rise so far as the world of those gods. Those who worship Me come direct to Me.

> Not knowing My transcendent, imperishable, supreme character, the undiscerning think Me who am unmanifest to have become manifest.[5]

1 VII, 20
2 VII, 21
3 VII, 22
4 VII, 23
5 VII, 24

"These persons of little intelligence do not know My unmanifest state," says Shri Krishna. "They mistake the manifest universe for the invisible reality behind. They do not know the best part of Me at all (the part beyond the manifest), do not know Me as the changeless, supreme Purushottama." If, for instance, we worship the Sun, who gives light and heat, we divide the divine power of God into its several aspects and worship one of them. Instead, we should try to know the highest, the invisible state of God. This visible universe is ever taking new shapes. The gods change their forms but God is ever the same.

[116]

July 25, 1926

Our intellect has not the power to tear up the veil from before the *atman* and set it free. One who has felt the desire to do this has no little intellectual power. So long as we have not reflected deeply over these matters, we imagine beings with as many as ten heads. Then someone may wake up and ask whether the *atman* can ever have heads. He would then remember his study [of the *Gita*], remember the verses in the Second Chapter and realize that the *atman* was unmanifest and could not be pierced or wetted. "Unthinking men," Shri Krishna says, "wish to measure Me with their little yardsticks, they make an image of Me and act as if it was Myself."

> Veiled by the delusive mystery created by My unique power, I am not manifest to all; this bewildered world does not recognize Me, birthless and changeless.[1]

"I do not vouchsafe light to all. Everyone cannot know Me, for I am veiled by the *maya* of My yoga." If God had not created such *maya*, we could not have existed in this visible universe. But, then, one may ask, why did God create this universe at all? To ask this question is like a clock asking why its maker made it. A creature must have complete faith in its creator. "The unthinking man enveloped in *maya*," says Shri Krishna, "does not know Me, the Unborn and the Immutable."

[117]

July 27, 1926

"I am not luminous to all, that is, everyone cannot see Me. Human beings are blinded by My light. Such is the power of My

[1] VII, 25

maya that people can truthfully say that at this moment some lives are being born and some are dying." But we should understand that these transformations are not real. Who can know that Reality which is veiled behind objects with name and form? If someone told us that in his country rivers get frozen and that human beings and vehicles pass over them, we would not easily understand his statement; this idea of Reality veiled behind these objects with name and form is similar to that. It is true, nonetheless. The Lord says that this is due to the power of His *yogamaya*, that His real essence is the Unmanifest.

> I know, O Arjuna, all creatures past, present and to be; but no one knows Me.
>
> All creatures in this universe are bewildered, O Parantapa, by virtue of the delusion of the pairs of opposites sprung from likes and dislikes, O Bharata.
>
> But those virtuous men whose sin has come to an end, freed from the delusion of the pairs of opposites, worship Me in steadfast faith.
>
> Those who endeavour for freedom from age and death by taking refuge in Me, know in full that *Brahman*, *adhyatma* and all karma.
>
> Those who know Me, including *adhibhuta*, *adhidaiva*, *adhiyajna*, possessed of even-mindedness, they know Me even at the time of passing away.[1]

Those who think of Me, even at the moment of death, as *adhibhuta*, *adhidaiva* and *adhiyajna*, are men who have become steady. They who know Me as the Lord of all creatures, of the gods and of *yajnas*, that is, as the Creator and Preserver of the whole universe, and know that this world of flux has no effect on Me whatever, are men united to Me in yoga."

[118]
Chapter VIII

July 28, 1926

In Chapter VII, Shri Krishna fulfilled his promise, explained both *jnana* and *vijnana* and assured Arjuna that once he had understood these he would never be touched by evil.

The *apara prakriti*, the world of visible objects, can be perceived with the senses and known through the intellect, but the *para prakriti* can be apprehended only when we go beyond the senses, the intellect and the ego. If we wish to know God's

[1] VII, 26, 27, 28, 29 & 30

transcendent essence, we should in some measure be what He is. We, too, have the two essences, *apara* and *para*, in us, of which we should subdue the *apara* and acquire better knowledge of the *para*.

The main question raised in Chapter I was, how can one kill one's kinsmen? The answer to this extended to seven Chapters. And now begins the eighth. Shri Krishna is making all this effort with the aim of removing the confusion of thought and the ignorance which had unsettled Arjuna's mind. He has been brought to the point of distinction between the *apara* and the *para prakriti*.

> What is the *Brahman*? What is *adhyatma*? What karma, O Purushottama? What is called *adhibhuta*? And what *adhidaiva*?
>
> And who here in this body is *adhiyajna* and how? And how at the time of death art Thou to be known by the self-controlled ?[1]

Arjuna asks Shri Krishna, "You have told me about *Brahman*, *adhyatma*, karma, *adhibhuta* and so on. But what do these terms mean? And what is *adhiyajna*? What is meant by saying that he whose mind is yoked to the Lord can know all this at the moment of death?"

[119]

July 29, 1926

Shri Krishna answers Arjuna's question.

> The Supreme, the Imperishable is *Brahman*; its manifestation is *adhyatma*; the creative process whereby all beings are created is called karma.[2]

That which never perishes and is the ultimate Reality is *Brahman*. Our nature is *adhyatma*.

The Lord of us all is the power which creates this *adhyatma*. Creating all beings and keeping them in existence is an act of renunciation and is known as karma.

[120]

July 30, 1926

We cannot have personal relation with all beings in the world, but can have spiritual relation with them.

Anyone who feels no desire to do good to others harms not only himself but others too. If a woman expecting a baby does

[1] VIII, 1 & 2
[2] VIII, 3

not protect it, she may die and the baby, too, may die. To protect it is her karma, which is a form of renunciation. If such a woman is not regular in eating, if she thinks evil thoughts and eats unwholesome food, both she and the baby would be harmed. We are continually harming ourselves in this manner. Some of us may be inclined to ask how the world is concerned if we harm ourselves. But in harming ourselves, we harm both ourselves and the world.

Karma here certainly does not mean an act of creation. Vyasa's writing of the *Gita* and the *Mahabharata* was a great *visarga* (an act of renunciation). It is impossible that the jewel of a work like the *Gita* would signify by the term karma the merely physical act of creation.

> *Adhibhuta* is My perishable form; *adhidaivata* is the individual self in that form; and O best among the embodied, *adhiyajna* am I in this body, purified by sacrifice.[1]

That is, Shri Krishna says that He is the Lord of *yajnas* and grants their fruit. The modes of being which belong to the living creatures in the world are perishable modes.

[121]

July 31, 1926

There is a saying in Latin which means that the way to Hell is paved with good intentions. Good intentions by themselves do not succeed, but the person doomed to Hell believes that they do, without his having to strive to realize them. We cannot give all that we wish to, but we can receive everything we would. However much I try, if you do not receive what I give, what can I do? If all of you make a serious effort, you can stop wasting others' time. If you but try to get up at four, you will most certainly not fail. What does it matter even if the effort breaks us? *Moksha* is for those who strive till they break.

Krishna is the Lord of *yajna*, and we worship Him because, though in human form, He worked all His life. He was awake every moment, awake even when the Pandavas slept. The latter's eyes were always fixed on Him. He did not wish to harm the Kauravas or help the Pandavas; His only aim was to see that right prevailed. He spent his body working ceaselessly all His life, but it retained its light till the last. The word *prayatna*[2] is just

[1] VIII, 4

[2] Effort, striving

an ordinary word, but the thing itself is such that the moment you resolve on it you will begin to reap the fruit. Krishna had resolved that the Pandavas should win and, therefore, their victory was certain. He was the very embodiment of disinterested service, and wished to harm none. When Parashuram[1] was lying with his head in Karna's lap, the latter was bitten by some deadly creature and was bleeding profusely, but he did not move an inch. Surely, he too was a human being, like any of us. We should, similarly, make good resolutions and strive to realize them, offering up the fruit of our effort to Shri Krishna.

By describing Arjuna as the best among beings endowed with a body, Shri Krishna suggests that he need not fear anyone at all.

[122]

August 1, 1926

> And he who, at the last hour remembering Me only, departs leaving the body, enters into Me; of that there is no doubt.
>
> Or whatever form a man continually contemplates, that same he remembers in the hour of death, and to that very form he goes, O Kaunteya.[2]

Hence they say, you will reap as you sow.

We should let no impurity enter our thoughts. Parents give us the human form, sometimes a form like their own. The subtle changes which take place within us become visible through our eyes. If we get a disease, we should believe that we ourselves are the cause of it. A person whose mind is so strong that he influences his surroundings, instead of being influenced by them, gets no disease. It is for our good, therefore, to believe that our illness is the result of our sins. If we have been repeating Ramanama from the depth of our heart, how can even a dream, if it is evil, leap over that protecting wall and enter our mind? If any does, we may believe that we have been uttering Ramanama only with our lips. If we have any fear whatever in our heart, that too is a form of evil and we suffer from many serious diseases because of it. Hence, as we free ourselves more and more from evil impulses and desires, we become less and less subject to disease. Even persons whose ears and noses and all other limbs had been infected are known to have recovered. The body possesses a natural power

[1] A Brahmin-warrior, one of the incarnations of Vishnu, from whom Karna learned the art and science of fighting

[2] VIII, 5 & 6

of recovery. Recovery brought about with the help of herbs lasts for some time only; and the man who has overcome his evil desires and cultivated devotion to God will refuse to be cured with the help of herbs and say that, when the evil in him has disappeared, he will be all right. If, as a result of this attitude, he dies, he will welcome death.

Anyone who thinks wicked thoughts will find that in one day his body has become ugly. Once a person charged with murder came to me. I merely looked at him and told him that he was trying to deceive me. He left at once.

[123]

August 3, 1926

Thinking is a form of karma. Thoughts have such power that sometimes their effects are more terrible than those of actions. If someone finds a pistol placed in his hand by another person and is forced to fire it, he cannot be said to have committed violence because he had acted under force. But he who harbours violence in his thoughts and, keeping himself in the background, incites others to do violence, is guilty of terrible violence. Besides, there are also enemies within which prompt us to commit violence. Despite our effort to think the best thoughts and act upon them, we are driven to commit sin. It is the desire and anger in us which are responsible for this. All the same, our efforts at self-control and good thoughts help us. If the God of death himself puts a pistol in a person's hands and forces him to commit violence, such violence will not harm him. He will ever have the name of Narayana on his lips and, when he dies, his end will be good. Ordinarily we do not see this happen, for our thoughts are those of miserable wretches. They ought ever to flow in a self-controlled stream. A person whose thoughts are of this kind repeats the name of Narayana while engaged in any work. His actions are not his, they are prompted by the Lord within.

Shri Krishna has packed in these two verses the essence of all philosophy: man will reap as he thinks.

> Therefore at all times remember Me and fight on; thy mind and reason thus on Me fixed thou shalt surely come to me.
>
> With thought steadied by constant practice, and wandering nowhere, he who meditates on the Supreme Celestial Being, O Partha, goes to Him.[1]

[1] VIII, 7 & 8

No one should believe that it will suffice if he does this at the moment of death. He who has been striving in this direction from his childhood will win the battle and the other will lose. We boarded a ship at Delagoa Bay to see Gokhale off. The latter was playing billiards. I had not joined him. He thought I did not like his playing that game and asked me: "Do you think I enjoy playing this?" "No," I said, "you are trying to prove the ability of our countrymen." In this way, even his playing was dedicated to Lord Krishna. I of course knew it. I am sure in my mind that my effort to learn dancing[1] was also not prompted by love of dancing. At that time, my only thought was to acquire all the accomplishments which make a gentleman. The point is that everything we do should be dedicated to Shri Krishna. We can so dedicate only the work which comes to us unsought, not that which we undertake of our own choice. Though the inmates of the Ashram attend to different tasks, dedicating them to Shri Krishna, in reality all of them are doing the same work if there is complete harmony in their thoughts. If that is not so, and only one person is earnest about spinning and others let their minds wander, then they cannot be said to join the former in spinning.

[124]

August 4, 1926

> Who so, at the time of death, with unwavering mind, with devotion, and fixing the breath rightly between the brows by the power of yoga, meditates on the Sage, the Ancient, the Ruler, subtler than the subtlest, the Supporter of all, the Inconceivable, glorious as the sun beyond the darkness, —he goes to that Supreme Celestial Being.[2]

He who knows all attains to that supreme, divine Purusha. At the moment of departing, that is, when dying, one should think on that Purusha Who is beginningless, Who rules the world and Who is in essence finer than the finest we can conceive.

In the sixth century B.C., there ruled in Lydia a king named Croesus[3]. He had immense wealth. The Greek saint and lawgiver, Solon[4], once went to see him. Croesus asked him whether anyone could be happier than he himself was. Solon's reply

[1] *Vide An Autobiography*, Pt. I, Ch. 15.

[2] VIII, 9 & 10

[3] The last king of Lydia, 560-546 B.C.

[4] *c.* 638-558 B.C.; Athenian statesman and poet. The story of their meeting is narrated by Herodotus, but is chronologically impossible.

was that only after a man has died can we say whether he had been happy. This same Croesus was afterwards attacked and defeated by King Cyrus of Persia. He was sentenced to be hanged. As he was being taken to the gallows, he shouted Solon's name thrice. On being asked by Cyrus why he did that, he repeated Solon's reply to his question. Cyrus freed him and kept him as his adviser. When the King died, he left his son in the care of Croesus. In much the same way, it is only after a man's death that we can say whether he has passed into a higher world.

Proceeding, Shri Krishna describes that supreme Purusha, Who is the Creator of everything that exists, Whose essence cannot be comprehended by our minds, Whom only the yogis see in their contemplation, Who has the glory of the sun (shines like the sun, with the light of timeless consciousness) and Who is beyond the darkness of ignorance. Our reason cannot conceive how infinitely small and how infinitely vast He is. He who, when leaving this world, thinks with a fixed mind on this Purusha,—only his mind is fixed who has yoked himself to the Lord in *bhakti* and who possesses the strength acquired by long *sadhana*—thinks of Him with *bhakti* and with the power of his yoga, who refuses any treatment or medicine to save his life—keeps his mouth shut,—who knows that he is leaving for a world where there is no darkness and no suffering or happiness, and who focuses his *prana* on the point midway between his brows and meditates, —such a person attains to the realm of the Supreme, the Divine Purusha described in this verse.

[125]

August 5, 1926

> That which the knowers of the Vedas call the Imperishable (*or* that word which the knowers of the Vedas repeat), wherein the ascetics freed from passion enter and desiring which they practise *brahmacharya*, that Goal (*or* Word) I will declare to thee in brief.
>
> Closing all the gates, locking up the mind in the *hridaya*, fixing his breath within the head, rapt in yogic meditation;
>
> Who so departs leaving the body uttering *AUM—Brahman* in one syllable—repeatedly thinking on Me, he reaches the highest state.[1]

While in the previous verse Shri Krishna referred to other states of mind, here He speaks only of meditation on the Lord.

[1] VIII, 11, 12 & 13

> That yogi easily wins to Me, O Partha, who, ever attached to Me, constantly remembers Me with undivided mind.
>
> Great souls, having come to Me, reach the highest perfection; they come not again to birth, unlasting and (withal) an abode of misery.[1]

Why is it misery to be born over and over again ?

A STUDENT: One may not be born a human being—in every life.

But what does it matter if one is born a monkey. We may enjoy our life dancing and jumping about all the time.

ANOTHER STUDENT: Can one be sure that, after one dies, in the next life, one will be born a Brahmin ?

Should we not welcome that state in which there is no death ? Are there any who like dying? Those who do, die again and again. He who does not want death gives up his attachment to bodily life, closes all the bodily doors without much thinking. If he forgets the body, mortifies it every moment, he will not have to die. It is because there is death for everyone who is born that life is a cause of suffering. The birds are ever happy, but then they have no knowledge and are not free. Would you like it if someone changed all the boys into birds ? That state in which there is no death and no birth, no disease, no attachment and no aversion, that supreme state is known as *moksha*.

[126]

August 6, 1926

Even big mountains, sun and moon and stars, all things are transient. If our lives were as long as one crore years, perhaps we would not feel the transience of our existence. We are not conscious of the transience of the sun, but science tells us that it is not eternal. Both from a profound and from a superficial view, it is transient. Ramanama alone is imperishable. Life and death are both transitory states; not only are they so, they are the cause of all suffering.

Why ? It is not because the *Gita* says so that we should regard them as the cause of suffering; we should feel in our own lives that they are so. The best way of ensuring that after death we pass to a higher world is to feel every moment that life in this world is from its very nature full of suffering, so that we give up attachment to it and free ourselves from the dualities of love and hatred.

[1] VIII, 14 & 15

We can understand even with our reason that life in this world is full of suffering. If we but think, we shall realize that the very process of birth of all creatures is something repulsive. This is what is meant by saying "I am sin", "I have my source in sin". This existence being enveloped in *maya*, we take pleasure every moment in what should repel us. We have no sense through which we can feel in all its intensity this pain [which the process of birth means]. Even our state after birth is, from the beginning to the end, one long imprisonment. We love fondling a child, because it smiles and laughs with pleasure. But, then, prisoners also laugh. We take pleasure in this slavery because it is a part of our existence, but in truth it is a state in which we cannot rest in peace even for a moment. Look at the physical frame of this body. It excretes dirt through countless pores, such dirt as we cannot bear touching. If only we reflect, we shall find nothing to attract us in this body. But, then, even this prison is a house through which we can win our freedom. If we come to regard it in that light, we shall make the minimum necessary use of it. The way to freedom, of course, does not lie in committing suicide. Anyone who kills himself will certainly be born again. He will yearn all the more to return to life. The ideal of self-control had its origin in the knowledge of the manner in which life comes into existence and of other facts of our physical life. This body is not to be pampered, but to be mortified and subjugated. If it sees that it does not get what it craves, it will on its own leave us in terror. If, Shri Krishna says, people realize the misery of this existence, the state to which He will raise them will be a little better than their present one. That supreme state is not to be conceived as one in which the higher bliss which we experience in this life will also vanish. On the contrary, we shall have it thousandfold in that other state. With this thought constantly in one's mind, one should get absorbed in the duties of this life, forget oneself altogether in them. One should see oneself in the whole world and the world in oneself, and act towards others accordingly. The ideal of non-violence also had its origin in this realization that, when human life as such is full of suffering, we should cause suffering to none.

> From the world of Brahma down, all the worlds are subject to return, O Arjuna; but on coming to Me there is no rebirth.[1]

[1] VIII, 16

All the worlds, including the world of Brahma[1], will return to their source. The sun, the moon, Brahma, Vishnu, all will perish. "But," Shri Krishna says, "once a human being comes to Me, he never perishes."

This is what I have tried to explain in my talk today.

[127]

August 7, 1926

There is great poetry in this verse. This little drop contains knowledge as vast as the sea, and the more that knowledge becomes part of our experience the more we discover its poetry. In such a verse, the poet soars on the wings of his imagination, released from the bondage of the body and the senses. His imagination works on what he has heard with his ears and seen with his eyes and, going beyond the certainties of reason, he says that all that is known through the senses is a product of the human mind; that is, he imagines that since we ourselves perish, this whole universe will perish too. All that the human mind can imagine or conceive is perishable, is subject to ceaseless change. He who has dedicated himself to truth will not be prepared to forsake it merely because the world does not agree with him, as if his truth depended on the world and he was acting in a play. Shri Krishna, therefore, the Prince of Yogis that He is, says here that we believe there is happiness in the world of Brahma but that there is no happiness even there.

He asks Arjuna to go to the world beyond all these worlds, the world in which He Himself dwells. This is simply beyond our imagination. But what is beyond our imagination does exist, nevertheless. If a person dies striving to reach that world, there is no rebirth for him.

> Those men indeed know what is Day and what is Night, who know that Brahma's day lasts a thousand *yugas* and that his night too is a thousand *yugas* long.[2]

[128]

August 8, 1926

A day and a night of ours are made up of 24 hours. They say that anyone who focuses his eyes on the tip of his nose and meditates will find bliss, but it is necessary to go beyond this.

[1] One of several heavens, distinct from the absolute, impersonal Brahma

[2] VIII, 17

In order to become a *jnani* one must learn to look deep into things. Anyone who practises this method but goes beyond it will study his self and draw far-reaching conclusions, will realize that things are not what they seem. We do not, thus, require a *Gita* to tell us that Brahma[1] must have a day different in length from ours; we can see this ourselves if we use our brains. It seems to us an absolute certainty that the Sun will always be there. He will be a *jnani* who understands the nature of time from a study of one object existing in time. Such a person will take into account all the factors, which ordinary men and women fail to do. The latter would generally reason that, since no one practises control of the senses, it is impossible to practise and ought not to be attempted; if we reason thus, we shall invite ruin upon ourselves. This is fallacious reasoning.

If we want to know what is a day and what a night, we should have a standard of measurement. How can we measure infinite time? A day as long as a thousand *yugas* and a night of equal length! We should know that there is a day and night of such length in order that we may learn patience, and that, if the result of our effort takes time to show itself, we may not give way to despair. We may have faith in the spinning-wheel, but what progress can we expect from devoted work of only four or five years? We may see no tangible result in our own life-time. Nonetheless, we should have faith and go on working. Having devoted ourselves to this work, we should not give way to despair, nor be proud of ourselves. Let us remember that a thousand *yugas* make one day, and out of a thousand Parvatis one succeeds. There were a great many Parvatis and Shambhus who failed, before one Parvati and one Shambhu succeeded. We should know that this is how the power of *tapas* works.

> At the coming of Day all the manifest spring forth from the Unmanifest, and at the coming of Night they are dissolved into that same Unmanifest.[2]

When Brahma's day[3] begins, the Unmanifest becomes manifest. All these creatures, which had vanished into nothingness, come to life again. When his night begins, the whole creation vanishes, that is, merges into the Unmanifest. In this way, all creation

[1] The Creator in the Hindu Trinity

[2] VIII, 18

[3] A day and a night of Brahma consist of 8,640,000,000 years or 2,000 *mahayugas*.

appears and vanishes, and does so endlessly. We have no reason to believe that the universe is fixed and motionless; in fact it is revolving, with a speed a thousand times greater than that of a spindle. The Earth will return into nothingness, will perish, but there will certainly be some who will survive that final destruction.

> This same multitude of creatures come to birth, O Partha, again and again; they are dissolved at the coming of Night, whether they will or not; and at the break of Day they are re-born.[1]

When the night comes, whether we wish it or not, the universe returns into nothingness, and when the day comes a new creation appears.

How long shall we remain caught in this endless cycle? To reassure us on this, Shri Krishna says:

> But higher than that Unmanifest is another Unmanifest Being, everlasting, which perisheth not when all creatures perish.[2]

There is another Unmanifest Reality beyond this Unmanifest[3] and it is immutable; it is the immutable Reality immanent in all perishable creatures. Everything which exists will perish, but the ground of all this existence is imperishable. Thus, we go a good deal further than the tip of our nose.

> This Unmanifest, named the Imperishable, is declared to be the highest goal. For those who reach it there is no return. That is My highest abode.[4]

Shri Krishna says: "You can come to Me by patient striving and living in this world only as a witness. Have faith and, devoting yourself to duty, work out the welfare of your soul." The substance of all this is that the supreme *Brahman* never perishes, everything else does.

[129]

August 10, 1926

The form in which the timeless essence which is God manifests itself is known as His incarnation. We can know that essence in every creature. The principle of oneness does not mean that all

[1] VIII, 19

[2] VIII, 20

[3] The source to which the visible universe returns at the end of the cycle; *vide* verse 18 above.

[4] VIII, 21

of us should become beasts; it means, on the contrary, that God is present in the heart of even the most wicked of creatures, and that the latter awakes to His presence when the time comes. Ramachandra's picture as a child is a product of the poet's imagination, but we may believe it as true, knowing that higher consciousness is present even at that age. If a little child is a *jnani* and still behaves as we know children do, we should say, "The *Brahman* sports before the *Brahman*."[1] Such a child would be a visible form of the *Brahman*, in the same sense that Parvati was the embodiment of *tapascharya* and Krishna of yoga, of the *Brahman*.

[130]

August 11, 1926

> This Supreme Being, O Partha, may be won by undivided devotion; in It all beings dwell, by It all is pervaded.[2]

"That supreme state, to be attained in yogic contemplation, is beyond my reach": so sang Raychandbhai.

> Now I will tell thee, Bharatarshabha, the conditions which determine the exemption from return, as also the return, of yogis after they pass away hence.[3]

"I shall now describe that state" (the word may also mean time) "after reaching which, or that path after treading which, there is no returning."

> Fire, Light, Day, the Bright Fortnight, the six months of the Northern Solstice—through these departing men knowing *Brahman* go to *Brahman*.[4]

It is often said that this and the next verse do not fit into the teaching of the *Gita*, but we will treat them as if they did.

The *Gita* did not drop down from heaven, nor is it as if every word that Krishna said to Arjuna was written down. Vyasa has given what the Lord said to a seeker and, in doing so, he would include even things which he himself did not understand from his own experience. It may have been a general belief in those times which made people particular that they did important things at particular hours of the day only, or welcomed death during a certain part of the day. The favourites of a king can approach him

[1] The line is from a poem by Narasinh Mehta
[2] VIII, 22
[3] VIII, 23
[4] VIII, 24

only at a fixed hour, and no one else can go to him at that time. Similarly, it may have been the prevalent belief in those days that only people who died in an auspicious hour would reach God; this, of course, did not mean that those who died in some other hour had not aspired and striven in their lives to reach God after death.

Those who die when there is fire and light, on any day in the bright half of one of the six months following the winter solstice, will reach the *Brahman*. This statement may be intended to have either a literal or an allegorical meaning. If the latter, it means that anyone who has attained a state like the bright half of the month, a state of knowledge as bright as light, will not return to this world after death. On the other hand:

> Smoke, Night, the Dark Fortnight, the six months of the Southern Solstice—therethrough the yogi attains to the lunar light and thence returns.[1]

Such a person lives in heaven and, when the merit earned by his virtuous deeds is exhausted, he returns to the earth.

We may, therefore, take either of the two meanings. Anyone who has not attained to full illumination will have to return to this earth; in other words, he who spends his life in disinterested work and prays daily to the Lord with love and devotion will not have to return, for he will have cut asunder the bonds of karma. Anyone who departs after a life of disinterested *bhakti* will not have to return.

[131]

August 12, 1926

Some persons treat these two verses as interpolated; we cannot do so, for the copies of the *Gita* which we use contain them. If the meaning of any verse contradicts the very meaning of the *Gita*, we may reject that verse, otherwise we should try to reconcile it with the rest of the teaching, as we did yesterday. *Kala* [in these verses] means state, condition. We do not know whether, in the age when the *Gita* was composed, the North and the South Poles were discovered. For those who live in the region of the North Pole, the day and the night are as long as our six months. The period following the winter solstice is a time of light and signifies a waking state, whereas the period following the summer

[1] VIII, 25

solstice signifies a state of ignorance. We have compared the latter state with the state full of desire and the former with that which is free from desire.

The Lord, Shri Krishna, now proceeds:

> These two paths—bright and dark—are deemed to be the eternal paths of the world; by the one a man goes to return not, by the other he returns again.[1]

These two paths, the bright and the dark, that which leads to a state from which there is no returning and the other which leads to a state which is impermanent, have existed from the beginning of time. The bright state is that of the illumination of knowledge and the dark state is that of ignorance. Dying in one state, a person never returns; dying in the other, he is bound to return.

> The yogi knowing these two paths falls not into delusion, O Partha; therefore, at all times, O Arjuna, remain steadfast in yoga.[2]

The yogi who knows the distinction between these two paths never succumbs to darkness. He realizes that disinterested *bhakti* is the best form of *bhakti*. If we have faith in the Lord and *bhakti* for Him, why should we forever be begging things from Him? Anyone who is filled with faith and love will feel that there is nothing for him to beg. He will have offered everything to the Lord, placed himself at His mercy. He may say: "All that is mine is yours." Such single-minded *bhakti* is *uttarayana*[3], it is light, and so on. What, again, is the significance of Krishna's advice to remain yoked to Him at all times? It means that one should cling to knowledge and single-minded devotion. The gods are immortal, but only compared to human beings. They, too, will perish in time. "Therefore," says Shri Krishna, "instead of going to the gods who will perish, if you come to Me, then alone will you get knowledge and in no other way." Arjuna should, Shri Krishna says, keep the knot in his heart, the little grains of dust which cover the knowledge within, so thoroughly cleaned that at the moment of death he will spontaneously have the right thoughts.

> Whatever fruit of good deeds is laid down as accruing from (a study of) the Vedas, from sacrifices, austerities, and acts of charity—all that the yogi transcends, on knowing this, and reaches the Supreme and Primal Abode.[4]

[1] VIII, 26
[2] VIII, 27
[3] Northward course of the sun
[4] VIII, 28

We saw in the verse beginning with *yavanartha udapane*[1] that he who has acquired this light and knowledge is in the condition of one who has secured that beyond which nothing else remains to be obtained.

[132]

Chapter IX

August 13, 1926

> I will now declare to thee, who art uncensorious, this mysterious knowledge, together with discriminative knowledge, knowing which thou shalt be released from ill.
>
> This is the king of sciences, the king of mysteries, pure and sovereign, capable of direct comprehension, the essence of dharma, easy to practise, changeless.[2]

There was a man who, whenever he got very angry, sat down to do sums in algebra; anyone else who tried to do this, when he ought to be repeating Ramanama, would find the effort a burdensome task. If someone is dying and cries for help, it would be unfeeling arrogance to tell him that you were busy doing sums in algebra, for it would be a moment when the Shastras could well be thrown into the sea. Doing a sum in algebra is not in itself a duty, but the aim behind it may be a duty. Through it, I may know who and where I am. Doing a sum is not by itself a duty, the first duty is service. For instance, eating is never a duty in itself. He is a true man who leaves the dinner table and runs to do an act of service.

The knowledge of this duty is *rajavidya.* It is the king of all secrets, it is sacred and the highest knowledge, it is dharma and worthy to be followed in action, and easy to follow besides; once acquired, it is never destroyed. "I will impart that knowledge to you," says Shri Krishna.

[133]

August 14, 1926

> Men who have no faith in this doctrine, O Parantapa, far from coming to Me, return repeatedly to the path of this world of death.
>
> By Me, unmanifest in form, this whole world is pervaded; all beings are in Me, I am not in them.[3]

[1] II, 46
[2] IX, 1 & 2
[3] IX, 3 & 4

So long as our eyes of knowledge have not opened, we have no choice but to see with the eyes of faith.

> And yet those beings are not in Me. That indeed is My unique power as Lord! Sustainer of all beings, I am not in them; My Self brings them into existence.
>
> As the mighty wind, moving everywhere, is ever contained in ether, even so know that all beings are contained in Me.[1]

Air fills space, but space is not identical with air. We can say that air fills space. Though space is empty, we can say that it is filled with air. And yet space is not air. The air which fills space is still not in it, so God who dwells in all creatures is still not in them. In one sense, He is not in them, for we can see other things with our eyes but not Him.

He who has faith and he who lacks it, both are sincere in their beliefs. God exists for him who has faith, but does not exist for him who lacks it.

A Shastri will be able to explain the point of these two verses.

The Ganga water does, and yet does not, contain dirt. Similarly, even the most wicked of beings exists in God. The cruellest of men, even a *Chandal*, exists in Him, and yet does not. God is above good and bad. Vyasa puts these contradictory statements together, for our reason knows its limitation in trying to describe the truth. It is enough if we understand that God pervades the entire universe.

[134][2]

August 15, 1926

Innumerable ways of falling are open to a man, he need not make any effort for the purpose; it is for rising that one has to strive. We may revere and always keep in a proper place a holy book which we believe helps us on the path of good; but anyone who goes no further than showing it outward reverence will find such reverence a means of bondage. There should, therefore, be discrimination even in reverence; only so will that reverence help us to advance. Outward reverence for a holy book is not all. We should go further than that. We should try to follow the teaching of the book in our life. God is omnipotent and we are His creatures. When, however, we, who are mere ants in His sight

[1] IX, 5 & 6

[2] The notes of this discourse were taken by Punjabhai.

try to eat Him up, He uses a part of His infinite power. He is so near that we feel we can touch Him this very moment, and yet we never do, so far away He is. As space and air exist one in the other, so do God and the universe. He who has faith certainly exists in God; he who lacks it does not. God does not force Himself on anyone, but He does not close the door, either, against anyone who aspires to be united to Him—such is His nature.

> All beings, O Kaunteya, merge into my *prakriti*, at the end of a *kalpa*, and I send them forth again when a *kalpa* begins.[1]

The holy books speak of such rise and disappearance of the worlds.

The individual soul, of course, passes through birth and death. But the universe, too, comes into existence and disappears. If the soul, therefore, wishes to know its essence, it will have to transcend the universe. We know for certain that this lamp will one day be destroyed, and yet it is the only thing we can use; it is essential, therefore, that we take care to keep it clean. This Ashram has buildings, which are its body, so to say. They will be destroyed one day. But the Ashram's soul, which is its ideals, will never perish. To realize that imperishable essence, we may even need to put up buildings of brick and mortar. In this way, we must use our reason and discrimination and keep working. If we wish to live in this world, we must put to use even things which will perish, but only with the aim of realizing the imperishable essence beyond them.

> Resorting to my *prakriti*, I send forth again and again this multitude of beings, powerless under the sway of *prakriti*.[2]

[135]

August 17, 1926

> But all this activity, O Dhananjaya, does not bind Me, seated as one indifferent, unattached to it.[3]

God acts according to His *prakriti*, and yet He does nothing since He is above even His *prakriti*.

If a king does sinful things, his subjects too suffer. But God, being omniscient, can do nothing without thought. Sin means only what is done without taking thought. How can a person who thinks before acting commit a sin? Likewise, how can one who is

[1] IX, 7
[2] IX, 8
[3] IX, 9

by nature inclined to sin act virtuously? If one does good spontaneously, in the same way that our eyes wink automatically, one will not have to suffer the fruits of such good actions. It is man's nature to do good, for all selves are one. That being so, the apparent separateness of each self has no significance. When this is realized, man's ego melts away. Man's essence, which is *atman*, is all-pervading, for he who has realized it will not see himself as different from others, but will see all in himself. For such a person, therefore, doing good becomes his nature. When he seems to be serving other creatures, he is doing so not out of kindness to them but is merely following his own nature. To us who are enveloped in *maya*, it may seem that he is practising virtue, but in truth it is not so; he is acting only according to his nature towards all creatures.

[136]

August 18, 1926

With me as Presiding Witness, *prakriti* gives birth to all that moves and does not move; and because of this, O Kaunteya, the wheel of the world keeps going.

Not knowing My transcendent nature as the sovereign Lord of all beings, fools condemn Me incarnated as man.[1]

"Creatures sunk in darkness, dwelling in the human body, do not know Me," says Shri Krishna, "they disregard Me" (Has not Tulsidas said that those who make a distinction between Rama and God are ignorant and know nothing? We project our ignorance on to God too.) "They do not know My supreme state, do not know Me as the Lord of all creatures. Labouring under the illusion that I am a human being, they do not know My real essence."

[137]

August 19, 1926

Vain are the hopes, actions and knowledge of those witless ones who have resorted to the delusive nature of monsters and devils.

But those great souls who resort to the divine nature, O Partha, know Me as the Imperishable Source of all beings and worship Me with an undivided mind.[2]

[1] IX, 10 & 11
[2] IX, 12 & 13

The mahatmas, who are ruled by their divine *prakriti*, like Vibhishana[1] and others, worship Me with their minds illumined by knowledge and with single-minded devotion—Me who am the Creator of all beings.

> Always declaring My glory, striving in steadfast faith, they do Me devout homage; ever attached to Me, they worship Me.
>
> Yet others, with knowledge-sacrifice, worship Me, who am to be seen everywhere, as one, as different or as many.[2]

"Others worship Me by striving for knowledge. Some of them worship Me as the only One (that is, believing that all this is Vasudeva), some others worship My different manifestations and others still worship Me in everything which exists.

We may take *vishvatomukham* to go with *mam*, and understand the line to mean that "they worship Me who am the same in all or dwell in all"; or we may interpret *ekatvena* to mean "with devotion" and *prithaktvena* to mean that "they look upon Me as the Lord and themselves as My devotees and worship Me in that spirit". Or, *ekatvena* may mean "worshipping Me as Impersonal Absolute" and *prithaktvena* may mean "worshipping Me as personal God". In any case, *vishvatomukham* taken as an independent, third term, yields no sense.

[138]

August 20, 1926

> I am the sacrificial vow; I am the sacrifice; I the ancestral oblation; I the herb; I the sacred text; I the clarified butter; I the fire; I the burnt offering.
>
> Of this universe I am Father, Mother, Creator, Grandsire; I am what is to be known, the sacred syllable *AUM*; the *Rig*, the *Sama* and the *Yajur*;
>
> I am the Goal, the Sustainer, the Lord, the Witness, the Abode, the Refuge, the Friend; the Origin, the End, the Preservation, the Treasure-house, the Imperishable Seed.[3]

I am *gati* which means *moksha*—the state which human beings strive to attain. I am the sustainer, the Lord, and the witness. I

[1] In the *Ramayana*; he tried to persuade his brother, Ravana, to restore Sita to Rama. Failing in this effort, he went over to Rama and was accepted by him.

[2] IX, 14 & 15

[3] IX, 16, 17 & 18

am the abode, and the shelter. I am *suhrid* which means a kind friend who serves me without expectation of reward.

> I give heat; I hold back and pour forth rain; I am deathlessness and also death, O Arjuna, Being and not-Being as well.[1]

I give heat, but in the form of the sun which gives happiness and the light of knowledge to all creatures. I draw the rains and release them. I am death and I am immortality; I am being and also non-being.

That is, every object and every state which we can think of in this universe are God. This means that God is not merely all that is good, He is also the evil. Nothing exists unless He wills it. It is not true that God is the Lord of light and Satan of darkness. While we live in this body, we may believe in these dualities. We should engrave Tulsidasji's words in our hearts, that while we are enveloped in *maya* all this, which is false, will seem as true. The nacre will appear as silver and the sun's rays will appear as the mirage. We shall continue to think in this way till a *jnani* opens our eyes and convinces us that the appearance of the rope as the serpent, of the nacre as silver and of the sun's rays as mirage, is but the work of our imagination. We believe that God is both good and evil and, believing that, some of us ask what harm there is in following evil. But it is quite wrong if we argue thus. The point is not that we should act like scorpions or centipedes, but that we should have goodwill for them, without ourselves becoming poisonous like them. The Lord has here stated a profound truth which is beyond the capacity of our reason to comprehend. What He has stated cannot possibly be true in this world. We can only imagine that it must be true in some sense. Being and non-being, virtue and sin, immortality and death, these are contradictory things. They cannot be true for human beings, they can be so only for God. That third state [in which contraries are reconciled] is not a mere mixture of the two. Hydrogen and oxygen together yield water, but water does not display the separate properties of either; it has characteristics of its own. Similarly, we must not imagine that God has in Him the qualities of both virtue and sin, but should think that He has something else which is different from either. If we had both virtue and sin in us, there would be an explosion, but Siva swallows both. The existence of the two in God is a miracle, and He alone knows its mystery. We should make no attempt to cultivate such a state. If we try to combine the two

[1] IX, 19

in us, such an attempt to imitate God will simply destroy us.

> Followers of the three Vedas, who drink the *soma* juice and are purged of sin, worship Me with sacrifice and pray for going to heaven; they reach the holy world of the gods and enjoy in heaven the divine joys of the gods.[1]

Those who perform the rituals enjoined in the three Vedas, who drink *somarasa* (in the region of the North Pole *somarasa* was food and it would be a crime to refuse it to anyone, for if given to a dying man it saved life), who wash away their sins and worship the Lord by performing sacrifices, pray that they should go to heaven. They go to the sacred realm of Indra and there enjoy divine pleasures such as gods do.

[139]

August 22, 1926

> They enjoy the vast world of heaven, and their merit spent, they enter the world of the mortals; thus those who, following the Vedic law, long for the fruit of their action earn but the round of birth and death.
>
> As for those who worship Me, thinking on Me alone and nothing else, ever attached to Me, I bear the burden of getting them what they need.[2]

Yoga means realization of God and *kshema* means safeguarding of the means which help us to attain it.

> Even those who, devoted to other gods, worship them in full faith, even they, O Kaunteya, worship none but Me, though not according to the rule.[3]

The right method is to have no intermediary between oneself and God. "But," Shri Krishna says, "those who seek Me through the gate-keepers that stand between, they too worship Me, for they worship these in order to reach Me."

> For I am the Acceptor and the Director of all sacrifices; but not recognizing Me as I am, they go astray.[4]

"I am," says the Lord "the recipient and the Lord of all *yajnas*." That is, he who does everything without thinking that he himself does it can say that not he but the Lord does every-

[1] IX, 20
[2] IX, 21 & 22
[3] IX, 23
[4] IX, 24

thing. "Those, however, who do not know the truth and, therefore, do not know Me, return again to the world."

The sinful man, so long as he is conscious of his ego, describes himself as the most wicked of men. Tulsidas says, on the one hand, that there could be none as lustful, lecherous, degraded and adulterous as he was and, on the other hand, attributes all his sins to God, for, since he had no ego in him, how could he have committed those sins? The river Ganga washes away all kinds of sins, but she receives no stain. Likewise, the timeless body in Rama is sinless. The physical Rama, of course, is subject to sin. If we pervert this idea and start committing sins and then say that sins cannot touch us, we shall be like the frog in the fable who tried to blow his body into the size of an ox and so burst. A *bhakta* will say: "I am a sinful man, but I am in your hands." Beyond this, our reason does not work. "Do not describe man as God; he is not God, but he is not different from the light of God."

[140]

August 24, 1926

> Those who worship the gods go to the gods; those who worship the manes go to the manes; those who worship the spirits go to the spirits; but those who worship Me come to Me.
>
> Any offering of leaf, flower, fruit or water, made to Me in devotion, by an earnest soul, I lovingly accept.[1]

The Lord did not accept the fruit sent by Duryodhana, for he had not sent it with love. His motive was to get his own aim served through Shri Krishna. He wanted the Lord's help on his own terms. He had not mastered the self. But Vidura, who was a man of simple heart, offered a plain dish of leafy greens and the Lord accepted it with love, for Vidura's *bhakti* was unrivalled and his heart was straightforward and clean. He felt no awe for the wealth of the mighty.

> Whatever thou dost, whatever thou eatest, whatever thou offerest as sacrifice or gift, whatever austerity thou dost perform, O Kaunteya, dedicate all to Me.
>
> So doing thou shalt be released from the bondage of action yielding good and evil fruit; having accomplished both renunciation and performance, thou shalt be released (from birth and death) and come unto Me.[2]

[1] IX, 25 & 26
[2] IX, 27 & 28

"If you live thus, you will be free from the bonds of karma which are sometimes good and sometimes evil in their fruit, for I shall be the recipient of all that you enjoy." He who has purified himself through sannyasayoga—who dedicates to the Lord all that he does, who keeps on doing useful work right till the end of his life, but in a spirit of dedication to the Lord, —such a one goes to Him after death.

> I am the same to all beings; with Me there is none disfavoured, none favoured; but those who worship Me with devotion are in Me and I in them.[1]

If we seek refuge in the Lord, He will give us all that we can wish. If we go to the Ganga, we can have the Ganga water, but we shall have only as much as fills our cupped palm if that is all we seek. The Lord provides a grain for the ant and a cart-load for the elephant.

[141]

August 25, 1926

> A sinner, howsoever great, if he turns to Me with undivided devotion, must indeed be counted a saint; for he has a settled resolve.[2]

A man like Ajamila may have resolved to purify himself of the evil in him, and he may sit down in a firm posture for yoga; maybe his thoughts do not leave him, but he is none the less a sadhu who keeps repeating *Om* and is firm in his resolution. But another person who is not firm in his mind and not regular in practice, who follows no method in his work, may be a good man and still he does not deserve to be called a sadhu.

> For soon he becomes righteous and wins everlasting peace; know for a certainty, O Kaunteya, that My *bhakta* never perishes.[3]

Such a person soon becomes a holy man, and attains inviolable peace of mind. We should not, therefore, regard even the most wicked of men as wicked. He can become good in this very life. Shri Krishna says: "Be certain, O Arjuna, that no *bhakta* of mine ever perishes."

This body perishes, but he dies after becoming a good man rather than a wicked one.

[1] IX, 29
[2] IX, 30
[3] IX, 31

> For finding refuge in Me, even those who though are born of the womb of sin, women, Vaisyas, and Sudras too, reach the supreme goal.[1]

"Anyone who surrenders himself or herself to Me," assures the Lord, "whether man or woman, Vaisya or Sudra, or one born among wicked people—in a family of the most wicked *Chandals*—even then such a person will attain the supreme state."

The Lord has given a great assurance to the world in these verses. This is His reply to those learned in the Vedas. Such persons argue that those who have not studied the Vedas cannot realize God. It was believed in those days that women, Vaisyas and Sudras cannot attain *moksha*. In fact, Krishna tended cows as a boy in Nanda's family and did the work of a Sudra. The Vaisya's function was rearing cows and agriculture. But in course of time those who were engaged in agriculture came to be regarded as Sudras. Shri Krishna says here that, even if Vaisyas and Sudras are not able to study the Vedas, they can certainly attain the blessed state. Anyone who, though ignorant of the Vedas, knows the *Brahman*, and has a pure heart is certain to attain this state.

> How much more then, the pure Brahmins and seer-kings who are my devotees? Do thou worship Me, therefore, since thou hast come to this fleeting and joyless world.
>
> On Me fix thy mind, to Me bring thy devotion, to Me offer thy sacrifice, to Me make thy obeisance; thus having attached thyself to Me and made Me thy end and aim, to Me indeed shalt thou come.[2]

"Forget yourself in Me," says Shri Krishna, "meditate constantly on Me, let your *atman* be in ceaseless communion with Me, and live with your heart ever united with Me; if you live thus, I shall draw you towards Me."

"You need only allow yourself to be drawn, and shall not resist. You may not draw Me, but I can draw you. You will be able to understand this riddle, no one else will."

This chapter has also been named *Rajavidya*[3] and *Rajaguhyayoga*[4]. Shri Krishna tells Arjuna that He has explained the highest knowledge and expounded the highest mystery—the meaning of yoga and *kshema*. The union of yoga is to be achieved with the Lord; one should not aspire to earn great riches or rise to a position of honour or win an empire in this world. All that is needed is a fixed determination to realize God. What is the good of any

[1] IX, 32
[2] IX, 33 & 34
[3] The sovereign science
[4] The yoga of sovereign mystery

pleasure we can get through the senses—the eyes, the nose, the ears and so on? We should not be allured by it, for such pleasure is short-lived. There were emperors, but they have passed away. He whom we seek dwells in our hearts, and the holy temple in which He sits opens only by the means of prayer. The Lord explained this by saying *manmana bhava madbhakto madyaji*[1]. "I am," He says, "the author and sustainer of all, I am the friend, I am the source, the cause of existence and of the final destruction—I am all this. There is nothing else. I am all that there is. You are of no consequence. The other gods in the worlds in between will also perish, like you. I alone never perish. If you wish that you should not perish, you should come to My world, and that you can do by surrendering your whole mind to Me. Whether you are engaged in bathing or washing or any other like activities, if you are repeating my name the while and if you dedicate to Me all that you eat, if you worship Me as you give your body its hire, you will surely come to Me."

[142]

Chapter X

August 26, 1926

> Yet once more, O Mahabahu, hear My supreme word, which I will utter to thee, gratified one, for thy benefit.
>
> Neither the gods nor the great seers know My origin; for I am, every way, the origin of them both.
>
> He who knows Me, the great Lord of the worlds, as birthless and without beginning, he among mortals, undeluded, is released from sins.[2]

Those who know Me as the Unborn, the Beginningless and the Supreme Lord of all creatures do not sink into the darkness of ignorance. A person who has sunk in darkness knows the night as day and the day as night. Among all these creatures who are bound to perish, the *jnani* becomes free from all sins, for he will have no vestige of aversion and attachment, no trace of egotism; he will remain unaffected by the pairs of opposites, will ever be humble and believe that it is the Lord who provides for his living.

> Discernment, knowledge, freedom from delusion, long suffering, truth, self-restraint, inward calm, pleasure, pain, birth, death, fear and fearlessness;[3]

[1] In IX, 34
[2] X, 1, 2 & 3
[3] X, 4

> Non-violence, even-mindedness, contentment, austerity, beneficence, good and ill fame,—all these various attributes of creatures proceed verily from Me.[1]

All the qualities mentioned in these two verses, intellect, knowledge, the absence of ignorant attachment, forgiveness, truthfulness, control of the senses, serenity, happiness and suffering, birth and death, fear and absence of fear, ahimsa, inward poise and contentment, *tapas*, making gifts, good name or evil reputation among men—these conditions exist in all creatures and I am the cause of each one of them.

The Creator of all beings is also the cause of all the good and evil which we see in these beings.

[143][2]

August 27, 1926

> The seven great seers, the ancient four, and the Manus too were born of Me and of My mind, and of them were born all the creatures in the world.
>
> He who knows in truth this My immanence and My yoga becomes gifted with unshakable yoga; of this there is no doubt.[3]

Everything which exists is created by the Lord. He who believes, not merely with his reason but with his heart, that no creature can live or act without His permission or except as He wills, yokes himself to Him in single-minded devotion, but he who forgets the Lord and believes in his pride that he rises by his own efforts labours under a delusion. There is no doubt at all that he who believes in God from the depth of his heart and obeys the Lord who dwells in him attains to a state of serenity which is never perturbed.

> I am the source of all, all proceeds from Me; knowing this, the wise worship Me with hearts full of devotion.
>
> With Me in their thoughts, their whole soul devoted to Me, teaching one another, with Me ever on their lips, they live in contentment and joy.
>
> To these, ever in tune with Me worshipping Me with affectionate devotion, I give the power of selfless action, whereby they come to Me.[4]

1 X, 5
2 The notes of this discourse were not taken by Mahadev Desai.
3 X, 6 & 7
4 X, 8, to 10

In this way, knowledge comes spontaneously to a *bhakta*. He does not have to wade through big volumes. But he who believes that he will acquire knowledge first and cultivate *bhakti* afterwards will fail miserably in his aim. No one can acquire knowledge in that way. Such knowledge breeds, if anything, pride. But he who lovingly cultivates devotion for the Lord and constantly thinks on Him gets knowledge without any special effort to that end.

> Out of every compassion for them, I Who dwell in their hearts, destroy the darkness, born of ignorance, with the refulgent lamp of knowledge.[1]

[144]

August 28, 1926

> Lord! Thou art the supreme *Brahman*, the supreme Abode, the supreme Purifier! Everlasting Celestial Being, the Primal God, Unborn, All-pervading.
>
> Thus have all the seers—the divine seer Narada, Asita, Devala, Vyasa —declared Thee; and Thou Thyself dost tell me so.
>
> All that Thou tellest me is true, I know, O Keshava, verily, Lord, neither the gods nor the demons know Thy manifestation.
>
> Thyself alone Thou knowest by Thyself, O Purushottama, O Source and Lord of all beings, God of gods, O Ruler of the universe!
>
> Indeed Thou oughtest to tell me of all Thy manifestations, without a remainder, whereby Thou dost pervade these worlds.
>
> O Yogi! constantly meditating on Thee, how am I to know Thee? In what various aspects am I to think of Thee, O Lord?
>
> Recount to me yet again, in full detail, Thy unique power and Thy immanence, O Janardana! For my ears cannot be sated with listening to Thy life-giving words.[2]

One who does engraving work every day does not tire of it. He returns to it whenever he is free. Similarly, Arjuna, who loves repeating Krishna's name in devotion, requests Him again and again to describe His powers till the latter can say no more.

[145]

August 29, 1926

> Yea, I will unfold to thee, O Kurushreshtha, My divine manifestations,—the chiefest only; for there is no limit to their extent.[3]

[1] X, 11
[2] X, 12 to 18
[3] X, 19

I am the *Atman*, O Gudakesha, seated in the heart of every being; I am the beginning, the middle and the end of all beings.

Of the *Adityas* I am Vishnu; of luminaries, the radiant Sun; of *Maruts* I am *Marichi*; of constellations, the moon.

Of the Vedas I am the *Sama* Veda; of the gods, Indra; of the senses I am the mind; of beings I am the consciousness.

Of *Rudras* I am Shankara; of *Yakshas* and *Rakshasas* Kubera; of *Vasus* I am the Fire; of mountains Meru.

Of priests, O Partha, know Me to be the chief Brihaspati; of army captains I am Kartikeya; and of waters, the ocean.

Of the great seers I am Bhrigu; of words I am the one syllable '*AUM*', of sacrifices I am the *Japa* sacrifice; of things immovable, the Himalayas.

Of all trees I am Ashvattha; of the divine seers, Narada; of the heavenly choir I am Chitraratha; of the perfected I am Kapila the ascetic.

Of horses, know Me to be Uchchaihshravas born with *Amrita*; of mighty elephants I am Airavata; of men, the monarch.

Of weapons I am *Vajra*; of cows, *Kamadhenu*; I am Kandarpa, the god of generation; of serpents I am Vasuki.

Of cobras I am Ananta; of water-dwellers I am Varuna; of the manes I am Aryaman; and of the chastisers, Yama.

Of demons I am Prahlada; of reckoners, the Time; of beasts I am the lion; and of birds, Garuda.

Of cleansing agents I am the Wind; of wielders of weapons, Rama; of fishes I am the crocodile; of rivers, the Ganges.

Of creations I am the beginning, end and middle, O Arjuna; of sciences, the science of spiritual knowledge; of debaters, the right argument.

Of letters, the letter A; of compounds I am the *dvandva*; I am the imperishable Time; I am the creator to be seen everywhere.

All-seizing Death am I, as also the source of things to be; in feminine virtues I am *Kirti* (glory), *Shri* (beauty), *Vak* (speech), *Smriti* (memory), *Medha* (intelligence), *Dhriti* (constancy) and *Kshama* (forgiveness).

Of *Saman* hymns I am *Brihat Saman*; of metres, *Gayatri*; of months I am *Margashirsha*; of seasons, the spring.[1]

"I am *Brihat Saman* among *Saman* hymns and *Gayatri* among metres. Among the months, I am *Margashirsha* (when in old times the Aryans lived in the region of the North Pole, this was regar-

[1] X, 20 to 35

ded as the first month of the year and that is why it is mentioned here). Among the seasons I am Spring."

[146]

August 31, 1926

> Of deceivers I am the dice-play; of the splendid, the splendour; I am victory, I am resolution, I am the goodness of the good.[1]

"I am the gaming of those who indulge in gambling." (This is merely intended to point out that God exists not only in what is good in the world, but also in what is evil. Shri Krishna could also have said that He was the sin of the wicked. He could certainly have said that He was Ravana among the demons, for He let Ravana have his way and enjoy himself only as long as He chose. The author's intention is only to assert that God is omnipotent. God's creation contains both good and evil. By saying this, Shri Krishna gives us some freedom to choose between the two. To us who are confined in the prison of this body, he grants that freedom. He gives us the freedom to shake off our bonds. If a prisoner condemned to imprisonment for life is permitted a seemingly unimportant condition by fulfilling which he can be free, it will be a great thing for him, for he can secure his freedom through it. We are in the same condition, for the Lord has assured us that we can be what we wish to be.) I am the splendour of the splendid. I am victory, resolution and the goodness of the good.

> Of *Vrishnis* I am Vasudeva; of Pandavas Dhananjaya; of ascetics I am Vyasa; and of seers, Ushanas.
>
> I am the rod of those that punish; the strategy of those seeking victory; of secret things I am silence, and the knowledge of those that know.
>
> Whatever is the seed of every being, O Arjuna, that am I; there is nothing, whether moving or fixed, that can be without Me.
>
> There is no end to my divine manifestations; what extent of them I have told thee now is only by way of illustration.
>
> Whatever is glorious, beautiful and mighty know thou that all such has issued from a fragment of My splendour.
>
> But why needst thou to learn this at great length, O Arjuna? With but a part of Myself I stand upholding this universe.[2]

[1] X, 36
[2] X, 37 to 42

If we have an idea of the infinite powers of the Lord, we shall become humble. We will not then follow the example of Narad who once felt proud of the one power which he possessed. The Lord has said that even being proud is His privilege. The substance of all that He has said is that we should learn to be the humblest of the humble. Knowing that there is no limit to the power of God, we should submit to violence if anyone attacks us, without offering violence in return. If we attempt to resist him with violence, God will humble our pride, for there has been no demon, from Ravana downwards, whom the Lord has not destroyed.

[147]

Chapter XI

September 1, 1926

This is regarded as an important chapter. The *Gita* is a poem with a profound meaning, and the eleventh Chapter is the most poetic of all. If we wish to learn true *bhakti*, we should know this Chapter by heart. If we do so, we shall feel, when reciting it, that we are bathing in a sea of *bhakti*.

> Out of Thy grace towards me, Thou hast told me the supreme mystery revealing the knowledge of the Supreme; it has banished my delusion.
>
> Of the origin and destruction of beings I have heard from Thee in full detail, as also of Thy imperishable majesty, O Kamalapatraksha!
>
> Thou art indeed just as Thou hast described Thyself, Parameshvara! I do crave to behold now that form of Thine as Ishvara.
>
> If, Lord, Thou thinkest it possible for me to bear the sight, reveal to me, O Yogeshvara, Thy imperishable form.

[148]

September 2, 1926

> Behold, O Partha, my forms divine in their hundreds and thousands, infinitely diverse, infinitely various in colour and aspect.
>
> Behold the *Adityas*, the *Vasus*, the *Rudras*, the two *Ashwins*, and the *Maruts*; behold, O Bharata, numerous marvels never revealed before.
>
> Behold today, O Gudakesha, in my body, the whole universe, moving, and unmoving, all in one, and whatever else thou cravest to see.[1]

"See the *Adityas*," Shri Krishna says, "the *Vasus*, the *Rudras*, the *Ashwins* and the *Maruts*, all together. See the entire world, animate and inanimate, all as one reality."

[1] XI, 1 to 7

This cosmic form includes, good and evil, Hindus and Muslims, believers and atheists, all.

"You may also see," Shri Krishna adds, "anything else you wish to see."

> But thou canst not see Me with these thine own eyes. I give thee the eye divine; behold My sovereign power!
>
> With these words, O King, the great Lord of Yoga, Hari, then revealed to Partha His supreme form as Ishvara.[1]

[149]

September 3, 1926

The teaching of the *Gita* was not meant to be merely preserved in a book; it was meant to be translated into action. Mahadev and Punjabhai take notes of what I speak, but had we arranged recording on a gramophone plate, every word could have been taken down. Could we have said, then, that the gramophone machine had understood the *Gita*? It is an inanimate object. Similarly, what will this knowledge profit us if we merely take down notes and do not put the teaching into practice? We should, therefore, serve the people among whom we live, and help our elders in their domestic chores. Why should Ba find it necessary to send for Kusum to help her? Why should she request Ramachandra, who is a guest here just for a few days, to help her wash the kitchen? Why should she, who is at present under a vow of eating only once a day, not get some time for rest? If you give her no help, you are like the gramophone in our example.

> With many mouths, and many eyes, many wondrous aspects, many divine ornaments, and many brandished weapons divine;
>
> Wearing divine garlands and vestments, anointed with divine perfumes, it was the form of God, all marvellous, infinite, seen everywhere.
>
> Were the splendour of a thousand suns to shoot forth all at once in the sky that might perchance resemble the splendour of that Mighty One.
>
> Then did Pandava see the whole universe in its manifold divisions gathered as one in the body of that God of gods.[2]

The whole universe, despite its manifold divisions, is gathered there in Him (Like a tree and its leaves. The tree is like the cosmic form of the Lord, the root and the leaves being one. The root contains the whole world of the tree, and the leaves represent that world divided into many forms.). Arjuna saw thus the [cosmic] form of the God of gods.

[1] XI, 8 & 9
[2] XI, 10 to 13

> Then Dhananjaya, wonderstruck and thrilled in every fibre of his being, bowed low his head before the Lord, addressing Him thus with folded hands:[1]

[150]

September 4, 1926

> Within Thy form, O Lord, I see all the gods and the divers multitudes of beings, the Lord Brahma on his lotus-throne and all the seers and the serpents divine.
>
> With many arms and bellies, mouths and eyes, I see Thy infinite form everywhere. Neither Thy end, nor middle, nor beginning do I see, O Lord of the Universe, Universal-formed![2]

(On the one hand, Arjuna says that Shri Krishna has a definite form and, on the other, he says that He is formless. In other words, His form is so vast that in truth He is formless.)

> With crown and mace and disc, a mass of effulgence, gleaming everywhere I see Thee, so dazzling to the sight, bright with the splendour of the fiery sun blazing from all sides,—incomprehensible.[3]

You bear crown, mace and disc. You are a mass of radiance which glows at all places.

(The sun gives some faint idea of the Lord's light, but it is no more than a dim point of light in comparison with the Lord's.) Thou art as lustrous as fire and the sun. Thou art dazzling to the sight because of thy immeasurable effulgence.

> Thou art the Supreme Imperishable worthy to be known; Thou art the final resting-place of this universe; Thou art the changeless guardian of the Eternal Dharma; Thou art, I believe, the Everlasting Being.[4]

Cannot we say that the rains yesterday were an aspect of this infinite cosmic form of God? He has placed the sun at such a great distance from us; what would have been our condition if it had been a little nearer? Can we, then, imagine Arjuna's condition with Shri Krishna standing near him, Krishna glowing with the light of a thousand suns?

> Thou hast no beginning, middle nor end; infinite is Thy might; arms innumerable; for eyes, the sun and the moon; Thy mouth a blazing fire, overpowering the universe with Thy radiance.[5]

[1] XI, 14
[2] XI, 15 & 16
[3] XI, 17
[4] XI, 18
[5] XI, 19

> By Thee alone are filled the spaces between heaven and earth and all the quarters; at the sight of this Thy wondrous terrible form, the three worlds are sore oppressed, O Mahatman![1]

(This Sabarmati, too, is an aspect of the infinite power of God. If the warning received yesterday comes true and there is a heavy flood, we would simply shake with fear.)

> Here, too, the multitudes of gods are seen to enter Thee; some awestruck praise Thee with folded arms; the hosts of great seers and *siddhas*, 'All Hail' on their lips, hymn Thee with songs of praise.[2]

[151]

September 5, 1926

One feels as though these verses were specially written for us.

We had information from the Collector that there would be a heavy flood in the Sabarmati. Naturally, I was agitated in my heart, not knowing what to do. But I reminded myself of the verses which I daily recite before the women: "*Govind, Dwarkavasin*" and so on. Krishna would be welcome if he flew to our help on His Garuda. Otherwise, if all these things were carried away in the flood, our honour would be saved. Let anyone who survives to witness the destruction live on faithful to our vows.

I had advised them to construct the loom-shed as far away as the road. "The weak will pretend to be good," as the saying goes, and so we have nothing to do but wait in patience. If the authorities of the [Sabarmati] jail invite us to take shelter in it, I will ask them if they have invited the people of Vadaj too. I will tell them that they should offer shelter to all others before they invite us.

You should eat, not to gratify your palate, but to keep yourselves alive to keep up your strength. As I sit here in peace, we heard the blowing of the mill whistles, and so I remarked, "No one can escape work." It is the same story: "We seek refuge with the Lord who is the ship that ferries us across this sea of creation." Shall we never be free from this affliction [of work]? When afflicted with other diseases, we may keep repeating the Lord's name, or the *dwadash mantra* or any other prayer which will bring us peace of mind. Which is a greater storm, the inward storm in the heart or this outward storm of work? Is this latter storm more of an affliction than that our eyes and ears should disobey us and

[1] XI, 20
[2] XI, 21

attend to things which they ought to shun? Every inmate of the Ashram has wings. I should like even the women to have them. Anyone who wishes to leave is certainly free to do so, either by train or to the city on the other side. As the headman of a village, this is all I can tell you. If you can think of anything better, please do.

The *Rudras*, *Adityas*, *Vasus*, *Sadhyas*, all the gods, the twin *Ashwins*, *Maruts*, Manes, the hosts of *Gandharvas*, *Yakshas*, *Asuras* and *Siddhas*—all gaze on Thee in wonderment.

At the sight of Thy mighty form, O Mahabahu, many-mouthed, with eyes, arms, thighs and feet innumerable, with many vast bellies, terrible with many jaws, the worlds feel fearfully oppressed, and so do I.

For as I behold Thee touching the sky, glowing, numerous-hued with gaping mouths and wide resplendent eyes, I feel oppressed in my innermost being; no peace nor quiet I find, O Vishnu!

And as I see Thy mouths with fearful jaws, resembling the Fire of Doom, I lose all sense of direction, and find no relief. Be gracious, O Devesha, O Jagannivasa!

All the sons of Dhritarashtra, and with them the crowd of kings, Bhishma, Drona, and that Karna too, as also our chief warriors—

Are hastening into the fearful jaws of Thy terrible mouths. Some, indeed, caught between Thy teeth are seen, their heads being crushed to atoms.

As rivers in their numerous torrents run headlong to the sea, even so the heroes of the world of men rush into Thy flaming mouths.

As moths, fast-flying, plunge into blazing fire straight to their doom, even so these rush headlong into Thy mouths, to their destruction.

Devouring all these from all sides, Thou lappest them with Thy flaming tongues; Thy fierce rays blaze forth, filling the whole universe with their lustre.

Tell me, Lord, who Thou art so dread of form! Hail to Thee, O Devavara! Be gracious! I desire to know Thee, Primal Lord; for I comprehend not what Thou dost.[1]

[152]

September 7, 1926

Doom am I, full-ripe, dealing death to the worlds, engaged in devouring mankind. Even without thy slaying them, not one of the warriors, ranged for battle against thee, shall survive.[2]

[1] XI, 22 to 31
[2] XI, 32

> Therefore, do thou arise, and win renown! Defeat thy foes and enjoy a thriving kingdom. By Me have these already been destroyed; be thou no more than an instrument, O Savyasachin![1]

"Savyasachin" means one who can use a bow with the left hand, that is, with either hand.

> Drona, Bhishma, Jayadratha and Karna, as also the other warrior chiefs—already slain by Me—slay thou! Be not dismayed! Fight! Victory is thine over thy foes in the field.
>
> Hearing this word of Keshava, crown-wearer Arjuna folded his hands, and trembling made obeisance. Bowing and all hesitant, in faltering accents, he proceeded to address Krishna once more.
>
> Right proper it is, O Hrishikesha, that Thy praise should stir the world to gladness and tender emotion; the *Rakshasas* in fear fly to every quarter and all the hosts of *Siddhas* do reverent homage.[2]

"And why should they not bow to you? You are the destroyer of the demons." The demons are our enemies, external and internal. What even if the river should swallow us and destroy us? How much more fearful is the flood inside us? Who will destroy the demons inside? And so Arjuna said:

> And why should they not bow down to Thee, O Mahatman? Thou art the First Creator, greater even than Brahma. O Ananta, O Devesha, O Jagannivasa, Thou art the Imperishable, Being, not-Being, and That which transcends even these.
>
> Thou art the Primal God, the Ancient Being; Thou art the final resting-place of this Universe; Thou art the Knower, the 'to-be-known', the supreme Abode; by Thee, O myriad-formed, is the Universe pervaded.
>
> Thou art *Vayu, Yama, Agni, Varuna, Shashanka, Prajapati,* and *Prapitamaha*! All hail to Thee, a thousand times all hail! Again and yet again all hail to Thee![3]

[153]

September 8, 1926

There was once a woman in Madras who was a devotee of the Lord. She used to worship Him with her back towards the idol. A learned man rebuked her for doing so, but she cited this

[1] XI, 33
[2] XI, 34 to 36
[3] XI, 37 to 39

verse in reply, and the learned pundit was speechless. If all space is pervaded by God, when we find his eyes, ears and noses on all sides, why should we sit facing in a particular direction to worship Him?

All hail to Thee from before and behind! All hail to Thee from every side, O All; Thy prowess is infinite, Thy might is measureless! Thou holdest all; therefore Thou art all.

If ever in carelessness, thinking of Thee as comrade, I addressed Thee saying, 'O Krishna!', 'O Yadava!' not knowing Thy greatness, in negligence or in affection.

If ever I have been rude to Thee in jest, whilst at play, at rest-time, or at meals, whilst alone or in company, O Achuta, forgive Thou my fault— I beg of Thee, O Incomprehensible one!

Thou art Father of this world, of the moving and the un-moving; Thou art its adored, its worthiest, Master; there is none equal to Thee; how then any greater than Thee? Thy power is matchless in the three worlds.

Therefore, I prostrate myself before Thee, and beseech Thy grace, O Lord Adorable! As father with son, as comrade with comrade, so shouldst Thou bear, beloved Lord, with me, Thy loved one.

I am filled with joy to see what never was seen before, and yet my heart is oppressed with fear. Show me that original form of Thine, O Lord! Be gracious, Devesha, O Jagannivasa!

I crave to see Thee even as Thou wast, with crown, with mace, disc in hand; wear Thou, once more, that four-armed form, O thousand-armed Vishvamurti!

It is to favour thee, O Arjuna, that I have revealed to thee, by My own unique power, this My Form Supreme, Resplendent, Universal, Infinite, Primal—which none save thee has ever seen.

Not by the study of the Vedas, not by sacrifice, not by the study of other scriptures, not by gifts, nor yet by performance of rites or of fierce austerities can I, in such a form, be seen by anyone save thee in the world of men, O Kurupravira!

Be thou neither oppressed nor bewildered to look on this awful form of Mine. Banish thy fear, ease thy mind, and lo! behold Me once again as I was.[1]

[1] XI, 40 to 49

[154]

September 9, 1926

Beholding again Thy benign human form I am come to myself and am once more in my normal state.

Very hard to behold is that Form of Mine which thou hast seen; even the gods always yearn to see it.

Not by the Vedas, not by penance, nor by gifts, nor yet by sacrifice, can any behold Me in the Form that thou hast seen.

But by single-minded devotion, O Arjuna, I may in this Form be known and seen, and truly entered into, O Parantapa![1]

First we should know the Lord, then see Him and then merge into Him. We may tell Him: "You may eat me up, I will not resist if You do. I am Yours, and I want to be one with You. What harm can it do even if You eat me up?" Telling us that He can grind us into paste with his teeth and throw it out, He tells us that we can know Him through *bhakti*. We can pass His test only through faith. When we know that everything takes place through Him and that we live and die as He wills, how can we be affected by anything?

He alone comes to Me, O Pandava, who does My work, who has made Me his goal, who is My devotee, who has renounced attachment, who has ill will towards none.[2]

The Lord has given the whole substance of Chapter XI in this last verse. "He who works for Me is ever devoted to Me, who is attached to nothing and bears ill will to none—not even to a person who may have committed a heinous sin—but ever blesses him instead,—such a person comes to Me."

[155][3]

Chapter XII

September 10, 1926

To love God means to be free from attachment to any work. We should of course do work, but without egotistic attachment to it, simply for the love of God. A lustful man forgets his love for parents and children when seeking gratification of his lust and abandons himself blindly to it. This also is a form of non-attachment. But the cause is a filthy one, whereas love for God is good.

[1] XI, 51 to 54
[2] XI, 55
[3] The notes of this discourse were not taken by Mahadev Desai.

And now for the meaning of the verse [with which we began].

> Of the devotees who thus worship Thee, incessantly attached, and those who worship the Imperishable Unmanifest, which are the better yogis?[1]

The Lord replies:

> Those I regard as the best yogis who, riveting their minds on Me, ever attached, worship Me, with the highest faith.
>
> But those who worship the Imperishable, the Indefinable, the Unmanifest, the Omnipresent, the Unthinkable, the Rock-seated, the Immovable, the Unchanging,
>
> Keeping the whole host of senses in complete control, looking on all with an impartial eye, engrossed in the welfare of all beings—these come indeed to Me.[2]

[156][3]

September 11, 1926

> Greater is the travail of those whose mind is fixed on the Unmanifest; for it is hard for embodied mortals to gain the Unmanifest Goal.[4]

Those who have fixed their minds on the Unmanifest, that is, who worship the formless *Brahman*, experience greater difficulty in their effort, for it is extremely difficult for us, embodied souls, to know the unmanifest state.

It is very difficult to meditate on *shunya.* The moment we attribute a single quality to God, we cease to worship the Unmanifest. We must all, nevertheless, realize that beyond the Personal God there is a Formless Essence which our reason cannot comprehend. The consummation of *bhakti* lies in the *bhakta* merging in God, so that ultimately nothing but One Formless God remains. Since, however, it is easier to reach this state through the worship of the Personal God, the Lord says that the other path of seeking the Formless Essence directly is difficult to follow.

> But those who casting all their actions on Me, making Me their all in all, worship Me with the meditation of undivided devotion,
>
> Of such, whose thoughts are centred on Me, O Partha, I become ere long the Deliverer from the ocean of this world of death.[5]

[1] XII, 1
[2] XII, 2 to 4
[3] The notes of this discourse were not taken by Mahadev Desai.
[4] XII, 5
[5] XII, 6 & 7

[157]

September 12, 1926

The verse beginning with *kleshodhikatarastesham*[1] has given me great light; for it says that devotion to the Unmanifest is difficult to cultivate and that it is a harder path to follow. The reason given is very significant. If one retires to a forest and meditates on God, one can certainly realize Him. Likewise, one who serves as an accountant or clerk or manager in a firm can also do that. Both may be in the same state of mind and can, therefore, reach the same goal.

If we are sincere in our devotion to the cause of the spinning-wheel movement, the country is bound to embrace it in course of time. This faith is an illustration of the path which human beings should adopt, this is the path of *bhakti*, of the worship of a Personal God, for the spinning-wheel is visible to us and we see power in it. If, however, we worship the spinning-wheel for itself, our worship will be like the worship of the Unmanifest *Brahman*. It will be so, that is, if we merely worship the spinning-wheel without spinning on it. In my view, however, even if a time comes when we decide to withdraw into complete silence, it will not mean that we have abandoned the spinning-wheel or forsaken our aspiration for the *Brahman*. If indeed we ever retire to some high peak on the Himalayas, it will not be because we shall have lost interest in the spinning-wheel or been disillusioned with the people. To retire with such a motive will be no way of worshipping the Unmanifest. Of course, we shall benefit in some way even if we do so. If a man decides out of disgust to observe *brahmacharya* or to give up immorality, he will certainly benefit. But his action will not have been prompted by true knowledge. Similarly, this idea of retirement is not meant for anyone who is disgusted with the spinning-wheel or with the people.

If a person, however, feels that there is an Essence beyond this universe of objects with name and form and that he must know it, and if he leaves this world and withdraws into solitude with that aim, that also is a legitimate path. But it is a difficult one even if one is sincere in one's aspiration to cultivate *bhakti* or the Unmanifest. The idea that the *Brahman* is real and that the visible universe is illusory is simply beyond the capacity of our reason to comprehend. How difficult it must be, then, to live according to it? It is only when our body is completely transform-

[1] XII, 5

ed into an armour that nothing will pierce it. The Shastras narrate the stories of Prahlad[1] and Sudhanva[2]. As these stories show, it is possible, even while one is physically alive, to live as if one had renounced one's body. It is extremely difficult for a man to cultivate such a state of mind and live for ever absorbed in the *atman*. All but one in a crore live in illusion and error. They will not break away from their ignorant attachment and will have to be born again in this world.

The path of karma is the easiest to follow. The path of reason can lead one into great error. The path along which we have the least danger of falling into error is the one described in the verse beginning with *nehabhikramanashosti*[3]. Neither Christians nor Muslims, nor certainly Hindus, have risen above the worship of the Personal God. There is a book by Shibli[4] in which he has discussed the question whether or not God has a body. Even a person who aspires to cultivate devotion exclusively for the Unmanifest worships some visible symbol. We can of course understand with our intellect the idea that the body is unconnected with the *atman*. To say that one can attain *moksha* while physically alive only means that, after death, one will not have to be born again. Has anyone ever been able to say what his state after death will be? The spiritualists and Theosophists are not correct, in my view, about what they say concerning spirits, in the sense that no one has been able to know and tell the whole truth.

For this reason, Shri Krishna told Arjuna that it would be better for him to take no interest in the problem at all. "Silence is golden in this matter," he says. "Don't you see, you dear simpleton, that I Myself have taken on a human body? And you ask Me, of all persons, whether worship of the Unmanifest is better, or that of the Personal God. You had better stop asking such questions and do as I tell you. Free yourself from all thoughts of violence and act towards all creatures with equal love and regard." If we understand this truth, we would escape many problems. We should not mind if, because we worship the Personal God, we

[1] A devotee of God who was persecuted by Hiranyakashipu, his unbelieving father

[2] Son of king Hansadhwaj in the *Mahabharata*, who defying his parents and adhering to truth and God, smilingly threw himself into a cauldron of boiling oil

[3] II, 40

[4] Presumably, *Life of the Prophet* by Maulana Shibli

are called idolaters and criticized for being so. And, therefore, proceeding, Shri Krishna says:

> On Me set thy mind, on Me rest thy conviction; thus without doubt shalt thou remain only in Me hereafter.
>
> If thou canst not set thy mind steadily on Me, then by the method of constant practice seek to win Me, O Dhananjaya.[1]

What is the difference between *abhyasayoga* and meditating on God? I think the former means listening to readings from holy books, reflecting on them and letting the mind dwell on their teachings. It means associating ourselves with men who are engaged in doing these things and listening to prayer songs and group devotions, for every little offering we make, leaf, flower, fruit or water, ultimately reaches God.

[158][2]

September 14, 1926

> If thou art also unequal to this method of constant practice, concentrate on service for Me; even thus serving Me thou shalt attain perfection.
>
> If thou art unable even to do this, then dedicating all to Me, with mind controlled, abandon the fruit of action.[3]

"Do not," Shri Krishna says, "be impatient to reap the fruit of your efforts."

> Better is knowledge than practice, better than knowledge is concentration, better than concentration is renunciation of the fruit of all action, from which directly issues peace.[4]

Here *jnana* does not mean mere learning, but it means genuine experience of truth in however limited a measure. Meditation, which means concentration of the mind [on God], is better than such *jnana*, but renunciation of the fruit of action is said to be better even than such meditation. Shri Krishna says this because a person practising meditation may possibly be deceiving himself. Moreover, *jnana* does not mean ultimate self-realization. *Jnana* and meditation are compared here in their restricted meanings and one is described as better than the other. Renunciation of the fruits of action is mentioned last, but in truth it should be the

[1] XII, 8 & 9
[2] The notes of this discourse were taken by Punjabhai.
[3] XII, 10 & 11
[4] XII, 12

first step. One who practises it becomes free from attachment to the ego.

Shri Krishna then proceeds to describe the characteristics of a man of this type.

> Who has ill will towards none, who is friendly and compassionate, who has shed all thought of 'mine' or 'I', who regards pain and pleasure alike, who is long-suffering;[1]

Friendship can exist only between equals, but one should feel compassion towards all. We cannot throw a cricket bat at a dog to hit it. How would we feel if our parents or teachers did that to us? Even if we are obedient sons of our parents, how would we feel towards them if they threw a bat at us to hit us? We shall not discuss here what our duty towards a dog is. It is certain, however, that it is not right for us to hit one. Forgiveness lies in not being angry even with a dog which may have bitten us. Tit for tat is a wrong principle. It is certainly not based on forgiveness. What can we gain by being wicked with the wicked? The good of both lies only in our showing love and compassion even for such persons.

We should understand the difference between selflessness and freedom from egotism. The first means not making a distinction between ourselves and others. It describes a person who regards the entire world as his family. The second term describes a person who believes that it is not he who has done a particular thing, that it is God who has done it.

[159]

September 15, 1926

> Who is ever content, gifted with yoga, self-restrained, of firm conviction, who has dedicated his mind and reason to Me—that devotee (*bhakta*) of Mine is dear to Me.
>
> Who gives no trouble to the world, to whom the world causes no trouble, who is free from exultation, resentment, fear and vexation, — that man is dear to Me.[2]

The meaning of this verse is already contained in the term *adweshta*[3].

[1] XII, 13
[2] XII, 14 & 15
[3] In XII, 13

> Who expects naught, who is pure, resourceful, unconcerned, untroubled, who indulges in no undertakings,— that devotee of Mine is dear to Me.[1]

The whole of Chapter XII describes the characteristics of a *bhakta*. If we compare the verses[2] which describe a *sthitaprajna* with these, we shall find them similar.

On whom does a *bhakta* of God rely except on Him? *Shuchi* means a person who is pure both in body and mind. *Daksha* means a person who does everything which he undertakes, wholly in a spirit of dedication to God. *Udasin* means one who remains unaffected even if all his many plans come to nothing. One who is a *sarvarambhaparityagi* will not go in search of work, work will come seeking him. God Himself will appoint his work and call him to it. Such a person, knowing that God shoulders the burdens of us all, leaves everything to Him. A slave need not go looking for work.

> Who rejoices not, neither frets nor grieves, who covets not, who abandons both good and ill—that devotee of Mine is dear to Me.
>
> Who is same to foe and friend, who regards alike respect and disrespect, cold and heat, pleasure and pain, who is free from attachment;
>
> Who weighs in equal scale blame and praise, who is silent, content with whatever his lot, who owns no home, who is of steady mind,— that devotee of Mine is dear to Me.[3]

"He does not get elated, though an emperor may bow to him," so sang Raychandbhai.

> They who follow this essence of dharma, as I have told it, with faith, keeping Me as their goal,—those devotees are exceedingly dear to Me.[4]

All of us have our appointed tasks, as Brahmins or Kshatriyas, Vaisyas or Sudras. Anyone who does his work without hope of reward and in a disinterested spirit is a *bhakta* of God. The Second Chapter contains verses describing a *sthitaprajna*. They describe the state of mind of a yogi living absorbed in a mystic world. This Chapter XII describes, in our ordinary language, the state of mind of a *bhakta*.

[1] XII, 16
[2] In II, 55 to 72
[3] XII, 17 to 19
[4] XII, 20

[160]

Chapter XIII

September 16, 1926

From Chapter XIII begins a new subject. It discusses the body and its nature.

> This body, O Kaunteya, is called the Field; he who knows it is called the knower of the Field by those who know.[1]

Pandavas and Kauravas, that is, divine and demoniacal impulses, were fighting in this body, and God was watching the fight from a distance. Please do not believe that this is the history of a battle which took place on a little field near Hastinapur; the war is still going on. This is the verse we should keep in mind in order to understand the meaning of the phrase *dharmakshetra.*

> And understand Me to be, O Bharata, the knower of the Field in all the Fields; and the knowledge of the Field and the knower of the Field, I hold, is true knowledge.[2]

Our bodily life will have been lived to some purpose if it is spent in thinking which of these two we should serve and which we should go to for refuge.

[161]

September 17, 1926

> What that Field is, what its nature, what its modifications, and whence is what, as also who He is, and what His power—hear this briefly from Me.
>
> This subject has been sung by seers distinctly and in various ways, in different hymns as also in aphoristic texts about *Brahman* well reasoned and unequivocal.[3]

This theme has been expounded analytically by seers in manifold ways in various hymns. It has been discussed in the *Brahmasutras*[4] with steps logically arranged and clearly explaining the connection between cause and effect; and every word has been weighed so that not a syllable could be altered.

[1] XIII, 1
[2] XIII, 2
[3] XIII, 3 & 4
[4] Aphorisms on Vedanta philosophy by Badarayana

The great elements, Individuation, Reason, the Unmanifest, the ten senses, and the one (mind), and the five spheres of the senses;

Desire, dislike, pleasure, pain, association, consciousness, cohesion—this, in sum, is what is called the Field with its modifications.[1]

The five *mahabhutas*, *ahamkar*, which sustains those *bhutas*, *buddhi*, the *avyakta* (*prakriti*), the ten senses, the mind and the objects of the five senses, so also desire, ill will, happiness, misery, association, consciousness, cohesion—this, in brief, is the Field with its modifications.

Sanghat means the power of the different elements in the body to co-operate with one another. *Dhriti* does not mean the abstract virtue of patience, but the property of the atoms in physical bodies to cohere. This property is made possible by *ahamkar*, which is latent in the unmanifest *prakriti*.

Freedom from pride and pretentiousness, non-violence, forgiveness, uprightness, service of the Master, purity, steadfastness, self-restraint;

Aversion from sense-objects, absence of conceit, realization of the painfulness and evil of birth, death, age and disease;

Absence of attachment, refusal to be wrapped up in one's children, wife, home and family, even-mindedness whether good or ill befall;

Unwavering and all-exclusive devotion to Me, resort to secluded spots, distaste for the haunts of men;

Settled conviction of the nature of the *atman*, perception of the goal of the knowledge of Truth,—

All this is declared to be knowledge and the reverse of it is ignorance.[2]

Shauch means outer and inner purity. It can be achieved by repeating Ramanama. This purity can be properly preserved only if the heart is constantly kept clean by repeating Ramanama. Every morning, we should weep with tears streaming from our eyes and ask ourselves why we did not remember to start repeating Ramanama, and why we, of all people, had a bad dream.

Absence of interest in the objects of senses means the awareness that certain things ought to be treated as forbidden by us, that they ought to be unacceptable to us.

The attributes described include the realization of the evils of birth and death, of old age, disease and suffering. One who realizes this starts with the thought: "I am sin." Why is it, we should ask ourselves, that we are afflicted with all manner of diseases? We ought to learn to cultivate equanimity of mind towards

[1] XIII, 5 & 6
[2] XIII, 7 to 11

everything which may happen, good and evil. What does living in solitude mean? Retiring into a cave to live there alone by oneself? Our effort will have been worthwhile only if we can feel solitude even in the midst of a huge crowd. To live in solitude means to sit in a spot meditating on one single thought.

[162]

September 18, 1926

> I will (now) expound to thee that which is to be known and knowing which one enjoys immortality; it is the supreme *Brahman* which has no beginning, which is called neither Being nor non-Being.[1]

Why does Shri Krishna say this, when they say that the *Brahman* is *sachchidananda* and that it alone is real? What he means to say is that *Brahman* does not mean being, the contrary of non-being. When we use the word *sat* in connection with the *Brahman*, its meaning transcends the two opposites and it signifies neither being nor non-being. It is, so to say, a neutral term. God cannot be described as evil, nor as good. He is above either. The reality which is God is beyond the three categories of time.

> Everywhere having hands and feet, everywhere having eyes, heads, mouths, everywhere having ears, It abides embracing everything in the universe.
>
> Seeming to possess the functions of the senses, It is devoid of all the senses; It touches naught, upholds all; having no *gunas*, It experiences *gunas*.
>
> Without all beings, yet within; immovable yet moving; so subtle that It cannot be perceived; so far and yet so near It is.
>
> Undivided, It seems to subsist divided in all beings; this *Brahman*—That which is to be known is the Sustainer of all, yet It is their Devourer and Creator.[2]

Though indivisible He seems to be there divided in all beings. He is worth knowing. He sustains all the creatures. He is their destroyer and yet the Creator of them all.

[163]

September 21, 1926

All contrary qualities are attributed to God because we cannot free our minds from dualities.

[1] XIII, 12
[2] XIII, 13 to 16

> Light of all lights, It is said to be beyond darkness; It is knowledge, the object of knowledge, to be gained only by knowledge; It is seated in the hearts of all.[1]

He is the Superlight. He is beyond darkness, that is, He is self-effulgent. . . .

He is Himself Knowledge. He is also the object of Knowledge to be realized only by Knowledge.

> Thus have I expounded in brief the Field, Knowledge and That which is to be known; My devotee, when he knows this, is worthy to become one with Me.
>
> Know that *prakriti* and *purusha* are both without beginning; know that all the modifications and *gunas* are born of *prakriti*.
>
> *Prakriti* is described as the cause in the creation of effects from causes; *purusha* is described as the cause of the experiencing of pleasure and pain.[2]

Karya (anything done under compulsion of desires) and *karan* (the desires)—*prakriti* is the cause of their creation. *Purusha* is the cause of the experience of happiness and misery.

God is described as having two aspects. Under one aspect we should know Him as *prakriti* and under the other as *purusha*. The world is ever changing, and is therefore *maya*. The *purusha* is not transient, for He is the witness.

> For the *purusha*, residing in *prakriti*, experiences the *gunas* born of *prakriti*; attachment to these *gunas* is the cause of his birth in good or evil wombs.[3]

[164]

September 22, 1926

It is enough if we look upon God as a king and if all of us become His slaves, that is, disclaim any right over our bodies.

> What is called in this body the Witness, the Assentor, the Sustainer, the Experiencer, the Great Lord and also the Supreme *Atman*, is the Supreme Being.[4]

The *purusha* dwelling in this body is *para*, that is, beyond *maya* but He witnesses and gives consent. He is the *bharta* who sustains

[1] XIII, 17
[2] XIII, 18 to 20
[3] XIII, 21
[4] XIII, 22

everything, and also the Enjoyer. He is, moreover, the God of gods and is described as *Paramatman.*

Fire has the power of burning, but it can burn nothing without God's consent.

> He who thus knows *purusha* and *prakriti* with its *gunas*, is not born again, no matter how he live and move.[1]

If anyone claims that he is a *bhakta* of God and that, therefore, the sins he may commit are committed by God, he is wrong. But it would be right if the world said of him that he was a man of God and that everything he did was done through him by God. If anyone asks us whether we have attained spiritual knowledge, our reply should be: "Only God knows; I do not know." Our reason may be carried away by pride at any time and become evil, but the man who has attained to perfect knowledge will never be misguided by his reason. Our belief is that Rama and Krishna were incarnations of God. How can we be sure that King Rama was not a hypocrite and his rule was not evil? How do we know that Krishna was not the most wicked of men? But we have no right to indulge in such doubts. Whomsoever we worship, we should look upon as *Purna Purushottam*[2], that is best. If we believe that the people of India have faith in God, we should worship Him accordingly.

This verse does not sanction self-indulgence, but points out the great value of *bhakti.* Every karma has the effect of binding the soul, but one can become free from the bonds of karma by dedicating all one's karmas to God. Thus, anyone who has become free from the egotistic idea of being the author of anything and who recognizes every moment of his life the authority of the Dweller within will never commit sin. It is in egotism that sin has its source. There is no sin where there is no consciousness of the "I". This verse explains how to act so that one may commit no sin.

> Some through meditation behold the *atman* by themselves in their own self; others by *Sankhya* Yoga, and others by Karma Yoga.[3]

[1] XIII, 23

[2] Perfect incarnation of God; the description is generally limited to Shri Krishna

[3] XIII, 24

[165]

September 23, 1926

> Yet others, not knowing (Him) thus, worship (Him) having heard from others; they too pass beyond death, because of devoted adherence to what they have heard.[1]

If, having heard it explained that we shall be saved by dedicating all our work to God, we act in this spirit, then we can say that "he who . . . is not born again, no matter how he live and move" applies to us.

> Wherever something is born, animate or inanimate, know, thou Bharatarshabha, that it issues from the union of the Field and the knower of the Field.[2]

If we examine things separately, human beings, grains of dust, water, and so on, our conclusions [about their origin] will be different in each case. If, instead, we go to the very first cause, we shall no more think of objects having their distinctive forms and names. The Ravana who invests things with such charm that we willingly submit to its spell is far more dangerous than the other one of the story who killed people physically.

> Who sees abiding in all beings the same *Parameshvara*, imperishable in the perishable, he sees indeed.[3]

Though things are ever perishing, there is an indestructible element in everything which remains unaffected by any change, He alone sees who sees this.

> When he sees the same *Ishvara* abiding everywhere alike, he does not hurt himself by himself and hence he attains the highest goal.[4]

When he sees the same God abiding alike at all places he does not destroy the self by the self—*believes that, with the destruction of his body, he himself does not perish*—and consequently he achieves the highest status.

> Who sees that it is *prakriti* that performs all actions and thus (knows) that *atman* performs them not, he sees indeed.[5]

[1] XIII, 25
[2] XIII, 26
[3] XIII, 27
[4] XIII, 28
[5] XIII, 29

Who realizes that *prakriti* is the doer of all actions and sees that *atman* is not the doer—*though all things take place through God's maya, the Supreme Purusha involved in the process is not their author*—he alone who does so sees indeed.

> When he sees the diversity of beings as founded in unity and the whole expanse issuing therefrom, then he attains to *Brahman*.[1]

[166]

September 24, 1926

The *Gita* is a work intended to be a guide in life and we should be able to find in it support for all our actions in practical life. Not all can understand Dr. Tribhuvandas's book[2]; a vaid or a doctor can understand it more easily than laymen. We are in the same position as the latter [in relation to the *Gita*].

> This Imperishable Supreme *Atman*, O Kaunteya, though residing in the body, acts not and is not stained, for He has no beginning and no *gunas*.
>
> As the all-pervading ether, by reason of its subtlety, is not soiled, even so *atman* pervading every part of the body is not soiled.
>
> As the one Sun illumines the whole universe, even so the Master of the Field illumines the whole field.
>
> Those who, with the eyes of knowledge, thus perceive the distinction between the Field and the knower of the Field, and (the secret) of the release of beings from *prakriti*, they attain to the Supreme.[3]

Who knows the difference between the Field and the knower of the Field, and who knows how creatures may become free from the bonds of *prakriti* and *maya*, he realizes *moksha*.

[167]

September 25, 1926

In Chapter XIII Shri Krishna explained the nature of the Field and the knower of the Field, the means of understanding the nature of each and the different characteristics of such knowledge. The very first characteristic of knowledge is stated to be *amanitva*. Hence, however great one's knowledge, if one is proud

[1] XIII, 30

[2] *Ma-ne Shikhaman* (Advice to a Mother); *vide An Autobiography*, Pt. III, Ch. VI.

[3] XIII, 31 to 34

of that knowledge, one has read the *Gita* in vain. Where there is pride, there is no knowledge. A man who has knowledge is always free from pride and ostentation, is straightforward, serves his guru, is pure and steady, is a man of self-control and is free from egotism, and he does not suffer because of old age and disease. He is not attached to his son or wife or home, is filled with unswerving devotion for the Lord, lives in solitude, takes interest in spiritual studies and is devoted to the pursuit of philosophic truth.

[168]
Chapter XIV

September 26, 1926

We assemble here for studying the *Gita*, that is, for learning to follow its teaching in daily life. When we have a stomachache, we consult a book of home remedies and use the medicine suggested. The *Gita* is such a book of home remedies for us. We find in it medicines for our spiritual disease. If we want to make the *Gita* our *Kamadhenu*, we should make it our only source as far as possible. We may consult any number of books in the world in support of what we derive from the *Gita*, but should be satisfied with its sole authority. For this, we should have single-minded devotion to it. Such devotion should become spontaneous in us.

In a certain place, people used secretly to catch fish from the village pond. The village committee decided that, since in any case people caught fish,—did so in secret and were then afraid of being discovered—they should be required to take out licences for catching fish and some revenue raised by that means. This led to a dispute between two parties and the dispute was brought to me for settlement. I was afraid to give a decision, for people are not content to leave it to others to exercise discrimination in religious matters and faith on their behalf. If we are guided by some other person's ideas about dharma, we would be lost when he was dead. It would have been much better if those village people had decided to consult the *Gita* or the Veda or the Koran, instead of asking me. We should look upon any of these works as the means of solving our spiritual problems. But I was told afterwards in reply [to my suggestion] that one could find support from a book for any idea. The true meaning of *Kamadhuk*, however, is that it satisfies a pure wish only. If the *Gita* satisfies any wish, it would not be a *Kamadhuk* but would be aunt

Putana[1]. When the authors of the Shastras said that Sudras and others should not read Vedas and other [sacred] works, probably their reason was that the latter might interpret these works to justify their own wishes in particular matters. Anyone who approaches the Shastras without scrupulous regard for truth and non-violence will derive no benefit from them. It is possible to draw any number of evil ideas from the Bible, the Vedas, the Koran and other scriptures. I have come across persons who justified even murder on the authority of these works. The *Gita*, however, will serve as a safe guide to anyone who reads it with truth and non-violence as his guiding principles. Everyone should decide for himself with its help. The work will not be a *Kamadhenu* to any person who consults Kishorelal or me, and accepts our interpretation of it. Instead of borrowing faith from others, one should have one's own faith and come to decisions accordingly. If the intention is sincere and there is no desire for outward show, any error that the decision may contain will be forgiven. A person acting in this manner learns a lesson from his error and discovers the right path.

> Yet again will I expound the highest and the best of all knowledge, knowing which all the sages passed hence to the highest perfection.
>
> By having recourse to this knowledge they became one with Me. They need not come to birth even at a creation, nor do they suffer at a dissolution.[2]

[169]

September 28, 1926

> The great *prakriti* is for me the womb in which I deposit the germ; from it all beings come to birth, O Bharata.[3]

Among the very first sentences in the Bible is; God said let there be light, and there was light; [that is,] let there be a universe, and a universe came into existence. A potter has to mould clay into a shape on his wheel and then put the thing into fire to bake; God does not have to act in that manner. He is a magician, He simply puts the seed in his imagination—which is *prakriti*, Lakshmi or Mother Goddess of the world—and the universe comes into existence.

[1] A female demon who attempted to kill the infant Krishna by suckling him, but was herself sucked to death by the child

[2] XIV, 1 & 2

[3] XIV, 3

> Whatever forms take birth in the various species, the great *prakriti* is their Mother and I the seed-giving Father.[1]

I am the *mahadyoni* of all the forms which take birth in the various species, as also the source of the seed—

> *Sattva*, *rajas* and *tamas* are the *gunas* sprung from *prakriti*; it is they, O Mahabahu, that keep the imperishable Dweller bound to the body.
>
> Of these *sattva*, being stainless, is light-giving and healing; it binds with the bond of happiness and the bond of knowledge, O sinless one.[2]

Those persons whose food, recreation and thoughts are *sattvik* are healthy. A person who merely eats *sattvik* food but is not *sattvik* in his general way of living and in his thoughts should be looked upon as a diseased person.

> *Rajas*, know thou, is of the nature of passion, the source of thirst and attachment; it keeps man bound with the bond of action.[3]

Know that *rajas* is associated with desire. This may mean either that it has its source in, or that it is the cause of, desire. It creates attachment for cravings. It keeps the embodied one (i.e., living being) bound with the bond of karma.

> *Tamas*, know thou, is born of ignorance, of mortal man's delusion; it keeps him bound with heedlessness, sloth and slumber, O Bharata.[4]

Pramad means all kinds of unworthy wishes arising in us. *Alas* is *pramad* in a worse form still. *Nidra*, which is next, is the state of mind natural to those sunk in darkness. A man who is established in *samadhi* and is always awake feels no need to recline for rest or stretch his limbs for relaxation. A lethargic person would not get up even from a place which had caught fire. It is his slumber that is referred to as part of the meaning of *tamas*.

[170]

September 29, 1926

> *Sattva* attaches man to happiness, *rajas* to action, and *tamas*, shrouding knowledge, attaches him to heedlessness.[5]

Sattva leads to happiness and the quality of *rajas* to karma. (This is not karma as it is defined in the *Gita*; it is the karma

[1] XIV, 4
[2] XIV, 5 & 6
[3] XIV, 7
[4] XIV, 8
[5] XIV, 9

of him who is always doing something or other without pausing to think.) *Tamas* covers up knowledge and leads to *pramad*.

> *Sattva* prevails, O Bharata, having overcome *rajas* and *tamas; rajas*, when it has overpowered *sattva* and *tamas*; likewise *tamas* reigns when *sattva* and *rajas* are crushed.[1]

If a person overcomes *rajas* and *tamas*, he can create *sattva*. (All the three exist in us. We should make a special effort to cultivate that which we want to strengthen.) If we wish to strengthen *rajas*, we should subdue the other two and, if the quality of *tamas*, we should stop the activity of both *sattva* and *rajas*.

> When the light—knowledge—shines forth from all the gates of this body, then it may be known that the *sattva* thrives.
>
> Greed, activity, assumption of undertakings, restlessness, craving—these are in evidence when *rajas* flourishes, O Bharatarshabha.
>
> Ignorance, dullness, heedlessness, and delusion—these are in evidence when *tamas* reigns, O Kurunandana.
>
> If the embodied one meets his end whilst *sattva* prevails, then he attains to the spotless worlds of the knowers of the Highest.[2]

That is, he attains spiritual welfare. When he is nearing death, such a person refuses to take any medicine which may be offered, and says that he will have nothing but Ganga water. He who awaits death in peace in this manner is a *sattvik* man.

> If he dies during the reign within him of *rajas*, he is born among men attached to action; and if he dies in *tamas*, he is born in a species not endowed with reason.[3]

The world of beings of action means the human world. The dark world means the world of brutes.

> The fruit of *sattvik* action is said to be stainless merit; that of *rajas* is pain and that of *tamas* ignorance.
>
> Of *sattva*, knowledge is born, of *rajas*, greed; of *tamas*, heedlessness, delusion and ignorance.
>
> Those abiding in *sattva* rise upwards, those in *rajas* stay midway, those in *tamas* sink downwards.
>
> When the seer perceives no agent another than the *gunas* and knows Him who is above the *gunas*, he attains to My being.[4]

[1] XIV, 10
[2] XIV, 11 to 14
[3] XIV, 15
[4] XIV, 16 to 19

When the *atman* dwelling as witness in this body sees none else, but knows only Him who is above the *gunas*, that person comes to Me.

> When the embodied one transcends these three *gunas* which are born of his contact with the body, he is released from the pain of birth, death and age and attains *moksha*.[1]

[171]

September 30, 1926

Arjuna asks:

> What, O Lord, are the marks of him who has transcended the three *gunas*? How does he conduct himself? How does he transcend the three *gunas*?
>
> He, O Pandava, who does not disdain light, activity, and delusion when they come into being, nor desires them when they vanish.[2]

The Lord replies:

He who transcends the three *gunas*, does not suffer because of light or activity or darkness—that is, when any of them predominates over the others—and does not wish that it should prevail or subside.

This is one of the few difficult verses in the *Gita*. Should not one wish to have knowledge? In fact, in the *gayatri mantra* itself—in the best Vedic prayer—we pray to the shining Being to purify our intellect, to make it *sattvik*. We also pray: *tamaso ma jyotirgamaya*[3]. We aspire to be lifted from the darkness of attachment to illumination, from darkness to light. What, then, should we make of the statement in this verse? If we, living in the Ashram, did not cherish the aspiration which we do, we would fail in our aims. We must teach every child to say this prayer the very first thing in the morning. We should pray, tears streaming from our eyes, to be saved from the army of Kauravas, the army of deep slumber.

What, then, does the *Gita* teach? That we should not mind even if the slumber becomes deeper, should not even wish to get out of it? Should we say, I have no wish, the three states are the same to me? If anyone feels thus, you may be sure he will be totally ruined. Either we should regard this verse as an inter-

[1] XIV, 20
[2] XIV, 21 & 22
[3] "Take me from darkness to light," an Upanishadic prayer

polation, or as the very key to the meaning of the *Gita*. If you remember, in the beginning Arjuna does not ask whether or not it is proper to kill, but asks what good he could expect from killing his kinsmen. And so the Lord asks him: "What is this distinction you make between kinsmen and others? Your duty is to do the job of killing, irrespective of whether they are your kinsmen or others." Similarly, Arjuna does not here ask Shri Krishna which of the three *gunas* is best. He knows that ultimately one must transcend all the three. We can know a person who possesses one of the three *gunas*. It is not difficult to distinguish among the three classes. But can we find anyone in this world who has risen above the *gunas* altogether? This verse gives the Lord's reply to that question. What other reply could He give? A person who has risen above the three *gunas* will not let himself be deceived by the threefold distinction of good, bad and indifferent, and we shall not see in him the effects of any of the three *gunas*, so rare will be his state of mind. But this is an important chapter, and we shall think more about it tomorrow.

[172]

October 1, 1926

We discussed one idea yesterday. Talking of a person who does not feel concerned whether light, activity or darkness prevails or subsides, we saw that we find no one of the sort in the world. We come across no person who does not wish to get rid of what we regard as evil—lethargy, inertia or excessive activity—or does not wish to acquire pure knowledge. On the contrary, we pray for such knowledge. The word *jijnasu*[1] came into use because of our aspiration for knowledge, and we should pray that this aspiration may ever grow. This verse, therefore, should fill us with greater enthusiasm for doing our duty. Our aim is to strive to end the suffering of the entire world.

It is a general rule that we should not take any statement of a writer in isolation, but should consider it in its total context.

Now, then, for whom is this verse meant? Well, it is meant for one who has risen above the *gunas*. It enumerates the characteristics of such a person. This is what he would appear to us to be. We do not know how he in fact acts. We say, for instance, that the sun is a blazing fire, but scientists say that it is utterly

[1] One who seeks knowledge

black. An English poet has said that things are not what they seem. This is Sankara's theory of *maya.* It means that things do not appear as they are, that they are not what they seem to be, for everything is known to us through the medium of the waves in our minds.

Surely, the rainbow is not in truth what it seems to be. It is mere appearance. That is why it has been said that this world is like waves in water, or like a rainbow.

By what sign shall we, who live in the three-coloured world, recognize the man who has transcended the three *gunas*? He will not feel unhappy if the world mistakenly labels a man bad, or regards him as a man of knowledge or a lethargic man. What does it matter if the world thinks that we are mere agitators?

Thus, one who has risen above the three *gunas* will not seem to the world to be happy when one sees activity or unhappy when one sees lethargy. Such a person has come out of the duality of happiness and misery. He has risen above the pairs of opposites. A person like this should seem to us untouched, unconcerned, by anything. He should be absolutely free from egotism.

There is, thus, a state which is different even from the middle one. The *Bhagavad Gita* has stressed this point again and again. It teaches you just one thing, to shed the thought of "I" in such matters. We say *neti, neti.* You think I am such a person. In truth, I am "yes" and you are "no".[1] A person who has risen above the three *gunas* should appear to the world to be a cipher, a mere stone. That is, he should have got rid of his "I". The world has looked upon Rama as God incarnate, for it could not do otherwise. Shankara asked Parvati how she could suppose that Rama felt miserable because of separation from Sita. He was, he said, pained to see that she had attributed ignorance to Rama, who had shed his egotism and worked like a cipher.

[173][2]

October 2, 1926

Every day we are born anew. *Ayurved* tells us that every seven years the whole body of a person changes into a new one, but that we are not aware of the change because it takes place slowly. The body does not change all of a sudden at the end of the seventh year, as if by magic, but the old body gradually

[1] Gandhiji meant that one was more conscious of one's own "I" than the "I" of another.

[2] The notes of this discourse were not taken by Mahadev Desai.

wears out and is replaced by a new one. Thus, creation and destruction follow upon the heels of each other. There is no point of space so completely empty that you can put anything there without displacing something else, that is, you cannot create without destroying. Even the mind becomes either stronger or weaker day by day. Everything in the world is in a state of flux. Nothing is fixed. Only God is both fixed and changing.

A person who has risen above the three *gunas* is one who has become a cipher. But when can one be in such a state? In his poem beginning with the words *apurva avasar*, Shri Rajchandra sings: "When the body has become as the burnt rope". That should be our condition. When a rope is burnt, only its form remains, and none of its other properties survive. Such a rope may be said to have risen above the three *gunas*, for it no longer has the property in virtue of which it can be used for connecting or binding things or drawing water from a well. A person who has risen above the three *gunas* is like such a rope. As a rope may produce on us the illusion of a snake, so we may think of such a person as being like inert stone or having no interest in any activity, but he does not care. It is our dharma to be like such burnt rope.

The only way of rising to this state beyond the three *gunas* is to cultivate the *sattvik* quality, for in order to rise to that state one is required to cultivate the virtues of fearlessness, humility, sincerity, and so on. So long as we live in the body, there is some evil, some violence. The most, therefore, that we can do is to be *sattvik* in the highest degree possible.

The state beyond the three *gunas* can only be imagined. It does not seem possible to maintain it in action. In concrete action, our state must be *sattvik* in the highest degree. We cannot say even of a seemingly perfect man that he has risen beyond the three *gunas*. We can only say that he seems to be like one who has so risen. Someone has said in English that, outwardly, we shall find no difference between a sinner and a man of virtue, but that the greater a sinner the more virtuous he can be. He ever thinks of his sinful life and gives up his vices one by one. To such a sinner, even a beautiful temptress like Rambha is but a wooden or stone figure. In this way, he becomes pure in no time.

If we wish to attain *moksha* any time, to rise above the three *gunas*, we should cultivate in us the *sattvik* qualities. That is why we pray: *tamaso ma jyotirgamaya*. So long as a person feels that he serves others, he is selfish. If he believes that he has risen above the three *gunas*, he is a great hypocrite. If we really serve others, people will certainly know that. How can we ourselves know it? It is said in the Bible: "Let not thy left hand know what thy right hand does." That is the mark of a person being *sattvik*. The characteristics of such a person are almost similar to those of one who has risen above the three *gunas*, though, of course, the latter is undoubtedly on a higher level than the former since he knows neither what his right hand nor what his left hand does.

> He, who, seated as one indifferent, is not shaken by the *gunas*, and stays still and moves not, knowing it is the *gunas* playing their parts;
>
> He who holds pleasure and pain alike, who is sedate, who regards earth, stone and gold, as all the same, who is wise and weighs in equal scale things pleasant and unpleasant, who is even-minded in praise and blame;
>
> Who holds alike respect and disrespect, who is the same to friend and foe, who indulges in no undertakings—that man is called *gunatita*.[1]

A person who has risen above the three *gunas* knows what it is to be in that state but cannot describe it. If anyone can describe his state, he is not a person who has so risen, for he is still conscious of his "I".

> He who serves Me with an unwavering and exclusive *bhaktiyoga* transcends these *gunas* and is worthy to become one with *Brahman*.
>
> For I am the very image of *Brahman*, changeless and deathless, as also of everlasting dharma and perfect bliss.[2]

A person who struggles ceaselessly and hard to overcome his shortcomings may not perhaps succeed, in this birth, in overcoming them all, but in the end he will surely benefit. Today the world will censure him for his shortcomings; if, however, he bears all that in patience, and strives ever harder, he is sure ultimately to get peace of mind. Peace lies in the very fact of struggling. It is a source of great reassurance. Hence, we should strive to cultivate *sattvik* qualities.

[174][3]

Chapter XV

October 3, 1926

The Lord said:

> With its root above and branches below, the *ashvattha* tree, they

[1] XIV, 23 to 25

[2] XIV, 26 & 27

[3] The notes of this discourse were not taken by Mahadev Desai.

say, is imperishable; it has Vedic hymns for leaves; he who knows it knows the Vedas.[1]

Shvah means "tomorrow". *Ashvattha,* therefore, means this transient world which will not last beyond tomorrow. It is changing every moment. That is why it is *ashvattha.* He is a man of spiritual knowledge who knows the real nature of this world and also knows dharma.

[175]

October 5, 1926

Above and below its branches spread, blossoming because of the *gunas,* having for their shoots the sense-objects; deep down in the world of men are ramified its roots, in the shape of the consequences of action.[2]

In the first verse, Shri Krishna shows the means of going beyond this world. In this verse, he has described the world from another point of view, that of the ignorant man.

Its form as such is not here perceived, neither is its end, nor beginning, nor basis. Let men first hew down this deep-rooted *Ashvattha* with the sure weapon of detachment:

Let him pray to win to that haven from which there is no return and seek to find refuge in the Primal Being from whom has emanated this ancient world of action.[3]

We shall remain apart from this world, while working in it, when we no longer look upon it as God's sport but, regarding it as the sphere in which people run after enjoyments, cut it off at the root with the weapon of non-co-operation. In no other way is it possible to cut it off at the roots, for it is without beginning and without end. That is why Shri Krishna has advised non-co-operation.

To that imperishable haven those enlightened souls go—who are without pride and delusion, who have triumphed over the taints of attachment, who are ever in tune with the Supreme, whose passions have died, who are exempt from the pairs of opposites, such as pleasure and pain.[4]

They who crave to win that haven are indifferent to honour or insult. They are absolutely free from delusion. They have

[1] XV, 1
[2] XV, 2
[3] XV, 3 & 4
[4] XV, 5

scored triumph over the taints of attachment. Those who are always *atmarthi* (that is, who are aware every moment that they are not their physical bodies but are the *atman*), whose cravings for objects of senses have subsided (who look not fear-struck but serene at the moment of death) are the enlightened souls that go to that imperishable haven.

On every leaf of the banyan tree are inscribed the Vedas, which means that Ramanama is inscribed on its every leaf. The world is a holy gift made by God out of His grace; the tree of the world grows from the navel of Brahma. But there is another world with its root below, whose leaves are the various objects of sense-pleasure; that world is the world of desire.

Adhyatmanityah means those whose thoughts dwell with love on Rama, who repeat His name and do His work.

[176]

October 6, 1926

> Neither the sun, nor the moon, nor fire illumine it; men who arrive there return not—that is My supreme abode.[1]

Its light is not borrowed from the sun or the moon or the fire, for it shines with its own light, men who reach it return not — that is my supreme abode.

> A part indeed of Myself which has been the eternal *Jiva* in this world of life attracts the mind and the five senses from their place in *prakriti*.[2]

"Every hair on the body chants the Vedas," so sang Tulsidas.

> When the Master (of the body) acquires a body and discards it, He carries these with Him wherever He goes, even as the wind carries scents from flower-beds.
>
> Having settled Himself in the senses—ear, eye, touch, taste, and smell—as well as the mind, through them He frequents their objects.
>
> The deluded perceive Him not as He leaves or settles in (a body) or enjoys (sense-objects) in association with the *gunas*; it is only those endowed with the eye of knowledge that see Him.[3]

We see only the world, but do not see God who is immanent in it.

[1] XV, 6
[2] XV, 7
[3] XV, 8 to 10

[177]

October 7, 1926

> Yogis who strive see Him seated in themselves; the witless ones who have not cleansed themselves see Him not, even though they strive.[1]

The first thing necessary, therefore, is the observance of the rules of *yama-niyama*.

One who has not observed them is apt to give wrong meanings to the verses of the *Gita*. Such a person would tell himself that, since the objects of senses are created by God, we should accept and enjoy them. They alone, who have become purified, who have suffered in the furnace of *tapas*, will read the right meanings.

> The light in the sun which illumines the whole universe and which is in the moon and in the fire—that light, know thou, is Mine.[2]

There is a story in an Upanishad which tells how some gods took the form of *yakshas* and went to test *Agni*, *Vayu*, etc., but were worsted.[3]

> It is I who, penetrating the earth, uphold all beings with my strength, and becoming the moon—the essence of all sap—nourish all herbs.[4]

Pervading the earth, I uphold all beings with my strength, and becoming the moon, the producer of all sap, nourish all herbs, food-crops and all else that grows in the fields.

> It is I who, becoming the *Vaishvanara* Fire and entering the bodies of all that breathe, assimilate the four kinds of food with the help of the outward and the inward breaths.[5]

Vaishvanara means the heat which digests food. The four types of food are what is sucked, what is licked, what is drunk and what is eaten.

> And I am seated in the hearts of all; from Me proceed memory, knowledge and the dispelling of doubt[6], it is I who am to be known in all the Vedas, I, the author of Vedanta and the knower of the Vedas.[7]

[1] XV, 11

[2] XV, 12

[3] Gandhiji had probably the *Kenopanishad* in mind. If so, he did not recollect the details of the story correctly.

[4] XV, 13

[5] XV, 14

[6] In his rendering Gandhiji has used the word "intellect" in place of "the dispelling of doubt".

[7] XV, 15

[178]

October 8, 1926

There are two Beings in the world: *kshara* (perishable) and *akshara* (imperishable). *Kshara* embraces all creatures and their permanent basis is *akshara*.[1]

In this world there are two Beings—*kshara* and *akshara*. *Kshara* means all beings which are subject to death, which have a name and form. The immutable reality behind them, the power of which sustains all, is *akshara*.

The Supreme Being is surely another—called *Paramatman* who as the Imperishable *Ishvara* pervades and supports the three worlds.

Because I transcend the *kshara* and am also higher than the *akshara*, I am known in the world and in the Vedas as *Purushottama* (the Highest Being).[2]

Because I transcend *kshara*, that is, the world of name and form and am also higher than *akshara*, the world and the Vedas know Me as the highest among all beings.

He who, undeluded, knows Me *Purushottama*, knows all, he worships Me with all his heart, O Bharata.[3]

He is above all opposites. Once we have risen above this world, which is but *maya*, need we think of God as its author?

Thus I have revealed to thee, sinless one, this most mysterious Shastra; he who understands this, O Bharata, is a man of understanding, he has fulfilled his life's mission.[4]

I have disclosed to thee this most secret (the best even of the best) Shastra; he who understands this becomes a man of understanding, fulfils his life's mission and also becomes free from his debt.

[179]

Chapter XVI

October 9, 1926

The Lord said:

Fearlessness, purity of heart, steadfastness in *jnana* and yoga—knowledge and action, beneficence, self-restraint, sacrifice, spiritual study, austerity, and uprightness;[5]

[1] XV, 16
[2] XV, 17 & 18
[3] XV, 19
[4] XV, 20
[5] XVI, 1

> Non-violence, truth, slowness to wrath, the spirit of dedication, serenity, aversion to slander, tenderness to all that lives, freedom from greed, gentleness, modesty, freedom from levity;
>
> Spiritedness, forgiveness, fortitude, purity, freedom from ill will and arrogance—these are to be found in one born with the divine heritage, O Bharata.[1]

Sattvasanshuddhi means purity of the self or inner purity. *Jnanayogavyavasthiti* means certainty of knowledge; *jnanavyavasthiti* means unceasing direct experience, and *yogavyavasthiti* means constant awareness of God, sense of identity with Him. Ahimsa also embraces violence deliberately committed out of compassion (When Dr. Nangi was to perform an operation, he used to fast on the day previous, so that no emotional disturbances in him, like anger, etc., might affect the patient.). A teacher who punishes his pupils without anger will have tears streaming from his eyes as he canes him. Consider Yudhisthira's forbearance—when, in King Virata's court, the King struck him, he did not let the drops of blood fall from his nostrils on the ground. Forbearance means returning good for evil, so profound is its significance.

[180]

October 10, 1926

> Pretentiousness, arrogance, self-conceit, wrath, coarseness, ignorance—these are to be found in one born with the devilish heritage.[2]

Dambha means pretending to possess what one does not. *Darpa* means boasting about something which one possesses in only a small measure. *Abhiman* means being proud of a quality which one possesses. Narad showed pride when he had vanquished Kamadeva[3], and he fell because of his pride. *Parushya* means harshness.

> The divine heritage makes for Freedom, the devilish for bondage. Grieve not, O Partha; thou art born with a divine heritage.
>
> There are two orders of created beings in this world—the divine and the devilish; the divine order has been described in detail, hear from Me now of the devilish, O Partha.
>
> Men of the devil do not know what they may do and what they may not; neither purity, nor right conduct, nor truth is to be found in them.[4]

[1] XVI, 2 & 3
[2] XVI, 4
[3] God of love
[4] XVI, 5 to 7

Those who lack purity and truthfulness and whose conduct is not moral are diseased men and women. There can be no disease unless there is mental evil or bodily error. A person whose *atman* is awake every moment of his life constantly prays that his body be filled with light. How did Ladha Maharaj overcome his leucoderma? Every time he applied the *bel* leaves on the affected parts, he prayed that light should enter his body. We can prevent unhealthy emotions from disturbing our body only if we daily pray for the flow of light into it. I would ask every person who suffered from a disease if he was free from attachments and aversions. Outwardly we may be clean and our conduct may be moral; but, in the absence of truthfulness, it is all as hollow as a drum. We gather here to cultivate that truthfulness.

[181]

October 12, 1926

> 'Without truth, without basis, without God is the universe,' they say; 'born of the union of the sexes, prompted by naught but lust.'
>
> Holding this view, these depraved souls, of feeble understanding and of fierce deeds, come forth as enemies of the world to destroy it.
>
> Given to insatiable lust, possessed by pretentiousness, arrogance and conceit, they seize wicked purposes in their delusion, and go about pledged to unclean deeds[1].
>
> Given to boundless cares that end only with their death, making indulgence or lust their sole goal, convinced that that is all.
>
> Caught in a myriad snares of hope, slaves to lust and wrath, they seek unlawfully to amass wealth for the satisfaction of their appetites.[2]

How can desire and anger overcome him who is protected by willing submission to holy authority?

Anger consumes many times more energy than does joy. It is because people spend more energy than they can afford that injustice and tyranny prevail in the world.

[182]

October 13, 1926

Anger involves expenditure of energy by thirteen muscles, whereas laughter by only ten. Enjoyment of sense-pleasure leads to death. *Brahmacharya* leads to immortality. Once Raychand-

[1] Gandhiji's rendering has "of sinful bent of mind" in place of "pledged to unclean deeds".

[2] XVI, 8 to 12

bhai was suffering from headache. I asked him to which theatre he had been to see a play. He replied that he had been witnessing a play at night, lying at home, and said that he did not wish to consume his energy in trying to cure his headache. It was good, he told me, that I saw him as he was. He was, he said, less powerful than God's law.

Sexual indulgence necessarily leads to death. If people gave themselves up to it, God's rule in the world would end, and Satan's prevail.

> This have I gained today; this aspiration shall I now attain; this wealth is mine; this likewise shall be mine hereafter.
>
> This enemy I have already slain, others also I shall slay; lord of all am I; enjoyment is mine, perfection is mine, strength is mine, happiness is mine.
>
> 'Wealthy am I, and high-born. What other is like unto me? I shall perform a sacrifice! I shall give alms! I shall be merry!' Thus think they, by ignorance deluded.[1]

Living in this way, man gambles away the *ratnachintamani*[2] of his body. Even Yudhishthira had gambled, and lost Draupadi too in the throw. We can, however, say that he had less of anger and desire in him than Duryodhana. We ourselves are full of that mixture. We must strive our best to raise ourselves to a higher level.

> And tossed about by diverse fancies, caught in the net of delusion, stuck deep in the indulgence of appetites, into foul hell they fall.
>
> Wise in their own conceit, stubborn, full of the intoxication of pelf and pride, they offer nominal sacrifices for show, contrary to the rule.[3]

Yajna is only a pretext; their real aim is to serve their own interests.

[183]

October 14, 1926

> Given to pride, force, arrogance, lust and wrath they are deriders indeed, scorning Me in their own and others' bodies.
>
> These cruel scorners, lowest of mankind and vile, I hurl down again and again, into devilish wombs.
>
> Doomed to devilish wombs, these deluded ones, far from ever coming to Me, sink lower and lower in birth after birth.[4]

[1] XVI, 13 to 15
[2] A precious stone which yields everything that is desired
[3] XVI, 16 & 17
[4] XVI, 18 to 20

> Threefold is this gate of hell, leading man to perdition,—Lust, Wrath and Greed; these three, therefore, should be shunned.[1]

One who keeps himself free from these does not devote himself to the pursuit of worldly happiness, but follows the path of spiritual welfare.

> The man who escapes these three gates of Darkness, O Kaunteya, works out his welfare and thence reaches the highest state.
>
> He who forsakes the rule of Shastra and does but the bidding of his selfish desires, gains neither perfection, nor happiness, nor the highest state.
>
> Therefore let Shastra be thy authority for determining what ought to be done and what ought not to be done; ascertain thou the rule of the Shastra and do thy task here (accordingly).[2]

In this context, we should say that we would obey our conscience. But, then, even Ravana would say that he obeyed his conscience. He alone can use this plea whose mind has become purified by knowledge acquired from Shastras. So the question is, what is Shastra? The Vedas, the works of history, the *Puranas* all these are Shastras. They, however, contain contradictory statements. Shastra comes from the root *shas*. Someone has argued that the *Gita* teaches the principle of "tit for tat", and quotes Shaikh Sadi in his support, who said that he who was good to the bad would be bad to the good. But Shastra is subject to the principles of truth and non-violence. Shastra rules, and does not aim at spreading anarchy. But of this more tomorrow.

[184]

October 15, 1926

Whenever we have a social problem to discuss, we should think of authorities and consult them; as, for instance, in connection with the problem of dogs which is unnecessarily agitating me. If, however, our foundations are not strong, consulting a Shastra will avail us nothing. If the foundations are strong, it should be our principle that we will cling to truth at any cost. We shall have read Shastras to some purpose if we are determined that, even if Yudhishthira told a lie, our ideal shall be truth.

If by Shastra we mean a book, the Bible, the Koran and other books have been before mankind for so many hundreds of years,

[1] XVI, 21
[2] XVI, 22 to 24

but no one has come to the end of these problems. The intention in this verse is to tell us not to look upon ourselves as an authority, that is, not to be guided by our wishes and feelings. So long as one's intellect has not become vigilant and the heart is not filled exclusively with Ramanama, one should be ruled by the authority of the Shastras. Here Shri Krishna refers to the struggle in us between divine and demoniac impulses. So long as we are in that condition, we should be guided by the authority of the Shastras. That Shastra means *shishtachara*[1], that is, we should follow the example of those forefathers of ours who were holy and fearless. The ideal of conduct among shepherds may be stealing sheep, and among meat-eaters eating meat. A boy once wanted to discuss with me whether or not we can eat meat, but his mother did not let me discuss the subject with him. She was right. She thought that nothing could be brought about by force. If the boy became a vegetarian, she thought, there would be a quarrel in the family. One must certainly fear *shishtachara*. It may be disregarded only if it requires one to violate truth, etc. Where the tradition of guru and disciple has disappeared, men will follow their own wishes. The *Gita* has advised us: *tadviddhi pranipatena*[2], but it is not so easy to find a guru. If we keep on the search for a guru, we shall always have some wholesome fear in our heart. With the thought of a guru constantly in our mind, it will remain pure. The *Gita* tells us that, if the divine impulse has quickened in us, we should be humble. [One should think] "I know nothing. I want to ask God, or a guru, but how may I see either?" We should, therefore, pray. He who prays with faith in God will one day be saved. He who talks as if *Brahman* was in him will not be saved. The literal meaning of the verse is that we should be guided by the authority of the Shastras. The derived meaning is that we should be guided by *shishtachara*. To be *shishta* means that, in the absence of a guru, we should be humble, and to be humble means to worship our personal God. That is, we should look upon ourselves as insignificant creatures, like bugs and fleas, and worship God. If you are humble, you will be saved. If you are humble and sincere, the veils before your eyes will be lifted one after another.

Chapter XVII begins with the idea explained in this verse.

[1] The prevailing social standard of right conduct

[2] Acquire knowledge by prostrating yourself (before a guru); in IV, 34

Chapter XVII

Arjuna said:

> What, then, O Krishna, is the position of those who forsake the rule of Shastra and yet worship with faith? Do they act from *sattva* or *rajas* or *tamas*?[1]

By disregarding the manner enjoined in the Shastras means by disregarding the *shishtachara*, or without the guidance of a guru, and with faith means with some little humility. Shri Krishna's reply to this is indirect. Not to accept Shastra as an authority and to have faith are inconsistent with each other. Faith consists in accepting the authority of Shastra.

Shri Krishna replies:

> Threefold is the faith of men, an expression of their nature in each case; it is *sattvik*, *rajas* or *tamas*. Hear thou of it.[2]

Arjuna and Shri Krishna are friends, but the former does not understand that Shri Krishna is playing with him. It is certainly not Arjuna's intention to corner Shri Krishna in argument. But the latter thinks that He might play with Arjuna a little. The Lord need not bother Himself why Arjuna put this question. He assumes that a person may disregard the manner enjoined in the Shastras, and then asks what kind of faith such a person has. Is it *sattvik* or *rajasik* or *tamasik* ?

[185]

October 16, 1926

> The faith of every man is in accord with his innate character; man is made up of faith; whatever his object of faith, even so is he.[3]

Faith can be enlightened. Everyone needs faith, provided one is not misguided by it. If anyone clings to a straw, he will certainly fall, but he will not fall who clings to the branch of a tree. Mrs. Besant has said that a person needs steps till he has climbed to the top. Shastra is such a step. Once a person has climbed to the top, he needs neither steps nor banisters. The top appears so perfectly flat to him that he pays no attention to what is below.

[1] XVII, 1
[2] XVII, 2
[3] XVII, 3

> *Sattvik* persons worship the gods[1], *rajasik* ones, the *Yakshas* and *Rakshasas*; and others—men of *tamas*—worship manes and spirits.
>
> Those men who, wedded to pretentiousness and arrogance, possessed by the violence of lust and passion, practise fierce austerity not ordained by Shastra.
>
> They, whilst they torture the several elements that make up their bodies, torture Me too dwelling in them; know them to be of unholy resolves.[2]

Those who do not even abide by the rules enjoined by Shastras but in their pride follow their self-chosen way fall into such a state.

If you put truth in one scale of the measure and *tapas*, Shastras and similar things in the other scale, the former will weigh heavier. That Shastra which seeks to suppress truth is of little use. Those who follow such a Shastra are men of demoniac inclination. If truth is timeless, so is untruth; and, likewise, if light is timeless, so is darkness too. We should embrace what is timeless only if it is combined with truth.

[186]

October 17, 1926

If a Shastra is not supported by truth and non-violence, it may even be the means of our fall. As they say, we should swim in our father's well, not drown ourselves in it. Father in this context means *shishtachara.* It is said that one cannot get knowledge without a guru. The moment you have found one, you know what the *shishtachara* is. But these are such hard times that one does not easily find a guru. If we are doing God's work, it is bound to be in harmony with *shishtachara.* That is why we are enjoined to keep repeating the Lord's name while doing any work. This verse explains in what spirit we should do this. Our faith must not be in ghosts and spirits or in demons. We ought to pray only to a beneficent deity.

> Of three kinds again is the food that is dear to each; so also are sacrifice, austerity, and charity. Hear how they differ.
>
> Victuals that add to one's years, vitality strength, health, happiness and appetite; are savoury, rich, substantial and inviting, are dear to the *sattvik.*[3]

[1] In his rendering Gandhiji has added here: "Gods mean *sattvik* powers or impulses".

[2] XVII, 4 to 6

[3] XVII, 7 & 8

> Victuals that are bitter, sour, salty, overhot, spicy, dry, burning, and causing pain, bitterness and disease, are dear to the *rajas*.
>
> Food which has become cold, insipid, putrid, stale, discarded and unfit for sacrifice, is dear to the *tamas*.[1]

If we cling to this classification, we shall not come to the right conclusion. Shri Krishna has first explained the qualities of the *sattvik* man, and then his taste, etc. *Ladu*[2]-lovers have included *ladus* in *sattvik* food. They do not help one to safeguard one's *brahmacharya*. In interpreting the meaning of *rasya*[3], too, we should use discrimination. There must have been a reason in that age for making such a classification, for there must have been persons even then who would eat a handful of chillies at a time. In the present age, there is no need for eating *snigdha*[4] foods. If here we start eating ghee, our food would be, not *sattvik* or *rajasik*, but such as a demon would love. The inclusion of bitter, sour and saltish foods is quite correct. Then the verse mentions food which has been left over. Stilton cheese (a food containing countless germs) is of this class. *Daliya*[5] and *mamara*[6] do not belong to this class.

[187]

October 19, 1926

> That sacrifice is *sattvik* which is willingly offered as a duty without desire for fruit and according to the rule.
>
> But when sacrifice is offered with an eye to fruit and for vain glory, know, O Bharatashreshtha, that it is *rajas*.
>
> Sacrifice which is contrary to the rule, which produces no food[7], which lacks the sacred text, which involves no giving up and which is devoid of faith is said to be *tamas*.[8]

A *yajna* without *dakshina* means one in which no gifts are made to the poor.

[1] XVII, 9 & 10
[2] A sweet shaped like a ball
[3] Relishing
[4] Containing fat
[5] & [6] Processed gram and rice
[7] Gandhiji's rendering has "grain" in place of "food".
[8] XVII, 11 to 13

> Homage to the gods, to Brahmins, to gurus and to wise men; cleanliness, uprightness, *brahmacharya* and non-violence—these constitute austerity (*tapas*) of the body.[1]

That is *tapas* in which one goes through physical discomfort or hardship.

> Words that cause no hurt, that are true, loving and helpful, and spiritual study constitute austerity of speech.
>
> Serenity, benignity, silence, self-restraint, and purity of the spirit —these constitute austerity of the mind.
>
> This threefold austerity practised in perfect faith by men not desirous of fruit, and disciplined, is said to be *sattvik*.
>
> Austerity which is practised with an eye to gain praise, honour and homage and for ostentation is said to be *rajas*; it is fleeting and unstable.
>
> Austerity which is practised from any foolish obsession, either to torture oneself or to procure another's ruin, is called *tamas*.[2]

A person who fasts for a hundred days or keeps standing on one foot performs not *sattvik* but *tamasik tapas*.

[188]

October 20, 1926

> Charity, given as a matter of duty, without expectation of any return,[3] at the right place and time, and to the right person is said to be *sattvik*.[4]

It may not in all circumstances be right to give what it is right to give in certain circumstances. This is also true about recipients. It is but right to give food to one who has lost the use of his limbs altogether. But suppose there is a blind man who is suffering from fever and comes begging. He would be an unworthy object of our charity if we gave him food. If we give him a blanket and he sells it, then also will our gift have been made to an unworthy person. In one place, it may be right to give food, in another something else, and in still another a third thing. The principle is the same in all cases, but its application will vary according to place, time and person. The same is true about *yajnas*.

[1] XVII, 14

[2] XVII, 15 to 19

[3] Gandhiji's rendering has: "to one who is not in a position to do good in turn".

[4] XVII, 20

Charity, which is given either in the hope of receiving in return, or with a view to winning merit, or grudgingly, is declared to be *rajas*.

Charity given at the wrong place and time, and to an undeserving recipient, disrespectfully and with contempt, is declared to be *tamas*.

AUM TAT SAT has been declared to be the threefold name of *Brahman* and by that name were created of old the *Brahmanas*, the Vedas and sacrifices.

Therefore, with AUM ever on their lips, all the rites of sacrifice, charity and austerity, proceed always according to the rule, by *Brahma-vadins*[1]. [2]

Those who seek knowledge of the *Brahman* dedicate all their *yajnas*, gifts and *tapas* to Shri Krishna. They do everything in the name of Hari[3], in the name of *Aum*.

With utterance of TAT and without desire for fruit are the several rites of sacrifice, austerity and charity performed by those seeking Freedom.

SAT is employed in the sense of 'real' and 'good'; O Partha, Sat is also applied to beautiful deeds.

[27][4] Constancy in sacrifice, austerity and charity, is called SAT; and all work for these purposes is also SAT.[5]

Aum comes first in all these actions. *Sat* signifies the process of their performance. If we wish that we should be steady in our *yajnas* and gifts, then *Aum* signifies the commencement and *sat* signifies the process. *Sat* signifies process and also stands for Hari. *Brahma satyam jaganmithya* has been stated in this sense.

Whatever is done, O Partha, by way of sacrifice, charity or austerity or any other work, is called *asat* if done without faith. It counts for naught hereafter as here.[6]

Aum tat sat means that all that exists is *Aum*, that our "I" is unreal, that God alone is and nothing else is real, that we are all running after things in vain.

We should even eat our food in a *sattvik* spirit. There are persons who eat as an act of worship. We should resolve that we

[1] Expounders of *Brahman*

[2] XVII, 21 to 24

[3] Vishnu

[4] Gandhiji has not given a translation of this verse. He has, however, referred to its content in the comment which follows.

[5] XVII, 25 to 27

[6] XVII, 28

wish to live as ciphers in this world. The world may kick us from one place to another as if we were a ball, but we will not let ourselves be so kicked. We will use our knowledge, our bodies, our strength and money, all for the service of others, and that too not with the desire to earn a good name for ourselves. Thus, *Aum tat sat* is a vow of humility. It teaches us to realize our utter insignificance, to be completely free from egotism. If the Imam Saheb[1] would recite it, here is a *kalama* for him.

[189]

October 21, 1926

The threefold classification of gifts, faith, *tapas*, etc., given in Chapter XVII is only an illustration. We can make as many categories as we like. The intention was to show that the reign of the three *gunas* prevails throughout the universe. A cooking or other utensil is an inert object, but it contains air inside; likewise, everything is pervaded by the spirit. Existing apart from the three *gunas* is God. We have to merge in Him. Even if we cultivate the *sattvik* qualities to their highest perfection in us, something of *rajasik* and *tamasik* will remain. But, without worrying ourselves about this, we should continue to strive and cultivate finer and finer *sattvik* qualities in us, for the impulses which agitate us the least and consume the least amount of our energy are *sattvik* impulses. Though Janaka was as good as a disembodied soul even while he lived in a body, the difference between him and us is only one of degree. It is true, of course, that for one like him there was no returning to this life after he was dead.

Chapter XVIII

In Chapter XVIII Arjuna requests Shri Krishna to explain to him the distinction between sannyasa and *tyaga*. He says:

> Mahabahu! I would fain learn severally the secret of *sannyasa* and of *tyaga*, O Hrishikesha, O Keshinishudana.[2]

The Lord replies:

> Renunciation of actions springing from selfish desire is described as *sannyasa* by the seers; abandonment of the fruit of all action is called *tyaga* by the wise.[3]

[1] Abdul Kadir Bawazeer
[2] XVIII, 1
[3] XVIII, 2

There is no real distinction between the two. *Kamya* karma seems to mean all karma—though I am not sure that I am right. Total renunciation of karma is not possible. The renunciation of all karma, then, is sannyasa, and *tyaga* means renunciation of fruits of karma.

[190]

October 22, 1926

Yesterday I interpreted *kamya* karma to mean all karmas. Surendra then reminded me of the explanation given by Vinoba, namely, karmas undertaken with definite motives. But every karma has some motive behind it. That we may be unattached to it is a different matter, but the motive is bound to be served. The existence of the body itself means karma. Though we live in the body, we can live unconcerned with it.

> Some thoughtful persons say: "All action should be abandoned as an evil"; others say: "Action for sacrifice, charity and austerity should not be relinquished."
>
> Hear my decision in this matter of *tyaga*, O Bharatasattama; for *tyaga*, too, O mightiest of men, has been described to be of three kinds.
>
> Action for sacrifice, charity and austerity may not be abandoned; it must needs be performed. Sacrifice, charity and austerity are purifiers of the wise.
>
> But even these actions should be performed abandoning all attachment and fruit; such, O Partha, is my best and considered opinion.
>
> It is not right to renounce one's allotted task; its abandonment, from delusion, is said to be *tamas*.
>
> He who abandons action, deeming it painful and for fear of straining his limbs, he will never gain the fruit of abandonment, for his abandonment is *rajas*.
>
> But when an allotted task is performed from a sense of duty and with abandonment of attachment and fruit, O Arjuna, that abandonment is deemed to be *sattvik*.
>
> Neither does he disdain unpleasant action, nor does he cling to pleasant action—this wise man full of *sattva*, who practises abandonment, and who has shaken off all doubts.
>
> For the embodied one cannot completely abandon action; but he who abandons the fruit of action is named a *tyagi*.[1]

[1] XVIII, 3 to 11

When we have resolved to renounce the fruits of all karmas, we will engage ourselves only in karma which is in the nature of a duty for us. By the sannyasa mentioned in the first verse, the poet meant renunciation of all karmas. The central idea of Chapter XVII was that one should work without selfish motives. The state of mind in which such motives will have disappeared most is the *sattvik* state. Total renunciation of karma is impossible while we live in the body, and the *atman's* connection with the body will remain right till the moment of death. What a person who has fallen into a state of *samadhi* can do is to stop the movements of the heart so that the heart-beat will not be perceived even with a stethoscope. The practitioners of yoga tell us that the soul can leave the body at will and fly away for a while. But to what purpose ? We can certainly reduce the pulse-rate at will. The truth is that if a yogi really wishes that his soul should leave his body, his faculty of speech and his mind, it will certainly do so. I have no doubt that, if we do not will that the body should endure, it will certainly fall. But our desire to give up the body is never intense, for we feel even a pin-prick. A person like Ramdas Swami can even dwell in another's body and feel his suffering, but he cannot be conscious of the bodies of all, except in imagination. All that we can do, therefore, is to shun karmas which have any trace of egotism in them.

[191]

October 23, 1926

Harishchandra's actions belonged to the category of *tyaga*. He was equally ready, when duty required him, to perform apparently evil as well as good actions.

> To those who do not practise abandonment accrues, when they pass away, the fruit of action which is of three kinds: disagreeable, agreeable, mixed; but never to the sannyasis.
>
> Learn, from me, O Mahabahu, the five factors mentioned in the *Sankhya* doctrine,[1] for the accomplishment of all action:
>
> The field, the doer, the various means, the several different operations, fifth and the last, the Unseen.[2]

When Fate was no longer favourable, Arjuna was robbed though he still had with him the same bow and arrows which he always had.

[1] Gandhiji's rendering adds here: "in which karma has been discussed".
[2] XVIII, 12 to 14

Whatever action, right or wrong, a man undertakes to do with the body, speech or mind, these are the five factors thereof.

This being so, he who, by reason of unenlightened intellect, sees the unconditioned *atman* as the agent—such a man is dense and unseeing.

He who is free from all sense of 'I', whose motive is untainted, slays not nor is bound, even though he slay all these worlds.[1]

If I put a pebble in . . .'s[2] hand and incite him to fling it at . . . [3], would the sin be on his head or mine? Arjuna dragged Krishna all the way from Dwarka [to Hastinapur] and was now saying that he did not wish to fight. Was that right? Shri Krishna tells Arjuna: "I ask you to fight." What harm need Arjuna fear, then? The sword in Harishchandra's hand was not his, nor was it Kashiraja's.[4] Harishchandra could have resorted to satyagraha, but should he have done that simply because the person in question was Taramati? When one's self-interest is involved, one should do an [unpleasant] thing irrespective of whether in itself it ought to be done. If, however, no self-interest had been involved, if it was not that the woman was his queen, if Harishchandra had been repelled by the deed itself, so much so that his hand would have refused to obey him, he could have resorted to satyagraha.

If read superficially, this verse is likely to mislead the reader. We shall not find anywhere in the world a perfect example of such a person; as in geometry we require imaginary, ideal figures, so in practical affairs, too, we require ideal instances when discussing ethical issues. This verse, therefore, can be construed thus only: "We may say [for the sake of argument] that he whose sense of 'I' has melted away altogether and whose reason is tainted with no trace of evil whatever can kill the entire world; but one who is completely free from the egotistic sense of 'I' has no body, and one whose reason is absolutely pure is simultaneously conscious of time in all its categories, past, present and future, and there is only one such being, God, Who does nothing though doing everything and Who is non-violent though He

[1] XVIII, 15 to 17

[2] & [3] The names are omitted in the source.

[4] Harishchandra was sold by sage Vishwamitra to recover the sacrificial gift due from him. When his wife, Taramati, came to the burning-ground to cremate her son, Harishchandra threatened to strike her with his sword because she prevented him from obeying his master and removing the shroud from the corpse.

kills." Man, therefore, has only one course open to him, that of not killing and of following the *shishtachara*—of following Shastra.

> Knowledge, the object of knowledge, and the knower compose the threefold urge to action; the means, the action and the doer compose the threefold sum of action.[1]

For instance, the idea that we must get swaraj is knowledge, and the person who deserves it is the knower. But this is not enough to bring us swaraj. There should be corresponding work for swaraj—the means of winning it. We can think out similar instances of any class of activities.

> Knowledge, action, and the doer are of three kinds according to their different *gunas*; hear thou these, just as they have been described in the science of the *gunas*.
>
> Know that knowledge whereby one sees in all beings immutable entity—a unity in diversity—to be *sattvik*.[2]

Things in this world seem distinct from one another, but in reality they are not so. If the jaundice in our eyes disappears, we would see all things as one, undivided reality.

> That knowledge which perceives separately in all beings several entities of diverse kinds, know thou to be *rajas*.[3]

That knowledge is *rajasik* which perceives separately in all beings different entities of various kinds.

It is through the *rajas* spirit that we make these three classes: I, mine and others. Attachments and aversions arise from this. The *sattvik* state has no room for attachments and aversions.

> And knowledge which, without reason, clings to one single thing, as though it were everything, which misses the true essence and is superficial is *tamas*.[4]

Tamas jnana is that in virtue of which a person does everything with attachment, without seeing any purpose in what he does and believing that it is without significance and of no consequence.

In *tamas* knowledge, all kinds of notions are mixed up and it is believed that there is no such Being as God.

[1] XVIII, 18
[2] XVIII, 19 & 20
[3] XVIII, 21
[4] XVIII, 22

That action is called *sattvik* which, being one's allotted task, is performed without attachment, without like or dislike, and without a desire for fruit.

That action which is prompted by the desire for fruit or by the thought of 'I', and which involves much dissipation of energy is called *rajas*.[1]

A *sattvik* person does not go seeking work. A *rajasik* person is engaged one day in inventing an aeroplane and is busy the next in discovering how to reach India from England in five hours. Such a person sets apart half an hour out of twenty-four to deceive his *atman*, and devotes the remaining twenty-three and a half to his body.

Is the charkha work *rajasik*, or is it *sattvik* too? This can be decided only by reference to the spirit in which it is done. If a person plies the charkha merely for the sake of money, his work is *rajasik*, but it will be *sattvik* if he does so for the good of the world, in the spirit of a *yajna*.

That action which is blindly undertaken without any regard to capacity and consequences, involving loss and hurt, is called *tamas*.[2]

In *tamas*, a person plunges into work without thinking of the consequences. One who works without desiring the fruit of his work knows what that fruit will be, but does not yearn for it.

[192]

October 26, 1926

That doer is called *sattvik* who has shed all attachment, all thought of 'I', who is filled with firmness and zeal, and who recks neither success nor failure.[3]

Free from the sense of "I" means one who works merely as an instrument. To say that he should have no attachment does not mean that he should be indifferent; on the contrary, such a person should be more active than others. The relation of God's devotee to God is, in one sense, that of the lover and the beloved, though in reality the two are as different from each other as north is from south. The devotee remains unattached [to sense-pleasures], whereas the lustful lover and beloved lose their vitality day by day. Do the British officials who come out to India lack

[1] XVIII, 23 & 24
[2] XVIII, 25
[3] XVIII, 26

anything in endurance and energy? They seem to be yogis, but they are not free from attachment. They believe in ends, and will adopt any means, fair or foul, for their sake. But one who is free from attachment is concerned with nothing but work and displays unfailing determination and energy. He displays determination and energy even in plying the charkha. A person who works in this spirit is a *sattvik* doer.

> That doer is said to be *rajas* who is passionate, desirous of the fruit of action, greedy, violent, unclean, and[1] moved by joy and sorrow.
>
> That doer is called *tamas* who is undisciplined, vulgar, stubborn, knavish, spiteful[2], indolent, woebegone, and dilatory.
>
> Hear now, O Dhananjaya, detailed fully and severally, the threefold division of understanding and will, according to their *gunas*.
>
> That understanding, O Partha, is *sattvik* which knows action from inaction, what ought to be done from what ought not to be done, fear from fearlessness[3] and bondage from release.
>
> That understanding, O Partha, is *rajas* which decides erroneously between right and wrong, between what ought to be done and what ought not to be done.
>
> That understanding, O Partha, is *tamas* which, shrouded in darkness, thinks wrong to be right and mistakes[4] everything for its reverse.[5]

[193]

October 27, 1926

> That will, O Partha, is *sattvik* which maintains an unbroken harmony between the activities of the mind, the vital energies and the senses.[6]

If a person clings to the decision he has made without being exercised about the consequences, does not change it from day to day, then we may say that he possesses a will that is unswerving. "By yoga" means in a spirit of dedication to God.

[1] Gandhiji's rendering has: "easily excited by joy or sorrow in success or failure".

[2] In place of "spiteful", Gandhiji's rendering has: "lacking firmness of decision".

[3] In place of "fear from fearlessness", Gandhiji's rendering has: "which things one should guard against and of which things one need have no fear."

[4] Gandhiji's rendering has: "sees everything in a wrong light".

[5] XVIII, 27 to 32

[6] XVIII, 33

> That will, O Partha, is *rajas* which clings, with attachment, to righteousness, desire and wealth, desirous of fruit in each case.[1]

The first signifies dedication to God and the second attachment. Because of that attachment, one pursues dharma, *artha*[2] and *kama*[3]. The decision of such a person may be faulty.

> That will, O Partha, is *tamas*, whereby insensate man does not abandon sleep, fear, grief, despair and self-conceit.[4]

Everything we do involves grief and ignorance and, at any rate, disappointment and fear.

> Hear now from Me, O Bharatarshabha, the three kinds of pleasure.
>
> Pleasure which is enjoyed only by repeated practice, and which puts an end to pain.
>
> Which, in its inception, is as poison, but in the end as nectar, born of the serene realization of the true nature of *atman*—that pleasure is said to be *sattvik*.[5]

One must do *tapascharya* for such happiness. It involves renunciation and, therefore, means hardship in the beginning. Everything in which one must sacrifice sleep and give up lethargy, for instance, study and learning and teaching, is a kind of *tapascharya*. But the reward is knowledge of the self. The bliss of knowing the *atman* is of the same character as the *atman*. The happiness of the body comes wholly from the satisfaction of desires, and because it depends on the satisfaction of desires it is transient. It is as transient as the life of a butterfly or a flash of lightning. The other happiness abides for ever. The happiness which springs from the serenity resulting from knowledge of the *atman* is like *amrita*.

> That pleasure is called *rajas* which, arising from the contact of the senses with their objects, is at first as nectar but in the end like poison.[6]

Suppose we have been to a play or some such show. We enjoy witnessing it, but afterwards suffer for loss of sleep and also on account of the effect of the play on our mind.

[1] XVIII, 34
[2] Wealth, power
[3] Pleasure
[4] XVIII, 35
[5] XVIII, 36 & 37
[6] XVIII, 38

That pleasure is called *tamas* which, arising from sleep and sloth and heedlessness, stupefies the soul both at first and in the end.

There is no being, either on earth or in heaven among the gods, that can be free from these three *gunas* born of *prakriti*.[1]

We should, therefore, strive to become free from these.

[194]

October 28, 1926

The duties of Brahmins, Kshatriyas, Vaisyas and Sudras are distributed according to their innate qualifications, O Parantapa.

Serenity, self-restraint, austerity, purity, forgiveness, uprightness, knowledge and discriminative knowledge, faith in God are the Brahmin's natural duties.[2]

Serenity, self-restraint, *tapas* (to keep body, speech and mind under control by hard discipline), purity, forgiveness (to wish well, from the heart, even to a person who may have hit us with a stone), straightforwardness (to have no impurity in one's eyes, to behave decently), knowledge and knowledge based on experience (not bookish, dry knowledge), faith in God—these are the natural duties of the Brahmin.

A person may have the qualities enumerated above, but may not believe in God, may be lacking in faith and devotion; if so, those very qualities will prove harmful. For instance, in Europe these days they train the body for prize competitions and wrestling matches. These persons, too, are required to exercise discipline over the body, but that is done without devotion to God and helps them in no way. Hence belief in and devotion to God should be among the most important characteristics of a Brahmin.

Valour, spiritedness, constancy, resourcefulness, not fleeing from battle, generosity[3], and the capacity to rule are the natural duties of a Kshatriya.[4]

A Brahmin, too, should have these qualities. For instance, Vashishtha and other sages had them. Likewise, a Kshatriya should have the qualities of a Brahmin; for example, Yudhishthira, Ramachandra, etc., were Kshatriyas but possessed the virtues of Brahmins. Bharata was the very ideal of what a Brahmin

[1] XVIII, 39 & 40

[2] XVIII, 41 & 42

[3] In place of "generosity", Gandhiji's rendering has: "being always ready to help the poor".

[4] XVIII, 43

should be. In this way every individual should display, in varying measure, the qualities associated with all the castes, and a person will belong to the caste whose virtues he possesses in a predominant measure. These will determine his natural karmas.

> Tilling the soil, protection of the cow and commerce are the natural functions of a Vaisya, while service is the natural duty of a Sudra.
>
> Each man, by complete absorption in the performance of his duty, wins perfection. Hear now how he wins such perfection by devotion to that duty.
>
> By offering the worship of his duty to Him Who is the moving spirit of all beings, and by Whom all this is pervaded, man wins perfection.[1]

Anyone who worships the *atman*—the *Brahman*—God that exists pervading the universe like its warp and woof,—reaches the goal; true success crowns him alone who sees prayer or worship in the karma which has fallen to his lot as his duty, who has made service and every karma of his a form of prayer.

> Better one's own duty[2], though uninviting, than another's[3] which may be more easily performed; doing duty which accords with one's nature, one incurs no sin.
>
> One should not abandon, O Kaunteya, that duty to which one is born,[4] imperfect though it be; for all action, in its inception, is enveloped in imperfection, as fire in smoke.[5]

This does not apply to actions like a stealing; it applies only to actions which have been described in the preceding verses as the natural karmas of the four castes. Even if one sees some evil in such karmas—as, for instance, Arjuna's shrinking from fighting because of his weakness of attachment—it is best to do them, for every karma, every beginning, is tainted with some evil.

> He who has weaned himself from attachments[6] of all kinds, who is master of himself, who is dead to desire, attains through renunciation the supreme perfection of freedom from action.[7]

[1] XVIII, 44 to 46

[2] Gandhiji's rendering adds here: "karma which is one's duty".

[3] Gandhiji's rendering adds here: "karma which is somebody else's duty".

[4] Gandhiji's rendering has: "which has come to one unsought".

[5] XVIII, 47 & 48

[6] Gandhiji's rendering has: "He who has given up attachment to everything, that is, has become free from attachment".

[7] XVIII, 49

Here by sannyasa is meant, not renunciation of all karmas but only the renunciation of the fruit of all karmas and it is such renunciation alone which can be successfully practised.

> Learn now from Me, in brief, O Kaunteya, how he who has gained this perfection, attains to *Brahman*, the supreme consummation of knowledge.[1]

[195]

October 29, 1926

> Equipped with purified understanding, restraining the self with firm will, abandoning sound and other objects of the senses, putting aside likes and dislikes.
>
> Living in solitude, spare in diet, restrained in speech, body and mind, ever absorbed in *Dhyanayoga*, anchored in dispassion.
>
> Without pride, violence, arrogance, lust, wrath, possession, having shed all sense of 'mine' and at peace with himself, he is fit to become one with *Brahman*.[2]

Ahankar, *bala* and *darpa* include one another, but it would not be like the *Gita* to use only one term. Its manner is to say the same thing over and over again in different ways. *Laghvashi*: I observe the vow of taking not more than five articles in my daily food, but, even if I keep it literally, I shall not have succeeded in keeping it well. Haridas mentioned dates and gave some good ones as gift. He watched my mood and offered me one to eat. I relished it, and immediately became conscious of a lapse. Even as it is, I told myself, you eat more than others do. I ate the date and it stuck in my throat. This is what should happen if we treat the body as something out of which we must take work.

In this verse, we are asked to purify the intellect and to be *laghvashi*. To be *laghvashi* does not mean merely to be moderate in eating, but to be satisfied with one article when we feel we can make do with two. It is as though this misfortune befell me because we would be discussing the word *laghvashi* today. A person may take a vow that he would live exclusively on milk, and then consume fifteen pounds a day, or convert it into *mava*[3] and eat it. Why is it that such a person won't add water to milk and drink it? A barrister friend in England used to read for

[1] XVIII, 50

[2] XVIII, 51 to 53

[3] Milk boiled till it becomes a thick paste

sixteen hours a day. He used to add water to his soup. Real hunger will prompt one to eat things that taste like *amrita.*

> One with *Brahman* and at peace with himself, grieves not, nor desires; holding all beings alike, he achieves supreme devotion to Me.
>
> By devotion he realizes in truth how great I am, Who I am; and having known Me in reality he enters into Me.
>
> Even whilst always performing actions, he who makes Me his refuge wins, by My grace,[1] the eternal and imperishable haven.
>
> Casting, with thy mind, all actions on Me, make Me thy goal, and resorting to the yoga of even-mindedness[2] fix thy thought ever on Me.
>
> Fixing thus thy thought on Me, thou shalt surmount all obstacles by My grace; but if possessed by the sense of 'I' thou listen not, thou shalt perish.
>
> If obsessed by the sense of 'I', thou thinkest, "I will not fight", vain is thy obsession; (thy) nature will compel thee.
>
> What thou wilt not do, O Kaunteya, because of thy delusion, thou shalt do, even against thy will, bound as thou art by the duty to which thou art born.[3]

"Hence," says Shri Krishna, "dedicate everything to me and, free from attachments and aversions and ever devoted to me, do the task which has fallen to your lot; so acting, you will remain untouched by sin."

[196][4]

October 30, 1926

> God, O Arjuna, dwells in the heart of every being and to His delusive mystery whirls them all, (as though) set[5] on a machine.[6]

We are sitting on this ball of earth, which does not stop from rotating or revolving even for a moment. It keeps rotating and revolving all the twenty-four hours. The stars and the sun do the same. Thus, nothing in the world is motionless. But things do not move through their own power; it is God's power which keeps everything in motion. Just as we keep a machine

[1] Gandhiji's rendering adds here: "not through his own strength".

[2] Gandhiji's rendering adds here: "knowledge and meditation".

[3] XVIII, 54 to 60

[4] The notes of this discourse were not taken by Mahadev Desai.

[5] Gandhiji's rendering has "the clay of the potter's wheel", in place of "set on a machine".

[6] XVIII, 61

in motion only as long as we choose and it has no power of its own to move, so also does God keep us in motion as He wills. We should not, therefore, be proud that we have done something. We should shed our egotism, become as a machine in God's hand and carry out His will, look upon Him as our all and obey His plan.

> In Him alone seek thy refuge with all thy heart, O Bharata. By His grace shalt thou win to the eternal haven of supreme peace.
>
> Thus have I expounded to thee the most mysterious of all knowledge; ponder over it fully, then act as thou wilt.
>
> Hear again My supreme word, the most mysterious of all; dearly beloved thou art of Me, hence I desire to declare thy welfare.
>
> On Me fix thy mind, to Me bring thy devotion, to Me offer thy sacrifice, to Me make thy obeisance; to Me indeed shalt thou come—solemn is My promise to thee, thou art dear to Me.
>
> Abandon all duties and come to Me, the only refuge. I will release thee from all sins, grieve not![1]

This verse is the essence of all Shastras and of the *Gita*. Shri Krishna tells Arjuna: "You should give up all arguing and take refuge in Me. That will be wholly for your supreme good. Only the service of the *atman* will advance a person's welfare."

> Utter this[2] never to him who knows no austerity, has no devotion, nor any desire to listen, nor yet to him who scoffs at Me.
>
> He who will propound this supreme mystery to My devotees, shall, by that act of highest devotion to Me, surely come to Me.[3]

All knowledge is preserved only when imparted to a person who is worthy of it, and not when imparted to one who is unworthy of it.

> Nor among men is there any who renders dearer service to Me than he; nor shall there be on earth any more beloved by Me than he.
>
> And who so shall study this sacred discourse of ours shall worship Me with the sacrifice of knowledge. That is My belief.[4]

That is, he who studies this intelligently will become free. Merely reciting the verses mechanically and without understanding their meaning will certainly not bring freedom.

[1] XVIII, 62 to 66
[2] Gandhiji's rendering has: "this knowledge".
[3] XVIII, 67 & 68
[4] XVIII, 69 & 70

[197]

October 31, 1926

And the man of faith who, scorning not,[1] will but listen to it,—even he shall be released and will go to the happy worlds of men of virtuous deeds.

Hast thou heard this, O Partha, with a concentrated mind? Has thy delusion, born of ignorance, been destroyed, O Dhananjaya?[2]

Arjuna said:

Thanks to Thy grace, O Achyuta, my delusion is destroyed, my understanding has returned, I stand secure, my doubts all dispelled; I will do Thy bidding.[3]

Arjuna's memory, which had become clouded, has become clear. He has understood what his nature and his duty are, and his doubt has gone.

Sanjaya said:

Thus did I hear this marvellous and thrilling discourse between Vasudeva and the great-souled Partha.

It was by Vyasa's favour that I listened to this supreme and mysterious Yoga as expounded by the lips of the Master of Yoga, Krishna Himself.

O King, as often as I recall that marvellous and purifying discourse between Keshava and Arjuna, I am filled with recurring rapture.[4]

If we do not feel a new interest in this every time we read it, the fault must lie with us, it cannot be that of the author of the *Gita*.

And as often as I recall that marvellous form of Hari, my wonder knows no bounds and I rejoice again and again.

Wheresoever Krishna, the Master of Yoga, is, and wheresoever is Partha the Bowman, there rest assured are Fortune, Victory, Prosperity and Eternal Right.[5]

To Shri Krishna has been attached the epithet *Yogeshvar* and to Arjuna *Dhanurdhara*; this means that there are fortune, victory and eternal right only where there is perfect knowledge joined with light and power. He who has knowledge should have the

[1] Gandhiji's rendering adds here: "one whose faith is blind may scorn".
[2] XVIII, 71 & 72
[3] XVIII, 73
[4] XVIII, 74 to 76
[5] XVIII, 77 & 78

fullest strength to use it; there should be perfection of knowledge and it should be fully translated into action.

We have taken this to be an imaginary conversation. The author of the *Mahabharata* has given us a wonderful work; he has displayed in it his perfect knowledge. He had entered into Krishna's heart. *Dhanurdhara* means a person devoted to duty. Is there anyone who has attained to absolute knowledge? For that person, however, who has the strength of spirit to act upon what seems certain knowledge to him, there is no such thing as defeat; he may even have prosperity, and more than that he does not wish. If he goes on acting in that spirit, even his errors will be corrected in course of time. We know that we should always speak the truth, but manage to tell only half the truth; but he who has pure knowledge and the necessary energy to act upon it, that is, has taken up a bow and arrow, will never depart from the path of morality.

We do not intend to give up the reading of the *Gita*; its reading at prayer time will continue, a few verses every day. We may also discuss some of them, if we wish to.

This is a work which persons belonging to all faiths can read. It does not favour any sectarian point of view. It teaches nothing but pure ethics.

CONCLUSION

[1]

November 4, 1926

The conclusion of our study of the *Gita* is that we should pray and read holy books, and know our duty and do it. If any book can help, it is this. Really, however, what help can a book or a commentary on it give? In the end, we achieve only as much as it is our good fortune to do. Our only right is to *purushartha*[1]. We can only strive and work. All human beings, and animals too, struggle. The only difference is that we believe that behind our struggle there is an intelligent purpose. What is the purpose, however? Merely to keep alive this body, or to know that which has taken on this body? To raise it or advance it, if that is possible? For the first object we work in any case, whether we wish or no. Our body itself is so made that it makes us work for it, even if we are unwilling. For instance, while the baby is still in the mother's womb, its organs do function in one way

[1] Striving or determined effort

or another. Though unconsciously, it does breathe. That also is a kind of effort. But it is not *purushartha*. Only effort aimed at the welfare of the *atman* can be described as *purushartha*. It has been described as the supreme *purushartha*. All else is futile expenditure of energy. For such *purushartha*, one of the means is reading the Shastras and reflecting and meditating on them. In order that our study may be really useful, it is necessary to repeat our recitation over and over again with attention to pronunciation, rhythm, etc. It is necessary to create an atmosphere of holiness round the *Gita*. If we are completely indifferent to it, then of course there is no question of attending to grammar, pronunciation, etc.

The truth about ourselves is that we strive for the supreme *purushartha* and know how to seek the means for it. We should honour and revere the *Gita*. It will certainly protect us. It is a deity of the mind. If so, we should read it daily as a part of our prayer.

What lesson shall we draw from all this? Today I will place before you only one idea. The *Gita* does not give the central importance to karma, nor to *jnana* nor to *bhakti*. It gives importance to all these. Oxygen is a very useful ingredient of air, but we cannot have only oxygen, other gases are equally necessary. Similarly, every element which the *Gita* includes is essential. Karma, *jnana* and *bhakti*, all three are essential, and each in its place is of central importance. Without *bhakti* human effort by itself will not succeed, and, without *jnana*, *bhakti* will not bear fruit. Hence we see at places *bhakti* or *jnana* treated as a means which helps us in doing the right karma.

We can, however, do without any of the three elements, thanks to something else which has been explained. We cannot easily understand *jnana* and can understand *bhakti*[1], but we can understand karma more easily than either. Decorating the image, repeating Ramanama, all this is karma. Activity of every kind is karma. Karma means body. When any thought takes on a body, assumes form, it becomes karma. Body is a visible thing. To the degree that we can see the body, we can see karma. We cannot, therefore, live without karma, and that is why, we can say, the *Gita* has stressed karma. However, *bhakti* and *jnana*, too, are essential. Let us suppose that we have boarded the ship; who is to give it motion now? Who will start it? We feel happy at the sight of the ship and board it, with faith

[1] The source has *jnana*, which seems to be a slip.

[that it will move]. Similarly, karma is indeed necessary, but we shall reach the goal only when an intelligent engineer starts and drives the ship. The idea of renouncing karma is a futile one. Even a sannyasi cannot live without karma. This argument, however, comes in later.

The *Gita's* karma is not karma done under compulsion; it must be prompted by some little measure at any rate of knowledge.

[2]

November 5, 1926[1]

Following the path of non-violence, we discovered the value of the spinning-wheel, as also of *brahmacharya*. Beyond the river [Sabarmati] is *bhogabhumi*[2], while this is *karmabhumi*[3]. We wish to follow the path of renunciation. But no renunciation is truly such unless it gives us joy. We cannot live without joy. It is but proper that we should celebrate Divali in a different manner from how it is done on that side of the river. We should today draw up a balance-sheet of our work. Our books of accounts are in our heart. We should have completely cleared the debit side. A business man always credits in his book at least one and a quarter rupee [on the New Year day]. We can follow him by making some good resolution. If we read the *Gita* regularly, we shall understand our duty easily.

The karma which the *Gita* advocates is done of one's own free will, and it is such karma as one cannot live without at all. There is another definition of karma besides this. Karma means body. So long as the body is connected with the soul, it has motion and acts. But karma also means violence. Hence complete freedom from karma, which means from the body, is *moksha*. We should seek an existence that dispenses with this body and is beyond this world full of violence. In this world which is all karma, we should strive to cultivate a state of *akarma*. The *Gita* has shown how we can do this. We shall discuss this by and by.

[1] This was Divali day.
[2] Place for enjoyment
[3] Place for duty

[3]

November 6, 1926

The peace of mind and the joy we feel when, with closed eyes, we recite the verses from memory are really great. We feel less joy when we read the verses.

Today is *padavo* (the New Year Day). May you succeed in the good resolutions which you made before coming here. Anyone who has not made a single resolution should make one at least, that he or she will be sincere. If you do not become so, the bright outer surface will be no more than gilt and the inside will be base metal. Nothing will shine without truth; let everyone, therefore, resolve that he will show himself as he is. The joy one can get by showing oneself as one is, is not to be had by decorating one's figure or beautifying oneself. There is untruth in wearing your cap at an angle, in wearing the sari in a particular style and dressing your hair smartly. Anyone who dresses himself in various fashions so that he may appear more handsome than he is starts learning a lesson in falsehood. We can build a palace on the foundation of truthfulness.

Chapter III deserves special attention. We saw yesterday that karma means the body, it means violence, and I told you then that I would discuss this idea further today. This Chapter dwells on the necessity of *yajna*. *Yajna* means work for the benefit of others. Afterwards, it is explained that every karma is tainted with evil, as it involves some measure of violence. However, violence committed for the sake of *yajna* is not violence. *Yajna* here does not mean that *yajna* in which they kill animals. There was a time when such *yajnas* were regarded as true *yajnas*, but now most people believe that they are not so. Since, however, every karma involves violence, I have divided violence into two categories. There is violence when the intention is to give pain, otherwise it is only an act of killing. Breathing involves killing, which is unavoidable violence and is, therefore, forgiven. Without such unavoidable violence, we cannot keep alive the body for its sacred pilgrimage. It is a principle of homoeopathy that the patient should take in the smallest possible quantity the very substance which has caused the disease. Similarly, if we wish to become non-violent in this violent world, we shall advance as we gradually become more and more non-violent. On the other hand, trying to overcome violence with violence leads to evil consequence. *Akarma* means reducing karma and the degree of violence involved in each karma. One who does that will not go seeking work to do. Such a person will ultimately reach a state in which his thought itself will be action. We cannot pursue even *bhakti* or *jnana* without some measure of karma—we shall see tomorrow how this is so.

[4]

November 7, 1926

Since every karma involves violence, our ideal is to escape all karma, which means to win deliverance from this life. This does not mean that the world in which we live should vanish or be destroyed; it means that one should voluntarily renounce activity and sit at home quietly, that is, live in *Vaikunth*[1], knowing that this world of name and form is transient and that it is unprofitable to take pleasure in it. This, however, is not possible. We cannot, through force of will, have this world vanish from before us, or bring about the *moksha* of all people in it. Everyone, then, should seek his *moksha*; but how? By committing suicide? One who kills himself will not escape the body. It is opposing the law of nature to seek escape in this manner. It is with the mind that we have to renounce the body. If every karma involves violence and evil, we can mentally renounce karma. Does it mean that, after renouncing karma in that manner, one can do any karma one chooses? No. At present we mentally draw to ourselves innumerable things. When we have mentally renounced all karmas, a great many of them will fall off on their own. Such a person will then use to his benefit, as much as he can, the world from which all air will have escaped. "Only the outward form surviving, as of the burnt rope"; however, the burnt rope will also occupy a little space. Even if it is reduced to dust particles and they fly away into air, they will certainly occupy some space somewhere! It is our belief that if the outward form vanishes and the dust particles, too, vanish, then everything will have vanished. Like the sea, God neither increases nor decreases. The dust particles, obeying their nature, will have merged in Him. When we have renounced karma mentally, all attachment to it will have ceased. Such a person will not even think what his duty is. He will be working only as directed by others. It is not he who will be doing the unavoidable, residual karma; God will be doing that. If I am not responsible even for my breathing, I am doing it under force, not willingly. A person who acts in such manner is non-

[1] The abode of Vishnu

violent. No one can be more non-violent than this while living in the body. Hence, as we saw in Chapter III, karma done in the spirit of *yajna*, that is, for the benefit of others, does not bind. To do karma for the benefit of others means to enlist ourselves as soldiers in God's army, to dedicate to Him our all, body, mind, wealth, intellect. I read a book by a protestant named Wallace. He saw that their activity of converting others to Christianity did no good. He decided to mix with our people. He fell in love with the religions of India, but he could not forget Jesus. He then embraced the Roman Catholic Church, and felt that he was nothing as an individual, that the Church was all. He made an image, Parthiveshwar Chintamani, and resolved to surrender himself to it. As for the line of guru and disciple [to which he should belong], he looked upon society as a whole as his guru. This idea has appealed to me. If the Pope is immoral, there is bound to be corruption in society, but any person who has decided that he will do nothing on his own but do only what the Pope asks him to do, will only benefit himself. A protestant would say that one should obey one's conscience, but this Wallace kept his conscience out and surrendered himself to the Pope. His giving up concern for his conscience was a great idea. He has narrated a story. A Hindu once advised him[1] that repeating Ramanama was good and a Muslim advised the name Khuda. He repeated the names Rama and Khuda by turn. He once saw that another person uttering Ramanama was floating on water. Thereupon, he started saying Khuda-Rama and began to sink. God then told him: "My friend, I am both Khuda and Rama." This man, Wallace, thus wanted to cultivate single-minded devotion. His worshipping another person wholeheartedly was itself worship of his conscience. Everything becomes easy only when one surrenders oneself to God and lives as a cipher. A person who does so will have renounced all karma. Suppose a woman regularly goes to the *haveli*[2], and that the other women who go there are immoral. This woman, however, will be saved. The man who taught the *mantra* of Ramanama could not float, but the other one who learnt it and used it with faith did. Similarly, this woman who goes to the temple sees no immoral figure in the image, she sees only God. She would swim across and be saved; the others would be drowned. In the same way, anyone who mentally renounces all

[1] It is not clear from the source who is meant.

[2] *Vaishnava* temple

karma will be doing even the unavoidable, residual karma unwillingly and, therefore, will not be responsible for them. If he eats, he does so unwillingly; he breathes, too, unwillingly. How smooth everything becomes as soon as we mentally renounce all karma. We shall discuss tomorrow the meaning of violence and non-violence and of bondage and *moksha*.

[5]

November 9, 1926

A person can be free from karma only when he gives up his body altogether. Even the wish to live in the body must be renounced. If it is not, one will have to pass through many more lives. The wish to live in this body is what is termed *dehadhyasa*. That is the sea of existence. While we remain in it, we shall ever be tossed about by the waves. In the course of time, then, we may perceive the deep truth that what we call happiness is not happiness but only an illusion of happiness, that misery is not misery but only an illusion of it. If a person mentally renounces karma, he becomes free from the sense of "I" and "Mine". He, therefore, resolves to work only in the spirit of *yajna* and for the benefit of others. Work done in such spirit is ahimsa, but only when two conditions are fulfilled by it. One is that there should be no element of selfishness in our motive, and the second is that there should be no self-interest of ours in it, that on the contrary it should be for the good and for the benefit of the world. If these two conditions are fulfilled then even the most dreadful-seeming act may be regarded as an act of ahimsa. We attribute ahimsa to an act, but we can do that only if the act is for the service of others. If a person can truthfully claim that he eats and performs other like acts in a disinterested spirit he is free from attachments. The wish to live in the body remains so long as I cling to it. We cannot hold a string in a disinterested spirit; holding it is an act of will. If a person has withdrawn his mind from the body as much as is humanly possible, he wins freedom from bondage to the body. What I am discussing is the question of violence and non-violence, of living in the body and being free from bondage to it. If this bodily life has no sense, use the body for the services of others, for a life of prayer to God. Those who advised us thus were not ignorant men, they spoke from experience. It is we who did not understand them. It is extremely difficult to give up our clinging to the body. Someone may well ask how we can explain this idea to a child. My reply is that it is only in young age that this idea is easily understood; one cannot understand it after one has lost one's teeth. A historian has said that there is no difference in outlook between youth and old age. Youth has desire and the capacity to satisfy it; in old age, the capacity is wanting and so the desire becomes stronger. If we do not follow the example of Menavati, who explained to Gopichand [the futility of attachment to bodily life], we shall invite misery upon ourselves. I go a step further and say that an old man is far more thoughtless than a young man. A prince is always surrounded by *hakims*[1] and consuming *yakutis*[2] but he is ever talking Vedanta[3]. Thus, boys and old men are the same in this regard. Anyone who imbibes something, however little that may be, from these verses—from the whole work, commencing with *Aum*—can attain complete peace. For him there will be only work undertaken for the service of others; the innumerable other karmas will have fallen away. If, while we live in this body, we keep it yoked to work like a bullock to the cart, it will run after fewer things to do and with very much less intensity. We shall, then, seem to be doing nothing, but in fact we shall be working with energy which it is impossible to describe. We should seek out one activity or karma from among the countless in the world, or rather one activity or karma should come seeking us. Anyone who wants to serve will find objects of service anywhere. At the end of all discussion, Shri Krishna asked Arjuna in Chapter XVIII: "Surrender yourself to Me, do this very thing, but in obedience to My command. Dedicate your all to Me and go on with it." How this can be done, we shall discuss later.

[6]

November 10, 1926

Today we are to have a bird's-eye view of the discussions, but I simply could not think out what to say. Right at the end of the work, in Chapter XVIII, Vyasa wondered what he had been making Krishna teach Arjuna, whether it was knowledge or ignorance, pure *bhakti* or something else. So he made Krishna brush aside all else and say: "Abandon all duties and come to Me, the

[1] Practitioners of *Unani* system of medicine
[2] *Unani* tonics
[3] Metaphysics (especially of the Upanishads)

only refuge."[1] He later made Arjuna also say that he had forgotten what he had been taught. The Lord replied that He, too, did not always remember the discussion and said that He would teach something new. And so He taught another *Gita*[2], which no one remembers.

Swami . . .[3] has been wandering for twenty-seven years, but till this day he has discovered nothing. Finally, now, he has joined the sect of . . . .[4] I am talking in a tone of despair, but what I am saying is true. How does one, and how should one, seek refuge in the Lord? Shri . . . '[5], the goldsmith, asked me to give him something, saying "Else, what could I carry back with me?" I looked at him for a while, unable to think of anything. Then I said: "Repeat Ramanama." What was it, however, that I gave him? And what did he receive? Things don't work that way. This is an old custom, but how many people following it seek refuge in Rama? The *Gita* was not the first work which advised us to seek refuge in the Lord. How, then, can we end our restless yearning? We must look inwards, not outwards, to discover the way. If we look outwards, where should we search? If God, on the other hand, is not outside of us but inside, how may we look inwards? How shall we blow up the big rock that lies across our way as we look inwards? To seek God means to sink into ourselves, that is, to renounce all activities. Since, however, it is not possible to renounce all activities, we should engage ourselves in as few activities as possible, reduce ourselves to the utmost insignificance. To seek God is not a Herculean task, as the world may think it is; all that is necessary is to make oneself humble and yoke the mind to work every minute for the welfare of the *atman*. It is we who obstruct ourselves in this effort. What should we do to overcome the obstructions? This is the first thing taught in the science of yoga. I have been thinking what education we should plan for boys and girls. They must get training in this. We should not deprive them of their right to get it. We wish to identify ourselves with the poor, but the children of the poor get nothing. From their infancy they work in the fields. Wherever the farmers' work is done systematically, their children are employed in such work right from their early years and few people

[1] In XVIII, 66

[2] The *Mahabharata*, "Ashvamedha Parva"

[3], [4] & [5] The names are omitted in the source.

think about the problems which exercise us. The way to realize God, which means the way to win swaraj too, is to do something which seems altogether unimportant, and that is, to show ourselves as we are even before children. If such behaviour becomes natural to us, the children will also watch it with admiration. I told you about Wallace. He said at the end: "I have still not surrendered my reason, and it is a protestant reason." But he did surrender his reason, his views, his all, and the salt was absorbed in the water of the sea. That is what the Buddha called nirvana. Such a person would not even remember that once he was an insignificant entity and think that he had now become the sea. We should, therefore, experience our insignificance, undertake the least important task and for its sake renounce everything, cultivate perfect disinterestedness.

We can achieve nothing by busily running about. The *Gita* advised Arjuna to give up concern with all dharma, that is, to take up the least important work and experience his insignificance. It tells us, in effect: "Live as a servant of the world; it is beyond your capacity to do more."

[7]

November 12, 1926

Can procreation for *yajna* be described as consistent with *brahmacharya*? Yes, it can. In it, however, the desire for progeny is more important than concern for *yajna*. Whereas the world simply cannot go on without non-violence practised as *yajna*, we cannot say that procreation is essential. If the *smritis*[1] say, nevertheless, that *brahmacharya* is possible for a householder, they use the term *brahmacharya* in a restricted sense which we have completely rejected in our discussions.

Besides, there is one more argument. If destruction is violence, creation, too, is violence. Procreation, therefore, involves violence. The creation of what is bound to perish certainly involves violence.

[8]

November 13, 1926

The *Mahabharata* is a unique work and in it the *Gita* has a unique place. Describing a physical battle, it gives an account

[1] Sacred books prescribing rules for personal conduct and social life

of an invisible fight and shows through it that in the physical battle not only those who lose but even those who win are defeated. The five or six who survived lived as though they were dead. Dhritarashtra becomes miserable, and so does Kunti[1]. We see in the Swargarohana Parva the fate which meets the five brothers and Draupadi. They die one after another. Yudhishthira, too, is hardly able to reach the end of the journey. And, therefore, Vyasa says that what they got from their victory was no better than dust.

This does not mean that we should stop striving. In one sphere, Fate is all powerful, and in another *purushartha*. *Purushartha* means striving, and supreme *purushartha* means escaping from the pairs of opposites. Living in the world of opposites is no better than collecting dust with our hands. It is, however, the purpose of the *Gita* to show that every particle of dust can become as valuable as a jewel in certain conditions. The three *gunas* are aiming arrows at you from all sides. If you remain unmoved as they pierce you, you can win. Those arrows may fall on the body and on the *atman* dwelling in the body, but, let them fall as long as they may, what harm can they do me so long as my *atman* is awake?

What is the condition under which this may be so? To explain who can understand this problem, Shri Vyasa gave the *Arjunavishadayoga*[2]. Arjuna here stands for the *atman* seeking knowledge. So long as the intellect is not aroused by circumstances, it will not feel the desire for knowledge. The *Gita* is not for the intellect so long as it remains ensnared by worldly allurements. Is the *Gita* for students? It is for all those who have faith, such faith that they wish to be Arjunas. A student who believes the statement of his teacher that India is 1,900 miles in length and 1,500 miles in breadth will not take up a rod and start measuring the distances. He takes the statement on trust. Similarly, when the teacher tells the pupils in the first standard that the earth is round, an intelligent pupil will believe him and start arguing with another who holds that it is flat. The pupil who is convinced of the truth of the statement will not question it. Such a pupil will also take on trust statements concerning dharma, which is also a kind of geography, as he does those about the physical science of geography. He will exercise his curiosity in regard to many problems, but some things have to be accepted on trust. For instance, the definition of a straight

[1] Mother of the Pandavas
[2] Chapter I

line. Afterwards, such things become clear as day-light. The years of student-life are a time when one should take things on trust. Why students, even grown-up people take things on trust. We have no choice but to have faith in the ultimate things which remain unexplained by reason. A student's reason is virgin, and it is not taxed much. As it sharpens and acquires light and power, he goes on solving problems with its help by repeatedly putting questions, bowing humbly to the teacher as he does so. The only condition is that the pupil should feel curiosity and be eager to know. That is why Chapter I is called *Vishadayoga*. The term means the path which unites one to God through despondency. If we wish to be filled with exclusive devotion to God, to win *moksha*, we should go through despondency. . . .[1] told me: "Cannot we see God through fasting? Is it not right that we should punish the body severely if we feel all the time distracted by evil thoughts?" "There are," he said, "so many *bawas*[2] in the country. Some of them lie on spikes in the fierce sun and derive great contentment; surely they cannot be thinking evil thoughts at that time?" We shall find such persons in Europe too. Fakirs also have that experience. There have always been people in the world who did *tapas*, and theirs is not a crazy notion. I have merely put before you my humble view. I do not ask you to do such things. Our aim is to mortify the mind, to teach it patience in order to purify it. Fasting and similar lashes are sufficient for that. If we could be certain that we would always succeed in our aim by fasting, everyone would fast. Do you think there are only a few in this world who seek knowledge? There are many such. People suffer a great many hardships to secure worldly things; do you think, then, that nobody would come forward to suffer being pierced with a nail in the neck for this purpose? I have seen persons who stabbed themselves with a knife as they begged for a pice. If people can do this to themselves for a pice, why should they not do it for a throne? But that path is not easy. We have a middle way open to us, which is the only one worth following. But there is a point in what . . .[3] told me, and that is that we should have a burning aspiration in this direction. We should have the same impatience and yearning for *moksha* which lustful men and women display for the gratification of their lust. Let us re-

[1] & [3] The names are omitted in the source.

[2] Mendicant sadhus

nounce our yearning for worldly things and cultivate yearning for *moksha* instead. The first condition for one to be like Arjuna is that one should feel a burning aspiration. People start making distinctions between "mine" and "others". There is no doubt about whether we may kill or not. We know that we may not kill. The eternal law is not the law of killing. Arjuna did not have the strength to follow that independent law, and merely asks how he could bring himself to aim his arrows at Drona and Bhishma. In this way, he made the false distinction between "his" and "others" and declared that he would not fight. But he is a mature man. He does not decide impulsively while sunk in darkness. He is all love for Krishna. Sinking with nervous fear, he asks Krishna to solve his problem. It is only when we feel nervous like him that we shall be cured. We shall not be cured till we feel a crisis. The experience is like the pangs of child-birth. Arjuna's experience is that which overwhelms one when one feels born again; may all of us have this experience. If the feeling endures, we would be saved.

[9][1]

In Chapter II, [we see that] the seeker should be eager. A person gets knowledge only when he suffers so much for it that his body becomes completely wasted and seems as if it would pass away any moment. We learn the same lesson from the story of *Gajendramoksha* and the narratives about Draupadi and others. When one has suffered so much, one gets knowledge and one's reason becomes purified. When Pilgrim felt that he was surrounded by fire on all sides, he ran without worrying about his wife and children. When we have such a feeling, we may say that our reason has become purified, and all veils will then be lifted. Arjuna's heart is in the right place, but it is enveloped in ignorance and, therefore, it cannot help him to decide. So Krishna explains the distinction between *atman* and the body. He advances one argument to convince Arjuna, till he is overwhelmed by it. Arjuna was worrying so much about the body; he should now worry equally for the *atman*. Krishna explains to him that the two things are distinct. The *atman* neither kills nor is killed. It is the body which perishes. Arjuna should know that in any case it will die, and should not worry about it. But this was only an argument. What should Arjuna actually do? "If you do," Shri Krishna tells him, "what I ask you to do, you will

[1] The date of this discourse is not given in the source.

have no cause to repent. Even if you make only a moderate effort, it will be rewarded. You should take my word that what you do, however small, will bear fruit." What type of person is he who works without worrying about the result? To answer this question, Shri Krishna describes the characteristics of such a person in Chapter II itself. The description creates so much interest in Arjuna, who was yearning for knowledge, that he feels eager to hear further. He has no inkling yet of *bhakti*. One cultivates it only when one forgets everything else. Mira was filled with *bhakti* when she realized that having seen the light of the sun and the moon, she did not need the light shed by a glow-worm. If such a person still needs to do karma, it is only for serving others and not for his own sake. A *bhakta* may do exactly what we do, but his reason will show him how to do it in a different manner. And so the Lord explains how to do karma, and thereafter He explains the secret of *bhakti*. [Understanding that], one's attachment to the body falls away, the *atman* becomes stronger and awakens more fully day by day, and ultimately one sees it in a divine vision.

[10][1]

When Arjuna becomes utterly weak, his intellect is awakened. Shri Krishna then tells him: "Your intellect by itself will not serve you. You will need to do yoga, karmayoga." Tilak Maharaj has demonstrated this with many convincing arguments. He has shown that the intellect needs, as it were, to take a partner to itself and be a householder. When Arjuna asked Shri Krishna to explain to him the characteristics of the person practising both forms of yoga, the latter enumerated the characteristics of a *sthitaprajna*. This confused Arjuna. Would such a person be a man of karma or a *jnani*?

In Chapter III, therefore, Shri Krishna explains the meaning of karma. No one can live at all without karma. Mirabai begged of the Lord that she should think on Him with every breath she took. We do not breathe consciously, but do so instinctively. A healthy person does all karmas with detachment in the same manner as he breathes. Karma may be a sign of health and it may also be a sign of disease. For instance, the manner in which a person suffering from asthma breathes indicates that he has a disease. This is also true of a man who feels suffocated.

[1] The date of this discourse is not given in the source.

Similarly, one's karma may be a sign of health in some other person, but not in oneself. After this, Shri Krishna gave the example of Janaka and others. Citing His own example, He said that He, too, had to work and keep the machine going. He could not so much as stretch His limbs for rest. Arjuna could sleep, Shri Krishna said, but He could not. Even then, He was always detached. If we follow this example, our intellect would retain its power till we are a hundred, or rather it would grow in strength with years. But human beings are attached to sense pleasures. If they were not, they would always attain perfect knowledge in course of time. If our experience is to the contrary, let us not pay attention to that. We are imperfect human beings and deduce imperfect principles from our imperfect experience. There should be, therefore, some flaw somewhere if experience tells us otherwise. Look at a fruit. As it grows bigger, it becomes more juicy and richer. The date has fallen off the tree and dried, but how sweet it is! Similarly, the intellect of a person who does not violate God's law should ripen and grow with years. In actual experience, however, we find that as a person grows older, he or she declines in strength and intelligence. Such a person has been a lover of gross pleasures in his life.

For an ordinary person, Chapter III is as valuable as a silver pot. It is extremely useful.

[11][1]

We have seen that God does not cease from karma even for a moment. How, then, can we win *moksha*? The reply was that the body should be left to do its karmas, that the *atman* was not involved in them. This teaching has been altogether misinterpreted by immoral people. But, truly speaking, it is easy enough to understand that the bond of the body itself involves karma. If there were no body, there would be no need to do karma, and God having no body He has no need to do karma. But the Lord says that, even though He has no body, He does not cease from karma. He should, therefore, be thought of as having one, for this entire visible creation is His body. When we think of Him as having no body, He is a Formless Reality. If the *atman* realizes that the body does its karma, it will be free from the bond of the latter. How can one feel that it is the body which goes on doing certain karmas? The body cannot do karma without the ego. Without the *atman*, the body itself can do nothing. This is

[1] The date of this discourse is not given in the source.

one more problem. This makes the *atman* a doer. It means, then, that the *atman*, joined to the ego, dwells in the body and does things. What we should do then was explained in Chapter III. "Service of others brings holy merit to one, and through harassment of others one incurs sin." We may unhesitatingly do what is most for the benefit of others. We shall, of course, assume that the person doing that will be as detached from it as he can be. When we take the least credit for such work, it will be done with the most efficiency. A person walking with his natural speed of a mile an hour will outdistance another running at a speed of sixty miles, for the former will have his joy in his *atman*, whereas the latter will be full of doubts. His running will on the whole serve no purpose. If our work is free from egotism, though our speed may be slow, we are certain to reach the goal. Let us by all means work in the spirit of *yajna* and for the benefit of others. All that we should concern ourselves with is whether it is the body or the *atman* that we serve. To say that man is born for service of others is true in one sense only, because all his work is prompted by self-interest. If this self-interest is the interest of the *atman*, then one's work is for the benefit of others. All the activities of such a person will be prompted by the motive of service.

Hence, the Lord concluded this part of the argument with the verse, "Better one's own duty, bereft of merit".[1] That means that, be one's own dharma what it is, even if it is seemingly without merit, it is better than another's which may have greater merit in it. Arjuna was attracted by the dharma of other people, and therefore, the Lord told him that, however good it was, it was not his dharma. Dharma well performed cannot be another's, for in fact such dharma cannot be well performed. Only one's own dharma can be well performed. The truth is that ultimately Arjuna will have to renounce both his own dharma and that of others, but he cannot have that *moksha* right now. *Swadharma* is what is natural to one. For him who works without egotism, his dharma lies clear before him. It grows and expands on its own. We can satisfactorily perform only our dharma, that which lies before us. We are deluded if we think that we can do teaching better than the work of cleaning lavatories which may have been assigned to us. We do as much good by cleaning lavatories as we would by teaching. From one point of view, the former is certainly without merit. What is cleaning lavatories in comparison with

[1] III, 35

studies? The Ganga stands nowhere in comparison with the sea. The Ganga's dharma is to let boats sail over her, the sea's to let ships sail over it. The Ganga's may seem to have no merit, but that is her true dharma. When we say that a dharma may be, or may seem to be, devoid of merit, "may be" is used ambiguously to mean "may seem to be". From one point of view a certain task may be better than another, and yet for us the latter is superior.

This truth is the source of the idea of *varna*. Today all the four *varnas* have forsaken their functions, and yet we believe in the idea, for it helps to have an ideal even if it is no more than an ideal. Anyone who wishes to become free from the body has no choice but to believe in *varna*, that is, in his own natural work. The Lord, therefore, told Arjuna that his work was to kill, and asked him to do it as *yajna*, without making a distinction between kinsmen and others. The words *viguna* and *svanushthitat* have an equal and like force.

[12][1]

The *Gita* is a valuable provision for the mind in one's life-journey, as the spinning-wheel is for the body. It is a provision which I am able to supply. Continue to receive it. Remember the resolution of the committee about the verses included in the prayers. Even if they seem to be without merit, their recitation must be continued. The Chapters from the *Gita* [for recitation] should change every fortnight. You will find it difficult to keep up the practice till you have memorized the verses; if so, by all means read from a book. If by and by only one person remains to keep up this practice, he should imagine the entire world to be his listeners and go on reciting the verses. This is the only right course for anyone who has dedicated his life to non-violence. This is for those who wish to enjoy a spiritual empire, not for those who crave for empires of other kinds. Follow the practice with greater zest and put greater life into it day by day. Today it is just a week-old baby. By and by it will, like the sun and the moon, rise and set periodically. Gradually, try to follow the meaning of the verses.

As I have told you, the *Gita* is a big knowledge-feast, it is the very *amrita* of knowledge. I must have had some point in saying that. Many can memorize the verses. It is something within the power of both a god and a demon. I have suggested memo-

[1] The date of this discourse is not given in the source.

rizing in order that you may make the right use of the *Gita* thereby, and not to enable you to make a show of your knowledge of it. If you know the verses by heart, you will get a little electrical energy from them at some hour of the day. You will think of some verse or other, and it will save you. These verses are like oxygen. For those who read the *Gita* with faith, it is like the fabled wish-yielding tree. It can end all of our threefold sufferings. We may not see such a result in this life, but our faith should not be shaken on that account. If the result does not come, the reason will be deficiency of our own effort and not want of truth in the idea itself. It is only if we read the *Gita* in this spirit that it will prove the *amrita* of knowledge.

[13][1]

How should we define *swadharma*? The *varnashrama* had its origin in this idea. It is not peculiar to Hinduism, but prevails all over the world. In view of this, it is necessary to consider what *swadharma* means. In Chapter XVIII, we were even told that following one's *swadharma* one attains perfection; that is, following one's *swadharma* one attains equality with all. In this transitory world, we see equality nowhere. No two leaves are equal. But the *Gita* shows the way to equality. We shall see tomorrow how it does that.

[14][2]

Swadharma, though devoid of merit, is better than *paradharma*, so much so that, if need be, one should prefer to die while doing one's *swadharma*. The reason is that *paradharma* may prove dangerous. We should be careful about this. No one should do work which belongs to another, for that may be dangerous. Suppose that there is a powerful minister in a country. Asquith was superior in authority to the commander-in-chief of the army, but his dharma was only to issue orders and it was for the latter to give effect to them. Obeying his orders, the commander-in-chief would order the army to march to the battle-field. Suppose Asquith became vain and himself wanted to lead the army; if he did that, the country would be destroyed. The minister is of course next to the King in authority, but his taking upon himself this *paradharma* would be fraught with danger. Now think of the commander-in-chief. Suppose he wanted to rise to a higher position of

[1] & [2] The dates of these discourses are not given in the source.

authority and to become a minister, so that he might order the next commander-in-chief. If he did, there would be a great struggle for power in the country and it would be destroyed. The commander-in-chief would lose the position he already enjoyed, without getting the one he wanted. One more condition is also essential. The commander-in-chief should do his work, and the minister his; neither is superior or inferior to the other. This requires a sense of dharma on the part of both. If they have it, neither would feel superior or inferior to the other, for each would do his own dharma well and earn 100 per cent marks.

In God's court, one's attitude to work will be given the highest importance. No one there will take into account who was superior and who inferior in status and authority. One should never believe that one's own dharma is superior and another's inferior. Or rather, one should believe that one's dharma is the best for one. Take the example of a mother's attitude to her child. If the latter is ugly, the mother will shower all the greater care on it and will quarrel with anyone who slights it. In the same way, one's own dharma helps one to win *moksha*. The *Mahabharata* contains many examples of this truth. In Tulsidas's work, too, Guha and Shabari were devoted to God as they did their own work, and so attained the supreme state.

Varnashrama had its origin in the idea of *swadharma*. We do not see today the true idea of *varna*. It is limited now to restrictions about inter-dining and inter-marriage. The idea of *varna* is not peculiar to Hinduism. Such dharma which was peculiar to one society would become narrow, and one need not die for it. If our dharma is universal and valid at all times, one should be ready to die for it. *Varna* does not consist in customary practices regarding inter-dining and inter-marriage; the division of society into *varnas* is a division of functions. The idea of pollution by touch was a later accretion. The distinctions of *varna* prevail all over the world. We find them in every country. Most parents have to think what they will do about their children when they grow up, and the boys and the girls, too, have to think about their future. Exercised over these problems, we sacrifice our interests in this world and our welfare in the next. Worried by them, we lose sight of our means of deliverance. Can anyone else show us what our *swadharma* is? Doing *swadharma* does not mean the freedom of the individual and subordination of society. If a man seeks *moksha* and still believes that he is independent, he will utterly fail in his aspiration. One who seeks *moksha* behaves as society's servant. To win *moksha* means to merge in the sea. To attain that state means to be one with an infinitely vast sea. We are but germs in society. That word "germs" signifies our subordination to it. We are, in truth, free in such subordination. Our duty is what society assigns to us. Of three persons who work together, one is bound to be the leader. A commander-in-chief must consult the minister in certain matters; and likewise the minister, too, should consult the former in some other matters. The definition [of *swadharma*], then, is that one must do the work assigned to one by one's superior. From this, we shall by and by rise to a higher stage.

[15][1]

How is that in this *Gita* which is concerned with *moksha* we are asked to do work which may have no great significance, and to concern ourselves with *swadharma* ? Can we win *moksha* in this manner? Yes, we can. In the *Mahabharata* there is Tuladhar's story. The Brahmin in search of knowledge got it from a butcher. The devotee whom Mahadev [Desai] mentioned was a potter, and Bhojo Bhagat[2] was a cobbler. In saying, "better is death in the discharge of one's duty."[3] Shri Krishna has not laid down a principle very difficult to follow. The idea of *swadharma* involves restrictions on oneself. *Swa* means that which one has been able to digest. If we are not able to digest [what we eat], many disturbances in the system will follow and we would get diseases. If, observing others round us consuming *dudhapak*[4] and growing fat, we also eat it, we would come to grief. *Swadharma* indeed helps everyone to win *moksha*. But, till we have won it, what should we do as human beings living in these physical bodies ? If we understand the body's dharma and do it, we shall have to voluntarily accept subordination in order that we may become perfectly ourselves. It is to God that we have to subordinate ourselves. Can we hope that, because we recite *antar mama*[5] every day, God who is asleep in our hearts will awake ? To wake Him, we shall have to seek someone's help. *Swadharma* means the work which falls to our lot from hour to hour. We should do the work assigned to us by others. We have to submit ourselves to our conscience, but what will a person do if he has no conscience? When we have elimi-

[1] The date of this discourse is not given in the source.
[2] Gujarati poet, 1785-1850
[3] In III, 35
[4] Boiled, sweetened milk cooked with a little rice
[5] A Bengali *bhajan* included in the *Ashram Bhajanavali*

nated the "I" from us, then will God take the place vacated by it. We have to accept subordination for His sake. Having accepted a job anywhere, we should do it with single-minded devotion and sense of duty; we should do it even if this work which falls to our lot is unattractive to us, repels us or smells of violence. If in a world like ours full of violence, such work falls to our lot, we must do it. A task of this kind fell to the lot of Harishchandra. When he raised his sword to kill his wife, he had no violence in him. Did he wish ill to his wife? His heart was filled with compassion. The poet says that he had hardened his heart, but in truth he had hardened only his hand. If we were painters, we would not draw him with a face distorted by a feeling of aversion. If he had in fact raised his sword with reluctance on his face, we would have to say that he was overcome by ignorant attachment and that, having risen so high, at last he fell; this blot would have remained on him. We cannot imagine any sign of suffering on his face. Following his example, we should do with perfect devotion and without hesitation any duty which falls to our lot. It is best, in the first instance, not to take up a task, but, having taken up one, we must not forsake it. Consider, for instance, a large black ant whose feet, if stuck in jaggery, will not let go their hold of it; they remain stuck to it. Not to forsake the task undertaken, that is but the definition of satyagraha itself. Everyone, from a child to an old man, should cling to the task undertaken till he or she breaks. This is internal meditation, this is Vedanta. Of course, the work done in this spirit should be dedicated to God. We should be totally absorbed in any work which we may be doing. If such absorption is inspired with a selfish interest in work, it will bring about our fall, and if with a sense of dedication to God it will lift us up.

[16][1]

So, then, this is one idea, that *swadharma* is better than *paradharma*. The next question is: if no one can escape doing karma, what is the difference between the karma of a wise man and that of an ignorant man? The former performs *yajna* for others, the latter works for himself. If we do karma as *yajna*, it would be as if we did no karma. Shri Krishna then advanced the argument of society's good, and told Arjuna that he should work on without wasting a single moment in idleness, should

[1] The date of this discourse is not given in the source.

work on without concern for the "I" and dedicating to God all that he did.

How does it happen that, though trying to act in this way, man sometimes commits sin? If, in doing *swadharma*, we follow our own wilful inclinations, do it in pride, we are not doing *swadharma*. What is the reason that, though most people in the world do their *swadharma*, the pile of sins in the world remains as huge as ever?

With Chapter III the *Gita* ends. It need not have been followed by anything more. Even in the third Chapter, there are five or six verses which are really important. The rest of the *Gita* is intended to explain more clearly what has been said in the first three chapters.

Shri Krishna tells Arjuna, in reply to his question, that desire and anger ride on our two shoulders. If they are with us while we do our *swadharma*, then we gain nothing. Can we say that many of those who enter the Councils act unworthily? They do it to serve others. But their action is prompted by desire, by the aim of getting the better of the Government; there is anger behind it and, therefore, it is not right. Desire and anger are blood-brothers. They dwell in the senses and the mind. We can, therefore, overcome them only by subduing these. Hence it is that the way to *moksha* is said to lie in becoming free from attachments and aversions. This is the reason why we are advised to become free from them. If we are enslaved by something, is there anything we would not do for its sake? Vishvamitra[1] did hard *tapas*, but afterwards he felt that his *tapas* was superior to Vasishtha's[2]; from that arose desire, which provoked anger. One should understand this with one's reason at any rate and move as slowly as a snail; one may then work on without fear of any kind.

[17]

November 23, 1926

We ought to cultivate such a state of mind that on no day can we have peace unless we have recited verses from the *Gita*. What a contrast between the noise at the evening and the peace in the early morning! We should not be satisfied merely with reciting the verses or leading their recitation anyhow. Day by day our recitation should improve in regard to pronunciation. One person's lapse in this matter is the lapse of all. As this is true of the music in a concert, so is it true of the music of life.

[1] & [2] Sages in the *Ramayana*

If we pray with the heart and the mind in unison, why should we care for the perishable body? Why should we be concerned whether it lives or falls? We may not mind the distance from others which this material thing imposes on us; after all, how far apart can a material thing keep us? If we have cultivated the unity of our self with the selves of others, with God as witness, if we treat the lapse of one as the lapse of all, it will be very good indeed. If we also pronounce the words correctly, we shall approach God with water in a vessel as clean as possible. We shall have placed a *bel* leaf in the water with utmost attention to cleanliness, and filled the vessel with water from the purest source. Such outward attentions are meaningless in themselves; but they lend grace where there is faith. A man of faith will make his gift as artistic as he can. Today's craftsmanship is lifeless and no craftsmanship at all. How much patience must the craftsmanship of olden days have required? How many years must have been spent on learning it? We have come across no engineer of the old school, one who had built palaces in his time. Our effort to master correct pronunciation is a sign of our heart-felt love; we should not, thus, let our recitation of the *Gita* become dry at any time.

In Chapter III, Shri Krishna explained the supremacy of karma. After explaining that, if we wish to practise yoga through karma, we should dedicate to God every karma which we do, He explained what other things should accompany karma. It should be enriched with knowledge. Let us think about the path of knowledge and the path of karma. Anyone who follows the former exclusively becomes heartless; he who follows the latter exclusively becomes dull in mind. For the right choice of karma we should combine the methods of both the paths. Both are excellent, but neither can be practised without the other. Is there anything as humble as a stone, or anything which does as much karma as it does? How utterly dedicated to God is its karma? It goes on working for ever in the same, unchanging manner; but, as a mere piece of stone, it never wins *moksha*. A stone should cease to be a stone and should become Ahalya[1], should come alive. On the one hand, we should be as inert as a stone, and, on the other, we should become the very image of knowledge, and this in such manner that no one can say whether the person is a man of karma or of knowledge. Then will his *purushartha* be complete. Where *jnana* and karma unite, *bhakti* will follow as a matter of course. For

[1] A character in the *Ramayana*. Her husband's curse had turned her into a stone, which regained her living form at the touch of Rama's feet.

the moment, we have seen that there should be a combination of the two. When we have understood the meaning of both, we shall see no difference between *sankhya* and yoga. That is the substance of Chapter IV. I shall not go into a discussion of the different types of *yajna*.

[18][1]

Hathayogis[2] believe Chapter VI to have been written for them. Their belief is that it was written because *hathayoga* has a place in the practice of yoga. I do not share this view, though I admit that *hathayoga* has some utility. We should avail ourselves of all possible means which help in self-realization. It is said about the purely physical processes described in *hathayoga* that those who go through them will attain self-realization. Jnanadeva went riding on a wall to receive someone who was coming to see him riding a lion. But what then? He thereby brought yoga into discredit. These processes do not necessarily take one to God. The secret of rising towards God lies in the mind. In this very Chapter there is the verse: *Uddharedatmanatmanam natmanamavasadayet.*[3] That is, this Chapter teaches the importance of controlling the self. Mortification of the body is also as much for the control of the mind as for the control of the self. Anyone who practises these processes, knowing that they help control of the mind, will certainly derive much profit from them. We have not taken them up because we have not met anyone who knows them. We have been visited by many who believed in them and recommended them to us, but none who knew them. Hence I have done nothing in that field. But I do have them in my mind. I mention this thing so that, if you come across a sadhu who is like me a seeker, you should avail yourselves of his services. Our bodies have become very weak. If we know these physical processes very well, they would be found to be far more effective exercises than what they teach in England. The sixth Chapter of course discusses the importance of rules. It also explains the means of doing karma in a disinterested spirit. *Jnana* signifies the knowledge of man who knows the Shastras and the term yogi means one who knows the science of karma.

This Chapter explains the conditions which must be fulfilled before we can do karma in a disinterested spirit. It is not possible

[1] The date of this discourse is not given in the source.

[2] Practitioners of yoga in its purely physical aspect

[3] In VI, 5

to do karma in that spirit without control of the self. Those who control themselves from hour to hour, only they can work in that spirit. Thieves, robbers and immoral men never talk about doing karma in a disinterested spirit. Many persons use the *Gita* to justify their actions. But disinterestedness is a state of the mind, and such a state can never be cultivated without effort and without self-control. One whose left hand does not know what his right hand does, such a one knows what it is to be equal-minded. Our yardstick is the ability to see others as ourselves. We should think whether we should be happy if others did to us what we do to them.

Disinterestedness can never be cultivated without a spirit of renunciation. That is the true meaning of Chapter VI.

[19][1]

The *Bhagavad Gita* is divided into three parts: six chapters for the syllable *tat*, six for *tvam* and six for *asi*[2].

In Chapter VI, Shri Krishna explains the means of controlling the senses. In the seventh chapter, he discusses the distinction between *jnana* and *vijnana*. *Vijnana* means knowledge of particulars. *Jnana* embraces God's *para prakriti*, and *vijnana* relates to His *apara prakriti*. Chapter VIII discusses further what is included in *vijnana*. The last verse in Chapter VII says that he who performs the three types of sacrifice, *adhiyajna*, *adhidaiva* and *adhibhuta*, goes to the Lord. Discussing *akshara*, Shri Krishna explained that one should meditate exclusively on that, for one becomes like that on which one meditates. He explained *adhidaiva* to mean that He was the *Parabrahman*, supreme above all, and asked why, since this was so, anyone should seek to please other deities lower or higher. It is God alone that one should worship and serve. But what does serving God mean? Shri Krishna said that He was both the invisible Reality and the visible world. If so, the karma which we do is also done by Krishna. If He is the master of the show, can we believe that we do anything? As the dirty water which falls into the Ganga is purified, so we should believe that the sins we commit are committed by God, for he who harbours no sinful thoughts cannot commit sin. Anything to which motion is imparted retains it for some time. If we fell a tree, for some time the leaves would remain green, but they would soon

[1] The date of this discourse is not given in the source.

[2] The three syllables constitute the great Upanishadic text *tat tvam asi*, "That thou art."

begin to wither. If a person has overcome both his conscious and unconscious desires, they will not rise again. In Chapters VII and VIII, Shri Krishna explains what Creation is and describes the visible world and the nature of karma, and shows that everything exists in God. Why does He lay so much stress on the necessity of doing karma in a disinterested spirit? These two chapters sufficiently explain the reason. A person who has plunged into water goes on swimming in it, but the latter is in no way concerned. Similarly, God is a sea of compassion. This too, however, is merely a conception of our mind. Truly speaking, God is neither a generous-hearted Being nor a sea of compassion. It is in such a God that we live and move.

[20][1]

Chapters IX and X are to be taken together. Shri Krishna says: "I dwell in all creatures, hence do all things for my sake." And so He said: "On Me fix thy mind, to Me bring thy devotion."[2] In Chapter X Arjuna asked Shri Krishna to show him His divine powers. The stream of *bhakti* which flows from Chapter VII onwards gathers volume from chapter to chapter. Shri Krishna shows Arjuna His divine powers and urges him again and again to dedicate everything to God. All the four chapters lead us towards *bhakti*. Chapter IX, especially, is about *rajavidya* and *rajaguhya*. It is really a great support for persons like us given to a life of sin. Even the most sinful person is promised help and support. The *Gita* would not approve anyone running down *mantras* from the Vedas. It says, on the contrary, that even the most sinful man will be saved if he dedicates everything to Shri Krishna. This knowledge is *guhya* only so long as it has not touched the heart.

[21]

[*November 27, 1926*][3]

Shri Krishna showed His cosmic form to Arjuna and explained to him that it could be seen, not by those who had studied the Vedas and gained other like qualifications, but only by those whose hearts were steeped in *bhakti*. What a vision it must have been! My enthusiasm for the *Gita* grows day by day. I agreed

[1] The date of this discourse is not given in the source.
[2] In XVIII, 65
[3] This date is given on the title page of *Gandhijinu Gitashikshan*.

to talk about the *Gita* and explain its meaning, and I liked the idea; but my pleasure in the discussion has grown from what it was when I started. I get daily more absorbed in it. We, who are given to self-indulgence, cannot always taste this joy. The real joy comes from *bhakti*, that is, it is spiritual. This interest is growing because it is like savouring food which is digested more and more completely from day to day, and it influences our conduct accordingly. Such is my state of mind. I feel that in this chapter the *Gita* reaches its highest point. We take twelve minutes to recite it, so that we are likely to feel tired by the time we have come half-way. If we let ourselves sink in it, we should be saved. Shri Vyasa has described the vision so vividly that we feel as if we see it with our own eyes. Beholding it, we wonder what our own place in this universe is. It is nothing. It is as small as a grain of dust. Where are we in this universe of stars, suns and planets? If a hair could speak, it would describe its place thus: "I have value so long as I am a part of the body; separate me from it and my value is lost. The essence of life in me cannot vanish; as for the material substance, even the vast universe is transient, existing only as name and form." We are nothing, compared with that visible manifestation of God, this vast universe. Being what they are, whom can we kill? Even if we kill anyone, we too shall die simultaneously. As we understand this more and more, we should become steeped ever more fully in *bhakti*.

Even those who go out visiting other places should keep up the daily practice.

[From Gujarati]

Gandhijinu Gitashikshan

87. LETTER TO C. NARAYANA RAO

THE ASHRAM,
SABARMATI,
November 27, 1926

DEAR FRIEND,

I have your letter.[1] Why do you want to leave your permanent service? I think it is quite possible for one to serve one's country no matter in what situation of life one may be, provided, of course, that the occupation itself is clean. In any case, in addition to the reason [for] wanting to leave service, please supply me with the following information:

What is your age? Are you married? Have you children? Are your parents alive? Have you any dependents? Are you keeping excellent health? Are you prepared to do continuous physical labour for 8 hours per day? Can you be satisfied with mere sanitation, field work or work in the kitchen or work at the spinning-wheel and the like? Do you know Sanskrit? How far have you studied? What languages do you know?

Yours sincerely,

SJT. C. NARAYANA RAO
CLERK, EXCISE DEPTT.
BERHAMPORE

From a microfilm: S.N. 11020

88. LETTER TO RICHARD B. GREGG

THE ASHRAM,
SABARMATI,
November 27, 1926

I see you are adding to my debt. I already owe you a reply to several questions in your previous letter.[2] And I have now before me another letter with quotations from Thomas Paine.[3]

[1] Writing on November 19, the correspondent had expressed a desire to leave his job and enter the Ashram for "leading a happy and peaceful life".

[2] For Gandhiji's earlier letters to Gregg, *vide* Vol. XXXI.

[3] *Vide* "Price of Freedom", 9-12-1926.

The quotations I hope to use as you suggest. I have not yet gone through them.

The articles on khaddar you may use just as you like.

I am glad you have appreciated the articles "Is This Humanity?"[1]. I felt that I should make my position clear irrespective of whether it sounded or was in fact tenable or not. It is enough that the views expressed therein represent my definite conclusions.

You will notice the flaw in your analogy. You compare duty towards the ward with your duty towards moral welfare of the assailant. Now the moral welfare of the assailant is not at stake when you are defending the ward. It is his physical existence that is at stake. And, if instead of the assailant being a stranger, it was another ward, but stronger than the one then under your protection, you would still have to defend the one under your protection against the other ward who is about to assail the former and whom you have no other means of overcoming. God will judge your duty in accordance with your intentions. Indeed, one may go a step further and assume the one who is to be protected not to be a ward, but an utter stranger who has sought protection. There is a beautiful tale in the *Mahabharata*. A great prince[2] had a pigeon flying to him for protection against a hawk. The hawk feels that the pigeon is his lawful prey duly appointed as such by God. The prince wards him off by saying that whilst pigeons ordinarily were a lawful prey for hawks, he cannot neglect the obvious duty of protecting those who sought his protection and the prince generously offered his own flesh as substitute. This, of course, is the most spiritual method of dealing with the hawk. But where one is too weak to adopt that method, one would be bound to carry out the law of protection by resisting the approach of the hawk by force. And this one would do in accordance with the law of ahimsa. I don't know whether I have made my position clear.

I see you are not coming to pass your winter in Sabarmati. I am sorry in two ways. First, because, though I shall be away, the Ashramites will miss you. Secondly, because, it is the fear of the Ashram climate and water that is deterring you. We, diet reformers, should really discover ways of bending climate to our will rather than succumb to them. I know, however, this is counsel of perfection. The step you are taking is prudent and therefore in the circumstances superior to the counsel of perfection

[1] *Vide* also Vol. XXXI.

[2] King Sivi of Ushinara, near Gandhara

which cannot be carried out without taking risk. I shall follow with considerable interest your researches in the tutorial line.

Devdas is quite well and strong. He has gone to nurse Mathuradas at Panchgani. I leave for Wardha on the 2nd December. My love to you and the Stokes and Sundaram and Savitri.

Yours,

R. B. GREGG
SIMLA

From a photostat: S.N. 12088

89. IS THIS HUMANITY?–VIII

[*November 28, 1926*]

Letters on this subject are still pouring in, but I fail to discover in them any new question or any fresh argument advanced. I would therefore ask those who have been thinking on this subject to read this series of articles over and over again. I do so without the slightest hesitation, inasmuch as they are the result not of ideas hastily formed, but of experience of many years. I have presented no new principles, but have tried to restate old principles. I cannot say how far the presentation is correct, but as it represents my honest conviction, and as many friends expect me to solve intricate problems in ahimsa, I can only ask them to turn to the series I have been writing. Some of my correspondents wrench my own sentences from their contexts and quote them against me, some quote part of them and omit the most essential remainder.

Thus I have never advocated the extirpation of dogs as a class. On the contrary my suggestions have been made for their betterment. I have repeatedly said that I have suggested the destruction of certain dogs under certain circumstances. Even this may be open to question. If it is, the objector should address himself only to that and nothing more.

I continue to be the same votary of ahimsa that I was before. I still continue to hold life not only in man and animal, but in plant and flower, as sacred, and yet make use of vegetables and flowers and fruit. Only the spirit behind the use is: 'He that soweth to his flesh shall of the flesh reap corruption; but he that soweth to the spirit shall of the spirit reap life everlasting.' Destruction of dogs, even as that of plant or vegetable, is advised only when it is a matter of imperative duty, and only when it is meant not to sow to the flesh, but to the spirit.

What torments me is the impotence of the votary of ahimsa. Ahimsa is not impotence. Ahimsa is not powerlessness. Ahimsa is unconquerable power. We shrink from it as we are dazed by its over-powering lustre. Only very few of us can catch a glimpse of it. Ahimsa is the distinguishing characteristic of an untrammelled spirit. It is at the root of a number of other qualities—discrimination, detachment, penance, equability and knowledge. It is the way of the brave, not of shrinkers. He who would understand ahimsa must understand the meaning of the inevitable *himsa* one sees about oneself. This statement, I know, is liable to abuse. But what is there free from this danger? Is not even God's name turned to the worst account? Have not rivers of blood been made to flow in His name? Have we not worshipped the Devil in His name? But that does not diminish His glory. That does not mean that we shall take His name in a secret corner.

All action is tainted inasmuch as it presupposes *himsa*. And yet we free ourselves from the bondage of action through action itself. This body is the receptacle of sin, and yet we seek to achieve salvation by making of that abode of sin God's own sanctuary. Even so with *himsa*.

And this *himsa*, calculated to take us on the onward path, must be spontaneous, must be the lowest minimum, must be rooted in compassion, must have discrimination, restraint, detachment at its back, and must lead us every moment onward to the path of ahimsa.

I propose to conclude this series with a brief reference by way of illustration to the way in which we are trying to solve the dog problem in the Ashram.

The problem is as old as the Ashram itself. The activity of the *Mahajan* has made it more serious, and we have put up with it not without reluctance. It is our practice to destroy rabid dogs. Two or three such cases have occurred during the last ten years. Healthy dogs have not been destroyed. They are being refused food. I see that, if the rule is strictly observed we would be all happy, but we cannot do so. Every inmate does not yet realize the necessity of it, and those who do are not sufficiently alive to the observance of the rule. And there are also employees in the Ashram,—how can they be made to observe the rule?

Some dogs we feed, there being no other alternative. Two bitches and their puppies are being maintained at present. The puppies have been kept in cosy boxes or baskets to keep them from cold, and are being given milk and the dams get specially prepared food.

On the other hand, we have applied to the *Mahajan* to remove stray dogs from here. The request has been accepted, though their cart has not yet come.

I have explained to the best of my light our duty to the dogs. Everyone has to act according to his own light. Let no one learn from me the *duty* of destruction. He may under certain circumstances permit himself to have recourse to it. I have laid down the limits. Everyone observes and will observe the law according to his own capacity. I have referred to the present practice at the Ashram simply to serve as an illustration of what my opinion means.

The religion of ahimsa consists in allowing others the maximum of convenience at the maximum of inconvenience to us, even at the risk of life. Everyone has to determine for himself the amount of inconvenience he is capable of putting up with. No third party can determine it for him. Religion, even as the soul, is both one and many.

Young India, 2-12-1926

90. *SPEECH AT CONVOCATION OF GUJARAT VIDYAPITH, AHMEDABAD*

November 28, 1926

I take it as God's favour that I have been able to be present here this year as I was last year, I congratulate the students who have received degrees and prizes and pray that their aspirations may bear fruit. I did not know what to say on this occasion. Just then Shri Chintaman Vaidya came to my rescue. The moment I received this week his letter saying that he would be coming here on business, the burden on me was lifted. His name is not unknown to students. His scholarship too is well known. He has published books on the *Mahabharata* and on Indian history. He has served his motherland not only through books but also through public work. Like our Vidyapith, there is a Vidyapith in Maharashtra also. He has been serving it. He holds the office of its Vice-Chancellor. The status of that Vice-Chancellor is higher than that of ours. Shankaracharya is the Chancellor there. Nanabhai[1] can work in consultation with me, while Shri Vaidya himself bears the entire responsibility there. It will certainly be worth your while to listen to what he has to say. And yet I have a few things to say to you.

All of you can see that in numerical strength the condition of the Vidyapith is deteriorating. But that does not frighten me in the least. Even today I have the same faith in its mission that I had when under good auspices I set up this Vidyapith in 1920. I may boldly say that my faith is being even strengthened. Numerical strength does count in the world, but so far as our movement is concerned we have to rely only on the strength of quality. When the numerical strength is small we need not be disheartened, but we must maintain special vigilance. Today a handful of British officials rule over India. Do they have that much self-confidence? As there are 250 districts in India, there must be 250 Collectors. How many men have to be controlled by a single Collector? And yet he can play tennis in the evening and enjoy sound sleep at night. He does not feel worried even in a forest. As we have to fight him, cultivate self-confidence even though you are a handful. If we have thousands of workers, we can afford indolence or neglect of duty, but when the number is small, everyone has to be particularly vigilant.

I assure you that I have not the slightest anxiety about the future of the Vidyapith. If you would remain vigilant in your work, the future is certainly bright. Even if there is but one student in the Vidyapith, he will definitely do his work. And for the sake of that one student—even if I were in Kashmir—I shall come here to award him a degree. You should never think that my enthusiasm at that time will be less even by an iota. I can say that I shall have all the greater enthusiasm in awarding a degree to that single student and I shall take greater pride in it—if I am entitled to take such pride.

The Vice-Chancellor has requested me to lead the Vidyapith along the lines of independent education. I welcome the ideals which he has set forth. Further I have been asked whether we shall retain the temptation of prizes. We have to make the students realize that education is itself a prize. The fruit of a sacrifice is the sacrifice itself. I welcome this idea also. But I am one who acts knowing one's limitations. We have to work against such a powerful wind that I dare make no changes.

[1] Nrisinhprasad Bhatt, then Vice-Chancellor of Gujarat Vidyapith

I have committed no folly in establishing the Vidyapith. You too should if you can have the same faith. I know our drawbacks, because I am full of them. Do not allow weaknesses to creep in.

[From Gujarati]

Sabarmati, Vol. V, Autumn Issue, 1926

91. LETTER TO BRIJKRISHNA CHANDIWALA

Monday [*November 29, 1926*][1]

CHI. BRIJKRISHNA,

Mirabehn will reach Delhi on Friday at about 10 or 11 and will be staying at Vidyavatiji's Gurukul. She goes there with the intention of learning Hindi. Meet her at the station and take her to Daryaganj.

Give her the help she needs. I am hoping that someone from the Gurukul will be at the station.

If you feel like coming to Wardha[2], do come over.

Blessings from
BAPU

From a photostat of the Hindi: G.N. 2353

92. LETTER TO PURUSHOTTAMDAS THAKURDAS

ASHRAM,
Monday [*November 29, 1926*]

BHAISHRI PURUSHOTTAM,

You have done what no one else has succeeded in doing. As I had promised, I have been studying currency this month.[3] Last week I finished reading the Royal Commission's report.[4] I was

[1] Mirabehn was in Delhi on Friday, December 3, 1926; *vide* "Letter to Mirabehn", 3-12-1926. The preceding Monday was November 29.

[2] On December 3, 1926, Gandhiji left Ahmedabad for Wardha, where he stayed up to December 20, 1926.

[3] *Vide* Vol. XXXI, p.367.

[4] The Royal Commission on Indian Currency, headed by Hilton Young, was announced by the Viceroy on August 20, 1926. In its report, the commission recommended fixing the value of the rupee at 1s 6d gold and the creation of a Central Bank. The addressee, who was a member of the Commission, differed from the majority on these two points.

very happy to read your minute. This does not mean that I understand the subject. You probably have no idea of my ignorance of the subject. The distinction between Gold Exchange standard, bullion standard and Exchange standard is still not clear to me. Just now I have been reading Madan's books. I do not know when I shall be ready to give my opinion. I am getting ready to display my ignorance. Meanwhile, from a distance I watch with admiration your fight.

Vandemataram from
MOHANDAS

From a microfilm of the Gujarati: S.N. 19970

93. *STRENGTH IN WEAKNESS*

I make no apology for reproducing General Smuts' great speech[1] on Emily Hobhouse at the time of burying the ashes of Emily Hobhouse in Bloemfontein. The speech makes clear what one individual with force of character can do; what a woman, miscalled the weaker sex, can do; what true patriotism means.

Young India, 2-12-1926

94. *THE WHEEL OF LIFE*

The headline is of my making but what follows is an abstract of C. Rajagopalachari's notes[2] submitted to the Royal Agricultural Commission[3]. The value of the notes lies in their being an accurate record of his experience. After a careful perusal of the note, the reader will answer for himself whether the spinning-wheel is or is not truly the Wheel of Life for India's millions. C. Rajagopalachari's second suggestion that the temptation of drink must be removed from the poor people is worthy of serious

[1] Not reproduced here

[2] Not reproduced here. The notes said that within a short time the number of spinning-wheels plying in Tamil districts alone had gone up to 30,000; that the average income from each wheel was Rs. 14-9-8 per year which, when compared with the Rs. 50/- that some of the agriculturist families got from their land per year, was a substantial amount.

[3] The Royal Commission on Indian Agriculture. The formation of the Commission headed by the Marquis of Linlithgow was announced by the Viceroy on January 20, 1926, and its sittings took place in the winter of 1926-27.

consideration by those who will solve the problem of economic distress. If the men will use up in drink the hard-earned coppers of their women spinners, even the spinning-wheel will be but a frail support.

Young India, 2-12-1926

95. *NOTES*

Currency

For the past many years, I have resisted the pressure of friends to study the currency question, not because it is not one of the most important questions engaging public attention but because I have more than enough to do and because I know nothing about the science and I never speak or write on subjects of which I have not acquired a knowledge to my own satisfaction. I am now no longer able to resist the pressure. The friends urge that I must assist in popularizing its study, and use such influence as I possess among the masses for their education in this vital matter. I do not share their enthusiasm. I am not sure that the masses can be made to understand the very intricate riddles of currency. But I dare not brush aside the weighty statement they make that the present currency policy of the Government if carried out means a strain upon the resources of the dumb millions of India which they are ill able to sustain. I have therefore promised to study the question, open the columns of *Young India* for its discussion and if possible to express my own opinion about it. In redemption of that promise I am in a position to publish elsewhere what I hope is the first instalment of a series of articles on currency from the pen of Professor P. A. Wadia. I have myself just finished a preliminary study of the report of the Royal Commission. I confess I do not understand it as I would understand say a work on the economics of the spinning-wheel. I am in search of a teacher who would make the language of currency almost as real to me as that of the spinning-wheel. Then but not till then shall I be able to express my own opinion on the problem. Meanwhile I promise to devote to its serious study all the odd moments I can spare.

Stray Dogs *v.* Village Dogs

A friend says: "You advocate the destruction of stray dogs. Do you include in the category the very useful village dogs?"

Most certainly I do not. I have made that perfectly clear in the pages of *Navajivan.* The village dogs are the cheapest and the most efficient police we have for protecting villagers against thieves at night and intruding dogs and other animals during the day. But I have not advocated an indiscriminate destruction even of stray dogs. Many other remedies have to be adopted before that drastic measure is resorted to. What I have insisted upon is a municipal bye-law authorizing municipalities to destroy unowned dogs. This simple legislation will protect the dogs from cruel neglect and put the *Mahajan* upon their mettle. It is the indiscriminate and thoughtless charity which has to be resisted. That charity which feeds dogs and indeed men who choose to become beggars harms the beggars and the society which encourages such false charity.

THE WORTHIEST LADY

A correspondent sends the following interesting cutting[1] taken from a history of Rome.

Young India, 2-12-1926

96. LETTER TO MIRABEHN

SURAT,
December 3 [1926]

CHI. MIRA[2],

Your telegram received. Delighted. God be with you.[3]
With love,

BAPU

SHRIMATI MIRABAI
KANYA GURUKUL
DARYAGANJ
DELHI

From the original: C.W. 5188. Courtesy: Mirabehn

[1] Not reproduced here. The extract described how four Romans disputed about whose wife was the worthiest of them all and discovered that it was Lucretia, wife of Lucius Tarquinius Collatinus, distinguished for her beauty and domestic virtues, who was working at the loom while the other three feasted.

[2] The superscription in this and other letters addressed to Mirabehn is in Devanagari.

[3] Gandhiji had sent Mirabehn to the Kanya Gurukul in Delhi to learn Hindi and to teach carding and spinning.

97. LETTER TO G. D. BIRLA

WARDHA,
Kartika Krishna 14, 1983 [December 4, 1926]

BHAI GHANSHYAMDASJI,

I have your letter. I have no difficulty in reading your letter. If no promise is broken by your not going to Europe, then it is my belief that this is not the time for you to go there.

I do not wish to write anything about your victory. There are certain battles in which defeat is victory. I do not know if what has happened now is good for you or not. My advice is for you to observe objectively everything that happens in the Assembly[1].

I know that I have served the country through my silence; however, I am not confident that I can unite the various parties. My heart shrinks from the idea of going to Gauhati.[2] I have even written to Srinivasa Iyengar and Motilalji asking to be excused. When I feel confident, I shall myself step into the arena.

I do not know where it would be proper for me to stay in Calcutta if I had to go there. Unless I am forced to go to some other place, I would like to live under your care.

Yours,
MOHANDAS

From the Hindi original: C.W. 6140. Courtesy: G. D. Birla

98. CULTURE

Elsewhere I reproduce almost word for word the talk Mahadev Desai gave on the *takli* during the Youth Week[3], for it embodies his inmost thoughts and the attendant circumstances are worthy of note. That speech was not delivered for its own sake. But some young men got bored listening to it and they started a disturbance. I have often written to say that the practice of causing disturbances does not become India's culture. In this country, at any rate, those who do not like someone's speech may

[1] Central Legislative Assembly

[2] For the annual session of the Congress

[3] Celebrated at Ahmedabad in November, 1926

not pay attention to it, and if they find it repugnant they may walk out. But they should not employ force to stop a speaker from speaking. To shout down someone is nothing but use of force. If intolerance grows among us, it will hamper our progress. We have no reason to believe that what we do not like must assuredly be bad. Certainly there are many things in the world which taste bitter in the beginning but turn out to be sweet in the end.

A nation whose youths discard restraint, courtesy, humility and tolerance courts destruction. The reins of national life are in the hands of youth alone. Their responsibility is greater than that of old people because the latter have given whatever they could or as much as they wished to give [to the nation]. Youths are today shaping the new order and making fresh contributions.

Those who had made noise forgot this responsibility of theirs. Mahadev Desai's speech was being communicated by his hands. Hence it was such as could be followed through the eyes. The youths were unable to stop the speech that was being conveyed by the hands. When they realized this inability of theirs, they stopped their shouting. But they certainly earned discredit by shouting. The next day the papers reported that the youths prevented Mahadev Desai from giving his speech on the *takli*. This brought discredit not to Mahadev Desai but to those who had shouted. But their discredit is tantamount to our country's. A country's credit is not distinct from that of its citizens.

Showing repugnance against the *takli* is like marching an army against an ant. It has been shown in *Navajivan* by extracts quoted from old books that the *takli* is one of man's oldest tools. The *takli* is poor people's machine, it is their asylum. Just as the plough is the means of producing food, so is the *takli* the means of producing cloth. Huge mills may arise out of the *takli*. A spinning-mill means a mill containing *taklis*. Just as a man who, plugging the pipe-connections to the different houses, trains them towards his own house and thereby makes others dependent on him for water supply, a spinning-mill too makes independent spinners dependent by getting within itself all the various *taklis*. Thus, a *takli* is a symbol of freedom, a mill that of dependence. How then can one dislike such a thing as a means of support? It is our duty to realize the power of that tiny thing. He who makes us realize its power deserves our gratitude, deserves a good turn from us.

Just as we should starve if we renounced the plough, we have become naked by giving up the *takli*. Because a few get clothes, we should not think that crores of people also get them. Records prove that lakhs of our brothers and sisters go about naked and suffer from hunger.

The *takli* has a twofold power—to cover the body and to feed it—because spinning provides us with cloth and the money saved thereby goes to augment our power of purchasing food. Hence I have given to the *takli* or the spinning-wheel the name of *Annapurna*[1].

The *takli* dispels our lethargy, covers our body and supports it. How can such an implement be disliked?

Moreover, a *takli* brings us into contact with our poor brethren and enables us to share their hardships.

The sages have given us through a story-poem an idea of the power of a tiny blade of grass. The wind could not blow it away. The fire could not burn it up. Someone may well ignore a blade of grass considering it worthy of contempt, but if countless numbers of them were not there we would get neither food nor water. The power that lies hidden in a tiny blade of grass also lies hidden in the *takli*. I request those who have scoffed at the *takli* to read the dialogue between Yaksha and the gods. Those who belittle the *takli* belittle the poor. Those who belittle the poor cut off their own legs, cut off the branch on which they are sitting. The rich exist because the poor are there. If there were no poor, how could there be room for the rich?

Young men, whether in a school or a college, whether non-co-operators or co-operators, whether among those who shouted and created disturbance or its unhappy witnesses, do not give up our old culture, do not give up courtesy, do not give up love of the poor. Just as the sword is a symbol of destruction, the *takli* is a symbol of sustenance. Those who used the sword in the form of shouting did no creditable thing. You should not discard the *takli* or calumniate it. Mahadev has drawn your attention to your duty. It is my firm faith that those who do not perform the *yajna* of spinning and do not wear khadi, which is its *prasad*[2], know neither the poor nor their ways. You too should have that faith.

[From Gujarati]

Navajivan, 5-12-1926

[1] Goddess of plenty

[2] Gift of grace

99. *LETTER TO BEHRAMJI KHAMBHATTA*

WARDHA,
December 5, 1926

BHAISHRI KHAMBHATTA,

I got your letter. Your coming here made me very happy indeed. Come again. As you progressively shed the love of the body, you will have more and more peace of mind. I have still not got hold of the name of that oil. I will find it.

Blessings from
BAPU

From a photostat of the Gujarati: C.W. 4367. Courtesy: Tehmina Khambhatta

100. *TELEGRAM TO CHHAGANLAL GANDHI*

December 6, 1926

TO
CHHAGANLAL GANDHI
ASHRAM, SABARMATI

AMERICAN FRIENDS WELCOME.

BAPU

From the original as delivered: S.N. 11249

101. *LETTER TO ASHRAM WOMEN*

WARDHA,
Silence Day, December 6, 1926

SISTERS,

As I had promised, the first thing I am doing in the morning after breakfast is to write this letter to you.

It is now five minutes to seven, and so all of you must be on your way to the prayer ground. Whatever time you fix, keep to it. I am sure that those of you who have agreed to attend [the prayers] would be doing that unless it be for very serious reasons. I have suggested to Ramniklal[1] that he should ex-

[1] Ramniklal Modi, a teacher in the Ashram School

plain to you one or two verses from the *Gita* every day. But you may make him read anything you like. Do not give up the practice of writing. Keep trying to improve your handwriting.

But all this is not dharma itself, it is only a help in following dharma. The definition of dharma is contained in the verses which we used to read daily. What we want to learn is how to follow dharma. It lies in altruism. Altruism means desiring and working for the good of others and serving them. Begin this service by loving one another like sisters and sharing one another's griefs. This is but one point. As I wish to write to you every week, let me end my speech here.

Dakshabehn, Kamalabehn and Chi. Rukhi are quite well. All of them travelled by third class but the train was not crowded and so they experienced no hardship. I was the only one to travel in the second class. Lakshmidas[1] is immersed in the charkha work. What happened there about reading from the *Gita* has also happened here. For the rest please read my letter to Chi. Purushottam.

Blessings from
BAPU

From a photostat of the Gujarati: G.N. 3629

102. LETTER TO MURIEL LESTER

WARDHA,
December 6, 1926

DEAR MISS LESTER,

I was able to finish reading your letter last night. I fear you will see more of the things you have described if you stay in India long enough. Religion is a complex problem, as complex as life itself. It is remarkable how much humbug can pass under its hallowed name. But what you have seen is a passing phase. The remote village life is in its way deeply spiritual, in my opinion more so than in the West. That is the permanent part of mass Hinduism. It will be finally judged by its influence on them. For ages the cult of violence has failed to produce any impression on them. History has no record of these villages having in a mass taken part in violence. Not therefore that they are totally nonviolent. But they are comparatively so. However, all this is futile

[1] Lakshmidas P. Asar

writing. What matters is how we live ourselves irrespective of what the whole world may do. The more I see of the world the more humbled I become and the more fully I learn to lean on God. I must not go beyond two pages.

Yours,

M. K. GANDHI

From a photostat: G.N. 6560

103. LETTER TO MIRABEHN

Monday [December 6, 1926][1]

CHI. MIRA,

I had expected to hear from you today. This is my second letter to you. The first was a card. I see that it is possible to send you the *Autobiography*[2] if it is written on Mondays, as I have done. Here is the translation therefore. Please revise and post here the same day in which case it will be in time. If you cannot revise the same day you may send direct to Swami. This should reach you on Wednesday and if it is posted even on Thursday, I should get it in time on Saturday. . . .The last day for posting to Ahmedabad for *Y. I.* is Sunday here. Now you know what you can do. This arrangement will continue so long as I am here.

Here is Rolland's letter.[3] Sparrow[4] has translated it for me. Here it is. If you think it is accurate, you need not translate anew for me.

Love,

BAPU

From the original. C.W. 5189. Courtesy: Mirabehn

[1] Date supplied by the addressee

[2] The *Autobiography* commenced appearing in instalments in *Young India*, 3-12-1925. Gandhiji used to send Mirabehn Mahadev Desai's translation of each chapter for revision.

[3] *Vide* Appendix II.

[4] Miss Helene Haussding

104. LETTER TO LALTA PERSHAD SHAD

WARDHA,
December 6, 1926

DEAR FRIEND,

You will forgive me for not acknowledging earlier your letter of 30th October. The reason for the delay in acknowledging it was that owing to the heavy correspondence, your letter was inadvertently put away in a file and was handed to me only last week.

Exactly the same pressure has been brought to bear upon me as you have put to go and see the Sat Gurus who the writers consider are likely to satisfy my craving. Only three or four days ago, I received a telegram from Madras Presidency "Come at once, show you the guru you want." Should I have gone there and should I respond to all such letters? In my opinion, that is not the way to follow out the search for a guru. When I say that at the proper time the guru will come to the seeker, it is not a sign of arrogance but a statement of a well-known truth. You do not move about on the earth in search of God. He is to be found in your heart. And so does the guru, the perfect man, seek out all those who are craving in all humility and sincerity. The problem before me, therefore, is not so simple as you put it, nor is it a case of wilfulness or obstinacy.

I made a commencement with the English book you have sent me, but I must tell you that I have not been able to make further progress, for the simple reason that the things already taken by me leave no moment's rest or interval.

Yours sincerely,

SJT. LALTA PERSHAD SHAD
KAYASTH MOHALLA
AJMER

From a photostat: S.N. 19761

105. LETTER TO V. V. DASTANE

WARDHA,
December 6, 1926

MY DEAR DASTANE,

I have your letter. Of course you know that my consent regarding the translation of the *Autobiography* into Marathi is subject to Swami's approval. But I think Swami was agreeable.

From what you have written, it seems to me that Munshiji is morally liable to support only his father. The rest are his sons and his wife and perhaps the three infants who are, I suppose, young children and not grown [-up] ones. The eldest son should be called upon to support himself. It will be a service to him and a burden off from Munshiji's shoulders. If the daughter-in-law cannot live with her husband, she can be accommodated in some Ashram where she can earn her own living. The 10-year-old boy should also be put in an Ashram. Munshiji himself should select some work suitable for him and which he should be bound to do. I wonder if the daughter-in-law is the housewife and housekeeper in the family. Even if it is so and if she consents, the son should be asked to leave the house unless he will work for his own living. In any way Munshiji himself should object to being a burden on the nation when there is no occasion for it.

Yours sincerely,

From a microfilm: S.N. 19762

106. LETTER TO MANIBEHN PATEL

WARDHA,
Monday [*December 6, 1926*][1]

I enclose a letter for the Ashram women's association. I was pained to find that you are still in an uncertain state of mind. I do not think any other place will suit you better than the Ashram. Even in the Ashram there may be something you do not like. If that is so, you may try to change it. If you are constipated, the remedy is in your own hands. Or you may get drinking water from Ahmedabad. Enough of it for one person to drink can easily

[1] As in the printed source

be brought from the city. If you boil the water from the river and then drink it, it will be as good as water from the city. You must make a firm resolve to remain cheerful. Do not change your mind about coming here after the 14th. You will certainly get help here in your Sanskrit studies at any rate. And the climate will of course suit you. Do not hesitate to write to me frankly.

Tell Ramniklal that I feel rather worried as I have no news about Punjabhai's[1] health. What is his address? If Ramniklal gets any news about Punjabhai's health, ask him to write to me.

[From Gujarati]

Bapuna Patro—Manibehn Patelne, pp. 41-2

107. LETTER TO PRABHASHANKAR PATTANI

SATYAGRAHA ASHRAM,
WARDHA,
Magsar Sud 1, 1983 [December 6, 1926]

SUJNA BHAISHRI,

You are welcome. I got your letter at Wardha. You give no news about your health. Write about it. I shall have to go to Kathiawar in March.[2] We shall certainly meet then. I will write if I have to come earlier. I also got a letter from you written from England.

Vandemataram from
MOHANDAS

From a photostat of the Gujarati original: C.W. 3217. Courtesy: Mahesh Pattani

[1] Punjabhai Shah, an inmate of the Ashram

[2] For a session of the Kathiawar Political Conference

108. LETTER TO DEVCHAND PAREKH

Monday [December 6, 1926][1]

BHAI DEVCHANDBHAI,

I send the accompanying for you to read and preserve. I have sent a suitable reply. I have written to tell him[2] that he need say nothing on the political situation, [and also that] we shall not ask him often to go to Kathiawar.

BAPU

From a photostat of the Gujarati: G.N. 5722

109. LETTER TO RAMDAS GANDHI

WARDHA,
Silence Day [December 6, 1926][3]

CHI. RAMDAS,

I got your letter. Where there is faith and straightforwardness, success follows sooner or later. Can one admire sufficiently Abbas Saheb's[4] straightforwardness? His faith is equally great, and so circumstances continue to favour him. Tell Abbas Saheb that I liked Rehana[5] very much this time. I spent hours with Mirabai. Soheli also met me at Baroda. She is grown up now and is engaged and so she was feeling very shy. She did not even talk to me. Manilal[6] will land in Bombay on the 11th. Most probably Omar Seth will insist upon his getting off at Porbandar.

Blessings from
BAPU

[1] The postmark bears the date December 9, 1926. The preceding Monday fell on December 6, 1926.

[2] Amritlal Thakkar, who had been invited to preside over the session of the Kathiawar Political Conference and who seems to have explained his difficulties in accepting the invitation

[3] From the postmark

[4] Abbas Tyabji

[5] Daughter of Abbas Tyabji

[6] Manilal Gandhi

[PS.]

Blessings to Abbas Saheb.

CHI. RAMDAS GANDHI
C/o CHI. GOURISHANKER VYAS
MANAVADAR
KATHIAWAR

From a photostat of the Gujarati original: G.N. 6851

110. LETTER TO MANIBEHN PATEL

WARDHA,
Wednesday [December 8, 1926][1]

CHI. MANI,

I have your postcard. Come by all means. The morning train is more convenient than the night train. But do what you like. I am not waiting to get married, so that I may change my mind every moment. This is the privilege of unmarried girls. Boys too exercise a little of it.

Blessings from
BAPU

[From Gujarati]
Bapuna Patro—Manibehn Patelne, p. 42

111. LETTER TO VASUMATI PANDIT

[December 8, 1926][2]

CHI. VASUMATI,

I got your letter. Ba is still in the Ashram. I have about ten people here—Mahadev, Subbiah, Keshu, Lakshmidas, Krishnadas, Kamalabehn, Dakshabehn (whom you do not know) and Rukhi. Over and above these, Rajagopalachari and other gentlemen have also arrived. Don't you want to come to Wardha? I believe I shall be here up to the 20th at least, I hope you are

[1] As in the printed source
[2] From the postmark

in good health. Miss Haussding is also with me. Mirabehn has gone to Delhi.

Blessings from
BAPU

From the Gujarati original: C.W. 473. Courtesy: Vasumati Pandit

112. LETTER TO RAJKISHORI MEHROTRA

Wednesday [December 8, 1926][1]

CHI. RAJKISHORI,

I have your letter. I would very much love to send you somewhere for education. But it would mean that you have given up the desire for further progeny, that you have resolved to observe *brahmacharya*, that you have vowed to spend your life in the service of others, and that you have given up the shelter of your own parents and parents-in-law. Have you their permission? To be self-reliant one has to forgo the attendance of servants and so on. Observing you, I find that you have not yet attained control of the palate; nor have you given up other pleasures. Consider all these things and then let me know your firm decision. Meanwhile you may put in a good deal of study even while you are in the Ashram. Do it.

Blessings from
BAPU

From the Hindi original: C.W. 4954; also G.N. 7479. Courtesy: Parashuram Mehrotra

113. HER OTHER SERVICES

In sending me a cutting from *Indian Opinion*, Phœnix (Natal), a friend drew my attention to an omission from General Smuts' tribute to Emily Hobhouse copied some time ago in these pages. It refers to her effort to introduce spinning and weaving industry amongst the distressed Boer women after the Boer War. Here is the passage[2] in question.

Young India, 9-12-1926

[1] From the postmark
[2] Not reproduced here

114. PRICE OF FREEDOM

Mr. Gregg sends me[1] the following extracts from a written address by Thomas Paine to the soldiers of General George Washington's American army in the Revolutionary War, December 1776, fighting against the British for the freedom of the thirteen American Colonies:

> These are the times that try men's souls. The summer soldier and the sunshine patriot will, in this crisis, shrink from the service of his country; but he that stands it *now* deserves the love and thanks of man and woman. Tyranny, like hell, is not easily conquered; yet we have this consolation with us, that the harder the conflict, the more glorious the triumph. What we obtain too cheap we esteem too lightly; 'tis dearness only that gives everything its value. Heaven knows how to put a proper price upon its goods; and it would be strange indeed, if so celestial an article as *Freedom* should not be highly rated....
>
> I once felt all that kind of anger, which a man ought to feel against the mean principles that are held by the Tories: a noted one, who kept a tavern at Amboy, was standing at his door, with as pretty a child in his hand, about eight or nine years old, as I ever saw, and after speaking his mind as freely as he thought was prudent, finished with this unfatherly expression, 'Well, give me peace in my day.' Not a man lives on the continent but fully believes that a separation must some time or other finally take place, and a generous parent should have said, 'If there must be trouble, let it be in my day that my child may have peace,' and this single reflection, well applied, is sufficient to awaken every man to duty. Not a place upon earth might be so happy as America. Her situation is remote from all the wrangling world, and she has nothing to do but to trade with them. . . .
>
> I call not upon a few, but upon all, not on this state or that state, but on *every* state; up and help us; lay your shoulders to the wheel; better have too much force than too little, when so great an object is at stake. Let it be told to the future world, that in the depth of winter, when nothing but hope and virtue could survive, the city and the country, alarmed at one common danger, came forth to meet and to repulse it. Say not that thousands are gone, turn out your tens of thousands; throw not the burden of the day upon Providence, but '*show your faith by your works*' that God may bless you. It matters not where

[1] *Vide* "Letter to Richard B. Gregg", 27-11-1926.

> you live, or what rank of life you hold, the evil or the blessing will reach you all. The far and the near, the home countries and back, the rich and the poor, will suffer or rejoice alike. The heart that feels not now is dead; the blood of his children will curse his cowardice, who shrinks back at a time when a little might have saved the whole, and made *them* happy. I love the man that can smile in trouble, that can gather strength from distress, and grow brave by reflection. 'Tis the business of little minds to shrink; but he whose heart is firm, and whose conscience approves his conduct, will pursue his principles unto death....
>
> There are cases which cannot be overdone by language, and this is one. There are persons too who see not the full extent of the evil which threatens them; they solace themselves with hopes that the enemy, if he succeed, will be merciful. It is the madness of folly to expect mercy from those who have refused to do justice; and even mercy, where conquest is the object, is only a trick of war; the cunning of the fox is as murderous as the violence of the wolf, and we ought to guard equally against both.

It is remarkable how similar are the qualities required of soldiers of peace and soldiers of war. Thomas Paine's speech could be addressed almost word for word and with complete appropriateness to the Congress volunteers of 1921 who enrolled under the Ahmedabad Congress pledge of complete non-violence in thought, word and deed. Whether you secure freedom by the use of physical force or spiritual force, i.e., through self-suffering, the price to be paid must be heavy, if it is to be a valuable article. Bravery and perseverance in the face of odds are as necessary, if not more, to the man of the spirit as to the man of the sword. Whether we will win swaraj by violent means or non-violent, we shall have to discard ease and comfort, not to speak of luxuries. Pratap reduced himself to penury for the sake of what he believed to be freedom. Prahlad delivered his body for free destruction for what he believed to be his freedom. But there are among us not a few who would gain swaraj for a song. Thomas Paine tells us that such a thing is not possible.

Young India, 9-12-1926

115. THE GREATEST GOOD OF ALL

A constant reader of *Young India* sends the following:[1]

I reproduce this letter for it helps me to elucidate my own position. If such a very careful reader of *Young India*, as I know this correspondent is, misunderstands my position as is evident from his letter, how many more occasional readers must have done likewise? Several readers did draw my attention to the danger of a misunderstanding arising owing to the traditional hardness of our hearts which makes us prone to seize every opportunity of doing violence. One can only be—one ought to be—most careful in the handling of delicate problems; but no fear of misuse of statements can be permitted to stop a free and honest discussion of fundamental truths. For me, I shall learn to be and do right only by prayerful discussion, elucidation and interchange of views. This letter I have quoted is an instance in point. The discussion has brought to light an honest misunderstanding of difference between the correspondent and myself in the interpretation of the same principle.

Whilst I am of opinion that Dr. Blazer was well acquitted, according to the test laid down by me, he was wrong in taking the life of his daughter. It betrayed want of faith in the humanity of those around him. There was no warrant for him to suppose that the daughter would not have been cared for by others. The position in the case of dogs under the circumstances assumed by me is materially different from the position in which Dr. Blazer found himself. Nor am I able to subscribe to the view that an idiot has no soul. I believe that even the lower creation have souls.

Weightier still is the difficulty which another earnest reader puts and which may be thus summarized:

> I appreciate the position you have taken up. It is the only true position. But does not your argument after all resolve itself into the utilitarian doctrine of the greater good of the greater number? And if that is your position, wherein

[1] Not reproduced here. The correspondent enclosed a newspaper cutting which carried a report of how a Dr. Blazer had chloroformed his imbecile daughter because he felt there would be no one to look after her once he was dead. It also carried the report of a French actress who shot her lover at his own request as he was suffering from an incurable disease. The jury in both cases acquitted the accused.

does the doctrine of non-violence differ from the utilitarian which makes no pretence to non-violence and which will not hesitate to destroy life if the destruction would lead to the greater good of the greater number?

In the first place even though the outward act may be the same, its implications will vary according to the motive prompting it. Thus as non-violence in the West stops at man and, even then, only where possible, there is no compunction felt either over subjecting animals to vivisection for the supposed greater good of mankind or over heaping up most destructive armaments also in the name of the same doctrine of utility. A votary of non-violence, on the other hand, might have done one act of destruction in common with the utilitarian, but he would prefer to die rather than make himself party to vivisection or to an endless multiplication of armaments.

The fact is that a votary of ahimsa cannot subscribe to the utilitarian formula. He will strive for the greatest good of all and die in the attempt to realize the ideal. He will therefore be willing to die so that the others may live. He will serve himself with the rest, by himself dying. The greatest good of all inevitably includes the good of the greater number, and therefore he and the utilitarian will converge at many points in their career but there does come a time when they must part company, and even work in opposite directions. The utilitarian to be logical will never sacrifice himself. The absolutist will even sacrifice himself. The absolutist, when he kills a dog, does so either out of weakness or in rare cases for the sake of the dog himself. That it is a dangerous thing to decide what is or is not good for the dog, and that he may therefore make grievous mistakes is irrelevant to the fact of the motive prompting the act. The absolutist's sphere of destruction will be always the narrowest possible. The utilitarian's has no limit. Judged by the standard of non-violence the late War was wholly wrong. Judged by the utilitarian standard each party has justified it according to its idea of utility. Even the Jallianwala Bagh massacre was justified by its perpetrators on the grounds of utility. And precisely on the same ground the anarchist justifies his assassinations. But none of these acts can possibly be justified on the greatest-good-of-all principle.

Young India, 9-12-1926

116. NOTES

Incongruity

With my resumed travelling, if it has to be continued, begins my sorrow—crowds coming to have *darshan* with unmistakable affection in their bright eyes and smiling faces, but doing nothing of what I have ceaselessly poured into their ears. On the 4th instant, girls and boys presented to me in the early morning hours at Jalgaon their neatly made strands of hand-spun yarn but with a few honourable exceptions, they themselves were dressed in mill-made cloth. I wonder if the girls and the boys knew why they were spinning at all. The girls had been spinning only for four months and they belonged to the municipal school.

Good Work

The report before me of their spinning tells me that the work of introducing spinning in certain schools of the municipality was entrusted to East Khandesh District Khadi Board. How businesslike it would be if this example was followed by the other municipalities and organization of hand-spinning was entrusted to Khadi Boards who are naturally expected to have experts for the work? In this school they have both the *takli* and the charkha. The maximum spun by a single girl on the wheel was 7,188 yards of yarn. The highest count was 22. The maximum per hour spun on the *takli* was 120 yards; on the charkha, 375 yards. The report says:

> *Takli*-spinning has so much fascinated the girls of standard IV that 15 of them learnt to spin on charkha and have spun during their spare time. Their example has induced some girls of standard III also to learn on charkha. The contagion is spreading and the number of such voluntary girl-spinners is steadily increasing. The spinning has become a pastime with some as they come to spin even on holidays. 12 prepare their own slivers while 2 have commenced even to learn carding.

It is to be hoped that before long every girl will card her own cotton and prepare her own slivers and that the teachers will induce the girls to take to wearing khaddar. The best way of doing it is fully to explain to the girls the reason for spinning and to place every facility for procuring khaddar at reasonable prices and of the type they need. The teachers should also establish contact with the parents of the girls and secure their active co-operation in the work. The fact is that all this work can only be thoroughly done when the organizers throw their whole soul into it, as witness the extraordinary success of the work among the Labour Union schools of Ahmedabad. All the spinning teachers would do well to make themselves the improvised testing appliance which has been described in these pages. Speed without strength is waste. To draw thread is not enough. It is necessary to draw thread that can be used for warp.

Young India, 9-12-1926

117. KHADDAR IN THE PUNJAB

The following is a summary[1] prepared in the A.I.S.A. office of an exhaustive report in Hindi received from the A.I.S.A. agency, Punjab. The original contains details which the summary has omitted for the sake of condensation. In the original I find that khaddar work is going on in 42 centres. I invite the reader to visualize what this means. It means a living contact with toilers in these villages and distributing wealth among them in exchange for their labour. 'So do the merchants' one may be thoughtlessly inclined to say. But there is a great difference between a merchant who goes in their midst to exploit them and a patriot who goes to them to invite them to work and receive wages for their labour. When the wheel is firmly established, its appeal will be irresistible. Its result will be banishment of starvation for those who would work without having to tear down their homes. The feature of the Punjab work is that it has now become almost self-supporting. It has practically no bad book debts. Exchange of yarn for khaddar at an additional charge of 2 as. per yard is a valuable feature fraught with great consequences. It is possible, I suppose, only in a place like the Punjab where, as the report says there is a large number of men and women still wearing khaddar. Lala Kishan Chand Bhatia naturally takes pride in the fact that he has been able to have sheets locally printed at reduced prices. He has also imported the Khadi Pratishthan wheel and copied it with effect. The cry in the Punjab as elsewhere is want of patronage. Khaddar cannot be sold as fast as it is produced. All may not die for the country, may we not for its sake even wear khaddar unless it is equal in appearance and price to the latest machine-made stuff from Manchester or Japan? If we will not even give

[1] Not reproduced here

one extra pice for khaddar or put some restraint upon our sartorial taste, what is our patriotism worth? The Punjab has cotton, spinning, weaving and commercial ability. Will it not have enough patriotism to buy up khaddar as fast as it can be made? It should not be necessary for Jamnalalji or me or anyone else to go to the Punjab, collect money for khaddar work or to sell it.

Young India, 9-12-1926

118. DOWN WITH SUPERNATURALISM![1]

TO

THE EDITOR,

Young India

SIR,

When you judge the action of a 'believer' like Aurangzeb in desecrating and demolishing a place of worship like the Kashi temple as 'belying' his 'belief', viz., Islam (in *Young India* of 4-11-'26), are you not presuming to know more of Islam than the Prophet of Islam himself? For you must know that Mahomed himself, the beau ideal of Aurangzeb, when he entered Mecca in triumph against the enemies, destroyed all the objects and places of 'idolatrous' worship in that city, leaving a few of them like the Kaaba stone which he himself believed in! So then you must either (i) say that Mahomed was one of those 'so-called believers who belied[2] their belief',—which will not be in keeping with your former dictum that the great religious teachers of mankind were men who had exhibited the image of God in their own persons (*vide Young India*, 8-7-'26, page 244, column 2); or (ii) allegorize away the iconoclastic career of the Arabian Prophet (May peace be on Him!), as you usually do with whatever in the scriptures of any sect taken literally you do not 'understand' or whatever in them similarly understood does not 'appeal to your reason'; or (iii) repudiate the universally received life story of Mahomed as spurious. If there is a fourth way, please point it out; but please remember that Aurangzeb has been styled a 'living saint' (Zinda Pir, etc.) by all Sunni divines and historians who have never a word to say against his temple destruction, so far as I know, but many of whom on the contrary have glorified him therefor.

Is this fact not remarkable, seeing how the Ulema of India are today divided on the subject of the desecrations, the demolitions and

[1] This appeared in the correspondence column of *Young India*.

[2] The source has "believed in" which was corrected in *Young India*, 23-12-1926.

massacres which Ibn Saud, the Wahabi, has been responsible for in Mecca, Medina and Taif, one section (the Ahle hadis) justifying those deeds as quite Islamic, and the other (Shias, Hanafis, etc.) declaring them un-Islamic? But I have yet to meet a member of that learned and pious fraternity who will wholeheartedly condemn Aurangzeb's high-handedness on the Hindus' holiest of holies. It is much like those Sanatanis who would lynch you for trying to do away with untouchability in India and at the same time lynch also, if they could, those white-coloured folk in South Africa who are maintaining untouchability with the Indians there.

I am thus led to think that conflict and inconsistency are in the nature of all non-rational faiths of supernatural pretensions. Hence, however much you try to 'liberalize' such religions, you will never have truly liberalized them before you have improved them out of existence altogether. To mend them is to end them, and can only one liberalize them *away*; that is my opinion in which, the more I think, the more I am confirmed.

Prince Yudhishthira seems to have glimpsed the truth when he answered the Yaksha in this wise:

> श्रुतिर्विभिन्ना स्मृतयश्च भिन्ना,
> नैको मुनिर्यस्य मतं प्रमाणम् ।
> धर्मस्य तत्त्वं निहितं गुहायाम् ।।

So in the cave where it lives we will do best to leave it!

Yours, etc.,
A SEEKER AFTER TRUTH

The reader will be glad to have this beautiful letter. The writer's hit at me is quite delicious. But I do not propose to adopt any of the three courses he thinks I usually take for defending the indefensible. There is so far as I know nothing in common between the Prophet's destruction of idols in Mecca and the reputed destruction by Aurangzeb. And should it turn out that the Prophet had erred on occasions, his error would but prove his fallible nature without in any way diminishing his glory as an inspired seer exhibiting on most occasions the image of God? He never himself claimed infallibility. On the contrary, he often consulted his companions and when he was once told by Omer that he need not consult anybody as he had direct dealings with God, it is recorded that he retorted that if he had on that occasion a message from God, he would not have consulted Omer. I know that "A Seeker after Truth" does not seriously mean that I "allegorize away", without good cause, whatever is inconvenient. I hope that his banter is meant merely to 'draw me'. Whatever the cause, I assure him and all concerned that whenever I regard any narrative as an allegory, I have substantial and intrinsic evidence for my belief. Nor do I repudiate without sufficient cause anything as spurious or apocryphal. As a fellow-seeker after Truth I hope I have courage enough to own my errors and limitations. There are things in all religious books which baffle me. I hope some day to have them made clear to me. Till then, I cultivate humility, patience to wait. Man need not know all.

The most serious part however of the writer's letter is his repudiation of the supernatural. I suggest to him that rationalists have as many conundrums and inconsistencies to account for as supernaturalists. Is the uniform testimony of some of the purest and noblest men so much humbug and hallucination when they say that according not to their belief, but experience, there is something beyond the senses? Is it not an arrogant claim to lay down the law that there is nothing beyond the five senses? Who does not *feel* that there are mysteries impenetrable by reason? Do not the daily and so-called sudden transformations of the character of those who worship in faith incontestably show that there are things that reason cannot understand or explain? The celebrated verse quoted by the writer after all presents the difficulty of knowing dharma except through the heart. And, after all, the author of the great book from which the verse has been taken was himself a believer in the supernatural. The mystery of creation and death is itself a living demonstration of the supernatural. It will be time enough to scoff at it when man has by his reason succeeded in creating life.

Young India, 9-12-1926

119. LETTER TO MIRABEHN

WARDHA,
December 9, 1926

CHI. MIRA,

Your two letters came into my hands the same day. I am glad you wrote so fully. Please continue the habit. I miss you in my walks here. We traverse the same old route. I hope you got my two letters. Nothing yet certain about going to Gauhati.[1] You will make it a point to see Hakimji and M. Mahomed Ali. You should see his wife and daughters too.

With love,

BAPU

From the original: C.W. 5190. Courtesy: Mirabehn

120. LETTER TO SHUAIB QURESHI

WARDHA,
December 9, 1926

MY DEAR SHUAIB,

The papers you sent me through Shankerlal about the Nigoi ground have been lying with me and in front of me all these long days. I have now read the whole of the thing carefully. The minutes of the meeting of the arbitrators, or whatever they may be called, have not been signed by all the parties. Messrs Bhopatkar and Dandekar were, therefore, strictly speaking, justified in making any corrections they chose. I am not going into the merits at all. Nor are the corrections made, I think, vitally different from the context.

So far as I can see there is only one material correction, namely, 'Hindus should ever have access to it as before.' Is that not contemplated by the original draft?

What is the cart track in clause 4 meant for ? Was it intended that the cart track will enable the people to visit Dehu but not so as to enable them also to visit the *paduka*? Having gone so far

[1] To attend the Congress session

as to retain the rights of Hindus to visit the *paduka*, everything else becomes, in my opinion, of little consequence.

If you are interesting yourself in this matter, I would advise you carefully to study the documents and then guide the trustees. If the Hindu arbitrators are still agreeable to the substance of the understanding set forth in D, I think that there is every prospect of a settlement.

What are you now doing? Do you propose to discharge the burden you have taken on your shoulders on behalf of the All-India Spinners' Association? You have to render an account of your doings in that behalf to the President and, what is more, to the still small voice within.

Yours sincerely,
M. K. GANDHI

From a photostat: S.N. 12381

121. LETTER TO GORDON LAW

AS AT THE ASHRAM,
SABARMATI,
December 9, 1926

DEAR FRIEND,

I have your letter[1] for which I thank you. The book[s] that I can recommend regarding Hinduism are Sir Edwin Arnold's translation of the *Bhagavad Gita* called the *Song Celestial,* his *Light of Asia,* Max Muller's *India: What It Can Teach Us,* Dutt's abridged *Ramayana* and *Mahabharata* in verses. There are several other books but I think that these give one a fair idea of Hindu thought.

Do you know that since 1915 I have discontinued giving sittings to photographers?[2] I have not one single copy of my own photograph. Those that are on sale at stationery shops and elsewhere are all snapshots. If you want me to get hold of one of these which friends tell me hardly represent me, I shall buy a copy and gladly sign it. But I would far rather like that the boys thought more of what I stand for than what my exterior

[1] Law, writing on November 5, had requested for information about what he should read from the Hindu scriptures (S.N. 10836).

[2] The correspondent had pleaded for one signed photograph of Gandhiji; *ibid.*

is like. But I do not wish to dogmatize. They shall make their own choice or you for them.

Here is my message to your boys: Above all think, speak and do the truth at any cost, with special emphasis on *any*.

Yours sincerely,

GORDON LAW, ESQ.
BOYS SECRETARY
YOUNG MEN'S CHRISTIAN ASSOCIATION
NEWBURG
NEW YORK, U.S.A.

From a photostat: S.N. 19756

122. LETTER TO DR. SURESH BANNERJI

WARDHA,
December 9, 1926

DEAR SURESH BABU,

I have your letter. I hope you will entirely get rid of your heart trouble.

I do not know whether to feel glad or sorry over Profulla Babu's decision. It all depends upon the motive behind it. I have written to him asking him to come to Wardha if he will. His severing the connection with the Pratishthan has given a severe shock to Satis Babu. You must some day come to Wardha and make Vinoba's acquaintance.

I have not forgotten the promise to pass a few days with you on my return from Gauhati if I go to Gauhati at all. I am yet undecided.

Yours sincerely,

DR. SURESH BANNERJI
ABHAY ASHRAM
COMILLA

From a microfilm: S.N. 19757

123. LETTER TO RAMDEV

WARDHA,
December 9, 1926

DEAR RAMDEVJI,

I have your letter. I do not remember having received the communication containing extracts about the 'pranks of anglicized Indians'. If you will send me a copy of that communication, I will see what I can do with it. I shall await your short article.

You may publish the scheme or do as you like with it.

I have in mind the forthcoming visit to the Gurukul to which I am really looking forward but you won't expect me to stay there for 13 days. Is that also the time of the Kumbha Mela?

The short article is received.

Yours sincerely,

SJT. RAMDEVJI
GURUKUL UNIVERSITY
P. O. GURUKUL KANGRI
(BIJNOR) U. P.

From a microfilm: S.N. 19758

124. LETTER TO DR. B. C. ROY

AS AT THE ASHRAM,
SABARMATI,
December 9, 1926

DEAR FRIEND,

I have purposely kept your telegram pending correspondence I am carrying on with Motilalji and other friends. I am not yet certain about my going to Gauhati. Motilalji just sends me a peremptory wire, but I am awaiting for his considered reply to my letter. In any event, if I do go to Gauhati, on my way going there I shall be in Calcutta only for a few hours pending the departure of the Assam Mail. I am therefore unable to give you any definite reply just now.

I hope the Hospital is flourishing.

Yours sincerely,

DR. BIDHAN ROY
CHITTARANJAN HOSPITAL
RUSSA ROAD
CALCUTTA

From a microfilm: S.N. 19759

125. LETTER TO HAKIM AJMAL KHAN

AS AT THE ASHRAM,
SABARMATI,
December 9, 1926

DEAR HAKIM SAHEB,

About the time I left the Ashram I got a letter from you. It was written by your secretary. I have not understood the letter. I do not know what Mr. C. Vijayaraghavachariar has written to you. Do you want me to write to him?

I hope that you are now thoroughly restored. I wonder if you are now taking any interest in public life. I came to Wardha 4 days ago and I am likely to be here for some time. I am trying to avoid going to Gauhati this time and I am trying to persuade Motilalji and others to let me off.

Yours sincerely,

HAKIM SAHEB AJMAL KHAN
SHARIF MANZIL
DELHI

From a photostat: S.N. 19760

126. *LETTER TO DR. N. S. HARDIKAR*

WARDHA,
December 9, 1926

DEAR DR. HARDIKAR,

I have not been able to reply to your letter earlier, for the simple reason that I have been overwhelmed with work and I had not the copy of *Young India* before me at the time I received your letter.

To draw me to Karnatak, you should really be able to sell one lakh worth of khaddar and collect one lakh for khaddar work. You say you would win me for remodelling the political life of Karnatak. Do you believe in the ability of khadi to remodel political life? Do you know that I have staked all upon khadi? The proposition enunciated is that you advance the political life in the country in exact proportion to the advance of khadi and no more. The moment I have driven this truth home, that moment will begin the forward movement.

Yours sincerely,

DR. N. S. HARDIKAR
HUBLI

From a microfilm: S.N. 19763

127. *LETTER TO H. C. HULL*

AS AT THE ASHRAM,
SABARMATI,
December 9, 1926

DEAR FRIEND,

I have your kind letter.[1] Yours is the fourth invitation I have received to visit America. Somehow or other, I do not think [*sic*] as yet the call within. If I am to be guided by the mere desire, I should straight away respond to your invitation. But something within me tells me that I could not deliver my message

[1] Hannah Clothier Hull had written on November 6 to say how warmly the Women's International League for Peace and Freedom would welcome Gandhiji's visit to the United States and added: We consider that your message for Peace and Goodwill is a message for people everywhere and that delivered personally would be a great help to the whole movement (S.N. 10837).

more effectively by going to America than by living it myself here, however inadequately it may be.

Yours sincerely,

HANNAH CLOTHIER HULL
NATIONAL CHAIRMAN
504, WALNUT LANE
SWARTHMORE, PENNA
U.S.A.

From a photostat: S.N. 19764

128. LETTER TO FRANCISCA STANDENATH

AS AT THE ASHRAM,
SABARMATI,
December 9, 1926

DEAR FRIEND,

I have your letter. I am so sorry that you did not get khaddar. I thought I had attended to it. On receiving your letter that you have not yet got it from Swami who was then travelling, I have now spoken to Swami and I hope that you received it before this letter.

I have not contributed anything whatsoever to the paper *Conscience* referred to by you. I came to know of its existence only through you. So many people are just now making use of all sorts of things in connection with me without my authority or knowledge.

You will let me know in due course whether the khaddar you received was of much use there. Of course, in that climate you will not hesitate to use all the warm clothing you need. The rule about khaddar is of local application, not of universal application. We in India dare not, when we have got our own cotton and ability to turn it into cloth, use cotton fabric which is not made here and which is imported from outside even though millions of people who are now idle for want of occupation could be usefully occupied in the khaddar industry.

Yours sincerely,

MRS. FRANCISCA STANDENATH
TRAUTMANSDORFGASSE NO. 1
GRAZ (IN STYRIA)
AUSTRIA

From a microfilm: S.N. 19765

129. LETTER TO S. B. SPILLENAAR

As at the Ashram,
Sabarmati,
December 9, 1926

DEAR FRIEND,

I have your letter.[1] There is no bar to anybody who enjoys good health and who is prepared to go through hardships of life, to live in poverty, and to do continuous labour, being admitted as a member of the Ashram. But I would advise you not to come to India whose climate is different from yours and where customs and habits are also so different. I think that you should try to reproduce the Ashram life there with such changes as may be found necessary. I cannot advise you to undertake the risk of coming to India and endangering your health or being otherwise disappointed.

Yours sincerely,

Sohanna Batteejee Spillenaar
61, P.W. 114th Street
New York City

From a photostat: S.N. 19766

130. LETTER TO ROLLO RUSSELL

As at the Ashram,
Sabarmati,
December 9, 1926

I was delighted to hear from you after so many years. I have got the book you have sent me. Much as I would like to read it, I do not know when I shall be able to read it.

Mine is a very difficult life—more so than when you saw it in Johannesburg. I have also after some experience come to see that it is not what you read but what you think that affects your life. I do hear about you from the Polaks now and then and it gives

[1] In the course of a lengthy letter dated October 20, Spillenaar, "a teacher of music and art" who had lost interest in her work and now evidently desired "spiritual enlightenment", had written to Gandhiji seeking admission to the Ashram for herself and her eleven-year-old son (S.N. 10931).

me delight to know that you were the same innocent soul that I knew in Johannesburg.

I am sending a line to Mrs. Russell.

Yours sincerely,

KENT HOUSE
1, NOTTINGHAM PLACE
W.I.

From a photostat: S.N. 19767

131. LETTER TO MRS. ROLLO RUSSELL

AS AT THE ASHRAM,
SABARMATI,
December 9, 1926

DEAR MRS. RUSSELL,

I was delighted to have the volume of verses written by your husband. I prize the gift though I am unable to say when I shall be able to read the volume. My time is all mortgaged.

Yours sincerely,

MRS. ROLLO RUSSELL

From a microfilm: S.N. 19768

132. TELEGRAM TO S. SRINIVASA IYENGAR[1]

[On or before *December 10, 1926*]

REACHING GAUHATI 24TH.

The Bombay Chronicle, 11-12-1926

[1] Srinivasa Iyengar had been elected President of the Congress session due to be held at Gauhati.

133. LETTER TO G. V. KETKAR

AS AT THE ASHRAM,
SABARMATI,
December 10, 1926

DEAR FRIEND,

I have your letter. The idea of a Gita Day and the manner in which you want it observed does not appeal to me at all. What is more, I do not agree with the interpretation you have sought to put upon it. I can't belittle the teaching of the Divine book by confining it to a description of a clash of arms between rival clans on an earthly battlefield.

Yours sincerely,
M. K. GANDHI

From the original: C.W. 982. Courtesy: G. V. Ketkar

134. LETTER TO A. A. PAUL

AS AT THE ASHRAM,
SABARMATI,
December 10, 1926

DEAR FRIEND,

I wonder what is going on about the contemplated Chinese visit.[1] The Indian programme before me for the next year is so heavy and there are many other such considerations that I should now like to know definitely, at the earliest possible moment, if and when I must go to China. You will please make it clear to the friends who are in correspondence with you that they are in no way bound to carry out the visit programme, because they have contemplated it and have in a way even given me the invitation. The visit, therefore, should be brought about only if there is a real felt want. I am sick of spectacular demonstrations. I have no desire for making speeches. The only thing I love is simple heart-to-heart conversation and an elucidation of difficulties. I would like you to cancel the contemplated visit without reference

[1] Through A. A. Paul, Gandhiji had received an invitation to visit China and had tentatively agreed to do so in the autumn of 1927; *vide* Vol. XXXI.

to me, if you arrive at the conclusion that not much good is to be expected out of it. My own opinion is, that in the present disturbed state of China,[1] the visit will miscarry. My message is one of unadulterated non-violence and truth. People are ill-fitted to receive such a message when feeling runs high and blood is hot. Nothing but a clear, proper call, therefore, should move me to China. Even if our friends in China are insistent and you also come to the conclusion that the visit should be paid, you will of course leave the final decision to me. Let there be the fullest material possible sent to me so as to arrive at a proper decision. In all such matters, it is the answer [to] the prayer that enables me to arrive at my decision.

Yours sincerely,

A. A. PAUL, ESQ.
KILPAUK
MADRAS

From a photostat: S.N. 11378

135. LETTER TO DR. B. C. ROY

WARDHA,
December 10, 1926

DEAR FRIEND,

I have seen your telegram to Mahadeo. I do not remember having received any letter from you and [to] the telegram I sent you a reply from Wardha by post[2] which I hope you have now received. It is now settled that I am going to Gauhati. I leave here on the 22nd, reach Calcutta on the 23rd morning and entrain the same day for Gauhati. I hardly think you want me to perform the ceremony[3] during the few hours that I am in Calcutta.

I propose to stay with a friend in Calcutta who used to come very often at Russa Road when I was there and who got me to

[1] China was, at this time, going through a phase of civil strife. Various provincial war-lords contended against one another for supremacy, and the Kuomintang under Chiang Kai-Sheik had not yet established itself as an effective central authority.

[2] *Vide* "Letter to Dr. B. C. Roy", 9-12-1926.

[3] This presumably refers to the laying of the foundation-stone of one of the wings of Chittaranjan Seva Sadan, which ceremony Gandhiji performed; *vide* "Speech at Chittaranjan Seva Sadan, Calcutta", 2-1-1927.

promise that I would stay with him next time I went to Calcutta. His name and address are: Sjt. Khandelwal, 50, Harish Mukerji Road, Calcutta.

Yours sincerely,

DR. B. C. ROY
36, WELLINGTON STREET
CALCUTTA

From a microfilm: S.N. 19754

136. LETTER TO D. K. PHADAKE

AS AT THE ASHRAM,
SABARMATI,
December 10, 1926

DEAR FRIEND,

I have your letter and the pages of your translation of Lokamanya's life by Mr. Kelkar.

I should like you to come to Wardha, hire some rooms nearby and watch me at my work from early morning to nine o'clock at night and if you find that there are any moments when I am free, you can inspan them for going through your book and then writing a preface. But if you cannot do so, you should take it from me that I have absolutely no leisure left to me and I have hardly time to go through the tasks that I have already undertaken. You must, therefore, please forgive.

Yours sincerely,

D. K. PHADAKE, ESQ.
6, KOCHIN STREET
FORT
BOMBAY

From a microfilm: S.N. 19755

137. LETTER TO MIRABEHN

Saturday [*December 11, 1926*][1]

CHI. MIRA,

I have your 4 letters. Two I have acknowledged already.

I suppose you know the meaning of *chi*[2]. It stands for *chiranjivi*[3] meaning 'long-lived'. That is the blessing which an elder prefixes to the names of the younger members of his family.

I like all your letters. I am glad you had an early opportunity of going to the Mussalman friend. Miss Grover's[4] name I had forgotten altogether. I was delighted that you went there. She is a good earnest soul, much devoted to her work.

You should give me your day's doings, and describe the prayers, the studies and the meals. Tell me what you are eating. How are your bowels acting? What is the quantity of milk you are taking ? What are the times of your meals ? Are there mosquitoes there ? Do you take your walks regularly ? Do you write any Hindi? Does anyone teach you? What fruit are you getting?

I duly got the corrected chapter.[5] You should find out the posting time.

I leave Wardha on 21st inst. Motilalji[6] insists on my going to Gauhati. I hope you will be getting your *Y. I.* regularly. If you do not, you should ask Swami and write to Mrityunjay to attend. I take it you will be getting Hindi *Navajivan* also.

You will not forget the Urdu script please.

The American friends, mother and daughter, are still here. I think I told you about their arrival. The daughter is a teacher in an important school. They are leaving tomorrow. Jamnalalji has over 40 guests on my account. Poor Jankibehn[7]!

I am keeping exceptionally good health. Exercise regularly morning and evening.

You can't complain of any brevity about this letter.

With love,

BAPU

[1] From the postmark

[2] & [3] In Devnagari in the source

[4] The name is not quite legible.

[5] Of the *Autobiography*; *vide* "Letter to Mirabehn", 6-12-1926.

[6] Motilal Nehru

[7] Jamnalal Bajaj's wife

Saturday

I was uncertain about the correctness of the passage in Rolland's letter[1] which you have now corrected. It reads perfectly intelligible now. Please do not return the original. File it among your papers.

B

From the original: C.W. 5191. Courtesy: Mirabehn

138. KATHIAWAR POLITICAL CONFERENCE

I congratulate the Committee of the Kathiawar Political Conference on choosing Shri Amritlal Thakkar as President of its forthcoming session[2].

Names of a number of luminaries in the political field had been suggested but when Amritlal Thakkar's name came up, no one had anything to say against it. As I understand it, the main consideration underlying this choice is that the president should be at least someone from Kathiawar and a man of character with a patriotic spirit. Shri Amritlal Thakkar could easily stand this triple test and come out successful. We cannot today find a worker who can excel Shri Amritlal Thakkar in point of character, whether in Kathiawar, in Gujarat or in India. His sacrifice for the sake of the country was perhaps earlier than that of all of us. His devotion has brought credit to him and his country and it is difficult to compete with him in dedicated service. Moreover, the field of activity which he selected for such service is as easy as it is difficult. It is easy because there are only a few who take interest in serving the communities whom he has chosen to serve and so he achieves quick results. It is difficult because if no results that startle the world are forthcoming, the raw or unseasoned workers would feel despondent. But Amritlal became the priest to Dheds[3] and Bhangis and not being satisfied with it became the servant and friend of the Bhils[4].

What will such a man do at a political conference? This point did not occur to those who selected him; but it did to Amritlal Thakkar. Taking me to task for allowing his name to come

[1] *Vide* Appendix II.

[2] Which was to be held at Porbandar in March 1927 but could be held only in January 1928.

[3] One of the communities traditionally regarded as untouchables

[4] Aboriginal tribe in Gujarat and Central India

up for selection, he writes to me a letter whose summary is given below:[1]

The fact that this question occurred to him points to the fine state of his mind. But does he not know that nowadays the Political Conference has made it its business to serve the *Antyajas* and others? Who can say that this service is not implied by and included in khadi? Not only that, but the Conference this year has directly rendered no mean service to the *Antyajas* and others and has spent no small amount of money for them. Thus the very activities which are dear to Shri Amritlal Thakkar constitute the present field of operation of the Conference. Moreover, Amritlal Thakkar is the pioneer of khadi work in Kathiawar. I do not, however, know whether his love of khadi or his faith in it is still the same as before. He will most probably clarify this point at the Conference.

Now there remains politics. In my opinion, there can be no conference or other politics outside of such constructive activities. I have visualized the same for the whole of India. If India leaves off the so-called politics and plunges itself only in constructive activities and works with the devotion of a Thakkar, swaraj will be secured very easily. Moreover, if I apply this principle to India I would naturally apply it in particular to Kathiawar. This does not mean that no political work should be done in Kathiawar or outside it. He who can only do political work and finds constructive activity futile will certainly plunge himself in politics alone. We shall take the cue from them and follow them. If we do not like their work, we shall allow them to go their way. When they will see that none of us follows them, they will doubt the correctness of their way and will retrace their steps. The Kathiawar Conference has taken to this golden way. I hope the Conference will not deviate from that path. I do not know of a single incident by reason of which the Conference should so deviate. If we become good, alert, free from fear, become united—the ruler too will easily become good, alert, loving and friendly towards his subjects. The divine rule "if one is good, the world is good" is no mere popular saying but a truth. "As the subjects so the ruler" is truer in this democratic age than "as the ruler so the subjects". Hence politics means a relationship among the people from the lowest to the highest strata and unity among all. This unity is a sort

[1] Not translated here. In the letter Thakkar had asked Gandhiji how he could fit in with politics when his field of work was with Dheds, Bhangis, Bhils, Kolis and others.

of constructive work wherein there is need of mutual relationship for all. Long speeches or articles cannot tell upon the rulers as the quiet, humble, modest work on khadi has been doing. But only the wise can listen to the silent eloquence of khadi. Earnest work and concentration are needed to listen to that sweet speech. Removal of untouchability means self-purification and union of hearts with the poor. To me speeches made in the Councils appear as nothing before this power.

But these are my own thoughts. I offer them to the Kathiawaris and to Shri Amritlal Thakkar. They may accept what they like out of them and reject the rest.

I had asked the Conference in Bhavnagar[1] to place me in charge of political work. The Conference did so. I believe the Conference has not erred therein. I have not been able to achieve anything that I can flaunt. I have suffered a defeat, I have been disappointed a little, but no other way occurred to me; there was and there is only that way. The Conference of entire Kathiawar can do only this much, can merely implore. That the people of the various States can do something special is a different matter. The workers of the various States who are familiar with the political conditions in their States can and should do the work there. I have deliberately set a limit to the field of activities of the Kathiawar Political Conference. Our President should consider whether we should cross this limit or not and should show us a new way if possible.

[From Gujarati]
Navajivan, 12-12-1926

139. ANTYAJ DIRECTORY

The Antyaj Directory which has been brought out by Shri Amritlal Thakkar's Antyaj Seva Mandal[2], has been purposely published by me, word for word, in the *Navajivan*[3]. I am afraid some of the readers must have got annoyed on seeing it, and those who were not annoyed might not have read it. If both these classes of readers exist then I would specifically recommend them to retrieve the previous issues and read the directory. The reader will get some idea of the amount of hard work put in compiling this

[1] At the session held there in 1925
[2] Association for service of untouchables
[3] In its issues of November 7, 14, 21, 28 and December 5, 1926

directory. Investigations were made in 88 villages of the Anand taluk itself. Such detailed investigation in each and every village demands the sacrifice of a great deal of time.

The facts found in the directory bring disgrace to those who follow Hindu dharma. One who reads this directory will realize immediately how much we have failed in our duty towards the *Antyajas*. A stranger may well say that the people of the place where *Antyajas* cannot have an adequate supply of even drinking water do not know the barest elements of religion.

The reader will note that in most of the villages Christian missionaries have been active. But this thing is as shameful for us as it is creditable to them. The service that we are now rendering to the Harijans may well be considered as satisfactory in view of the fact that formerly we were doing nothing at all. But it is a matter of shame for us as long as there is even a single village without a Hindu worker for the Harijan or without proper facilities of drinking water.

Shri Amritlal Thakkar assigned the work of this directory to Shri Parikshitlal[1]. Shri Parikshitlal is a graduate of the Vidyapith. This vast field is open for every graduate of the Vidyapith. Service to the villages is true service to the nation, because the people of India live in the seven lacs of her villages. India does not exist in her cities which are mere degraded images of Europe's cities. And those who have realized that the service of villages starts with khadi and the cause of the *Antyajas* have known almost everything there is to know.

[From Gujarati]

Navajivan, 12-12-1926

[1] Parikshitlal Mazmudar, later President of the Gujarat Harijan Sevak Sangh

140. LETTER TO HARI-ICHCHHA

WARDHA,
Magsar Sud 7, 1983 [*December 12, 1926*]

CHI. HARI-ICHCHHA,

I had certainly preserved this song of yours. Send me an acknowledgment. I am sure you are continuing your Hindi studies and attending prayers regularly. Chandan and others must have improved their health. Do all the women spin?

Blessings from
BAPU

From the Gujarati original: C.W. 4909. Courtesy: Hari-ichchha Kamdar

141. LETTER TO DR. KARL THIEME

AS AT THE ASHRAM,
SABARMATI,
December 13, 1926

DEAR FRIEND,

I have your letter. Here are my answers to your questions:

(1) The attempts at solving the Hindu-Muslim question have not yet been successful. It is a matter of time.

(2) I am unable to endorse any scheme of co-operation with the British Government until the system is adequately changed, i.e., until military expenditure is very considerably reduced to the advantage of India and prohibitive tariff imposed upon all foreign cloth and until prohibition is declared. I have no select material to send you but you can gather all the information on these points in the pages of *Young India* whose principal writings are now available in book-form. The book can be had of Mr. S. Ganesan, 29, Pycrofts Road, Triplicane, Madras.

Yours sincerely,

DR. KARL THIEME
LEIPZIG
GERMANY

From a photostat: S.N. 12319

142. LETTER TO DR. B. C. ROY

AS AT THE ASHRAM,
SABARMATI,
December 13, 1926

DEAR FRIEND,

The enclosed has remained with me for a long time, buried among the papers which I was then unable to attend to. As I have a few moments to spare to go through arrears, I have come across the enclosed which I send you for such remarks as you may wish to make.

Yours sincerely,

From a microfilm: S.N. 19750

143. LETTER TO DHIREN

AS AT THE ASHRAM,
SABARMATI,
December 13, 1926

MY DEAR DHIREN,

Your letter of 9th instant has lain with me for some time. But pressure of work has been so overwhelming that much of my correspondence has remained in arrears. I know your letter ought not to have so remained. But you will believe me when I tell you that there has been of late not one moment for me to spare and I have been obliged to put off many things which I otherwise might not have.

I hear from Urmila Devi that you are keeping good health and that you are keeping yourself busy. I hope, too, that you have made considerable progress in spinning. I wish you would learn carding also there if you are permitted to do so. If you have even seen the process of carding, you could easily learn it even without any tuition.

Now for your question. An innocent prisoner need not starve and, in my opinion, he does not lose his dignity by accepting maintenance money from his custodians. But I do think that he may not take anything beyond his bare sustenance. But he need not stint himself to the extent of damaging his health or starving his relatives if the custodians pay him enough to enable him to support those who were depending upon him. Thus, after all, the question of amount is a matter for each individual to settle for himself. But I have no doubt whatsoever about the propriety of accepting maintenance money.

Yours sincerely,

SJT. DHIREN
C/O SUPERINTENDENT
CENTRAL JAIL
MIDNAPORE (BENGAL)

From a photostat: S.N. 19751

144. *LETTER TO S. K. JAIN*

AS AT THE ASHRAM,
SABARMATI,
December 13, 1926

DEAR FRIEND,

Your letter of 3rd October last has lain with me without attention for want of time. If the young man will correspond with me giving me all the particulars about his life and tell me whether he will be prepared to go through the discipline at the Satyagraha Ashram for six months before he is put to any work, I shall see what can be done. As a matter of fact, there is no difficulty about accommodating any number of young men of character and ability.

I am in Wardha up to the 20th instant, after which date, it would be better to address your letter to my permanent address.

Yours sincerely,

SJT. S. K. JAIN
15, NAGJI BUNGALOWS
MATUNGA, G. I. P.
BOMBAY

From a microfilm: S.N. 19752

145. *LETTER TO T. N. NATHANI*

AS AT THE ASHRAM,
SABARMATI,
December 13, 1926

DEAR FRIEND,

I have your letter. I do not remember the swami or the incident. But it is quite likely that I asked him, if he came to the Ashram, whether he spun. But I could not have turned my back towards him as he must have found me busy at the time. It is my habit now to receive visitors whilst I am spinning so as to save time. I talk and spin at the same time.

I do remember having received a complaint about my having been represented in some photo prints as Lord Krishna. I do also remember having written strongly against it. But I have no recollection of how many lines I wrote about the incident. I do not think that the weight of a writing is to be justified by its length.

I have not yet found a single swami coming to me whom I could instinctively tell as my guru.

Yours sincerely,

TARACHAND NANAKRAM NATHANI
HALANI, (*via*) MEHRABPUR, N. W. RLY.

From a photostat: S.N. 19753

146. *LETTER TO PRABHASHANKAR PATTANI*

WARDHA,
Monday [December 13, 1926][1]

SUJNA BHAISHRI,

You know that Chi. Mathuradas[2] stays in your bungalow at Panchgani. He has not so far paid any rent. He and I earnestly desire that something should be paid. I have also told him that he should vacate the bungalow during the season; they are therefore, getting ready to vacate it by the end of February. I wish

[1] From the postmark

[2] Mathuradas Trikumji

you to let me know the amount of the rent. Write to me about your health.

Vandemataram from
MOHANDAS

From a photostat of the Gujarati: C.W. 3208. Courtesy: Mahesh Pattani

147. LETTER TO ASHRAM WOMEN

WARDHA,
Magsar Sud 11, 1983, December 13, 1926

Today also I am thinking of you after my breakfast. It is exactly 6.50, your time for prayers. You may miss everything else but not this. It means co-operation among ourselves, and between ourselves and God. It is a real purifying bath. As the body becomes dirty if we do not bathe, so also the pure soul appears impure unless the heart is washed with the water of prayer. Do not, therefore, miss prayers any time. At 4 o'clock in the morning, there is an opportunity for co-operation among all. Not all the women, however, are able to attend the prayer. But the 7 o'clock prayer is an occasion of co-operation among women. It should be possible for all of them to attend it. Co-operation among Ashram women is very essential.

The two American ladies who had stayed with you for a day came here. They left yesterday after staying here for three days. They are mother and daughter. The daughter is unmarried and is twenty-five years of age. She teaches one of the higher classes in a college of five hundred girls. Her Principal has sent her on tour to study how moral education is given in different parts of the world. Her mother accompanies her as her guardian. The two go everywhere in the world fearlessly. How I wish that we had such fearlessness, and this young woman's devotion to service!

Mirabehn's life should set all of you thinking. You must be receiving letters in Hindi from her. From her letters to me I see that she has won over the hearts of the Gurukul girls with her simplicity and affectionate nature. She has made herself one with the girls, and has been teaching them carding and spinning very well. She does not waste a single moment. I expect such devotion, sacrifice and purity from you. Is it too much to hope that you should become experts in your work, live a pure life and take yourselves to all parts of the country? Every moment I realize the need for women workers. We find many self-sacrificing men. But do we see anywhere self-sacrificing women coming out for public work ? Woman is an embodiment of self-sacrifice. But at present her self-sacrifice is confined to the family. Why should she not make for the nation even greater sacrifices than what she does for her family ? Any woman who dedicates herself to dharma will ultimately make such sacrifice for the whole world. But one's country represents the first stage. And when the interest of one's country is not in conflict with the interests of the world, service in the cause of one's country takes one towards *moksha*.

My request to you this week is that all of you should think seriously of this.

I address this letter to Tarabehn[1] since Manibehn may not be there. But I should like you to appoint a leader from among yourselves.

Blessings from
BAPU

From a photostat of the Gujarati: G.N. 3632

148. A LETTER[2]

WARDHA,
December 15, 1926

DEAR FRIEND,

Your letter has been placed in my hands only just now. Much as I should like to speak to your hostel on ahimsa, I fear I shall have no time on the 21st when I shall be in Nagpur only for a few hours. I may not leave Wardha before that date.

Yours sincerely,
M. K. GANDHI

From a photostat: C.W. 4505. Courtesy: Mrs. Lumsden

[1] Wife of Ramniklal Modi

[2] The addressee is not known.

149. FROM HIS HIMALAYAN HEIGHTS

A friend who has all his life lived in the plains of India and who is now combining work with recreation in the Himalayas, being lost in admiration over the snowy range, sends me the following quotation:

> Lifted above the world in silence, terrible in their cold and their distance, yet beautiful beyond all words, what are the Himalayas like? Why, they are like a great monk, clothed in ashes, lost in meditation, silent and alone! They are like the great god himself, Siva Mahadeva.

and ends with Holmes' 'tribute to silence':

> Silence is the true language of cosmic adoration.

Young India, 16-12-1926

150. SOUTH AFRICAN SITUATION

Mr. Andrews cables as follows from Pretoria:

> Prayer day endorsed by Dutch Church nineteenth. Hertzog receives delegates[1] seventeenth. Then retires. First session twentieth.

The endorsement of the prayer day by the Dutch reformed Church is a great step towards securing an atmosphere favouring a just solution of the difficult question. The Dutch Church is a most conservative body in South Africa. It has rarely taken a broad view of the Indian or the general colour question as it is called in South Africa. The reception that is to take place on the seventeenth by General Hertzog of the delegates to the Conference is a step in recognition of the tremendous importance of the Conference and of the issues that are to be discussed by the Conference.

I hope that the Indian public will back wholeheartedly the noble effort of this single-minded Englishman. One may thoughtlessly say that it costs nothing to offer prayers and that the pressmen will announce that prayers were offered for the success of the mission at so many places. But in reality, it is a most difficult thing that Mr. Andrews has asked us to do. One can give

[1] The members of the Indian deputation who were visiting South Africa to discuss with the Union Government problems of South African Indians

of one's possessions willingly or unwillingly or even for a show. One may give unwilling intellectual assent to a proposition. But there is no such thing as unwilling or showy heart co-operation. And what Mr. Andrews wants is heart co-operation, for, prayer is nothing else but an intense longing of the heart. You may express yourself through the lips; you may express yourself in the private closet or in public; but to be genuine, the expression must come from the deepest recesses of the heart. Let those who can, that is those who believe in the cause of the Indians of South Africa and who believe in God and therefore in prayer, set apart some time on the nineteenth instant for the heart co-operation with the Indian settlers of South Africa and invoke God's blessings on the deliberations of the Conference.

If there is anybody in India who still does not know what the Indian cause in South Africa is, let him or her understand that the very existence of the Indians in South Africa is at stake. Specifically, the Asiatic Bill[1] that was suspended during the last session of the Union Parliament and which will be subject matter of discussion is a bill which is so designed as to make it impossible for any self-respecting Indian to remain in South Africa. Let those who do not know the legal position of Indians in South Africa realize that they have practically no political status whatsoever within the Union. They have no rights even of residence in Orangia except as domestic servants. In many parts they cannot become owners of landed property. Throughout South Africa, the trading rights have been considerably curtailed and the administration of the existing legislation regarding trading rights is becoming more and more severe against Indian traders, even against those who are holders of trading licenses of long standing. I say nothing about the social barriers that have been erected against them and consequent difficulties about freedom of travelling, etc. They have hardly any facility for the education of their children worth the name. The position, therefore, it will be seen, is precarious enough as it is. The Asiatic Bill if it is passed will put the finishing touch. The Conference has been brought about after tremendous difficulties to ease the situation and to secure the barest justice for the Indian settler. And it is on this effort that C. F. Andrews seeks to invoke the blessing of God on the nineteenth instant. Let those who believe, in all humility, tender their heart co-operation.

Young India, 16-12-1926

[1] The Class Areas Bill; *vide* Vol. XXXI.

151. NOTES

"Prosperous" India

Mr. A. M. Samuel, Minister for Overseas Trade, is reported to have thus spoken to the Lincoln Chamber of Commerce:

> India is our best customer. She buys about £ 90,000,000 worth of goods from us a year, mostly manufactured goods of high finish containing a large amount of British labour. Any increase of trade with India, therefore, would be welcome because by increasing the employment of labour we would be carrying out the main policy of the present Government, namely, the reduction of unemployment figures.
>
> India bought from us immense quantities of iron and steel goods and railway material. She was prosperous and had large sums with which to purchase imported goods. She only awaited a level of prices which would suit her views. The credit of India stood very high, second only to the credit of Great Britain herself. Many firms in the Lincoln district already possessed properly equipped sales and technical organizations in India, but the Government representatives in India asked firms to provide efficient and technical representation upon the spot. The sale of highly complex machinery and plant called for an increased backing up by technical advisers. The salesman needed a technical adviser at his right hand always to assist him in obtaining contracts. It was necessary that the British technical representatives should be in touch with the buying engineers in India to explain the details of the machines offered or sold. We still supplied 80 per cent of the machinery imported into India, and most of the British firms had their own technical agents in India, but he still came across reports of Indian purchasing authorities complaining that they did not get the services from the British expert staffs that they desired. They also complained that we did not maintain an adequate supply in India of stocks and spare parts.
>
> As regards the Indian market for agricultural machinery, he knew that British firms had gone to great trouble and expense to develop this market without any considerable success. The Indian Government, however, was striving to assist the Indian cultivator, and one of the best methods to do so was to put better agricultural implements into his hands. Agricultural and co-operative credit departments were being set up in India to show the people how to use and repair modern implements and to assist them to purchase them.

There is no doubt that Mr. Samuel honestly believes that we are prosperous, and that it would add to our prosperity to buy all the machinery that England can manufacture, whether agricultural or otherwise, as also technical skill. How far from truth both these statements appear to us to be. We know that India is not prosperous; that it is daily growing poorer, and some of us know also that the problem of poverty will never be solved by an indiscriminate importation of machinery and technical skill from England, or any other foreign land. As Gokhale put it years ago, this kind of importation stunts our growth. We become more and more hewers of wood and drawers of water. What we need to do is to add to our capacity for labour with our hands and feet the necessary technical skill, so that we may devise our own machinery suitable to our requirements. A slavish imitation of the West can but kill all initiative or skill and therefore the capacity for living with anything like decent comfort. It is such speeches like Mr. Samuel's which arouse suspicions about the object of Commissions like the Royal Agricultural Commission, as was recently adverted to in these pages.

Young India, 16-12-1926

152. KHADI PRATISHTHAN

Last week I published a comprehensive summary of the report upon the progress of khadi in the Punjab.[1] I now give below a similar report from the Khadi Pratishthan omitting the balance-sheet, because the items that the reader would be interested in are included in the body of the report. Khadi workers will carefully study the reports I am publishing so that they can compare the methods of work adopted in different provinces. The reader will note that magic lantern lectures for popularizing khadi are a special feature introduced by the Khadi Pratishthan and are being now taken up in other parts of India. The technical department is also a strong feature of the Pratishthan. After considerable difficulty, the Pratishthan has secured its own premises, where extensive experiments are being carried on in dyeing and bleaching all of which makes khadi more attractive.

Young India, 16-12-1926

[1] *Vide* "Khaddar in the Punjab", 9-12-1926.

153. LETTER TO SHIVABHAI PATEL

WARDHA,
Thursday, December 16, 1926

BHAI SHIVABHAI,

I have your letter.

There is no reason for you to worry. Strictly speaking, I do regard a violation of the vow to have occurred, but our responsibility for that is slight. You did not consciously desire that the thing should happen, and, therefore, no elaborate atonement is necessary. Whenever you have an involuntary discharge in dreams, you should take light food or even forgo a meal the next day. Or, when you become conscious that it has occurred, you should get up and take a hip-bath. If this is not possible, you should clean the wet part, and repeat Ramanama. This cleaning will be enough atonement. What you should do depends on the state of your mind at the moment. After cleaning yourself in this manner, you should not make yourself unhappy about the occurrence or brood over it. If you have slipped either in regard to eating, reading, thinking or selecting your company, see that you do not commit a similar error in future. Only a person who is completely free from desire can escape involuntary ejaculation, and that too with ceaseless effort.

You should give up your evening meals and casual snacks. Nothing should be taken just to gratify the palate. You should be content with whatever pleasure you get from the food that you must take.

Blessings from
BAPU

[PS.]

There is no news about your brother yet.

I have not gone through the letter after writing it.

From a photostat of the Gujarati: S.N. 9491

154. LETTER TO HARDAYAL NAG

[*December 17, 1926*][1]

DEAR FRIEND,

I have your letter[2] which I was delighted to receive. I do not know what I shall be doing at Gauhati. I shall act as the Spirit leads me.

Charkha is surely not dying in Bengal. It may be in Chandpur. The output of khaddar in Bengal is steadily increasing and so are the sales.

If you are not keeping very good health, I certainly do not think it is worth while troubling [you] to come to Gauhati. Whatever I do there will undoubtedly be known to the public. But I have advised all non-co-operators not to trouble about coming to Gauhati with the expectation of any fireworks display or even the expectation of any non-co-operation programme being discussed, apart from khaddar.

Forward, 24-12-1926

155. LETTER TO S. HIGGINBOTTOM

AS AT THE ASHRAM,
SABARMATI,
December 17, 1926

DEAR FRIEND,

I have your letter. It is evident that thoughts produce effects, perhaps, more powerful than the spoken word; for, if you have thought so much of me, for which many thanks, I have thought none the less of you and I have spoken to so many about you and your acts.

I do not think there is any chance of my passing through Allahabad in the near future and I have in front of me a prolonged tour. But I am likely to be at the Ashram at the end of February when, if you could come over and pass a day or two,

[1] As in the source

[2] The correspondent had asked for Gandhiji's programme at the Gauhati Congress.

we could have a quiet time together and you could see the Ashram activities and also give us the benefit of your valuable advice in the agricultural work we are doing.

Yours sincerely,
M. K. GANDHI

SAM HIGGINBOTTOM, ESQ.
ALLAHABAD AGRICULTURAL INSTITUTE
ALLAHABAD

From a photostat: G.N. 8935

156. MESSAGE TO PUBLIC MEETING, WARDHA[1]

December 19, 1926

I am glad you are having a prayer meeting in response to the appeal of that good soul Andrews. The problem in South Africa is the problem of the removal of untouchability. The work of the conference now [being] held in South Africa will have a far-reaching effect not only on Indians but on all Asiatics, Negroes and others. Let us pray to God that He may inspire the members of the conference with wisdom and that justice may be done.

The Bombay Chronicle, 22-12-1926

157. LETTER TO MIRABEHN

December 19, 1926

CHI. MIRA,

I have been having your delightful letters. I dare not attempt a long letter just now. When I write to Rolland, it shall go through you. But do you think it is necessary to write? I am glad you have come in touch with Mrs. Gadodia. You must take long walks.

With love,

Yours,
BAPU

From the original: C.W. 5192. Courtesy: Mirabehn

[1] Gangadharrao Deshpande presided at the meeting. The message was read out by Mahadev Desai.

158. LETTER TO RAJKISHORI MEHROTRA

WARDHA,
Monday [On or before *December 20, 1926*][1]

CHI. RAJKISHORI,

I had been intending to talk to you in detail but could not get the time. Parasram tells me your mind is not at peace in the Ashram. Parasram does not intend to keep you there under compulsion. If you wish to stay somewhere else you may do so. You should not force Parasram to leave the Ashram. He is bound to provide you a maintenance but not to stay with you if you do not like to stay where he does. The wife follows the husband but the husband cannot follow the wife because he is often obliged to go to various places for earning a livelihood or for self-improvement.

I hope you and the boys are in good health. Write to me what you feel without any hesitation.

Blessings from
BAPU

From the Hindi original: C.W. 4953. Courtesy: Parashu Ram Mehrotra

159. LETTER TO PARASHU RAM MEHROTRA[2]

Silence Day [On or before *December 20, 1926*][3]

"Adhere to work entrusted. Sending instructions."

You must have got the above telegram. Remain absorbed in your work. Keep sending money to your parents as you used to. Do the *Young India* work and that of Hindi teaching. More when I come. Stop worrying.

Blessings from
BAPU

[PS.]

Neither you, nor Rajkishori, nor the children should fall ill. Mind.

I leave Wardha on the 21st.

From the Hindi original: C.W. 4957. Courtesy: Parashu Ram Mehrotra

[1] & [3] The date is based on the recollection of Parashu Ram Mehrotra.
[2] The first sheet of the letter is not available.

160. LETTER TO ASHRAM WOMEN

Silence Day, Magsar Sud 1, [19]83 [December 20, 1926]

DEAR SISTERS,

I got Chi. Radha's[1] letters written on behalf of all of you. It is good that you have chosen Gangabehn as your leader. But may I draw your attention to the necessity of your helping her to discharge her duties well, now that you have made her your leader? By appointing an illiterate sister of yours as your leader, you have given due importance to character and sacrifice. This is as it should be. Knowledge is useless without character. Have no doubt whatever about this.

A leader means the most important servant. A king acquires the right to issue orders only when he has risen above all others in his ability to serve. His orders would then be, not for serving his self-interest, but for the good of the community. These days irreligion parades as religion. Kings, therefore, run after pleasures instead of living as men of self-sacrifice, and exercise authority only to that end. But you have appointed Gangabehn as your leader with a religious aim. This means that you have decided Gangabehn to be the chief servant among you all who are trying to become servants.

Please remember that all of you are tied to Mother India with a cord of hand-spun yarn. If you give up spinning, you give up service too. Do not, therefore, neglect the spinning-wheel. Today Rama dwells in the spinning-wheel. The fire of starvation is raging all around. I do not see any other help against it except through the spinning-wheel. God always reveals Himself to us in some concrete shape. That is why we sing of Draupadi that for her God took the form of garments. Anyone who desires to see God today may see Him in the form of the spinning-wheel.

I have exceeded my limits. I did not wish to write more than two sheets. I cannot cope with my work if I become too greedy to write to you.

I send to Chi. Maganlal all the letters of Mirabehn. I want all you sisters to listen to them carefully, try to understand them and reflect over them. In my view she is at present the ideal woman worker among us.

[1] Daughter of Maganlal Gandhi

By asking me to write to you on good paper with a margin, Radha has laid on me a fairly heavy burden. I shall bear it as far as I can.

I say nothing regarding my health, since it is very good. Jamnalalji and Janakibehn are sheltering me and giving me plenty of quiet. It seems I have gained four pounds. I am able to eat well. At every meal I eat a little of what Ba prepares for me. I have still some of it left.

I shall leave this place tomorrow. Mithubehn[1], Jamnabehn and Perinbehn[2] are coming here from Bombay for khadi work. I shall meet them at Gondia.[3] You should find out from the map where Gondia is.

Dakshabehn and the German lady left yesterday, the former for Bardoli and the latter for Banaras.

Blessings from
BAPU

From a photostat of the Gujarati: G.N. 3630

161. LETTER TO G. D. BIRLA

Monday [December 20, 1926][4]

BHAI GHANSHYAMDASJI,

Received your two letters. I am returning Bhai Shriprakash's original letter.

I was glad to read the plain story of your department. Elections have polluted our atmosphere. I have seen enough of this. After all the trouble taken, the country is not going to gain but lose. But I cannot advise you to leave the Assembly. The idea of being neutral is that not even a vote should be cast under pressure from anyone, as usually happens.

The assurance you gave me was needless because I have faith in your earnest efforts. Even then your assurance is gratifying.

[1] Mithubehn Petit

[2] Perinbehn Captain

[3] Gandhiji visited Gondia, now in Madhya Pradesh, on December 22, 1926.

[4] The reference in the letter to Gandhiji's arrival on 23rd in Calcutta *en route* to Gauhati suggests that the letter was written on the preceding Monday, which fell on this date.

I shall arrive in Calcutta on the 23rd and leave for Gauhati the same day. I shall stay at Bhai Khandelwal's. When I was in Calcutta he used to call often. I had told him that, when I went to Calcutta again and if it was not for political reasons, I would stay with him, and he insists on it now. And so I shall have to stay at his place. You aren't going to Gauhati, are you?

Yours,
MOHANDAS

From the Hindi original: C.W. 6141. Courtesy: G. D. Birla

162. SPEECH AT PUBLIC MEETING, WARDHA[1]

[December 20, 1926][2]

. . . I do not know what else I am expected to do. During the year of silence, I have given my most earnest thought to it and have come to the conclusion that we can have swaraj, even *Ramarajya,* if we fulfil the triple programme—a programme in which men and women, young and old, Hindus, Mussalmans, Christians, Government servants and all can alike take part. I am, if possible, more convinced than ever that swaraj is impossible to be attained if there is no Hindu-Muslim unity, if we still suffer from the curse of untouchability and if our middle classes refuse to understand the gospel of swadeshi. Don't think that I am sticking on to this programme out of obstinacy or perversity. There is nothing on earth that I would not give for the sake of the country excepting, of course, two things and two only, viz., Truth and Non-violence. I would not sacrifice these two for all the world. For, to me Truth is God and there is no way to find truth except the way of Non-violence. And I do not seek to serve India at the sacrifice of Truth or God. For I know that a man who forsakes Truth can forsake his country, and his nearest and dearest ones. . . . Now is the time to act. For how long is a man to go on talking? He may do so once, twice, aye, a hundred times, but action or example is his last resort. . . . Even if the whole of India ranged on one side were to declare that Hindu-Muslim unity is impossible, I will declare that it is perfectly possible, I will say that, if there is anything like God or Truth on earth, Hindu-Muslim unity is also possible. Even if

[1] Extracted from Mahadev Desai's "Weekly Letter". A Gujarati report of what appears to be the same speech was published in *Navajivan*, 26-12-1926.

[2] As given by Mahadev Desai

masses of people were to burn khadi publicly and say that it is an insane programme, I will declare that those people have gone mad. In the same way, even if all the Hindus of India were to be ranged against me in declaring that untouchability, as we know it today, has the sanction of the Shastras or the *smritis*, I will then declare that these Shastras and these *smritis* are false. Everywhere shall I go forth thus uttering the three articles of my creed—my *kalma* and my *gayatri*,—so that I may be true to myself and my Maker.

Young India, 30-12-1926

163. LETTER TO RAMESHWARDAS PODDAR

ON THE TRAIN,
Tuesday [*December 21, 1926*][1]

BHAI RAMESHWARJI,

I got your letter as well as Rs. 50. You have done nothing wrong by not coming to Wardha. Even if you have done something wrong, you have made up for it by sending the money. I am passing the money to Amritlalji. Repeat Ramanama.

Yours,
MOHANDAS

From a photostat of the Hindi: G.N. 187

164. LETTER TO MANIBEHN PATEL

GONDIA,
[*December 21, 1926*][2]

CHI. MANI,

I am aware of your affection for me. But surely you do not expect to stay with me all your life. But you can live with my work. That means that you should prepare yourself for it. Do not waste a single minute there. Write to me regularly. I too shall write as often as I can.

[From Gujarati]

Bapuna Patro—Manibehn Patelne, p. 39

[1] The postmark bears the date 22-12-1926, which was a Wednesday.

[2] The source has "1926". Gandhiji was in Gondia for a few hours on December 21.

165. *SPEECH AT OPENING OF GYMNASIUM, AMRAOTI*[1]

[*December 21, 1926*][2]

You know that I am a man conscious of my limitations and it is not in my nature to have more things than I can attend to. But I could not resist Dr. Patwardhan's request. I was glad to be told that this gymnasium was open to Hindus and Mussalmans alike, and that not only Mussalmans but untouchable youths are members of it. I rejoice to see that the institution is thus free from communalism.

Our Shastras say that a boy who would keep his body fit and strong and make the best use of it should observe *brahmacharya*. I have travelled all over the country and one of the most deplorable things I have noticed is the rickety bodies of young men. So long as we labour under the curse of child-marriage, and so long as many members of our society are children of such marriages, so long much bodily exercise is an impossibility. Who will recommend physical exercise to consumptives? We should therefore lay the axe at the root of this curse, if we would see our young men and women strong and healthy and India on the path of vigorous and healthy growth. Manu has laid down that a student should observe *brahmacharya* up to his 25th year at least. All physical exercise will be futile so long as these conditions are not satisfied.

But there is another thing to which I should like to draw your attention. You know that I am pledged to have nothing to do with things even remotely connected with violence. Whatever others may say, I am convinced that the way of non-violence is the only way and the highest and permanent religion for me. How is it then, someone might ask, that an avowed votary of non-violence like me has at all associated himself with an institution like this? The reason is clear. Ahimsa or non-violence means the renunciation of the capacity to use violence. He who has not that capacity is therefore incapable of exercising non-violence. Non-

[1] Extracted from Mahadev Desai's "Weekly Letter".

[2] Mahadev Desai says: "The year's silence was broken on the evening of the 20th at the same place [Wardha], and active touring began yesterday. Amraoti, Nagpur and Gondia being the places visited. . . " Gandhiji was at Nagpur on December 21. It is likely that he visited Amraoti earlier on the same day.

violence is a mighty spiritual force but its votary should have the power to use physical force and should consciously and deliberately refuse to exercise that force. Not that physical training is a *sine qua non* for acquiring capacity for violence, but we may not encourage our youths to have feeble physiques in order to be capable of ahimsa. You cannot make a man non-violent by depriving him of arms. One of the many crimes of the British rule in India is that we have been forcibly deprived of our arms—not indeed with a view to making us non-violent even if such a thing was possible but to emasculating us. I want India to be strong and free to exercise its strength and yet to renounce it.

Thus I like institutions like these for physical training. But let me utter a word of warning. No institution that has as its object the subjection of a community, whether Hindu, Mussalman, Parsi, or Christian, can have my blessings. Only that institution can have my blessings which aims at the growth of the physical culture of all communities, of all the youths of the nation, to whatever creed or community they belong. I should not have come here, did I not know that the gymnasium I have opened belonged to the latter type, and whilst once more congratulating you I wish and pray that you may all be true and pure, and your lives may be consecrated to the service of our nation and of our religions.

Young India, 30-12-1926

166. SPEECH AT PUBLIC MEETING, NAGPUR[1]

December 21, 1926

Mahatmaji exhorted the people to help the Tilak Vidyalaya with money. He reiterated his faith in khaddar and said that, if the people were willing to follow his advice, they could get swaraj in a few years. Mahatmaji was pained to see people wearing foreign cloth and said that he was tired of hearing *Mahatma Gandhiki Jai*. What he wanted was real work. From this morning he had assumed active work and would travel through the length and breadth of India to preach his message of the charkha.

Forward, 22-12-1926

[1] The meeting was held at Chitnis Park on the seventh anniversary of the Tilak Vidyalaya.

167. THE MESSAGE OF GANGA AND JUMNA

A friend thus writes:[1]

We have more Gangas and Jumnas than the two. It is true they bear other names. They are, however, watering our vast plains from the North to the South and the East to the West. The message that the Ganga and the Jumna gave to this friend is not the only message that the mighty rivers of India are giving to her inhabitants. They remind us of the sacrifice we must make for the sake of the land we are living in. They remind us of the process of purification that we must continuously go through as the rivers themselves are going through from moment to moment. I wrote nearly 10 years ago that the *gayatri*, the common prayer of Hinduism, was one of the precious gifts of the Ganga. Her shining waters must have given the *rishis* of old the inspiration. In the modern rush, the chief use we have for our rivers is to empty our gutters in them and to navigate our cargo vessels, and in the process make them dirtier still. We have no time, as the friend had, to stroll down to these rivers, and in silent meditation listen to the message they murmur to us.

Young India, 23-12-1926

168. NOTES

A. I. S. A. Resolutions

The following resolutions were passed by the Council of the All-India Spinners' Association at its meeting held at Wardha from 13th to 16th December 1926.

> I. Resolved that all sale depots conducted directly by the All-India Spinners' Association or through provincial departments be instructed strictly to avoid all sales on credit whether they be retail sales or wholesale transactions with other depots.
>
> II. Resolved that cash securities be insisted on from hawkers covering the amount of stock taken by them for sales. In special cases, however, where desirable hawkers are unable

[1] The letter is not reproduced here. The correspondent had described the feelings of ecstasy that the river Jumna had inspired in him.

to furnish such security, personal sureties may be taken from them. In all cases hawkers should be strictly warned that they should make no credit sales on any account and periodical settlements of accounts should be made. If at any time a hawker is unable to pay up the cash for the stock sold or the balance of stock does not tally, the hawker should be at once discharged and steps should be taken against him for recovery of the monies due.

III. Whereas it is not desirable that the sale depots should be run in places where the public does not give adequate support enabling them to be conducted without loss, all provincial departments are instructed to close down depots where, after two years' experience, it is found that the charges incurred exceed $6\frac{1}{4}\%$ of the total sales effected per year, and to open new depots only where they expect this standard to be reached at least in the course of a year.

IV. Whereas it is necessary, at present, to concentrate our efforts on such centres, where, by reason of greater unemployment or special adaptability to the industry of hand-spinning and hand-weaving, there are greater facilities for the production of khadi, it is resolved that, in proposing schemes of work, provincial agents and secretaries should not undertake to open or maintain centres of production which can be run only at a loss. But where it is considered desirable in the interests of the movement that any centres should be run or maintained at a loss, it should be borne in mind that no more than 10 % of the total capital invested for production in the province should be invested in such pioneer effort.

KENYA INDIANS

In another column is published a letter from Mr. D. B. Desai, a settler of Kenya, referring to an increase in the poll tax which Indians of Kenya have been made to pay for the past twelve years and more.[1] The letter is remarkable for the wealth of details it contains. If the facts set forth in it are true, it is a serious reflection upon the Europeans of Kenya and the Kenya Government. The reader will recollect that the Indians of Kenya did not submit to the poll tax without protest. Of course the protest was useless. But one would have thought that there would be no further addition to the iniquitous tax. If, however, my correspondent is right, by a currency trick the tax was raised by 50 per

[1] For the text of the letter, *vide* Appendix III.

cent., i.e., it went up from 20 shillings to 30 and now the amending legislation raises it to 50 shillings. The reasons given for the rise would seem to be utterly absurd. The reader must read the letter to know how the tax is to be utilized. The Kenya Indians have certainly every reason for hoping that the public and the Government will come to their assistance and demand a veto of this discriminating and unjust legislation.

Young India, 23-12-1926

169. *KHADI SERVICE*

The Council of the All-India Spinners' Association, after most careful and exhaustive discussion and after considering all the opinions that had been received upon the draft published some time ago in these pages, has recast the rules which the reader will find published elsewhere. Forms of application and contract of service are also published. This service provides those who want to serve the cause of khadi an opportunity of so doing and, at the same time, a modest remuneration for themselves.

The Board of Studies will also be the Examination Board. It does not mean necessarily that all the Examiners will examine all the candidates. But the various examinations required under the rules will be conducted by one or more of the examiners selected by the Chairman of the Board.

Suggestions were received that the course which extends to 3 years is altogether too long for the remuneration promised. But all the members came to the conclusion that 3 years were none too long for the subjects to be studied and the practical work to be done. Experience gained during the last five years has shown that continued practice is necessary to learn the various arts that are included in the course. Those who have gone out to organize khadi work in the different villages with less experience and knowledge have found themselves handicapped. The science of hand-spinning is capable of progressive improvement. Researches that are being made from time to time show that there is room for the best among us to apply themselves to the development of the art so that without extra effort or time the income of the millions, for whom hand-spinning is designed, may be almost doubled.

It is an unfortunate fact that in our schools and colleges handicrafts find no place. All the knowledge, therefore, gained in the schools and colleges is of little use for the training required for khadi service. Therefore a graduate has to start almost on equal terms with a raw youth. Indeed, it is possible for the former even to labour under a handicap, if he has developed, as many do develop, a repugnance towards physical exertion.

The second question that came up for anxious consideration was that of remuneration. The Khadi Service is designed for meeting the need of paupers. It is impossible to hold out bright pecuniary prospects in such a service. I have no doubt whatsoever that the scale of salaries devised by the Government is out of all proportion to the condition of India's masses. It has relation to the requirements of the inhabitants of a rich island and therefore means an almost unbearable burden upon the poor millions. Let no one, therefore, compare the remuneration offered under the Khadi Service with that obtainable under the Government service. At the same time, I make bold to say that the start offered is as good as that offered by the Government. Where the Khadi Service fails in comparison is in the ultimate prospect. The maximum attainable under the Government may reach four figures whereas Khadi Service offers an increase amounting to Rs. 20 at the most. For those, therefore, who have received an English education to enter this service is undoubtedly a sacrifice. But is it too much to ask the English-educated youths of the country to make what after all is a very small sacrifice? I consider it to be very small, for it should be remembered that they have received their English education at the expense of the masses. It is an exclusive education which the masses can never get. And it is an education which, if it has given us a few self-sacrificing patriots, has also produced many more men who have been willing accomplices with the Government in holding India in bondage.

It will also be noted that to the poor and deserving, the service offers a suitable scholarship and at the end of the training, while the rules bind the Association to keep those who may be found properly qualified employed for 10 years, they leave it open for them to serve the Association or to seek prospects elsewhere. This relaxation has been purposely made in order to induce young men to come and learn the art of spinning and all it means even though they may not join the Service.

Young India, 23-12-1926

170. HAND-WEAVING AMONG PARSIS

A correspondent extracts for me the following passage from the Gazetteer of the Bombay Presidency, Volume VII, Page 155, edition 1883:

> The Parsi weavers of Gandevi were of special note, and in 1787-88 Dr. Hove, a European traveller, visited that town for the express purpose of learning from the Parsis some knowledge of their art. The industry has died out for above fifty years. The Parsi women of the priestly class still, however, make a large number of sacred threads *kusti* or *kasti*, worn by Parsi men and women. These find a large sale in Bombay and cost Rs. 3 or more according to the labour displayed. Some of the Parsi women also make tape for cots and rough dhoti and khadi to order for local traders, but the Parsis as a rule have quite abandoned the weaving in which they excelled.

What a great boon to India and to themselves it would be if the Parsis who are conducting liquor shops were to exchange the immoral liquor traffic for the uplifting and productive occupation of weaving in which they excelled only 50 years ago! The reference to the hand-spun *kasti* reminds me of the stalwart Parsi sister whom I met in Navsari and who told me that the Parsi ladies of Navsari who made their livelihood out of *kasti*-spinning and whose sacred fingers gave the religious touch to the *kasti* were hounded out by those who had gone there under the guise of reformers to substitute the hand-spun thread with the machine-spun.

Young India, 23-12-1926

171. ALL-INDIA SPINNERS' ASSOCIATION

The annual report of the All-India Spinners' Association has been just published. It is brief enough for any busy man to go through. A spinners' association means an association not of but for the poorest. It cannot be of the poorest, for they have no knowledge of what an association is and have not even labour to save which they can give to their association. It follows therefore that if there must be an association for them, others who live on their labour make some small return to the poorest of their brothers and sisters. Of such then is this Association made.

They are all too few for the purpose. I wish there were more. But whether they are few or many, their work is substantial. It has on its record 110 carders, 42,959 spinners and 3,407 weavers among whom were distributed over 9 lakhs of rupees at the lowest computation. This distributing work was done at 150 production centres catering to the needs of roughly 1,500 villages. I have mentioned these salient facts merely to whet the reader's appetite. There is not an idle word in the report. It is simply a fairly well arranged catalogue of facts and figures. The reader, if he cares to look at it, will find therein the quantity of khadi produced and sold during the year. He will find too how many young men are earning their living in this growing organization, and how many other ancillary activities are undertaken by it. The report can be had by writing to the All-India Spinners' Association office, Ahmedabad, and sending 4 annas stamps.

Young India, 23-12-1926

172. *INTERVIEW TO THE PRESS*

CALCUTTA,
December 24, 1926

Before he left for Gauhati, Mahatma Gandhi, interviewed on the question of a new programme, said it was too early to talk because the programme had to be settled by the Congress. He said:

Everyone may have his own views, but it is difficult to say what the Congress will accept. So far as I am aware, the people are going with an open mind and a sincere desire to arrive at some workable programme which can be accepted by different groups, but it is too risky to prophesy anything about what the programme is going to be, even roughly.

On the working of the Reforms, Mahatmaji remarked:

So far as I can say, there will be certainly strongest disinclination to work the Reforms until, naturally, the sore point that Bengal feels, namely, indefinite detention of political prisoners, is honourably and satisfactorily settled.

The Bombay Chronicle, 25-12-1926

173. TELEGRAM TO LAJPAT RAI[1]

December 24, 1926

RECEIVED STUNNING NEWS. YOU SHOULD GO DELHI PREVENT EXCITEMENT OR RESENTMENT. WIRE PARTICULARS.

The Leader, 28-12-1926

174. TELEGRAM TO INDRA VIDYAVACHASPATI[2]

[*December 24, 1926*]

HAVE RECEIVED STUNNING WIRE. FATHER DIED LIKE A HERO.

[From Hindi]
Hindi Navajivan, 6-1-1927

175. SPEECH AT A.I.C.C. MEETING, GAUHATI[3]

[*December 24, 1926*]

A press reporter had come to me and asked me to say something. I told him I could not. I felt too overwhelmed to be able to say anything. Mrs. Naidu also pleaded with me for a message. I again refused. Since I have been, this time, ordered to speak, I shall try to express what I feel. But I am in no condition really to say anything. I can, however, tell you how the news affected me. As soon as I received Lalaji's wire I conveyed the news to Malaviyaji and others and sent telegrams

[1] The news of Swami Shraddhanand's assassination was received by Lajpat Rai at Calcutta on December 23, and the next day he conveyed it to Gandhiji, who was on his way to Gauhati to attend the A.I.C.C. meeting. The telegram reached him at Sorbhog, a wayside station. Gandhiji sent this telegram to Lajpat Rai who, along with M. R. Jayakar, left Calcutta for Delhi the same night.

[2] Mahadev Desai, in his "Gauhati Letter", says that Gandhiji sent this telegram on hearing of the assassination of Swami Shraddhanand.

[3] The text of the speech has been extracted from Mahadev Desai's "Gauhati Letter".

to Lalaji and Swamiji's son Indra. In that telegram, rather than express sorrow or grief, I said that this was no ordinary death, that I should not weep over it. Unbearable as it is, my heart refuses to grieve; it rather prays that all of us may be granted such a death.

From Swami Shraddhanand's point of view what has happened may be called a blessed event. He had been ill. I had not been aware of it but a friend told me that it would be a miracle if Swamiji survived. Later, in reply to a telegram of mine his son wired that he was slowly improving. I was assured that Dr. Ansari was looking after him with solicitude. Thus he was in bed gravely ill and in bed he was murdered. All men, of course, must die but of what worth is their dying? In India and wherever there are Hindus and Mussalmans, the death of Swamiji before his time will produce an effect very different from what would have been produced if Swamiji had died a natural death. I have not sent brother Indra any telegram or letter expressing sympathy with him. There was nothing I could say to him except that the death his father had met was a blessed death.

But I have said all this from the point of view of Swamiji and from my own point of view. I have repeatedly said that I make no distinction between Hindus and Mussalmans. I am a Hindu by birth and I find peace in the Hindu religion. Whenever peace seemed to elude me, it was in the Hindu religion that I found it. I studied other religions also and I decided that, whatever its defects and drawbacks, Hinduism alone could be the religion for me. That is what I feel and that is why I call myself a *sanatani* Hindu. Many *sanatanis* feel exasperated by this claim of mine and say: How can this man who has come back from England with all these new-fangled ideas be a Hindu? But this does not weaken my claim to being a Hindu, and Hinduism tells me to abide in friendship with all. So I have to think of the viewpoint of Mussalmans also.

And when I look at this matter from the Mussalmans' viewpoint, things are different. This deed was done through the hand of a Mussalman. Entering the house under the pretext of having a religious discussion with Swamiji he committed this monstrous act. The servant had told him that Swamiji was ill and could not see him. There was some argument at the door. When Swamiji heard it, he said: "Well, let him come." And although Swamiji need not have talked with him, he did so. He had not the strength, in fact, to talk much. All he wanted was gently to persuade him to go away. So he called him and said: "My friend, you can talk with me to your heart's content after I get well. But now I am bed-ridden." At this the visitor asked for water to drink. Swamiji told Dharam Singh to get him some. As soon as the faithful servant turned his back, he took out a revolver. He fired two shots, not satisfied with one. Swamiji died then and there. Hearing the shots Dharam Singh ran to save his master, but it was too late! It was not God's will that Swamiji's body should be saved. Dharam Singh was also hit and is now in hospital. The killer, Abdul Rashid, is in police custody. It pains me to imagine the feeling that this will evoke among the Hindus. Without doubt this will create ill feeling for Mussalmans among the Hindus. Today there is no love between the two communities. There is no trust. Both do realize that at the end they have to live together like brothers, but meanwhile each, conscious of its weakness, wants to fight with the other, become strong and then unite. In these circumstances, and with the poison that is spread in the newspapers, it is difficult to say what this deed will lead to. That was why I wanted to keep silent. I cannot calm the storm that is raging within me, I cannot suppress it and I cannot express it before you.

We should learn a lesson from the fact that Swamiji died by the hand of Abdul Rashid. Let this make us try to understand each other. It would be wonderful if we realized that we cannot live together in perpetual conflict. But the atmosphere that prevails today holds out no hope that we shall escape with only one murder.

I shall say nothing at the moment of my personal relationship with Shraddhanandji. He opened out his heart to me. About six months ago when he visited the Ashram, he said to me: "I get many letters holding out threats to my life. But they do not worry me." You see, he was a brave man. In all the world I know no one braver than Swamiji. He had no fear of death for he had faith in God. That is why he used to say: "Even if they take my life what would it matter?" There is nothing to be wondered at that he was killed. There would be nothing to be wondered at if there were more murders. Today it is a Mussalman who has murdered a Hindu. We should not be surprised if a Hindu killed a Mussalman. God forbid that this should happen but what else can one expect when we cannot control our tongue or our pen? I must, however, say that if any Hindu imitated this act he would only bring disgrace to Hinduism.

I have said that it would be better if, instead of ignorant people fighting among themselves, the leaders who harbour enmity towards each other were to do the fighting. But it should not be that an individual from among the ignorant folk takes the life of a leader.

Let us pray to God that we may understand the real meaning of this assassination. This is a testing time for Hindus and Mussalmans. Let the Hindus remain peaceful and refrain from seeking revenge for this murder. Let them not think that the two communities are now enemies of each other and that unity is no longer possible. If they do, they will be committing a crime and bringing disgrace upon their religions. And, in my opinion, if a Mussalman thinks that Abdul Rashid did well he will be disgracing his religion. For that is not his religion. His religion is something else. Now is the opportunity for the Mussalmans to show the real teachings of Islam. Shraddhanandji and the Hindus have, of course, got what they had to, but as a man and as a friend and brother of Mussalmans, I must tell them that it will do both our communities good if we would understand this in the right spirit. May God give us faith and wisdom to survive this test and to behave towards each other, after this deed, in such a way that God can say that the two communities did what they ought to have done.

[From Hindi]

Hindi Navajivan, 6-1-1927

176. SPEECH AT SWADESHI EXHIBITION, GAUHATI[1]

December 25, 1926

Mahatmaji said that his faith in the charkha was intense and was increasing day by day. He, therefore, welcomed all opportunities of doing propaganda for organizing the charkha movement. For swaraj he had laid down three conditions, of which he held the spread of spinning-wheel to be the foremost. Indeed, this was the one platform where crores could work together—juveniles, adults, men and women could all contribute their mite. And more than this, it was a platform which offered women the best scope for taking their due share in the national movement for swaraj. He was, indeed, sure that

[1] The opening of the Swadeshi Exhibition by Gandhiji drew large crowds who lined the route and shouted "*Mahatma Gandhiki Jai*" as he entered the exhibition grounds. The attendance within the enclosure was large and on the dais, besides Gandhiji, were seated Malaviya and Sarojini Naidu. Other leaders present included Srinivasa Iyengar, Dr. Moonje, Motilal Nehru, Abul Kalam Azad, B. G. Horniman, V. J. Patel, Mohamed Ali, Swami Satyadev, Mrs. Aney and Lala Girdharilal.

success in the charkha programme would itself go a great deal towards the fulfilment of the second condition, namely, Hindu-Muslim unity.

He was studying the currency problem with a view to forming his own opinion on the controversy that was going on in respect of the exchange ratio. But from what he had read, he felt that really towns lived on villages and middlemen were helping to bleed the peasants and the country and were sending out of the country crores of rupees. He stated on the testimony of the Government Collectors' reports that villages were being ruined and that at least one-tenth of the people of India did not have enough to eat. For one hundred years the town people had bled the villager white. Why then would not they give the villager some return by taking to khaddar and thereby encouraging a movement which was full of the greatest possibilities for the uplift of the country? The Congress was a great institution, but it had not reached the villagers to any appreciable extent.

The Spinners' Association, organized under the Congress, had been given by the Congress complete swaraj and the Association had already secured touch with 1,500 villages and was providing work for 50,000 women and 4,000 weavers. Those who visited places of pilgrimage knew the state of beggary there. He held it a crime to give charity to the people capable of doing work if they were provided proper employment. The fifty thousand women who had been provided work by the Spinners' Association were those who had had no employment and did not earn a penny. If their operations could be extended and if he could be backed by the knowledge that leaders like Pandit Motilal, Pandit Malaviya and Maulana Mohamed Ali were taking to the spinning-wheel, his message would be heard and the problem of beggary could as well be tackled. A vast field remained to be covered as there were something like seven lakhs of villages in India. The price of khaddar today was practically half of what it was in 1921 and certainly it was untrue to say that there was less of khaddar produced.

Forward, 27-12-1926

177. ALL-INDIA COW-PROTECTION ASSOCIATION

It is said that the work of this Association proceeds but sluggishly. Its Working Committee met in Wardha on the 17th of this month. A resolution was passed to start the work of the committee meeting after postponing it for half an hour, due to want of quorum; in the meantime Dr. Moonje arrived and then the meeting commenced its work with the requisite quorum. This sort of thing should not happen in any organization. But as we have little or no interest in the constructive programme, only a few people attend such meetings if there is no financial gain in doing so.

This Association has to secure cow-protection through institutions selling milk and hides; hard work, finance, talent, etc., are therefore necessary. Who would like to attend a meeting of such an Association?

And yet, the question of cow-protection is very important from the religious and economic points of view. Agriculture is not possible without the well-being of cattle and man cannot live without agriculture. Moreover, we cannot have milk without cattle and the life of the people becomes difficult without milk.

The well-being of cattle depends entirely on their intelligent rearing and such knowledge cannot be gained without effort. Hence the object of the All-India Cow-protection Association is to spread such knowledge through experiments and to remove the repugnance that people have towards the trade in hides and tanning.

Who should take interest in this? Every thinking man and woman should. Whether many take interest or a few, such associations should continue their work with determination and prove their faith in it.

Hence the Committee has passed four resolutions.

Since an expert in the art of dairy management is available, the President has been authorized to spend up to Rs. 50,000 in order to implement the experiment of a dairy.

A gentleman is available for running the leather workshop and hence expenditure up to another Rs. 50,000 has been sanctioned to run this experiment.

The Association does not yet have so much money. The Association would hardly have Rs. 10,000. As for the rest, it is uncertain. There is a hope that the remaining amount will be provided. Friends have offered to help. And I have the faith that money will be positively available if the work as well as the workers are good. Hence I have taken the above-mentioned authority from the Committee. Those interested in the welfare of the cow should render such help as they may wish to offer. Every pie is and will be accounted for. Accounts will be regularly published. Success or failure in the work depends on circumstances. It is hoped that at the end of the experiment both the activities can be shown to be self-supporting.

I wish to introduce the workers engaged in this work after I am well acquainted with this work. If these experiments succeed, they would, I think, provide the key to cow-protection.

The other resolutions are to make the Association self-sufficient in membership. The society is in need of workers and not officers. Hence there is a resolution to the effect that if a member of the Committee absents himself from three consecutive meetings, membership lapses automatically. This resolution is essential because only those who can give the benefit of their views while the Committee formulates resolutions deserve to continue as members. How can those who do not remain present give such benefit? The Secretary will start correspondence with every member in this behalf.

The fourth resolution applies to the members. Those members who do not pay in their subscription for the following year will not remain members. This is just to give a reminder. The members and representatives of this Association should be responsible individuals. Really speaking, these two principles should be regarded as inevitable in all institutions that members must pay the subscription and that the representatives must be present at the meeting.

It is my hope that those who subscribe to the objectives of the Association will welcome all these four resolutions and help the Association as much as possible.

It may be said that the Committee had just to approve the arrangement regarding the Secretary. Shri Valji Govindji Desai was appointed Secretary on a salary of Rs. 200 a month. Shri Valji Desai is a *go-sevak*[1] and a learned man. He did not ask for Rs. 200 out of greed but because his family responsibilities were large. I could not find a more qualified Secretary than Shri Desai. According to the constitution of the Association the responsibility for the choice rested with me. When Shri Valji Desai was appointed for this work, it was felt that he would have to devote

[1] One who serves the cause of cow-protection

all his time to the work of cow-protection. Later it was found that he could spare some time. So we both decided that he should utilize that time in literary activities and earn some income out of it. Since he can get that type of work, he informed the Association that he would not receive from it more than Rs. 50 a month. He has been taking this amount since July last. The Association has accepted his decision with thanks. He has been granted permission to do during his spare time any outside work available to him. I must say that the work that Shri Valji Desai is doing in his spare time may not be regarded as done for the Association itself, but it is, to a large extent, definitely connected with the work of cow-protection. It does not appear necessary to pass on this information to the readers of *Navajivan.*

[From Gujarati]
Navajivan, 26-12-1926

178. SPEECH AT FLAG-HOISTING CEREMONY, GAUHATI[1]

December 26, 1926

DR. HARDIKAR AND VOLUNTEERS,

I am glad to see you here this morning. I hope that the National flag unfurled by me this morning will be kept flying for ever and you will all do works befitting the honour of the great flag. I bless you for your service to the Motherland.

Forward, 27-12-1926

179. RESOLUTION AND SPEECH AT CONGRESS SESSION, GAUHATI[2]

December 26, 1926

RESOLUTION

This Congress expresses its horror and indignation at the cowardly and treacherous murder of Swami Shraddhanand and places on record its sense of the irreparable loss the nation

[1] Delivered in Hindi after unfurling the Congress flag in front of the Congress *pandal* in the morning. Dr. N. S. Hardikar was in charge of the volunteers.

[2] The text of the speech was also published in *Young India*, 13-1-1927, under the heading "Hero among Heroes".

has sustained by the tragic death of a brave and noble patriot who dedicated his life and his great gifts to the service of his country and of his faith and espoused with fearless devotion the cause of the lowly, the fallen and the weak.

BROTHERS AND SISTERS,

You must have noticed that the resolution I have moved originally stood in Maulana Mohamed Ali's name. But I am here to move it in obedience to the President's summons. We see from the newspapers that the assassination of Swamiji has evoked grief and horror throughout the land. I said speaking on the same subject at the All-India Congress Committee that we should not mourn over Swamiji's death. He had died the death of a hero, and every one of us might wish for such a death. But I want to make a slight correction in that last statement. Every brave man welcomes such a death whenever it comes to him. He greets it as a friend. But let no one therefore invite or hanker after such a death, let no one desire that someone else should be in the wrong and err against God and man, so that he might become a martyr. It is wrong to wish anyone to go astray. Let us all be brave enough to die the death of a martyr, but let no one lust for martyrdom.

Swamiji was a hero among heroes, the bravest of the brave. He had astonished the nation with an unbroken record of bravery. I am witness of the pledge he had taken to sacrifice himself at the altar of the country.

But need anyone speak at length on Swamiji's services to the nation? Swamiji, as everyone knew, was the help of the helpless, the friend of the weak and the oppressed and the work he had done for the untouchables was unsurpassed. I well remember his having told me once that, unless every Hindu member of the All-India Congress Committee had an untouchable servant in his home, the work of the Congress for the uplift of the untouchables would not be complete. This may sound as an impracticable proposal, but it shows his unbounded love for the untouchables.

I shall not refer here to his many other services. Whilst the assassination of such a great hero and patriot, such a servant and devotee of God as Swamiji, can be made to serve the country's cause, imperfect men as we are, it is natural for us to mourn over his sad death. And when one thinks of the circumstances under which he met his death, one is naturally filled with horror and indignation. The assassin sought an interview with Swamiji to have a discussion on Islam. His faithful servant refused to admit him as he had Dr. Ansari's orders to allow no interviews so long as Swamiji was seriously ailing. But God had evidently ordered otherwise. Swamiji, when he overheard the request, asked Dharam Singh to let the man in. Brother Abdul Rashid was shown in. I purposely call him brother, and if we are true Hindus you will understand why I call him so. Swamiji asked his servant to admit Abdul Rashid, because God had willed to show therethrough the greatness of Swamiji and the glory of Hinduism. Swamiji was, of course, too ill to discuss religious topics and he asked the stranger to seek another occasion. But he would not go. He said he was thirsty and asked for water. Swamiji asked Dharam Singh to fetch water for him and taking advantage of his absence, the man deposited bullet shots in Swamiji's breast.

This is a thing which should not have happened in India—India where both Hindus and Mussalmans are proud of their faiths. I have studied the Koran with the same reverent attention as I give the *Gita*, and I say that the Koran nowhere sanctions or enjoins such murders. The murder has been possible because the two communities look upon each other with feelings of hatred and enmity. Many Mussalmans believe that Lalaji and Malaviyaji are the sworn enemies of Islam as was Swamiji in their opinion. On the other hand, many Hindus regard Sir Abdur Rahim and other Mussalmans as the enemies of Hinduism. To my mind both are wholly wrong. Swamiji was no enemy of Islam nor are Lalaji and Malaviyaji. Lalaji and Malaviyaji have a right to express their opinion freely and even if we disagree with them, no one may excite feelings of hatred against them. And yet, what do we see today? There are few Mussalman papers today which do not use foul language against these patriots. Now I ask in all humility what is the wrong they have done. We may not see eye to eye with them in their methods of work. But I am sure that it is his great service that has earned for Malaviyaji the name, Bharat Bhushan. Lalaji too has a great record of service. Then take the Mussalman leaders. Sir Abdur Rahim may think that Hindus are in advance of the Mussalmans in every respect, that they are rich, they are educated, and the Mussalmans are poor and uneducated. Sir Abdur Rahim thinks that his community should have a preference in the services. It is open to us to feel and say that he is mistaken in his views, but why should we abuse him for his opinions? If Maulana Mahomed Ali says that although he has respect for Gandhi he holds that the faith of a Muslim who believes in the Koran is greater than the faith of Gandhi, why should we be angry? Do not some Christian clergymen say that a Christian regularly going to church and serving Jesus is better than a Hindu however pious he may be? What does that matter to us? I therefore appeal to you that if you hold dear the memory of Swami Shraddhanandji, you would help in purging the atmosphere of mutual hatred and calumny, you would help in boycotting papers which foment hatred and spread misrepresentation. I am sure that India would lose nothing if 90 per cent of the papers were to cease today. Many Mussalman papers today subsist on hatred of the Hindu and many Hindu papers subsist on hatred of the Mussalman. Swamiji has left for us a rich lesson written in his blood. "Do you know the liberality of the Arya Samaj?," he once asked me. "Do you know how Maharshi Dayanand forgave the man who poisoned him?" I knew it. How could I be ignorant of it, knowing as I did that the Maharshi had before him the example of Yudhishthira and the teaching of the *Gita* and the Upanishads? But Shraddhanandji in his overflowing reverence for the Maharshi dilated upon his forgiveness. I tell you the disciple had no less of that noble quality than his great master. Speaking once about the implications of *shuddhi* he told me that his *shuddhi* excluded any feeling of ill will for the Mussalman, that it meant purification of self and of the great community to which he belonged, and that his ideal was the ideal of the *Gita* — "See thyself in every one of the created beings." But he emphasized that the Hindu also was no less a friend of his than the Mussalman and that it was his duty to serve him. Even if the whole Muslim world were to turn against me, I would declare that Malaviyaji is my friend and elder brother. I declare also in the same breath that none of the Mussalman leaders is an enemy of Hinduism. Sir Abdur Rahim is not an enemy of the Hindus, nor is Mian Fazli Hussain. When I met him he assured me that he was an old Congressman, that he loved the Hindus no less than the Mussalmans, but that as a Mussalman he wanted to serve the latter. We may disagree with him in his views, we may not like his demands for the Mussalmans, but why should we therefore swear at him and say that he is an enemy of the Hindus? Why should we not express our dissent from his views and fight them, if necessary, even as I do with Malaviyaji, in many respects, in a satyagrahi way? I repeat, therefore, with all the emphasis I can command that Sir Abdur Rahim or Mr. Jinnah or the Ali Brothers are no enemies of the Hindus. Let not the lesson of Swami Shraddhanandji's death be lost on us. You will all be accepting this resolution standing while, at this moment perhaps, there are Hindu-Muslim disturbances going on in Delhi. But I tell you that, if every one of you understands and lays to his heart the lesson that Swami Shraddhanandji has left for us, it is again possible to win swaraj in no time. I am a mad man, you will say, accustomed to giving rash promises. Well, I tell you I am not mad, I am still as much in earnest about my programme as I was in 1920, but those who made pledges in 1920 broke them and made swaraj impossible then. We are all children of the same Father—whom the Hindu and the Mussalman and the Christian know by different names. What if Sankara declared his faith in one God in his formula *Ekamevadvitiyam* or Ramanuja in his dual doctrine or Mahomed in his *La Illah Illillah*? All meant one and the same thing. If we cleanse our hearts, we shall be able to see that Swamiji has served us in his death as much as he served us when living. Let us purify our hearts with his blood, and fight, if need be, for our rights in a peaceful and satyagrahi way. Let every Mussalman also understand that Swami Shraddhanandji was no enemy of Islam, that his was a pure and unsullied life, and that he has left for us all the lesson of peace written in his blood.

Now you will, perhaps, understand why I have called Abdul Rashid a brother, and I repeat it, I do not even regard him as guilty of Swami's murder. Guilty, indeed, are all those who excited feelings of hatred against one another. For us Hindus, the *Gita* enjoins on us the lesson of equality; we are to cherish the same feelings towards a learned Brahmin as towards a *Chandal*, a dog, a cow and an elephant.

This is no occasion for mourning or tears, it is an occasion that should burn in our hearts the lesson of bravery. Bravery is not the exclusive quality of the Kshatriyas. It may be their special privilege. But, in our battle for swaraj, bravery is essential as much for the Brahmin and the Vaisya and the Sudra as for the Kshatriya. Let us not therefore shed tears of sorrow, but chasten our hearts and steel them with some of the fire and faith that were Shraddhanandji's.

Report of the Indian National Congress, Forty-first Session, Gauhati (Assam), 1926, pp. 42-5

180. RESOLUTION AND SPEECH AT CONGRESS SESSION, GAUHATI

December 26, 1926

RESOLUTION

This Congress welcomes the Round Table Conference now sitting in South Africa to deliberate upon the best method of dealing with the question of the status of Indian settlers in that sub-continent and prays for divine blessing and guidance upon its deliberations.

This Congress once more tenders its thanks to that good Englishman, Mr. C. F. Andrews, who has been chiefly instrumental in preparing in South Africa a calm atmosphere suitable for the holding of the Conference.

This Congress authorizes the President to cable the text of the Resolution to General Hertzog, Sir M. Habibulla and Mr. C. F. Andrews.[1]

Mahatmaji addressed the assembly in Hindi and the following is a summary of his speech:

He said that Mr. C. F. Andrews had kept him in touch with the position in South Africa through correspondence. Mr. Andrews had emphasized in his letters that prayers should be held all over for divine guidance of the Round Table Conference. Need for such prayer was paramount. They knew that the Indian Government had no power to force its will on South Africa. The recent Imperial Conference had conceded to the dominions even greater freedom and independence in the field of imperial relations. They could, therefore, only pray to God to shower His blessings on those engaged in the discussions of the Round Table Conference so that enlightened by the divine blessings, the Conference might concede justice to the Indian settlers in South Africa.

He then drew the attention of the audience to the fact that the untouchability of South Africa, from which their countrymen were suffering, was nothing but a repercussion of Indian untouchability. It therefore behoved them to put their own house in order.

He reminded the South African statesmen that history showed those who having power abused it prepared for their own ruin, and implored them to

[1] The resolution was seconded by Abul Kalam Azad, and passed unanimously.

grant the Indian settlers elementary justice which they desired. They did not ask for favours; in fact they had forgone, for the sake of peace, things they need not have in strict justice.

Report of the Indian National Congress, Forty-first Session, Gauhati (Assam), 1926, pp. 51-2

181. LETTER TO ASHRAM WOMEN

GAUHATI,
Monday, December 27, 1926

DEAR SISTERS,

Instead of writing to you in the morning as usual, I am writing this just before the mail is cleared. Here it is cleared early.

The scenery around here is lovely. Our hut is put up right on the bank of the Brahmaputra; Kaka Saheb would be tempted by the very sight of the hut to stay here. There is a thatch of straw by way of roof. The walls are made of pieces of bamboo that grows all round here. The bamboo is plastered with mud. The inside of the wall is covered with khadi made in Assam. There is no cot inside, but there is an improvised platform, a wooden plank with bamboo legs. Over it is spread straw, on the hay a carpet and on the carpet a khadi sheet. On this I sit, dine and sleep. It is big enough to accommodate four more, but no one else sleeps on it. The ground in the hut, too, is spread over with hay, on which is spread a carpet, which again is covered with khadi. Who would not like to stay in such a hut? Of course, the life of such a hut is very short. It is useless in the rainy season. But it costs very little, takes only a day or two to put up, and requires no great skill. This is so with all true art. It is always simple and natural.

It is quite damp and cold here, but if one moves about briskly one does not get ill.

More next time, whatever comes to my mind then.

Blessings from
BAPU

From a photostat of the Gujarati: G.N. 3631

182. *SPEECH AT CONGRESS SESSION, GAUHATI*[1]

December 27, 1926

Mr. Gandhi said an appeal had been made to him for sense of justice. His sense of justice would restore the yarn franchise and make spinning also obligatory.[2] Personally he believed in quality rather than in quantity, but if Congressmen believed in quantity rather than in quality, he suggested that the fewer the restrictions the better for the Congress. If, on the other hand, they believed in quality, then they must impose certain restrictions upon membership which promoted quality and thereby promoted national regeneration. The Congress wanted all the parties within its fold, but they wanted them not at any cost, and let it not be a charge either against the No changers or against the Swarajists that they wanted to keep the Congress as a close corporation; but, after all, national organizations had their own restrictions which regulated their growth. It was, therefore, for the committee to decide whether khaddar was essential or not. In his opinion it was the only binding tie between the Congress and the masses. There were on the Spinners' Association's register more than fifty thousand men and women who were provided with work. Congress must harness this power of khaddar and increase it in order to achieve swaraj. Swaraj would not drop from the Downing Street but by linking the Congress with the masses through that slender cotton thread. He granted that the present franchise could not work because as it stood it was humiliating. What had happened in a number of cases was that a few yards of khaddar hired or purchased were kept near the Congress Committee's offices and the members, while entering the offices in order to participate in committee discussions and registering their votes, put on the khaddar cloth.

[1] Gandhiji was speaking in the Subjects Committee on a motion by Motilal Nehru which read: "Resolved that the following amendment be made in Article 7 of the Congress constitution: Substitute the following for sub-Clause 4. 'No person shall be entitled to vote at the election of the representatives or the delegates or any committee or sub-committee or any Congress organization whatsoever or to be elected as such or to take part in any meeting of the Congress or Congress organization or any committee or sub-committee thereof if he has not complied with sub-Section (1) hereof and does not habitually wear hand-spun and hand-woven khaddar.'"

[2] Mahadev Desai's report in his "Weekly Letter" has this here: "Let me say my sense of justice will be reconciled only by the restoration of the spinning franchise. If a stiffening of the franchise is, as I think it certainly is, necessary for national growth, am I not justified in laying down conditions for it? If any member should charge me with motives to exclude any party, I should feel deeply sorry, if not insulted."

Please do not insult the masses who are dumb. They are already sufficiently insulted. If you believe in the number and not on the quality of Congressmen, then we may as well urge the Congress to remove this yarn franchise completely; but if you believe in quality, then we must stiffen the franchise. Not that I want Congressmen to go out of Congress but because this stiffening is necessary for the growth of the Congress organization.

The amendment of Pandit Motilal is a plea for honesty. If you do not believe in the wearing of khaddar then it is your bounden duty to unhesitatingly vote against it, but the existing clause is nothing but humiliation. In voting on this question, consideration of person must be avoided. Khaddar must stand on its own bottom or it should be destroyed. Please, therefore, eliminate me from your considerations. I do not care whether khaddar remains or not, but I do care for honour of the Congress, because Congress is a mighty name. No success at the polls will achieve swaraj. Yesterday you had to raise the delegate's fee from one to five rupees. Why? Has the Congress chest become so empty? If we had faith in Congress, our financial position would have been brighter. Was not our financial position far better in 1920-21? Is it khaddar that has brought our finances so low? I would ask you to put your hands on your heart and ask yourself why is this downfall. My individual opinion is that this proposition must be carried without any dissentient but if you carry the proposition, you must carry it with all the implications, that is, we must carry on the education of the people in the use of khaddar. You must do nothing to placate me. I do not need your patronage. I am an humble servant of the nation exactly on the same basis as you are, on the terms of absolute equality. I reserve all the rights of a member to myself and, as I am a lover of liberty, I give you the same right to exercise your liberty.

Amrita Bazar Patrika, 28-12-1926

183. LETTER TO MIRABEHN

[*December 27, 1926*][1]

CHI. MIRA,

I have all your love letters. The one about the repugnance against Mussalmans is disturbing. It is the fear of conversion that has caused this repugnance.

You are doing the right thing there. Watch everything. Mend where you can. Be still, where you are helpless. You have gone there only as a learner. Your *business* is to finish your Hindi. You will teach and reform only by the way. You will not therefore become a participator in anything that goes on in your school which the Gurukul is for you, even as I cannot be a participator in the sins of a drunkard who may teach me how to shave. But this is not to criticize anything you have hitherto done. This is merely to assure you that you are doing quite well.

Why apologize about the expenses ? We do want to be stingy. But we do not want to deny ourselves the things we need for keeping us fit for service. You know that you can get what funds you need from Mr. Gadodia.

Rita is *aritha* the soap-nut.

You will see many more Miss Rams. May your contact open their eyes. Raisina[2] is all you describe it to be and much worse. It is built with blood money. Instead of the blood circulating down to the feet, it is all being sucked by the head. Presently there will be meningitis and—!

Here the scenery is beautiful. Our hut is on the edge of the bank of the mighty Brahmaputra. It is damp and cold; very windy. But the weather is most bracing if one would take vigorous exercise. I generally walk to the Congress tent—one mile and a little over.

I leave tomorrow for Calcutta where I expect to be for four days.

With love,

BAPU

From the original: C.W. 5193. Courtesy: Mirabehn

[1] From the postmark

[2] New Delhi

184. SPEECH AT CONGRESS SESSION, GAUHATI[1]

December 28, 1926

You are seeking to inculcate a spirit of complete independence among those who are divided amongst themselves. A wise man does not attempt to take a bigger bite than he can digest. Supposing complete independence was something infinitely superior to swaraj, even then I suggest to you to be patient and attain what is possible at the present moment and then mount further steps. One step is now enough for me, but coming to the rock-bottom, I suggest to you that swaraj includes complete independence, and because it included this, Mr. Jinnah and Pandit Malaviya resisted it, and Mr. Jinnah even went out. We want to make it absolutely clear that we want to remain within the Empire if it may be possible. Why do you lose all faith in human nature and in yourself? Why do you lose faith in your ability to bend down the haughtiness of the Englishmen and make them serve you? If you have repugnance against the white skin, do you want to drive away every Englishman and not keep any, even for teaching you English? Take the instance of South Africa; there is that haughty nation the Dutch Boer. Even they do not bring in such a resolution. General Hertzog has returned from London completely converted. He knows, if he wants to declare independence today he can get it. I shall not be satisfied with any constitution that we may get from the British Parliament unless it leaves that power with us also. So that if we choose to declare independence we could do so. ("Hear, hear.") Do not impair the effect that the word carries. Do not limit its interpretation. Who knows somebody may give us a still better definition. The potency of the word increases because it is undefined and is, I would say, undefinable.

Mahatma Gandhi at this stage made a statement about his views confidently on the Nabha question in the light of the fact that the Congress should not take up questions concerning Indian States. He wanted this question to be reopened and also felt that the currency issue was so important from the point of view of the masses that he was surprised to hear that last night [Subjects] Committee dismissed it summarily.[2]

The Searchlight, 2-1-1927

[1] Gandhiji was speaking on the Independence Resolution in the Subjects Committee.

[2] After Gandhiji, Motilal Nehru and Sambamurti spoke.

185. SPEECH AT CONGRESS SESSION, GAUHATI[1]

December 28, 1926

Mahatma Gandhi congratulated Mr. Banerjee on this sentiment.[2] They should not mind the galaxy of Mahatmas throughout the length and breadth of the country. It was better to get out of their clutches (laughter).

But I am not a Mahatma. I am an humble servant of the nation and you won't easily get out of my clutches (laughter). Because I do not yield to the fiery anarchist in my capacity for self-sacrifice, I am never frightened of even the most forward programme; but I would like you to consider and weigh the words from the lips of a man who has seen many a battle in his life and who knows how forward marches can be performed. If you define the word 'swaraj' today, you will be simply limiting its potency. I may say complete independence is included in the word 'swaraj'. It also includes something else which is repugnant to your sense of self-respect today. I say it does include a close association with the British people on terms of absolute equality. Those to whom this association is unbearable because of the atrocities of the Jallianwala Bagh and because of what has gone on even after the inauguration of the Reforms, I sympathize with them, but I say you are impatient and my advice to you is *festina lente* (hasten slowly).

If this resolution is not withdrawn and is challenged to division and rejected by an overwhelming majority, you will still have before you a most forward programme I have given, but do not delude yourself even with the distant hope that I will lead even you in the Council programme. There is no if about it today. When the spirit within me tells me that I shall go to the battle-ground in the Council, I shall on my knees apply to Panditji to take me into his fold and give me his secretaryship (laughter), but that is not yet. You should not say or think that the time may never come. I have never erased out of my mind the Council programme. Those who have a long memory may recall that, at the special session in Calcutta, I said that they must

[1] Gandhiji was speaking for a second time on the Independence Resolution.

[2] Upendranath Banerjee had said that the mere fact that Gandhiji was opposed to the resolution should not be an argument against the resolution.

not think that the Councils might never be considered by us, but if I went to the Council or sent people to the Council, and Lord Reading asked me, 'You come to my Council,' I would say, 'Yes, but do these things and I come.' Just as I accepted the Champaran Commission of enquiry, I am quite capable of accepting office in the Council and capable of becoming an Executive Councillor (laughter), but when I become an Executive Councillor you may depend upon me that swaraj has come (laughter) and Mr. Sambamurti's complete independence also.

I have acquired and achieved my own personal independence. Now I want every Indian to acquire that independence and the sum-total of that is complete independence. I can tell you negatively that, until the All-India Congress Committee really becomes the working body of the men determined to complete the work, when India has really completed one of its promises, namely, the boycott of foreign cloth, when you have very nearly achieved the boycott of foreign cloth, you will find me going to Pandit Motilal and saying, 'Please sir, may I be admitted into your Council party?' But that boycott cannot be achieved unless you really become determined men. I want every one of you to join this Khadi Service. I can give you thirty rupees a month and training, but I will send you to the villages and you achieve the boycott of foreign cloth. Then, you will have me to work the Council programme also.

Today we are not a disciplined body. You put your hand on your heart and say that you are. We do not yield with willing obedience to the Chair that we ought to. We should lift up our Chairman and say, 'Yes, we shall march with you shoulder to shoulder.'

Do you know that threatening letters are being received that now that Swami Shraddhanand has lost his life, some Mussalman should also lose his? There is a postcard which is now in the hands of the Chairman. It is anonymous. There is nothing in it, but the sum-total of these anonymous letters gives us the clue as to where the country is going. Can I have any time for shouldering the Council programme when the atmosphere around us is surcharged?[1] If it is possible for so many of us to cleanse the atmosphere, you will find me giving my attention to the Council programme. Please eliminate me from your mind. If you summarily reject this amendment, you will do so on your

[1] The source has "surfeited".

own responsibility and its merits without the slightest bargaining and without the slightest mental reservation.[1]

The Searchlight, 2-1-1927

186. SPEECH AT MEETING OF MUNICIPAL BOARD, GAUHATI[2]

December 28, 1926

Mahatmaji, in a brief reply, thanked the Board for the honour done to him and stated that he was very much pleased that spinning and weaving had not yet lost their hold on the people of Assam. He was conscious that even today it was essential for every girl of marriageable age among them to have the knowledge of weaving. He wanted the Gauhati Municipal Board to set an example to other local bodies by introducing teaching of spinning, weaving and Hindi to the boys and girls in primary schools under their control and for this purpose he wanted them to get trained teachers. If Gauhati gave the lead, others would follow.

Amrita Bazar Patrika, 30-12-1926

187. INTERVIEW TO ASSOCIATED PRESS[3]

GAUHATI,
December 28, 1926

He informed the Associated Press representative that his business in the coming year would be to spread the message of the charkha and use of khaddar and also collect funds for the All-India Deshbandhu Memorial, the central factor of which is spread of khaddar.

Forward, 30-12-1926

[1] The amendment was rejected by a large majority.

[2] Gandhiji was presented an address of welcome by the Municipal Board.

[3] The interview took place before Gandhiji's departure for Calcutta the same day in the afternoon.

188. ABHOY ASHRAM KHADI WORK

The following report[1] of khadi work done by the Abhoy Ashram, Comilla, for 1925-26 will be read with interest. I would urge the reader to study the reports I am publishing. They prove, as nothing else can, the progress and potentiality of khadi in a cumulative and compelling manner. The reports make not an isolated case nor a case for one province only, but they present cases from almost all the provinces. Those provinces that show nothing or little are the provinces that await workers. 'The harvest is, indeed, rich, the labourers are few.' The report of the Abhoy Ashram gives one an idea how khadi has gone down in prices. It shows that khadi prices will drop still further as the skill of spinners and weavers increases. The most remarkable fact about this enterprise is that khadi has been self-supporting from the very beginning. The reason is not far to seek. The majority of the members are volunteers and take only a subsistence wage. I would like those who draw up reports to avoid 'about' and 'nearly' whenever they are giving figures. 'About 8,000 spinners' carries but a vague idea. Each centre must be able to give the exact number of spinners, weavers and carders, etc. In a great movement of a universal character, one cannot be too careful, too accurate. The movement depends for its success upon the strictest adherence to truth and purity of character on the part of workers. It has no bounty save the honour, character and sacrifice of its workers. And no movement that has this backing needs any other bounty.

Young India, 30-12-1926

[1] Not reproduced here

189. *SHRADDHANANDJI—THE MARTYR*

The expected has happened. Swami Shraddhanandji passed a day or two at the Satyagraha Ashram at Sabarmati, now about six months ago, and told me, in the course of his conversations, that he often received letters threatening his life. Where is the reformer who has not a price put upon his head? There was, therefore, nothing untoward in his getting the letters. And there is nothing untoward in the assassination having taken place.

Swamiji was a reformer, he was a man of action, not of words. His was a living belief. He had suffered for it. He was bravery personified. He never quailed before danger. He was a warrior. And a warrior loves to die, not on a sick-bed, but on the battle-field.

Shraddhanandji became seriously ill about a month ago. Dr. Ansari was, as his physician, giving him all the loving attention he was capable of giving. The telegram I received from his son, Indra, in reply to my inquiry[1] at the beginning of month, was that he was better and that he wanted my 'love and prayer' both of which he had before the asking.

God had willed for him a martyr's death and so, though he was still on the sick-bed, he died at the hands of an assassin who had asked to be admitted to the Swamiji's presence for the purpose of holding a religious discourse on Islam, who was admitted at the Swamiji's instance, and who, under pretence of wanting water to quench his thirst, had Swamiji's faithful servant, Dharam Singh, sent out to fetch water, and who, in the absence of the servant, deposited two death wounds in the patient's breast, as he was lying in his bed. We have not the last words of the Swamiji, but if I knew him at all, I have no doubt that he prayed to his God to forgive him who knew not that he was doing anything wrong. In the language of the *Gita*, therefore, 'Happy the warrior who achieves such a blessed death.'

Death is at any time blessed, but it is twice blessed for a warrior who dies for his cause, i.e., truth. Death is no fiend, he is the truest of friends. He delivers us from agony. He helps us against ourselves. He ever gives us new chances, new hopes. He is like sleep, a sweet restorer. Yet it is customary to mourn when a friend dies. The custom has no operation when the death is that

[1] This communication is not available.

of a martyr. I cannot, therefore, mourn over this death. He and his are to be envied. For though Shraddhanandji is dead, he is yet living. He is living in a truer sense than when he moved about in our midst in his giant body. The family in which he was born, the nation to which he belonged are to be congratulated upon so glorious a death as this. He lived a hero. He has died a hero.

But there is another side to the shield. I regard myself as a friend of the Mussalmans. They are my blood-brothers. Their wrongs are my wrongs. I share their sorrows and their joys. Any evil deed done by a Mussalman hurts me just as much as that done by a Hindu. This foul deed has been done by one who bears a Mussalman name. As a friend of the Mussalmans, therefore, I deeply regret the event. The joy of the death is thus tempered by the sorrow that an erring, misguided brother has been the cause of it. Martyrdom can, therefore, never be wished for. It becomes a thing of joy only when it comes unsought. We may not gloat over the errors of the least of our fellows.

But the fact is that an error often refuses to become patent until it becomes atrocious. It dies only after being completely disgraced.

This tragedy has a national importance. It draws pointed attention to an evil that is eating into the vitals of the nation. Both Hindus and Mussalmans have the choice before them. We are both on our trial.

Hindus may, by being resentful, disgrace Hinduism and postpone the unity that must come. They can by self-restraint show themselves to be worthy of the message of the Upanishads and of Yudhishthira who was the embodiment of forgiveness. Let us not ascribe the crime of an individual to a whole community. Let us not harbour the spirit of retaliation. Let us not think of the wrong as done by a Mussalman against a Hindu, but of an erring brother against a hero.

Mussalmans have an ordeal to pass through. There can be no doubt that they are too free with the knife and the pistol. The sword is no emblem of Islam. But Islam was born in an environment where the sword was and still remains the supreme law. The message of Jesus has proved ineffective because the environment was unready to receive it. So with the message of the Prophet. The sword is yet too much in evidence among Mussalmans. It must be sheathed if Islam is to be what it means—peace. There is danger of Mussalmans secretly endorsing the mad deed. It will be a calamity for them and the world. For ours is after all a world problem. Reliance upon the sword is wholly inconsistent with reliance upon God. There should be, on their part, unequivocal mass condemnation of the atrocity.

I wish to plead for Abdul Rashid. I do not know who he is. It does not matter to me what prompted the deed. The fault is ours. The newspaper man has become a walking plague. He spreads the contagion of lies and calumnies. He exhausts the foul vocabulary of his dialect, and injects his virus into the unsuspecting, and often receptive minds of his readers. Leaders 'intoxicated with the exuberance of their own language' have not known to put a curb upon their tongues or pens. Secret and insidious propaganda has done its dark and horrible work, unchecked and unabashed. It is, therefore, we the educated and the semi-educated class that are responsible for the hot fever which possessed Abdul Rashid.

It is unnecessary to discriminate and apportion the blame between the rival parties. Where both are to blame, who can arbitrate with golden scales and fix the exact ratio of blame? It is no part of self-defence to tell lies or exaggerate.

It is too much to hope, but Swamiji was great enough to warrant the hope that his blood may wash us of our guilt, cleanse our hearts and cement these two mighty divisions of the human family.

I must deal with the life of Swamiji as I knew him in the next issue of *Young India*.

Young India, 30-12-1926

190. COMPARISON IN UNTOUCHABILITY

During my stay in Wardha, I had occasion to visit the untouchable quarters. The inmates seemed happy but the awakening that has come into being amongst them has made them dissatisfied with the progress of the campaign against the curse of untouchability. They resent the fact that they are still being debarred from the use of temples, wells and public schools in general. They cannot, they will not, understand that progress is 'lame' and, therefore, tantalizingly slow. They can see no reason, there is none, for the insufferable disabilities under which they are labouring.

Two days after this interesting visit I discovered that in Wardha, thanks to the efforts of Jamnalalji, they were better off than anywhere else. They have several public wells open to them. They were freely admitted to the Municipal schools. As orphans they had the same facilities as the others. They had free use of public water-taps. And a continuous attempt was being made to break down completely the wall of prejudice against them.

About the same time that I was having experiences of the thought-current of the untouchable brethren, I had to rehearse to myself the incidents of the untouchability of South Africa. I had to do so in view of the Round Table Conference that is deliberating there at present. We who are responsible for Indian untouchability are ourselves victims of it in South Africa. It is a case over again of 'the biter bitten'. We have sown the wind in India, we are reaping the whirlwind in South Africa.

The Conference is now sitting to consider whether there is a way out. Andrews is making herculean efforts to bring about a happy result. He has mobilized the purest forces of South Africa in favour of the cause.

Let us, however, see the difference between the two untouchabilities. The Indian is withering. The axe has been laid at its root. Enlightened public opinion is against it. No one whose opinion carries any weight defends it. The chains that bind the 'untouchables' are daily being broken. Law does not countenance it. What there is of it is all due to the persistence of custom. Customs die hard, they long survive the withdrawal of legal sanction, especially if they are ancient. The disappearance of Indian untouchability is now purely a question of time.

The South African species on the other hand is growing into a hardy tree. It is being daily armed with fresh legal sanctions. The legal disabilities of the Indian untouchables of South Africa have grown with every sitting of the Union Parliament since 1915 in spite of the final settlement of 1914. It is spreading in other parts of the British Empire, as was made plain by the Kenya letter printed last week in these columns.

It is against this growing evil that Andrews is fighting almost single-handed in South Africa. Let us hope that his efforts will be crowned with success.

But the very best way of dealing with the evil no doubt is to rid ourselves of it in India. The members of the Union Deputation[1] were heard to say more than once that it would be time

[1] The Parliamentary deputation from South Africa headed by F. W. Beyers, which arrived in India on September 18, 1926, on a three weeks' visit at the invitation of the Government of India

for Indians to agitate for the removal of the bar in South Africa when they had got rid of it in India. No doubt they forgot or did not know that with us here, there was no legislative bar against the untouchables. But it would ill become us to advance an argument of that nature when we are seeking justice. There is a fine legal maxim which is applicable to our case. Those who seek justice must come with clean hands. The best case therefore that we can prepare against South African untouchability is to put our own house in order. Till then, I suppose, we will have to be content with what palliatives the Round Table Conference secures for us.

There is the other side to the question. The untouchables owe something to themselves and to India. But I must deal with this phase of the question in another article.

Young India, 30-12-1926

191. NOTES

Sir Habibulla Deputation

Mr. C. F. Andrews cables:

> Advisable delegation stay till February to tide over provincial election and keep atmosphere calm.

I do hope that it would be possible for Lord Irwin to comply with Mr. Andrews' advice and permit the Deputation to stay in South Africa till the elections are over. The elections in South Africa, as everywhere else, raise not the best thoughts but the worst passions and create bad blood. There is no doubt that the Deputation's will be a restraining influence. But that, of course, from a South African point of view, may be the best reason for sending the Deputation away before the elections begin. The candidates may resent the courteous curb that the presence of the Deputation must impose upon a free flow of their eloquence.

"Happy Despatch"?

The esteemed correspondent whose letter evoked the article "The Greatest Good of All"[1] (*Young India*, 9-12-1926) writes:

> Of the three cases, you have dealt only with the first, that of Dr. Blazer and expressed no opinion on the merits of the other two—the Paris case and the Danish law. I and many others of your readers, I

[1] *Vide* pp. 401-2.

am sure, would be grateful if you could enlighten us as to how you would judge these matters also from your own ethical standpoint.

The cases referred to are:

> At about the same time last year I remember I read about the Paris case in which an actress shot and killed her lover at his own importunate request, as he was suffering excruciating pain from a disease from which there was no hope of recovery. The actress was tried for manslaughter, but acquitted on the jury's verdict that no crime had been committed in view of the circumstances. Though there appears to be no law in France to justify such a verdict, I have read that in Denmark there has been actually a law passed making it no crime for certain authorized persons in cases like the above to put an end to a human life with 'happy despatch'.

In my opinion, such killing, if it is done *bona fide*, will certainly not count as *himsa* as understood and defined by me. But I could not take it upon my shoulders to justify such action on the part of a third party, as I would never have sufficient material to judge such a case. The defence will rest solely upon the intention. And since no one but God is the infallible judge of intentions, everyone must act on his own responsibility and take all the consequences. It follows, therefore, that the Danish law cannot be defended. And I should hold it to be most dangerous to justify any act of killing on the ground of the desire of the victim to be killed. There are many cases in which a man may for the moment, being overwhelmed with pain, desire to be killed rather than live in agony. But he would be most grateful upon recovery to know that his wish was not complied with. The better thing would, in my opinion, be boldly to put an end to a life which we may absolutely know to be past saving. Such a case would be that of a comrade on the battle-field who has received a fatal wound and who has no possibility of receiving any medical aid. In this case, it will not be his wish that would determine the act of killing but the certain knowledge of a lingering death in utter helplessness and without hope even of loving nursing. For it is assumed that the soldier who ends the agony by killing is not able even to nurse his wounded comrade.

Control of Evil Thoughts

A correspondent sends me an essay in support of the view propounded in these columns in the series of articles "Towards Moral Bankruptcy". There is nothing new in it, but it contains a quotation from Buddha's teachings which should help those who are trying to control evil thoughts. Here is the passage:

> When by reason of a phase of mind, there arise in a brother bad and wrong thoughts associated with appetite, hatred and delusion, then he should divert his mind from that to another phase associated with what is right. If they still arise, then he should study the perils they entail, marking how wrong and depraved such thoughts are and how they ripen into ill. If they still keep on rising, he should ignore them and not let his mind dwell on them. And if they still continue, he must bethink him how to allay all these modes and fashions of thoughts. As he does so, these thoughts will pass away and disappear, so that his heart stands firm, is steadfast, is focussed and concentrated. And lastly, if, allay as he may, these thoughts continue to rise, then with his teeth clenched and with his tongue pressed against his palate, he should by sheer force of mind, restrain, coerce and dominate his heart. As he does so these thoughts will pass away and disappear. He will think only such thoughts as he wishes and not those he wishes not to think.

Young India, 30-12-1926

192. SPEECH AT PUBLIC MEETING, CALCUTTA[1]

December 31, 1926

Mahatmaji, addressing the gathering in Hindi, said that Swami Shraddhanand's death was not an easy thing. It was not the death of an ordinary man. The heroes died not the death of an ordinary man. Swamiji was immortal by sacrificing his life for the cause of Hindu religion. They had assembled there to perform some "tarpan" for the memory of the late Swami. A memorial fund had been opened and he hoped that everybody would contribute his mite to it. They had chalked out a proposal that ten lakhs of rupees would be raised for the memorial fund half of which would be spent for untouchability work and half for *shuddhi* and *sangathan*. Swamiji had done much for the Hindu religion and he was one of the foremost religious workers. Swamiji, continued Mahatma Gandhi, had no differences with him in respect of removing untouchability. To speak the truth, the late Swamiji lived for the untouchables and if they meant to do proper honour to his memory, they could only do it by taking up the mission of Swami Shraddhanand's life.

Speaking on *shuddhi* and *sangathan* Mahatmaji said that the mission taken up by the late Swami was on the proper way. Every religion had a legitimate

[1] The meeting was held at Maheshwari Bhavan, Barrabazar, to pay tribute to Swami Shraddhanand's memory and to collect funds for *shuddhi* and *sangathan* movement. Madan Mohan Malaviya also spoke on the occasion.

right of conversion and self-organization so long as it was not based on force. Swami Shraddhanand was not ever for forcibly converting anybody and he could claim to know Swamiji fully well.

Amrita Bazar Patrika, 1-1-1927

193. LETTER TO MAGANLAL GANDHI

Monday [*December 1926*][1]

I have your two letters. It is good that you have started taking your meals in the common mess.

Please let me know about Keshu's[2] condition. Nobody can manufacture or sell the Ramchandra lift. Have you renewed the registration of its patent? If you received any communication from the Patents Office, please pay up the arrears. We can pay Best & Co. only after the formalities about the patent are completed, when we start selling the lifts.

Kakasaheb should prepare a report of the prayer for South Africa and send it to Andrews. I have no more time to write; it is about 10 p.m.

Blessings from
BAPU

From the Gujarati original: C.W. 7749. Courtesy: Radhabehn Chowdhari

194. LETTER TO MANIBEHN PATEL

[*1926*][3]

CHI. MANI,

I got your letter. Well, if unmarried girls fall ill, to whom shall I complain about it? It is as if the sea had caught fire. We should master the art of preserving good health if only for being able to serve others. I think that all of you must use mosquito-nets at night as a matter of course even as you wear clothes. For the rest, read my letter to the Ashram children.

[1] December 19, 1926 was observed as a day of prayer for success of the Round Table Conference in South Africa. Reference in the letter to this day suggests that the letter was written sometime in December.

[2] Son of the addressee

[3] As in the source

I hope that by the time you get this letter you will have completely recovered from your illness.

Blessings from
BAPU

[From Gujarati]
Bapuna Patro—Manibehn Patelne, p. 37

195. LETTER TO MANIBEHN PATEL

Silence Day [*1926*][1]

CHI. MANI,

I have not heard from you lately. I hope you are quite well now. Your illnesses will become fewer as you cease worrying needlessly and your mind becomes trusting like a little child's. You should understand the meaning of "trusting". It means that one with such a mind never takes offence, nor takes notice of anyone's misconduct nor sees wrong anywhere. This is a noble state of mind. Let me tell you straightway that I for my part have not attained it. I wish to reach it, but I am still far away from it. It is reached earlier by men and women who observe inviolate *brahmacharya*. I have known such people. Andrews has nearly reached it. Men who look upon him as a fool are fools themselves. You must cultivate such a trusting nature.

Blessings from
BAPU

[From Gujarati]
Bapuna Patro—Manibehn Patelne, p. 38

[1] As in the printed source

196. LETTER TO MANIBEHN PATEL

Silence Day [1926][1]

CHI. MANI,

I got your letter. I heard the news from father too. I do not write more about [your] illness, for I hope to meet you on Saturday at the latest. But you should get well and strong immediately.

Blessings from
BAPU

[From Gujarati]
Bapuna Patro—Manibehn Patelne, p. 39

197. LETTER TO MANIBEHN PATEL

Silence Day [1926][2]

CHI. MANI,

I have your letter. Upon a chance remark by me, Mahadev [Desai] showed me your letter to him without waiting to get your permission. No one should expect Mahadev to keep anything from me. That is beyond his power. Once we have formed a habit, we are unable to do anything different. This virtue is worth cultivating so far as good habits are concerned. One who sincerely meditates over non-violence becomes in the end incapable of violence, not in deed but in thought. Thought is the father of action. When thought disappears, action automatically becomes impossible.

What if separation from you has been as painful to me as separation from me is to you? You chose what was for your good, and I chose what was good for me. In acting thus lies your welfare, mine and the world's. Education should enable us to find our happiness in our good. If, therefore, you think that living in the Ashram is good for you, you should feel happy in doing so. And in this do not deceive yourself or me. You may be sure that the moment you do not like to stay in the Ashram, I shall willingly let you go elsewhere. Write to me without reserve. Never

[1] & [2] As in the printed source

mind if I do not understand you or lecture to you in reply. Learn to bear with the lectures of seniors.

Blessings from
BAPU

[From Gujarati]
Bapuna Patro—Manibehn Patelne, p. 40

198. LETTER TO MANIBEHN PATEL

Monday [*1926*][1]

CHI. MANI,

I got your letter. You did well to go to Ahmedabad city at the time of uncle's (Vithalbhai's)[2] visit.

Manu[3] and Manilal[4] can be brought round only with patience.

Ba again said she would start on Sunday. She must reach [Sabarmati] on Wednesday at the latest.

I am writing this just before retiring to bed. So I will not write more.

Blessings from
BAPU

[From Gujarati]
Bapuna Patro—Manibehn Patelne, p. 41

199. LETTER TO LAKSHMI[5]

THE ASHRAM,
SABARMATI,
[*1926*][6]

CHI. LAKSHMI,

This time, it may be said, your letter was late. Your hand-writing has improved. There should not be two kinds of writing

[1] As in the printed source

[2] Vithalbhai Patel visited Ahmedabad after his election as President of the Central Legislative Assembly.

[3] Grand-daughter of Gandhiji

[4] One of the Ashram students

[5] Daughter of Dudabhai, a Harijan inmate of the Ashram

[6] The addressee was born in 1914. Reference to entering her 13th year suggests that the letter was written in 1926.

in one letter. There is nothing to worry if you are inclined to play. Children are bound to be playful. But they should have the same heart for work too. Those children whose mind is always engrossed in play can't help lying some time or other. Now you will be entering your 13th year. It is not so young an age. You should get from here new clothes if those you are using wear out. If they can be stitched there, that is, if Danibehn knows how to sew, khadi can be sent from here; but if she is unable to do so, the clothes can be made here and sent to you. Take a vow to do some good deed on your birthday.

Rukhi[1] and Anandi[2] are ill. Both have fever. I hope they will be all right in two or three days.

From a microfilm of the Gujarati: S.N. 19627

200. LETTER TO PRABHASHANKAR PATTANI

THE ASHRAM,
SABARMATI,
Friday [*1926*][3]

SUJNA BHAISHRI,

After you wrote about the fever, there has been no letter from you; I trust there is nothing to worry about. I wish you to recover the strength you have lost even if you have to try hard. Can you disentangle yourself from administration till you completely regain strength? I may be tempted to come to Trapaj if you take complete rest and make a vow to get back your full strength. If I do so, I would place you in the custody of a guard. Will an unrestricted authority tolerate this restriction?

Vandemataram from
MOHANDAS

From a photostat of the Gujarati: C.W. 3200; also G.N. 5886. Courtesy: Mahesh Pattani

[1] Daughter of Maganlal Gandhi

[2] Daughter of Lakshmidas Asar

[3] Reference in the letter to the addressee's indifferent state of health and his stay at Trapaj suggests this year.

201. LETTER TO PRABHASHANKAR PATTANI

THE ASHRAM,
SABARMATI,
Saturday [*1926*][1]

SUJNA BHAISHRI,

I have your letter. Looking at your meagre weight, you cannot be said to have really recovered. Nor do you seem to have improved much in Abu. Your acceptance of my condition for coming to Trapaj is lukewarm. Such acceptance will not tempt me to pay the visit. The weather here at present is not inviting to an ailing man. The afternoons are very sultry. The sky is overcast; and it would not rain. In such weather even otherwise healthy people may fall ill. Why not take your family and go to Panchgani? Of course, I do wish you to spend a few days at Panchgani.

Vandemataram from
MOHANDAS

From a photostat of the Gujarati: C.W. 3201. Courtesy: Mahesh Pattani

202. TALKS TO ASHRAM WOMEN[2]

[*1926*]

O Govinda, O Krishna residing in Dwarka, O beloved of all Gopis, how is it that you do not know that I am oppressed by the Kauravas, i.e., wicked passions?

O Lord, O husband of the Goddess of Beauty, O Lord of Vraja, the destroyer of all distresses, O Janardana, rescue me submerged in the ocean of the Kauravas.

O Krishna, Krishna, O great sage, Soul of the universe, Creator of the universe, O Govinda, save me who seek your help, drooping in the midst of the Kurus.

My ideal is this: A man should remain man and yet should become woman; similarly a woman should remain woman and yet become man. This means that man should cultivate the gentle-

[1] Year inferred from contents; *vide* preceding item.

[2] Notes taken by Manibehn Patel at Gandhiji's morning prayer meetings for women during 1926

ness and the discrimination of woman; and woman should cast off her timidity and become brave and courageous.

It is said that women are jealous, but this does not mean that men are free from this failing or that all women are jealous. Women have to stay indoors for all the twenty-four hours and therefore their jealousy becomes more conspicuous. That is all.

* * *

My patience in teaching you will be endless. It will end only when your readiness to learn ends.

* * *

Both man and woman can become fearless. Man thinks that he can be fearless, but it is not always true; similarly woman thinks she is weak and allows herself to be called so; this too is not right. Women have no need at all for fear. I will tell you what I heard about Mirabai the day before yesterday. Mirabai went to Vrindavan and knocked at the door of a sadhu. The sadhu replied from inside that he never looked at a woman. Mirabai asked him, "Who are you? I know only one man, and that is Krishna." On hearing this, the sadhu opened the door, fell at the feet of Mirabai and said, "You have opened my eyes today. I have been saved from an abyss."

* * *

Man and woman are characterized by fear as long as both are subject to passions.

Draupadi showed as great a strength as Yudhishthira did.

Draupadi had five husbands at one time and yet has been called 'chaste'. This is because in that age, just as a man could marry several wives, a woman (in certain regions) could marry several husbands. The code of marriage changes with time and place.

But from another point of view, Draupadi is a symbol of the mind. And the five Pandavas are the five senses brought under its control. And it is indeed desirable that they are so controlled. Since all the five senses were under the control of the mind and had become refined, the mind (Draupadi) can be said to have wedded the five senses (Pandavas).

The strength which Draupadi showed was immense. Even Bhima and the Dharmaraja Yudhishthira were afraid of her.

While in jail, as I read the prayer of Draupadi to Krishna at this time, as given in the *Mahabharata,* I wept bitterly.

To my mind, this prayer of Draupadi has extraordinary strength in it. Countless men in North India recite these verses.

The power of words too increases or decreases in proportion

to the penance underlying them. What is there in the word 'ॐ'? It is simply made up of three syllables अ, उ and म्. And yet its value lies in the penance associated with it. When there is greater penance behind the word, its value becomes greater. The same is the case with Draupadi. She may even be regarded as an imaginary character created by Vyasa. Such a woman may or may not have existed. But the great strength of Vyasa's penance and the recitation by crores of people of the prayers put into Draupadi's mouth by him have raised the value of that prayer.

'Govinda' means the master of the senses; by Gopis are meant the thousands of sense-organs. *Gopijanapriya* means one who is the beloved of the masses or, say, of the weak. Draupadi was surrounded by the Kauravas. The Kauravas are our evil desires. Draupadi cries, "O Keshava, how is it that you do not know me?" It is the cry of the distressed, the voice of the aggrieved. Do not we all have evil desires? When are we free from passions? Draupadi says that she has been surrounded by Kauravas. Here 'Kauravas' may also mean wicked persons. But we are overpowered even more by our evil desires than by wicked persons. So it is better to interpret 'Kauravas' to mean evil desires.

Draupadi is a servant of God and as such she has the right even to quarrel with Him. She cries, "Oh Master, Oh Lord, Oh Ramanath, i.e., Lakshmipati, i.e., Lord of the World, He who gives salvation, He who brings about self-realization, Vrajnath, i.e., Lord of the universe, Artinashana, i.e., Dispeller of grief, I am drowning in a sea of Kauravas, i.e., I am sinking in a multitude of desires; I am full of wicked passions. Save me."

Draupadi repeats the call "Krishna, Krishna". When a person is either in great joy or in great misery, he calls out to God twice. Draupadi says, "I come to you for refuge; save me; I am beset with evil passions, and have become weak; my limbs are giving way. Save me."

In Bombay there is a woman named Janakibai. In 1915 when I was staying with Revashankarbhai she came to see me. She boasted a great deal about herself. At that time I did not believe her. Then when I went to Dwarka, she also was there. I made particular inquiries in regard to her and found that she moved quite freely among the most wicked of men. Her idea was that she should be able to preserve her chastity even while living in the midst of the worst men. It so happens that no one even in anger addresses her with a disrespectful 'thou'. She moves amongst them like a lioness.

* * *

We are helpless like Draupadi, because we are all full of impurities and evil desires. Our fear of serpents and such like is a proof of our weakness. I am regarded as the highest in the Ashram; even then I, too, feel afraid. It means that I also am more helpless than Draupadi.

Dwarka means the whole world, or we ourselves, not the dirty little town near Porbandar in Kathiawar.

* * *

What can women have done that even men like Tulsidas have used insulting epithets for them? Whether it was the fault of Tulsidas or of the times, the blemish is nevertheless there.

The ancient laws were made by seers who were men. The women's experience, therefore, is not represented in them. Strictly speaking, as between man and woman, neither should be regarded as superior or inferior. The place and functions of both are different, and God has defined both.

* * *

Only the self can raise the self; the self is the help of the self. Only women can raise women. This requires *tapascharya* and hard work. It is true that women are more capable of it than men; but the *tapascharya* must be intelligent. Today women merely toil on in a helpless condition like drudges.

It may be agreed that no one can save woman except herself. But it may be asked, 'Can she be self-supporting?' My heart says that she can. If she learns satyagraha, she can be perfectly independent and self-supporting. She will not have to feel dependent upon anyone. This does not mean that she shall not take any help from others. She will certainly. But if such help be not forthcoming she will not feel destitute. If we are detached, even while we use the articles which we receive, we are self-dependent. In such a state, even though receiving help from all the world we in fact never become dependent on anyone. And if help were refused, we would say, it was good that it was not given, and would not get angry, nor blame anyone. This is called satyagraha. It is not enough merely to be convinced that we should be fearless. We should become fearless at heart. Casting off fear does not mean that we should not care for the world's opinion.

One should give up the idea that one is helpless. God is the help of all. It is possible to throw the blame for the present sorry condition of women on their husbands. But women should think how best they can themselves cast off their own weakness.

* * *

There can be only one prayer for us all. If we offer this prayer daily, understanding it properly, it will get embedded in our minds. Keshava (God) is always with us. He is not in some Dwarka. That is only the language of the poet. Draupadi forgot that Keshava was with her. He clothed her body again and again remaining beside her. Whenever evil thoughts or evil desires spring in our mind, we should say to ourselves: oh, why do such thoughts come to me? We should then think of these verses of prayer.

* * *

This[1] is not a mere political book. I have used the language of politics, but I have really tried to offer a glimpse of dharma. What is the meaning of 'Hind Swaraj'? It means rule of dharma or *Ramarajya.* I have addressed as many meetings of women as of men. At women's meetings I have always used the word *Ramarajya* in place of swaraj.

This book is the gist of my thinking for several years. Just as one cannot help speaking out when one's heart is full, so also I have been unable to restrain myself from writing the book since my heart was full. The book is meant mainly for the illiterate masses.

* * *

Whatever character we have inherited from our parents is our real inheritance. It may be said to be our spiritual inheritance, and it is our duty to add to it. If a father leaves an inheritance of a lac of rupees and the son increases it to a million and then says "What kind of man my father was who collected only a lac and how clever I am that I amassed a million", he is a wicked son; there is pride in what he says. We do not wish to add to money inherited from our parents, but to character, to our spiritual inheritance, and we should not feel proud about it, for spiritual inheritance is not possible without humility.

* * *

In abstaining from a thing we have not been used to from birth—for example, meat-eating—we make no sacrifice. Such a thing is quite natural for us, and we perform no heroic act thereby.

* * *

Man's beauty is in his character, that of a beast in its body. In the case of a cow, for instance, we may say how good it is

[1] *Hind Swaraj*

because of its skin, or hair, or feet, or horns; in the case of a man, on the other hand, we do not say that he is good because he is five feet and a half, or bad because he is four feet and a half, or better if he is an inch more than five feet and a half. Being good or bad in the case of man lies in his heart, not in his body or even in his accumulated wealth. Here in the Ashram, we have regarded it our dharma to build up the virtues of the heart. We eat and drink, and construct buildings with sand and mortar. That is because we have to do these things. We have not despised mud huts, we would not be ashamed to live in one but we should indeed feel ashamed to live in luxury. We should hang our heads in shame if we add to our wealth. Indeed, we may possess wealth for service; we have to accumulate such wealth, much against our will. But some people accumulate wealth regarding greed as their religion. This is not proper. In proportion as we make our outer life more and more elaborate, we harm our moral progress, and we injure our dharma.

* * *

Our merchants earn crores of rupees in the markets of Bombay. That is no cause for delight to us. It is rather a matter for regret. Because when a Bombay merchant earns five crores by way of brokerage, the Britisher gets ninety-five crores and that too he takes away from the country through bleeding the poor man white. We do not realize this, because after all it takes time to bleed a nation of thirty-three crores of people.

* * *

If a labourer does all his work dedicating it to God, then thereby he can attain self-realization. Self-realization means purity of self. Strictly speaking, only those who do bodily labour get self-realization; because 'God is the strength of the weak'. By 'weak' is not meant 'weak in body', though for them also their strength is God—but we should take it to mean weak in means and materials. The labourer must cultivate humility, for mere developing of intelligence may lead to the development of an *asuri* intelligence. By doing merely intellectual work, we develop *asuri* tendencies. It is, therefore, that the *Gita* says that one who eats without labour eats stolen food. Humility is inherent in labour. And that is why it is karmayoga or activity that leads to salvation. Doing physical work simply for wages is no karmayoga, since the idea is simply to earn money. Cleaning of latrines for earning money is no *yajna* (sacrifice). But the same work if done by way of service, for the sake of sanitation and for the good of others, becomes *yajna*.

One who does bodily labour out of a spirit of service, in all humility and for self-realization, gets self-realization. Such a one should never feel reluctant to work. He should be ever awake.

* * *

How can the pot call the kettle black when both are of practically the same colour? In the same way what can man say to woman or how can he criticize her? If numerous suspicions, doubts, passions and fears characterize women, they exist also in men. Some pundits say that woman cannot attain salvation. But as I see it, that is not so. The *Vaishnavas* believe that there has not been a greater devotee than Mirabai. My view is that if Mirabai cannot get salvation, no man can ever get it.

* * *

The farmer sleeps in the field. Are you or the British officer ever likely to sleep there? But who cares for the poor man's feelings? What joy does he get out of life? He has to work in the field from early morning. So he also spreads his bed there. He may die of snake-bite. But the farmer leads such a life by compulsion. If it is at all called sacrifice on his part, it is sacrifice forced on him. It is not as though he refused to travel by train; if someone provided him the opportunity, he would travel. But if he leads his particular kind of life in full knowledge of it, his life would indeed be blessed. Some sages lead a life like this farmer, or like Jada Bharat. But in their case they have taken to such life purposely.

* * *

I would certainly worship an idol made of clay, if thereby my mind becomes lighter. If my life becomes fruitful, then only the worship of young Krishna's idol has meaning. The stone is no God; but God resides in the stone. If I besmear the idol with sandal paste, make an offering of rice, and pray to it for strength to cut off so many heads, one of you should throw the idol into a well, or break it into pieces.

* * *

If we wish to develop in us the capacity to look on all with an equal eye, we should aim at getting only what the rest of the world gets. Thus if the whole world gets milk, we may also have it. We may pray to God and say, "O God, if you wish me to have milk, give it first to the rest of the world." But who can pray thus? Only he who has so much sympathy for others and who labours for their good. Even if we cannot practise this principle, we must at least understand and appreciate it. For the present, our only prayer to God should be that since we are fallen so low He may accept whatever little we do. We may not progress in this direction but He should give us strength to lessen our *parigraha*. If we repent of our sins, they will not increase further. We should not keep anything with us thinking it belongs to us, but should strive to give up as much of our *parigraha* as we can.

* * *

If man needs the help of the whole world before he can follow truth and non-violence, then he would indeed become dependent. But God has arranged things so beautifully, that even if the whole world is against him, he can still follow truth and non-violence himself. If we do not wish to quarrel, the other person can certainly not quarrel with us. In the end he will get tired and will be quiet. On the other hand, if we become angry, we increase anger. It is like adding fuel to the fire.

* * *

How can he rise, in whose mind there is never any problem?

* * *

From the fact that . . .[1] committed suicide, we should learn that we should not allow sorrow or troubles to prey constantly upon our minds. We should not brood over them. If we have felt hurt by someone, we should tell him so straightway. Then the pain will not remain in our hearts. Even brooding sorrowfully within oneself is a kind of suicide.

Self-condemnation is desirable to some degree. In a way it is good to remain dissatisfied with oneself. If a man's dissatisfaction is within limits he will rise. But if he always needlessly goes on finding fault with himself and says, he has not been able to do this or that, then he will really not be able to do anything and will become a fool. We should at the same time be contented and discontented. Then only can we rise.

The body is sometimes called a *ratnachintamani*. If we remain devoted to God, it would really prove to be so. But to become wholly devoted to God, we have to control the body.

Man has to move about out of doors. His work is outside the house. So he does not quickly become despondent. But woman has to stay all the time inside the house. So she is lonely and falls an easy prey to despondency. If she finds another woman to

[1] Name omitted in the source

talk to, she becomes so talkative that she fails to discriminate between what she should say and what she should not. Being always in the house she develops such defects. Of course, in a sense such loneliness is desirable. It saves her from many temptations. But it is fruitful only if we learn to turn our eyes inward, search our hearts, and become introspective.

* * *

Suppose there is a woman who is entirely illiterate yet remains devoted to her duties. She does not touch even a blade of grass that does not belong to her. She does not steal even in her dreams. If you ask her what the *Bhagavata* is, she stares you in the face. But she loves every human being as though she were the mother of all mankind.

Suppose there is another woman, who knows everything, has all the Upanishads by heart, whose pronunciation is excellent, but who steals, lies, is clever in making others work for her and is adept in almost everything. There is not the slightest doubt that the former is superior to the latter. Of course if she learns reading and writing, she would be better still.

* * *

Of what use is knowledge in which there is no humility or tenderness? Sage Kaushika became angry when a bird eased itself over him. The bird was consumed to ashes by his anger. The sage felt somewhat proud at the power of his penance. He then went to a house as a guest. The lady of the house was busy serving her husband, and so kept the visitor waiting. After she had finished her work she went to the sage with some food for him and stating the cause of her delay apologized to him. The sage got angry. The lady said, "I am not a bird that you can burn me with an angry look; besides, such anger cannot be called wisdom." The sage learnt a lesson and said, "You have given me two kinds of food—food to eat and the food of wisdom."

* * *

A man who does the work that falls to his lot in the natural course of things can remain unattached to it. He does not get false attachment for such work.

Real knowledge and true education can be had by devoted performance of one's duty.

It is disgusting to see people that throng the hospitals. Doctors treat them, but it is also their duty to teach them how to remain healthy. But hardly any doctor does this. Most doctors pamper the body. By doing this they harm man's character and degrade his soul. Besides, by pampering the body they do not really save it.

To kill living animals for medicinal purposes to learn suturing, is this the work of a human being? It is the work of the devil.

* * *

Passion is common both to man and woman. The mind of a passionate person always wanders about seeking objects of pleasure. We must understand that our life is not for enjoying or giving such pleasures, but for self-realization.

The marriage of Siva and Parvati is regarded as an ideal marriage. One who wants to wed like Parvati should think of a man like Siva who is free from all passions. It is not Parvati alone that was destined to get such a husband. Every woman holds that fate in her own hands.

In choosing a husband, one must not go by the kind of clothes he puts on, or the turban he wears. One must see how educated he is, and how good he is in character. Once you have decided to marry, marry one who has good character, and whose mind is compatible with yours. If you find such a person, well and good; otherwise resolve to remain unmarried. One should not think of marrying anyone that comes along. Parvati had resolved that she would marry only one who was free from all passions like Siva, otherwise she would remain unmarried. Every girl should cherish the ideal of Parvati.

* * *

Not to ride on another's back is also service. Not to accept service from another, and to develop an attitude of not making others work for one is also service.

* * *

The world is such that if we put three stitches at one place thirteen others give way elsewhere. Then how can we improve it? Real progress consists in recognizing Truth which exists within us as our Soul.

If you are good, the world is good. Bhagawan Patanjali has written that the desire for revenge disappears in the presence of non-violence. If we are ourselves slaves we regard all others also as slaves. In short, who wants to cheat an innocent man? One who tries to play false with such a person will ultimately only hurt himself. If we do not retaliate, if we do not oppose the misdeeds of a wicked person, his misdeeds themselves will bring about his downfall. He will fall and then correct himself.

* * *

If we achieve swaraj in our own Ashram, we would obtain swaraj for the whole of India. It means we would all be straight like a stick. None of us would look upon another with suspicion. If we have no mutual distrust swaraj is at hand.

Swaraj means rule over one's own self, not over another. It means controlling one's self. He who has gained control over his sense organs, has obtained almost everything.

He who believes in punishment and violence has necessarily to resort to deceit. Deceit is a necessary accompaniment of such belief.

* * *

Our temple is in our Ashram, nay, it is in our hearts. A temple constructed of a few stones has no meaning. Only a temple raised in our hearts is useful.

If our Ashram goes on well like this and does not produce any bad people, it will become a place for pilgrimage.

* * *

Every pebble on the bank of the Narmada is said to be Siva. By the Narmada we do not mean only the river near Broach, but all rivers. If we wash clean a pebble on the bank of a river and offer *bilva patra*[1] to it, the pebble becomes Siva for us. Going a step further, if we take a lump of earth and mould it into the shape of a Siva Linga it also becomes Siva for us. On going still further, we may think that Siva resides in the hearts of us all.

We are idolators as well as iconoclasts. We destroy the stone in the idol, but we worship the image of God in it.

I expect all the women in the Ashram not to do a single piece of work without giving it proper thought. To this end, women should acquire knowledge. At present, the women of India have become dull and lifeless.

* * *

A girl who wishes to remain unmarried should be wedded to independence. A girl dependent upon others can never remain unmarried.

If the ghost dies, the spirit will rise. If we rob someone, someone else is ready to rob us. There is a proverb in Gujarati

[1] The leaf of a tree regarded sacred by Hindus

which says that there is always something mightier than a lion to subdue a lion.

* * *

Just as when we do not know cooking, and yet prepare half-cooked things and eat them we get indigestion, in the same way if we cannot understand what we read and yet go on reading, we shall get literary indigestion.

* * *

Even the greatest are punished if they do things they ought not to do.

* * *

Devotees of God carry on activities dictated by their inner voice. But this inner voice also may sometimes deceive. So devotees must always remain vigilant.

* * *

A person who tells a half-lie tells one lie and a half, because he deceives also his own mind; whereas a person who tells an absolute lie knows that he is telling one.

* * *

Education of children mainly depends on mothers. Howsoever I may try to educate children in the Ashram, my efforts would prove futile without the co-operation of mothers. We have to educate our children to be helpful to others.

Even when a child goes to a teacher for studying, he takes with him a string attached to his mother's heart. He is always thinking when he can return to his mother. The mother draws the child to herself by means of this string.

We may read the *Gita*, or the *Ramayana* or the *Hind Swaraj*. But what we have to learn from them is desire for the welfare of others. We have to teach this to our children also.

* * *

Those forefathers of ours who gave up liquor did a manly thing. But for us who have never drunk liquor, there is only negative kind of merit in not drinking. We simply do not incur the sin of drinking—that is all. We may be said to have really given up drinking only when we understand all the evils that result from drinking.

In the same way, there is no meaning in our observing sacred days and vows without understanding their significance. Such observance becomes useful both to us and to society if we understand and can explain to others their significance. Such observance becomes useful both to us and to society if we understand and can explain to others their significance. Our women observe Nagapanchami, Janmashtami and other holy days. But they should understand their significance. It is possible that the meaning of Nagapanchami is that considering the serpent as a symbol of the enemy, it was sought through this means to inculcate the principle of not killing even one's enemies. In this world, excepting perhaps man, there is no other creature so poisonous as a serpent. If we regard anyone as so full of venom as a serpent, we should learn to love him, as though he were full of nectar. From doing this, we shall learn that every human being is worthy of worship, i.e., of service.

* * *

This world is held together by bonds of love. History does not record the day-to-day incidents of love and service. It only records incidents of conflict and wars. Actually, however, acts of love and service are much more common in this world than conflicts and quarrels. We see innumerable villages and towns flourishing in the world. If the world were always full of discord, they could not possibly exist.

* * *

We must necessarily abolish those laws that destroy dharma. Not only should we not abide by such laws, but we should even actively resist them. Now there are two ways of doing this—either through violence or through satyagraha. We should follow only the path of satyagraha. We cannot commit violence in the name of dharma. We may allow ourselves to be hanged or to be killed rather than kill others in the name of dharma.

* * *

It is often asked how women may protect their honour. It is even suggested that they should carry daggers on them. If they do carry daggers, the daggers could of course be used against their own persons. One has to be very tough to be able to wield a dagger. One would have to change one's whole mode of life, for a person who has never seen blood drawn, or drawn blood himself, can never use a dagger. In order to be able to use a dagger, we shall have to take to hunting, kill quantities of sheep —so hard shall we have to make our hearts before we can thrust a dagger into someone.

So instead of teaching women to use a dagger, it is better to teach them to be fearless. God's protecting hand is always over us. If we really believe in the existence of God, whom shall we fear? Even if the most wicked of persons assaults you, recite Ramanama.

Most wicked persons would run away at this earnest cry to God. But if that does not happen, what does it matter? We should learn to die on such an occasion. If a child is on its death-bed, do we not almost kill ourselves in looking after it? If even after the mother's greatest efforts, the child dies in her lap, she has the satisfaction that she did her best for it. It is our duty to be ever prepared thus to lay down our life. However wicked the man, if we die rather than yield to his physical strength, what after all can he do to us? It is possible that a wicked man may give up his wickedness when faced with a pure-minded person, who is quite prepared to die. Thus satyagraha is twice blessed. It blesses him who offers it and also him against whom it is offered.

[From Gujarati]

Bapuna Patro—Ashramni Behnone, pp. 77-97

203. LETTER TO MANIBEHN PATEL

[*January 1, 1927*][1]

CHI. MANI,

I have your letter. Read the letter[2] on the reverse. I am thinking of sending you for this work. Only you or Mirabehn can work there. The girls there would be Sindhi and so knowledge of English and Hindi would be necessary. We cannot send Mirabehn as yet. I, therefore, should like you to go. If you decide to do so let me know.

Whether you feel happy or not, you have to stay in the Ashram, that is to say, with me. Pour out your heart to me and exact from me a mother's duties. Are you sure that the reason for your lack of interest is not the absence of a life-companion? A well-wisher of yours emphatically advised me that I should get you married. The suggestion was made as we were talking about a certain young man. He is not a Patidar, but is a deserving youth. I said that I had no fear on your account. I see no signs at present to suggest that you may wish to get married. He then told me that I did not know you. You can see from my language that I am not joking this time. Reply to me without any fear. One thing is certain, that a girl who wants to

[1] As in the printed source

[2] Dated 20-12-1926, from Narayandas Anandji of Karachi, asking Gandhiji to depute a competent lady from Gujarat to teach *takli*-spinning in the Municipal Girls' Schools of Karachi

remain unmarried all her life should be brave. She should remain cheerful otherwise people would say that she should be married off.

Blessings from
BAPU

CHI. MANIBEHN PATEL
SATYAGRAHA ASHRAM
SABARMATI

[From Gujarati]
Bapuna Patro—Manibehn Patelne, pp. 43-4

204. *SPEECH AT MEETING OF DEPRESSED-CLASS SCHOOLS, CALCUTTA*[1]

January 2, 1927

Mahatmaji in reply said that he never knew that the members of the depressed classes would present him with an address. He felt their troubles and untold miseries and he sometimes wanted to become an untouchable so that he would clearly realize their position in the country. Mahatmaji was sorry to say that the members of the Hindu community were not helping them in any way. On the other hand, they were having their service in the way of labour. The country would be ruined if that feeling prevailed in the Hindu community. Swami Shraddhanand who had sacrificed his valuable life in removing untouchability from the country had said that, if he saw that the Hindus were keeping at least one depressed-class boy in their house, he would think that the Hindus were really feeling for the untouchables in the country. Before that Swamiji expected that they should give up the habit of drinking, gambling, and other vices which always kept them behind the other communities in the country.

Continuing, Mahatmaji said that Pandit Madan Mohan Malaviya had issued an appeal to collect five lakhs of rupees to complete the *shuddhi* and *sangathan* movement of Swami Shraddhanand. Malaviyaji did not expect any money from them as he knew the members of the Hindu community would fulfil his desire for their good. Still as a mark of respect to the sacred memory of Swami [Shraddhanand] they should collect some money among themselves and approach Malaviyaji with the purse.

Amrita Bazar Patrika, 4-1-1927

[1] Gandhiji was replying to an address of welcome presented by the students of sixteen depressed-class schools in Calcutta and Howrah. The meeting was held at Mirzapur Park, Calcutta.

205. SPEECH AT CHITTARANJAN SEVA SADAN, CALCUTTA[1]

[*January 2, 1927*][2]

In declaring the foundation to be well and truly laid,[3] Gandhiji emphasized what Dr. Nilratan Sarkar had described as the spiritual unity between Deshbandhu and Gandhiji which had become, if possible, more real after Deshbandhu's death. He had no doubt that, if Deshbandhu's energies had not been absorbed, like all other political leaders', by politics owing to the peculiar conditions of enslaved India, he would have entirely devoted himself to religious reform and to the service of *Daridranarayana*[4]. But Deshbandhu believed, said Gandhiji, in following the lesson of the *Gita*—Do your immediate duty, even though other duties may seem to be superior—and if he seemed that day to be laying the foundation of an ordinary maternity home, he was sure that from the point of view of Deshbandhu it was a step forward to swaraj. He then alluded to the suspicion expressed in some quarters that the Bengalis being of a parochial outlook, the memorial would also take a parochial character.

I would not mind the Bengalis absorbing the whole of India in Bengal, for then the old Panditji[5] from the U.P. and myself, an old Bania from Gujarat, would be left free to have some rest. I would not mind in the least the whole of India being absorbed in Bengal that gave birth to Rabindranath, Ram Mohan Roy, Keshub Chundra Sen, Ramakrishna Paramahamsa and Vivekanand, Bengal which was hallowed by the sacred feet of Chaitanya, Bengal which is sanctified by the sacred rivers the Ganges and the Brahmaputra. But the fear is baseless, as Dr. Bidhan Roy has declared on behalf of the trustees, that Seva Sadan would be conducted on the same broad lines as [those on which] Deshbandhu served the Motherland. The institution is a living tribute to one who had the emancipation of women at heart, those down-trodden sisters of ours who are the victims of our lust and passion. It does not belong to this or that

[1] Extracted from Mahadev Desai's "Weekly Letter"

[2] The date is taken from the *Forward* report.

[3] Two annexes for the Obstetric Ward and X-Ray Block of the Seva Sadan—the Deshbandhu Memorial Hospital

[4] God in the form of the destitute

[5] Madan Mohan Malaviya

trustee, it belongs to the nation. Let us strive to make it worthy of Deshbandhu and let it immortalize his memory in India.

Young India, 13-1-1927

206. SPEECH AT KEORAHTALA CREMATION GROUND, CALCUTTA[1]

January 2, 1927

Mahatma Gandhi made a short speech on the occasion. He said that he laid the foundation of a memorial in honour of one of the greatest patriots of Bengal, nay, of whole India. Mahatma Gandhi thought himself very fortunate in performing the ceremony. He regretted that he could not come into intimate acquaintance with Aswini Babu. When Mahatmaji was in South Africa, he used to read newspapers during the Bengal Partition days and it was there that he got acquainted with Aswini Babu's works through the papers.

On his return to India, Mahatmaji continued, he had the privilege to have *darshan* of the late Aswini Kumar Dutt and that was during his Bengal tour when he went to Barisal. At Barisal, as soon as he got down from the steamer, he was told that Aswini Babu was lying on sick-bed and hence could not come to welcome him. So he thought it his first and foremost duty to go directly and see the great patriot on his sick-bed. He still remembered that loving look when he met Aswini Babu and he could never forget it.

Mahatmaji next recognized that the lesson we learnt from the life of Aswini Kumar was that only those could be the worshippers of the motherland who had given up all pleasures of life and sacrificed all their desires for the cause of the country. Mahatmaji advised young Indians to learn the spirit in which Aswini Kumar led his life, and that was the lesson that every young man should learn from the life of the great men of the world.

Mahatmaji further said that many things could be heard about many people in the papers, but until and unless one could come in contact with those men, one was not able to get the truth about them. When Mahatmaji came in close contact with Aswini Dutt, he realized the absolute truth of what he had read in the papers.

Mahatmaji, in conclusion, appealed to young men to mix with such great men and follow in their footsteps if they wanted to serve the country, and the only true memorial that they could raise in the name of such great men was only to follow in their footsteps.

Amrita Bazar Patrika, 4-1-1927

[1] Gandhiji was laying the foundation for a memorial to Aswini Kumar Dutt.

207. *SPEECH AT KHADI PRATISHTHAN, SODEPUR*[1]

[*January 2, 1927*][2]

You will see that he[3] has staked his all on khadi. Many of you will think that he has gone mad, but I tell you it is faith that moves mountains, and Satis Babu has faith in khadi, and the determination that he must stop, as much as he can, the lakhs of rupees worth of foreign cloth that is dumped every day in the Calcutta market.

In response to his appeal for collections, Rs. 500 were collected on the spot and Rs. 3,000 and odd were promised.

Young India, 13-1-1927

208. *LETTER TO GANGABEHN VAIDYA*

[After *January 2, 1927*][4]

CHI. GANGABEHN,

I find that you make mistakes in gender. In the Kutchhi dialect there are only [two] genders—feminine and masculine. But in Gujarati there is a third, the neuter gender. You say *ghar kevo*[5], while in Gujarati we say *ghar kevun*[6], you say *tamaro sharir*[7], while in Gujarati we would say *tamarun sharir*[8]. You will find it interesting to compare the two languages in this manner and will be able to correct your mistakes more easily. Such mental exercise will also develop your intellect.

Blessings from

BAPU

From the Gujarati original: C.W. 8703. Courtesy: Gangabehn Vaidya

[1] Gandhiji was opening the Kalashala of Khadi Pratishthan, established by Satis Chandra Das Gupta, at Sodepur, near Calcutta. The report is extracted from Mahadev Desai's "Weekly Letter".

[2] The date is taken from the *Hindu* report.

[3] Satis Chandra Das Gupta

[4] The letter was in reply to one from the addressee dated January 2, 1927.

[5], [6], [7] & [8] Gujarati expressions for "What kind of a house" and "Your body"; in each pair, the adjective in the first expression is in the masculine gender and in the second expression in the neuter gender.

209. TELEGRAM TO PARASHU RAM MEHROTRA

CALCUTTA,
January 3, 1927

PARASHU RAM
SATYAGRAHA ASHRAM
WARDHA

YOU MAY DEVOTE FOR [TNIGHT][1] "STREEDARPAN"[2].

BAPU

From a photostat: G.N. 7487; also C.W. 4962

210. LETTER TO MIRABEHN

January 3, 1927

CHI. MIRA,

I have your two letters. I see what you are passing through and I am glad of it. You have to love humanity in spite of itself. The Ashram is finally not at Sabarmati but in yourself. The vilest beings must enter there purified. That is the meaning of treating all alike and in this universe of opposites remaining unaffected even as the lotus remains unaffected by water though immersed in it.

I understand your programme. You may carry it out. I continue to send you letters to Kanya Gurukul till I hear from you again.

I suppose in the circumstances related by you, you will not advise me to send anybody to the place as a pupil.

I am writing this at Sodepur, a suburb of Calcutta, where Satis Babu has built his Khadi Works. It is a great effort. It has cost nearly Rs. 80,000.

We leave for Comilla tomorrow as per programme sent to you. But for future guidance, it would be well to note that when in doubt send to the last address.

[1] This part of the original is damaged.

[2] *Streedarpan* was a Hindi magazine devoted to social topics, edited by Mehrotra before he joined the Ashram. He had sought leave of absence from Gandhiji for attending to its financial problems.

You will be interested in the enclosed which was handed to me by a friend.

With love,

BAPU

From the original: C.W. 5194. Courtesy: Mirabehn

211. LETTER TO MANIBEHN PATEL

[SODEPUR,]
Monday [January 3, 1927][1]

CHI. MANI,

I had hoped to get a letter from you but so far I have not had any. I hope you are keeping good health, both of body and mind. You must be making rapid progress in Sanskrit. Write to me in detail. I shall be in Comilla till the 6th, and in Kashi till the 9th. In Kashi, address the letter at "Gandhi Ashram, Banaras Cantonment". Write to Father. He seems to be worrying about you. We are all well.

Blessings from
BAPU

SHRIMATI MANIBEHN
SATYAGRAHA ASHRAM
WARDHA, B. N. RLY

[From Gujarati]
Bapuna Patro—Manibehn Patelne, p. 44

212. LETTER TO ASHRAM WOMEN

SODEPUR,
Monday, Magsar Vad 0[2]*, January 3, 1927*

DEAR SISTERS,

This time I have not yet received your weekly letter. We have shifted today to the new buildings erected on the land purchased by the Khadi Pratishthan. They have built many small houses here. The houses took only nine months to build. The processes of washing, bleaching and dyeing khaddar with the aid of machines are now carried on here. There was a big gathering

[1] As in the printed source
[2] The new moon day

here yesterday. The attendance was very good. I thought that I should ask for a collection from the audience; I did, and got about Rs. 3,500/-.

Prayers are held here just as we hold them there. The verses which they recite are also the same. But their recitation is out of tune, compared to ours, and so it jars a little on the ear. But gradually they will improve.

Perinbehn, Mithubehn and Jamnabehn are still with me. They are carrying on their khadi work. They have sold about half the stock they had brought with them.

It is a very good thing that your prayers are held regularly. I note that they are also well attended. Do not forget that spinning is *yajna.* The *Gita* says that he who eats food without offering *yajna* eats stolen food. '*Yajna*' *means work done for the good of others*. For us spinning is such public work.

Blessings from

BAPU

From a photostat of the Gujarati: G.N. 3633

213. LETTER TO PRABHASHANKAR PATTANI

ON THE TRAIN,
January 4, 1927

BHAISHRI,

You ask me not to write merely to acknowledge your letters, and want to know when I am going to Kathiawar. I must reply, then. I am hoping that I shall be there in the beginning of March.[1]

Look after your health.

Vandemataram from

MOHANDAS

[PS.]

If the Hindus forgive Abdul Rashid[2], what can be more welcome than that?

From a photostat of the Gujarati: C.W. 3210. Courtesy: Mahesh Pattani

[1] The Kathiawar Political Conference was to be held at Porbandar in March.

[2] Assassin of Shraddhanand

214. LETTER TO RAMDAS GANDHI

Tuesday [January 4, 1927][1]

CHI. RAMDAS,

I write this on the train. Regarding towels . . .[2] to Pattani Saheb and others. There are many hospitals in Kathiawar. All the towels can be easily sold among them. After buying from Gondal did you not buy khadi at all or did you buy it from somewhere else? I am making arrangements for the rent to be paid by aunt. I will not leave her without any means of support. Manilal[3] is going to the Ashram.

Blessings from
BAPU

From a photostat of the Gujarati: G.N. 6852

215. PRAYER DISCOURSE AT ABHOY ASHRAM[4], COMILLA

[January 5, 1927][5]

You are the pioneers and like the Jamnotri and Gangotri.[6] Be you as those two streams. As I think of you I picture to myself two fine horses running abreast and drawing the khadi carriage at full speed, vying with each other. You have achieved a unique success inasmuch as you do not depend on extra-provincial help for the sale of your products. You have bent the women of Bengal to your will—all honour to them—and they are proud today to wear saris that you supply to them. Let then the strength and weakness of each be the strength and weakness of the other,

[1] From the postmark

[2] Some words are missing in the source.

[3] Manilal Gandhi who had come to India from South Africa

[4] Institution run by Dr. Suresh Chandra Bannerji. The Ashram conducted seven schools for untouchables and also ran a khadi store. Only the concluding remarks of a long talk at the prayer are available.

[5] The report is extracted from Mahadev Desai's "Weekly Letter" where no date has been assigned to it, but it is placed before the report of the public meeting, which took place on January 5.

[6] The reference is to the Khadi Pratishthan and the Abhoy Ashram.

and let the Khadi Pratishthan look in its hour of difficulties to the Abhoy Ashram, and *vice versa*.

Young India, 13-1-1927

216. SPEECH AT VILLAGERS' MEETING, COMILLA

January 5, 1927

The Mahatma with his party visited two Namsudra villages, viz., Rajapura and Muradpur, near about the Ashram and addressed the inhabitants in Hindi. The Mahatma was received by the villagers, men, women and children with *hullas*[1], and the blowing of conch-shells and *sankirtans*[2]. His message to them was not to consider themselves lower than others and not to imitate the bad habits of the so-called higher classes. He asked them to give up drinking and to lead a simple and honest life. He specially dwelt upon the importance and utility of khaddar and exhorted them to follow the examples of the members of the Abhoy Ashram. . . .

Amrita Bazar Patrika, 7-1-1927

217. SPEECH AT PUBLIC MEETING, COMILLA[3]

January 5, 1927

You have been so kind to me in giving me permission to speak in Hindi. If only because I want to show you my appreciation of your kindness, I propose to say a few words to you in English. Every time that I am obliged to speak in the English language before an audience of my countrymen, I feel humiliated and ashamed. I have urged upon Bengali audiences several times not to put an undue strain upon my loyalty, not to put an undue strain upon Bharatamata herself. It is the easiest thing possible for every Indian north of the Vindhya range to pick up Hindi inside of a month. Try it and tell me if what I say is not true. Let us not say that our mother tongue is only Bengali or Gujarati or Punjabi, as the case may be. These are provincial languages. When we sing that ode to the Motherland—*Bande Mataram*, we sing it to the whole of India. When Bankim[4] wrote

[1] Sound uttered by women of Bengal on auspicious occasions as a sign of welcome

[2] Devotional mass singing

[3] The meeting was held at Mahesh Prangan.

[4] Bankim Chandra Chatterji

the inspired song he said *saptakoti bhujaih*[1]. But you and others deliberately said *dwi-trimshatkoti bhujaih*[2] and it was proper. It was proper and dignified on your part to sing of *dwi-trimshatkoti bhujaih*, and it was proper and dignified for the whole of India to accept that magnificent ode. Shall we not then live up to it and sing with all our hearts and say we are sons of Mother India, not merely sons of Bengal? I ask you, therefore, next time I happen to come here or you invite me to come, to insist upon my speaking to you in Hindi and Hindi alone. That is one thing.

We have seen the last of the last session of the Congress. On the sacred banks of the Brahmaputra, in the midst of that magnificent foliage and scenery almost unrivalled in the world, our leaders deliberated. They have evolved a Council programme. But how many of us can take a direct part in the working of that programme? How many of us can enter Councils and the Legislative Assembly? How many of us are entitled to elect members to these legislative bodies? Are the millions of the villagers of India enfranchised? Is India living in her 10 or 20 cities, or is she living in her 700,000 villages? What then is the programme that can weld together the 30 crores of people scattered on a surface 1,900 miles long and 1,500 miles broad in 700,000 villages? What is it that every villager, man, woman and child, Hindu and Mussalman, can do with profit and, at the same time, uplift the whole of India? The one and unequivocal answer is the spinning-wheel and khaddar. The message of khaddar can penetrate to remotest villages if we only will that it shall be so. The spinning-wheel can be turned by millions of the villagers of India who have been reduced to pauperism, who have been ground down to dust, not merely under the foreigner's heels but under your heels, under my heels. We the city-dwellers are living upon the labour, upon the wealth of these millions of villagers; not like the Americans, not like the Englishmen, who live upon the exploitation of Asiatic races or the so-called weaker races of the earth. Even they would be obliged to take up the spinning-wheel or any equivalent if they were not able to exploit India, China, Africa and other parts of the earth. We do not exploit them, because it is a virtue of necessity with us. But I hope that a time is coming when out of the fullness of our hearts, out of a wider national outlook, we shall disdain of our own free will to exploit a single nation of the earth, no matter how weak. I hope that in

[1] Seven crore arms—a reference to the population of Bengal at the time

[2] Sixty crore arms—a reference to the population of India

your lifetime and mine that time is coming when we shall reach our freedom and having reached it, we shall say to all the nations of the earth that they need not fear us, as we have lived in perpetual fear of the so-called civilized races of the earth. You may not believe me today. You may call me, if you like, a mad man. But the time is coming when you will say that what this old man said was right and that, if India was really to prosper in her villages and not in her cities, the spinning-wheel was the only instrument of India's prosperity and India's freedom.

And hence it was that you saw the phenomenon at Gauhati, which I did not expect, which I had not asked for, however much I desired it. But you saw at Gauhati the extraordinary phenomenon of the Congress franchise being improved along khaddar lines. I know there were bickerings about it. But I also know that it was the pressure of the popular mind that extorted that improvement in the franchise. The leaders made that important improvement because they saw that khaddar and khaddar alone was the only passport to the hearts of the villagers. Let me assure you that it was khaddar that won the elections for the Swarajists. You may not know, or perhaps you know, that in Madras even those who were otherwise opposed to khaddar were obliged to take it up at the time of appealing to the electorate, and as the days roll on, you will find that khaddar will gain in importance, because it has intrinsic worth about it; and because no national popular organization contains for its working so many self-sacrificing, able, young, educated men as the khaddar organization; because no organization is capable of giving employment to an almost unlimited number of patriotic youths who will be content with an honourable livelihood and who will be content to pass their lives in the closest touch with the villagers and share their food, their sorrows and joys. I invite you to show me a single other organization which has that capacity in it.

Believe me, khaddar is not a dying cult. There is no fall in the barometer of khaddar. Five years' experience shows that it has been an undoubtedly gradual, but a steady and hopeful rise. It could not have been otherwise. Because India wants it, because India's millions require full means in order to sustain their energy, therefore the Congress has passed the resolution making it necessary for Congressmen to wear khaddar habitually and not merely on ceremonial occasions. They may wear mill-cloth on rare occasions, when it is absolutely necessary for their bread and butter; but they dare not, if they are honest Congressmen, habitually wear anything but hand-spun and hand-woven khaddar.

And now a word about untouchability. A great hero and patriot Swami Shraddhanandji died for the sake of the untouchables. He loved them as dearly as his own life. He regarded them as his own children, and, if it was in his power, he would have banished untouchability from the shores of India. And what does that banishment mean? It means universal love. It means translating into action the great message of the *Bhagavad Gita* which is: Treat the Brahmin and the Bhangi alike, if you would but know God. But how are they alike? A Brahmin is any day superior to the Bhangi in learning, and how am I to treat both alike? The *Bhagavad Gita* says that you should treat them even as you would wish to be treated by them, or even as you would treat yourself:

आत्मवत्सर्वभूतेषु यः पश्यति स पश्यति ।[1]

That is the teaching of the *Bhagavad Gita*. That hero and martyr translated this teaching into action in his own life and he has sanctified it, and sealed it with his blood. Let that blood purify us, and let it remove the last taint of any isolation or aloofness that we may be harbouring against those brothers of ours whom in our arrogance we call untouchables. They are not untouchables, we are untouchables. Let them have every attention, every kindness that they deserve from us. During my Comilla visit, I have seen two villages which are predominantly occupied by the so-called untouchables. Had I not been told, I should not have known that the people I saw were untouchables. I could see no difference between them and the others who were standing with them there. They eat and drink and think and feel even as we do. If a sum-total of their virtues and vices and the privileges they are denied were to be made and compared with our virtues and vices and the privileges we enjoy and deny to them, I am sure in God's books we should find our debit side far heavier than theirs. Let us then think no more of any single person on earth as an untouchable. That is the lesson that comes down to us from South Africa too. Ajust Nemesis has descended upon us there. Just as we are treating our brothers here, our kith and kin are being treated as pariahs and Bhangis in South Africa. The moment we purge ourselves of the sin, the moment we are free from the curse of untouchability, you will find the shackles dropping off our countrymen in South Africa.

[1] This is not to be found in the *Bhagavad Gita*; cf., however, VI, 29 & 32, with one of which, it is possible, Gandhiji confused it.

I dare not touch the problem of Hindu-Muslim unity. It has passed out of human hands, and has been transferred to God's hands alone. Even as Draupadi, forsaken by her husbands, forsaken by men and gods alike, asked God and God alone to come to her help, and God gave her unfailing help, so it is with me and so should it be with every one of us. Let us ask for help from God, the Ail-Powerful and tell Him that we His tiny creatures have failed to do what we ought to do, we hate one another, we distrust one another, we fly at one another's throat and we even become assassins. Let our heart's cry then ascend to His throne, and let us wash His feet with tears of blood and ask Him to purge our hearts of all hatred in us. We are disgracing His earth, His name and this sacred land by distrusting and fearing one another. Although we are sons and daughters of the same motherland, although we eat the same food, we have no room for one another. Let us ask God in all humility to give us sense, to give us wisdom.

You have listened to me with the greatest attention. I have given you also what I don't willingly give to the audience—an English speech, and that also at some length. I now want my reward. I want you tomorrow to come to the Abhoy Ashram and denude it of every yard of khaddar in its store, if my message, the message of the paupers of India, has gone home to you. There you will see a band of workers working for them and for you. They are the link between you and the villagers. They are trying to do their level best to serve the motherland. I want you to put your hands into your pockets and give me what you have and what you can and what you will, not out of shame, not out of any pressure that you may feel because you are in this meeting, not out of patronage for me or affection for me. I shall use your affection for other work if you will give me your affection. But I want you to give me what you can and what you have for the sake of paupers, for the sake of those who do not even get one square meal a day. If you are satisfied that this organization is being worked well, and with ability and self-sacrifice, and if you are convinced that it is not sinful to wear khaddar and it cannot be wrong to wear khaddar woven and spun by your starving countrymen, and that it is right and proper and necessary to do so, you will give your coppers and silver and gold, whatever you may have.

If you have any suspicion about it, any doubts in the matter, I ask you to restrain your hands and not to give me a single pie. If not today, at least on some near date, you will be convinced of the message. But if you are convinced that this is the right thing—although you may not have the strength to carry out the message fully into practice—you will support this great, aye the greatest, national industry. There is no better way of industrializing the villages of India than the spinning-wheel. No man has yet been able to show a better or more effective substitute—I say even an equal substitute—than the spinning-wheel for the millions of Indians who are idle for at least four months in the year, who are starving for want of a square meal, and for whom even one anna a day means a fortune. I plead on behalf of them. May God help you to understand this simple message.

You will recall that last time I was in Bengal, I collected for the All-Bengal Deshbandhu Memorial[1]. That was for what is now the Seva Sadan. I announced then that, in due course, I would collect for the All-India Deshbandhu Memorial. You know that its object was to promote the message of the spinning-wheel. You will thus be contributing to the Memorial by contributing to khaddar.

Amrita Bazar Patrika, 7-1-1927; also *Young India*, 13-1-1927

218. SWAMIJI AS I KNEW HIM

My first acquaintance with Swamiji was when he was Mahatma Munshiram, and that by letter. He was then Governor of Kangri Gurukul, his great original contribution to education. He was not satisfied with the orthodox Western method. He wanted his boys to be saturated with Vedic teaching, and he taught through Hindi, not English. He wanted them to be and remain *brahmacharis* during their training. He had inspired his boys to contribute to the fund that was then being collected for the Satyagrahis of South Africa. And he wanted them to do so by themselves labouring as coolies for hire; for, was it not a coolies' fight in South Africa? The boys rose to the occasion, earned full wages and sent them to me. The letter he wrote to me about this incident was written in Hindi. I was addressed as 'my dear brother'. It endeared me to Mahatma Munshiram. We had never met each other before.

Andrews was the link between us. He was anxious that whenever I returned home, I should make the acquaintance of

[1] *Vide* Vol. XXVII.

what I used to call his trinity—the Poet, Principal Rudra and Mahatma Munshiram.

From the time of the receipt of that letter, we became brothers-in-arms. We met each other in 1915 at his favourite Gurukul and with each meeting we came closer and knew each other better. His love of ancient India, Sanskrit and Hindi was remarkable. He was undoubtedly a non-co-operator before non-co-operation was born. He was impatient to gain swaraj. He hated untouchability and was anxious to raise the status of the untouchables. He could not brook any restriction upon their freedom.

When the Rowlatt agitation was started, he was among the very first to hail it. He wrote a very warm letter to me. But the suspension of Satyagraha after the Amritsar and Viramgam tragedies he could not understand. From that period our differences commenced but they never once disturbed the brotherly relations that subsisted between us. The differences showed to me his childlike nature. He blurted out the truth as he knew it without regard to consequences. He was daring to a fault. I observed more and more the temperamental differences between us as time progressed but they only proved to me the goodness of the soul in him. To think audibly is no crime, it is a virtue. It is the hallmark of truth. Swamiji thought audibly.

The Bardoli decision broke his heart. He despaired of me. His open protest was most energetic. His private letters to me were still more so but with the emphasis on the differences there was an equal emphasis on love. He was not satisfied with an avowal of love in mere letters. He sought me out as opportunity offered and explained his own position, tried to understand mine. But the real reason, as it seems to me, for seeking me out was to assure me, as if any such assurance was necessary, of undiminished love for me as for a younger brother.

My remarks about the Arya Samaj[1] and its great author and my references to him hurt him deeply; but our friendship was strong enough to bear the strain. He could not understand that it was possible to reconcile my general estimate of the Maharshi with the quality of forgiveness that he had in a boundless measure for personal injury. His devotion to the Maharshi was too great to brook any criticism of him or his teachings.

He has been severely criticized and maligned in the Mussalman Press for his *shuddhi* movement. I myself could not accept

[1] *Vide* Vol. XXIV.

his standpoint. I do not accept it even now. But, in my opinion, he had a complete defence of his own position from his own standpoint. *Shuddhi* is entitled to the same toleration that is claimed for *tabligh* so long as either remains within moral and legitimate bounds. But this is not the occasion for entering into an examination of that highly controversial question. Both the *tabligh* and the *shuddhi* which is a reply to the former, have to undergo a radical change. Progress of liberal study of religions of the world is bound to revolutionize the existing clumsy method of proselytizing which looks to the form rather than the substance. It is the transference of allegiance from one fold to another and the mutual decrying of rival faiths which gives rise to mutual hatred.

Swamiji's assassination can be turned to good account by us if we both Hindus and Mussalmans could possibly realize the deeper meaning of *shuddhi*.

I cannot close the reminiscences of the life of a great reformer without recalling his last visit to the Satyagraha Ashram only a few months ago. Let me assure my Mussalman friends that he was no hater of Mussalmans. He undoubtedly distrusted many Mussalmans. But he bore them no ill will. He thought that Hindus were cowed down and he wanted them to be brave and be able to defend themselves and their honour. In this connection he told me that he was much misunderstood and that he was absolutely innocent of many things that were said against him. He told me he had several threatening letters. He was warned by friends not to travel alone. But this man of faith said, "What protection shall I seek but of God? Not a blade of grass perishes without His will. I know therefore that nothing can happen to me so long as He wishes me to serve through this body."

During this stay of his he spoke to the boys and girls of the Ashram school. He said the best protection of Hinduism must come from within, from self-purification. He put the greatest emphasis on the need of *brahmacharya* for the building of character and body.

Young India, 6-1-1927

219. *NOTES*

Shraddhanand Memorial

It is in the fitness of things that there should be an appeal on behalf of the Hindu Mahasabha for funds to perpetuate the memory of the late Swami Shraddhanandji. I congratulate the Sabha on having decided upon inviting collections for carrying on the work for which the Swamiji chiefly lived after his sannyasa. This was removal of untouchability, *shuddhi* and *sangathan*. The appeal has been made for five lakhs for untouchability and as many for *shuddhi* and *sangathan*. For my own part I still remain unconvinced about the necessity of the *shuddhi* movement, taking *shuddhi* in the sense it is generally understood. *Shuddhi* of sinners is a perpetual inward performance. *Shuddhi* of those who can be identified neither as Hindus nor as Mussalmans or who have been recently declared converts but who do not know even the meaning of conversion and who want to be known definitely as Hindus is not conversion but *prayaschitta* or penance. The third aspect of *shuddhi* is conversion properly so called. And I question its use in this age of growing toleration and enlightenment. I am against conversion whether it is known as *shuddhi* by Hindus, *tabligh* by Mussalmans or proselytizing by Christians. Conversion is a heart-process known only to and by God. It must be left to itself. But this is no place for airing my views on conversion. Those who believe in it have a perfect right to follow their own course without let or hindrance, so long as it is kept within proper limits, i.e., so long as there is no force or fraud or material inducement and so long as the parties are free agents and of mature age and understanding. Those, therefore, who believe in *shuddhi* have a perfect right to subscribe to the appeal.

Sangathan is really a sound movement. Every community is entitled, indeed bound, to organize itself if it is to live as a separate entity. I have kept myself aloof from it because of my peculiar ideas of organization. I believe in quality rather than quantity. The fashion nowadays is to rely upon quantity even at the cost of quality. Quantity has its place no doubt in social and political economy. Only I am ill-fitted for organizing quantity in the way it is done at present. Therefore, for me the appeal only for funds for the removal of untouchability has a value. It comes with a force all its own. For reform of Hinduism and for its real protection, removal of untouchability is the greatest thing. It is all-inclusive and, therefore, if this the blackest spot on Hinduism is removed, you have automatically all that *shuddhi* and *sangathan* can be expected to yield. And I say this, not because of the vast number of untouchables whom every Hindu should seek to embrace as one of his own but because consciousness of having broken down a barbarous and ancient custom and consequent purity it necessarily implies gives a strength which is irresistible. Removal of untouchability therefore is a spiritual process. Swamiji was a living embodiment of that reformation because he had no half measures about it, because he would not compromise, he would give no quarter. If he could have had his way, he would have made short work of untouchability in Hinduism. He would have opened every well and every temple to every untouchable on conditions of absolute equality and he would have braved all consequences. I can conceive no more fitting memorial to Swami Shraddhanandji than that every Hindu should henceforth purge his heart of the uncleanliness which untouchability undoubtedly is and deal with the untouchable as with his own kith and kin. His monetary contribution to the memorial, therefore, will, in my opinion, be merely an earnest of his irrevocable resolution to root out the evil and cast it away once and for all from Hinduism.

The 9th day of January is the day appointed for doing public and religious reverence to the memory of the Swamiji. I hope that the ceremony will be performed in every city and every village. But the ceremony will lose its real significance, if at the same time those who take part in it do not purge themselves of the taint of untouchability. Every untouchable should, therefore, take part in the ceremony; and what a great thing it would be if every temple were thrown open to the untouchables on that day. If an organized effort is made, the collections could be finished without the slightest difficulty before the sun sets on the 9th January.

KHADI BOARD OF STUDIES

In selecting the Board of Studies the Council of the All-India Spinners' Association had included Dr. Profulla Chandra Ghosh's name in the Board subject to his acceptance of the office. But as his acceptance was not received owing to his absence from his headquarters in time for publication, the name was withdrawn at the last moment. Dr. Ghosh has now kindly accepted the office. The reader will be glad to learn that the Board will have the assistance of one who has made a study of and has practical experience of the science of charkha and khadi.

PRIZE ESSAY ON HAND-SPINNING

The Prize Essay on Hand-spinning and Hand-weaving issued by the All-India Spinners' Association and written by Professor S. V. Puntambekar and Sjt. N. S. Varadachari is a publication which I commend to the attention both of the khadi worker and the sceptic. The khadi worker will find many things in this volume occupying 235 pages of bold type in octavo size, which he perhaps had not known before. It has four chapters. The first gives the history of hand-spinning and hand-weaving in India before the advent of the British. The second deals with the complete ruin of hand-spinning, the greatest national industry, and almost complete ruin of hand-weaving, the second great national industry. The third deals with the possibilities of hand-spinning and hand-weaving and incidentally sets up a comparison between mill-spinning and mill-weaving and hand-spinning and hand-weaving. And the fourth deals with exclusion or boycott of all foreign cloth through the spinning-wheel. The authors give facts and figures for every statement made by them.

The price of the book is one rupee. Copies can be had from the office of the All-India Spinners' Association, Ahmedabad, or from Mr. S. Ganesan, Current Thought Press, Triplicane, Madras, by sending one rupee and two annas to cover postage.

Young India, 6-1-1927

220. THE CONGRESS

When, in Cawnpore, the Assam delegates gave the invitation to hold the Congress of 1926 at Gauhati and the Congress accepted the invitation I was filled with misgivings. I felt that Assam was too far away, too unorganized and too poor to shoulder the heavy burden of holding a Congress session. Gauhati has a population of only 16,000. No place with such a small population has, before Gauhati, had the temerity to invite the Congress. Gauhati, however, beat all previous records, and in an incredibly short space of time erected, in the midst of surroundings of great natural beauty on the banks of the great Brahmaputra, a city under khadi canvas. The huge Congress pavilion itself was made of pure Assam khadi. The Reception Committee had to import material and men from outside in order to provide for the varied tastes of delegates and visitors from different provinces. Leaders' quarters were isolated from the delegates' quarters. When I resented the isolation, I was told that it was not done intentionally, but it had to be done because there was not enough ground available in one single spot to provide accommodation for all. The construction of the cottages was incredibly simple,—Assam bamboo, Assam mud, Assam straw, Assam khadi and Assam labour were responsible for the very simple but artistic huts erected on the Brahmaputra bank. And as Mr. Phookan led me to one of these beautiful huts, he said, "Now it must delight your heart in that we are giving you not a palace miscalled hut, as you had remarked in Belgaum[1], but we are giving you a proper hut, only we cannot claim any merit for it because it is a virtue of necessity; for we could have given you nothing more, nothing less." I was, however, more than glad for this virtue of necessity. Let not the reader however imagine for one moment that there was in any degree whatsoever less comfort in these artistic huts than in the palatial-looking structure that was provided in Belgaum. All the other arrangements so far as I gather were in keeping with this artistic simplicity.

The address of the Chairman[2] of the Reception Committee was equally simple and equally artistic and therefore naturally brief.

Proceedings commenced punctually at the advertised time. No time was lost in ceremonial functions. In a few minutes Mr. Phookan's brief address was finished, the President[3] amidst shouts of applause walked to the rostrum and read his address. The suppressed gloom cast over the assembly through the news of the assassination of Swami Shraddhanandji was no doubt there, but it was not allowed to be made visible. The delegates knew that Swamiji had died a hero's death and it therefore demanded no tears but action and so the business part of the Congress went on as if nothing had happened. The ceremonial was severely cut off including the usual presidential procession. The address of the President for the matters it covers is brief enough. I pass by the references to the Councils and the defence of the Swarajist attitude which occupies half of the address.

The constructive programme has its due share given to it. The place of honour is assigned to khaddar. The President trusts that the All-India Spinners' Association will become a nation-

[1] The venue of the Congress session in 1924, over which Gandhiji presided

[2] Phookan

[3] S. Srinivasa Iyengar

wide labour organization which, if it cannot be identical with swaraj, will go some way towards it. It can become that if every Congressman and every Congresswoman will do his or her duty.

> The spinning-wheel has by its persuasiveness affected to a visible extent the national psychology, and has lent a new dignity to our manhood and womanhood.

This was more than exemplified by the enthusiastic manner in which the amendment in the franchise clause regarding khaddar was accepted by the Congress in spite of stubborn opposition offered to it. No wonder that the President considers that "khaddar is at once the radiant symbol of our self-reliance and of our power of resistance".

In the constructive programme the second place is given to prohibition and the President correctly pleads guilty to the charge that we have not lately paid much attention to the question of total prohibition. He says,

> The movement will gain in moral grandeur if we successfully organize the will of the nation in that behalf.

He remarks that

> No minister has during the past six years been found, and I doubt whether a minister will now be found, to be courageous enough to bring in a bill for total prohibition and to resign his office on its rejection or disallowance.

There is something somewhere utterly wrong if, in a place like India which is overwhelmingly dry, ministers are unwilling to provide what is the nation's due, namely, total prohibition. There is as much flaw in the argument that it is an interference with the right of the people, as there would be in the argument that the laws prohibiting theft interfere with the right of thieving. A thief steals all earthly possessions, a drunkard steals his own and his neighbour's honour. It surprises me to discover that the President has failed to suggest the obvious method of providing for the deficit of revenue. There is a huge military expenditure, so much of which is utterly useless and based upon distrust of the nation. It is capable of reduction by more than 25 crores which is the revenue from drinks and drugs.

Untouchability comes next. He does not think that it is necessary to wait for swaraj till untouchability is removed. He cites the capital instance, in his favour, of the United States of America achieving freedom long before the abolition of a very real and widespread slavery. But he hastens to add,

> We must all agree that we must make an end of untouchability, apart from any question of swaraj and whether we ever win swaraj or not.

And then this Brahmin philosopher lays down that

> the higher philosophy of Hinduism as well as the history of the religious dissidence in our country emboldens me to claim that the rule regarding untouchability has neither part nor lot with the indestructible soul of Hinduism. Judged by any test humanitarian, rational or spiritual, patriotic or democratic, we cannot with decency uphold in Hinduism the dogma of an immutable untouchability. It clouds our vision, limits our experience, hardens our heart, narrows our sphere of responsibility and prevents our ideals of justice, love and sincerity from being perfect.

I congratulate the President for this eloquent and severe condemnation of the curse that has descended upon Hinduism.

The next heading is labour and unemployment. I am inclined to think that this needs more diligent study than appears to have been given to it. It requires, in my opinion, considerable revision. I suggest that the charkha movement with all its implications provides the largest form of relief to the unemployment of millions.

The currency policy of the Government has also claimed a paragraph in his address. The President 'cordially' welcomes the formation of the Indian Currency League and trusts that it will adequately educate public opinion on the question of the ratio, the gold standard, gold currency and other cognate questions. He says:

> But I am certain the League will be able to achieve nothing, either by debate and vote in the Assembly or by protest outside, unless it comes into line with the Congress and unless its members harness themselves to the dynamic politics of the Congress.

Indian States have also found a paragraph in the address.

Greater India naturally follows the paragraph on Indian States.

> The status of Indians abroad, whether in South Africa or Kenya, in Fiji or Guiana, in Ceylon or Malaya, in America or Australia, depends inevitably upon the status of Indians in their own land; and swaraj for India depends in its turn upon the brave and unfaltering spirit of our kith and kin across the seas.

I suppose the presidential suggestion "of the holding once in a way of a session of the Congress in South Africa" is merely a pious wish. The subject deserves better examination than it has received. I presume the absence of any reference to Mr. Andrews's signal services is an unintentional oversight due to the many local pre-occupations of the very busy President.

The Asiatic Federation comes in too for a few lines. Mr. Iyengar deplores that "we have too long neglected the possibilities of a cultural and business union with all Asiatic countries." I venture to suggest that the cultural union is being sufficiently attended to by our great Poet and the business union by the great commercial firms.

The irrepressible optimism of the President is to be observed in the paragraphs upon Communalism and Nationalism. He says:

> I am confident that wherever intensive propaganda, sincere and persuasive, clearly analyses the fallacies underlying it, communalism will go to the wall. Happily, prejudice and suspicion are not deep-seated amongst Indians and communalism is but their offspring.

Under the heading 'Plea for Tolerance', one reads the following pregnant sentences:

> Though each community should be free to make conversions, no resort to conversion is really any longer useful or necessary. For the lives of the best and most pious men in each community are a fitter and more effective propaganda in that behalf than definite missionary effort. But wherever the latter is made, it should be open and general and neither secret nor directed to the converting of particular men or women. Let us realize that no great and long-established religion gains in truth, beauty or spirituality with any increase in its census figures.

He winds up the paragraph by quoting the following beautiful passage from Ashoka's inscriptions:

> He who does reverence to his own sect while disparaging the sects of others wholly from attachment to his own, with intent to enhance the splendour of his own sect, in reality by such conduct inflicts the severest injury on his own sect.

The President is evidently against communal representation. He says:

> That much abused expression "communal representation" is a misnomer; for all the communities are equally interested in all public questions and in the country's problems and in particular solutions of them.

Again he says:

> Let us realize clearly that to uphold justice between man and man is to uphold justice between community and community. As a safeguard a

negative rule against members of any community or caste monopolizing offices is all that is required.

The President remarks:

> The intrusion into politics of religion, and very often of dogmatic religion, must be resisted as a primitive or mediaeval idea, born of theocracies, and disastrous alike to religion and to politics.

But he adds:

> I do not speak of morality or of that spiritual quality which is common to all religions; for thereby politics and organizations are cleansed and made sweet and wholesome.

Sjt. Iyengar adds:

> Let us not forget, in the fever of political controversy, that the strength of each religion is derived from God and rooted in the souls of Prahlads. Not all the tortures of a Torquemada[1], nor all the burning at the stakes, nor all the forms of persecution have been able to destroy the mystic quality of the human soul. Neither Hinduism nor Islam derives or requires strength either from the present or from any future Government. Both stand far, far above swaraj which is not comparable to them. Neither foreign governments nor self-governments, neither democracies nor autocracies, can destroy that seed of faith which is in every one of us, that inspired interpretation of the universe to which one clings for guidance and solace in this world and for salvation in the next.

The last three pages of the address are devoted to a fervent appeal for unity.

> There can be only two parties in India, the party of the Government and its adherents that obstruct swaraj, and the party that fights visibly and unceasingly for swaraj . . . I deprecate the philosophy of individualism in a supreme struggle for freedom against a powerful people with their trained bureaucracy and with unlimited material resources. On a question whether a particular course is wise or unwise, will succeed or fail, will accelerate swaraj or retard it, to make one's opinion or judgment or feeling a matter of conscience is false philosophy. On a point of religion, of morality, of honour, one's own conscience must be the arbiter, but in transacting the affairs of a country, when a decision is not irreligious, immoral or dishonourable, I fail to see how we may rely on our right to differ from one another and yet uphold the discipline necessary for an organization fighting for swaraj.

[1] Thomas Torquemada (1420-1498); Inquisitor-General of Spain who is said to have condemned more than 10,000 people to be burned at the stake

The conclusion is in keeping with the fervency of the appeal and the deep emotion that underlies every line of this address. He says:

> Swaraj is not an intellectual but an emotional proposition. We must cherish it in our hearts with unquenchable faith. . . . We must become possessed by a passion for swaraj that is not warped by fallacies and impulses, that will stand for a uniform and rapid corporate advance in serried masses, that will know no obstacles, that will not wax and wane with the seasons, that will not be daunted by imprisonments or depressed by failures.

Let me hope that the appeal will find an echo in the hearts of us all.

The resolutions do not require an elaborate examination. Besides the condolence resolutions, there is of course the Council resolution for the guidance of Council-wallas, then the resolutions about South Africa and Kenya, the Bengal detenus and the Gurdwara prisoners. The khaddar clause in the constitution is, in my opinion, altered for the better. The ceremonial wear had become the laughing stock of all. Habitual wear of khaddar is the right thing if khaddar wear should find a place in our franchise qualifications. It is to be hoped that every Congress worker will enforce this resolution in his own person and induce others to do likewise. But I must deal more fully in a subsequent issue with many other things that were discussed in the Subjects Committee in connection with the resolutions withdrawn or rejected.

Young India, 6-1-1927

221. *INTERVIEW TO FREE PRESS OF INDIA*

COMILLA,
January 6, 1927

With reference to the statement[1] issued by Mr. T. C. Goswami[2] on the habitual khadi wear resolution passed by the Congress at Gauhati the following interview was granted to a representative of the Free Press of India by Mahatma Gandhi:

I tender my congratulations to Mr. Goswami upon his frank statement on khaddar. It should clear the atmosphere of cant, hypocrisy and humbug. Khaddar must stand or fall on its

[1] Not reproduced here

[2] Member of the Legislative Assembly from Bengal

own merits. Mr. Goswami betrays a mental attitude which no doubt makes any mention of khaddar repugnant to him. His is not an objection to khaddar as a fetish but it is an objection to khaddar even as an economic factor, because he says that khaddar may be even an economic waste and permanent exclusion of foreign cloth may not be a desirable thing. If I thought like Mr. Goswami I should also object to the khaddar clause as strongly as he does. The change from ceremonial to habitual wear was not due to my prompting. But I have no hesitation in endorsing the change as desirable and even necessary for the growth of a true national life. Politics apart from nationalism I do not understand. I consider boycott of foreign cloth not merely as a political expedient but as a permanent duty. I regard it as immediately possible in terms of khaddar if we have the will.

I go a step further and say that boycott of foreign cloth through khaddar is the only thing the nation is capable of achieving within a measurable distance of time, and since the economic aspect of khaddar includes organization of the whole nation towards one *single* effort, it has tremendous political consequences. If, therefore, it is right and proper to restrict the membership of the Congress to those who desire swaraj and to exclude those who wish to retain the present British domination, it is equally right to restrict the membership to those who desire and work for the boycott of foreign cloth, through active, continuous and persistent khaddar production and sale. It is the beauty of khaddar and not its limitation, as Mr. Goswami suggests, that it is no respecter of persons and that it can adorn the body of a government spy as much as that of a saintly servant of India, whoever he may be. For the nation includes all the highest and the lowest, the healthy and the unhealthy, the good as well as the wicked. But it should be the privilege of the good to reform the wicked and serve them.

Forward, 7-1-1927

222. SPEECH AT WOMEN'S MEETING, COMILLA

January 6, 1927

. . . Next he addressed a big gathering of ladies, where he said that they must have swaraj, which meant *Ramarajya* which again could not come without Sita. He exhorted all to attain the virtues of Sita and to wear clothes made by their own hands as Sita used to do, and also to follow the examples of Sita by leading a simple and pure life. He concluded by saying that the charkha was the only cure for pauperism.

When he appealed for funds for the All-India Deshbandhu Memorial, the ladies contributed some money and some of them even gave away their gold ornaments.

Amrita Bazar Patrika, 8-1-1927

223. LETTER TO MANIBEHN PATEL

[KASHI,]
Saturday [*January 8, 1927*][1]

CHI. MANI,

I have your letter. It is good that you are studying with Valjibhai's help. You will learn much from him.

I do not know why you have been relieved of your teaching work, for I could not understand the reasons from the letter in which the news was conveyed to me. You yourself should be bold and ask the reason. I thought that the reason must have been explained to you. I remained unconcerned by the news because, irrespective of whether or not you teach, you continue to stay in the Ashram, and the salary, or whatever you name it, will continue to be paid to you. The responsibility for you is mine. You should not get angry with the teachers. They have to run the institution, and so they may act as they think proper. But you have a right to know the reason, and you shall know it.

You should now get ready to learn spinning. You should learn everything that goes with it, that is to say, repairing the spinning-wheel, recognizing the different varieties of cotton, ginning, pressing, carding, spinning, moistening the yarn, making skeins,

[1] As in the printed source

joining the broken thread—all these processes. You should learn to make a *mal*[1] and to wind the *sadi*[2] round the spindle. Moreover, wherever you go you should learn what else you can besides these processes, and as part of this programme of studies you should improve your proficiency in Hindi and Sanskrit. In studying Sanskrit, you should know the meaning of every verse in the *Gita* along with its syntax. And of course, you should learn to spin on the *takli*. There was a telegram from Karachi to say that your name has been sent to the Board. I am happy.

Write to me regularly and go on working very cheerfully. Now, from the 2nd to the 8th I shall be in Gondia, Nagpur, Wardha, Akola and Amaravati. I am not certain about the towns on the programme. It will be better to address your letters to Wardha.

Blessings from

BAPU

[From Gujarati]

Bapuna Patro—Manibehn Patelne, pp. 45-6

224. *COMPLICATIONS OF UNTOUCHABILITY*

I publish in this issue Shri Govindji Jadavdas's letter under the heading which he has himself given to it, viz., "The Downfall of Hinduism". The purport of his letter is this: If untouchability is to be removed, then why have separate schools, temples and wells for the untouchables? This argument is certainly not pointless. Similar problems have arisen and still arise in South Africa. I had raised the argument myself, in South Africa, that setting up of separate schools for the Indians means prolonging the life of untouchability. Only those who have themselves suffered can realize the pain of other sufferers; in the same way I can appreciate Shri Govindji's unhappiness.

But where I realized that it would be considered foolish on my part to ignore the existence of a thing which does exist, I did my work with full realization of the discrimination which was there. So I accepted the proposal of having separate schools. I had also accepted [in S. Africa] the proposal for separate first and second-class compartments in trains for Indians. Like Govindji I too had opposed such a discrimination there. But when

[1] Belt or cord passing round the wheel and the spindle

[2] Cotton thread moistened with gum

the mere existence of a community was in danger, I accepted such a discrimination which would virtually lead to lightening the discrimination in spite of its continuance. For example, the Indians could formerly travel only by the third class; as a result of the agitation an order was issued allowing them to travel in first and second-class compartments. Simultaneously it was decided to have for the Indians separate first and second-class coaches. We accepted this provision even after we had opposed discrimination. The government authorities can make arrangements [for common coaches] but how can others be forced to sit with us?

I yielded to this line of thinking and came to the conclusion that as long as the *Antyajas* are not able to make use of common temples, etc., it is better to have for them separate institutions by which they may benefit, rather than totally to deprive them of the amenity. Theoretically, untouchability has disappeared. Still many are not yet ready to discard it altogether in practice. What should the friends of the untouchables do so long as such a situation persists? How else can they prove their sincerity of purpose? The answer should be that it can be done by constructing temples, etc., for the untouchables.

Shri Govindji says that such temples, etc., may be built, but why label them with unpleasant words, "for the untouchables only"? No one has assigned such unpleasant labels. The temples, etc., which are being built are used by those who have made donations towards their cost as well as by other friends of the untouchables. From this viewpoint the institutions built for the benefit of the untouchables are in fact for the general public. But the untouchables have the first claim upon them. In the matter of using these institutions, the untouchables are given the first preference, and their requirements looked to first.

Though I can fully realize the unhappiness of an *Antyaja* like Shri Govindji, I wish him to believe that the Antyaj Directory[1] and the underlying motive to build temples, etc., is pure, laudable and in the interests of the *Antyajas*.

[From Gujarati]

Navajivan, 9-1-1927

[1] *Vide* "Antyaj Directory", 12-12-1926.

225. INTERVIEW TO BHAGWANDAS[1]

BANARAS,
January 9, 1927

BHAGWANDAS: Mahatmaji, I wish very much to know what you think of certain measures which seem to me very helpful, or indeed indispensable, for the welfare and progress of India in political as well as other respects. I have been trying my feeble best to place them before the public for the last six years, but more or less in vain. If they could secure your approval, the country would look at them with more consideration, and might attempt to put them into operation, for the force of your *tapasya* (asceticism and self-denial) is very great, and the country rightly places great faith in you because of your great selflessness. I put these measures into the form of Proposals for Resolutions, and requested my dear friend, Shri Shiva Prasad Gupta, to try to get them placed before the Gauhati Congress. But nothing more could be done than to place copies in the hands of the members of the A.I. Congress Committee. With your permission I will put the same in the form of questions to you.

First of all, do you think, or not, that the essence of true swaraj, true self-government, is that all the laws should be made by the elected representatives of the people, and that these elected representatives should embody the higher self, and not the lower self, of the people, that is to say, they should be the wisest, the most experienced, the most unselfish and philanthropic persons available?

MAHATMA GANDHI: This also is among the essential features.

What other essential features are there, if any?

My ideal is that every person should realize dharma. In that case, there will be no need left for any representatives. That is the ideal swaraj. There are no rulers and no ruled in that swaraj; no government servants; all are the servants of all. This is the ideal swaraj. If this ideal swaraj is kept in view, mistakes would be avoided, or, at least, minimized. It is certain that such ideal swaraj can never be attained; but we will be able to make a near approach to it.

This is no doubt the highest kind of swaraj. Apparently the Republic of the Uttara-Kuru as described in the *Mahabharata* was something like this.

But the inhabitants of that happy land were all supermen and superwomen, god-and-goddess-like *Jivanmuktas* and *Yoga-Siddhas*, perfect, final, men

[1] The original Hindi report of the interview was published in *Aaj*, 19-2-1927.

and women, *insan-ul-ka-mil, mard-wa-zan-i-mam* ("Be ye perfect, even as your Father in Heaven is perfect"), according to the tradition of that epic. In view, obviously, of our present condition, however, you yourself said at the Ahmedabad Congress of 1921 that you could lead this country to Dominion Home Rule. Would not that be the preliminary or intermediate form of swaraj which would be suitable for us now?

Yes.

There must be legislatures in such swaraj?

Yes.

Representatives would have to be elected for them?

Yes.

These representatives should be the wisest, most experienced, most selfless, most philanthropic persons available?

Yes.

Electors should always keep this ideal, this guiding principle, in view?

Yes.

Should this guiding principle be followed in making elections for District Boards, Municipal Boards, and other local elective bodies, as well as for the Congress Committees of all grades?

Certainly.

Is this guiding principle recognized by, is this ideal spread among, the Indian public?

To some extent.

Looking at the elections made to the Congress Committee and the various elective bodies, what inference can we draw as to the extent to which this principle is recognized and acted on? Is the extent very small, or sufficient?

It is less than it ought to be.

This same principle should guide the elections to the legislative bodies, should it not?

It should guide all the elections that are made nowadays.

Has sufficient effort been made by leaders, individually, or by the Congress as a body, to spread this ideal among the public?

It would not be enough to say yes or no in reply to this question. I believe that the present atmosphere is not favourable for this purpose.

You said before that the principle had been recognized to some extent by the public. What was the cause of the spread of the ideal to that small extent?

So far the effort has been individual. When the atmosphere becomes favourable, then all persons begin to act according to such ideals without any effort.

Should effort be made to create such a favourable atmosphere or not?

It should be made unceasingly.

What kind of effort would be helpful?

The number of the individuals who make this effort should increase constantly. And there is, and has always been, only one way to bring about this increase, viz., that those who believe in this ideal should cling to it in the face of all difficulties.

That is to say, individuals should spread the ideal by teaching and preaching, in speech and writing?

Individuals should preach by the example of their conduct. Speeches and writings are also of help. Conduct includes speaking and writing.

I entirely agree that preaching has no force if the preacher does not act up to his own advice. But while you have been putting on khaddar and working the charkha yourself, you have also, side by side, with the setting of this personal example, been preaching them very extensively and very diligently. And that is why they are spreading. So too you have been preaching assiduously and widely various measures connected with non-violent non-co-operation. Do you not think that in this very important matter also it is very necessary to give advice to and remind the public persistently as thus: "Whenever you have to elect representatives, you should elect persons of such-and-such qualifications"? Without such advice, will not the general public remain in darkness, without any guide, in this exceedingly important matter?

This question is right. But really the answer to it is included in my previous answer. I regard advising and preaching as part of conduct generally. I do not give a separate place to precept because when a person cannot set a good example his precept is useless, and often becomes harmful. And he who keeps his conduct right does as a fact give advice also whenever there is an opportunity.

But so far as I am aware, you have not advised the Indian public as yet, in your speeches and writings, as to the qualifications they should look for in the persons they elect.

Not once but many times have I given this advice, in speech and writing.

Should I find writings on the subject in *Young India*?

Yes.

I will search. In the meanwhile, will you kindly tell me what means should be employed, what rules followed, to secure properly qualified representatives? So far as I can see, the general complaint is that the representatives chosen are not of the right quality, either in the self-governed countries of the West or in present-day India under the new election system. This is the one chief and serious defect in current systems of self-government, is it not?

And this is the reason why I strongly oppose Council-entry. So long as the people do not realize *swatva* (i.e., spirituality), so long as their intelligence is not awake, so long it will not be possible to secure purity in elections by any laws. And this purity has a large part in my present efforts. From the very beginning my endeavour has been directed towards the increase of the power, the soul-force of the people, by self-purification and *tapasya* (self-denial, *riyazat*, *nafs-kushi*). By such *tapasya* their intelligence will be purified and rectified. Because of this, the persons who were elected for Municipal Boards, etc., after the commencement of the non-co-operation movement, were good persons, and they were elected without trouble and expense. When that atmosphere disappeared, confusion began.

By the ancient tradition of this land, *tapasya* (self-denial, *riyazat*, *zohd*) and *vidya* (right knowledge) are two distinguishable (though more or less interdependent) things, and only by the combination of both is achieved that true humanity, true spirituality, or realization of God or Self or *Brahman* or Allah or *Brahmanhood*, or Kamal, however it may be called, which is what I believe you mean by *swatva* (selfness). In the Puranic story we read that Ravana and others made great *tapasya*, but the result of that was tyrannical earthly power and excessive luxury to them, for some time, and groaning to the rest of the world. They made *tapasya* without *vidya* (right knowledge). What I feel is that in the atmosphere created by the N.C.O., there was the element of *tapasya*, but not of *vidya* (emotion and enthusiasm and self-denial but not clear intelligence and right knowledge of the essential feature of the object to be striven for); and that this was the reason why the atmosphere could not gain permanence, but dispersed in two or three years. Do you think this belief of mine to be right or wrong?

It is generally right. A little modification is needed. Our *tapasya* at that time was not sufficient in amount. Had it been sufficient, we should certainly have achieved the *vidya* also. The Lord has said in the *Gita* that God gives right understanding to the person of firm devotion.

I too believe so, but devotion brings such wholesome fruit only when it is rightly directed, when its aim, its object, its ideal, is the Right Object, not otherwise. The *Gita* also says: "They who worship other gods go to the other gods; they who worship *Me* (the Higher Self) come to *Me*." Also: "There is no purifier like unto knowledge." My belief has therefore always been that from the very beginning of *tapasya* (self-denying effort), right knowledge of the essential features of the true Goal is also absolutely indispensable; otherwise the soul-force, the power, of whatever kind, gathered by *tapasya*, will certainly err away into wrong paths, as that of Ravana, etc. Is that belief of mine wrong or right?

Entirely right.

Just for this very reason have I been endeavouring, from the very beginning of the N.C.O. movement, that side by side with the *tapasya* (self-sacrifice) of N.C.O., appropriate *vidya* (right knowledge) should be particularly imparted to the people, by the Congress and the leaders, as to the *essential* of this intermediate swaraj, i.e., Dominion Home Rule, viz., the election of *duly qualified* representatives. Was this wish of mine wrong?

If it meant that any *yojana* (detailed constitution) should be placed before the people, then I have arrived at the opinion that it would be of no use. But it is quite right and proper that such knowledge should be given to the people, that they should be so awakened as will make them able to elect duly qualified representatives only. What the qualifications of the representatives should be—I do not like to fix this now. All this should be left to the intelligence of the electors.

In respect of the charkha, the cultivation of cotton, the storing of yarn, the weaving of cloth, the selling of it, etc., you yourself and through your co-workers, are constantly giving instruction and information to the people in much detail. Do you not think it necessary to give to the people, similarly, in respect of this very important matter even some little specific indication as to the marks by which the fitness of representatives might be recognized? Even such self-evident truths, as that two and two make four, have to be taught to children with much labour. That the charkha should be worked in leisure hours is also an almost self-evident proposition; yet this also, and with all the labour you have spent on it, is not yet so widespread among the people as it ought to be. Now then can you leave for the unaided understanding of the electors the decision of the fitness of representatives, without any instruction and guidance? If you think it undesirable to fix any age-limit, you might give indications in some other respects at least.

I have written something in this respect, and will write as I find time. But there is no need to speak about it in the Congress.

When the people come to the occasion for electing representatives, then advice will have to be given to them about it, as is done now regarding the charkha. Everything has its own fit time.

Which of the qualifications suggested by me in No. 2 of my proposals for the Gauhati Congress do you think to be desirable, if any at all, for persons to be elected?

Almost all, but not for legislative enactment. It is a matter essentially for the education of the electors.

I will now ask about another matter. Is it possible to bring about unity and peace between the followers of the several religions without explaining to them that the essentials of all these religions are one and the same? Without showing that the various religions are one at heart, is it possible to make the various religionists one at heart?

No.

Only when it is explained to the followers of the several religions that the heart of all religions is the same, will it become possible to make peace between the followers thereof?

Yes.

What should be done to bring this about?

All the good and true followers of the several religions should preach and promulgate this fact.

What special effort have you made, or intend to make, in this behalf?

I have made enough individual effort; and it continues to be made even today. There is a lack of persons amongst us for this *prachara* (propaganda), i.e., there are very few persons amongst us who might separate the merits and demerits of the various religions, bring together all the merits, and put them before the people.

Do you not think that an influential leader like yourself should bring together into a committee elected representatives, large-hearted and broad-minded, of the several religions current in India, who might preach such essential unity of the religions by speech, writings, and conduct?

I think I have made efforts to the extent of my powers; but it seems I have not the ability to bring together educated and learned persons for such work. I have, therefore, contented myself with my own individual efforts.

As the time is short, I pass on to another subject. The Hindu Sabha is laying stress on *shuddhi* and *sangathan*. Can the work of *shuddhi* be done effectively without accepting the principle of "class-caste by temperament and functions (and not by birth)"? And is the work of *sangathan* possible without first abolishing the mutual untouchability which prevails at present in respect of dining among the thousands of sub-castes of Hindus?

I have explained my views as regards *shuddhi* and *sangathan* in *Young India* in the articles I wrote in appreciation of Shraddhanandji. I am unable to say more. I may say here, however, that even *panktibheda* (separate seats at dinner) is destructive of *sangathan*, without a doubt.

You have said in *Young India* of 6-1-1927: "Both the *tabligh* and the *shuddhi* which is a reply to the former, have to undergo a radical change. Progress of liberal study of religions of the world is bound to revolutionize the existing clumsy method of proselytizing which looks to the form rather than the substance. It is the transference of allegiance from one fold to another and the mutual decrying of rival faiths which gives rise to mutual hatred. . . ." "The third aspect of *shuddhi* is conversion properly so called. And I question its use in this age of growing toleration and enlightenment. I am against conversion, whether it is known as *shuddhi* by Hindus, *tabligh* by Mussalmans, or proselytizing by Christians."

I most heartily subscribe to all this; in saying it you have completely endorsed the first two objects of the Theosophical Society, which has been working for fifty-one years, and of which I have been a member for forty-three. But the "growing toleration and enlightenment" are obviously growing very very slowly, and the "liberal study of the religions of the world", which "is bound to revolutionize the existing clumsy methods of proselytizing" which seek simply to change the labels and signboards on the foreheads of persons, has failed to produce its due effect, so far, on the *practice* of the highly educated men who are at the back of these conversion movements. Therefore is it not desirable that a great leader like yourself should diligently help to quicken the growth of the toleration and enlightenment and the progress of the liberal study of religions, in more specific and express ways, as suggested in No. 6 of my proposals for the Gauhati Congress, by organizing committees for the purpose all over the country, to do this vitally important work, which has been rather put aside latterly by the Theosophical Society?

When I asked in my previous question whether the principle of caste according to character-and-functioning (*karmana varnah*) was not the only legitimate basis as well as completion of *shuddhi*, my implication was just this that if the principle was accepted, the whole of mankind would at once be "converted" to essential Hinduism without anyone having to change his particular religious label or signboard.

I can only answer in the words of the seer: "The distant scene I do not care to see, one step enough for me." After all, the future is determined by the sum-total of the present activities, often contradictory, of mankind.

You do not, presumably, think it undesirable to form an army of volunteers for public work in connection with the Congress. If so, do you not think that if the qualifications mentioned in No. 5(a–b) of my proposals for the Gauhati Congress were prescribed and adopted, the army would become much more efficient? If you consider any particular qualification out of these inappropriate, or any other as more appropriate, would you very kindly mention it?

It would be desirable to form such a corps if it is possible. The qualifications too are good. But my experience shows that we are not in a position to form any such body for all India. It will not come into being by means of resolutions.

The Hindustan Times, 4-10-1927

226. *SPEECH AT BENARES HINDU UNIVERSITY*[1]

BANARAS,
January 9, 1927

"You have had your say now. No one is listening to you. Why not stop talking of khaddar?" That was the advice that was being given him in some quarters. Gandhiji said:

But why should I stop reciting my favourite *mantra* when I have before me the example of Prahlad of old refusing to give up Ramanama in the teeth of tortures worse than death? And I have not had to go through any tortures yet. How can I give up the only message that the condition of my country has been whispering to me? Panditji[2] has collected and has been still collecting lakhs and lakhs of rupees for you from Rajas and Maharajas. The money apparently comes from these wealthy princes, but in reality it comes from the millions of our poor. For unlike Europe the rich of our land grow rich at the expense of our villagers the bulk of whom have to go without a square meal a day. The education that you receive today is thus paid for by the starving villagers who will never have the chance of such an education. It

[1] The meeting was attended by about 2,000 students and was held under a *shamiana* specially erected for the Viceregal visit which preceded Gandhiji's by just a week. The report is extracted from Mahadev Desai's "Weekly Letter".

[2] Madan Mohan Malaviya

is your duty to refuse to have an education that is not within the reach of the poor, but I do not ask that of you today. I ask you to render just a slight return to the poor by doing a little *yajna* for them. For he who eats without doing his *yajna* steals his food, says the *Gita*. The *yajna* that was required of the British civic population during the War was for each household to grow potatoes in its yard and for each household to do a little simple sewing. The *yajna* of our age and for us is the spinning-wheel. Day in and day out I have been talking about it, writing about it. I shall say no more today. If the message of the poor of India has touched your hearts I want you to raid Kripalani's khaddar store tomorrow and denude it of all its stock, and to empty your pockets tonight. Panditji has cultivated the art of beggary. I have learnt it from him, and if he specializes in laying the princes under tribute, I have learnt to be equally shameless in emptying the pockets of the poor, for the benefit of those who are poorer than they.

* * *

Malaviyaji's one object in begging millions for you, in raising these palatial buildings, is to send out to the country gems of purest ray, citizens healthy and strong to serve their motherland. That purpose will be defeated if you allow yourselves to be swept with the wind that comes today from the West—the wind of impurity. Not that the methods have the general sanction of Europe. There are friends in Europe, a very few, who are fighting hard to counteract the poisonous tendency. But if you do not wake up betimes, the immoral wave that is fast gathering strength might soon envelop and overwhelm you. I cry out to you, therefore, with all the strength at my command: Be warned, and flee from the fire before it consumes you.

Young India, 20-1-1927

227. SPEECH AT SHRADDHANAND MEMORIAL MEETING, BANARAS

January 9, 1927

It is a sacred day today and the meeting is taking place at a very good spot, where temple and mosque stand side by side. If any Mussalman considers Swami Shraddhanand to have been an enemy, he is in error. Swamiji died as a hero. He pursued his mission according to truth and dharma with great courage.

[From Hindi]

Aaj, 10-1-1927

228. SPEECH AT MEETING OF UNTOUCHABLES, BANARAS

January 9, 1927

I thank you for the address you have presented to me. If Mussalmans will only realize it, this is for them too a sacred day. We have today paid homage to the memory of Swami Shraddhanand and have bathed in the Ganga. We took the holy bath in the hope that we too might gain some of the qualities of Swamiji. Swamiji was a friend of the untouchables. He suffered in their suffering. And it was for their sake that he sacrificed his life. It was all to the good. If someone gets killed for the sake of religion it brings him only good. He cannot die a nobler death. Swamiji was so firm that he found it painful himself to go where untouchables were not allowed to go—just as Yudhishthira would not go even to heaven without his companion, the dog. The untouchables too have faults. Some of them drink. This they should give up. They should not argue that after all caste Hindus drink too. For the untouchables have got to go forward. They should imitate virtues, not vices. They should not gamble. They should not lie. They should maintain cleanliness. Every morning and evening they should repeat the name of Rama and thus cleanse their souls. We should all wear khadi. For this gives livelihood to the poor. Contributions will be raised all over the country today for the emancipation of the untouchables. I want that you should also contribute at least one pice each. I pray to God that the hearts of the so-called untouchables may become pure and they may be pillars of the Hindu community.

[From Hindi]

Aaj, 10-1-1927

229. SPEECH AT MEETING OF WOMEN, BANARAS[1]

January 9, 1927

Sisters, I have just come from one meeting and am on my way to another, a bigger one. Please listen peacefully to the few words I have to say to you. The first thing is that if you want swaraj or *Ramarajya* in India you have to become pure as Sita. Sita was pure in body and mind. When she was put through the ordeal on her return from Lanka, the flames did not even touch her. Why? Because she was pure not only in body but also in mind. No cloth was imported from England at the time, English cloth was not worn. All women plied the charkha and wore khadi. Foreign cloth does not add to your beauty. Real beauty consists in making body and mind pure. Only a woman who keeps body and mind pure can be worthy of our reverence. Therefore, sisters, wear khadi, ply the charkha and become pure. Make your sons and daughters pure by having them wear khadi. If you wish to give me something make some donation for khadi.

The other thing I wish to talk to you about is the death of Swami Shraddhanand. Swamiji is not dead: he lives in our hearts. He was brave; he had a noble soul. We have taken a bath in the Ganga and we have paid tribute to Swamiji. May God impart to us some of his qualities so that we can carry on his work.

[From Hindi]

Aaj, 12-1-1927

[1] The meeting was held in the Kashi Naresh Hall of the Hindu School.

230. SPEECH AT PUBLIC MEETING, BANARAS

January 9, 1927

Mahatmaji thanked the Municipal Board for the address presented to him and said it had been suggested to him that he should start his new programme from Banaras. He said:

I am sorry I have not come here to enunciate some new programme. Nor am I aware of any new programme. I am afraid therefore that those who have come to this meeting looking for a new programme will have to be disappointed. I put before the people only what I feel is to their good. There is nowhere else in the world such stark poverty as prevails in India. The poor want work. The peasantry want work for four months of the year. The purpose is not fulfilled by simply distributing money among the poor. This will make beggars of them. The best occupation for them, the best work for the peasantry is the charkha. No one has told me that there can be any simpler occupation than the charkha. I therefore appeal to you to wear khadi, ply the charkha and help in this programme. I appeal to you to go and see the khadi exhibition after this meeting. You will then know what fine khadi is now being produced. If people were to help in this, ten times as much could be accomplished.

God dwells in our hearts. If we listen to Him we shall know that it is our duty to wear cloth made by poor people. Foreigners would even distribute their cloth free to make it acceptable to us. Those who grudge paying a little extra money for the poor cannot be either true Hindus or true Mussalmans. For those who will not help the poor, it is futile to think of God.

I have just come from Bangali Tola and a meeting of women at the Hindu School. Women have made donations. Some of them have parted with even their jewellery. Here at this meeting also there are some sisters. I ask them too to be pure as Sitaji. When she was put through the ordeal, when she entered the fire, she did not get burnt, the flames did not so much as touch her. No foreign cloth ever came in contact with Sitaji's body. Sitaji and her maid both plied the charkha. During that age yarn was spun with hand and people wore hand-spun cloth. I appeal to the ladies to ply the charkha and wear khadi.

I am asked why I keep silent on the Hindu-Muslim question.

We have now lost grip of this question. Today is the *jalanjali*[1] day of Swami Shraddhanand. Let us today commune with his soul. A brother of ours became mad and killed him. In truth he is not dead. He lives yet. Had the assassin not become mad this tragedy would not have occurred. I receive letters saying that there are a number of people behind this. I do not know. But I know that this killing is against the teachings of the Koran. I cannot accept that Shraddhanandji was an enemy of the Mussalmans. I did not agree with all his views. All the same I have repeatedly said the Mussalmans should not consider Shraddhanandji, Malaviyaji and Lalaji their enemies. All have the right freely and fearlessly to express their views. All can preach their several religions. Swamiji was full of compassion for all living things. Now of course the untouchables are treated much more humanely than before. In this respect we have made some progress. Swami Shraddhanand had been associated with this work from a very early stage. Emancipation of the untouchables was the main part of his programme. The time is now coming when Hindus and Muslims will cleanse their hearts and God will be pleased. The only way in which we can please Swamiji's soul is for all of us to help in the work for the emancipation of the untouchables.

I must tell the Hindus to wash off the stain of untouchability. This will be true *shuddhi*. They should not think of revenge. If they do, they will cause pain to the soul of Shraddhanandji and disgrace Hinduism. Madness cannot be answered by madness. I appeal to the Hindus not to seek revenge, not to think of it. Otherwise they would cause pain to the soul of Shraddhanandji.

To the Mussalmans I have to say this. Let there not be a single Mussalman who approves this killing of Shraddhanandji even privately. There is nothing in the Koran to support this. If we wish to free India, we must cleanse our hearts.

[From Hindi]

Aaj, 12-1-1927

[1] Offering of water as part of obsequies

231. LETTER TO MIRABEHN

Unrevised

BANARAS *alias* KASHI,
January 10, 1927

CHI. MIRA,

I have your letter, or letters is it? I am writing this against my time for going to the station.

I am glad of all the varied experiences you are having. I shall not be angry so long as you keep your health and your mental balance. For the rest we learn through mistakes. Not that I know of mistakes made by you. But where there is consciousness of mistakes, readiness to mend is sufficient penance and antidote in a majority of cases.

I had rich experiences in Kashi, but of these I have no time to speak.

With love,

BAPU

From the original: C.W. 5196. Courtesy: Mirabehn

232. LETTER TO ASHRAM WOMEN

KASHI,
Silence Day, Pausa Sud 6 [January 10, 1927][1]

DEAR SISTERS,

Only yesterday I got the letter written by Chi. Radha. I see that your 7 o'clock prayers are going on regularly and that all of you feel interested in them. I am happy. What Kaka Saheb has said is certainly worth bearing in mind. Instead of replying by a mere yes or no, we should develop the ability to understand and explain the reasons for our reply.

Yesterday was the day of homage to Shraddhanandji. Pandit Malaviyaji is here in Kashi at present. He sent word at the last moment that we ought to go to the Ganga-ghat for a bath and prayers. I got ready and took with me the students of the Rash-

[1] *Pausa Sud* 6 seems to be a slip for *Pausa Sud* 7 which was a Monday.

triya Vidyapith who had come to see me. We formed ourselves in twos and started. Malaviyaji joined us and slowly our procession swelled. I have not time for describing the scene at the Ganga-ghat. It was simply grand. The ghat is not as clean as I would wish it to be.

After bath, we went for the *darshan* of Kashi Vishwanath. Mahadev will perhaps give you a description of other things there. The German lady was with us. It was doubtful whether she would be permitted to enter. She is a Buddhist and hence can be regarded as a Hindu. How could she be denied admittance? *I had decided that if she was stopped, I too would not go in.* But the priest kept quiet when he was told that she was a Hindu.

How can I describe the dirtiness of the street leading to the Kashi Vishwanath temple?

Blessings from
BAPU

From a photostat of the Gujarati: G.N. 3634

233. LETTER TO MANILAL GANDHI

KASHI,
Monday [January 10, 1927][1]

CHI. MANILAL,

I have your letter. There is no harm if Ba reads it. I have not given it to her so far, but I intend to. You would have done a good turn to Harilal if you had not given him even the ten rupees which you gave. But don't mind, since you have given it. I don't think you have made any big mistake. Often strictness results in real kindness and kindness turns out to be cruelty. If all people become strict with Harilal with a loving heart, his eyes would soon open. But all of us are full of weaknesses and, therefore, cannot cultivate such loving strictness. Being ourselves in need of false kindness, we show such kindness to others. I am not reproaching you for giving him ten rupees but am only trying to teach you wisdom. You will still have many ordeals to pass through.

I have been trying to do something for you. Have no worry on that account. But make yourself worthy. Do not waste a single

[1] Gandhiji was in Banaras on Monday, January 10, 1927.

moment. If you have time, write an article about E. A. either for *Young India* or *Navajivan* and send it to me immediately.

Blessings from
BAPU

From the Gujarati original: C.W. 1118. Courtesy: Sushilabehn Gandhi

234. LETTER TO MIRABEHN

January 10, 1927

CHI. MIRA,

I have your letter describing the drive with Hakimji. I do not mind either your tasting the dishes at Brijkishen's or the *pan* from Hakimji. The latter's tempting you with *pan* distresses me. It is bad stuff and he should never have offered it to you. But opinions differ. He evidently considers it to be harmless. However, the reasoning that you have employed for justifying the tasting of the dishes and the *pan* is in my opinion faulty. Why should one *know* the taste of what one does not need or wish to take? Do you know that this is the reasoning that has been applied to justify every form of vice? It is the million times told story of the forbidden apple: why should I not know the taste of the thing I am asked not to take or touch? But you must not worry. If you do not understand my reasoning, you must argue with me patiently. If you appreciate my reasoning, it is to serve as warning in the future. But it must not result in self-reproach. There is no cause for it. The incident is trivial. But trivialities possess deadly potentialities. Hence the paternal warning.

Now about your analysis of the Kanya Gurukul. I hope you have spoken about it to Vidyavati. But you must discuss it freely with Principals Ramdev and Sethi. Principal Ramdev is her guide and if he is convinced, immediate improvement can be made. I propose to send him the relevant extract from your letter. That will make your position quite clear. The insanitation, the indiscipline must go. The anti-Muslim feeling is a more difficult proposition. But you have to do your duty. Little girls' minds must not be poisoned if we can help it. But whilst you will talk about these things, you will remember your limits. You have gone out to learn Hindi and to observe and gain experience, not to reform or teach. Yours will, therefore, be remarks only by the way and merely as suggestions either for acceptance or rejection. Your own conduct is sufficient effort for reform otherwise.

I am writing this on the moving train during my silence which finishes at 9 p.m.

With love,

BAPU

[PS.]

Yes, when you go back to Delhi to inspect *takli*-spinning you may stay with Brijkishen.

BAPU

[PPS.]

Can you decipher my writing?

From the original: C.W. 5195. Courtesy: Mirabehn

235. LETTER TO NANABHAI I. MASHRUWALA

ON THE TRAIN,
Monday [January 10, 1927][1]

BHAISHRI NANABHAI,

I have your letter. I feel that Dastane's demand is reasonable. Just now I am touring for collecting funds. Hence I should go in the main to places where I can expect to obtain some contributions. But I think Akola is bound to be included in the itinerary. There is no question of my not visiting a place which has a devoted lover of khadi like you. Formerly I used to tour with the idea which you have explained. If you do not follow the difference, ask me again. Gomatibehn[2] must be free from her fever and Kishorelal must have left by now.

Blessings from
BAPU

SHRIYUT NANABHAI ICHCHHARAM MASHRUWALA
AKOLA DISTRICT

From a photostat of the Gujarati: C.W. 4319. Courtesy: Kanubhai Mashruwala

[1] The postmark bears the date January 13, 1927. Monday fell on January 10.

[2] Wife of Kishorelal Mashruwala

236. LETTER TO GANGABEHN VAIDYA

[After *January 10, 1927*][1]

CHI. GANGABEHN,

Never mind if you commit mistakes. If you keep on trying to avoid them, they will cease by and by.

Spiritual progress is easy for one whose mind is always occupied with thoughts of serving others. Since you are constantly engaged in such service, everything will be well with you.

Blessings from

BAPU

From the Gujarati original: C.W. 8704. Courtesy: Gangabehn Vaidya

237. LETTER TO COW-PROTECTION COMMITTEE, MYSORE

AS AT THE ASHRAM,
SABARMATI,
January 11, 1927

DEAR FRIEND,

I must apologize to you for the very long delay in acknowledging your letter of 27th November, 1926. I duly received your first intimation which I thought was purely formal and as I had nothing effective to say, I did not send you a reply. From your second letter, however, I observe that you were anxious to have my opinion. But when I received it I was so overwhelmed with work that I had no time to collect my thoughts and give you a considered reply. Even as it is, I am sending you this reply in the midst of my Bihar tour. I hope you will accept these facts as sufficient excuse for the delay that has been caused in sending you my reply. Probably now it is of no use, even so I gave myself the satisfaction of telling you that there was no discourtesy intended by me in the first instance in not replying and now in replying at a time when my reply may prove too late.

In matters of religion I am against any State interference, and the cow question is in India a mixed matter of religion and

[1] The letter was in reply to the addressee's dated January 10, 1927.

economy. So far as economy is concerned, I have no doubt that it is the concern of every State, whether Hindu or Mussalman, to conserve the cattle supply. But, if I have understood your questionnaire rightly, the underlying note is whether the State would be justified in interposing itself between Hindus and Mussalmans and regulating cow slaughter even for purposes which Mussalmans consider to be religious. In India which I consider to be as much the land of Hindus born in it as of Mussalmans, Christians and others born in it, even a Hindu State may not prohibit cow slaughter for purposes considered to be religious by any of its subjects without the consent of the intelligent majority of such subjects so long as such slaughter is conducted in private and without any intention of provoking or giving offence to Hindus. That the very knowledge of any such slaughter would give offence to Hindus is inevitable. But unfortunately we know that in India cow slaughter is often resorted to to defy and wound Hindu sentiment. This should be put down by every State that has the slightest regard for its subjects. But in my opinion the economic side of the cow question, if it is properly handled, automatically provides for the delicate religious side. Cow slaughter should be and can be made economically impossible, whereas unfortunately, of all the places in the world, it is the sacred animal of the Hindus which has become the cheapest for slaughter. To this end I suggest the following:

(1) The State should in the open market buy out every [head of] cattle offered for sale by outbidding every other buyer.

(2) The State should run dairies in all principal towns ensuring a cheap supply of milk.

(3) The State should run tanneries where the hides, bones, etc., of all dead cattle in its possession should be utilized and should offer to buy again in the open market all privately-owned dead cattle.

(4) The State should keep model cattle farms and instruct the people in the art of breeding and keeping cattle.

(5) The State should make liberal provision . . .[1]

From a microfilm: S.N. 12667

[1] The letter is incomplete.

238. LETTER TO A. C. C. HARVEY

As at the Ashram,
Sabarmati,
January 11, 1927

DEAR FRIEND[1],

Your letter written on Christmas Day has followed me in my travels and I am able to overtake it only today. I would ask you to believe me when I tell you that I have nothing against General Dyer or even Sir Michael O'Dwyer.[2] They were both creatures[3] and symptoms of a deep-seated disease of which I had not sufficient knowledge when I pleaded for co-operation at Amritsar. Whatever force there was in my plea was in my honest belief behind it. The Rowlatt Act and the subsequent events having opened my eyes, I cannot summon to my aid the fervour of Amritsar. My belief is shaken. Nothing has happened to restore it, though I am eager for its restoration. It gives me no pleasure to disbelieve men and measures. But I shall be false if I shut my eyes to facts as I see them. I think that non-co-operation is a fundamental fact in God's plan, even as darkness is. There is no such thing as co-operation if there is no non-co-operation.[4] If we give our co-operation for the prosecution of that which is good, we must withdraw it from that which is evil. I believe that the present British administration of India is

[1] A.C.C. Harvey was on the staff of the Khalsa College, Amritsar, during 1919-20, and met Gandhiji when he visited the institution (S.N. 12094).

[2] Harvey had referred to a meeting at Bombay on December 21, at which Sir Chimanlal Setalwad and Jinnah had "urged the policy of 'back to Amritsar' ", whereas Gandhiji, he recalled, had persuaded the Congress at Amritsar to adopt a 'policy of moderation and co-operation'. Harvey had observed that "worse things were done on the nationalist side than that of the Government". *Ibid.*

[3] The source has "preachers".

[4] Criticizing the policy of non-co-operation as not being right "in the light of the universal religion", Harvey had commended "the policy of co-operation, of friendly discussion, of 'getting together' to talk over things, to explain viewpoints, quietly, sincerely and with desire to understand, as so ably exemplified by such men as Lord Reading, Lord Irwin". Further, Harvey had described the policy of non-co-operation as not only negative and therefore barren, "not only politically wrong, but also *irreligious*, contrary to the will of God". He had appealed to Gandhiji "to ponder over these words so that you may perhaps be helpful to them to give a right lead" (S.N. 12094).

on the whole not good but positively evil. The military policy and the revenue policy which includes the hideous traffic in drink and drugs and the preference given to English interests over Indian are causing progressive deterioration both moral and material of the people of this unhappy country. English people are not all conscious of this tremendous wrong that is being done to the country and they will never be if we continue to give our co-operation whether through ignorance, through hypocrisy or through weakness. Non-co-operation, therefore, is the only alternative to an armed rebellion. It has been suggested that the object can be achieved by persuasion and argument. In my opinion, which is based upon extensive experience, argument has only a limited place in an endeavour to persuade people. In deepest matters argument hopelessly fails. But whilst I feel so strongly about my position, let me assure you that my non-co-operation is itself designed to bring about co-operation. I need hardly assure you. . . .[1]

[A. C. C. Harvey
Government Intermediate College
Ludhiana
Punjab]

From a photostat: S.N. 12804

239. A LETTER[2]

As at the Ashram,
Sabarmati,
January 12, 1927

DEAR FRIEND,

I do not propose to deal with your letter in the columns of *Young India*, because I think the average reader has not the difficulty that has presented itself to you. I could certainly call myself a votary of non-violence, if in spite of the consciousness that I kill thousands of invisible creatures, I incessantly long to be free from the necessity of so killing and avoid every occasion possible for so doing. And, I therefore long to be free from the bondage of the flesh which is birth and death. My refusal to live the present life does not end the agony. But refusal to have

[1] The text in the source is incomplete.

[2] The addressee is not known.

another body after the dissolution of the existing one, is a possibility capable of realization.

Yours sincerely,

From a photostat: S.N. 12805

240. SPEECH AT DHANBAD[1]

January 12, 1927

He said that on an enquiry from Babu Rajendra Prasad about the inclement weather he had come to know that rains even in winter were not quite unusual in the province and that that was to some extent necessary too. He was no doubt conscious of the immense difficulties the audience had to face on account of the rain; his own difficulties were no less. But he was capable of working in the midst of all sorts of difficulties, his life had been only a prolonged story of his fight with difficulties of every description.

After announcing the meeting to be addressed by him at six next evening, he proceeded to explain the purpose of his visit. He said that they were perhaps aware that his tour was specially intended to preach the message of the charkha and khaddar. He admitted that there was enough field in the country for other activities with a view to the attainment of swaraj but he had taken to the charkha because he had found that that could be prescribed with equal force for all—Hindus and Muslims, males and females, men and boys, touchables and untouchables. The charkha was the universal thing and as such it was to be taken up by all according to the capacity of each individual. Working at the wheel was the sacred business of every Indian; everyone was required to join this universal *yajna*. But if that was not possible for all, they could do one thing. They could at least put on khaddar.

Continuing, he said that khaddar work to be conducted on a large scale throughout India demanded a large sum of money to be spent over it. That money was to be supplied by the country. Nearly 16 lakhs were already collected and spent and as a result, nearly 50 thousand women who had formerly nothing to do, and about 4,000 men who also formerly had almost nothing to do, had got employment. Weavers, many of whom were compelled to give up their profession on account of hard competition with Lancashire weavers, had once more found occupation, while large sums had already gone to the carders and ginners. Spinning, therefore, was the saviour of the poor, while the middle-class men also could derive much benefit from it. Without humbly approaching the Government, without supplicating the rich, middle-class young men could solve a good deal of their unemployment

[1] The meeting was held in a local hall.

problem by taking to the charkha. Riches were of course not to be expected from this work, but young men could very well earn an honest living by reverting to khaddar work.

Proceeding, he said that the fund, for which he was appealing for money, was called Deshbandhu Memorial Fund, started to commemorate the sacred memory of the late Deshbandhu. Khaddar was very dear to his heart. He had realized that the charkha was the thing for the whole of India and through that alone one could approach the masses for village reconstruction work which was the unrealized dream of his life. A few days before his death, he had expressed his wish to the speaker to accompany him (Mahatmaji) on his tour for khaddar work. But "man proposes, God disposes". Before he could begin to work according to his plan, he was snatched away by the cruel hand of death. It was in order to fulfil his last wish, said Mahatmaji, that the All-India Deshbandhu Memorial Fund, to be utilized by the All-India Spinners' Association, was inaugurated. He referred to the circumstances under which the All-Bengal Deshbandhu Memorial Fund was allowed to be spent over the Hospital, while at the very time he had appealed for money for the All-India Memorial Fund for khaddar work. It was time, said the speaker, that each one of them contributed his quota to fulfil the last wishes of Deshbandhu. By contributing to this fund the donor might serve two useful purposes at the same time; firstly they would honour the sacred memory of Deshbandhu who lived and died for them, and, secondly, they would be helping the poor with work and money.

Proceeding, Mahatmaji said that to purchase one yard of khaddar was to help the poor men of their country to the extent of about four annas, whereas spending money over foreign cloth was to send the same abroad to the untold miseries of their own people. To purchase Indian mill-made cloth did not mean helping the poor, for it was the capitalists who used to enjoy the largest amount of profit, doling out a negligible amount to the labourers, which was not sufficient for them even to keep their body and soul together. Three-fourths of the money spent over Indian mill-made cloths, said the speaker, filled the already overflowing coffers of the capitalists, while the labourers who were really in need of money did not get collectively more than one-fourth of the profit. The charkha was the only effective weapon to fight the poverty of the country to a successful close.

Mahatmaji then appealed for money. He wanted everyone present to contribute his mite for this noble work and asked them to send the money to the proper authority if they had not it with them at that time. He exhorted the audience to solemnly promise in that hall to put on khaddar habitually for all time to come. He said that he would ask them even to burn their foreign clothes, if they had any. But if they could not go so far as that, they must henceforward boycott all foreign clothes without the least hesitation. Khaddar had become the burning passion of his life because he had found that and that alone could give food to the poor. People might call him mad, but he could not give up that work for anything. He asked everyone present in that hall to pay what little he could. He did not want that people should pay money out of fear or shame; he wanted every one of them to feel the nobility of the cause and then do whatever lay in his power.

Referring to untouchability, he said that that was the greatest blot upon Hindu society and that should be wiped out at the soonest possible date. Hinduism never taught one man to consider another man as untouchable. By observing the custom of untouchability, Hindus were committing a sin. Swami Shraddhanand gave his life for the sake of the removal of untouchability. It was their duty to take up that work of service to the poor and the untouchables.

Incidentally he referred to the Hindu-Muslim tension and deplored the murder of Swamiji. But Swamiji's death could be turned to good account, if both the Hindus and the Muslims cleansed their hearts with his blood. That would be the work of purification, that would be a real *shuddhi* work. What was the duty of the Hindus ? They should not seek to retaliate. The teaching of all religions was not to return evil for evil but good for evil. All the religions taught that the greatest conquest was the conquest of one's own self. The Hindus should attain that self-possession. Abdul Rashid was a poor creature; he alone was not responsible for this diabolical deed. The bulk of the Muslim Press in Delhi and all those who had been holding up Swami Shraddhanand, Lala Lajpat Rai and Pandit Madan Mohan Malaviya as the enemies of Islam collectively contributed to the murder. The results of those things were before them. The whole atmosphere of the country demanded purification. Enthusiasm like that of 1922 was necessary for their success in the battle they had undertaken, but that could not come until the process of purification had reached its completion. Everyone should, therefore, concentrate all his attention upon self-purification. It was wholly unwise to be inimical to the enemies, one should rather pity them.

The Searchlight, 16-1-1927

241. *INDEPENDENCE*

Year after year a resolution is moved in the Congress to amend the Congress creed so as to define swaraj as complete independence and year after year happily the Congress throws out the resolution by an overwhelming majority. The rejection of the resolution is proof of the sanity of the Congress. The moving of the resolution betrays the impatience (pardonable in the circumstances) of some ardent Congressmen who have lost all faith in the British intentions and who think that the British Government will never render justice to India. The advocates of independence forget that they betray want of faith in human nature and therefore in themselves. Why do they think that there can never be change of heart in those who are guiding the British people? Is it not more correct and more dignified to own that there is no change of heart because we are weak? Nature abhors weakness. We want from the British people and the world at large not mercy but justice that is our due. And justice will come when it is deserved by our being and feeling strong.

I am sure that the staunchest votary of independence does not mean that he will not have any British association on any terms whatsoever. Even when he says so, he means, as one of the supporters of the resolution admitted in answer to my question, that the British people will never accept association on equal terms. This is totally different from rejecting British association on any terms.

Indeed the word swaraj is all-embracing. It does include complete independence as it includes many other things. To give it one definite meaning is to narrow the outlook, and to limit what is at present happily limitless. Let the content of swaraj grow with the growth of national consciousness and aspirations. We may be satisfied today with dominion status. The future generations may not be, may want something better. Swaraj without any qualifying clause includes that which is better than the best one can conceive or have today. Swaraj means even under dominion status a capacity to declare independence at will. So long as we have not achieved that capacity, we have no swaraj. This is the least it should mean. South Africa has achieved that status today. It is a partnership at will of free peoples. Between Britain and the Dominions there is a partnership at will on terms of equality and for mutual benefit. What India will finally have is for her and her alone to determine. This power of determination remains unfettered by the existing creed. What therefore the creed does retain is the possibility of evolution of swaraj within the British Empire or call it the British Commonwealth. The cryptic meaning of swaraj I have often described to be within the Empire if possible, without if necessary. I venture to think that it is not possible to improve upon that conception. It is totally consistent with national self-respect and it provides for the highest growth of the nation.

After all, the real definition will be determined by our action, the means we adopt to achieve the goal. If we would but concentrate upon the means, swaraj will take care of itself. Our exploration should, therefore, take place in the direction of determining not the definition of an indefinable term like swaraj but in discovering the ways and means.

Young India, 13-1-1927

242. NOTE

Indians in Panama

The Legislative Assembly of the Republic of Panama recently passed an Immigration Restriction Act prohibiting the entry of British Indians among others. President Chiari had in a well-considered message returned the Bill to the Assembly advising considerable amendments and reconsideration. But the Assembly refused to make the amendments recommended except in matters that were inevitable. The Assembly defended its restriction upon the liberty of British Indians on the ground of protection of the rights of posterity. There are at present not more than perhaps thirty Sindhi Indian merchants of fancy goods. It was acknowledged that their presence was no menace to the inhabitants of Panama. Nevertheless the law is retrospective in its effect with the exception that those who can prove continuous previous domicile of ten years may receive exemption certificates. I hardly think there are many settlers there who can prove continuous residence in Panama for such a long period. If African experience is any guide, Indian settlers abroad are not in the habit of staying out of India for such a long period. The matter is now, I understand, before the Foreign Office. It remains to be seen how far that office is able to protect the rights of the resident Indian population and of those who may choose to emigrate to Panama in search of an honest livelihood.

Young India, 13-1-1927

243. MESSAGE TO CONGRESSMEN

Have faith. Along with intellectual capacity develop strength of character.

[From Hindi]

Aaj, 13-1-1927

244. SPEECH AT DHANBAD[1]

January 13, 1927

Mahatma Gandhi in replying thanked the commissioners for the welcome addresses they had presented him. He thanked particularly the commissioners of the Municipality for frankly confessing that khaddar and charkha were not much in use in the jurisdiction of their municipality. He said that he used to take keen interest in municipal affairs even when he was in South Africa. He knew that towns played a prominent part in the affairs of the country and that almost all movements in the modern world sprang from the towns. He was aware further that sense of civic responsibility was to be awakened in their young men. But in the peculiar condition of India, towns were at the most only of secondary importance. India lived in villages and towns, sank into insignificance when compared with seven lakhs of villages. This importance of village life in India was not to be lost sight of by the commissioners of the municipalities. There was a growing tendency in this country on the part of the educated men to cut off all their connection with villages and wipe them out of their memory. This tendency was to be checked. In Europe the villages depended for everything upon the towns which were the centres of all sorts of activities. But in India it was the villages which nourished the towns and as such it was the duty of every townsman to see that the healthy growth of the villagers was not interfered with in any way. One wondered how India could be so poor in spite of her exports exceeding her imports. The

[1] At the meeting, held in the morning in the Dhanbad town hall, Gandhiji was presented addresses by the Dhanbad Municipality and the Local Board. Gandhiji addressed altogether five meetings at Dhanbad, Jharia and other places.

reason was that crores of rupees went out of this country to add to the prosperity of other people while the majority of their own men did not know what it was to have two full meals a day. Whatever little money was left in this country went to the coffers of merchants and middle men. He (Mahatmaji) did not envy their lot but the poor villages were not to be forgotten. They themselves were starving while they were supplying the townspeople not only with food but also with other luxuries. It was to find out a few morsels of food for these hungry millions that he was asking them to take to the charkha. The poor, weak, miserable villagers could eat and live if only they all used khaddar in preference to all other cloth. He wished them all to work at the charkha as a sacred duty but if they could not do so they could wear khaddar at least. He said that he was glad that they had introduced spinning on a small scale in their jurisdiction but the work remained still incomplete. All their activities would remain incomplete until they perfected the khaddar organization. He himself would not be satisfied till then. To work for khaddar was to work for the poor. That was why he had been devoting all his time and energy to the work. It was their duty to take up that work for the sake of the poor, for the country and for God.

Concluding, he thanked them once more for the warm reception they had accorded him.

The Searchlight, 16-1-1927

245. SPEECH AT PUBLIC MEETING, KATRAS[1]

January 13, 1927

He said that he was glad to see them there. Last time when he was at Jharia, he had no opportunity to go to that place [Katras]. Jharia, he said, was a place which attracted people, both capitalists and labourers, from all parts of India. Labourers were the chief inhabitants of that place and as such he wanted to speak a few words to them.

Continuing, he said that he used to call himself also a labourer. If anybody enquired about his calling, he used to say that he was a weaver, or a cultivator. He would rather like to be called a scavenger. The profession of a scavenger was not to be looked down upon. He did a great benefit to human society. His profession was to cleanse the most dirty portion of a house. Society was, therefore, highly indebted to him. His was a profession of service and it was unwise to consider him low. His (speaker's) mother, in fact, every mother, did the same thing as a scavenger. Did they hate their mothers for that reason? If his own mother had not done the work

[1] The meeting was held in a spacious *pandal*. Gandhiji spoke after an address of welcome in Hindi was presented to him.

of a scavenger for him in his boyhood, he could not have lived so long and come in their midst to address them. It was not due to the profession that a scavenger should be looked down upon. Unless the heart of a man was dirty, there was no reason why he should be considered low, no matter how low his profession might be. His appeal, therefore, to the scavengers as a matter of fact, to all labourers, was that they should begin to cleanse themselves simultaneously with cleansing the household of other persons. He was aware that the labourers were addicted to drinking, gambling, smoking and other evil habits. They must be free of all these vices. He was in favour of total prohibition, but as long as that could not be achieved, they should themselves try to get rid of that pernicious habit. Credit lay in a man's abstinence in the midst of all sorts of temptations. He appealed to them to give up drinking for God's sake as well as for their own sake.

Referring to gambling, he said that that was a most vicious practice. The Pandavas lost their all on that account. But they recovered at last because they were on the side of truth. Yudhishthira was himself repentant for what he did. Referring to their lustful habit, he said that he was aware that there were people who used to leave their wives and destroy their health and wealth after vile prostitutes. That was a very bad habit. All women, other than one's wife, were to be considered as sisters.

Smoking of *bidi* and *ganja* was also to be given up. He could not understand why people smoked *ganja*. He knew that even rich and learned men smoked cigarettes and *bidis*. But that was no reason why they also should be addicted to the same. There was no reason why one man should be addicted to vicious habits because another man was used to them. His appeal to even the educated men was that they should give up smoking.

Continuing, he said that labourers should remember that there were men who were poorer than them. They (the labourers) had money to spend over wine, gambling, smoking and all that, but there were people in villages who could not get even sufficient food and clothing to keep themselves alive. They could at least earn about 15 to 20 rupees, but their brothers in villages could seldom see the face of a pice. Had they any feeling for them? They themselves were poor. Was it not very reasonable, then, that they should realize the miseries of those who were poorer than even them, he asked. If they felt like that, it was their duty to wear khaddar exclusively. They should clothe themselves with khaddar woven with pure yarn spun by their poor sisters in villages. Whatever they paid for khaddar was paid to those poor creatures. Women who could not earn even a penny were earning about two annas a day each. He was appealing to them for that money to be paid to their poor fellow beings. They could help them with that money by wearing khaddar. The law of God was that man should sympathize with his fellow-creatures in distress. He appealed, therefore, in God's name to them to exclude all clothes except khaddar and help him with money in cash, no matter how little it was, to carry on that work. Khaddar worth Rs. 96 thousand was produced in Bihar the previous year and about 60 thousand worth was sold within a period of six months. All this money went to the homes of the poor. A good deal of money was now spent over the selling of khaddar. If they purchased khaddar as they purchased foreign cloth, much of that money could be saved and utilized for the purpose of production. If they decided to do that, the entire amount of khaddar required in the country could be produced here without any difficulty. What was necessary was their sympathy and support; would they deny that?

Addressing the ladies he said that, if they wanted swaraj, which term was synonymous with *Ramraj*, they should each be like Sita. Sita was pure of heart, she kept her body clean by wearing hand-spun and hand-woven khaddar. She lived at a time when the charkha was to be found in every household and every woman used to spin. That time was to be revived again. The charkha should even now find as important a place as the household hearth.

Addressing others, the Mahatma said that, if they wanted freedom they would have to undergo considerable sacrifice. The minimum they could do was to put on khaddar. The khaddar movement must receive their whole-hearted support; they must render every possible financial support to that cause. He then narrated the circumstances in which the All-India Deshbandhu Memorial Fund was inaugurated and appealed to the audience to honour the sacred memory of the departed great by contributing to that fund.

Continuing, he said that the Deshbandhu Memorial Fund was to be utilized for the purpose of spreading khaddar. They had already got some money for the Fund but the work they had undertaken demanded more and more money. Sixty crores of rupees annually went out of the country; their aim was to keep that money here. A huge sum was, therefore, to be spent over that. Their task was great, but he hoped to fulfil it with their help. Everyone could pay to that fund without any difficulty; even Government servants could contribute to that. He hoped that he would not go disappointed from that place.

Referring to untouchability, he said that Swami Shraddhanand sacrificed his life for that cause. They should remove this blot at least for the sake of Swamiji. Hinduism had nothing to do with that pernicious system. The *Gita* never taught a man to consider another as untouchable.

Referring to Hindu-Muslim unity, he said that both the communities were to go through the process of purification before they could hope to attain that unity. To the Muslims, he said that, if anyone of them considered the murder of Swamiji as a praiseworthy act on the part of the murderer, it was a great mistake. He claimed to be a *sanatani* Hindu, but he had studied the Koran with as much reverence as the *Gita*. But he had nowhere found in the Koran any approval of such dastardly deeds. On the contrary, there were passages there distinctly against violence. If violence was to be committed, it was to be committed upon one's own self for the purpose of fighting the evils in oneself, not upon another person. Hindus had become weak and cowardly; how could they expect to rise in spite of their weaknesses? The real *shuddhi* work was the work of self-purification and it was the duty of everyone of them to go through that process. He prayed to God to help them in their work.[1]

The Searchlight, 19-1-1927

246. SPEECH AT PUBLIC MEETING, JHARIA[2]

January 13, 1927

Mahatma Gandhi, in addressing the meeting, said that he was glad that the president of the Employees' Association had complied with his request and did not read the address written in English. He had received two addresses in the morning which were written in English. But he objected to the third, because there were few people in the meeting who could understand that language. He would have very much appreciated the address if it was written either in Hindi or in Bengali. He had no quarrel with the English language; it was, indeed, a good language. He claimed to have some knowledge of it. If he had any ill feeling against the English language, he would not have conducted an English paper. But all occasions were not favourable for using that language. They had their lingua franca, that is, Hindi. They could very well use that language on interprovincial matters no matter if it was faulty. A man was not to be judged by his words, they were to see whether his heart was sincere. He himself might speak grammatically incorrect Hindi, but his motive was honest and that was enough to recommend his speech to them.

Continuing, he said that Jharia was a place where people, Hindus, Muslims, Sikhs, Christians, Marwaris, Gujaratis, Bengalis, Biharis, in fact, people from all provinces of India flocked together. He hoped that they all lived together on friendly terms without bearing ill will to anyone.

Proceeding, he narrated the havoc caused to India by imported cloth. He said that it was but natural and desirable that man should try to do good to all, irrespective of their nationality and religion. But it was monstrous for a man to help others in such a way as to incur irreparable loss to his own house. Why did they put on foreign cloth then? Was it to help the weavers of Manchester? Certainly not. The one answer he had found to this question was that it was a fashion to put on foreign clothes and that khaddar was rough and coarse. But would they refuse the bread prepared by their mothers if it was bad and go begging from door to door for better bread? Khaddar was the

[1] At the meeting, a purse of Rs. 885 was presented to Gandhiji and some money collected on the spot.

[2] At the meeting an address of welcome was presented to Gandhiji by the members of the Indian Colliery Employees' Association, Jharia.

gift of their motherland and therefore sacred to them. They might demand of their mothers for better bread; but, as long as that was not ready, they had no other alternative but to take that contentedly. Similarly, they might try to improve the quality of khaddar but as long as that could not be done, they had to remain content with what was available, no matter how coarse it was.

Proceeding, he said that a characteristic feature of Indian civilization was that a man was to help his fellowmen in distress. By wearing khaddar, they could perform their religious duty, namely, helping the poor. Their *Gita* taught them that a man who did not perform *yajna* committed sin thereby. Spinning at the wheel was *yajna* for them; a spinning-wheel was to be kept in every household as a sacred altar. He said that he was just coming from the local Khadi Bhandar. He had seen that khaddar worth only Rs. 1,000 was kept in stock in that shop and even that could not be consumed. He did not know how many rupees worth of foreign cloth was sold in Jharia, but he was sure that the sale of foreign cloth exceeded that of khaddar many times. It was a matter of great regret to him that even such a small khaddar shop could not be conducted in Jharia. He appealed to all to make it a point to wear khaddar. He requested them to solemnly promise to discard all foreign cloth and habitually wear khaddar.

Addressing the labourers, he asked them to observe temperance and put on khaddar in preference to all other cloth. They would thereby be giving food and clothing to hundreds of their own hungry men and women who could not earn even a single pice for want of occupation. Mahatmaji next touched upon untouchability and Hindu-Muslim tension.

Replying to the address, he said that he was glad that the work of the association was improving and he congratulated the organizers on their success. As to the second, namely, the relations between the capitalist and the labourer, he assured them that his sympathy was always with the poor labourers and that his aim was to establish harmony and peace between the employer and the employee. He said that he had, of course, done something for the labourers of Jamshedpur but he was not fully aware of local conditions. In Jamshedpur the leaders of the labourers included some of his own men and even his friend and brother, Mr. Andrews. Nevertheless, if his help was at any time necessary, he would try to do what little he could. He, of course, did not believe that all capitalists were bad and oppressive; on the contrary, he knew many who had really the good of the employees at heart. He was for equal and legitimate rights for all. He advised the labourers to be on the right path and said that he was sure that truth would triumph at last. He concluded his speech by once more appealing for money.[1]

The Searchlight, 19-1-1927

[1] At the end of the speech Gandhiji was presented a purse of Rs. 1,001.

247. *SPEECH AT PUBLIC MEETING, AURANGABAD*[1]

January 14, 1927

He said that when he toured in Bihar on a previous occasion he had not the opportunity to come to that place. He was glad, therefore, to meet them there and thanked them for coming over to that place from distant villages. He said that his visit was intended to appeal to them to do some little work for India and for themselves and hoped that they would not disappoint him.

India, he said, was a poor country. Those who lived in the towns could scarcely imagine how poor the villagers were; even those villagers who had come to the meeting did not know that there were men living in far-off villages who were poorer than them even. These poor people lived in woeful obscurity dragging somehow or other their miserable existence to a melancholy close. The people of the towns depended for their livelihood upon the villagers who, in their turn, got money from those miserable creatures. They produced wealth for the whole country, while they themselves had no means to keep their bodies and souls together. The railways of India might bring some amount of wealth to a fortunate few, but they deprived the real producers of wealth of even their means of livelihood. He appealed to them in the name of God for those poor, wretched and miserable villagers who were the very backbone of Indian society.

Continuing, he described how the imports of foreign cloth had contributed to the misery and poverty of their people and explained how a check on that unlimited import might give an effective check to the growing poverty of the country. The most effective weapon he had devised to fight the course of such unnatural events was the spinning-wheel and he said he had come to recommend that to them. He was confident that if they could effectively boycott foreign cloth and take exclusively to khaddar, they could proceed a long way towards their goal, namely, swaraj. But if the political significance of khaddar was not recognized, there were other grounds strong enough to recommend it. If khaddar was not to be used as a political weapon, they might use it with a view to helping thousands of their poor countrymen. The charkha, he said, was their *Annapurna* because it had the power to give food and drink to almost an unlimited number of poor men. The poverty of their people was a universally recognized fact; even English chroniclers had in their books testified to the fact that there were thousands of people in India who did not know what it was to have two full meals a day. He himself had seen with his own

[1] About 10,000 people were present at the meeting which was held in the open maidan near the Dak Bungalow and which Gandhiji addressed for about half an hour.

eyes in Orissa what he had so long read only in books. People in Orissa were so poor that they had really no means of subsistence. Was it not their duty to help them?—he asked. If they could not help them in any other way, they might help them by wearing khadi. The work of khaddar could be done by all —Hindus and Muslims, males and females, men and boys. The Bengalis and the Punjabis, all could join this work and contribute their mite to its success. There was no ban even upon Government servants in respect of wearing khadi. Khaddar produced by their own brothers and sisters in the peaceful atmosphere of villages situated far off from the din and bustle of modern industrialism, deserved every sympathy and encouragement from them. It was sanctified with their memories of the past; it was their religious duty to put on khaddar in preference to every other kind of cloth.

Continuing, he said that money spent on foreign cloth went into the pockets of the weavers of Manchester and Lancashire, while that spent over Indian mill-made cloth filled the already-full coffers of the Ahmedabad merchants. It pained him to think that in spite of there being expert manufacturers in India, Indians had to pay so much money to foreign manufacturers. The East India Company might have been responsible for the extinction of their industry during the first period of their reign. They might have put an end to their textile industry by violence and their undesirable methods. But who was responsible for the continuance of that state of things, he asked. If they even now began to patronize khaddar, Indian cloth might once more become the observed of all observers of the world. They should take to spinning and khaddar as a means of *prayashchitta*. Even the rich men should begin to spin, not for money, but for setting an example to the credulous and imitative people of the villages. Hinduism strictly enjoined upon everyone to perform *yajna*. *Yajna* was that which was performed not in the interest of one's own self, but in the interest of others. In the present circumstances of India, no other work could be more beneficial to the poor villagers than spinning and it was therefore the best possible *yajna* for the Indians.

Proceeding, the Mahatma said that in Bihar alone they had distributed Rs. 29,000 and Rs. 36,000 among the spinners and weavers, respectively. It seemed to him that the people of Bihar had love for khaddar, but if all of them had patronized it they might have distributed more wealth among the poor inhabitants of the province. About one hundred years ago, Patna used to produce very fine khadi which was exported to foreign countries and the people of those countries used that cloth as an object of luxury. The wheel had turned and India instead of exporting fine cloth to foreign countries consumed imported cloth worth crores of rupees and the people of India felt proud to wear fine foreign cloth. They as people of Bihar must remember the progress that the textile industry had made in Patna in the past and it was their duty to revive those good old days. They could do so by patronizing khaddar in every possible manner. Khaddar had made much progress; fine khaddar was now available and the price also had considerably gone down as compared with what it was in 1921. If the people made adequate response it might still be made cheaper.

He then appealed for funds for the All-India Spinners' Association and then dealt with the problem of untouchability and the problem of Hindu-Muslim unity.

He said that swaraj which had ever been the dream of his life had almost come in 1921-22. The real *shuddhi* work, namely, the process of purification, had begun at that time. A wave of enthusiasm had swept over the country and that was why they could come almost near their goal. The same chapter was to be repeated again, but that could not be done till dissensions and disunions kept them hopelessly divided.

Proceeding, he said that those who entered the Councils did it with the sincere desire of doing good to the country and they might do some good work as well. But how many could go to the Councils and how many were there who had the right of voting, he asked. Sixty lakhs of voters did not constitute the whole of India; his aim was to raise the thirty crores of Indian people. Khaddar, he believed, might serve as a link between the rich and the poor; the spinning-wheel might bring about unity and harmony among the entire population of India. He appealed once more to the people to contribute to the funds of the All-India Spinners' Association and prayed to God to help them in doing their duty.[1]

The Searchlight, 21-1-1927

248. ENTRY IN VISITORS' BOOK[2]

GAYA,
Pausa Sud 12, 1983 [*January 15, 1927*][3]

I feel very happy to see this library. While thanking the donor, I pray for the progress of the library.

From a photostat of the Hindi: G.N. 2509

[1] At the end of the meeting, Gandhiji was presented a purse of Rs. 2501.

[2] Of the Munnalal Library at Gaya

[3] There was no *Pausa Sud* 12 in this year. Gandhiji was in Gaya on January 15, 1927 which corresponded to *Pausa Sud* 13.

249. TELEGRAM TO MANIBEHN PATEL

GAYA,
January 15, 1927

YOUR DELIGHTFUL LETTER. MASTER CARDING GINNING SOON.

BAPU

[From Gujarati]
Bapuna Patro—Manibehn Patelne, p. 46

250. SPEECH AT MEETING, GAYA[1]

January 15, 1927

Mahatmaji, speaking in Hindi, regretted that the address presented to him on behalf of the municipality was written in English. He said that whenever he found an opportunity he had repeatedly asked the people to present him addresses either in the vernacular of their province or in the national language of India, namely, Hindi. He had no spite against the English language; he himself used that language on special occasions, but it was undesirable that they should use it while addressing their own men. He requested the municipality to use Hindi whenever they presented any address, not merely to himself, but to any other Indian leader.

Continuing, he said that Gaya was really a sacred place to the Hindus, a place of pilgrimage for them. But it pained him to see the deplorable state of the roads of that sacred city which was frequented by people from all parts of the country. He had occasion that morning to see some of the roads in Gaya. They surpassed in dirtiness even the roads of Ahmedabad, which was an old city and home of many poor people, which fact might be an excuse for the municipality of that place. He regretted to say that he had never before seen such dirty roads in any part of India. Gaya, being a place of all-India interest, its municipality ought to have been an ideal one, but he was sadly disappointed. He said that the commissioners should be up and doing in reforming the municipal arrangements of that great city. How could they do so? In order to achieve that end, the commissioners should themselves take up the work. Mere dependence upon paid sweepers and scavengers would not better the situation. He would rather request the chairman and the commissioners of the Board to take the broomsticks and buckets of water

[1] At the meeting, Gandhiji was presented addresses by the Municipality and the District Board.

themselves and proceed to cleanse the roads and latrines of the city. Towns were of considerable importance to the development of a country. Growth of civic responsibilities in the people was an urgent necessity for their political emancipation. He said that the case of Gaya was not an exception. There were many other municipalities in India which were guilty of such bad administration. But the exceptional character of Gaya city demanded it to be free from these evils. There was nothing to be ashamed of in sweeping the streets; he himself had done it in many places; he had done it even in Bihar, in Champaran. He was no lover of Western civilization; he would rather oppose all Western influences which tended to injure the vital interests of India. But he would welcome all that was good in Western culture. In respect of municipal administration, they had much to learn from the Western people. Glasgow and Birmingham were formerly as dirty as Gaya, or perhaps even worse. But the way in which the municipal administrators of those two places had reformed them was worthy to be imitated by the municipal commissioners of India. He hoped that the Gaya Municipality will be prompt in reforming the state of that city.

Continuing, he regretted that the Chairman of the Municipality did not inform him in the morning that he and his colleagues could not agree on two points, namely, khaddar and removal of untouchability. In that case he might make time to try to convince them on those two points. If they wanted to create a link between them and the villagers, the charkha and khaddar were unavoidable for them. As regards untouchability, he did not think that there was any necessity of arguing on that point, after the death of Swami Shraddhanand. He claimed to be a *sanatani* Hindu. But he had never found any of the Hindu scriptures sanctioning untouchability in the form in which it was practised by them. If untouchability was not removed, Hindu society might altogether perish in the near future. There were only three religions in the world, namely, Christianity, Islam and Hinduism. He would regard Buddhism and Sikhism as branches of Hinduism, as the Hindu Mahasabha had defined it. But the mighty Hindu society was fast disintegrating. Christianity and Islam, in fact, the entire non-Hindu population of the world, were keenly watching the movements of the Hindu society. If they wanted to justify their existence and revive their old glory, it was their clear duty to remove that blot from Hinduism.

He had received that morning a cable from Mr. Andrews. If they continued to tyrannize upon the so-called untouchables, how could they expect to receive proper treatment at the hands of the white men in South Africa? Sjt. Gokhale had rightly said in one of his addresses that it was but quite natural that the white people should look down upon the Indians who so inhumanly treated certain sections of their own people. So long as the removal of untouchability was not achieved and the khaddar movement was not made to succeed, all their works would remain incomplete.

Continuing, he thanked the District Board for taking up khaddar work, although he was sorry that spinning could not be made popular with school-children. He was not surprised, for he knew the habit of children. In order to make them spin regularly, the teachers should have to spin themselves. The example of teachers might prompt the students to cling to the charkha as a plaything and they might create wonders while playing with the same. He reminded the people of the good old days of their textile industry and asked them to endeavour their best to bring back those days.

The Searchlight, 21-1-1927

251. SPEECH AT PUBLIC MEETING, RAMNA[1]

January 15, 1927

He said that he was reminded by the chairman of the municipality as well as by the president of the Hindu Sabha that Gaya was a sacred place of pilgrimage, hallowed by the association of Lord Buddha. But it pained him to see the miserable state of the latrines and the roads of Gaya dirtier than those which he had ever seen in his life. He said that he had reminded the commissioners of their duty, but, if the people had not developed sufficient sense of responsibility, it was impossible for the municipality to discharge its duty. Where the people were alert, the commissioners could not neglect their duty, for it was in the hands of the people themselves to replace those commissioners by new and better ones. He had advised the commissioners to sweep and cleanse the roads, he would advise all the people to join them in their work. Keeping the roads clean was as much the duty of the citizens as of the scavengers; the latter could not discharge their duty if the former did not heartily co-operate with them.

Referring to the Hindu Sabha address, he said he was glad that the Sabha was trying to free the Hindus of cowardice. But he had found that the Hindus alone were not cowards. Cowardice had become the attribute of Indians as a whole. If they could get rid of this evil, there could be no power on earth to check their forward march.

He thanked the Hindu Sabha for working for khaddar and removal of untouchability. Untouchability, he had told them on a former occasion, was no part of Hinduism. They should hang down their head in shame before the world for indulging in that sin. The *Gita* taught them that man should not differentiate between a Brahmin and a *Chandal*. The interpretation which he would give to that verse was that man should serve both Brahmin and *Chandal* alike

[1] Over 10,000 people attended the meeting at which an address of welcome was presented to Gandhiji by the local Hindu Sabha.

and hate none. According to Hinduism, there were only four *varnas*; there could not be a fifth one.

Proceeding, he said that *shuddhi* with him was synonymous with *atma-shuddhi*, self-purification. They would work this *shuddhi* by loving the untouchables. Swami Shraddhanand had died for religion. The one burning passion of his life had been the regeneration of the untouchables. They should do away with that evil at least for the sake of the great Swami. He (the Mahatma) had of course his honest difference of opinion with Swamiji with regard to *shuddhi* as he (Swamiji) understood it. He said:[1]

I have made no secret of the fact that I did not approve of all aspects of the *shuddhi* work. After much prayerful study of the Hindu Shastras I have come to the conclusion that there is no room in them for conversions such as they have in Islam and Christianity. I am also certain on a prayerful reading of the Koran that there is no warrant for the *tabligh* that is being promoted today. It is possible that I may be mistaken. Let God correct me in that case. I for myself would love to protect my religion with *tapascharya*—the way of prayerful suffering which is the royal road to success in any noble object. The real memorial that the Hindus can raise to Swamiji is to rid Hinduism of the curse of untouchability. Let both Hindus and Mussalmans cleanse their hearts with the purifying blood of Swamiji's sacrifice. I must be free to read the *Gita* or the Koran of my own accord. Why should a Hindu compel me to read the one or a Mussalman to read the other? Why should I need a Christian to compel me to read the Bible? No one may stand between a man and his religion or God. He who has no inkling of religion, whose heart is arid and purified—how dare he purify (by proselytizing) others? But that is my opinion. And as I am a votary of liberty I have in spite of my opinion insisted that Shraddhanandji had as much right to propagate the Vedic dharma as a Mussalman to propagate that of the Koran. And if Shraddhanandji was assassinated for his *shuddhi* work, it did no credit to Islam. Hinduism is proud of the sacrifice and has been enriched by it. Let no Mussalman secretly approve of the act or believe that it has done any good to Islam. Let not a single Hindu harbour any thought of retaliation. If the Hindu and the Mussalman rid themselves of mutual distrust and fear, there is no power that can stop their freedom. We are the makers of our own slavery. I had sealed my lips up to now on this burning

[1] The paragraph that follows has been extracted from Mahadev Desai's "Weekly Letter" in *Young India*.

topic. It is Shraddhanandji's sacrifice that has compelled me to open them to a certain extent. But I can give no guidance in this atmosphere. I shall only send my prayers to God that He may rid us of fear and hatred and distrust, and make us rely solely on the strength of love.

Referring to the protection of cows, he observed that it was a non-controversial matter and he was glad that they were doing so. The Hindus themselves were responsible for the present condition of Indian cows. If they did not sell their cows to the butchers for money, if they took proper care of the milch cows, their condition could not be so deplorable. He had heard that there was a *goshala* in Gaya. There were many such in India. If they could properly conduct them, they could easily maintain old and decrepit cows out of the income derived from milk, milk-products and hides of dead cows which could be made payable by establishing tanneries.

Continuing, Mahatmaji appealed to the people to help the poor villagers by habitually wearing khadi. Charkha, he said, was their *kamadhenu*. It had the power to feed thousands of poor, starving villagers. He regretted that even a small khaddar shop could not be conducted in a town like Gaya. It pained him to see a small khaddar shop amidst a number of big shops full of foreign cloth. He longed to see that day when all the big shops in the market would be stocked with khaddar, while there would remain only one or two small shops with foreign and Indian mill-made cloth and even those few not properly conducted.

Concluding, he appealed to the people in the name of God, to contribute what little they could to the Deshbandhu Memorial Fund for khaddar work and thus give financial help to the poor people of their country. . . .

The Searchlight, 21-1-1927; also *Young India*, 27-1-1927

252. LETTER TO MIRABEHN

[*January 16, 1927*][1]

CHI. MIRA,

I have your letter giving a description of your mishap, etc. I thought that the Bihar itinerary was sent to you, but I now remember it was not even ready when the first dates were sent. The Bihar dates were sent to you yesterday. I take it that you are using your map to locate the places and I suggest your writing

[1] From the postmark

the stations in Hindi characters as an interesting and useful exercise.

With love,

BAPU

[PS.]

This is being written just after prayer time 5 a.m. for we are just going far away.

From the original: C.W. 5197. Courtesy: Mirabehn

253. *LETTER TO DAHYABHAI M. PATEL*

ON TOUR,
[*January 16, 1927*][1]

BHAISHRI DAHYABHAI,

I got your letter. There is no doubt that the condition of the cultivators is deteriorating in these times. But the causes of that deterioration go deeper than you think. Impatience will harm the cause. Anger does not mend matters. If you realize that the remedy lies not with the Government but with the cultivators, you will go ahead with your work without feeling unhappy all the time. If I get even a moment free, I will write about the subject in *Navajivan*. I got the cutting from the *Prajabandhu*[2]. I did not get the one you say you sent before this. I think I shall come upon it by and by.

Blessings from
BAPU

From the Gujarati original: C.W. 2698. Courtesy: Dahyabhai M. Patel

[1] From the postmark

[2] A Gujarati weekly of Ahmedabad

254. LETTER TO V. G. DESAI

Sunday [January 16, 1927][1]

BHAISHRI VALJI,

I got your letter. I had also got your telegram. Every effort is being made to send you all the original writings.

I wish to engage you for translation work. I am writing to Kaka about it. The series being contributed by Shankerlal's brother-in-law will continue for a long time and I feel that you can be utilized in that work. I am writing to Kaka as he is the editor.

I suppose you remember that March 11 is the date fixed for the meeting of [All-India] Cow-protection [Association][2]. You must have found the names of the members and written to them. Sunday — you must have despatched the Association circular regarding the meeting, and finalized the accounts by obtaining details from Revashankerbhai[3], the Ashram[4], etc.

Are you taking care of your health ?

Vandemataram from
MOHANDAS

BHAISHRI VALJI DESAI
SATYAGRAHA ASHRAM
SABARMATI

From a photostat of the Gujarati: C.W. 7390. Courtesy: V. G. Desai

[1] From the postmark
[2] The addressee was then secretary of the Association.
[3] Revashanker J. Zaveri, who was then the treasurer of the Association
[4] The Sabarmati Ashram, the headquarters of the Association

255. SPEECH AT WOMEN'S MEETING, SONEPUR[1]

January 16, 1927

Think of Sita. Do you imagine she went about with Rama in his 14 years' forest wanderings with heavy ornaments like you? Do you think they add to your beauty ? Sita cared for the beauty of her heart and covered her body with pure khaddar. The heavy ornaments you wear are not only ugly but harmful inasmuch as they are the permanent receptacles of dirt. Free yourselves of these shackles and relieve the poverty of people who have no clothes, much less ornaments, to wear.

Young India, 27-1-1927

256. SPEECH AT PUBLIC MEETING, CHHAPRA[2]

January 16, 1927

Mahatmaji made a joint reply. After having thanked the Boards for kindly presenting him the addresses, he said that although he would speak a few words on other subjects also, his visit was mainly intended to preach the message of khaddar and charkha. He said that one of the addresses referred to his efforts to root out the evil of untouchability. It was the burning desire of his heart to wipe out that blot from Hindu society. Swami Shraddhanand, he said, who died in his attempts to do so, used to say that unless one untouchable was kept as family member in the house of each and every Indian leader, they could not say that untouchability was removed. The fifth *varna* was their own creation; the Shastras never sanctioned it. If the leaders kept the untouchables in their houses, there was no reason why people should blame them. 'Serve the untouchables' was the lesson of Swami Shraddhanand's life. They should learn further the lesson of fearlessness from his life and that of the evils of communalism from his death. He said that Hindu-Muslim unity was a dire necessity for them. Unless that was attained they could not even dream of swaraj.

Continuing, he said that the poverty of their country was a universally admitted fact. If they were true to their religion and true to their country,

[1] Extracted from Mahadev Desai's "Weekly Letter"

[2] At the meeting, which was attended by about ten thousand people, Gandhiji was presented addresses in Hindi by the Municipality and the District Board. He later addressed a women's meeting at the Town Hall before proceeding to Ekma.

they could not but have sympathy with the poor. The best way they could help the poor was by wearing khadi. They should not spend even a cowrie over foreign or Indian mill-made clothes.

He appealed once more to them to put on khaddar in preference to all other clothes.

He then announced that he would himself sell khaddar in that meeting, and, with a few pieces of khadi in his hand, he stood on the dais and called for purchasers. . . .

The Searchlight, 21-1-1927

257. *SPEECH AT PUBLIC MEETING, SEWAN*[1]

[*January 16, 1927*][2]

I am glad you say that your sub-division is better than other parts so far as Hindu-Muslim unity is concerned. But can you say that you are so united that your unity will stand the strain of anything happening elsewhere? I wish there can be at least one province, one district, one sub-division in this vast land which can proudly say that no power on earth can foment a Hindu-Muslim quarrel there. We may think we are living but disunited we are worse than dead. The Hindu thinks that in quarrelling with the Mussalman he is benefiting Hinduism, and the Mussalman thinks that in fighting a Hindu he is benefiting Islam. But each is ruining his faith. And the poison has spread as among the members of the communities themselves. And no wonder. For one man cannot do right in one department of life whilst he is occupied in doing wrong in any other department. Life is one indivisible whole.

I said at Comilla that the problem had passed out of human hands, and that God had taken it into His own. Maybe the statement springs from my egotism. But I do not think so. I have ample reason for it. With my hand on my breast, I can say that not a minute in my life am I forgetful of God. For over twenty years I have been doing everything that I have done as in the presence of God. Hindu-Muslim unity I had made a mission of my life. I worked for it in South Africa, I toiled for it here, I did penance for it, but God was not satisfied, God did not want me to take any credit for the work. And so I have now

[1] Condensed summary of a speech delivered in Hindi

[2] Sewan is a sub-divisional town in the district of Saran, which, according to *The Searchlight*, 21-1-1927, Gandhiji covered on January 16.

washed my hands. I am helpless. I have exhausted all my effort. But as I am a believer in God, as I never for a moment lose faith in Him, as I content myself with the joy and sorrow that He wills for me, I may feel helpless, but I never lose hope. Something within me tells me that Hindu-Muslim unity must come and will come sooner than we might dare to hope, that God will one day force it on us, in spite of ourselves. That is why I said that it has passed into the hands of God. This, I said, might be taken to be an arrogant utterance—arrogant inasmuch as it implies that it is not in the power of any other man to achieve the work, as if no one has worked for it more than I. But there is no arrogance in the statement. Hundreds may have done the work with the same earnestness, love and energy, but none with more. And I believe that all of them must be feeling as helpless as I. In 1920, I said that not even the British Empire with all the resources of its armed strength, diplomacy and organization could efface us, make us slaves, or divide Hindus from Mussalmans. But that was because I thought we were godfearing then. We trusted one another and we relied on one another's strength. But how am I to prevail upon you today to cast off all fear, hatred and distrust? Shraddhanandji was not the enemy of Mussalmans. He was a warrior, he had the courage of his convictions. Assassination was not the way to fight him. Let us Hindus and Mussalmans both wash the sins of our heart with his blood.

And what is it that we should be fighting for? We Hindus may be idol-worshippers. We may be mistaken. But when God gave every man the right to make mistakes, when God suffers us to live although we are idol-worshippers, why should not the Mussalmans suffer us too? And if a Mussalman thinks that he must slaughter the cow, why should a Hindu stay his hands by force? Why should he not fall on bended knees before him and plead with him? But we will do no such thing. Well then, God will one day make the Mussalman and the Hindu do what we will not do today. If you are believers, I beseech you to retire into yourselves and pray to the In-dweller to stay your hands from wrong and to make them do the right thing. Let that be our prayer every morning and evening. There is no other way.

Young India, 27-1-1927

258. *LETTER TO MIRABEHN*

January 17, 1927

CHI. MIRA,

We are now on the north of the Ganges and therefore letters will for the time being take longer to reach you. We are on Rajendra Babu's ancestral property in a remote village[1] though not remote from the railway line.

What is your progress in Hindi now? Are you speaking it without reserve? Do you get much time to talk in Hindi? Or do you have to carry on your work through English? I hope you have continued your weekly Hindi letter to the Ashram. It is fairly cold here. It is never warm in the shade. The weather is also damp but bracing. One feels like walking all day long and yet I can get but little [time].

I am there somewhere about 20th March. I suppose you would want to be there till then but in no case if the place does not suit you.

With love,

Yours,

BAPU

[PS.]

I hope you have got the itinerary. If not, address your letters Khadi Office, Muradpore, Patna. It is incessant wandering. By the [time you]r reply to this reaches me, it will be quite 10 days, I fear. I reach Patna 30th inst.

From the original: C.W. 5198. Courtesy: Mirabehn

[1] Jeeradei

259. *LETTER TO MANIBEHN PATEL*

Silence Day [*January 17, 1927*][1]

CHI. MANI,

I got your letter. There is nothing in your letter which you need keep back from others. However, no one else except Mahadev has read it.

Surely, I will never force you to marry, nor will Father. If I could have my way I would rather force girls to remain unmarried. It is the girls themselves who compel me to force them to marry. You are, therefore, safe so far as I am concerned. I was being harassed by people who did not understand you and so I wrote to you to ascertain your desire and that too because I had observed your restlessness. I do know of young women (girls) whose restlessness is due to their desire to get married, though they themselves are not aware of this. I am sure that it cannot be so in your case. Still it was my duty to draw your attention to the problem, and I also wished to suggest that there was no harm in thinking of getting married even after having expressed one's intention not to do so. Of course it would be different if you had taken a vow. In that case, the heavens may fall but the vow must not be violated. Since, however, you have not taken a vow, even a person like me may ask you what you desire. Others may even urge you to get married. This does not mean that I want you to take a vow. That you may do when you feel that it is absolutely necessary. I shall never feel compelled again to mention the subject of marriage to you; not only that, but I shall even prevent others from doing so. You should, however, get over your restlessness and so live always that your unmarried state may win people's respect. *Brahmacharya* should be understood in a spiritual sense, and in order that it may bring you spiritual benefit, you should observe it in the manner recently complained by me in my autobiography[2] in *Navajivan.* You should, therefore, maintain a calm and cheerful temper, be industrious in your habits and cultivate a tolerant outlook.

Read *Margopadeshika*[3] several times over till you have master-

[1] As in the printed source

[2] Pt. III, Ch. VII and VIII

[3] Sanskrit Reader written by Dr. R. G. Bhandarkar

ed it. Understand the meaning of every word in the *Gita* with the help of the rules explained in that book.

I have sent a wire to you asking you to master ginning and carding. I have sent a wire to Narayandas too at Karachi. But have not received a reply from him; whether or not I hear from him, I have received similar requests from others too. I intend to send you to various places from time to time for teaching spinning. I have asked for a salary of Rs. 50 and travelling expenses. This will give you good experience too. We shall think afterwards what to do then. You should not take up any work there for the present. You should, however, continue drawing Rs. 30/-. You may save what you can from it. I will ask for an account later on.

Blessings from
BAPU

CHI. MANIBEHN PATEL
SATYAGRAHA ASHRAM
SABARMATI

[From Gujarati]
Bapuna Patro—Manibehn Patelne, pp. 47-51

260. LETTER TO JAMNALAL BAJAJ

Silence Day, Pausa Sud 14 [January 17, 1927][1]

CHI. JAMNALAL,

I have your letter. I have sent you a telegram regarding the stores at Gondia and Amaravati. If I have to visit Gondia, I may be able to go there too. I have to leave Patna on the 31st evening. I can catch the Bombay Mail at Mogulsarai on the 1st. I shall be reaching Jabalpur . . .[2] on the same day. That means that I shall be arriving in Gondia on the 2nd. I shall get a seat in the Bhusaval [Mail] at any rate on the 3rd.

Now about Manilal. I have written to Kishorelal in that connection and have asked him to show the letter to you. My suggestion just now is that either Gomatibehn or Vijayalakshmi should ask Sushila, without mentioning the name, whether she

[1] The itinerary of Gandhiji's tour mentioned in the letter suggests that the letter was written in January 1927. Although *Pausa Sud* 14 corresponded to January 16, Monday was January 17.

[2] Omission is in the source.

intends to get married. I gather from Kishorelal's letter that none of the girls is yet thinking of getting married. If this is true, why should we persuade her to marry? Kishorelal believes that, if at all, Sushila may be thinking of getting married. That is why it seems to me that we can proceed further in the matter after ascertaining whether she wishes to get married. Meanwhile I will definitely come there. Perhaps we shall then know more clearly what to do.

My tour in these parts is going on at great speed . . .[1] is arranged well. Better arrangements . . .[2] can be made though today we are in Rajendra Babu's village.

Although Janakibehn's complaint of piles has become less acute, it is better to consult a doctor and do as he suggests. I should not like you to postpone consulting a doctor.

I hope Vinoba is keeping good health. I wish to hear about Shivaji's health too.

Blessings from
BAPU

From a photostat of the Gujarati: G.N. 2879

261. LETTER TO ASHRAM WOMEN

Silence Day, Pausa Sud 14 [January 17, 1927]

DEAR SISTERS,

I have your letter.

I always write to you on Mondays; but as I keep moving from town to town, the day on which you receive my letters may vary. Till now I was to the south of the Ganga. Yesterday I came over to the north, crossing the river. From Patna we crossed over to the other side by means of a boat. A car awaited us there and took us to Sonepur. Soil here is not sticky like mud; it has a mixture of sand in it. It, therefore, feels soft to the feet like velvet. Ba and I walked for about a mile. We were not wearing sandals. We liked to walk on the sand very much indeed. Mother Ganga prepares new soil every year in this part of the country. For hundreds of miles she carries mud and silt with her and, depositing them here, she runs along to the sea as though she wanted to avoid feeling embarrassed by being told by anyone of the great good she was doing to the land.

[1] & [2] omissions are in the source.

Today we are in Rajendra Babu's village. Rajbansi Devi is here. Chandramukhi and Vidyavati are at present in Chhapra, the town where he (i.e., Rajendra Babu) lives. We met them in Chhapra. Both are in relatively good health—Chandramukhi slightly worse than she was in the Ashram and Vidyavati slightly better.

In a women's meeting yesterday I started educating them on a new subject. The women here wear heavy silver ornaments; they keep their children dirty and do not comb their hair. I, therefore, criticized their habit of wearing ornaments. The result was that some of them gave away their anklets, necklaces and so on to me, and promised that they would neither buy nor wear others in future. While doing this, I thought of all of you. Ba is giving me great help in this work, but that is because she agrees with me in this. You can do work of this kind better than I. But that requires self-sacrifice, enthusiasm, and opportunities. All this you can have there. Do we not sing *atmavatsarvabhuteshu*[1]? We should regard all as ourselves. Then, on finding somebody's children dirty, we would feel as if our own children were dirty and so would feel ashamed; on finding someone else suffer would ourselves suffer and seek a remedy for the suffering.

But I have exceeded my limit. Much as I like to exceed, I feel nervous when I look at the pile of correspondence lying before me.

Find out from a map where Patna, Sonepur, and Chhapra are situated. This is the land where King Janaka lived.

Blessings from
BAPU

[PS.]

With whose permission did Gangabehn Zaveri let her foot be sprained? Well, God's will be done! If one is negligent, one deserves punishment.

BAPU

From a photostat of the Gujarati: G.N. 3635

[1] (He sees rightly who) in all things sees himself.

262. *LETTER TO MIRABEHN*

[*January 18, 1927*][1]

CHI. MIRA,

I have two more letters from you. Yes, you may go to Hardwar as soon as you wish. You need not stay there for teaching carding and spinning unless it is a help to learning Hindi. As you do not seem to be getting much Hindi, it is better to go away at once. In no case must you endanger your health. You will therefore judge for yourself and do what you think is best. You will of course tell Vidyavati exactly as you feel.

Your letter about the assassination makes me sad. I am hoping that you probably did not understand what your informers were saying or feeling. Hatred is of course there or there would have been no strife. But to think that youngsters can be infected makes one shudder.

Did you go to Swamiji's house?

With love,

Yours,

BAPU

From the original: C.W. 5199. Courtesy: Mirabehn

263. *KHADI IN BIHAR*

Sjt. Rajendra Prasad has sent me the report on the work of the Bihar branch of the A.I.S.A. for the year ending September 1926. It is a record of steady progress. After mentioning the vicissitudes the organization had to pass through in the early stages, the report says:[2]

There are 8 production and sale centres and 11 sale depots. Besides these there are sale agencies at 6 places and more are being established. The agency has 65 wholetime workers including two honorary workers. Their average earnings are Rs. 25 per month. During the year under review 2,698 spinners earned Rs. 29,519; 489 weavers, Rs. 36,862; 6 tailors, Rs. 230 during two

[1] From the postmark

[2] The statement, which gave figures of the production and sale of khaddar, is not reproduced here.

months; 8 dyers and printers Rs. 2,273 during six months including the cost of dyes; and 40 washermen Rs. 1,951 during six months. It goes without saying that the spinners and weavers too were not wholetime workers. They worked only during their spare time and irregularly.

The report then says:

> The progress that has been made is not only in regard to increased production and sale but also in regard to the quality of khaddar and reduction in its price.

The average price in 1923 was Rs. 1-0-5 per yard of fine cloth. It was reduced to As. 13 in 1926. When the yarn was very weak the weaving charge was 3 annas 3 pies per yard of 45 inches width. On account of the improvement in the yarn, it has now been reduced to 2 annas 3 pies per yard of the same width. Nor is there any difficulty about getting sufficient weavers to weave hand-spun yarn. Some of these weavers weave even up to 72 inches width and the variety of weaving includes twills, coatings of various designs, etc. Dyeing and printing is being developed under the special care of a graduate of the Bihar Vidyapith.

The report, after mentioning the work in different branches of the organization, says:

> If we could dispose of our present stock, it is expected that we shall be able to reduce our prices still further by about 10 p.c.

It naturally dwells upon the successful peripatetic exhibitions that were held during the year, of which a detailed account has appeared from time to time in these pages. The interesting report contains the following pregnant reflections:

> The province of Bihar is particularly suited for khaddar work. The population is agricultural; there is no industry in the province worth the name, outside the coalfields of Chhotanagpur and apart from the great Tata Iron and Steel Works at Jamshedpur. The tradition of spinning is still extant in most parts of it and the number of weavers and looms is large enough to supply almost the entire requirement of cloth of the province. Cotton, though of an inferior quality, is also produced in many parts of it. The work of production of khaddar is, therefore, not very difficult, although it requires organization and technical skill to improve its quality. It can be extended almost indefinitely, if sufficient capital and organizing and technical skill are forthcoming.
>
> The above narrative will show the progress made in reviving the ancient but practically all but dead industry of spinning in Bihar. We have succeeded in touching but the merest fringe of the vast area in

which spinning can be revived and made to furnish a much-needed occupation for the idle hours of our great agricultural population. That its possibilities are vast can hardly be denied. That some supplementary occupation, not to speak of income, is necessary for the population will be apparent from the fact that the average quantity of land actually cultivated with food and non-food crops is less than three-quarters of an acre per head. It is the yield of this small quantity of land, nearly four-fifths of which are unirrigated and depend upon the freaks of the monsoon, that is expected not only to keep the body and soul together of every individual but also to supply him with cloth and other necessaries of life and to meet among others all demands of the zamindar, the society and the State. Looked at from this point of view the admittedly scanty earning of 7 pies per day by charkha is not after all so small and does afford, as experience has shown, substantial relief to a class of people who need such relief but cannot get it through forced unemployment. It is believed that agriculture does not require more than a hundred days' labour in the year but the work is so distributed that the agriculturist cannot leave his farm and seek work elsewhere at a distance. In fact, the nature of the work is such that it allows plenty of leisure but at short intervals and a supplementary industry, which is not capable of being taken up and put aside to be resumed later at the stage at which it was left, cannot be usefully taken up. Experience has shown that the charkha alone can serve the purpose.

It is hoped that the appeal made in the report to the public for the purchase of khaddar will meet with the liberal response it deserves.

Young India, 20-1-1927

264. HINDI v. *ENGLISH*

Organizers of meetings seem to require constant reminders that not English but Hindi or Hindustani is the common medium of expression among the masses. I have observed that unlike as in 1921 the addresses hitherto presented to me during the tour have been in most cases in English. The absurdity became patent when an address in English on behalf of the employees of Jharia collieries was sought to be read to me and that, at a big mass meeting attended by thousands, hardly fifty of whom could possibly understand English. The vast majority could have easily followed Hindi and a very large number could have understood Bengali. The officers of the association were from Bengal. If the

English drafting was meant for me, it was wholly unnecessary. They might have written the address in Bengali and given me a translation in Hindi or even in English. But to inflict English on that big audience would have been an insult to them. I hope that the time is coming when, if the proceedings are conducted in a language the majority cannot understand, they would leave such meetings. Be it said to the credit of the chairman at this meeting that he saw the absurdity as soon as I drew his attention to it and very courteously allowed the address to be taken as read. May the incident serve as a warning to all the organizers but more especially those in the Andhradesh, Tamil Nadu, Kerala and Karnatak. I know their difficulty. But they have had now for six years in their midst an efficient organization for the spread of Hindi. Their addresses should be in the vernaculars of their respective provinces with a Hindi translation for my benefit. I have always made an exception in Dravida land and delivered my speeches in English wherever they have so desired. But I do think that the time has come when they should dispense with English for big public meetings. Really it is the English-speaking leaders who are blocking the way to our rapid progress among the masses by their refusal to learn Hindi which can be easily picked up inside of three months even in Dravida land, if the learners will give three hours per day. Let those who doubt give a trial to the Hindi Prachar Karyalaya conducted in Madras under the aegis of the Hindi Sahitya Sammelan, Prayag. They will find at the head office in Triplicane and the branches in Andhradesh and elsewhere books and teachers that will satisfy them. There is no excuse save idleness or disinclination for not knowing Hindi which is understood by over twenty crores of the people of Hindustan.

Young India, 20-1-1927

265. NOTES

All-India Deshbandhu Memorial

I hope the readers of *Young India* have not forgotten the All-India Deshbandhu Memorial. When I suspended touring after the Cawnpore Congress for one year, I knew that the collection of funds for the All-India Deshbandhu Memorial to which I had pledged myself would be suspended. But it was inevitable. At the time of suspension I had stated that, if God willed it, at the end of the year I would resume my tour for the collection. I resumed it at Calcutta and all the collections that I am now making will be for the All-India Deshbandhu Memorial except where the donors otherwise specify the object of their donations. And since the object of the All-India Deshbandhu Memorial is village organization and that through the spinning movement, all these collections automatically become part of the All-India Spinners' Association which is the agency through which the Memorial collections are to be utilized for the purpose. A resolution to this effect was passed by the All-India Deshbandhu Memorial Committee at Cawnpore in 1925. I trust, therefore, that those who are in charge of the organization of meetings in connection with my tour will take good care to inform those who may attend meetings of the object of the tour. There should be no desire to spring a surprise upon those who attend meetings by asking for subscription. The honest course is to let them know beforehand that they will be asked to pay. No one need pay unless he believes in the Memorial and its object. I know, too, that a man may revere the memory of Deshbandhu and still not believe in the spinning movement. But I would venture to remind such people of what were Deshbandhu's last wishes expressed to his wife, his sister and his trusted lieutenants and Satis Chandra Das Gupta of Khadi Pratishthan and to me almost exactly 7 days before his death. He said that as soon as he descended from Darjeeling, he would throw himself heart and soul into the spinning movement. He could see that that was the greatest constructive movement we could undertake and that it was the most effective method of village organization and village reconstruction. It was for that reason that he had asked me to send for Satis Babu with whom he had discussed the plan of working the spinning movement and it was for the spinning movement that he had intended to spend the largest part of the money that had been collected for village reconstruction. The Spinners' Association, therefore, is the natural outcome, if I may say so, of Deshbandhu's wishes.

To Organizers

If all goes well, I hope during the year to cover, besides Bihar, part of Maharashtra, Madras Presidency including Karnatak, U.P., Bengal and Orissa. I should love to visit the other provinces also if time and health permit and if they intend to subscribe to the Memorial, that is, khadi work.

To Orissa I have promised to go and pass there, so far as it is humanly possible, the month of November, not because I expect to make large collections but because it is to my mind an epitome of our distressful condition. Orissa regenerate is to me the regeneration for the whole of India. It is a land which need not be the poorest in the country. Its people are in no way inferior to those of the other parts of India. They have a fine history all their own. They have magnificent temples. They have the Lord of the Universe in their midst who knows no distinction between his creatures. And yet, sad to relate, under the very shadow of the mighty temple people die of hunger in their thousands. It is a land of chronic poverty, chronic famine, and chronic disease. Nowhere have I seen in the eyes of people so much blankness, so much despair so much lifelessness as in Orissa. I therefore look forward to my stay in November with sad pleasure.

It is a province that can be, ought to be, easily organized for spinning, because the people have no work. The whole of Orissa cannot be transplanted to the factories of Bengal or the factories of all India put together. It would be wrong even if it was possible. Happily it is not possible. The people must live on their own land and learn to be resourceful, industrious, and learn even to be happy. They have forgotten what happiness can be. Let the workers in Orissa, therefore, understand their responsibility. I expect them to throw themselves heart and soul into the spinning movement. Let them not think of the whole of Orissa. Let them think of single villages where they will establish themselves, and where they may, by prayerful and persistent effort, lift the people out of the Slough of Despond into which they have stuck.

And though, as I have said, I do not expect to make large collections, I shall welcome the only pies of the people who will attend meetings, even as I welcomed them when I travelled in 1921. The sight of old people with their trembling fingers untying the knots which firmly held their pies and willingly surrendering them to me is never to be forgotten. I want to see it again and renew, if a renewal is necessary, the determination that this winter of despair is to be changed into the summer of hope and happiness within a measurable distance of time.

May I ask the organizers also to bear in mind that the tour is to be almost incessant and that I must do my editing and attend to my correspondence during the hours they may leave for me and in the trains? Besides Mondays, at least three hours should be left for me in addition to the time required for ablutions and meals. All night demonstrations must be avoided. It is impossible after a strenuous day's work to stand the strain of disturbance during sleeping hours.

And as this is to be a purely business tour, the meetings should be so arranged and the audiences should be so seated as to leave passages for collectors to pass to and fro. All shoutings and noises should be avoided. I have observed that where management is efficient, collections mount up. The audiences have invariably been found by me to be responsive. Though the thousands of the rich are welcome, I know that it is the coppers and the single rupees of the poor people that bless the movement. It is theirs and let them freely contribute to it their mite.

Young India, 20-1-1927

266. THE CENTRAL FACT

During my tour in so far as it has progressed up to now, I have observed that spinning organizations have not an accurate register of spinners and that the figures supplied and published by me from time to time in these pages were based upon the deductions drawn from the actual wages paid to the spinners. For statistical information the calculation is sound enough because it must err on the right side, i.e., of understatement. But it is not good enough for the movement itself. The spinning movement depends for its permanence upon a vital and direct contact being established between the workers and the spinners; for then and then only shall we be able to understand the wants, aspirations and limitations of the spinners. The object is to penetrate the remotest Indian homes in the innumerable villages of India and to introduce a ray of hope and light into these homes. This we shall never do, if we do not establish a living touch with the spinners. We cannot, therefore, be satisfied with the work of middlemen whom we may not and do not know. We must be able to trace the course of every pie till it is safely deposited in the hands of the spinners. And let it be remembered that spinning is the central fact of the movement, not weaving, not dyeing, not printing, not even carding and ginning, anterior though the last two processes are to spinning. For the economic solution depends upon a supplementary employment being found for the largest number of the semi-starved millions. That employment by far the best is spinning and that alone, as will be seen by a study of the figures for the various provinces given in these pages.

The Bihar figures reproduced in this issue show 489 weavers against 2,698 spinners. My own observation is that ten spinners are required to feed one weaver both working for the same amount of time. The ultimate ambition is to teach the spinners carding and ginning so as to enable them to increase their earnings as spinners without much effort and without much training. This is being done on a fairly large scale in Bihar, Bengal and the Madras Presidency. The Spinners' Association can justify its existence therefore only upon its achieving a progressive amelioration in the economic condition of the vast masses who can be reached in no other way in a shorter time. The movement depends also for its increasing influence and vitality upon this fact of its tender care for the millions of whom it has as yet only touched but a small part.

Workers have suggested to me that, if an accurate register is to be kept of every spinner, it would involve extra cost. Possibly, it will. Not being in charge of a single centre, I am unable fully to understand the difficulty of keeping such registers. But I can say without any fear of challenge that, whatever the cost may be, a complete register of spinners is an absolute necessity until spinning has become an automatically working movement beyond risk of destruction. The extra cost that the keeping of such a register may involve will be worth undertaking if we are to put the movement on a stable foundation. What an accurate and simultaneous entry of every pie received and spent in a banking corporation is to its honest existence and steady growth, an accurate register of spinners is to the honest existence and steady growth of the spinning movement. I hope therefore that every spinning organization will without any loss of time set about keeping a full and up-to-date register of its spinners. Needless to say that the workers who will be in charge of the registers and who will come in contact with the spinners must be men—and how nice if they were women ?—of unimpeachable character and purity. The discovery of this flaw in the movement was made by me through the hypersensitiveness of the workers of Bengal. In my notice of the Abhoy Ashram report,[1] I made an incidental observation that our statements of figures must not contain "abouts" and "nearlies" and then I made a general observation about the necessity of purity of character. I had in making that observation no one in particular in mind but owing to the juxtaposition of the general remark to the mention of the work of the Abhoy Ashram some of its inmates suspected that my remarks were aimed at them. I had no difficulty in disabusing their minds of the suspicion; but the conversation enabled me to understand and convince the members of the Ashram of the necessity of keeping an accurate up-to-

[1] *Vide* "Abhoy Ashram Khadi Work", 30-12-1926.

date register of spinners. I am therefore not sorry for the paragraph that I wrote in my notice of the Abhoy Ashram, if only because it has led to the discovery of the flaw in our human account-keeping. But let me reiterate for the information of all concerned that in this spinning movement which is fraught with tremendous consequences, we cannot put too much stress upon the absolute necessity of members of our organizations being and remaining beyond suspicion, and if we are to attain this standard of purity, we will have to develop a thick skin enough to stand and take in good part well-meant suggestions, criticisms and observations.

Young India, 20-1-1927

267. A CANDID CRITIC

I must not withhold the following letter from the readers:

> I have perused your article 'Swamiji the Martyr' with the care and reverence it deserves. I have read it five times before attempting to criticize it. This is to avoid hasty criticism.
>
> The article is undoubtedly written in fascinating language. I envy your style. It attracts, but to me it appears, that it is rather dangerously attractive.
>
> My criticism is based on my estimation of your character. I have often debated with some friends on this subject. They hold that you are a statesman in the garb of a saint—ready to forgo truth in the cause of your country. I have on the contrary maintained that you are a saint—who has entered politics in fulfilment of your mission, to practise truth in the face of most trying and perplexing circumstances. I shall be very obliged to know if my estimation is correct. For if it is not, the criticism that follows has little value. I am of the opinion that a man of policy is within his rights to write in the manner you have done.
>
> You will agree with me that to suppress truth is a form of falsehood; to refuse to call a spade a spade when you feel it like that is cowardice; and that fearlessness and truth go together.
>
> Do you feel, Mahatmaji, that the murder of Swamiji was an inhuman, barbarous and cruel act of a Muslim ruffian and that the entire Muslim community should be ashamed of it? Why do you refuse to characterize it as such? Instead of condemning the deed and the doer, and those who are responsible for this act (those who describe Hindu leaders as Kafirs—the hot Muslim propagandists and the mad Muslim priests), you have begun to defend the murderer and hold an apology for the

community. You never defended Dyer. Is not a European a brother too?

You say further, Islam means peace. Is this truth? Islam as taught by the Koran and practised by Muslims ever since its birth never meant peace. What makes you write a thing so patently wrong? Buddhism, Christianity, Hinduism of course teach peace, but not Islam. May I know what makes you think and write like this?

You never minced matters when condemning the wrongs of the Government, you never minced matters when you condemned Arya Samaj, why fear to condemn Muslims for even proved wrongs?

I am sure if such a black act had been committed by a Hindu against a Muslim leader (which Heaven forbid!), you would have condemned the murderer and the community in unsparing terms. You would have asked Hindus to repent in sack-cloth and ashes, to offer fasts, hold hartal, raise memorial to the departed Muslim and many other things. Why do you accord preferential treatment to your 'blood brothers' the Muslims?

A truth-teller knows no fear, not even of the sword of Islam and I trust you will oblige me by giving reply to above in the columns of your esteemed weekly.

The writer is frank and obviously in earnest and reflects the prevalent mood.

To clothe me with sainthood is too early even if it is possible. I myself do not feel a saint in any shape or form. But I do feel I am a votary of Truth in spite of all my errors of unconscious omission and commission. The correspondent has judged rightly that I am not "a statesman in the garb of a saint". But since Truth is the highest wisdom, sometimes my acts appear to be consistent with the highest statesmanship. But I hope I have no policy in me save the policy of truth and ahimsa. I will not sacrifice truth and ahimsa even for the deliverance of my country or religion. This is as much as to say that neither can be so delivered.

In writing about the assassination of Swamiji, I have not suppressed truth. I do believe the act to be all that the correspondent describes. But I feel pity for the murderer even as I felt for General Dyer. Let not the correspondent forget that I refused to be party to any agitation for the prosecution of General Dyer. I do claim that a European is just as much brother to me as a Mussalman Indian or a Hindu.

What I do feel about the assassin is that he is himself a victim of foul irreligious propaganda in the name of religion. Hence it is that I have held the newspapers that have corrupted the public mind to be responsible for the murder. I do hold the maulvis and all those who have indulged in exciting hatred against Swamiji to be responsible.

But I do regard Islam to be a religion of peace in the same sense as Christianity, Buddhism and Hinduism are. No doubt there are differences in degree, but the object of these religions is peace. I know the passages that can be quoted from the Koran to the contrary. But so is it possible to quote passages from the Vedas to the contrary. What is the meaning of imprecations pronounced against the Anaryas[1]? Of course these passages bear today a different meaning but at one time they did wear a dreadful aspect. What is the meaning of the treatment of untouchables by us Hindus? Let not the pot call the kettle black. The fact is that we are all growing. I have given my opinion that the followers of Islam are too free with the sword. But that is not due to the teaching of the Koran. That is due in my opinion to the environment in which Islam was born. Christianity has a bloody record against it, not because Jesus was found wanting, but because the environment in which it spread was not responsive to his lofty teaching. These two, Christianity and Islam, are after all religions of but yesterday. They are yet in the course of being interpreted. I reject the claim of maulvis to give a final interpretation to the message of Mahomed as I reject that of the Christian clergy to give a final interpretation to the message of Jesus. Both are being interpreted in the lives of those who are living these messages in silence and in perfect self-dedication. Bluster is no religion nor is vast learning stored in capacious brains. The seat of religion is in the heart. We Hindus, Christians, Mussalmans and others have to write the interpretation of our respective faiths with our own crimson blood and not otherwise.

Young India, 20-1-1927

[1] Non-Aryans

268. *SPEECH AT MADHUBANI*[1]

January 20, 1927

Mahatmaji in replying thanked the Boards for presenting him addresses. He thanked the boys of the Brahmacharya Ashram also for singing before him the sweet Vedic hymns. He said that there was neither any necessity, nor had he so much time at his disposal to reply separately to all the addresses presented to him. But one thing had drawn his attention. He said that he was told in three or four addresses that attempts were being made to start Ayurvedic dispensaries in many parts of the province. It seemed to him that the people of Bihar were interesting themselves in the Ayurvedic system of treatment. He had expressed his opinion on the subject on many occasions and he would like to draw their attention to that. He believed that there was a good deal of truth in that system, but he believed none the less that the practitioners of that system had their own defects and joined the profession without proper training. He admitted that the Western system of medical treatment was very defective, but he knew this also that the Indians did not do even half of what the people of Europe were doing for the success of their medical science. But they had great opportunity to work for the improvement of that science. He requested the Municipalities and District Boards to see to this matter. He further requested the *vaidyas* to make a scientific study of the system. If there were defects in the system, and defects there certainly were, they should not try to conceal them; on the contrary, every effort should be made to remove them.

Continuing, he said that he was glad to learn that the organizers of the Madhubani *goshala* agreed with his views on the utilization of the hides of dead cattle for the improvement of the cattle themselves. *Goshalas,* he said, had two aspects, one economic and the other religious. The question of cow-protection was a non-controversial matter. He did not understand why there should be any quarrel with the Muslims on that point. His views on *kurbani,* he said, remained unchanged.

Continuing, he said that the existing line of work of the *goshala* had also many defects in it. They should be maintained in the right and proper way. The organizers of these houses should be thoroughly acquainted with the treatment of animal diseases. They should know how to house and feed the cows, how to make milk cheaper for the poor village purchasers; in fact, the con-

[1] At the meeting, addresses were presented to Gandhiji on behalf of the Municipality, the District Board, the *goshalas,* the Youngmen's Debating Club and the Arya Samaj.

ductors of *goshalas* must thoroughly study the science of cattle-keeping and then alone could the purpose of *goshalas* be served.

Proceeding, he said that he had done all he could for the attainment of Hindu-Muslim unity but had failed. For that reason he had given up reading newspapers even. He had no time to read them either. His condition, he said, had become like king Janaka of Mithila who had looked indifferently when his own city was burning, for he had done all he could to prevent the fire. Similarly his (Mahatmaji's) attitude towards Hindu-Muslim differences was that of indifference for he knew that it was not in his power to remedy it. He said he did not know how or when Hindu-Muslim unity would come. The people of this country had gone mad; they were unhesitatingly cutting the throats of each other. He could not be a party to it. His religion was of non-violence, his faith in non-violence remained as unshaken as it was before, although attempts were made by his friends to convince him of the utility of violence on special occasions. To him all things were not as they seemed and he believed firmly that non-violence was the religion through which alone one could triumph ultimately. For all those reasons, he said, he had stopped dealing with the subject altogether. But he believed that the unity would certainly come one day, if not through the agency of man, through the agency of God.

Referring to khaddar, he said that he was glad that a purse was presented to him for khaddar work. But from Madhubani he expected much more. Madhubani, he said, was a big khaddar centre. He saw that many poor spinners of the place came four or five miles walking on foot with their yarn to take cotton or money from the workers. He knew that there were people who were even poorer than they. While he was at Champaran he had heard a lady complain that she could not take her bath in the Ganges and clean her clothes because she had no additional clothes to spare. This might have been an exaggeration but such cases were not absent. There was no other way to relieve the poverty of those people except by giving them an occupation and the best possible occupation they could give them was spinning.

Continuing, he said that he had just heard a hymn from the *Isopanishad* which meant that those who did not work stole other men's property. What did it mean, he asked. It did not mean that he actually stole other men's property but it meant that he lived on the food earned by other men's labour. As a matter of fact, no man had any right to live, unless he worked not only for himself but for all men alike, for an individual is but a drop in the great ocean of humanity. Similarly, the *Gita* taught him that no man should eat unless he had performed *yajna* and of the many *yajnas* sanctioned by that sacred book, that of working for others was the best. Spinning, then, was the only work which could help thousands of people; it was the universal *yajna* which could be performed by all.

Addressing the ladies, he said that to him all who were clad in foreign clothes were naked, for nothing but khaddar could cover the nakedness of Indians.

Mahatmaji appealed to the people to look into the affairs of the local national school and of the *goshala* and help them with money if they deserved it. It was the duty of a citizen, he said, to help his fellow-beings and institutions in distress.

He concluded by appealing once more for money for khaddar work and asking people to purchase khadi which was stocked at the meeting.

The Searchlight, 26-1-1927

269. SPEECH AT PUBLIC MEETING, SAMASTIPUR

January 20, 1927

He said that he was glad to see them once more. It was impossible for him to forget the people of Samastipur who had once brought him there in a special train with Babu Brajkishore Prasad and others. He had, therefore, come to Samastipur with great hope. His tour, he said, was intended to preach the message of khaddar. It pained him very much to see that most of the people who had come to see him had not put on khaddar. He had preached the message of khaddar for five long years from thousands of platforms but still the people were reluctant to use khadi. Bihar had the capacity to produce as much khaddar as could be consumed in the province and if only the people patronized that great cottage industry, thousands of their unemployed men and women—ginners, carders, spinners, weavers, and even bleachers and washermen—could be provided with food and clothing. Every farthing that they could spend on khadi would go to the homes of their poor countrymen. It was their religious duty, therefore, to put on khadi and khadi alone.

Continuing, he said that by purchasing mill-made cloth they were helping only the rich mill-owners of either Lancashire or Ahmedabad. He was intimately acquainted with the condition of labourers through Anasuyabehn. He knew it definitely that the labourers were little benefited by the huge amount of money that people spent over mill-made cloth. The rich mill-owners were not in need of money and they had a wide market even outside India, but the poor countrymen of theirs were dying for a bit of rough bread. He knew how poor the people of Bihar were, for he had been in Champaran for a long time. Would they not be kind and sympathetic to these poor people, he asked.

Proceeding, he said that money was necessary for the furtherance of khaddar work. In order to save crores of money permanently in the country, crores of money were to be invested in the beginning. He had come to their door to beg of them that money. He regretted that no khaddar was stocked at the place of the meeting, although he was told on his arrival that there were khaddar shops in the town and that some khaddar would surely be stocked on the spot. Nevertheless he requested the people to go at once to the khaddar shop and clothe themselves in khadi.

Concluding, Mahatmaji spoke a few words on the evils of untouchability and paid an eloquent tribute to Shraddhanand, the martyr, who had embraced death in his attempt to regenerate the untouchables.

An address of welcome on behalf of the Municipality was then read by Babu Giriwardhar, Chairman, to which Mahatmaji made a short reply. He expressed his satisfaction that there was no ill-feeling between the Hindus and the Mussalmans of Samastipur. It was a great thing. He hoped that that state of things would continue to exist.

Referring to their desire to have a khaddar-producing centre at Samastipur, he said that if they sincerely desired such an organization, Rajendra Babu would surely look into the matter. He hoped that if requisite amount of money was advanced by the people themselves, Rajendra Babu would be coming to their help with all the energy he possessed.

Referring to the national school, he regretted that it was not what it ought to have been. He saw there certain charkhas and the students were also seen sitting by them, but it was all a mockery, a mere show. Neither the teacher nor the students knew anything about spinning. He had given proper instructions to the head master and he (the head master) had agreed to work according to that plan. He hoped that they would send him a satisfactory report within a month.

Continuing, he said that the municipalities could do a good deal of work if they so desired. They could push on the khaddar work to the great profit of not only the work but of themselves also.

A purse of Rs. 2,000 was then presented to him on which he remarked that Samastipur should not have contributed such a small amount.

The Searchlight, 26-1-1927

APPENDICES

APPENDIX I

GANDHIJI'S QUESTIONS TO RAJCHANDRA AND HIS REPLIES[1]

1. Q. What is the Soul? Does it perform actions? Do past actions impede its progress or not?

A. (1) As there are physical objects like a pot, a piece of cloth, etc., so there is an entity called the *atman* whose essence is knowledge. The former are impermanent. They cannot exist through all time in the same form. The *atman* is an imperishable entity which exists eternally in the same form. Anything which is not the product of a combination of other elements is imperishable. We cannot think of the *atman* as being such a product, for, no matter in how many thousand different ways we combine material substances, such combinations cannot possibly produce life and consciousness. Every one of us can know from experience that by combining several elements we cannot produce in the compound a property which is not present in any of those elements. We do not find knowledge to be the essence of physical substances. If we change the forms of such substances and combine them, or if they change and combine by chance, the products will be of the same kind as they are; that is, they will be of a material nature and will not have knowledge as their essence. It is not possible, then, that the *atman*, which the seers describe as having knowledge as its essential character, can be produced by any combination of the elements (earth, water, air, space) of which physical substances like a pot, a piece of cloth, etc., are composed. The *atman* has knowledge as its essential character, whereas material substances are characterized by its absence. These are the eternal natures of the two.

This and a thousand other reasons prove the *atman* to be imperishable. Further reflection on the subject enables us to realize that the *atman* from its nature is imperishable. There is, therefore, no error or logical difficulty in believing that the *atman*, the existence of which is the cause of our experiencing happiness and suffering which also withdraws itself from either, and which is conscious of something which thinks and impels, is characterized by awareness as its essential nature and that, in virtue of this nature, it is an imperishable entity which exists eternally; on the contrary, belief in the *atman* has this merit of accepting truth.

(2) When the *atman* has attained a state of knowledge, the state resulting

[1] The translation of the questions is reproduced from Vol. I, pp. 90-1. The letter accompanying Rajchandra's replies is dated Bombay, Saturday, *Aso Vad* 6, *1950* [October 20, 1894].

from a true understanding of its essence, it is the *karta*[1] of that state, the state of illumination (determination of what it truly is) and of the resulting state of pure awareness, which is its true nature. In a state of ignorance, it is the *karta* of the emotions of anger, love of honour, attachment, greed, etc., and, when enjoying the fruits of these emotions, becomes, as the occasion may require, the *karta* of physical objects like a pot, a piece of cloth, etc., that is, he is not the creator of the original substance of those objects, but is only the *karta* of the action of imposing some form on it. This latter state is described in Jainism as karma, and in Vedanta as illusion or in other similar terms. If we reflect carefully on the matter, we shall clearly see that the *atman* cannot be the *karta* of physical objects or emotions like anger, that it is *karta* only of the state of self-realization.

(3) The karmas performed while in the state of ignorance are like seed in the beginning and grow into a tree in course of time; in other words, the *atman* has to suffer the consequences of those karmas. Just as contact with fire produces the experience of heat, the natural end of which is pain, so the *atman*, being the *karta* of emotions of anger, etc., has to suffer, as consequence, pain in the form of birth, old age and death. You should carefully reflect over this idea and ask me any question which may arise in your mind about it, for an understanding of the state from which the soul must withdraw itself and the effort to withdraw will bring deliverance to it.

2. Q. What is God? Is He the creator of the universe?

A. (1) You, I and others are souls suffering the bondage of karma. The soul's existence in its natural state, that is, in freedom from karma and purely as the *atman* that it is, is the state of being Ishvar[2]. That which has the *aishvarya*[3] of knowledge, etc., may be described as Ishvar. This Ishvarhood is the natural state of the *atman*, which is not revealed when it is engaged in karmas. When the *atman*, however, realizes that being engaged in karma is not its real nature and fixes its attention on itself, then alone do omniscience, power, etc., manifest themselves in it and we can see nothing among all the objects in the universe with greater power than the *atman's*. It is, therefore, my positive belief that Ishvar is another name for *atman* and does not signify a different Being of greater power.

(2) Ishvar is not the creator of the universe, that is, atoms, space, etc., can be conceived only as imperishable entities and not as created from some other substance. If it is stated that they came into being from Ishvar, that, too, does not seem likely; for, if we believe that Ishvar is a spirit, how can atoms, space, etc., come into being from Him? For it is impossible that matter can come into existence from that which is spirit. If Ishvar is regarded as material,

[1] Author, doer
[2] Ruler, God
[3] Power

He will then lose His Ishvarhood; also, a spiritual entity like the soul cannot come into being from such an Ishvar. If we regard Him as being both matter and spirit, that only means that we are pleased to call the world, which is both matter and spirit, by another name, Ishvar. Instead of doing that, it is better to call the world the world: If we hold that atoms, space, etc., are imperishable entities and that Ishvar only awards the fruits of karma, this, too, cannot be proved. Convincing reasons have been given in support of this view in *Shatdarshan Samuchchaya*[1].

3. Q. What is *moksha*?

A. While the *atman* is in the state of ignorance, characterized by anger, etc., it is under the bondage of the body, and complete cessation of such a state, deliverance from it, is described by seers as *moksha*. A little reflection shows this to be logical and convincing.

4. Q. Is it possible for a person to know for certain, while he is still living, whether or not he will attain *moksha*.

A. If our arms are tied with a rope wound several times round them and if the twists of the rope are loosened one after another, we feel the loosening of each twist and in the end become conscious of the rope having been removed. In like manner as the innumerable bonds, the products of ignorance, which bind the *atman* loosen one by one, the latter becomes conscious of progressing towards *moksha*, and when the bonds are about to fall off, the *atman* shines forth with the light of its essence and knows beyond doubt that it is about to be delivered from the bonds of ignorance. While still dwelling in this body, it comes out of the state of ignorance, etc., and becomes conscious of its pure essence and of its absolute otherness and freedom from all relations. In other words, it is possible to experience the state of *moksha* even while living.

5. Q. It is said that after his death, a man may, according to his actions, be reborn as an animal, a tree or even a stone. Is this a fact?

A. After the soul has left the body, it attains a state according to the merit it has earned through its actions; hence, it may be born even as a lower creature, or may have even to assume a body of earth[2] and, devoid of the other four senses, suffer the fruits of its karma [through the sense of touch alone]. This does not mean, however, that it becomes pure stone or earth. The soul assumes a body of stone, but, even then, it exists as soul, though its existence is not manifest to us. Since, in that condition, the other four senses are unmanifest, the soul may be described as having an earth-body. In the course of time, the soul leaves such a body after it has enjoyed the fruits of its karmas and then the stone material exists merely as atoms and, because the soul has

[1] A philosophical treatise; Rajchandra had earlier sent a copy of it to Gandhiji.

[2] Probably as a particle of organic matter present in the earth

left it, does not possess the instinct of food, etc. In other words, the idea is not that stone itself, which is pure matter, becomes a soul. It is in order to enjoy the fruits of those karmas which, because of their hard nature, compels the soul to take on a body possessing only one sense, the sense of touch, the other senses remaining unmanifest, that it is born in an earth-body; it does not, however, become pure earth or stone. The body is like a garment to the soul, and is not its essence.

[6. & 7.][1] The answer to Q. 6 is contained in the reply given above as also the answer to Q. 7 which is that earth or stone as such cannot be the *kartas* of any karma. It is the soul which has entered them and lives in them that is the *karta* of karmas, and even so, the relation between the two is like milk and water. Just as, even when they are mixed, milk is milk and water is water, so also the soul, through the binding effect of its karmas which confines it to the possession of one sense only, seems to have become stone or mere matter, but, in its essential nature, it is a soul and even in that state it possesses the instincts of hunger, fear, etc., though they remain unmanifest.

8. Q. What is Arya Dharma? Do all Indian religions originate from the Vedas?

A. (1) In defining Arya Dharma, everyone has his own religion in view. Commonly a Jain describes Jainism, a Buddhist describes Buddhism and a Vedantin describes Vedanta as Arya Dharma. But seers describe only that Arya—noble—path as Arya Dharma which enables the soul to realize its true nature, and rightly so.

(2) It is impossible that all religions had their origin in the Vedas. I know from experience that great souls like the [Jain] Tirthankars[2] have revealed knowledge of a thousand times deeper import than what the Vedas contain. I, therefore, believe that, since something imperfect cannot be the origin of a perfect thing, we are not justified in asserting that all religions had originated from the Vedas. We may believe that Vaishnavism and other sects had their origin in the Vedas. It seems that the latter existed before the time of the Buddha and Mahavira, the last teacher of Jainism; it also seems likely that they are really ancient works. But we cannot say that only that which is ancient is true or perfect, nor that what came later is necessarily untrue or imperfect. Apart from this, the ideas propounded in the Vedas and in Jain doctrines have existed from the beginning of time; only the outward forms changed. There is no totally new creation or absolute destruction. Since we may believe that the ideas propounded by the Vedas and in the doctrines of Jainism and other religions have existed from the beginning of time, where is the room for controversy? All the same, it is only right that you and

[1] The questions are not given in the source in Gandhiji's words and, therefore, they are not included in the questions translated in Vol. I.

[2] Self-realized men whose teachings evolved into Jainism

I and others should reflect and consider which of these systems of ideas has more power—truth—in them.

9. Q. Who composed the Vedas? Are they *anadi*[1]? If so, what does *anadi* mean?

A. (1) The Vedas were probably composed a long time ago.

(2) No scripture, considered as a book, is *anadi*; but with respect to the ideas propounded in them, all scriptures are *anadi*, for there have been souls at all times who taught them in one form or another. It cannot be otherwise. The emotions of anger, etc., are *anadi* and so are those of forgiveness, etc. The way of violence, too, is *anadi*, as is the path of non-violence. What we should consider is which of these conduce to the welfare of the soul? Both classes of things are *anadi*, though sometimes the one and sometimes the other may be predominant.

10. Q. Who is the author of the *Gita*? Is God its author? Is there any evidence that He is?

A. (1) The replies given above partly answer this question; if by God we mean a person who has attained illumination—perfect illumination—then we can say that the *Gita* was composed by God. If, however, we accept God as being all-pervading, like the sky, eternally existing and passive, the *Gita* or any other book cannot have been composed by Him. For, writing a book is an ordinary activity undertaken at a particular point in time and is not *anadi*.

(2) The *Gita* is believed to be the work of Veda Vyasa and, since Lord Krishna had propounded this teaching to Arjuna, He is said to be its real author. This may be true. The work is indeed great. The ideas it propounds have been taught from time immemorial, but it is not possible that these same verses have existed from the beginning of time. Nor is it likely that they were composed by God Who does nothing. They can have been composed only by an embodied soul, who acts. There is no harm, therefore, in saying that a perfectly illuminated person is God, and that a Shastra taught by him is one revealed by God.

11. Q. Does any merit accrue from the sacrifice of animals or other things?

A. It is always sinful to kill an animal to give it as an offering in sacrifice or injure it in any way, even if this is done for the purpose of a sacrifice or living in the very abode of God. The practice of giving gifts at the time of a sacrifice does earn some merit, but since this is accompanied with violence it, too, deserves no commendation.

12. Q. If a claim is put forward that a particular religion is the best, may we not ask the claimant for proof?

A. If no proof is required and if any such claim is made without proof in its support, reason and unreason, dharma and *adharma*, everything will have

[1] Without a beginning

to be accepted as "the best". Only the test of proof can show what is the best and what is not. That religion alone is the best and is truly strong, which is most helpful in destroying the bondage of worldly life and can establish us in the state which is our essence.

13. Q. Do you know anything about Christianity? If so, what do you think of it?

A. I know something in general about Christianity. Even a little study of the subject will show that no other country has gone so deep as India and discovered a religious path which can rival the one discovered by the great seers of India. Among the other religions, Christianity asserts the eternal subjection of the soul, even in the state of *moksha*. It does not give a true description of the *anadi* state of the soul, of the law of karma or of the cessation of karma, and I am not likely, therefore, to accept the view that it is the best religion. It does not seem to offer a satisfactory solution of the problems which I have mentioned. I am not making this statement in a sectarian spirit. If you wish to ask more questions on this, you may, and then it will be possible for me to resolve your doubts still further.

14. Q. The Christians hold that the Bible is divinely inspired and that Christ was an incarnation of God, being his son. Was He?

A. This is a matter of faith and cannot be proved rationally. What I said above concerning the claim that the *Gita* and the Vedas are divinely inspired may be applied to the Bible too. It is impossible that God, who is free from birth and death, will incarnate Himself as a human being; for it is the changes of attachment, aversion, etc., which are the cause of birth and it does not appeal to reason that God, who has no attachment and aversion, will take birth as a human being. The idea that Jesus is, and was, the son of God may perhaps be acceptable if we interpret the belief as an allegory; otherwise, tested by the canons of reason, it is difficult to accept. How can we say that God, Who is free, has or had a son? If we assert that He has or had one, what was the manner of the son's birth? If we believe that both God and His son are *anadi*, how can we explain their being father and son? These and other objections deserve examination. If we reflect over them, I think the belief will not be found acceptable.

15. Q. Were all the Old Testament prophecies fulfilled in Christ?

A. Even if they were, that should only make us think about the two scriptures. Nor is the act of the prophecies having been fulfilled a sufficiently strong reason to justify us in asserting that Jesus was an incarnation of God, for the birth of a great soul can also be predicted with the help of astrology. Even if, however, someone foretold the event by virtue of his knowledge, unless it is established that that person had perfect knowledge of the path to *moksha*, the fact of his having predicted a future event appeals only to faith as proof of a thing and we cannot believe that no reasoning on the opposite side can diminish its force.

[16.][1] *A*. In this question you ask about the miracles attributed to Jesus Christ. If it is said that he put a soul back into the body which it had left, or that he put another soul in its place, this could not possibly have been done. If it could be done, the law of karma would lose its meaning. Apart from this, mastery of yoga techniques enables a person to perform certain miracles, and if it is claimed that Jesus had such powers we cannot assert that the claim is false or impossible. Such yogic powers are of no consequence compared to the power of the *atman*; the latter is infinitely greater than the powers attained by yoga. You may ask more questions on this subject when we meet.

17. Q. Can anyone remember his past lives or have an idea of his future lives?

A. This is quite possible. One whose knowledge has become pure may be able to do so. We can infer the possibility of rain from certain signs in the clouds; similarly, from the actions of a soul in this life, we can understand, perhaps partially, their causes in its previous existence. We can also judge from the nature of the actions what results they are likely to have. On further reflection, we can also know what kind of a future existence the soul is likely to have or what kind of a past existence it had.

18. Q. If yes, who can?

A. The answer to this is contained in the reply above.

19. Q. You have given the names of some who have attained *moksha*. What is the authority for this statement?

A. If you have addressed this question personally to me, I may say in reply that one can to some extent infer from one's own experience how a person whose involvement in earthly existence is about to end is likely to speak or act, and on the basis of this one can assert whether or not such a person attained *moksha*. In most cases, we can also get from Shastras reasons in support of our conclusion.

20. Q. What makes you say that even Buddha did not attain *moksha*?

A. On the basis of the teachings of Buddhist scriptures. If his views were the same as these, then they seem to have been inconsistent with one another, and that is not a mark of perfect illumination. If a person has not attained perfect illumination his attachments and aversions are not likely to disappear so long as he is in such a state; earthly existence is a necessary consequence. One cannot, therefore, claim such a person to have attained absolute *moksha*. Moreover, it is impossible for you and me to know from independent sources that the Buddha's views were different from those contained in the teachings attributed to him. Even so, if it is asserted that his views were in fact different and proof given in support of the assertion, there is no reason why we should not accept that as possible.

[1] This is omitted in the translation of the questions in Vol. I.

21. Q. What will finally happen to this world?

A. It does not seem rationally possible to me that all souls will attain absolute *moksha* or that the world will perish completely. It is likely to continue to exist for ever in the same state as at present. Some aspect of it may undergo transformation and almost disappear, and another may grow; such is the nature of the world that, if there is growth in one sphere, there is decline in another. Having regard to this fact, and after deep reflection, it seems impossible to me that this world will perish completely. By "world" we do not mean this earth only.

22. Q. Will the world be morally better off in the future?

A. It would not be proper to encourage any soul which loves immorality to take wrong advantage of the answer to this question. All modes in this world, including morality and immorality, have existed from the beginning of time. But it is possible for you and me to eschew immorality and accept morality, and it is the duty of the *atman* to do that. It is not possible to assert that immorality will be given up by all and morality will prevail, for such an extreme state cannot come about.

23. Q. Is there anything like total destruction of the world?

A. If by *pralaya* is meant total destruction, that is not possible, for complete destruction of all that exists is impossible. If by *pralaya* is meant the merging of everything in God, the belief is accepted in some doctrines but that does not seem possible to me. For, how can all objects and all souls arrive in an identical state so that such a thing may happen? If they ever do, then diversity cannot develop again. If we accept the possibility of *pralaya* on the supposition of unmanifest diversity in the souls and manifest sameness, how can diversity exist except through connection with a body? If we believe that such connection exists [in the state of *pralaya*], we shall have to believe further that all souls will have one sense only and in doing so we shall reject, without reason, the possibility of other modes of existence. In other words, we shall have to suppose that a soul which had attained a higher state and was about to be free for ever from the contingency of existence with one sense only had none the less to be in such a state. This and many similar doubts arise. A *pralaya* involving all souls is impossible.

24. Q. Can an illiterate person attain *moksha* through *bhakti* alone?

A. *Bhakti* is a cause of knowledge and knowledge of *moksha*. If by an illiterate person we mean one without knowledge of letters, it is not impossible that he may cultivate *bhakti*. Every soul has knowledge as its essence. The power of *bhakti* purifies knowledge, and pure knowledge becomes the cause of *moksha*. I do not believe that, without the manifestation of perfect knowledge, absolute *moksha* is possible. Nor need I point out that knowledge of letters is contained in perfect [spiritual] knowledge. It cannot be true that knowledge of letters is a cause of *moksha* and that, without it, self-realization is not possible.

25. Q. Rama and Krishna are described as incarnations of God. What does that mean? Were they God Himself or only a part of Him? Can we attain salvation through faith in them?

A. (1) I, too, am convinced that both were souls of great holiness. Each of them, being an *atman*, was God. If it is a fact that all the coverings over their *atman* had fallen off, there need be no dispute about their having attained absolute *moksha*. I do not think that any soul can be a portion of God, for I can think of a thousand reasons against such a belief. If we believe a soul to be a portion of God, the belief in bondage and *moksha* will have no meaning. For then God Himself will be the cause of ignorance, etc., and, if that is true, He ceases to be God. In other words, in being regarded as Lord of the soul God actually loses something from His status. Moreover, if we believe that the soul is a portion of God, what motive will a person have to strive for anything? For in that case the soul cannot be regarded as the *karta* of anything. In view of this and other objections, I am not prepared to believe any soul to be a portion of God; how, then, can I believe that such was the case with great and holy souls like Rama and Krishna? There is no error in believing that these two were unmanifest God, but it is doubtful whether perfect Godhood had become manifest in them.

(2) The question whether we can attain *moksha* through faith in them can be easily answered. *Moksha* means absence of or deliverance from all forms of attachment, ignorance, etc. It can be attained when we cultivate faith in a person whose teaching will enable us to win such freedom from attachment and ignorance, and, reflecting on our true essence, come to have the same faith in our *atman* that we have in the teacher and identify ourselves with his personality. Worship of any kind other than this cannot win absolute *moksha*. It may help one to win the means of *moksha*, but even that cannot be asserted with certainty.

26. Q. Who were Brahma, Vishnu and Siva?

A. If people believed in three *gunas*[1] as the cause of creation and personified them [as Brahma, Vishnu and Siva], this or similar explanations may make the belief plausible. But I am not particularly disposed to believe that they are what the *Puranas* describe them to be, for some of the descriptions appear to be allegories intended for religious instruction. Even so, I think it would be better that we, too, try to profit from the instruction they contain rather than attempt in vain to ascertain the principles embodied in the personification of Brahma, and so on.

27. Q. If a snake is about to bite me, should I allow myself to be bitten or should I kill it, supposing that that is the only way in which I can save myself?

A. One hesitates to advise you that you should let the snake bite you.

[1] Modes of cosmic energy

Nevertheless, how can it be right for you, if you have realized that the body is perishable, to kill, for protecting a body which has no real value to you, a creature which clings to it with love? For anyone who desires his spiritual welfare, the best course is to let his body perish in such circumstances. But how should a person who does not desire spiritual welfare behave? My only reply to such a question is, how can I advise such a person that he should pass through hell and similar worlds, that is, that he should kill the snake? If the person lacks the culture of Aryan character, one may advise him to kill the snake, but we should wish that neither you nor I will even dream of being such a person.

[From Gujarati]

Shrimad Rajchandra

APPENDIX II

ROMAIN ROLLAND'S LETTER TO GANDHIJI

DEAR FRIEND,

I have your good letter[1] that Mira has sent me. I thank you cordially for it. But I do not understand at all what the Poet could have told you. I never said or wrote anything to Tagore regarding your article in the *Liber-Amicorum.* I have never spoken about it to any of the Poet's party. If I had done so, it would have only been to express joy which those words have given me and the gratitude I have felt. How could the idea have entered my mind to complain of a judgment like yours? I consider it an honour of my life to have been able to place myself at your service and to have spread your thoughts in the world.

I claim this role of *free servitor*—far far from protesting against it! And I am grieved to see that such thoughts have been attributed to me.

I cannot understand this at all. These are without doubt baseless reports which start without cause and are magnified in circulation, and lead to so much misunderstanding. This one must be entirely [ef]faced, for it has absolutely no basis.

Dear friend, I love you and revere you. Pray remain to the end of your life towards me and all others what you always have been, the absolutely sincere man who does not seek to please or flatter, who says not one word more than he thinks. All *amour propre* disappears in your presence.

From a photostat of the draft in Mahadev Desai's handwriting: S.N. 13288

[1] *Vide* Vol. XXXI, pp. 540-1.

APPENDIX III

KENYA INDIANS: D. B. DESAI'S LETTER

BROACH,
December 12, 1926

SIR,

I think you are by now aware that Kenya (British East Africa) Government has decided to levy an additional tax of one pound on every Indian, as a non-native Poll Tax. The Indian Citizens' Association has sent me now the following cable:

"Additional Poll Tax one pound Asiatics only. Move Press, platform, Congress and Government."

From this cablegram, I gather that things have become worse and they ask help of the people of India as well as the Government of India, and I have no doubt that both will readily give assistance to Kenya Indians in the matter.

I think it will be of some use if I give you some history as regards this non-native Poll Tax. The ordinance for the collection of this non-native Poll Tax was passed by the British East Africa Government in the year 1912 to collect from every non-native male adult a sum of fifteen rupees per annum from the 1st of January 1913. At this time, i.e., in 1912, there was no Indian Representative—either nominated or elected—on the Kenya Legislative Council; so according to that popular maxim "no taxation without representation", this non-native Poll Tax of fifteen rupees was both bad and unjust as against Indians.

Further up to 1920 in Kenya (then British East Africa) the Indian rupee was a current and legal coin, and from 1912 till the day the currency was changed, a rupee there was equivalent to one shilling and four pence; so Indians used to pay every year Rs. 15 equal to 20s Subsequently rupee currency was changed to florin currency, making a florin equal to a rupee (or in other words substituting "florins" wherever the word "rupees" appeared in all the local laws and ordinances in British East Africa). By this change of currency florins 15 were charged for this non-native Poll Tax. In the year 1922, a further change in currency was effected in British East Africa (Kenya) whereby shilling currency was introduced in place of florin currency making two shillings equal to a florin. So under the later change of currency 30s were charged for this tax, thus making this tax of 30 shillings instead of 20 shillings without any fault of the tax-payers. This shows an increase of 50 per cent, which is really, one must admit, unjust.

I further think, it will be of interest to you to know that in the territories now known as the "Colony and Protectorate of Kenya" there is included a ten miles coastal strip of land which is under the suzerainty of H.H. the Sultan of Zanzibar and for which the Kenya Government, from the day it assumed the administration in that country, is paying an annual rent to H. H. the Sultan of Zanzibar. And under the treaty which has been made by the British Government with the Sultan of Zanzibar, it has been agreed *inter alia* that no new taxes will be imposed, save and except those enumerated and mentioned in the said treaty upon the residents residing in this ten miles strip and it is understood that the British Government has not got the sanction of H.H. the Sultan of Zanzibar with regard to the levy of this non-native Poll Tax.

Last month the Kenya Legislative Council has passed the Non-Native Poll Tax (amendment) Ordinance whereby the Government will charge every non-native male Asiatic 50 instead of 30 shillings stated above. The reason advanced for this and other taxation (of which particulars will be found mentioned below) is to provide for educational facilities to European and Indian children. But the Government of Kenya, it seems to me, has forgotten, when advancing the above reason, that from the beginning till now the Government of Kenya has spent considerably large amounts after European children's education neglecting and at the cost of Indian children's education, and the provision was hithertofore made from "General Taxation". But now in order to tax the Indian community, it seems to me, the Government has engineered this new device which, in my opinion, is both inequitable and unjust.

From the Minority Report which has been submitted by the Hon. Messrs J. B. Pandya and Shamsud Deen, the two nominated Indian members to the Kenya Legislative Council, it appears that the Kenya Government requires £ 52,000 for education purposes and this sum is to be earmarked as follows:

Europeans	£ 32,000 for 960 children, i.e., about £ 33 17s per head
Indians	£ 20,000 for 2,318 children, i.e., about £ 8 12s per head

So from this one could easily understand how Indian education in Kenya is neglected. Over and above the number of children mentioned above there are 2,547 Indian children without any means of education. Further, I think, it will not be out of place here to mention to you that school-going children pay 2s, 4s and 8s per month according to the standard in which they study, which will also mean that Indian children are contributing much more than their European brothers and sisters and this fact the Government of Kenya has omitted to take into its consideration.

As stated in the Majority Report (which is signed by the Colonial Secretary to the Government of Kenya as one of the Members of the Committee), which is submitted to the Kenya Government (and of which report the Governor has spoken in very high terms) and which is passed by the Kenya Legislative Council, the said amount of £ 52,000 has been raised in the following way:

Spirits £ 25,000; Wines £ 7,000; Champagnes £ 500;

Male domestic servants £ 7,000 (from Europeans only) and Asiatic Poll Tax £ 12,000.

It is alleged and assumed in the said Majority Report that for the first three items which are to produce £ 32,500 in taxation, £ 24,500 will be contributed by the Europeans and the rest by the Indians. But as the Kenya Government keeps no record to show the proportion, it will be unwise to arrive at any assumption. Barring this £ 32,500 there remains £ 19,000 in the new taxation which are divided between the Europeans and the Indians; the former contribute £ 7,000 and the latter £ 12,000.

The domestic servants' tax which is mentioned in the above paragraph is to be payable "at the rate of two shillings per mensem on every *male domestic* servant above the apparent age of *sixteen* and in *excess* of *two* servants per household" which will mean that there will be many families which will not be burdened with this tax, which is not an *individual* tax, while in the case of the additional Asiatic Poll Tax every male adult Asiatic will have to pay 20s extra. Here too there is an open injustice.

One of the members who has signed the said Majority Report has stated during the debate in the Kenya Legislative Council, "With regard to the Poll Tax, this was *especially* put in to meet the requirements of the Indian community, as it was felt that the Indian community did not spend money in the country on *luxuries* like Europeans did, *but sent it out of the country*". From the above statement one naturally gathers the prejudices which are working in the matter of levying of this new tax. The only motive for the new additional one pound poll tax, to my mind, is to harass the law-abiding Indian citizens of Kenya by the Kenya Government which is in the hands of the Kenya white settlers practically speaking.

On behalf of the Kenya Indians I have to request you to take this matter up and do the needful justice to this subject as occasions require. Your advice to Kenya Indians will be appreciated. I may in the end mention that if the people in India and the Government of India will not take steps to cause this new additional tax to be removed, the Kenya Government will start collecting it from the 1st January 1927 and if it is once collected it will be very difficult, as I understand it, to get it removed. I think the Gauhati Congress should take this matter up.

Yours, etc.,
D. B. DESAI

Young India, 23-12-1926

SOURCES

Aaj: Hindi daily published from Varanasi.

Amrita Bazar Patrika: English newspaper of Calcutta which first appeared as a Bengali weekly in 1868; a daily since 1891.

Bapuna Patro—Manibehn Patelne (Gujarati): Ed. Manibehn Patel, Navajivan Publishing House, Ahmedabad, 1957.

(*The*) *Bombay Chronicle*: English daily published from Bombay.

Forward: English daily started by C. R. Das from Calcutta.

GANDHI SMARAK SANGRAHALAYA, NEW DELHI: Central Museum and Library of Gandhian Literature and Documents; *vide* Vol. I, p. 349.

Gandhijinu Gitashikshan (Gujarati): Ed. Narahari Parikh, Sabarmati Ashram Trust, 1955.

Hand-spinning and Hand-weaving: S. V. Puntambekar and Varadachari, the All-India Spinners Association, Ahmedabad, 1926.

(*The*) *Hindu*: English newspaper issued from Madras started as a weekly in 1878, became a tri-weekly in 1883 and a daily since 1889.

(*The*) *Hindustan Times*: English daily published from New Delhi.

(*The*) *Leader*: English daily published from Allahabad.

Navajivan (1919-31): Gujarati weekly (with occasional bi-weekly issues) edited by Gandhiji and published from Ahmedabad; first issued on September 7, 1919. It was converted from *Navajivan ane Satya*, Gujarati monthly (1915-19). Also issued in Hindi from August 19, 1921.

Report of the Forty-first Session of the Indian National Congress, 1926.

Sabarmati, Vol. V, Autumn Issue, 1926: Manuscript magazine of the National School at Sabarmati Ashram, Ahmedabad.

SABARMATI SANGRAHALAYA: Library and records containing documents relating to Gandhiji's South African period and Indian period up to 1933; *vide* Vol. I, pp. 349-50

(*The*) *Searchlight*: English daily published from Patna.

Shrimad Rajchandra: Compiled by Mansukhlal Mehta, published by Revashanker Zaveri.

Young India (1918-31): English weekly founded by Jamnadas Dwarkadas at Bombay; from May 7, 1919, published bi-weekly under Gandhiji's supervision; from October 1919, issued as a weekly from Ahmedabad with Gandhiji as Editor.

CHRONOLOGY

(*November 5, 1926—January 20, 1927*)

November 5: Gandhiji in Satyagraha Ashram, Sabarmati.

November 21: V. S. Srinivasa Sastri met Gandhiji in the afternoon.

November 28: Gandhiji spoke at the convocation of Gujarat Vidyapith, Ahmedabad.

December 3: Left Ahmedabad for Wardha.
Stopped at Surat on the way and visited Vinay Mandir.

December 4: Reached Wardha.

December 19: Sent message to public meeting, Wardha.

December 20: Addressed public meeting at Wardha.

December 21: Left Wardha for Gauhati. Addressed public meetings at Amraoti and Nagpur. Stayed for a few hours at Gondia.

December 23: Reached Calcutta.
Swami Shraddhanand assassinated.

December 24: Gandhiji left for Gauhati. Spoke at the A.I.C.C. meeting at Gauhati.

December 25: Spoke at opening ceremony of Swadeshi Exhibition, Gauhati.

December 26: Spoke at flag hoisting ceremony at the Congress *pandal.*
Proposed resolutions and spoke on death of Swami Shraddhanand and on status of Indians in South Africa.

December 27: Spoke in Subjects Committee on desirability of stiffening franchise so that no one who does not wear khaddar should be entitled to vote.

December 28: Spoke twice on Independence Resolution in the Subjects Committee.
Addressed meeting of Municipal Board, Gauhati.
In interview to Associated Press, said that his business in the coming year would be to spread message of charkha and khadi.
Left Gauhati for Calcutta.

December 31: Spoke at public meeting held at Maheshwari Bhavan, Barra Bazar, Calcutta.

January 2: Spoke at gathering of students of sixteen depressed-class schools of Calcutta and Howrah.
Spoke at Chittaranjan Seva Sadan, Calcutta.
Laid foundation for memorial to Aswini Kumar Dutt.
Spoke at opening ceremony of Kalashala of Khadi Pratishthan, at Sodepur.

January 4: Left for Comilla.

January 5: Spoke at Abhoy Ashram and public meeting at Comilla.

January 6: At Comilla gave interview to the Free Press of India on the khadi resolution.
Spoke at a women's meeting, Comilla.

January 9: In Banaras gave interview to Dr. Bhagwandas on the question of swaraj.
In Banaras delivered speeches at Benares Hindu University, Shraddhanand's Memorial meeting, meeting of untouchables, women's meeting and at public meeting.

January 10: Left Banaras for Allahabad.

January 11: In Daltenganj.

January 12: Spoke at public meeting in Dhanbad.

January 13: Addressed meetings at Dhanbad, Katras, Jharia.

January 14: Spoke at public meeting in Aurangabad.

January 15: Addressed meetings at Gaya and Ramana.

January 16: Spoke at women's meeting in Sonepur and at public meetings in Chhapra and Sewan.

January 17: Took rest in Rajendra Prasad's house, in Chhapra

January 18: Visited Ekma and Maharajganj

January 19: Visited Darbhanga.

January 20: Addressed meetings at Madhubani and Samastipur.

INDEX OF TITLES

INDEX

ERRATA

PAGE		FOR	READ
15	*Line 11 from bottom	117	1117
33	*Item 17, line 2	Dr. Faret	Dr. Paret
69	*para 1, line 6	assure	assume
	*para 2, line 5	uses	used
103	*Line 10 from bottom	noting	nothing
108	*Line 8 from bottom	minds	mind
116	*line 24	warrior	warriors
173	line 23	as being a slender thread	as being pulled by a slender thread
188	*line 3	Ikshavaku	Ikshvaku.”
	*line 2 from bottom	exist if	exist; if
220	*line 8	need	used
241	*line 9	*Atmanam unjita*	*Atmanam yunjita*
243	*line 17	God	food
350	*line 13	half the truth but he	half the truth; but he
375	*para 1, last line	lie	live
483	*Footnote 6, line 1	her 13th birthday	entering her 13th year
569	*para 3, line 4		Sunday may be treated as dateline.

*Due correction made.